D0398338

Writing
Los Angeles

A Literary Anthology

Writing
Los Angeles
A Literary Anthology

Edited by David L. Ulin

A Special Publication of
The Library of America

Introduction, headnotes, and volume compilation © 2002 by Literary Classics of the United States, New York, N.Y. All rights reserved. No part of this book may be reproduced commercially by offset-lithographic or equivalent copying devices without the permission of the publisher. Some of the material in this volume is reprinted with the permission of holders of copyright and publication rights. Acknowledgments are on page 875. Distributed to the trade by Penguin Putnam Inc. and in Canada by Penguin Books Canada. Design by Doyle Partners. The text is Cochin, with BeLucian Ultra headings.

Library of Congress Cataloging-in-Publication Data:
Writing Los Angeles: a literary anthology/edited by David L. Ulin
      p.   cm.
ISBN 1-931082-27-8
1. American literature—California—Los Angeles. 2. Los Angeles (Calif.)
—Literary Collections. I. Ulin, David L.
PS572.L6 W74 2002
810.8'0979494—dc21   2002069352

10 9 8 7 6 5 4 3 2 1

Printed in the United States

Contents

Introduction

Los Angeles is not a new city. Established in 1781 as a Spanish pueblo, it is nearly as old as the United States, and like America's, its history is one of self-invention. As the historian Kevin Starr has written, it did not so much evolve as will itself into being. Originally a tiny settlement—as recently as 1844 barely three thousand people occupied the "Los Angeles District," which at the time extended from the San Fernando Valley into Orange County—it briefly became the capital of Mexican California under Governor Pío Pico. During the Mexican War it was the site of several battles. After California entered the Union in 1850, L.A. incorporated as a U.S. city, and with the completion of the first transcontinental railroad spur lines in the 1870s, its identity as a quintessentially American promised land began to take shape.

Starting with the real-estate boom of the 1880s, during which its population nearly tripled, Southern California became a huckster's paradise. "From 1900 to 1920," the pioneering historian and social critic Carey McWilliams wrote in *Southern California Country: An Island on the Land*, "Los Angeles was essentially a tourist town. Like most tourist towns, it had its share of freaks, side-shows, novelties, and show-places. Ducks waddled along the streets with advertisements painted on their backs; six-foot-nine pituitary giants with sandwich-board signs stalked the downtown streets; while thousands of people carrying Bibles in their hands and singing hymns marched in evangelical parades." This period peaked with the Long Beach oil boom, which inspired more than one and a quarter million new residents to move to Southern California during the 1920s before the bubble burst when the Julian Petroleum scandal shook the region. This massive stock fraud debacle, just two years before the onset of the Great Depression, did much to tarnish Los Angeles's public image and to usher in a more disillusioned era.

If L.A. has often seemed like a city without history it is perhaps because so much of its past has been recycled into myth. As early as the 1880s, inspired in part by Helen Hunt Jackson's 1884 novel *Ramona*, civic boosters and real estate promoters began to disseminate a legendary version of the mission era. The period of Hispanic rule was a pastoral world where a cultured Spanish elite lived in civilized luxury on *ranchos* cultivated by Indian laborers. This was the beginning of a long tradition of nostalgia for the good old days in Southern California. The mission legend spread widely, and has lingered tenaciously; its influence can still be found in art and architecture, street names, even public spaces such as Olvera Street in downtown Los Angeles, a Mexican marketplace that purports to offer visitors an authentic taste of the old pueblo, although it was actually created in 1930 as a tourist site.

The successive boom periods and the region's rapid commercial development encouraged the development of such mythologies. It was all part of a remarkably successful sales campaign to spur investment and settlement, a campaign that used phrases like "America's Mediterranean" to extol a climate at once mild and invigorating, and that idealized Southern California as a place where, in Charles Dudley Warner's phrase, "nature seems to work with a man, and not against him." The thousands who flocked to L.A. in response to such descriptions saw it as a place where they would find whatever they were looking for, and where in turn they could reinvent themselves, leaving the past behind. The earliest selections in this book—which include Helen Hunt Jackson gently reminiscing about the mission days and Stewart Edward White and Harris Newmark commenting from different angles on the freewheeling hype of the boom period—show the roots of a literature that would blossom in the 1920s and 1930s.

The emergence of Los Angeles as a modern city owes much to two developments: the relocation of the motion picture industry (previously centered on the East Coast) to Southern California and the purchase in 1904 of vast tracts of the San Fernando Valley (largely worthless land at the time) by a syndicate comprising the *Los Angeles Times*'s Harry Chandler and other local leaders. The land deal would ultimately yield over $100 million in profits because of the purchasers' secret knowledge of a plan to irrigate the arid Valley with water hijacked from the Owens River Valley, a few hundred miles to the north. Without that Owens Valley water, Southern California could not have spread out far enough to require the network of roads and freeways that made it possible for the city's car culture to take hold. As for the movie business: well, it's impossible to imagine what the Southland would have been like without it. Cars and movies, after all, are the essential icons of Los Angeles, emblems of speed and light and movement; but they also reside at the heart of our national mythology, and this is perhaps why Los Angeles has come to occupy such a singular place among American cities, a symbol of the country's most expansive dreams and its most streamlined technologies. This quintessentially twentieth-century metropolis was to prove an irresistible subject for a startlingly diverse group of writers.

The movies contributed in a more direct way to the literary culture embodied in this anthology: they encouraged the arrival of writers, thousands of them, who began to flood Southern California in the 1920s, looking for work in film. Much has been made over the years of Hollywood's role in the evolution of Southland culture. For the poet Vachel Lindsay, in his 1915 book *The Art of the Motion Picture*, movies represented a new American art form, one that would make Los Angeles a kind of Athens of the modern age. Other writers were more typically inclined to see Hollywood as a commercial behemoth swallowing everything in its path. In any event the film industry transformed the region by offering paying work to a wide variety of writers from elsewhere. For these newcomers, L.A. was exotic territory, full of outsized ambitions and outsized fantasies, a funhouse mirror offering grotesquely exaggerated reflections of America itself. If, prior to the motion picture era, Los Angeles literature had been provincial, based on local iconography and the glories of a half-imaginary past, the writing of the 1920s and 1930s focused on the freaks and side-shows that Carey McWilliams described, displaying L.A.'s most eccentric curiosities and evangelical excesses for a national audience. "Here," wrote Bruce Bliven in *The New Republic* in 1927, "is the world's prize collection of cranks, semi-cranks, placid creatures whose bovine expression shows that each of them is studying, without much hope of success, to be a high-grade moron, angry or ecstatic exponents of food fads, sun-bathing, ancient Greek costumes, diaphragm breathing and the imminent second coming of Christ."

Bliven was not the first and far from the last outsider to write about Los Angeles in such terms. As recently as 1960, in "Superman Comes to the Supermarket," Norman Mailer could note, "One gets the impression that people come to Los Angeles in order to divorce themselves from the past, here to live, or try to live in the rootless pleasure world of an adult child"—a comment that has the same quality of generalizing condescension as Bliven's statement of a quarter century before. In the first half of the twentieth century, Los Angeles writing can be seen as dominated by the accounts of those who arrived from elsewhere. This is still true, in some ways, although the new immigrants to L.A. come not from other parts of the United States, but from Latin America and the Pacific Rim, a transformation reflected in works like Garrett Hongo's *Volcano* or Sandra Tsing Loh's "Coming Home to Van Nuys." But as the city has developed, it has become less a place people *go to* than one they *come from,* and by now there have been several generations of Los Angeles–born writers who don't see the city as exotic and have focused less on the ephemeral and carnival-like aspects of L.A. life than on its more enduring qualities.

The story of Los Angeles has always been, on the most basic level, the story of the interaction between civilization and nature. Mary Austin's early essay "The Land" delineates in unblinking detail just how unforgiving is the desert ecosystem on which the city was superimposed. As Lawrence Clark Powell's *"Ocian in View"* and Gary Snyder's "Night Song of the Los Angeles Basin" indicate, L.A. continues to be an idiosyncratic hybrid of the urban and the elemental, a metropolis carved from desert and ringed by ocean and mountains, whose pure, flat light (described so eloquently by Lawrence Weschler in "L.A. Glows") can lend a deceptively tranquil quality to an environment where uncontrollable forces remain at work. There is a geographic instability that may prefigure some of the emotional and social instability that has so often provided subject matter for Los Angeles writers; in a landscape where nothing can be certain, there is the inevitable feeling that anything goes. In "Fire Season," Joan Didion ponders this fluidity by suggesting that to live in Los Angeles is to do a constant dance with a disaster-prone environment. The same notion surfaces in John McPhee's "The Control of Nature" and, to some extent, in Cedric Belfrage's historical novel *Promised Land.* Raymond Chandler's "Red Wind," with its memorable opening description of the Santa Ana winds and their effects on people—"Meek little wives feel the edge of the carving knife and study their husbands' necks"—is as ominous an encapsulation of L.A.'s relationship to the elements as has ever been written.

"Red Wind" also figures here as a representative slice—early but very choice—of the work of Raymond Chandler, a writer who in his day looked like a better-than-average pulp writer but who now seems more like the inventor of a mythic Los Angeles and the progenitor (with his predecessor Dashiell Hammett) of a school of noir writers who have flourished everywhere but most especially in L.A. Chandler's mix of clipped description, aphoristic wisecracks, and disappointed romanticism came together with the hardboiled, hard-luck Depression-era mood of writers like James M. Cain to spawn one of the signature modes of L.A. writing, which would evolve and flourish in the work of Ross Macdonald, Walter Mosley, and James Ellroy (all of them featured in this book). The disillusioned, world-weary sensibility of Chandler and his successors is of course not limited to crime fiction; in the same year that Chandler's first novel, *The Big Sleep*, appeared, two other masterful books— John Fante's *Ask the Dust* and Nathanael West's *The Day of the Locust*—explored similarly dark territory, dismantling the glittering promises of the dream city and finding unsettling realities underneath. In the decades since, a comparably disillusioned sensibility has marked the work of writers as different as Chester Himes, Joan Didion, Gavin Lambert, and Robert Towne. As Carolyn See put it, "Southern California bespeaks alienation. The West Coast is the end of the road for the American Dream. We're up against a blank wall out here, and we can't go any farther. So even if you get what you want, then what? There is no out, you're here. It looks good, but that's it."

One of the corners of L.A. culture where noir has nestled deepest is Hollywood. Throughout the 1940s and 1950s, *film noir* was a genre charged with creative excitement, and a host of noir writers, from Cain and Chandler to David Goodis and Jim Thompson, found gainful employment in the industry. Noir provided a gritty counterweight to the dreamier aspects of the movies' fantasy life, a corrective to the endless happy endings promised by celebrity and glamour. For writers in general, noir or otherwise, the relationship with Hollywood has always been complicated and often conflicted. Authors like William Faulkner, F. Scott Fitzgerald, and Tennessee Williams could hardly regard their film assignments as anything but a commercial sideline distracting them from their real work, and European emigrés like Bertolt Brecht were often inclined to see themselves as exiles in a vulgar marketplace. Yet all these writers also found unique material in the Southland, and as the excerpts in this book from the diaries of Christopher Isherwood and the memoirs of Salka Viertel indicate, the intellectual scene was far from barren. The movie writers also had the inestimable advantage of being able to observe the dream factory behind the scenes, and those hidden machinations and power struggles fired the imaginations of writers as different as Nathanael West, Budd Schulberg, John O'Hara, and Horace McCoy. The Hollywood novel, a genre pioneered by the brothers Carroll and Garrett Graham in their long-lost 1930 satire *Queer People*, evolved into a vibrant form of L.A. writing, one that in its fatalistic cynicism is a kind of literary cousin to noir crime fiction.

The rediscovery of a book like *Queer People*, with its scabrous portrait of a vanished Hollywood, has been one of the great pleasures of editing *Writing Los Angeles*. It is satisfying to be able to reclaim, for instance, a piece like James M. Cain's "Paradise," published in 1933 in *The American Mercury*, a surprisingly mellow take on Los Angeles by a writer better known for depicting its harsher side. It is even more satisfying to juxtapose the elements of a book like this and to see how the often conflicting angles of vision work together to form a portrait of a constantly changing, always surprising city. There is a strand of homegrown social criticism that runs from Louis Adamic to Mike Davis, by way of such distinctive voices as Carey McWilliams and Joan Didion; there are those who, like Reyner Banham and David Hockney, have celebrated Los Angeles without apology; and there are those who, like Carol Muske or Charles Bukowski or Wanda Coleman, have brought to life the close-up details of lives often hidden from public view. In a city where myth-making is an industry, L.A.'s writers have often felt the need to resist imposed narratives, preferring to carve out their own version of reality, no matter how fragmentary.

I wish this book could have been even longer than it is; there are certainly many significant Los Angeles writers whom it wasn't possible to include, whether for reasons of space or because their writing doesn't deal directly with the city. The handful of excerpts from novels in these pages can only scratch the surface of a long tradition that includes Myron Brinnig's *The Flutter of an Eyelid*, Steve Erickson's *Days Between Stations* and *Rubicon Beach*, Rudolph Wurlitzer's *Quake*, Peter Viertel's *In the Canyon*, Wallace Thurman's *The Blacker the Berry*, John O'Hara's *Hope of Heaven*, and Horace McCoy's *I Should Have Stayed Home*. An anthology like this can only hint at the cumulative density of Los Angeles's literary record; it is intended as a starting point for exploring the rich and diverse perspectives of a century of writing. I hope that at the very least it will spark a recognition of just how variously Los Angeles can be reimagined, in ways that go far beyond the commonplaces of movies and guidebooks.

No anthology on this scale can be the work of any one individual; throughout the long months of its preparation, I've been blessed by the assistance of a wide range of interested parties, both in Los Angeles and beyond. For their input and suggestions, I'd like especially to thank to Stephen Cooper, Rae Dubow, David Fine, Lynell George, Erik Himmelsbach, David Kipen, Bonnie Nadell, Tom Nolan, David Reid, Susan Salter Reynolds, Richard Schickel, Carolyn See, Kevin Starr, and Louise Steinman. I feel a special gratitude to the Rare Book Room of the Los Angeles Public Library, where I spent a dozen or so mornings reading my way through nearly seventy years of *Westways* magazine, a search that not only yielded M.F.K. Fisher's delightful essay "Pacific Village," but also offered a rare and unexpected window onto Southern California as it is and as it was.

David L. Ulin
Los Angeles, 2002

Helen Hunt Jackson

When Helen Jackson (1830–1885) published her novel *Ramona* in 1884, she wanted to draw attention to the suffering and exploitation of California's Indians at the hands of rapacious white settlers. Jackson, a native of Amherst, Massachusetts, and a close friend of Emily Dickinson, had become interested in the American West following her marriage to a Colorado banker. *Ramona*—which is where the literary culture of Los Angeles really begins—did indeed make a tremendous impact, but not as a political tract: it was Jackson's nostalgic evocation of the Spanish mission era, a supposedly halcyon time marked by unspoiled nature and a social order characterized by beneficent dons and noble, hardworking Indians, that caught the public's attention. For many decades, the novel's afterlife extended into place names, tourist souvenirs, advertising campaigns, and a celebrated annual pageant in the town of Hemet. In "Echoes in the City of the Angels," first published in *The Century* in 1883 and later reprinted in *Glimpses of California and the Missions* (1902), Jackson devotes her considerable literary gifts to a similarly soft-focused account of the surviving traces of the original Los Angeles, which were beginning to fade into the past even as she wrote: turning history into an elegant pastoral fable, she makes the present into something like the aftermath of a dream.

from

ECHOES IN THE CITY OF THE ANGELS

The tale of the founding of the city of Los Angeles is a tale for verse rather than for prose. It reads like a page out of some new "Earthly Paradise," and would fit well into song such as William Morris has sung.

It is only a hundred years old, however, and that is not time enough for such song to simmer. It will come later, with the perfume of century-long summers added to its flavor. Summers century-long? One might say a stronger thing than that of them, seeing that their blossoming never stops, year in nor year out, and will endure as long as the visible frame of the earth.

The twelve devout Spanish soldiers who founded the city named it at their leisure with a long name, musical as a chime of bells. It answered well enough, no doubt, for the first fifty years of the city's

1

life, during which not a municipal record of any sort or kind was written, — "Nuestra Señora Reina de los Angeles," "Our Lady the Queen of the Angels;" and her portrait made a goodly companion flag, unfurled always by the side of the flag of Spain.

There is a legend, that sounds older than it is, of the ceremonies with which the soldiers took possession of their new home. They were no longer young. They had fought for Spain in many parts of the Old World, and followed her uncertain fortunes to the New. Ten years some of them had been faithfully serving Church and king in sight of these fair lands, for which they hankered, and with reason.

In those days the soft, rolling, treeless hills and valleys, between which the Los Angeles River now takes its shilly-shallying course seaward, were forest slopes and meadows, with lakes great and small. This abundance of trees, with shining waters playing among them, added to the limitless bloom of the plains and the splendor of the snow-topped mountains, must have made the whole region indeed a paradise.

Navarro, Villavicencia, Rodriguez, Quintero, Moreno, Lara, Banegas, Rosas, and Canero, these were their names: happy soldiers all, honored of their king, and discharged with so royal a gift of lands thus fair.

Looking out across the Los Angeles hills and meadows to-day, one easily lives over again the joy they must have felt. Twenty-three young children there were in the band, poor little waifs of camp and march. What a "braw flitting" was it for them, away from the drumbeat forever into the shelter of their own sunny home! The legend says not a word of the mothers, except that there were eleven of them, and in the procession they walked with their children behind the men. Doubtless they rejoiced the most.

The Fathers from the San Gabriel Mission were there, with many Indian neophytes, and Don Felipe, the military governor, with his showy guard of soldiers.

The priests and neophytes chanted. The Cross was set up, the flag of Spain and the banner of Our Lady the Queen of the Angels unfurled, and the new town marked out around a square, a little to the north of the present plaza of Los Angeles.

If communities, as well as individuals, are happy when history finds nothing to record of them, the city of the Queen of the Angels must have been a happy spot during the first fifty years of its life; for not a written record of the period remains, not even a record of grants of land. The kind of grant that these worthy Spanish soldiers and their sons contented themselves with, however, hardly deserved recording, — in fact, was not a grant at all, since its continuance depended entirely on the care a man took of his house and the improvement he put on his land. If he left his house unoccupied or let it fall out of repair, if he left a field uncultivated for two years, any neighbor who saw fit might denounce him, and by so doing acquire a right to the property. This sounds incredible, but all the historical accounts of the time agree on the point. They say: —

> "The granting authorities could, and were by law required, upon a proper showing of the abandonment, to grant the property to the informant, who then acquired the same and no better rights than those possessed by his predecessor."

This was a premium indeed on staying at home and minding one's business, — a premium which amounted to coercion. One would think that there must have been left from those days teeming records of alienated estates, shifted tenures, and angry feuds between neighbor and neighbor. But no evidence remains of such strifes. Life was too simple, and the people were too ignorant.

Their houses were little more than hovels, built of mud, eight feet high, with flat roofs made of reeds and asphaltum. Their fields, with slight cultivation, produced all they needed; and if anything lacked, the rich vineyards, wheat-fields, and orchards of the San Gabriel Mission lay only twelve miles away. These vineyards, orchards, and granaries, so near at hand, must have been sore temptation to idleness. Each head of a family had been presented, by the paternal Spanish king, with "two oxen, two mules, two mares, two sheep, two goats, two cows, one calf, an ass, and one hoe." For these they were to pay in such small installments as they were able to spare out of their pay and rations, which were still continued by the generous king.

In a climate in which flowers blossom winter and summer alike, man may bask in sun all the year round if he chooses. Why, then, should those happy Spanish soldiers work? Even the king had thought it unnecessary, it seems, to give them any implements of labor except "one hoe." What could a family do, in the way of work, with "one hoe"? Evidently they did not work,—neither they, nor their sons, nor their sons' sons after them; for, half a century later, they were still living a life of almost incredible ignorance, redeemed only by its simplicity and childlike adherence to the old religious observances.

———

With the beginning of the prosperity of the City of the Angels, came the end of its primeval peace. Spanish viceroys, Mexican alcaldes and governors, United States commanders, naval and military, followed on each other's heels, with or without frays, ruling Californian through a succession of tumultuous years. Greedy traders from all parts of the world added their rivalries and interventions to the civil and military disputation. In the general anarchy and confusion, the peaceful and peace-loving Catholic Fathers were robbed of their lands, their converts were scattered, their industries broken up. Nowhere were these uncomfortable years more uncomfortable than in Los Angeles. Revolts, occupations, surrenders, retakings, and resurrenders kept the little town in perpetual ferment. Disorders were the order of the day and of the night, in small matters as well as in great.

The Californian fought as impetuously for his old way of dancing as for his political allegiance. There are comical traditions of the men's determination never to wear long trousers to dances; nor to permit dances to be held in houses or halls, it having been the practice always to give them in outdoor booths or bowers, with latticework walls of sycamore poles lashed together by thongs of rawhide.

Outside these booths the men sat on their horses looking in at the dancing, which was chiefly done by the women. An old man standing in the centre of the enclosure directed the dances. Stopping in front of the girl whom he wished to have join the set, he clapped his hands. She then rose and took her place on the floor; if she could not dance, or wished to decline, she made a low bow and resumed her seat.

To look in on all this was great sport. Sometimes, unable to resist the spell, a man would fling himself off his horse, dash into the enclosure, seize a girl by the waist, whirl around with her through one dance, then out again and into the saddle, where he sat, proudly aware of his vantage. The decorations of masculine attire at this time were such as to make riding a fine show. Around the crown of the broad-brimmed sombrero was twisted a coil of gold or silver cord; over the shoulders was flung, with ostentatious carelessness, a short cloak of velvet or brocade; the waistcoats were embroidered in gold, silver, or gay colors; so also were the knee-breeches, leg-gings, and stockings. Long silken garters, with ornamented tassels at the ends, were wound round and round to hold the stockings in place. Even the cumbrous wooden stirrups were carved in elaborate designs. No wonder that men accustomed to such braveries as these saw ignominy in the plain American trousers.

They seem to have been a variety of Centaur, these early Cali-fornian men. They were seldom off their horses except to eat and sleep. They mounted, with jingling silver spur and glittering bridle, for the shortest distances, even to cross a plaza. They paid long visits on horseback, without dismounting. Clattering up to the win-dow or door-sill, halting, throwing one knee over the crupper, the reins lying loose, they sat at ease, far more at ease than in a house. Only at church, where the separation was inevitable, would they be parted from their horses. They turned the near neighborhood of a church on Sunday into a sort of picket-ground, or horse-trainers' yard, full of horse-posts and horses; and the scene was far more like a horse-fair than like an occasion of holy observance. There seems to have been a curious mixture of reverence and irreverence in their natures. They confessed sins and underwent penances with the simplicity of children; but when, in 1821, the Church issued an edict against that "escandalosisima" dance, the waltz, declaring that whoever dared to dance it should be excommunicated, the merry sinners waltzed on only the harder and faster, and laughed in their priests' faces. And when the advocates of decorum, good order, and indoor dancing gave their first ball in a public hall in Los Angeles, the same merry outdoor party broke every window and door in the building, and put a stop to the festivity. They per-sisted in taking this same summary vengeance on occasion after occasion, until, finally, any person wishing to give a ball in his own house was forced to surround the house by a cordon of police to protect it.

The City of the Angels is a prosperous city now. It has business thoroughfares, blocks of fine stone buildings, hotels, shops, banks, and is growing daily. Its outlying regions are a great circuit of gardens, orchards, vineyards, and corn-fields, and its suburbs are fast filling up with houses of a showy though cheap architecture. But it has not yet shaken off its past. A certain indefinable, delicious aroma from the old, ignorant, picturesque times lingers still, not only in byways and corners, but in the very centres of its newest activities.

Mexican women, their heads wrapped in black shawls, and their bright eyes peering out between the close-gathered folds, glide about everywhere; the soft Spanish speech is continually heard; long-robed priests hurry to and fro; and at each dawn ancient, jangling bells from the Church of the Lady of the Angels ring out the night and in the day. Venders of strange commodities drive in stranger vehicles up and down the streets; antiquated carts piled high with oranges, their golden opulence contrasting weirdly with the shabbiness of their surroundings and the evident poverty of their owner; close following on the gold of one of these, one has sometimes the luck to see another cart, still more antiquated and rickety, piled high with something—he cannot imagine what— terra-cotta red in grotesque shapes; it is fuel,—the same sort which Villavicencia, Quintero, and the rest probably burned, when they burned any, a hundred years ago. It is the roots and root-shoots of manzanita and other shrubs. The colors are superb,—terra-cotta reds, shading up to flesh pink, and down to dark mahogany; but the forms are grotesque beyond comparison: twists, querls, contortions, a boxful of them is an uncomfortable presence in one's room, and putting them on the fire is like cremating the vertebræ and double teeth of colossal monsters of the Pterodactyl period.

The present plaza of the city is near the original plaza marked out at the time of the first settlement; the low adobe house of one of the early governors stands yet on its east side, and is still a habitable building.

The plaza is a dusty and dismal little place, with a parsimonious fountain in the centre, surrounded by spokes of thin turf, and walled at its outer circumference by a row of tall Monterey cypresses, shorn and clipped into the shape of huge croquettes or bradawls standing broad end down. At all hours of the day idle boys and still idler men are to be seen basking on the fountain's stone rim, or lying, face down, heels in air, in the triangles of shade made by the cypress croquettes. There is in Los Angeles much of this ancient and ingenious style of shearing and compressing foliage into unnatural and distorted shapes. It comes, no doubt, of lingering reverence for the traditions of what was thought beautiful in Spain centuries ago; and it gives to the town a certain quaint and foreign look, in admirable keeping with its irregular levels, zigzag, toppling precipices, and houses in tiers one above another.

One comes sometimes abruptly on a picture which seems bewilderingly un-American, of a precipice wall covered with bird-cage cottages, the little, paling-walled yard of one jutting out in a line with the chimney-tops of the next one below, and so on down to the street at the base of the hill. Wooden staircases and bits of terrace link and loop the odd little perches together; bright green pepper-trees, sometimes tall enough to shade two or three tiers of roofs, give a graceful plumed draping at the sides, and some of the steep fronts are covered with bloom, in solid curtains, of geranium, sweet alyssum, heliotrope, and ivy. These terraced eyries are not the homes of the rich: the houses are lilliputian in size, and of cheap quality; but they do more for the picturesqueness of the city than all the large, fine, and costly houses put together.

Moreover, they are the only houses that command the situation, possess distance and a horizon. From some of these little ten-by-twelve flower-beds of homes is a stretch of view which makes each hour of the day a succession of changing splendors, — the snowy peaks of San Bernardino and San Jacinto in the east and south; to the west, vast open country, billowy green with vineyard and orchard; beyond this, in clear weather, shining glints and threads of ocean, and again beyond, in the farthest outing, hill-crowned islands, misty blue against the sky. No one knows Los Angeles who does not climb to these sunny out-lying heights, and roam and linger on them many a day. Nor, even thus lingering, will any one ever know more of Los Angeles than its lovely outward semblances and mysterious suggestions, unless he have the good fortune to win past the barrier of proud, sensitive, tender reserve, behind which is hid the life of the few remaining survivors of the old Spanish and Mexican *régime*.

Once past this, he gets glimpses of the same stintless hospitality and immeasurable courtesy which gave to the old Franciscan establishments a world-wide fame, and to the society whose tone and customs they created an atmosphere of simple-hearted joyousness and generosity never known by any other communities on the American continent.

In houses whose doors seldom open to English-speaking people, there are rooms full of relics of that fast-vanishing past, — strongholds also of a religious faith, almost as obsolete, in its sort and degree, as are the garments of the aged creatures who are peacefully resting their last days on its support.

In one of these houses, in a poverty-stricken but gayly decorated little bedroom, hangs a small oil-painting, a portrait of Saint Francis de Paula. It was brought from Mexico, fifty-five years ago, by the woman who still owns it, and has knelt before it and prayed to it every day of the fifty-five years. Below it is a small altar covered with flowers, candlesticks, vases, and innumerable knick-knacks. A long string under the picture is hung full of tiny gold and silver votive offerings from persons who have been miraculously cured in answer to prayers made to the saint. Legs, arms, hands, eyes, hearts, heads, babies, dogs, horses, — no organ, no creature, that could suffer, is unrepresented. The old woman has at her tongue's end the tale of each one of these miracles. She is herself a sad cripple; her feet swollen by inflammation, which for many years has given her incessant torture and made it impossible for her to walk, except with tottering steps, from room to room, by help of a staff. This, she says, is the only thing her saint has not cured. It is her "cross," her "mortification of the flesh," "to take her to heaven." "He knows best." As she speaks, her eyes perpetually seek the picture, resting on it with a look of ineffable adoration. She has seen tears roll down its cheeks more than once, she says; and it often smiles on her when they are alone. When strangers enter the room, she can always tell, by its expression, whether the saint is or is not pleased with them, and whether their prayers will be granted. She was good enough to remark that he was very glad to see us; she was sure of it by the smile in his eye. He had wrought many beautiful miracles for her. Nothing was too trivial for his sympathy and help. Once when she had broken a vase in which she had been in the habit of keeping flowers on the altar, she took the pieces in her hands, and standing before him, said: "You know you will miss this vase. I always put your flowers in it, and I am too poor to buy another. Now, do mend this for me. I have nobody but you to help me." And the vase grew together again whole while she was speaking. In the same way he mended for her a high glass flower-case which stood on the altar.

Thus she jabbered away breathlessly in Spanish, almost too fast to be followed. Sitting in a high chair, her poor distorted feet propped on a cushion, a black silk handkerchief wound like a turban around her head, a plaid ribosa across her shoulders, contrasting sharply with her shabby wine-colored gown, her hands clasped around a yellow staff, on which she leaned as she bent forward in her eager speaking, she made a study for an artist.

She was very beautiful in her youth, she said; her cheeks so red that people thought they were painted, and she was so strong that she was never tired; and when, in the first year of her widowhood, a stranger came to her "with a letter of recommendation" to be her second husband, and before she had time to speak had fallen on his knees at her feet, she seized him by the throat, and toppling him backward, pinned him against the wall till he was black in the face. And her sister came running up in terror, imploring her not to kill him. But all that strength is gone now, she says sadly; her memory also. Each day, as soon as she has finished her prayers, she has to put away her rosary in a special place, or else she forgets that the prayers have been said. Many priests have desired to possess her precious miracle-working saint; but never till she dies will it leave her bedroom. Not a week passes without some one's arriving to implore its aid. Sometimes the deeply distressed come on their knees all the way from the gate before the house, up the steps, through the hall, and into her bedroom. Such occasions as these are to her full of solemn joy, and no doubt, also, of a secret exultation whose kinship to pride she does not suspect.

In another unpretending little adobe house, not far from this Saint Francis shrine, lives the granddaughter of Moreno, one of the twelve Spanish soldiers who founded the city. She speaks no word of English; and her soft black eyes are timid, though she is the widow of a general, and in the stormy days of the City of the Angels passed through many a crisis of peril and adventure. Her house is full of curious relics, which she shows with a gentle, half-amused courtesy. It is not easy for her to believe that any American can feel real reverence for the symbols, tokens, and relics of the life and customs which his people destroyed. In her mind Americans remain to-day as completely foreigners as they were when her husband girded on his sword and went out to fight them, forty years ago. Many of her relics have been rescued at one time or another from plunderers of the missions. She has an old bronze kettle which once held holy water at San Fernando; an incense cup and spoon, and massive silver candlesticks; cartridge-boxes of leather, with Spain's ancient seal stamped on them; a huge copper caldron and scales from San Gabriel; a bunch of keys of hammered iron, locks, scissors, reaping-hooks, shovels, carding-brushes for wool and for flax: all made by the Indian workmen in the missions. There was also one old lock, in which the key was rusted fast and immovable, which seemed to me fuller of suggestion than anything else there of the sealed and ended past to which it had belonged; and a curious little iron cannon, in shape like an ale-mug, about eight inches high, with a hole in the side and in the top, to be used by setting it on the ground and laying a trail of powder to the opening in the side. This gave the Indians great delight. It was fired at the times of church festivals, and in seasons of drought to bring rain. Another curious instrument of racket was the matrarca, a strip of board with two small swinging iron handles so set in it that in swinging back and forth they hit iron plates. In the time of Lent when all ringing of bells was forbidden, these were rattled to call the Indians to church. The noise one of them can make when vigorously shaken is astonishing. In crumpled bundles, their stiffened meshes opening out reluctantly, were two curious rush-woven nets which had been used by Indian women fifty years ago in carrying burdens. Similar nets, made of twine, are used by them still. Fastened to a leather strap or band passing around the forehead, they hang down behind far below the waist, and when filled out to their utmost holding capacity are so heavy that the poor creatures bend nearly double beneath them. But the women stand as uncomplainingly as camels while weight after weight is piled in; then slipping the band over their heads, they adjust the huge burden and set off at a trot. "This is the squaw's horse," said an Indian woman in the San Jacinto valley one day, tapping her forehead and laughing good-naturedly, when the shopkeeper remonstrated with her husband, who was heaping article after article, and finally a large sack of flour, on her shoulders; "squaw's horse very strong."

———

In the western suburbs of Los Angeles is a low adobe house, built after the ancient style, on three sides of a square, surrounded by orchards, vineyards, and orange groves, and looking out on an old-fashioned garden, in which southernwood, rue, lavender, mint, marigolds, and gillyflowers hold their own bravely, growing in straight and angular beds among the newer splendors of verbenas, roses, carnations, and geraniums. On two sides of the house runs a broad porch, where stand rows of geraniums and chrysanthemums growing in odd-shaped earthen pots. Here may often be seen a beautiful young Mexican woman, flitting about among the plants, or sporting with a superb Saint Bernard dog. Her clear olive skin, soft brown eyes, delicate sensitive nostrils, and broad smiling mouth, are all of the Spanish madonna type; and when her low brow is bound, as is often her wont, by turban folds of soft brown or green gauze, her face becomes a picture indeed. She is the young wife of a gray-headed Mexican señor, of whom—by his own most gracious permission—I shall speak by his familiar name, Don Antonio. Whoever has the fortune to pass as a friend across the threshold of this house finds himself transported, as by a miracle, into the life of a half-century ago. The rooms are ornamented with fans, shells, feather and wax flowers, pictures, saints' images, old laces, and stuffs, in the quaint gay Mexican fashion. On the day when I first saw them, they were brilliant with bloom. In every one of the deep window-seats stood a cone of bright flowers, its base made by large white datura blossoms, their creamy whorls all turned outward, making a superb decoration. I went for but a few moments' call. I stayed three hours, and left carrying with me bewildering treasures of pictures of the olden time.

Don Antonio speaks little English; but the señora knows just enough of the language to make her use of it delicious, as she translates for her husband. It is an entrancing sight to watch his dark weather-beaten face, full of lightning changes as he pours out torrents of his nervous, eloquent Spanish speech; watching his wife intently, hearkening to each word she uses, sometimes interrupting her urgently with, "No, no; that is not it,"—for he well understands the tongue he cannot or will not use for himself. He is sixty-five years of age, but he is young: the best waltzer in Los Angeles to-day; his eye keen, his blood fiery quick; his memory like a burning-glass bringing into sharp light and focus a half-century as if it were a yesterday. Full of sentiment, of an intense and poetic nature, he looks back to the lost empire of his race and people on the California shores with a sorrow far too proud for any antagonisms or complaints. He recognizes the inexorableness of the laws under whose workings his nation is slowly, surely giving place to one more representative of the age. Intellectually he is in sympathy with progress, with reform, with civilization at its utmost; he would not have had them stayed or changed, because his people could not keep up and were not ready. But his heart is none the less saddened and lonely.

This is probably the position and point of view of most cultivated Mexican men of his age. The suffering involved in it is inevitable. It is part of the great, unreckoned price which must always be paid for the gain the world gets when the young and strong supersede the old and weak.

A sunny little southeast corner room in Don Antonio's house is full of the relics of the time when he and his father were foremost representatives of ideas and progress in the City of the Angels, and taught the first school that was kept in the place. This was nearly a half-century ago. On the walls of the room still hang maps and charts which they used; and carefully preserved, with the tender reverence of which only poetic natures are capable, are still to be seen there the old atlases, primers, catechisms, grammars, reading-books, which meant toil and trouble to the merry, ignorant children of the merry and ignorant people of that time.

The leathern covers of the books are thin and frayed by long handling; the edges of the leaves worn down as if mice had gnawed them: tattered, loose, hanging by yellow threads, they look far older than they are, and bear vivid record of the days when books were so rare and precious that each book did doubled and redoubled duty, passing from hand to hand and house to house. It was on the old Lancaster system that Los Angeles set out in educating its children; and here are still preserved the formal and elaborate instructions for teachers and schools on that plan; also volumes of Spain's laws for military judges in 1781, and a quaint old volume called "Secrets of Agriculture, Fields and Pastures," written by a Catholic Father in 1617, reprinted in 1781, and held of great value in its day as a sure guide to success with crops. Accompanying it was a chart, a perpetual circle, by which might be foretold with certainty what years would be barren and what ones fruitful.

Almanacs, histories, arithmetics, dating back to 1750, drawing-books, multiplication tables, music, and bundles of records of the branding of cattle at the San Gabriel Mission, are among the curiosities of this room. The music of the first quadrilles ever danced in Mexico is here: a ragged pamphlet, which, no doubt, went gleeful rounds in the City of the Angels for many a year. It is a merry music, simple in melody, but with an especial quality of light-heartedness, suiting the people who danced to it.

There are also in the little room many relics of a more substantial sort than tattered papers and books: a branding-iron and a pair of handcuffs from the San Gabriel Mission; curiously decorated clubs and sticks used by the Indians in their games; boxes of silver rings and balls made for decorations of bridles and on leggings and knee-breeches. The place of honor in the room is given, as well it might be, to a small cannon, the first cannon brought into California. It was made in 1717, and was brought by Father Junipero Serra to San Diego in 1769. Afterward it was given to the San Gabriel Mission, but it still bears its old name, "San Diego." It is an odd little arm, only about two feet long, and requiring but six ounces of powder. Its swivel is made with a rest to set firm in the ground. It has taken many long journeys on the backs of mules, having been in great requisition in the early mission days for the firing of salutes at festivals and feasts.

Don Antonio was but a lad when his father's family removed from the city of Mexico to California. They came in one of the many unfortunate colonies sent out by the Mexican Government during the first years of the secularization period, having had a toilsome and suffering two months, going in wagons from Mexico to San Blas, then a tedious and uncomfortable voyage of several weeks from San Blas to Monterey, where they arrived only to find themselves deceived and disappointed in every particular, and surrounded by

hostilities, plots, and dangers on all sides. So great was the antago-
nism to them that it was at times difficult for a colonist to obtain food
from a Californian. They were arrested on false pretences, thrown
into prison, shipped off like convicts from place to place, with no one
to protect them or plead their cause. Revolution succeeded upon
revolution, and it was a most unhappy period for all refined and cultivated persons who had joined the colony enterprises. Young men
of education and breeding were glad to earn their daily bread by any
menial labor that offered. Don Antonio and several of his young
friends, who had all studied medicine together, spent the greater
part of a year in making shingles. The one hope and aim of most of
them was to earn money enough to get back to Mexico. Don Antonio, however, seems to have had more versatility and capacity than
his friends, for he never lost courage; and it was owing to him that
at last his whole family gathered in Los Angeles and established
a home there. This was in 1836. There were then only about eight
hundred people in the pueblo, and the customs, superstitions, and
ignorances of the earliest days still held sway. The missions were still
rich and powerful, though the confusions and conflicts of their ruin
had begun. At this time the young Antonio, being quick at accounts
and naturally ingenious at all sorts of mechanical crafts, found profit
as well as pleasure in journeying from mission to mission, sometimes spending two or three months in one place, keeping books,
or repairing silver and gold ornaments. The blowpipe which he made
for himself at that time his wife exhibits now with affectionate pride;
and there are few things she enjoys better than translating to an
eager listener his graphic stories of the incidents and adventures of
that portion of his life.

While he was at the San Antonio Mission, a strange thing happened. It is a good illustration of the stintless hospitality of those old
missions, that staying there at that time were a notorious gambler
and a celebrated juggler who had come out in the colony from Mexico. The juggler threatened to turn the gambler into a crow; the
gambler, after watching his tricks for a short time, became frightened, and asked young Antonio, in serious good faith, if he did not
believe the juggler had made a league with the devil. A few nights
afterward, at midnight, a terrible noise was heard in the gambler's
room. He was found in convulsions, foaming at the mouth, and

crying, "Oh, Father! Father! I have got the devil inside of me! Take him away!" The priest dragged him into the chapel, showered him with holy water, and exorcised the devil, first making the gambler promise to leave off his gambling forever. All the rest of the night the rescued sinner spent in the chapel, praying and weeping. In the morning he announced his intention of becoming a priest, and began his studies at once. These he faithfully pursued for a year, leading all the while a life of great devotion. At the end of that time preparations were made for his ordination at San José. The day was set, the hour came: he was in the sacristy, had put on the sacred vestments, and was just going toward the church door, when he fell to the floor, dead. Soon after this the juggler was banished from the country, trouble and disaster having everywhere followed on his presence.

On the first breaking out of hostilities between California and the United States, Don Antonio took command of a company of Los Angeles volunteers to repel the intruders. By this time he had attained a prominent position in the affairs of the pueblo; had been alcalde and, under Governor Michelorena, inspector of public works. It was like the fighting of children, — the impetuous attempts that heterogeneous little bands of Californians here and there made to hold their country. They were plucky from first to last; for they were everywhere at a disadvantage, and fought on, quite in the dark as to what Mexico meant to do about them, — whether she might not any morning deliver them over to the enemy. Of all Don Antonio's graphic narratives of the olden time, none is more interesting than those which describe his adventures during the days of this contest. On one of the first approaches made by the Americans to Los Angeles, he went out with his little haphazard company of men and boys to meet them. He had but one cannon, a small one, tied by ropes on a cart axle. He had but one small keg of powder which was good for anything; all the rest was bad, would merely go off "pouf, pouf," the señora said, and the ball would pop down near the mouth of the cannon. With this bad powder he fired his first shots. The Americans laughed; this is child's play, they said, and pushed on closer. Then came a good shot, with the good powder, tearing into their ranks and knocking them right and left; another, and another. "Then the Americans began to think, these are no pouf balls; and when a few more were killed, they ran away and left their flag behind them. And if they had only known it, the Californians had only one more charge left of the good powder, and the next minute it would have been the Californians that would have had to run away themselves," merrily laughed the señora, as she told the tale.

This captured flag, with important papers, was intrusted to Don Antonio to carry to the Mexican headquarters at Sonora. He set off with an escort of soldiers, his horse decked with silver trappings; his sword, pistols, all of the finest: a proud beginning of a journey destined to end in a different fashion. It was in winter time; cold rains were falling. By night he was drenched to the skin, and stopped at a friendly Indian's tent to change his clothes. Hardly had he got them off when the sound of horses' hoofs was heard. The Indian flung himself down, put his ear to the ground, and exclaimed, "Americanos! Americanos!" Almost in the same second they were at the tent's door. As they halted, Don Antonio, clad only in his drawers and stockings, crawled out at the back of the tent, and creeping on all fours reached a tree, up which he climbed, and sat safe hidden in the darkness among its branches listening, while his pursuers cross-questioned the Indian, and at last rode away with his horse. Luckily, he had carried into the tent the precious papers and the captured flag: these he intrusted to an Indian to take to Sonora, it being evidently of no use for him to try to cross the country thus closely pursued by his enemies.

All night he lay hidden; the next day he walked twelve miles across the mountains to an Indian village where he hoped to get a horse. It was dark when he reached it. Cautiously he opened the door of the hut of one whom he knew well. The Indian was preparing poisoned arrows; fixing one on the string and aiming at the door, he called out angrily, "Who is there?"—"It is I, Antonio."—"Don't make a sound," whispered the Indian, throwing down his arrow, springing to the door, coming out, and closing it softly. He then proceeded to tell him that the Americans had offered a reward for his head, and that some of the Indians in the rancheria were ready to betray or kill him. While they were yet talking, again came the sound of the Americans' horses' hoofs galloping in the distance. This time there seemed no escape. Suddenly Don Antonio, throwing himself on his stomach, wriggled into a cactus patch near by.

Only one who has seen California cactus thickets can realize the desperateness of this act. But it succeeded. The Indian threw over the cactus plants an old blanket and some refuse stalks and reeds; and there once more, within hearing of all his baffled pursuers said, the hunted man lay, safe, thanks to Indian friendship. The crafty Indian assented to all the Americans proposed, said that Don Antonio would be sure to be caught in a few days, advised them to search in a certain rancheria which he described, a few miles off, and in an opposite direction from the way in which he intended to guide Don Antonio. As soon as the Americans had gone, he bound up Antonio's feet in strips of rawhide, gave him a blanket and an old tattered hat, the best his stores afforded, and then led him by a long and difficult trail to a spot high up in the mountains where the old women of the band were gathering acorns. By the time they reached this place, blood was trickling from Antonio's feet and legs, and he was well-nigh fainting with fatigue and excitement. Tears rolled down the old women's cheeks when they saw him. Some of them had been servants in his father's house, and loved him. One brought gruel; another bathed his feet; others ran in search of healing leaves of different sorts. Bruising these in a stone mortar, they rubbed him from head to foot with the wet fibre. All his pain and weariness vanished as by magic. His wounds healed, and in a day he was ready to set off for home. There was but one pony in the old women's camp. This was old, vicious, blind of one eye, and with one ear cropped short; but it looked to Don Antonio far more beautiful than the gay steed on which he had ridden away from Los Angeles three days before. There was one pair of ragged shoes of enormous size among the old women's possessions. These were strapped on his feet by leathern thongs, and a bit of old sheepskin was tied around the pony's body. Thus accoutred and mounted, shivering in his drawers under his single blanket, the captain and flag-bearer turned his face homeward. At the first friend's house he reached he stopped and begged for food. Some dried meat was given to him, and a stool on the porch offered to him. It was the house of a dear friend, and the friend's sister was his sweetheart. As he sat there eating his meat, the women eyed him curiously. One said to the other, "How much he looks like Antonio!" At last the sweetheart, coming nearer, asked him if he were "any relation of Don Antonio." "No," he said. Just at that moment his friend rode up, gave one glance at the pitiful beggar sitting on his porch, shouted his name, dashed toward him, and seized him in his arms. Then was a great laughing and half-weeping, for it had been rumored that he had been taken prisoner by the Americans.

From this friend he received a welcome gift of a pair of trousers, many inches too short for his legs. At the next house his friend was as much too tall, and his second pair of gift trousers had to be rolled up in thick folds around his ankles.

Finally he reached Los Angeles in safety. Halting in a grove outside the town, he waited till twilight before entering. Having disguised himself in the rags which he had worn from the Indian village, he rode boldly up to the porch of his father's house, and in an impudent tone called for brandy. The terrified women began to scream; but his youngest sister, fixing one piercing glance on his face, laughed out gladly, and cried, "You can't fool me; you are Antonio."

Sitting in the little corner room, looking out through the open door on the gay garden and breathing its spring air, gay even in midwinter, and as spicy then as the gardens of other lands are in June, I spent many an afternoon listening to such tales as this. Sunset always came long before its time, it seemed, on these days.

Occasionally, at the last moment, Don Antonio would take up his guitar, and, in a voice still sympathetic and full of melody, sing an old Spanish love-song, brought to his mind by thus living over the events of his youth. Never, however, in his most ardent youth, could his eyes have gazed on his fairest sweetheart's face with a look of greater devotion than that with which they now rest on the noble, expressive countenance of his wife, as he sings the ancient and tender strains. Of one of them I once won from her, amid laughs and blushes, a few words of translation: —

> "Let us hear the sweet echo
>   Of your sweet voice that charms me.
>   The one that truly loves you,
>   He says he wishes to love;
>   That the one who with ardent love adores you,
>   Will sacrifice himself for you.

Do not deprive me,
Owner of me,
Of that sweet echo
Of your sweet voice that charms me."

Near the western end of Don Antonio's porch is an orange-tree, on which were hanging at this time twenty-five hundred oranges, ripe and golden among the glossy leaves. Under this tree my carriage always waited for me. The señora never allowed me to depart without bringing to me, in the carriage, farewell gifts of flowers and fruit: clusters of grapes, dried and fresh; great boughs full of oranges, more than I could lift. As I drove away thus, my lap filled with bloom and golden fruit, canopies of golden fruit over my head, I said to myself often: "Fables are prophecies. The Hesperides have come true."

Mary Austin

The story of Southern California has always been a story of land and water: the conflict between the drive to develop a desert terrain and the need to conserve diminishing water resources. In "The Land," originally published as the first story in her collection *Lost Borders* (1909), Mary Austin (1868–1934) captures the unforgiving nature of the physical landscape upon which the elaborately enticing superstructures of California are built. Austin drew on firsthand experience. Raised in Illinois, she moved west at the age of twenty, homesteaded near Fort Tejon, and settled for a time in the Owens Valley, some 250 miles northeast of Los Angeles; later, she opposed the notorious scheme by which the city diverted water from the valley, a process that led to the destruction of many farming communities. Her 1917 novel *The Ford* dramatizes the valley's fate, although oddly Austin changed the setting to Northern California. Austin's prolific literary output encompassed novels, memoirs, poetry, and religious writings, and she maintained an energetic correspondence with figures as varied as Sinclair Lewis, Isadora Duncan, H. G. Wells, Theodore Roosevelt, and Marianne Moore.

THE LAND

When the Paiute nations broke westward through the Sierra wall they cut off a remnant of the Shoshones, and forced them south as far as Death Valley and the borders of the Mojaves, they penned the Washoes in and around Tahoe, and passing between these two, established themselves along the snow-fed Sierra creeks. And this it was proper they should do, for the root of their name-word is Pah, meaning water, to distinguish them from their brothers the Utes of the Great Basin.

In time they passed quite through the saw-cut cañons by Kern and Kings rivers and possessed all the east slope of the San Joaquin, but chiefly they settled by small clans and family groups where the pines leave off and the sage begins and the desert abuts on the great Sierra fault. On the northeast they touched the extreme flanks of the Utes, and with them and the southerly tribes swept a wide arc about that region of mysterious desertness of which you shall presently hear more particularly.

The boundaries between the tribes and between the clans within the tribe were plainly established by natural landmarks — peaks, hill-crests, creeks, and chains of water-holes — beginning at the foot of the Sierra and continuing eastward past the limit of endurable exis-tence. Out there, a week's journey from everywhere, the land was not worth parcelling off, and the boundaries which should logically have been continued until they met the cañon of the Colorado ran out in foolish wastes of sand and inextricable disordered ranges. Here you have the significance of the Indian name for that country — Lost Borders. And you can always trust Indian names to express to you the largest truth about any district in the shortest phrases.

But there is more in the name than that. For law runs with the boundary, not beyond it; it is as fast to the given landmarks as a limpet to its scar on the rock. I am convinced most men make law for the comfortable feel of it, defining them to themselves; they shoulder along like blindworms, rearing against restrictions, turn-ing thereward for security as climbing plants to the warmth of a nearing wall. They pinch themselves with regulations to make sure of being sentient, and organize within organizations.

Out there, then, where the law and the landmarks fail together, the souls of little men fade out at the edges, leak from them as water from wooden pails warped asunder.

Out there where the borders of conscience break down, where there is no convention, and behavior is of little account except as it gets you your desire, almost anything might happen; does happen, in fact, though I shall have trouble making you believe it. Out there where the boundary of soul and sense is as faint as a trail in a sand-storm, I have seen things happen that I do not believe myself. That is what you are to expect in a country where the names mean some-thing. Ubehebe, Pharanagat, Resting Springs, Dead Man's Gulch, Funeral Mountains — these beckon and allure. There is always a tang of reality about them like the smart of wood smoke to the eyes, that warns of neighboring fires.

Riding through by the known trails, the senses are obsessed by the coil of a huge and senseless monotony; straight, white, blinding, alkali flats, forsaken mesas; skimpy shrubs growing little and less, starved knees of hills sticking out above them; black clots of pines high upon rubbishy mountain-heads — days and days of this, as if Nature herself had obscured the medium to escape you in her secret operations.

One might travel weeks on end and not come on any place or occasion whereby men may live, and drop suddenly into close hives of them digging, jostling, drinking, lusting, and rejoicing. Every story of that country is colored by the fashion of the life there, breaking up in swift, passionate intervals between long, dun stretches, like the land that out of hot sinks of desolation heaves up great bulks of granite ranges with opal shadows playing in their shining, snow-piled curves. Out there beyond the borders are the Shivering Dunes, heaps upon heaps of blinding sand all acrawl in the wind, drifting and reforming with a faint, stridulent rustle, and black, wall-sided box-cañons that give the stars at midday, scored over with picture-writings of a forgotten race. There are lakes there of a pellucid clearness like ice, closed over with man-deep crystals of pure salt. Long Tom Bassit told me a story of one of these which he had from a man who saw it. It was of an emigrant train all out of its reckoning, laboring in a long, hollow trough of desolation between waterless high ranges, arriving at such a closed salt-pit, too much spent to go around it and trusting the salt crust to hold under their racked wagons and starveling teams. But when they had come near the middle of the lake, the salt thinned out abruptly, and, the forward rank of the party breaking through, the bodies were caught under the saline slabs and not all of them recovered. There was a woman among them, and the Man-who-saw had cared — cared enough to go back years afterward, when, after successive oven-blast summers, the salt held solidly over all the lake, and he told Tom Bassit how, long before he reached the point, he saw the gleam of red in the woman's dress, and found her at last, lying on her side, sealed in the crystal, rising as ice rises to the surface of choked streams. Long Tom wished me to make a story of it. I did once at a dinner, but I never got through with it. There, about the time the candles began to burn their shades and red track of the light on the wine-glasses barred the cloth, with the white, disdainful shoulders and politely incredulous faces leaning through the smoke of cigarettes, it had a garish sound. Afterward I came across the proof of the affair in the records of the emigrant party, but I never tried telling it again.

That is why in all that follows I have set down what the Borderers thought and felt; for that you have a touchstone in your *own* heart, but I should get no credit with you if I were to tell what really became of Loring, and what happened to the man who went down into the moaning pit of Sand Mountain.

Curiously, in that country, you can get anybody to believe any sort of a tale that has gold in it, like the Lost Mine of Fisherman's Peak and the Duke o' Wild Rose. Young Woodin brought me a potsherd once from a kitchen-midden in Shoshone Land. It might have been, for antiquity, one of those Job scraped himself withal, but it was dotted all over with colors and specks of pure gold from the river bed from which the sand and clay were scooped. Said he:

"You ought to find a story about this somewhere."

I was sore then about not getting myself believed in some elementary matters, such as that horned toads are not poisonous, and that Indians really have the bowels of compassion. Said I:

"I will do better than that, I will *make* a story."

We sat out a whole afternoon under the mulberry-tree, with the landscape disappearing in shimmering heat-waves around us, testing our story for likelihood and proving it. There was an Indian woman in the tale, not pretty, for they are mostly not that in life, and the earthenware pot, of course, and a lost river bedded with precious sand. Afterward my friend went to hold down some claims in the Coso country, and I north to the lake region where the red firs are, and we told the pot-of-gold story as often as we were permitted. One night when I had done with it, a stranger by our camp-fire said the thing was well known in his country. I said, "Where was that?"

"Coso," said he, and that was the first I had heard of my friend.

Next winter, at Lone Pine, a prospector from Panamint-way wanted to know if I had ever heard of the Indian-pot Mine which was lost out toward Pharump. I said I had a piece of the pot, which I showed him. Then I wrote the tale for a magazine of the sort that gets taken in camps and at miners' boarding-houses, and several men were at great pains to explain to me where my version varied from the accepted one of the hills. By this time, you understand, I had begun to believe the story myself. I had a spasm of conscience, though, when Tennessee told me that he thought he knew the very squaw of the story, and when the back of the winter was broken he meant to make a little "pasear" in search of the lost river. But Tennessee died before spring, and spared my confessing. Now it only needs that some one should find another sherd of the gold-besprinkled pot to fix the tale in the body of desert myths. Well—it had as much fact behind it as the Gunsight, and is more interesting than the Bryfogle, which began with the finding of a dead man, clothless as the desert dead mostly are, with a bag of nuggets clutched in his mummied hands.

First and last, accept no man's statement that he knows this Country of Lost Borders well. A great number having lost their lives in the process of proving where it is not safe to go, it is now possible to pass through much of the district by guide-posts and well-known water-holes, but the best part of it remains locked, in-violate, or at best known only to some far-straying Indian, sheep-herder, or pocket hunter, whose account of it does not get into the reports of the Geological Survey. But a boast of knowledge is likely to prove as hollow as the little yellow gourds called apples of Death Valley.

Pure desertness clings along the pits of the long valleys and the formless beds of vanished lakes. Every hill that lifts as high as the cloud-line has some trees upon it, and deer and bighorn to feed on the tall, tufted, bunch grass between the boulders. In the year when Tonopah, turning upon itself like a swarm, trickled prospectors all over that country from Hot Creek to the Armagosa, Indians brought me word that the men had camped so close about the water-holes that the bighorn died of thirst on the headlands, turned always in the last agony toward the man-infested springs.

That is as good a pointer as any if you go waterless in the coun-try of Lost Borders: where you find cattle dropped, skeleton or skin dried, the heads almost invariably will be turned toward the places where water-holes should be. But no such reminders will fend men from its trails. This is chiefly, I am persuaded, because there is something incomprehensible to the man-mind in the concurrence of death and beauty. Shall the tender opal mist betray you? the airy depth of mountain blueness, the blazonry of painted wind-scoured buttes, the far peaks molten with the alpen glow, cooled by the ris-ing of the velvet violet twilight tide, and the leagues and leagues of stars? As easy for a man to believe that a beautiful woman can be cruel. Mind you, it is men who go mostly into the desert, who love it past all reasonableness, slack their ambitions, cast off old usages, neglect their families because of the pulse and beat of a life laid bare to its thews and sinews. Their women hate with implicitness the life like the land, stretching interminably whity-brown, dim and shadowy blue hills that hem it, glimmering pale waters of mirage that creep and crawl about its edges. There was a woman once at Agua Hedionda—but you wouldn't believe that either.

If the desert were a woman, I know well what like she would be: deep-breasted, broad in the hips, tawny, with tawny hair, great masses of it lying smooth along her perfect curves, full lipped like a sphinx, but not heavy-lidded like one, eyes sane and steady as the polished jewel of her skies, such a countenance as should make men serve without desiring her, such a largeness to her mind as should make their sins of no account, passionate, but not necessitous, patient—and you could not move her, no, not if you had all the earth to give, so much as one tawny hair's-breadth beyond her own desires. If you cut very deeply into any soul that has the mark of the land upon it, you find such qualities as these—as I shall presently prove to you.

Stewart Edward White

Of all America's cities, none has ever hyped itself quite so shamelessly as Los Angeles. The booster myth has been a central aspect of L.A.'s self-image since as far back as the 1870s, when the first transcontinental railroads rolled into town. In an episode from *The Rules of the Game* (1910), the popular and prolific novelist Stewart Edward White (1873–1946) offers an early example of that ethos in action, portraying a Los Angeles where everything is bigger, stranger, and endlessly promoted—less an urban landscape than, in the words of Carey McWilliams, "a great circus without a tent." It is perhaps surprising to see, in White's early sketch, so much of Los Angeles's trademark image already in place. Ironically, in view of his skeptical presentation of the young city's burgeoning cults and newfangled religions, White himself became a fervent proponent of spiritualism.

from

THE RULES OF THE GAME

B ob went on to Los Angeles with the sprightly Baker. At first glance the city seemed to him like any other. Then, as he wandered its streets, the marvel and vigour and humour of the place seized on him.

"Don't you suppose I see the joke?" complained Baker at the end of one of their long trolley rides. "Just get onto that house; it looks like a mission-style switch engine. And the one next to it, built to shed snow. Funny! sure it's funny. But you ain't talking to me! It's alive! Those fellows wanted something different from anybody else—so does everybody. After they'd used up the regular styles, they had to make 'em up out of the fresh air. But anyway, they weren't satisfied just to copy Si Golosh's idea of a Noah's Ark chicken coop."

They stopped opposite very elaborate and impressive iron gates opening across a graded street. These gates were supported by a pair of stone towers crowned with tiles. A smaller pair of towers and gates guarded the concrete sidewalk. As a matter of fact, all these barriers enclosed nothing, for even in the remote possibility that the inquiring visitor should find them shut, an insignificant détour would circumvent their fenceless flanks.

"Maudsley Court," Bob read sculptured on one of the towers.

"That makes this particular subdivision mighty exclusive," grinned Baker. "Now if you were a homeseeker wouldn't you love to bring your dinner pail back to the cawstle every night?"

Bob peered down the single street. It was graded, guttered and sidewalked. A small sentry box labelled "office," and inscribed with glowing eulogiums, occupied a strategic position near the gates. From this house Bob immediately became aware of close scrutiny by a man half concealed by the indoor dimness.

"The spider," said Baker. "He's onto us big as a house. He can spot a yap at four hundred yards' range, and you bet they don't get much nearer than that alone."

A huge sign shrieked of Maudsley Court. "Get a grin!" was its first advice.

"They all try for a catchword—every one of 'em," explained Baker. "You'll see all kinds in the ads; some pretty good, most of 'em rotten."

"They seem to have made a start, anyway," observed Bob, indicating a new cottage half way down the street. It was a super-artistic structure, exhibiting the ends of huge brown beams at all points. Baker laughed.

"That's what it's intended to seem," said he. "That's the come-on house. It's built by the spider. It's stick-um for the flies. 'This is going to be a high-brow proposition,' says the intending purchaser; 'look at the beautiful house already up. I must join this young and thriving colony.' Hence this settled look."

He waved his hand abroad. Dotted over the low, rounded hills of the charming landscapes were new and modern bungalows. They were spaced widely, and each was flanked by an advertising board and guarded by a pair of gates shutting their private thoroughfares from the country highways. Between them showed green the new crops.

"Nine out of ten come-on houses," said Baker, "and all exclusive. If you can't afford iron gates, you can at least put up a pair of shingled pillars. It's the game."

"Will these lots ever be sold?" asked Bob.

"Out here, yes," replied Baker. "That's part of the joke. The methods are on the blink, but the goods insist on delivering themselves. Most of these fellows are just bunks or optimists. All hands are surprised when things turn out right. But if *all* the lots are ever sold, Los Angeles will have a population of five million."

They boarded an inward-bound trolley. Bob read the devices as they flashed past. "Hill-top Acres," he read near a street plastered against an apparently perpendicular hill. "Buy before the rise!" advised this man's rival at its foot. The true suburbs strung by in a panorama of strange little houses—imitation Swiss châlets jostling bastard Moorish, cobblestones elbowing plaster—a bewildering succession of forced effects. Baker caught Bob's expression.

"These are workingmen's and small clerks' houses," he said quietly. "Pretty bad, eh? But they're trying. Remember what they lived in back East."

Bob recalled the square, painted, ugly, featureless boxes built all after the same pattern of dreariness. He looked on this gay bewilderment of bad taste with more interest.

"At least they're taking notice," said Baker, lighting his pipe. "And every fellow raises *some* kind of posies."

A few moments later they plunged into the vortex of the city and the smiling country, the far plains toward the sea, and the circle of the mountains were lost. Only remained overhead the blue of the California sky.

Baker led the way toward a blaring basement restaurant.

"I'm beginning to feel that I'll have to find some monkey-food somewhere, or cash in," said he.

They found a table and sat down.

"This is the place to see all the sights," proffered Baker, his broad face radiating satisfaction. "When they strike it rich on the desert, they hike right in here. That fat lady thug yonder is worth between three and four millions. Eight months ago she did washing at two bits a shirt while her husband drove a one-man prospect shaft. The other day she blew into the big jewelry store and wanted a thirty-thousand-dollar diamond necklace. The boss rolled over twice and wagged his tail. 'Yes, madam,' said he; 'what kind?' 'I dunno; just a thirty-thousand-dollar one.' That's all he could get out of her. 'But tell me how you want 'em set,' he begged. She looked bewildered. *'Oh, set 'em so they'll jingle,'* says she."

After the meal they walked down the principal streets, watching the crowd. It was a large crowd, as though at busy midday, and variously apparelled, from fur coat to straw hat. Each extreme of costume seemed justified, either by the balmy summer-night effect of the California open air, or by the hint of chill that crept from the distant mountains. Either aspect could be welcomed or ignored by a very slight effort of the will. Electric signs blazed everywhere. Bob was struck by the numbers of clairvoyants, palm readers, Hindu frauds, crazy cults, fake healers, Chinese doctors, and the like thus lavishly advertised. The class that elsewhere is pressed by necessity to the inexpensive dinginess of back streets, here blossomed forth in truly tropical luxuriance. Street vendors with all sorts of things, from mechanical toys to spot eradicators, spread their portable layouts at every corner. Vacant lots were crowded with spielers of all sorts—religious or political fanatics, vendors of cure-alls, of universal tools, of marvellous axle grease, of anything and everything to catch the idle dollar. Brilliantly lighted shops called the passer-by to contemplate the latest wave-motor, flying machine, door check, or what-not. Stock in these enterprises was for sale—and was being sold! Other sidewalk booths, like those ordinarily used as dispensaries of hot doughnuts and coffee, offered wild-cat mining shares, oil stock and real estate in some highly speculative suburb. Great stores of curios lay open to the tourist trade. Here one could buy sheepskin Indian moccasins made in Massachusetts, or abalone shells, or burnt-leather pillows, or a whole collection of photographic views so minute that they could all be packed in a single walnut shell. Next door were shops of Japanese and Chinese goods presided over by suave, sleepy-eyed Orientals, in wonderful brocade, wearing the close cap with the red coral button atop. Shooting galleries spit spitefully. Gasolene torches flared.

Baker strolled along, his hands in his pockets, his hat on the back of his head. From time to time he cast an amused glance at his companion.

"Come in here," he said abruptly.

Bob found himself comfortably seated in a commodious open-air theatre, watching an excellent vaudeville performance.

He enjoyed it thoroughly, for it was above the average. In fifteen minutes, however, the last soubrette disappeared in the wings to the accompaniment of a swirl of music. Her place was taken by a tall, facetious-looking, bald individual, clad in a loose frock coat. He held up his hand for silence.

"Ladies 'n' gentlemen," he drawled, "we hope you have enjoyed yourselves. If you find a better show than this in any theatre in town, barring the Orpheum, come and tell us about it and we will see what we can do to brace ours up. I don't believe you can. This show will be repeated every afternoon and evening, with complete change of programme twice a week. Go away and tell your friends about the great free show down on Spring Street. Just tell them about it."

Bob glanced startled at his companion. Baker was grinning.

"This show has cost us up to date," went on the leisurely drawl, "just twenty-eight hundred dollars. Go and tell your friends that. *But"* — he suddenly straightened his figure and his voice became more incisive — "that is not enough. We have decided to give you something *real* to talk about. We have decided to give every man, woman and child in this vast audience a first-night present of Two Silver Dollars!"

Bob could feel an electric thrill run through the crowd, and every one sat up a little straighter in his chair.

"Let me see," the orator went on, running his eye over the audience. He had resumed his quieter manner. "There are perhaps seven hundred people present. That would make fourteen hundred dollars. By the way, John," he addressed some one briskly. "Close the gates and lock them. We don't want anybody in on this who didn't have interest enough in our show to come in the first place." He winked humorously at the crowd, and several laughed.

"Pretty rotten, eh?" whispered Baker admiringly. "Fixed 'em so they won't bolt when the show's over and before he works off his dope."

"These Two Silver Dollars, which I want you all to get, are in these hampers. Six little boys will distribute them. Come up, boys, and get each a hatful of dollars." The six solemnly marched up on the stage and busied themselves with the hampers. "While we are waiting," went on the orator, "I will seize the opportunity to present to you the world-famed discoverer of that wonderful anæsthetic, Oxodyne, Painless Porter."

At the words a dapper little man in immaculately correct evening dress, and carrying a crush hat under his arm, stepped briskly from the wings. He was greeted by wild but presumably manufactured applause. He bowed rigidly from the hips, and at once began to speak in a high and nasal but extremely penetrating voice.

"As far as advertising is concerned," he began without pre-amble, "it is entirely unnecessary that I give this show. There is no man, woman or child in this marvellous commonwealth of ours who is not familiar with the name of Painless Porter, whether from the daily papers, the advertising boards, the street cars, or the elegant red brougham in which I traverse your streets. My work for you is my best advertisement. It is unnecessary from that point of view that I spend this money for this show, or that this extra money should be distributed among you by my colleague, Wizard Walker, the Medical Marvel of Modern Times."

The tall man paused from his business with the hampers and the six boys to bow in acknowledgment.

"No, ladies 'n' gentlemen, my purpose is higher. In the breast of each human being is implanted an instinctive fear of Pain. It sits on us like a nightmare, from the time we first come to consciousness of our surroundings. It is a curse of humanity, like drink, and he who can lighten that curse is as much of a philanthropist as George W. Childs or Andrew Carnegie. I want you to go away and talk about me. It don't matter what you say, just so you say something. You can call me quack, you may call me fakir, you may call me charletan — but be sure to call me SOMETHING! Then slowly the news will spread abroad that Pain is banished, and I can smile in peace, knowing that my vast expenditures of time and money have not been in vain, and that I have been a benefit to humanity. Wizard Walker, the Medical Marvel of Modern Times, will now attend to the distribution, after which I will pull a few teeth gratis in order to demonstrate to you the wonderful merits of Oxodyne."

"A dentist!" gasped Bob.

"Yup," said Baker. "Not much gasoline-torch-on-the-back-lot in his, is there?"

Bob was hardly surprised, after much preamble and heightening of suspense, to find that the Two Silver Dollars turned out finally to be a pink ticket and a blue ticket, "good respectively at the luxurious offices for one dollar's worth of dental and medical attention FREE."

Nor was he more than slightly astounded when the back drop rose to show the stage set glitteringly with nickel-mounted dentist chairs and their appurtenances, with shining glass, white linen, and with a chorus of fascinating damsels dressed as trained nurses and standing rigidly at attention. Then entered Painless himself, in snowy shirt-sleeves and serious professional preoccupation. Volunteers came up two by two. Painless explained obscurely the scientific principles on which the marvellous Oxodyne worked—by severing temporarily but entirely all communication between the nerves and the brain. Then much business with a very glittering syringe.

"My lord," chuckled Baker, "if he fills that thing up, it'll drown her!"

In an impressive silence Painless flourished the forceps, planted himself square in front of his patient, heaved a moment, and triumphantly held up in full view an undoubted tooth. The trained nurses offered rinses. After a moment the patient, a roughly dressed country woman, arose to her feet. She was smiling broadly, and said something, which the audience could not hear. Painless smiled indulgently.

"Speak up so they can all hear you," he encouraged her.

"Never hurt a bit," the woman stammered.

Three more operations were conducted as expeditiously and as successfully. The audience was evidently impressed.

"How does he do it?" whispered Bob.

"Cappers," explained Baker briefly. "He only fakes pulling a tooth. Watch him next time and you'll see that he doesn't actually pull an ounce."

"Suppose a real toothache comes up?"

"I think that is one now. Watch him."

A young ranchman was making his way up the steps that led to the stage. His skin was tanned by long exposure to the California sun, and his cheek rounded into an unmistakable swelling.

"No fake about him," commented Baker.

He seated himself in the chair. Painless examined his jaw carefully. He started back, both hands spread in expostulation.

"My *dear* friend!" he cried, "you can save that tooth! It would be a crime to pull that tooth! Come to my office at ten to-morrow morning and I will see what can be done." He turned to the audience and for ten minutes expounded the doctrine of modern dentistry as it stands for saving a tooth whenever possible. Incidentally he had much to say as to his skill in filling and bridge work and the marvellous painlessness thereof. The meeting broke up finally to the inspiring strains of a really good band. Bob and his friend, standing near the door, watched the audience file out. Some threw away their pink and blue tickets, but most stowed them carefully away.

"And every one that goes to the 'luxurious offices' for the free dollar's worth will leave ten round iron ones," said Baker.

After a moment the Painless One and the Wizard marched smartly out, serenely oblivious of the crowd. They stepped into a resplendent red brougham and were whisked rapidly away.

"It pays to advertise," quoted Baker philosophically.

They moved on up the street.

"There's the inventor of the Unlimited Life," said Baker suddenly, indicating a slender figure approaching. "I haven't seen him in three years—not since he got into this graft, anyway."

"Unlimited Life," echoed Bob, "what's that? A medicine?"

"No. A cult. Hullo, Sunny!"

The approaching figure swerved and stopped. Bob saw a very slender figure clad in a close-fitting, gray frock suit. To his surprise, from beneath the wide, black felt hat there peered at him the keenly nervous face of the more intelligent mulatto. The man's eyes were very bright and shrewd. His hair surrounded his face as an aureole of darkness, and swept low to his coat collar.

"Mr. Baker," he said, simply, his eyes inscrutable.

"Well, Sunny, this is my old friend Bob Orde. Bob, this is the world-famous Sunny Larue, apostle of the Unlimited Life of whom you've heard so much." He winked at Bob. "How's the Colony flourishing, Sunny?"

"More and more our people are growing to see the light," said the mulatto in low, musical tones. "The mighty but simple principles of Azamud are coming into their own. The poor and lowly, the humble and oppressed are learning that in me is their salvation—" He went on in his beautiful voice explaining the Colony of the Unlimited Life, addressing always Bob directly and paying little attention to Baker, who stood aside, his hands in his pockets, a smile on his fat, good-natured face. It seemed that the Colony lived in tents in a cañon of the foothills. It paid Larue fifty dollars a head, and in return was supported for six months and instructed in the mysteries of the cult. It had its regimen. "At three we arise and break our fast, quite simply, with three or four dry prunes," breathed Larue, "and then, going forth to the high places for one hour, we hold steadfast the thought of Love."

"Say, Sunny," broke in Baker, "how many you got rounded up now?"

"There are at present twenty-one earnest proselytes."

"At fifty a head—and you've got to feed and keep 'em some-how—even three dried prunes cost you something in the long run"—ruminated Baker. He turned briskly to the mulatto: "Sunny, on the dead, where does the graft come in?"

The mulatto drew himself up in swift offence, scrutinized Bob closely for a moment, met Baker's grin. Abruptly his impressive manner dropped from him. He leaned toward them with a captivating flash of white teeth.

"You just leave that to me," he murmured, and glided away into the crowd.

Baker laughed and drew Bob's arm within his own.

"Out of twenty of the faithful there's sure to be one or two with life savings stowed away in a sock, and Sunny's the boy to make them produce the sock."

"What's his cult, anyway?" asked Bob. "I mean, what do they pretend to believe? I couldn't make out."

"A nigger's idea of Buddhism," replied Baker briefly. "But you can get any brand of psychic damfoolishness you think you need in your business. They do it all, here, from going barefoot, eating nuts, swilling olive oil, rolling down hill, adoring the Limitless Which-ness, and all the works. It is now," he concluded, looking at his watch, "about ten o'clock. We will finish the evening by dropping in on the Fuzzies."

Together they boarded a street car, which shortly deposited them at an uptown corner. Large houses and spacious grounds indicated a district of some wealth. To one of these houses, brilliantly lighted, Baker directed his steps.

"But I don't know these people, and I'm not properly dressed," objected Bob.

"They know me. And as for dress, if you'd arrange to wear a chaste feather duster only, you'd make a hit."

A roomful of people were buzzing like a hive. Most were in conventional evening dress. Here and there, however, Bob caught hints of masculine long hair, of feminine psyche knots, bandeaux and other extremely artistic but unusual departures. One man with his dinner jacket wore a soft linen shirt perforated by a Mexican drawn-work pattern beneath which glowed a bright red silk undergarment. Women's gowns on the flowing and Grecian order were not uncommon. These were usually coupled with the incongruity of parted hair brought low and madonna-wise over the ears. As the two entered, a very powerful blond man was just finishing the declamation of a French poem. He was addressing it directly at two women seated on a sofa.

"Un r-r-rêve d'amour!"

He concluded with much passion and clasped hands.

In the rustle ensuing after this effort, Baker led his friend down the room to a very fat woman upholstered in pink satin, to whom he introduced Bob. Mrs. Annis, for such proved to be her name, welcomed him effusively.

"I've heard so much about you!" she cried vivaciously, to Bob's vast astonishment. She tapped him on the arm with her fan. "I'm going to make a confession to you; I know it may be foolish, but I *do* like music so much better than I do pictures."

Bob, his brain whirling, muttered something.

"But I'm going to confess to you again, I like artists so much better than I do musicians."

A light dawned on Bob. "But I'm not an artist nor a musician," he blurted out.

The pink-upholstered lady, starting back with an agility remarkable in one of her size, clasped her hands.

"Don't *tell* me you write!" she cried dramatically.

"All right, I won't," protested poor Bob, "for I don't."

A slow expression of bewilderment overspread Mrs. Annis's face, and she glanced toward Baker with an arched brow of interrogation.

"I merely wanted Mr. Orde to meet you, Mrs. Annis," he said impressively, "and to feel that another time, when he is less exhausted by the strain of a long day, he may have the privilege of explaining to you the details of the great Psychic Movement he is inaugurating."

Mrs. Annis smiled on him graciously. "I am home every Sunday to my *intimes*," she murmured. "I should be so pleased."

Bob bowed mechanically.

"You infernal idiot!" he ground out savagely to Baker, as they moved away. "What do you mean? I'll punch your fool head when I get you out of here!"

But the plump young man merely smiled.

Halfway down the room a group of attractive-looking young men hailed them.

"Join in, Baker," said they. "Bring your friend along. We're just going to raid the commissary."

But Baker shook his head.

"I'm showing him life," he replied. "None but Fuzzies in his tonight!"

He grasped Bob firmly by the arm and led him away.

"That," he said, indicating a very pale young man, surrounded by women, "is Pickering, the celebrated submarine painter."

"That what?" demanded Bob.

"Submarine painter. He paints fish and green water and lobsters, and the bottom of the sea generally. He paints them on the skins of kind-faced little calves."

"What does he do that for?"

"He says it's the only surface that will express what he wants to. He has also invented a waterproof paint that he can use under water. He has a coral throne down on the bottom which he sits in, and paints as long as he can hold his breath."

"Oh, he does!" said Bob.

"Yes," said Baker.

"But a man can't see three feet in front of his face under water!" cried Bob.

"Pickering says he can. He paints submarinescapes, and knows all the fishes. He says fishes have individual expressions. He claims he can tell by a fish's expression whether he is polygamous or monogamous."

"Do you mean to tell me anybody swallows that rot?" demanded Bob indignantly.

"The women do—and a lot more I can't remember. The market for calf-skins with green swirls on them is booming. Also the women clubbed together and gave him money enough to build a house."

Bob surveyed the little white-faced man with a strong expression of disgust.

"The natural man never sits in chairs," the artist was expounding. "When humanity shall have come into its own we shall assume the graceful and hygienic postures of the oriental peoples. In society one must, to a certain extent, follow convention, but in my own house, the House Beautiful of my dreams, are no chairs. And even now a small group of the freer spirits are following my example. In time—"

"If you don't take me away, I'll run in circles!" whispered Bob fiercely to his friend.

They escaped into the open air.

"Phew!" said Bob, straightening his long form. "Is that what you call the good society here?"

"Good society is there," amended Baker. "That's the joke. There are lots of nice people in this little old town, people who lisp our language fluently. They are all mixed in with the Fuzzies."

They decided to walk home. Bob marvelled at the impressive and substantial buildings, at the atrocious streets. He spoke of the beautiful method of illuminating one of the thoroughfares—by globes of light gracefully supported in clusters on branched arms either side the roadway.

"They were originally bronze—and they went and painted them a mail-box green," commented Baker drily.

At the hotel the night clerk, a young man, quietly dressed and with an engaging air, greeted them with just the right amount of cordiality as he handed them their keys. Bob paused to look about him.

"This is a good hotel," he remarked.

"It's one of the best-managed, the best-conducted, and the best-appointed hotels in the United States," said Baker with conviction.

The next morning Bob bought all the papers and glanced through them with considerable wonder and amusement. They were decidedly metropolitan in size, and carried a tremendous amount of advertising. Early in his perusal he caught the personal bias of the news. Without distortion to the point of literal inaccuracy, nevertheless by skilful use of headlines and by manipulation of the point of view, all items were made to subserve a purpose. In local affairs the most vulgar nicknaming, the most savage irony, vituperation, scorn and contempt were poured out full measure on certain individuals unpopular with the papers. Such epithets as "lickspittle," "toad," "carcass blown with the putrefying gas of its own importance," were read in the body of narration.

"These are the best-edited, most influential and powerful journals in the West," commented Baker. "They possess an influence inconceivable to an Easterner."

The advertising columns were filled to bursting with advertisements of patent medicines, sex remedies, quack doctors, miraculous healers, clairvoyants, palm readers, "philanthropists" with something "free" to bestow, cleverly worded offers of abortion; with full-page prospectuses of mines; of mushroom industrial concerns having to do with wave motors, water motors, solar motors, patent couplers, improved telephones and the like, all of whose stock now stood at $1.10, but which on April 10th, at 8.02 P.M., would go up to $1.15; with blaring, shrieking offers of real estate in this, that or the other addition, consisting, as Bob knew from yesterday, of farm acreage at front-foot figures. The proportion of this fake advertising was astounding. One in particular seemed incredible — a full page of the exponent of some Oriental method of healing and prophecy.

"Of course, a full-page costs money," replied Baker. "But this is the place to get it." He pushed back his chair. "Well, what do you think of our fair young city?" he grinned.

"It's got me going," admitted Bob.

"Took me some time to find out where to get off at," said Baker. "When I found it out, I didn't dare tell anybody. They mob you here and string you up by your pigtail, if you try to hint that this isn't the one best bet on terrestrial habitations. They like their little place, and they believe in it a whole lot, and they're dead right about it! They'd stand right up on their hind legs and paw the atmosphere if anybody were to tell them what they really are, but it's a fact. Same joyous slambang, same line of sharps hanging on the outskirts, same row, racket, and joy in life, same struggle; yes, and by golly! the same big hopes and big enterprises and big optimism and big energies! Wouldn't you like to be helping them do it?"

"What's the answer?" asked Bob, amused.

"Well, for all its big buildings and its electric lights, and trolleys, and police and size, it's nothing more nor less than a frontier town."

"A frontier town!" echoed Bob.

"You think it over," said Baker.

Harris Newmark

A price war in the late 1880s between the Santa Fe Railroad and the Southern Pacific made Los Angeles a suddenly affordable destination: ticket costs plummeted, the city was inundated with new arrivals, and thus began a real estate boom of epic proportions. Everyone from housewives to clergymen got caught up in the frenzy, and by the time the boom tapered off at the decade's end, more than a hundred new towns had been established in Southern California. In *Sixty Years in Southern California, 1853–1913* (1915) Harris Newmark (1834–1916), one of early L.A.'s leading entrepreneurs and philanthropists, chronicles the boom's excesses, not the least of them in the realm of advertising.

from

SIXTY YEARS IN SOUTHERN CALIFORNIA
1853–1913

As the final sequence to the events of three or four preceding years, Los Angeles, at the time when I left for Europe, had already advanced beyond the threshold of her first really violent "boom;" and now symptoms of feverish excitement were everywhere noticeable in Southern California. The basis of real estate operations, heretofore sane enough, was quickly becoming unbalanced, a movement that was growing more and more intensified, as well as general; and as in the case of a mighty stream which accumulates overwhelming power from many feeders, there was a marshalling, as it were, in Los Angeles of these forces. The charms of climate and scenery (widely advertised, as I have said, at the Philadelphia Centennial and, later, through the continuous efforts of the first and second Chambers of Commerce and the Board of Trade), together with the extension of the Southern Pacific to the East and the building of the Santa Fé Railroad, had brought here a class of tourists who not only enjoyed the winter, but ventured to stay through the summer season; and who, having remained, were not long in seeking land and homesteads. The rapidly-increasing demand for lots and houses caused hundreds of men and women to enter the local real-estate field, most of whom were inexperienced and without much responsibility. When, therefore, the news of their phenomenal activity got abroad, as was sure to be the case, hordes of would-be speculators—some with, but more without knowledge of land-manipulation, and many none too scrupulous—rushed to the Southland to invest, wager or swindle. Thousands upon thousands of Easterners swelled the number already here; dealers in realty sprang up like mushrooms. It was then that the demand for offices north of First Street, exceeding the supply, compelled many an agent unwillingly to take accommodations farther south and brought about much building, even to—Second Street! It also happened that a dozen or more competitors occupied a single storeroom. Selling and bartering were carried on at all hours of the day or night, and in every conceivable place; agents, eager to keep every appointment possible, enlisted the services of hackmen, hotel employees and waiters to put them in touch with prospective buyers; and the same properties would often change hands several times in a day, sales being made on the curbstone, at bars or restaurant tables, each succeeding transfer representing an enhanced value. Although I was abroad during the height of this period, psychologically so interesting, newspapers, letters and photographs from home—supplemented, on my return, by the personal narratives of friends—supplied me with considerable information of the craze.

As I have already remarked, the coming of the Santa Fé—as well as the ensuing railroad war—was a very potent factor in this temporary growth and advance in values; and soon after the railroad's advent, a dozen towns had been laid out on the line between Los Angeles and San Bernardino, the number doubling within a few months. Indeed, had the plan of the boomers succeeded, the whole stretch between the two cities would have been solidly built up with what in the end proved, alas! to be but castles in the air. Wherever there was acreage, there was room for new towns; and with their inauguration, thousands of buyers were on hand to absorb lots that were generally sold on the installment plan. More frequently than otherwise, payments became delinquent and companies "went broke;" and then the property reverted to acreage again. This sometimes led to serious complications, especially when the contract between the landowner and the so-called syndicate allowed the latter to issue clear title to those who paid for their lots. In such cases, the acreage when recovered by the original owner would be dotted here and there with small possessions; and to reinstate his property was, as a rule, no easy task. This, of course, refers to the failures of which there were more than enough; on the other hand, many of the towns inaugurated during the Boom period not only have survived and prospered, but have become some of our most attractive and successful neighbors.

If every conceivable trick in advertising was not resorted to, it was probably due to oversight. Bands, announcing new locations, were seen here and there in street cars, hay and other wagons and carriages (sometimes followed by fantastic parades a block long); and for every new location there was promised the early construction of magnificent hotels, theaters or other attractive buildings that seldom materialized. When processions filled the streets, bad music filled the air. Elephants and other animals of jungle and forest, as well as human freaks—the remnants of a stranded circus or two— were gathered into shows and used as magnets; while other ingenious methods were often invoked to draw crowds and gather in the shekels. The statements as to climate were always verified, but in most other respects poor Martin Chuzzlewit's experience in the Mississippi town of Eden affords a rather graphic story of what was frequently in progress here during the never-to-be-forgotten days of the Boom. As competition waxed keener, dishonest methods were more and more resorted to; thus schemers worked on the public's credulity and so attracted many a wagon-load of people to mass-meetings, called ostensibly for the purpose of advancing some worthy cause but really arranged to make possible an ordinary sale of real estate. An endless chain of free lunches, sources of delight to the hobo element in particular, drew not only these chronic idlers but made a victim of many a worthier man. Despite all of this excitement, the village aspect in some particulars had not yet disappeared: in vacant lots not far from the center of town it was still not unusual to see cows contentedly chewing their cud and chickens scratching for a living. In 1889, however, the Council governed this feature of domestic life by ordinance, and thenceforth there was less of the "cock's shrill clarion."

Extraordinary situations arose out of the speculative mania, as when over-ambitious folks, fearful perhaps lest they might be unable to obtain corner- and other desirably-situated lots, stationed themselves in line two or three days before the date of anticipated land-sales; and even though quite twenty selections were frequently the limit to one purchase, the more optimistic of our boomers would often have two or three substitutes waiting in a line extending irregularly far down the sidewalk and assuming at night the appearance of a bivouac. I have heard it said that as much as a hundred dollars would be paid to each of these messengers, and that the purchaser of such service, apprehensive lest he might be sold out, would visit his representative many times before the eventful day. Later, this system was improved and official place-numbers were given, thus permitting people to conduct their negotiations without much loss of time.

So little scientific consideration was given to actual values that they were regulated according to calendar and clock; lots in new subdivisions remaining unsold were advertised to advance to certain new prices at such and such an hour, on such and such a day. After these artificial changes, investors would gleefully rub their hands and explain to the downcast outsider that they had "just gotten in in time;" and the downcast outsider, of whom there were many, yielding after repeated assaults of this kind, would himself become inoculated with the fever and finally prove the least restrained boomer of them all. From what I read at the time and heard after my return, I may safely declare that during the height of the infection, two-thirds of our population were, in a sense, more insane than sane.

Syndicates, subdivisions and tracts: these were the most popular terms of the day and nearly everybody had a finger in one or the other pie. There were enough subdivisions to accommodate ten million people; and enough syndicates to handle the affairs of a nation. And talking about syndicates: the disagreement of members themselves as to values frequently prevented the consummation of important sales and resulted in the loss of large profits to the objectors as well as to their associates. In many a well-authenticated case, the property remained on the owners' hands until it became almost worthless.

Wide-awake syndicates evolved new methods, one of which—
the lottery plan—became popular. A piece of land would be prepared for the market; and after the opening of streets, as many
chances would be sold as there were lots in the tract. On the eventful day, the distribution took place in the presence of the interested
and eager participants, each of whom made a selection as his number was drawn. To increase the attractiveness of some of these
offers, cottages and even more elaborate houses were occasionally
promised for subsequent erection on a few lots. The excitement at
many of these events, I was informed, beggared description. Among
others sold in this manner at the beginning, or possibly even just
before the Boom, were the Williamson Tract, beginning at the corner of Pico and Figueroa streets and once the home-place of the
Formans, and the O. W. Childs orchard on the east side of Main
Street and running south from what is now about Eleventh. Both of
these drawings took place in Turnverein Hall, and the chances sold
at about three hundred and fifty dollars each.

Tricksters, of whom at such times there are always enough,
could exercise their mischievous proclivities; and the unwary one,
who came to be known as the tenderfoot, was as usual easily hood-
winked. Land advertised as having "water privileges" proved to be
land *under water* or in dry creeks; land described as possessing scenic
attractions consisted of—mountains and chasms! So situated were
many of these lots that no use whatever could be made of them; and
I presume that they are without value even now. One of the effects
of subdividing a good part of the ten thousand or more acres of agricultural land in the city then irrigated from the *zanjas* was both to
reduce the calls for the service of the city *Zanjero*, and to lessen considerably the importance and emoluments of his office.

Advertisers tried to outdo themselves and each other in original
and captivating announcements; with the result that, while many
displayed wit and good humor, others were ridiculously extravagant. The Artesian Water Company came onto the market with
three hundred acres of land near Compton and the assurance that
"while the water in this section will be stocked, the stock will not be
watered." Alvan D. Brock, another purveyor of ranches, declared:

I mean business, and do not allow any alfalfa to grow under my feet.

A. F. Kercheval, the poet, to whom I have already referred, relieved himself of this exuberance regarding the Kercheval Tract (on Santa Fé Avenue, between Lemon and Alamo streets):

HE OR SHE
That Hesitates is Lost!
An axiom that holds good in real estate,
as well as in affairs of the heart.
Selah!

Another advertisement read as follows:

HALT! HALT! HALT!
Speculators and Homeseekers, Attention!
$80,000 — Eighty Thousand Dollars — $80,000
Sold in a Day at the Beautiful
McGarry Tract
Bounded by Ninth and Tenth and Alameda Streets.
Come Early, before they are All Gone!

Still another was displayed:

Boom!   Boom!
ARCADIA!
Boom!   Boom!

And now and then, from a quarter to a full page would be taken to advertise a new town or subdivision, with a single word — the name of the place — such as

RAMIREZ!

Vernon and Vernondale were names given to subdivisions on Central Avenue near Jefferson Street. Advertising the former, the real-estate poet was called into requisition with these lines:

Go, wing thy flight from star to star,
From world to luminous world as far
As the universe spreads its flaming wall,

> Take all the pleasure of all the spheres,
> And multiply each through endless years,
> One Winter at Vernon is worth them all!

while, in setting forth the attractions of the Lily Langtry Tract, the promoter drew as follows from the store of English verse:

> Sweet Vernon, loveliest village of the plain,
> Where health and plenty cheers the laboring swain,
> Where smiling Spring its earliest visit paid,
> And parting Summer's lingering blooms delayed;

concluding the announcement with the following lines characteristic of the times:

> Catch on before the whole country rushes to Vernondale!
> Every man who wishes a home in Paradise should locate in this,
> the loveliest district of the whole of Southern California.

> This is where the orange groves are loveliest!
> This is where the grapes are most luxuriant!
> This is where the vegetation is grandest!
> This is where the flowers are prettiest!

Vachel Lindsay

By 1915, the motion picture business had staked its claim to Southern California, drawn by sun and light and the availability of a wide variety of natural settings. After some initial resistance Los Angeles overcame its doubts about the "movie colony," which in just seven years had evolved from a civic nuisance to an industry with an annual payroll of $20,000,000. In "California and America," a chapter from his pioneering *The Art of the Moving Picture* (1915), the poet Vachel Lindsay (1879–1931) offers a not-yet jaded impression of the young Hollywood. Lindsay, the proponent of a visionary populism of near-messianic proportions, saw movies as a new language. He also had a propensity for falling in love (unrequitedly) with the goddesses of the silent screen, writing for instance of Mae Marsh: "She is madonna in an art/As wild and young as her sweet eyes."

CALIFORNIA AND AMERICA

The moving picture captains of industry, like the California gold finders of 1849, making colossal fortunes in two or three years, have the same glorious irresponsibility and occasional need of the sheriff. They are Californians more literally than this. Around Los Angeles the greatest and most characteristic moving picture colonies are being built. Each photoplay magazine has its California letter, telling of the putting-up of new studios, and the transfer of actors, with much slap-you-on-the-back personal gossip. This is the outgrowth of the fact that every type of the photoplay but the intimate is founded on some phase of the out-of-doors. Being thus dependent, the plant can best be set up where there is no winter. Besides this, the Los Angeles region has the sea, the mountains, the desert, and many kinds of grove and field. Landscape and architecture are sub-tropical. But for a description of California, ask any traveller or study the background of almost any photoplay.

If the photoplay is the consistent utterance of its scenes, if the actors are incarnations of the land they walk upon, as they should be, California indeed stands a chance to achieve through the films an utterance of her own. Will this land furthest west be the first to capture the inner spirit of this newest and most curious of the arts? It certainly has the opportunity that comes with the actors, producers, and equipment. Let us hope that every region will develop the silent photographic pageant in a local form as outlined in the chapter on Progress and Endowment. Already the California sort, in the commercial channels, has become the broadly accepted if mediocre national form. People who revere the Pilgrim Fathers of 1620 have often wished those gentlemen had moored their bark in the region of Los Angeles rather than Plymouth Rock, that Boston had been founded there. At last that landing is achieved.

Patriotic art students have discussed with mingled irony and admiration the Boston domination of the only American culture of the nineteenth century, namely, literature. Indianapolis has had her day since then, Chicago is lifting her head. Nevertheless Boston still controls the text-book in English and dominates our high schools. Ironic feelings in this matter on the part of western men are based somewhat on envy and illegitimate cussedness, but are also grounded in the honest hope of a healthful rivalry. They want new romanticists and artists as indigenous to their soil as was Hawthorne to witch-haunted Salem or Longfellow to the chestnuts of his native heath. Whatever may be said of the patriarchs, from Oliver Wendell Holmes to Amos Bronson Alcott, they were true sons of the New England stone fences and meeting houses. They could not have been born or nurtured anywhere else on the face of the earth.

Some of us view with a peculiar thrill the prospect that Los Angeles may become the Boston of the photoplay. Perhaps it would be better to say the Florence, because California reminds one of colorful Italy more than of any part of the United States. Yet there is a difference.

The present-day man-in-the-street, man-about-town Californian has an obvious magnificence about him that is allied to the eucalyptus tree, the pomegranate. California is a gilded state. It has not the sordidness of gold, as has Wall Street, but it is the embodiment of the natural ore that the ragged prospector finds. The gold of California is the color of the orange, the glitter of dawn in the Yosemite, the hue of the golden gate that opens the sunset way to mystic and terrible Cathay and Hindustan.

The enemy of California says the state is magnificent but thin. He declares it is as though it were painted on a Brobdingnagian piece of gilt paper, and he who dampens his finger and thrusts it through finds an alkali valley on the other side, the lonely prickly pear, and a heap of ashes from a deserted campfire. He says the citizens of this state lack the richness of an æsthetic and religious tradition. He says there is no substitute for time. But even these things make for coincidence. This apparent thinness California has in common with the routine photoplay, which is at times as shallow in its thought as the shadow it throws upon the screen. This newness California has in common with all photoplays. It is thrillingly possible for the state and the art to acquire spiritual tradition and depth together.

Part of the thinness of California is not only its youth, but the result of the physical fact that the human race is there spread over so many acres of land. They try not only to count their mines and enumerate their palm trees, but they count the miles of their sea-coast, and the acres under cultivation and the height of the peaks, and revel in large statistics and the bigness generally, and forget how a few men rattle around in a great deal of scenery. They shout their statistics across the Rockies and the deserts to New York. The Mississippi Valley is non-existent to the Californian. His fellow-feeling is for the opposite coast-line. Through the geographical accident of separation by mountain and desert from the rest of the country, he becomes a mere shouter, hurrahing so assiduously that all variety in the voice is lost. Then he tries gestures, and becomes flamboyant, rococo.

These are the defects of the motion picture qualities also. Its panoramic tendency runs wild. As an institution it advertises itself with the sweeping gesture. It has the same passion for coast-line. These are not the sins of New England. When, in the hands of masters, they become sources of strength, they will be a different set of virtues from those of New England.

There is no more natural place for the scattering of confetti than this state, except the moving picture scene itself. Both have a genius for gardens and dancing and carnival.

When the Californian relegates the dramatic to secondary scenes, both in his life and his photoplay, and turns to the genuinely epic and lyric, he and this instrument may find their immortality together as New England found its soul in the essays of Emerson. Tide upon tide of Spring comes into California through all four seasons. Fairy beauty overwhelms the lumbering grand-stand players. The tiniest garden is a jewelled pathway of wonder. But the Californian cannot shout "orange blossoms, orange blossoms; heliotrope, heliotrope!" He cannot boom forth "roseleaves, roseleaves" so that he does their beauties justice. Here is where the photoplay can begin to give him a more delicate utterance. And he can go on into stranger things and evolve all the Splendor Films into higher types, for the very name of California is splendor. The California photoplaywright can base his Crowd Picture upon the city-worshipping mobs of San Francisco. He can derive his Patriotic and Religious Splendors from something older and more magnificent than the aisles of the Romanesque, namely: the groves of the giant redwoods.

The campaign for a beautiful nation could very well emanate from the west coast, where with the slightest care grow up models for all the world of plant arrangement and tree-luxury. Our mechanical East is reproved, our tension is relaxed, our ugliness is challenged every time we look upon those garden paths and forests.

It is possible for Los Angeles to lay hold of the motion picture as our national text-book in Art as Boston appropriated to herself the guardianship of the national text-books of Literature. If California has a shining soul, and not merely a golden body, let her forget her seventeen-year-old melodramatics, and turn to her poets who understand the heart underneath the glory. Edwin Markham, the dean of American singers, Clark Ashton Smith, the young star treader, George Sterling, that son of Ancient Merlin, have in their songs the seeds of better scenarios than California has sent us. There are two poems by George Sterling that I have had in mind for many a day as conceptions that should inspire mystic films akin to them. These poems are The Night Sentries and Tidal King of Nations.

But California can tell us stories that are grim children of the tales of the wild Ambrose Bierce. Then there is the lovely unforgotten Nora May French and the austere Edward Rowland Sill.

Edison is the new Gutenberg. He has invented the new printing. The state that realizes this may lead the soul of America, day after to-morrow.

Louis Adamic

The early boosterism that typified Los Angeles also found early detractors. One of the first was Louis Adamic (1899–1951), a writer and labor activist who emigrated from Slovenia at the age of fourteen. On arriving in Southern California in the 1920s, he eked out a living at such jobs as fire-watcher in the San Gabriel forests and watchman in the pilots' office in San Pedro harbor. Adamic saw a ruthless Los Angeles where unscrupulous self-promoters got rich off the unfulfilled hopes of deluded dreamers looking for a paradise that didn't exist. His description of Los Angeles as an enormous village—what Richard Meltzer later called "the biggest HICK Town (per se) in all the hick land"—is echoed in the work of critics and debunkers from Carey McWilliams and Nathanael West through Joan Didion and Mike Davis. In this 1926 diary entry, included in *Laughing in the Jungle* (1932), Adamic offers up a road map of a city on the make.

from
LAUGHING IN THE JUNGLE

Los Angeles is probably one of the most interesting spots on the face of the earth. Some one should write a book about it; an honest-to-goodness book, not a mere booster pamphlet. . . . In its advertisements, the Realty Board calls the town "The City Beautiful," "The Wonder City," "The Earthly Paradise," and other fancy names, none of which is exactly inaccurate. It *is* beautiful and wonderful in spots, and I guess for some people it is paradise. But that isn't coming anywhere near the truth about it. . . .

The people on the top in Los Angeles, the Big Men, as elsewhere in America, are the business men, the Babbitts. They are the promoters, who are blowing down the city's windpipe with all their might, hoping to inflate the place to a size that it will be reckoned the largest city in the country—in the world. Throughout the town one sees huge electric signs—"2,000,000 population by 1930." These signs represent the spirit of Los Angeles. They were put up by the men who own most of the lots and subdivisions.

These men are the high priests of the Chamber of Commerce whose religion is Climate and Profits. They are—some of them—grim, inhuman individuals with a great terrifying singleness of purpose. They see a tremendous opportunity to enrich themselves beyond anything they could have hoped for ten or even five years ago, and they mean to make the most of it. They have their fingers in every important pie, not only in the city, but everywhere in southern California and even below the border. They work hard. I hear that Harry Chandler, publisher of the *Times*, spends sixteen hours daily in his office. They are possessed by a mad drive which—so far as I can make out—is not deeply rooted in their own personalities, but is rather a part of the place, this great region of eternal spring which stretches between the Sierras and the sea, and which, of late years, has begun to capture the imagination of millions of people, who for various reasons have become dissatisfied with what life offers them in Gopher Prairies in the East, in the South, and the Middle West.

And trailing after the big boys is a mob of lesser fellows, whom the former awe with their superior economic advantages and control through the Chamber of Commerce and other *pay*-triotic organizations: thousands of minor realtors, boomers, promoters, contractors, agents, salesmen, bunko-men, officeholders, lawyers, and preachers—all driven by the same motives of wealth, power, and personal glory, and a greater Los Angeles. They exploit the "come-ons" and one another, envy the big boys, live deliriously for business, bigger and better business, while their wives gather in women's clubs, listen to *swamis* and *yogis* and English lecturers, join "love cults" and Coué clubs in Hollywood and Pasadena, and their children—boys and girls in their teens: "beautiful but dumb"—jazz and drink and rush around in roadsters. . . .

Then there are the Folks—oh, the *dear* Folks! They are the retired farmers, grocers, Ford agents, hardware merchants, and shoe merchants from the Middle West and other parts of these United States, thousands and tens of thousands of them. They are coming in by trains and automobiles. They have money. They made it during the war. Not that they are not entitled to it. Most of them worked harder than any one should work through their best years. They were the pioneers back in Ioway and Nebraska. No doubt they swindled a little, but they always prayed a little, too, or maybe a great deal. And they paid taxes and raised young ones. They are old and rheumatic. They sold out their farms and businesses in the Middle West or wherever they used to live, and now they are here in California—sunny California—to rest and regain their vigor, enjoy climate, look at pretty scenery, live in little bungalows with a palm-tree or banana plant in front, and eat in cafeterias. Toil-broken and bleached out, they flock to Los Angeles, fugitives from the simple, inexorable justice of life, from hard labor and drudgery, from cold winters and blistering summers of the prairies. . . .

Of course, there are other kinds—many kinds—of people in Los Angeles, but the Folks predominate in numbers and give the place the aspect of a great, overgrown village. They brought with them their preachers, evangelists, and Sunday-school superintendents. They are half-educated, materially prosperous but spiritually and mentally starving. They are retired; they have nothing to do all day; they are a bit exhilarated by climate—and so they follow any fake who possesses personality and looks in any way strange and impressive and can say words which they don't understand in a thrilling voice.

They have money, these Folks, and so, besides the more or less legitimate real-estate business, there are all kinds of bunko promotion schemes—mining, oil, and others—in which the Folks invest their money and never see it again. The financial editor of the *Times* remarked the other day that a sensible person should not get indignant over the existence of bunko schemes in the city. What's the difference, he said, whether the crooks or the idiots had the money? No matter who had it, the money helped to build up Los Angeles. . . .

Most of the Folks are unwell, old, rheumatic men and women. Next to "Where do you come from?" the most frequently asked question is, "Now, how do you feel today?" Health is a big thing in Los Angeles. Most of the people come here to be sun-kissed and made well, and so healing is one of the big industries in town. Besides thousands of more or less regular doctors, there are in Los Angeles no end of chiropractors, osteopaths, "drugless physicians," faith-healers, health lecturers, manufacturers and salesmen of all sorts of health "stabilizers" and "normalizers," psychoanalysts, phynotists, mesmerists, the glow-of-life mystics, astro-therapeutists, miracle men and women—in short, quacks and charlatans of all descriptions. . . . My mind goes back to the Old Country. In Carniola, as I recall, "How do you feel today?" was an unusual question; in fact, I believe that I never heard it asked. There, good health was the rule, rather than the exception, even among elderly people, and so there was little interest in it. . . . In Los Angeles health is the leading topic of conversation.

And Los Angeles is America. A jungle. Los Angeles grew up suddenly, *planlessly*, under the stimuli of the adventurous spirit of millions of people and the profit motive. It is still growing. Here everything has a chance to thrive—for a while—as a rule only a brief while. Inferior as well as superior plants and trees flourish for a time, then both succumb to chaos and decay. They must give way to new plants pushing up from below, and so on. This is freedom under democracy. Jungle democracy!

In Panama, I remember, I once saw a great stretch of jungle country from a mountain top. It was beautiful from the distance. Looking at it, I could not believe that actually it was a dank, unhealthy, dangerous region, into which one should not venture except if properly equipped with mosquito netting and armed with guns and bolos.

The same goes for Los Angeles (*i.e.* America). From Mount Hollywood, Los Angeles looks rather nice, enveloped in a haze of changing colors. Actually, and in spite of all the healthful sunshine and ocean breezes, it is a *bad* place—full of old, dying people, and young people who were born old of tired pioneer parents, victims of America—full of curious wild and poisonous growths, decadent religions and cults and fake science, and wildcat business enterprises, which, with their aim for quick profits, are doomed to collapse and drag down multitudes of people. . . . A jungle. . . .

Hence, if one lives in Los Angeles—in America—one would best be properly equipped and armed—not with guns and bolos and mosquito netting, but with knowledge and understanding of the scene, with a sense of humor—with laughter. Otherwise the place is very apt to get the better of one, both materially and spiritually. . . .

Aldous Huxley

Los Angeles has long been a magnet for British visitors who often became residents; Hollywood's English colony constituted a subculture in its own right, and to this day Santa Monica is a plentiful source of marmite, Ovaltine, and afternoon tea. When Aldous Huxley (1894–1963) visited in 1925 — recounted in "Los Angeles. A Rhapsody," which appeared in *Jesting Pilate* (1926) — he was very much the outsider, registering the jangling, kaleidoscopic chaos of the "City of Dreadful Joy" with a mixture of fascination and disdain. (His impressions of the Los Angeles variety of mass hedonism almost certainly found their way into his dystopian 1932 novel *Brave New World*.) Whatever his misgivings, Huxley eventually succumbed to the pleasures of the place, and from 1937 was a permanent resident. He extended his satirical dissection of Southern California in *After Many a Summer Dies the Swan* (1939) and *Ape and Essence* (1948), while exploring more utopian possibilities in *Island* (1962) and in his accounts of his psychedelic experiments, *The Doors of Perception* (1954) and *Heaven and Hell* (1956).

LOS ANGELES. A RHAPSODY

FIRST MOVEMENT

Daylight had come to the common folk of Hollywood, the bright California daylight. But within the movie studio there shone no sun, only the lamps, whose intense and greenish yellow radiance gives to living men and women the appearance of jaundiced corpses. In a corner of one huge barn-like structure they were preparing to "shoot." The camera stood ready, the corpse-lights were in full glare. Two or three cowboys and a couple of clowns lounged about, smoking. A man in evening dress was trusting to his moustache to make him look like an English villain. A young lady, so elegant, so perfectly and flawlessly good-looking that you knew her at once for the Star, was sitting in a corner, reading a book. The Director — it seemed a waste that such a profile should be *au-dessus de la mêlée* instead of in the pictures — gave her a courteous hail. Miss X looked up from her literature. "It's the scene where you see the

55

murder being committed," he explained. Miss X got up, put away the book and beckoned to her maid, who brought her a comb and a mirror. "My nose all right?" she asked, dabbing on powder. "Music!" shouted the Director. "Make it emotional." The band, whose duty it is in every studio to play the actors into an appropriate state of soul, struck up a waltz. The studio was filled with a sea of melodic treacle; our spirits rocked and wallowed on its sticky undulations. Miss X handed back her powder puff to the maid and walked up to the camera. "You hide behind that curtain and look out," the Director explained. Miss X retired behind the curtain. "Just the hand first of all," the Director went on. "Clutching. Then the face, gradually." "Yes, Mr. Z," came the quiet voice of the Star from behind the hanging plush. "Ready?" asked the Director. "Then go ahead." The camera began to purr, like a genteel variety of dentist's drill. The curtain slightly heaved. A white hand clutched at its edge. "Terror, Miss X," called the Director. The white hand tightened its clutch in a spasm of cinematographic fear. The Director nodded to the bandmaster. "Put some pep into it," he adjured. Pep was put in; the billows of treacle rose higher. "Now the face, Miss X. Slowly. Just one eye. That's good. Hold it. A little more terror." Miss X heart-rendingly registered her alarm. "That's good. That's very good. O.K." The camera stopped purring. Miss X came out from behind the curtain and walked back to her chair. Reopening her book, she went on quietly reading about Theosophy.

We moved on and, after halting for a few moments on our way to watch some more terror being registered (by a man this time and under a different Director), penetrated into the secret places of the studio. We pronounced passwords, quoted the Manager's permission, disclaimed connections with rival companies and were finally admitted. In one room they were concocting miracles and natural cataclysms—typhoons in bathtubs and miniature earthquakes, the Deluge, the Dividing of the Red Sea, the Great War in terms of toy tanks and Chinese fire crackers, ghosts and the Next World. In another they were modelling prehistoric animals and the architecture of the remote future. In cellars below ground, mysteriously lighted by red lamps and smelling of chemicals, a series of machines was engaged in developing and printing the films. Their output was enormous. I forget how many thousands of feet of art and culture they could turn out each day. Quite a number of miles, in any case.

SECOND MOVEMENT

Emerging, I bought a newspaper. It was Saturday's; a whole page was filled with the announcements of rival religious sects, advertising the spiritual wares that they would give away, or sell on the Sabbath. "Dr. Leon Tucker with the Musical Messengers in a Great Bible Conference. 3 Meetings To-morrow. Organ Chimes, Giant Marimbaphone, Vibraphone, Violin, Piano, Accordeon, Banjo, Guitar and other Instruments. Wilshire Baptist Church." The Giant Marimbaphone was certainly tempting. But in the First Methodist Church (Figueroa at Twentieth) they were going to distribute "Mother's Day Flowers to all Worshippers." (On Mother's Day you must wear a red carnation if your mother is alive, a white one if she is dead. The florists are everywhere the most ardent of matriolaters.) Moreover they had booked the exclusive services of Dr. James H. Maclaren, Dramatic Orator, who was going to give his well-known stunt, "Impersonations of Lincoln and Roosevelt." "Dr. Maclaren," we were informed, "comes with a unique, original, eloquent, instructive and inspiring Message concerning two of our Great Presidents. Uplifting and inspiring. It will do your soul good. The wonderful Messages of these two Great Presidents will be brought home with new emphasis and you will feel that you have spent the evening in the company of great Spirits. Hear the great organ, Quartet of Artists and Vested Chorus." At the Hollywood Congregational Church there were to be moving pictures of Jackie Coogan in his crusade to the Near East; the prospect was a draw. But then so was the photograph of Miss Leila Castberg of the Church of Divine Power (Advanced Thought); her performance might not be very interesting — she was scheduled to preach at the Morosco Theatre on Divine Motherhood — but the face which looked out from her advertisement was decidedly pleasing. Less attractive, to the devout male at any rate, were the photos of Messrs. Clarke and Van Bruch; but the phrasing of their ad. was enough to counteract in the mind of the reader the effect produced by their portraits. "IT'S ON, FOLKS, IT'S ON," so the announcement ran. "The tide is rising at an OLD-FASHIONED REVIVAL. Every night except Monday, 7.30 P.M. Soul-stirring sermons and songs. Special to-night! Hear 10 Evangelists — 10. Van Bruch-Clarke Evangelistic Party."

Jazz it up, jazz it up. Keep moving. Step on the gas. Say it with dancing. The Charleston, the Baptists. Radios and Revivals. Uplift and Gilda Gray. The pipe organ, the nigger with the saxophone, the Giant Marimbaphone. Hymns and the movies and Irving Berlin. Petting Parties and the First Free United Episcopal Methodist Church. Jazz it up! "N. C. Beskin, the CONVERTED JEW, back from a successful tour, will conduct a tabernacle campaign in Glendale. "WHY I BECAME A CHRISTIAN?" Dressed in Jewish garb. Will exhibit interesting paraphernalia." Positively the last appearance. The celebrated Farmyard Imitations. 10 Evangelists — 10. The finest troupe of Serio-Comic Cyclists ever. Onward Christian Soldiers. Abide with me. I'm gonna bring a watermelon to my girl to-night.

THIRD MOVEMENT

Mother's Day. (Mr. Herring of Indiana, "The Father of Mother's Day.") But why not Flapper's Day? It would be more representative, more democratic, so to speak. For in Joy City there are many more Flappers — married as well as unmarried — than Mothers.

> Nunc vitiat uterum quae vult formosa videri,
> Raraque in hoc aevo est quae velit esse parens.

Thousands and thousands of flappers, and almost all incredibly pretty. Plumply ravishing, they give, as T. S. Eliot has phrased it, a "promise of pneumatic bliss." Of pneumatic bliss, but of not much else, to judge by their faces. So curiously uniform, unindividual and blank. Hardly more expressive — to the foreign eye, at any rate — than any of the other parts of that well-contoured anatomy which they are at such pains to display.

On the beaches of the Pacific that display was indeed superb. Mack Sennett Bathing Beauties by the hundred. They gambolled all around us, as we walked up and down in the windy sunlight along the sands. Frisking temptations. But we were three St. Anthonies —

Charlie Chaplin and Robert Nichols and I—three grave theologians of art, too deeply absorbed in discussing the way of cinematographic salvation to be able to bestow more than the most casual attention on the Sirens, however plumply deserving.

FOURTH MOVEMENT

Cocktail time. (We've dealt with the same bootlegger for upwards of two years now. A most reliable man.) Ice rattles in the shaker—a dance of miniature skeletons—and the genuinely reliable liquor is poured out. *À boire, à boire!* Long live Pantagruel! This is dry America. We climbed into our host's car and drove, it seemed interminably, through the immense and sprawling city. Past movie palaces and theatres and dance halls. Past shining shops and apartments and enormous hotels. On every building the vertical lines of light went up like rockets into the dark sky. And the buildings themselves—they too had almost rocketed into existence. Thirty years ago Los Angeles was a one-horse—a half-horse—town. In 1940 or thereabouts it is scheduled to be as big as Paris. As big and as gay. The great Joy City of the West.

And what joy! The joy of rushing about, of always being busy, of having no time to think, of being too rich to doubt. The joy of shouting and bantering, of dancing and for ever dancing to the noise of a savage music, of lustily singing.

> (Yes, sir, she's my Baby.
>   No, sir, don't say "Maybe."
> Yes, sir, she's my Baby now.)

The joy of loudly laughing and talking at the top of the voice about nothing. (For thought is barred in this City of Dreadful Joy and conversation is unknown.) The joy of drinking prohibited whisky from enormous silver flasks, the joy of cuddling provocatively bold and pretty flappers, the joy of painting the cheeks, of rolling the eye and showing off the desirable calves and figure. The joy of going to the movies and the theatre, of sitting with one's fellows in luxurious and unexclusive clubs, of trooping out on summer evenings with fifty thousand others to listen to concerts in the open air, of being always in a crowd, never alone. The joy of going on Sundays to hear a peppy sermon, of melting at the hymns, of repenting one's sins, of getting a kick out of uplift. The joy in a word, of having what is technically known as a Good Time.

And oh, how strenuously, how whole-heartedly the people of Joy City devote themselves to having a Good Time! The Good Times of Rome and Babylon, of Byzantium and Alexandria were dull and dim and miserably restricted in comparison with the super-latively Good Time of modern California. The ancient world was relatively poor; and it had known catastrophe. The wealth of Joy City is unprecedentedly enormous. Its light-hearted people are unaware of War or pestilence or famine or revolution, have never in their safe and still half empty Eldorado known anything but prosperous peace, contentment, universal acceptance. The truest patriots, it may be, are those who pray for a national calamity.

On and on we drove, through the swarming streets of Joy City. (One automobile, sir, to every three and a quarter inhabitants.) The tall buildings impended, the lights whizzed up like rockets. On and on. Across an open space there suddenly loomed up a large white building, magically shining against the intensified blackness of the sky behind. (Just finished, sir, The Temple of the Elks.) From its summit the beams of half a dozen searchlights waved to heaven. They seemed the antennae of some vast animal, feeling and probing in the void—for what? For Truth, perhaps? Truth is not wanted in the City of Dreadful Joy. For Happiness? It is possessed. For God? But God had already been found; he was inside the shining Temple; he *was* the temple, the brand new, million-dollar Temple, in which at this moment the initiates of the venerable Order of Elks were con-gregated to worship, not the effetely aristocratic Lady Poverty, but plain American Mrs. Wealth. Five or six hundred motor-cars stood parked outside the doors. What *could* those luminous antennae be probing for? Why, for nothing, of course, for nothing! If they waved so insistently, that was just for fun. Waving for waving's sake. Movement is a joy and this is the great Joy City of the West.

FIFTH MOVEMENT

The restaurant is immense. The waiters sprint about, carrying huge dishes of the richest food. What Gargantuan profusion! Great

ten pound chops, square feet of steak, fillets of whale, whole turkeys
stewed in cream, mountains of butter. And the barbarous music
throbs and caterwauls unceasingly. Between each juicy and sati-
ating course, the flappers and the young men dance, clasped in an
amorous wrestle. How Rabelais would have adored it! For a week,
at any rate. After that, I am afraid, he would have begun to miss the
conversation and the learning, which serve in his Abbey of Thelema
as the accompaniment and justification of pleasure. This Western
pleasure, meaty and raw, untempered by any mental sauce —
would even Rabelais's unsqueamish stomach have been strong
enough to digest it? I doubt it. In the City of Dreadful Joy Pantagruel would soon have died of fatigue and boredom. *Taedium lau-
damus* — so reads (at any rate for the inhabitants of Rabelais's continent) the triumphant canticle of Californian joy.

The restaurant is suddenly plunged into darkness. A great beam
of light, like the Eye of God in an old engraving, stares down from
somewhere near the ceiling, right across the room, squinting this
way and that, searching — and at last finding what it had been looking for; a radiant figure in white, the singer of the evening. A good,
though not superlatively good singer in the style of Ethel Levey or
Jenny Golder.

> You gotta feed a chicken corn,
> You gotta feed a seal fish,
> You gotta feed a man (significant pause and *oeillade*) Love.

And so on. The enthusiasm which greets these rhymed lectures in
elementary physiology is inordinate. Being enthusiastic is a joy. We
are in Joy's metropolis.

There is a final burst of applause. The divine eyelid closes down
over God's shining eye. The band strikes up again. The dancing re-
begins. The Charleston, the fox-trot. "There is only one first-class
civilisation in the world to-day. It is right here, in the United States
and the Dominion of Canada." Monkeyville, Bryan, the Ku Klux
Klan. "Europe's is hardly second-class, and Asia's is fourth to sixth
class." Jazz it up; jazz it up! And what did late, great Ambassador
Page have to say? "The whole continent (of Europe) is rotten, or
tyrannical, or yellow dog. I wouldn't give Long Island or Moore
County for the whole continent of Europe." And with Coney Island

added to Long Island and Los Angeles in the scale along with Moore County, he might have thrown in all Asia and the British Empire. Three cheers for Page! Yes, sir, "American idealism has made itself felt as a great contributory force to the advancement of mankind." Three cheers for George F. Babbitt and the Rotary Club! And three cheers for Professor Nixon Carver! "Prosperity," the Professor has said, "is coming to us precisely because our ideas are not materialistic. All these things (*e.g.,* the Elks' Temple, the jazz bands, the movie palaces, the muffins at breakfast) are added to us precisely because we are seeking the Kingdom of God and His righteousness." Three cheers more—thrice three! The Prof. deserves them.

It is almost midnight. A few minutes and it will be the Sabbath. A few hours and the Giant Marimbaphone will be proclaiming the glory of the new billion dollar God. At the Ambassador Hotel (alas, too expensive for me to stay at) Dr. Ernest Holmes will be preaching on "The Science of Jesus." It is time to go home. Farewell, farewell. Parting is such sweet sorrow. Did Tosti raise his bowler hat when he said "Good-bye"?

H. L. Mencken

Among the most flamboyant figures in 1920s Los Angeles was the evangelist Sister Aimee Semple McPherson. Preaching the doctrine of the Four Square Gospel at her Angelus Temple in Echo Park, Sister Aimee at the peak of her popularity had over 40,000 loyal followers, and was worth more than a million dollars in property and assets. In May 1926, she disappeared while swimming near Santa Monica, only to reappear five weeks later in the Mexican desert, claiming to have been kidnapped. The truth was more lurid: she had run off with the Angelus Temple's radio operator, a married man with whom she'd been having an affair. McPherson stood trial on charges (later dropped) of obstructing justice. In the midst of the scandal, H. L. Mencken (1880–1956)—no friend either to evangelism or to the emerging culture of Los Angeles—arrived in Southern California to report on Sister Aimee for the *Baltimore Evening Sun.*

SISTER AIMÉE

The Rev. sister in God, I confess, greatly disappointed me. Arriving in Los Angeles out of the dreadful deserts of Arizona and New Mexico, I naturally made tracks to hear and see the town's most distinguished citizen. Her basilica turned out to be at a great distance from my hotel, far up a high hill and in the midst of a third-rate neighborhood. It was a cool and sunshiny Sunday afternoon, the place was packed, and the whisper had gone around that Aimée was heated up by the effort to jail her, and would give a gaudy show. But all I found myself gaping at, after an hour, was an orthodox Methodist revival, with a few trimmings borrowed from the Baptists and the Holy Rollers—in brief, precisely the sort of thing that goes on in the shabby suburbs and dark back streets of Baltimore, three hundred nights of every year.

Aimée, of course, is richer than most evangelists, and so she has got herself a plant that far surpasses anything ever seen in shabby suburbs. Her temple to the One God is immensely wide—as wide, almost, as the Hippodrome in New York—and probably seats 2,500 customers. There is a full brass band down in front, with a grand piano to one side of it and an organ to the other. From the vast gallery, built like that of a theater, runways run along the side walls to what may be called the proscenium arch, and from their far ends stairways lead down to the platform. As in many other evangelical bull-rings, there are theater seats instead of pews. Some pious texts are emblazoned on the wall behind the platform: I forget what they say. There are no stained-glass windows. The architecture, in and out, is of the Early Norddeutscher–Lloyd Rauchzimmer school, with modifications suggested by the filling-stations of the Standard Oil Company of New Jersey. The whole building is very cheaply made. It is large and hideous, but I don't think it cost much. Nothing in Los Angeles appears to have cost much. The town is inconceivably shoddy.

As I say, Aimée has nothing on tap to make my eyes pop, old revival fan that I am. The proceedings began with a solemn march by the brass band, played about as well as the average Salvation Army could have done it, but no better. Then a brother from some remote outpost filed down the aisle at the head of a party of fifty or sixty of the faithful. They sang a hymn, the brother made a short speech, and then he handed Aimée a check for $500 for her Defense Fund. A quartet followed, male, a bit scared, and with Army haircuts. Two little girls then did a duet, to the music of a ukulele played by one of them. Then Aimée prayed. And then she delivered a brief harangue. I could find nothing in it worthy of remark. It was the time-honored evangelical hokum, made a bit more raucous than usual by the loud-speakers strewn all over the hall. A brother who seemed to be a sort of stage manager held the microphone directly under Aimée's nose. When, warmed by her homiletic passion, she turned this way or that, he followed her. It somehow suggested an attentive deck steward, plying his useful art on a rough day. Aimée wore a long white robe, with a very low-cut collar, and over it there was a cape of dark purple. Her thick hair, piled high, turned out to be of mahogany brown. I had heard that it was a flaming red.

The rest of the orgy went on in the usual way. Groups of four, six, eight or twenty got up and sang. A large, pudgy, soapy-looking brother prayed. Aimée herself led the choir in a hymn with a lively tune and very saucy words, chiefly aimed at her enemies. Two or three times more she launched into brief addresses. But mostly she simply ran the show. While the quartets bawled and the band played she was busy at a telephone behind the altar or hurling orders in a loud stage-whisper at sergeants and corporals on the floor. Obviously, a very managing woman, strongly recalling the madame of a fancy-house on a busy Saturday night. A fixed smile stuck to her from first to last.

What brought this commonplace and transparent mountebank to her present high estate, with thousands crowding her tabernacle daily and money flowing in upon her from whole regiments of eager dupes? The answer, it seems to me, is as plain as mud. For years she had been wandering about the West, first as a side-show wriggler, then as a faith healer, and finally as a cow-town evangelist. One day, inspired by God, she decided to try her fortune in Los Angeles. Instantly she was a roaring success. And why? For the plain reason that there were more morons collected in Los Angeles than in any other place on earth—because it was a pasture foreordained for evangelists, and she was the first comer to give it anything low enough for its taste and comprehension.

The osteopaths, chiropractors and other such quacks had long marked and occupied it. It swarmed with swamis, spiritualists, Christian Scientists, crystal-gazers and the allied necromancers. It offered brilliant pickings for real estate speculators, oil-stock brokers, wire-tappers and so on. But the town pastors were not up to its opportunities. They ranged from melancholy High Church Episcopalians, laboriously trying to interest retired Iowa alfalfa kings in ritualism, down to struggling Methodists and Baptists, as earnestly seeking to inflame the wives of the same monarchs with the crimes of the Pope. All this was over the heads of the trade. The Iowans longed for something that they could get their teeth into. They wanted magic and noise. They wanted an excuse to whoop.

Then came Aimée, with the oldest, safest tricks out of the pack of Dr. Billy Sunday, Dr. Gipsy Smith and the rest of the old-time hell-robbers, and to them she added capers from her circus days. In a month she had Los Angeles sitting up. In six months she had it in an uproar. In a year she was building her rococo temple and her flamboyant Bible College and the half-wits were flocking in from twenty States. Today, if her temple were closed by the police, she could live on her radio business alone. Every word she utters is carried on the air to every forlorn hamlet in those abominable deserts, and every day the mail brings her a flood of money.

The effort to jail her has disingenuousness in it, and the more civilized Angeleños all sympathize with her, and wish her well. Her great success raised up two sets of enemies, both powerful. One was made up of the regular town clergy, who resented her raids upon their customers. The other was composed of the town Babbitts who began to fear that her growing celebrity was making Los Angeles ridiculous. So it was decided to bump her off, and her ill-timed morganatic honeymoon with the bald-headed and wooden-legged Mr. Ormiston offered a good chance. But it must be manifest to any fair observer that there is very little merit in the case against her. What she is charged with, in essence, is perjury, and the chief specification is that, when asked if she had been guilty of unchastity, she said no. I submit that no self-respecting judge in the Maryland Free State, drunk or sober, would entertain such a charge against a woman, and that no Maryland grand jury would indict her. It is unheard of, indeed, in any civilized community for a woman to be tried for perjury uttered in defense of her honor. But in California, as everyone knows, the process of justice is full of unpleasant novelties, and so poor Aimée, after a long and obscene hearing, has been held for trial.

The betting odds in the Los Angeles saloons are 50 to 1 that she will either hang the jury or get a clean acquittal. I myself, tarrying in the town, invested some money on the long end, not in avarice, but as a gesture of sympathy for a lady in distress. The local district attorney has the newspapers on his side, and during the progress of Aimée's hearing he filled one of them, in the chivalrous Southern California manner, with denunciations of her. But Aimée herself has the radio, and I believe that the radio will count most in the long run. Twice a day, week in and week out, she caresses the anthropoids of all that dusty, forbidding region with her lubricious coos. And twice a day she meets her lieges of Los Angeles face to face, and has at them with her shiny eyes, her mahogany hair, her eloquent hips, and her lascivious voice. It will be a hard job, indeed, to find twelve men and true to send her to the hoosegow. Unless I err grievously, our Heavenly Father is with her.

Upton Sinclair

The Long Beach oil boom of the early 1920s was a transformative event, ushering in a decade of excess that encompassed political scandals all the way up to the White House and ended only with the 1927 collapse of the Julian Petroleum Company, which had issued more than three million shares of phony stock. In that same year Upton Sinclair (1878–1968) published his *Oil!*, a muckraking novel that traces the corrupting effects of the boom through the travails of a father-and-son team of independent oil operators. Sinclair, best known for *The Jungle*, his 1906 exposé of the meatpacking industry, had settled in Pasadena in 1916 and was for many decades a singular presence in Southern California political life as socialist candidate for congressman, senator, and governor. He came closest to success in his tumultuous 1934 race for the governorship on the EPIC (End Poverty in California) ticket, but was defeated due in part to a well-orchestrated smear campaign led by, among others, MGM mogul Louis B. Mayer.

from

OIL!

Well, they made the trip back to the old field; and Bunny remembered all the adventures of the last ride, the place where they had had lunch, and what the waitress had said, and the place where they had stopped for gas, and what the man had said, and the place where they had run into the "speed-cop." It was like fishing—that is, for real fish, like you catch in water, not in oil-wells; you remember where you got the big fish, and you expect another bite there. But the big fish always come at a new place, said Dad, and it was the same with "speed-cops." A cop picked them up just outside Beach City, passing a speed-trap at forty-seven miles; and Dad grinned and chaffed the cop, and said he was glad he hadn't been really going fast.

They got to Lobos River that evening; and there was the rig, fishing away—screwing the stands of pipe together and working down into the hole with some kind of grabbing device on the end, and then hauling up and unscrewing—stand after stand, fifty or sixty of them, one after another—until at last you got to the bottom one, only to find that you had missed your "fish!"

Well, Dad said his say, in tones that nobody could help hearing. If he couldn't find men who would take care of their own bones, it was doubtless too much to hope they would take care of his property. They stood there, looking like a lot of school-boys getting a birching—though of course the "rough-neck" who was wholly to blame had been turned loose on the road long ago.

There was a salesman from a supply house there with a patent device which he guaranteed would bring up the obstacle the first run; so they tried it, and left the device in the hole—it had held on too tight! Evidently there was a pocket down there, and the crow-bar had got wedged crossways; so they'd have to try a small chunk of dynamite, said Dad. Ever listen to an explosion four thousand feet under the ground? Well, that was how they got the crowbar loose; and then they had a job of cleaning out, and drilling some more, and setting a casing to cover the damaged place in the hole.

Thus, day by day, Bunny got his oil lessons. He wandered about the field with Dad and the geologist and the boss driller, while they laid out the sites for future wells; and Dad took an envelope and pencil, and explained to Bunny why you place your wells on the four corners of a diamond, and not on the four corners of a square. You may try that out for yourself, drawing a circle about each well, to indicate the territory from which the oil is drained; you will see that the diamond shape covers the ground with less overlapping. Wherever you overlap, you are drilling two holes to get the same barrel of oil; and only a dub would do that.

They drove back to Beach City, and found that Bertie had come home. Bertie was Bunny's sister, two years his senior, and she had been visiting the terribly fashionable Woodbridge Rileys, up north. Bunny tried to tell her about the fishing-job, and how things were going at Lobos River, but she was most cruelly cutting—described him as a "little oil gnome," and said that his fingernails were a "dead give-away." It appeared that Bertie had become ashamed of oil; and this was something new, for of old she had been a good pal, interested in the business, and arguing with Bunny and bossing him as any older sister should. Bunny didn't know what to make of it, but

gradually he came to understand that this was a part of the fashionable education Bertie was getting at Miss Castle's school.

Aunt Emma was to blame for this. She had granted Jim's right
to confine Bunny's training to the making of money, but Bertie at
least should be a young lady—meaning that she should learn how
to spend the money which Dad and Bunny were going to make.
So Aunt Emma got the name of the most expensive school for
young female money-spenders, and from that time on the family
saw little of Bertie; after school she went to visit her new rich
friends. She couldn't bring them to her home, there being no real
butler—Rudolph was a "farm-hand," she declared. She had picked
up some wonderful new slang; if she didn't like what you said, she
would tell you that you were "full of prunes"—this was away back
in history, you understand. She would give a pirouette and show off
her fancy lingerie, with violet-colored ribbons in it; she would laugh
gleefully: "Aren't I a speedy young thing?"—and other phrases
which caused grandmother to stare and Dad to grin. She would be
pained by her father's grammar: "Oh, Dad, *don't* say 'jist'!" And
Dad would grin again, and reply: "I been a-sayin' it jist fifty-nine
years." But all the same, he began a-sayin' it less frequently; which
is how civilization progresses.

Bertie condescended to drive out to the field, and see the new
derricks that were going up. They went for a walk, and whom
should they meet but Mrs. Groarty, getting out of her elderly Ford
car in front of her home. Bunny was naively glad to see her, and
insisted upon introducing Bertie, who displayed her iciest manner,
and, as they went on, scolded Bunny because of his horrid vulgar
taste; he might pick up acquaintance with every sort of riff-raff if he
chose, but certainly he need not make his sister shake hands with
them! Bunny could not understand—he never did succeed in
understanding, all his life long, how people could fail to be interested in other people.

He told Bertie about Paul, and what a wonderful fellow he was,
but Bertie said just what Dad had said, that Paul was "crazy." More
than that, she became angry, she thought that Paul was a "horrid
fellow," she was glad Bunny hadn't been able to find him again.
That was an attitude which Bertie was to show to Paul all through

Paul's life; she showed it at the very first instant, and poor Bunny was utterly bewildered. But in truth, it was hardly reasonable to expect that Bertie, who was going to school in order to learn to admire money—to find out by intuition exactly how much money everybody had, and to rate them accordingly—should be moved to admiration by a man who insisted that you had no right to money unless you had earned it!

Bertie was following her nature, and Bunny followed his. The anger of his sister had the effect of setting Paul upon a lonely eminence in Bunny's imagination; a strange, half-legendary figure, the only person who had ever had a chance to get some of Dad's money, and had refused it! Every now and then Bunny would stop by and sit on a rabbit-hutch, and ask Mrs. Groarty for news about her nephew. One time the stout lady showed him a badly scrawled note from Ruth Watkins—Paul's sister, whom he loved—saying that the family had had no word; also that they were having a hard time keeping alive, they were having to kill a goat now and then—and Mrs. Groarty said that was literally eating up their capital. Later on there was another letter from Ruth, saying that Paul had written to her; he was up north, and still on the move, so no one could get hold of him; he sent a five-dollar bill in a registered letter, and specified that it was to go for food, and not for missions. It wasn't easy to save money when you were only getting a boy's pay, Paul said; and again Bunny was moved to secret awe. He went off and did a strange secret thing—he took a five-dollar bill, and folded it carefully in a sheet of paper, and sealed it up in a plain envelope, and addressed it to "Miss Ruth Watkins, Paradise, California," and dropped it into a mail-box.

Mrs. Groarty was always glad to see Bunny, and Bunny, alas, knew why—she wanted to use him for an oil-well! He would politely pay her with a certain amount of information. He asked Dad about Sliper and Wilkins, and Dad said they were "four-flushers"; Bunny passed this information on, but the "medium lots" went ahead and signed up with this pair—and very soon wished they hadn't. For Sliper and Wilkins proceeded to sell the lease to a syndicate, and so there was a tent on the lot next to the Groarty home, and free lunches being served to crowds of people gathered up in the streets of Beach City by a "ballyhoo" man. "Bonanza Syndicate

No. 1," it was called; and they hustled up a derrick, and duly "spud-ded in," and drilled a hundred feet or so; and Mrs. Groarty was in heaven, and spent her thousand dollars of bonus money for a hun-dred units of another syndicate, the "Co-operative No. 3." The crowds trampled her lawn, but she didn't care—the company would move her home when they drilled the second well, and she was going into a neighborhood that was "much sweller"—so she told Bunny.

But then, on his next visit, he saw trouble in the stout lady's fea-tures. The drilling had stopped; the papers said the crew was "fish-ing," but the men said they were "fishing for their pay." The selling of "units" slowed down, the "ballyhoo" stopped, and then the syndi-cate was sold to what was called a "holding company." The drilling was not resumed, however, and poor Mrs. Groarty tried pitifully to get Bunny to find out from his father what was happening to them. But Dad didn't know, and nobody knew—until six months or so later, long after Dad had brought in his Ross-Bankside No. 1 with triumphant success. Then the newspapers appeared with scare headlines to the effect that the grand jury was about to indict D. Buckett Kyber and his associates of the Bonanza Syndicate for fraudulent sales of oil stock. Dad remarked to Bunny that this was probably a "shake-down"; some of the officials, and maybe some of the newspaper men, desired to be "seen" by Mr. Kyber. Presumably they were "seen," for nothing more was heard of the prosecution. Meantime, the owners of the lease could not get anyone to continue the drilling, for the block next to them had brought in a two hun-dred barrel well, which was practically nothing; the newspapers now said that the south slope looked decidedly "edgy."

So Bunny, in the midst of his father's glory, would pass down the street and encounter poor Mr. Dumpery, coming home from the trolley with dragging steps, after having driven some thousands of shingle-nails into a roof; or Mr. Sahm, the plasterer, tending his lit-tle garden, with its rows of corn and beans that were irrigated with a hose. Bunny would see Mrs. Groarty, feeding her chickens and cleaning out her rabbit-hutches—but never again did he see the fancy evening-gown of yellow satin! He would go inside, and sit down and chat, in order not to seem "stuck-up"; and there was the stairway that led to nowhere, and the copy of "The Ladies' Guide:

A Practical Handbook of Gentility," still resting on the centre-table, its blue silk now finger-soiled, and its gold letters tarnished. Bunny's eyes took in these things, and he realized what Dad meant when he compared the oil-game to heaven, where many are called and few are chosen.

Scattered here and there over the hill were derricks, and the drilling crews were racing to be the first to tap the precious treasure. By day you saw white puffs from the steam-engines, and by night you saw lights gleaming on the derricks, and day and night you heard the sound of heavy machinery turning, turning—"ump-um—ump-um—ump-um—ump-um." The newspapers reported the results, and a hundred thousand speculators and would-be speculators read the reports, and got into their cars and rode out to the field where the syndicates had their tents, or thronged the board-rooms in town, where prices were chalked up on blackboards, and "units" were sold to people who would not know an oil-derrick from a "chute the chutes."

Who do you think stood first in the newspaper reports? You would need to make but one guess—Ross-Bankside No. 1. Dad was right there, day and night, knowing the men who were working for him, watching them, encouraging them, scolding them if need be—and so Dad had not had a single accident, he had not lost a day or night. The well was down to thirty-two hundred feet, and in the first stratum of oil-sand.

They were using an eight-inch bit, and for some time they had been taking a core. Dad was strenuous about core-drilling; he insisted that you must know every inch of the hole, and he would tell stories of men who had drilled through paying oil-sands and never known it. So the drill brought up a cylinder of rock, exactly like the core you would take out of an apple; and Bunny learned to tell shale from sandstone, and conglomerate from either. He learned to measure the tilt of the strata, and what that told the geologist about the shape of things down below, and the probable direction of the anticline. When there were traces of oil, there had to be chemical analyses, and he learned to interpret these reports. Every oil-pool in the world was different—each one a riddle, with colossal prizes for the men who could guess it!

Dad guessed that he was right over the pool, and so he had ordered his "tankage." There was going to be a rush for this, as for everything else, and Dad had the cash—and still more important, the reputation for having the cash! He would get his "tankage" onto the lease, and if he were disappointed in his hopes for oil—well, somebody else would get it, and they would be glad to take the "tankage" off his hands. So there came a stream of heavy trucks, and stacked up on the field were flat sheets of steel, and curved sheets, all fitting exactly.

You may be sure the buyers of "units" did not fail to make note of that! They were hanging round the derrick day and night, trying to pick up hints; they followed the men to their homes, and tried to bribe them, or to get into conversation with their wives. As for Bunny, he was about the most popular boy in Beach City; it was wonderful how many kind gentlemen, and even kind ladies there were, anxious to buy him ice-cream, or to feed him out of boxes of candy! Dad forbade him to say a word to strangers, or to have anything to do with them; and presently Dad banned discussions at the family table—because Aunt Emma was chattering in the ladies' clubs, and the ladies were telling their husbands, besides gambling "on their own!"

The core showed more signs, and Dad gave orders to build the foundations of the tanks; then he ordered the tanks put up, and the clatter of riveting machines was heard, and magically there rose three ten thousand barrel tanks, newly painted with flaming red lead. And then—hush!—they were in the real oil-sands; Dad set a crew of Mexicans to digging him a trench for a pipe line; and the lease-hounds and the dealers in units discovered that, and the town went wild. In the middle of the night Dad was routed out of bed, and he called Bunny, and they jumped into their old clothes and went racing out to the well, and there were the first signs of the pressure, the mud was beginning to jump and bubble in the hole! The drilling had stopped, and the men were hastily screwing on the big "casing-head" that Dad had provided. He wasn't satisfied even with that—he set them to fastening heavy lugs to the head, and he hustled up a couple of cement men and built great blocks of cement over the lugs, to hold her down in spite of any pressure. There wasn't going to be a blow-out on Ross-Bankside No. 1, you bet; whatever oil came through that hole was going into the tanks, and from there into Dad's bank account!

It was time for the "cementing-off," to make the well water-proof, and protect the precious oil-sands. Down there under the ground was a pool of oil-sands. Down there under the ground was a pool of oil, caught under a layer of impermeable rock, exactly like an inverted wash-basin. The oil was full of gas, which made the pressure. Now you had drilled a hole through the wash-basin, and the oil and gas would come to you—but only on condition that you did not let any surface water down to kill the pressure. All the way down you had been tapping underground streams and pools of water; and now you had to set a big block of cement at the bottom of the hole, solid and tight, filling every crevice, both inside and outside your casing. Having got this tight, you would drill a hole through it, and on down into the oil sands, thus making a channel through which the oil could flow up, and no water could leak down. This was the critical part of your operation, and while it was going on the whole crew was keyed up, and the owner and his son, needless to say.

First you put down your casing, known as the "water-string." If you were a careful man, like Dad, you ran this "string" all the way up to your derrick-floor. Next you began pumping down clean water; for many hours you pumped, until you had washed the dirt and oil out of the hole; and then you were ready for the cement-men. They came with a truck, a complete outfit on wheels, ready to travel to any well. Another truck brought the sacks of cement, a couple of hundred of them; the job called for pure cement, no sand. They got everything ready before they started, and then they worked like so many fiends—for this whole job had to be put through in less than an hour, before the cement began to set.

It was an ingenious scheme they had, very fascinating to watch. They fitted inside the casing a cast-iron "packer," having rubber discs at the top and bottom, so that it floated on the water in the casing; the cement went on top of this. The sacks were jerked open, and dumped into the hopper of the mixing machine, and the mixer began to revolve, and the river of grey liquid to pout into the hole. It ran fast, and the heavy pumps set to work, and drove it down, stroke after stroke. In half an hour they had filled several hundred feet of the casing with cement; after which they put on a rubber "packer," fitting tight to the casing; and again the heavy pumps went to work, and drove the mass of cement, between the two "packers," down into the hole. When they came to the bottom, the bottom packer would drop, and the cement would pour in, and the pressure of the top packer would force it into every cranny of the hole, and up between the outside of the casing and the earth—one or two hundred feet high it would rise, and when it set, there you would have your "water shut-off."

What could be more fun to watch than a job like this? To know what was going on under the ground; to see the ingenuity by which men overcame Nature's obstacles; to see a crew of workers, rushing here and there, busy as beavers or ants, yet at the same time serene and sure, knowing their job, and just how it was going!

The job was done; and then you had to wait ten days for your cement to get thoroughly set. The state inspector came and made his tests, to be sure you had got a complete "shut-off"; if you hadn't, he would make you do it over again—some poor devils had to do it twenty or thirty times! But nothing like that happened to Dad; he knew about "cementing off"—and also about inspector, he added with a grin. Anyhow, he got his permit; and now Ross-Bankside No. 1 was drilling into the real oil-sands, going down with a six-inch hole. Every few hours they would test for pressure, to be sure they had enough, but not too much. You were right on the verge of triumph now, and your pulse went fast and you walked on tip-toe with excitement. It was like waiting for Christmas morning, to open your stocking, and see what Santa Claus had brought! There were crowds staring at the well all day, and you put up rude signs to make them keep their noses out.

Dad said they were deep enough now, and they proceeded to set the last casing—it was known as the "linear," and had holes like a sieve, through which the treasure would flow. They were working late into the night, and both Dad and Bunny had old clothes on, and were bathed in oil and mud. At last they had the "liner" all ready, and the tools out, and they started to "wash" the well, pumping in fresh water and cleaning out the mud and sand. That would go on for five or six hours, and meantime Dad and Bunny would get their sleep.

When they came back, it was time to "bail." You understand, the pressure of the gas and oil was held down by the column of water, two thirds of a mile deep. Now they had what they called a "double-section bailer," which was simply a bucket fifty feet long. They would let that down, and lift out fifty feet of the water-column, and dump it into the sump-hole. Then they would go down for another fifty; and presently they would find they didn't have to go down so far, the pressure was shoving the column of water up in the hole. Then you knew you were getting near to the end; one or two more trips of the bailer, and the water would be shot out of the hole, and mud and water and oil would spout up over the top of the derrick, staining it a lovely dripping black. You must drive the crowds off the lease now, and shout "Lights out!" to the fools with cigarettes.

There she came! There was a cheer from all hands, and the spectators went flying to avoid the oily spray blown by the wind. They let her shoot for a while, until the water had been ejected; higher and higher, way up over the derrick—she made a lovely noise, hissing and splashing, bouncing up and down!

It was just at sundown, and the sky was crimson. "Lights out!" Dad kept calling—nobody must even start a motor-car while she was spouting. Presently they shut her off, to try the valve of the casing-head; they worked on, late into the night, letting her spout, and then shutting her off again; it was mysteriously thrilling in the darkness. At last they were ready to "bring her in"—which meant they would screw up the "flow-line" between the casing-head and the tank, and let the oil run into the latter. Just as simple as that— no show, no fuss, you just let her flow; the gauge showed her coming at the rate of thirty thousand gallons every hour, which meant that the first tank was full by noon the next day.

Yes, that was all; but the news affected Beach City as if an angel had appeared in a shining cloud and scattered twenty-dollar gold pieces over the streets. You see, Ross-Bankside No. 1 "proved up" the whole north slope; to tens of thousands of investors, big and little, it meant that a hope was turned into glorious certainty. You couldn't keep such news quiet, it just didn't lie in the possibility of human nature not to tell; the newspapers bulletined the details—Ross-Bankside was flowing sixteen thousand barrels a day, and the gravity was 32, and as soon as the pipe-line was completed—which would be by the end of the week—its owner would be in possession of an income of something over twenty thousand dollars every twenty-four hours. Would you need to be told that the crowds stared at Dad and at Bunny, everywhere they went about the streets of the city? There goes the great J. Arnold Ross, owner of the new well! And that little chap is his son! Say, he's got thirteen dollars coming to him every minute of the day or night, whether he's awake or asleep. By God, a fellow would feel he could afford to order his lunch, if he was to have an income like that!

Bunny couldn't help but get a sense of importance, and think that he was something special and wonderful. Little thrills ran over him; he felt as if he could run up into the air and fly. And then Dad would say: "Take it easy, son! Keep your mouth shut, and don't go a-gettin' your head swelled. Remember, you didn't make this here money, and you can lose it in no time, if you're a light-weight." Dad was a sensible fellow, you see; he had been through all this before, first at Antelope, and then at Lobos River. He had felt the temptation of grandeur, and knew what it must be to a boy. It was pleasant to have a lot of money; but you must set up a skeleton at the feast, and while you quaffed the wine of success, you must hear a voice behind you whispering, "Memento mori!"

Carroll & Garrett Graham

The "Hollywood novel" dates back to the late teens and early twenties, but it was only with the publication of *Queer People* (1930) by the brothers Carroll and Garrett Graham that the form began to come into its own. Cynical and biting (and, it must be said, pervasively anti-Semitic), it was, Budd Schulberg wrote, "the kind of thing you would not dare to bring into a motion picture studio unless you hid it in a brown wrapper and locked it in your middle desk drawer." This satirical take on a film community awash in its own excess gives a glimpse behind the respectable veneer offered up by Hollywood publicists and movie magazines, and its publication scandalized the industry. In the excerpt that follows, Whitey, the Grahams' hard-bitten protagonist, gains entry into the inner circles of the movie world.

from

QUEER PEOPLE

And so the film star called the bootlegger.

It was the only logical thing for Gilbert Vance to do. All in one day, his wife had left him, Colossal Pictures had renewed his contract, his mistress had returned unexpectedly from location, his lawyer had informed him that a charge of driving while intoxicated had been "fixed," and his tests—both film and Wassermann—had turned out favorably.

He had rather expected his wife to leave him, and he had been hoping that she would do it sooner. He had not been quite so sure about the contract, and it was naturally a source of immense relief to know that his magnificent salary was to continue for another year. But his joy was complete when Peanuts Oliver turned up in Hollywood. She was to have been away two weeks longer, and she would have been had her director been content with mere perpetual intoxication. But when he lapsed into delirium tremens, the company decided that while this would probably make no difference in the quality of the production, it would be a good excuse to call the troupe home and save money.

All of these things, naturally, called for a party.

Almost simultaneously with the arrival of the bootlegger, guests, guided by that occult sense which most Hollywood guests seem to possess, began to drop in.

Joe Greet, directing a comedy at Culver City, heard of the budding brawl in some mysterious fashion, dismissed his mimes for the afternoon, and hurried to Vance's home.

A leading man, apprised of the festivities, rushed over from the studio, without bothering to remove his grease-paint or change from the evening dress in which he had been performing.

Wind of it eddied to the Y.W.C.A. Studio Club. A bulletin was posted in the lobby for all hands to stand by the telephone and await invitations.

A blond young extra man driving by the house was seized because he could play the piano. He sent for his heart of the moment, a tempestuous Mexican girl who had lately abandoned a Tia Juana honky-tonk for a career on the screen.

There came divers others—scenario writers, a director or two, a minor studio official, two gagmen, extra girls, a real estate salesman, a casting director, and an unemployed press agent.

It assumed the aspect of particularly high festivities as the guests began to plow steadily through Gilbert Vance's Scotch. As the afternoon shadows lengthened and the din increased, an untrained ob-server might have thought that the utmost had been achieved in Hollywood wassail.

But the guest who was to prove the party's most spectacular member had not yet arrived. He had not even met any of those present. They had never heard of him.

Hollywood had no adequate means of coping with Whitey, nor Whitey with Hollywood. His invasion was in the nature of a surprise attack—a surprise to both Hollywood and Whitey.

He alighted from a Santa Fe transcontinental train, dusty and bored with three days of staring at Kansas, New Mexico and Arizona.

A taxi-driver seized his bags (one of which had been borrowed from a friend without permission) and whisked Whitey to the Rosslyn Hotel in downtown Los Angeles.

Whitey registered, somewhat grandiosely, as Theodore Anthony White, indicated Chicago as his place of residence, bought copies of all the afternoon papers, and followed the boy to his room.

After a bath had removed the railroad grime from his chubby body, Whitey settled down to survey his probable future in Los Angeles.

Unpacking his bags was no great task. They contained another suit, a battered pair of tan shoes, bedroom slippers belonging to the friend who owned the bag, an old and frayed beach robe, a bathing suit two sizes too small for him, manuscripts of five unfinished short stories, a deck of marked cards from which the seven of spades was missing, a snapshot of himself and a plump maiden taken on the beach of Miami, two volumes of James Branch Cabell and a copy of Hecht's *Count Bruga*, an assortment of rumpled linen, a revolver which he had removed from the body of a slain Chicago gangster, shirt and shoes to go with evening dress which he did not possess and divers odds and ends, including an empty gin bottle, the last contents of which had been consumed as the train passed through Hutchinson, Kansas.

Whitey, to his knowledge, had not an acquaintance in town and was heartily glad of it. In his roving career as a newspaperman he had touched upon such ports as the Denver *Post*, the New Orleans *Times-Picayune*, the Omaha *Bee*, the Chicago *Herald-Examiner*, the Washington *Star*, the Cleveland *Plain-Dealer* and, returning to Chicago, the *Tribune*.

Until this day he had let Los Angeles remain unsmirched by his presence. He had fled to it now because the police had frowned upon a business venture which had seemed quite ingenious to Whitey at the time. The venture had embraced the manufacture and sale of police badges in wholesale lots without official sanction.

Whitey had thirty-six dollars in bills and silver amounting to about two dollars and seventy cents when he settled down in his hotel. He had no qualms whatsoever as he prepared to hurl himself against the city editors. He had attacked many a town with weaker financial reserves.

He glanced critically at the afternoon papers of Los Angeles and decided to try the morning publications first, because the pay was generally higher and also because he preferred the odd working hours, being a strange creature at best.

At six o'clock that evening he presented himself at the door leading into the editorial rooms of the *Examiner*. His way was barred by an unfriendly and impertinent boy.

"What's the name of the city editor?" Whitey asked.

"Van Ettisch. Why?"

"I want to see him."

"What about?"

"I'll discuss that with Mr. Van Ettisch."

"If it's a job you're after, he says not to let in any more of these hungry-looking reporters."

"My lad, just such young whelps as you have been trying to keep me out of city rooms from coast to coast. You can't win."

"Them's my orders."

Whitey appeared dismayed, but was not. He departed, walking humbly until he had turned the corner of the hallway and was out of sight. Then he began a thorough search for the back door which instinct and experience told him was there. A whirr of linotypes led him to the composing room. He threaded his way unerringly through it to a door which led to a vast chamber filled with typewriter desks. A number of the desks were occupied by earnest young men, but it was easy for Whitey to pick his way to the throne of the city editor. Van Ettisch looked exactly like a city editor, for one thing, and for another, his desk was in a remote corner, and he sat facing the door.

"Mr. Van Ettisch?" Whitey began, trying to inject dignity, deference and importance into his tone.

"Yes." The reply was neither friendly nor forbidding. It was a bare statement of fact.

Whitey leaped to his recitation. He must get it all out, he knew, before the editor could chill him with the stock reply, "Sorry, but we're all full."

"Mr. Van Ettisch, my name is White. I just got in from Chicago, where I've been doing re-write on the *Herald-Examiner*, and Mr. Duffy Cornell said to look you up and he would recommend me if you want recommendation."

This was untrue. It had been some years since Whitey had

worked for that paper, and if Mr. Cornell remembered him at all he certainly would have recommended him as nothing more than an unreliable reporter and a thoroughly bad egg. But Whitey knew that editors do not check up on such things.

"How long since you worked there?" Van Ettisch asked.

"Two months ago."

"Ever work on any other papers?"

"Oh, sure," Whitey rattled off a list of them glibly; not too many, for that would have branded him as a drifter.

"Just do re-write?"

"Oh, no, sir. Assignments, re-write, copy desk. Did make-up down in New Orleans."

This latter was also untrue.

"Married?"

"No, sir."

"Booze hound?"

"Oh, no, sir." Whitey's round face became angelic.

Van Ettisch paused to survey the candidate, after the manner of an expert horse-trader. He saw a stocky, plump man of medium height, with a round, pink, beaming face—a pleasant face, almost always lighted by a smile. His eyes were small and piggy, but they were alert and intelligent. His black hair was parted in the middle and plastered to his head. He was neither well-dressed nor unkempt. In short, he looked typically the reporter.

"Might use you on re-write, temporarily at least," Van Ettisch said. "Can't pay much."

"I don't care about that."

"Fifty a week to start."

"That's fine."

Thus did Theodore Anthony White become a member of the editorial staff of the *Examiner*. He was handed four stories to re-write from the afternoon papers. He acquitted himself satisfactorily, and convinced his employer immediately that he was a man of experience.

Nothing more happened to him until almost nine o'clock. His name was called out, and he scurried to the city desk.

"I've decided to send you on an assignment," Van Ettisch said, handing him a slip of paper on which an address was written.

"North Las Palmas Street. That's in Hollywood. Gilbert Vance lives there. You know—the movie actor. We have a tip his wife has left him. If she hasn't, she should. He won't answer the phone, but he's probably there. He'll lie about it, so demand to see Mrs. Vance. If she isn't there call back, and we'll bust the story."

"How do I go? Taxi?"

"Taxi, my eye! Catch a red car on Hill Street marked Gardner Junction. It goes out Hollywood Boulevard. Get off at Las Palmas. You can take a cab from there."

And thus began Whitey's invasion of Hollywood itself.

The surface car pushed slowly through the evening tangle of traffic on Hill Street, darted through the tunnel and turned on Sunset Boulevard. Rows of cheap houses and tawdry shops passed in review. Whitey had heard vaguely that Sunset was a prominent street, and he peered out curiously.

"If this is it, Hollywood's not so hot," he told himself.

He changed his mind gradually. Large apartment buildings, and smart shops and cafés replaced the frame dwellings and boarding houses. He noted by a signpost that the car had now swerved into Hollywood Boulevard.

A few minutes more and he had come upon another business district, the raucous traffic as heavy and disordered as in downtown Los Angeles. Office buildings and theaters came into view upon the real "Broadway" of the city. Flashing signs proclaimed the Music Box, the Vine Street Theater, the Hollywood Playhouse, the Egyptian, the glittering Chinese Theater, the Plaza Hotel, the Roosevelt and El Capitan.

Whitey scrambled to his feet when the conductor shouted, "Las Palmas." A moment later he stood on the pavements of Hollywood Boulevard and surveyed the oddest city in America.

A tremendous uproar was taking place across the street. A truck, bearing a huge generator, was providing power for giant arc-lights which played about the sky and into windows and spectators' eyes. One shop was ablaze with studio "broad" lights. A wheezy tenor, boosted to Gargantuan proportions, was bawling over the radio. Perhaps three hundred persons were milling about the street.

"What are they doing?" Whitey asked another observer. "Making a movie?"

"No. An opening for some beauty shop. A guy can't start a cigar store here any more without raising a row about it."

Whitey found a cab, gave the driver Gilbert Vance's address and was carried away toward his first encounter with a movie star. He did not hear the whirr of a maniacal Destiny's machinery en route.

The cab whined up a badly lighted street. Abruptly, the road bounced against the Hollywood hills and they began to climb. The driver was forced to shift into second gear.

"What a place for a house," Whitey muttered as they began to twist and duck among the hills.

"Her'y'are," the driver announced, jamming on the brakes without warning. Whitey peered out dubiously and saw only a wooden gate in the darkness. No lights were visible.

"Are you sure this is the place?" he asked.

"You want Gilbert Vance's house, don't you?"

"Yes, but it's all dark."

"You can't see the house from here. Go through that gate and up those stone steps. I oughta know the place. I've carried Vance up to it enough times."

"Well, you better wait for me," said Whitey. He pushed through the gate and began to feel his way around the winding steps, hoping fervently that Vance was not a lover of police dogs. A final turn, after a brief steep climb, brought a flood of light from a large studio window. Whitey could hear a jumble of voices, mingled with a phonograph playing *That's My Weakness Now.*

It was a very odd house, he decided from what he could see of it as he beat the large bronze knocker upon the futuristic half-Chinese, half-Grand Rapids door. His pounding at length brought a highly suspicious Japanese youth who peered out, barely opening the door.

"What you want?"

"I want to see Mr. Vance."

"Not here."

"Nuts; of course he's here. I'm from the *Examiner.*"

"Wait."

Whitey quickly slipped his foot in the door to prevent its being locked. After a brief struggle, the servant gave it up and disappeared to carry the message. He returned, followed by a large and rather handsome man, coatless and tieless, his thin, high voice contrasting oddly with his muscular frame.

"Whataya want?"

"Are you Gilbert Vance?"

"Yeah. What of it?"

"My name is White. I'm from the *Examiner* and . . ."

"The hell you are. Where's Jim Mitchell?"

"How do I know? I don't even know Jim Mitchell."

"He's the guy from the *Examiner* that's always around Hollywood."

"Oh, yes," Whitey explained, lying easily. "I remember. I'm a new man on the paper. This is Mitchell's night off."

"Well, what do you want? Let's have it."

"It's this, Mr. Vance. We got a tip down at the office that you and Mrs. Vance are separated, and that she's not living with you any more."

"It's a damned lie."

"Well, that's what we wanted to check up on. Is Mrs. Vance here?"

Vance did not reply for a moment, but studied Whitey carefully. When he did answer, his manner had changed.

"So you're a new man, huh?"

"Yes."

"Been in town long?"

"Poke him in the nose, Gil," came an alcoholic voice from the innards of the house.

Vance ignored the advice.

"I say, you haven't been here long?"

"About six hours."

"I see. Just a minute. I'll bring Mrs. Vance out, and she'll deny that there's any truth in this."

Vance was gone for some moments. He returned with a kittenish blonde, a good many years his junior, whom he led affectionately by the arm.

"Mabel, this is Mr. . . . . at . . ."

"White."

"Yes; Mr. White, of the *Examiner.* He has an absurd report that we have separated. I want you to deny it to his face."

The kittenish blonde giggled and lisped her reply.

"How perfectly ridiculous. Why, I wouldn't think of leaving Mr. Vance."

"You have no intention of separating?"

"Oh, no," they both chorused.

"That's fine. Can I use your telephone?"

"Bust him in the nose, Gil," came the alcoholic voice again.

"Sure, step right in," said Vance.

Whitey followed them into a large and gaudily furnished drawing room, somewhat dishevelled. The blond extra man was playing the piano. His Mexican inamorata was winding the phonograph, by way of providing competition. The leading man, in full evening dress, was asleep on a couch, breathing loudly. Three couples were dancing to the piano. A swarthy man was telling a long and apparently bawdy story to a mixed group. On a pile of cushions in one corner was sprawled a stocky, red-faced and rather morose gentleman with heavy and curiously assorted features. He was quite drunk, obviously, and glared at Whitey who assumed, correctly, that here was the source of the nose-busting advice.

At one end of the large and over-furnished room was a long table, crowded with bottles, tall glasses, ginger ale, seltzer bottles, a bowl of cracked ice and other appurtenances of the bar. On the floor were empty bottles, their straw wrappers strewn indiscriminately about.

"Telephone right here in the hall," said Vance, pointing. "Have a highball?"

As Whitey sat down at the telephone, Vance poured an almost lethal portion of Scotch whiskey into a tall glass, dumped in a chunk of ice, haphazardly added seltzer water, and placed the mixture at Whitey's elbow.

"Mr. Van Ettisch, this is Whitey," the reporter said, when his call eventually reached the city desk. "I'm calling from Vance's house. Yes, both Mr. and Mrs. Vance are here. They deny the separation. What? No, that's the only statement they will make. There's nothing to it. All right, I'll start back right away."

Vance had been listening carefully.

"There won't be anything in the paper about this?" he asked.

"Nope; not a word."

"That's great. Nice of you to fix things up like that. Have another drink?"

"Sure."

He led Whitey back into the center of things. Vance was more than a little intoxicated, Whitey observed, but was concealing it admirably.

"Boys and girls," Vance called, waving his arm like a prize-fight announcer, "want you to meet my old friend, Mr. White, from the *Examiner.*"

"Poke him in the nose," came the voice of the man on the floor.

"Now, listen, Joe," Vance said, soothingly. "You lay off, see? This guy is all right, and he just did me a favor. Don't get on one of your fighting jags."

"Never saw a reporter in my life who wasn't a double-crosser," the bellicose guest muttered.

"That's Joe Greet," Vance whispered to Whitey. "A comedy director. He's always talking about fighting, but he's harmless. He hates newspapermen because they sort of jammed him up when he got tight and drove into a street car a little while ago."

Another puissant highball was forced into Whitey's hand.

"Make yourself at home," Vance said. "You don't need to be introduced to anybody. There's the bar, and it's cafeteria style. Just a quiet little family gathering, with everybody friends."

"I'm going back to work as soon as I finish this," Whitey said.

But he was wrong.

Arna Bontemps

Early civic promoters liked to describe Los Angeles as a landscape of racial purity, or (in the words of *Los Angeles Times* city editor Charles Fletcher Lummis) "a new Eden for the Saxon homemaker." In fact, by 1930, L.A. had the largest African-American population on the West Coast. But the literary documentation concerning black life in early twentieth-century Southern California is scarce. Arna Bontemps' engaging novel *God Sends Sunday* (1931) is almost unique in its portrait of an otherwise neglected corner of L.A. life. (The novel was later adapted into the 1946 musical *St. Louis Woman*, with music by Harold Arlen.) Bontemps (1902–1973) came to Los Angeles in 1906, at the age of three, and was raised in Watts. He remained there until he moved to New York in 1924, where he participated in the first stirrings of what became the Harlem Renaissance. In later years he published a steady stream of novels, poems, historical works, and children's books, while working as librarian of Fisk University in Nashville. With his close friend Langston Hughes he edited the influential anthology *The Poetry of the Negro: 1746–1949.*

from

GOD SENDS SUNDAY

An incredible orange moon was rising over a world that seemed tiny by comparison, a world of low fences, dark shrubbery, and little, crooked shacks.

Augie, standing against a whitewashed picket gate, beneath the street lamp, suggested a comic little man cut with scissors from black paper. His preposterous luggage, his battered top-hat, were both far out of proportion with his small, aged body. He had rested a moment to re-fill his pipe and to cast a few nervous glances over the strange dark neighborhood.

"Dis de place a'right," he told himself. "But how's I'm gonna find Leah at dis time o' night? I ain't seen a livin' soul whut could enlighten me."

There was not a lighted window in sight, no sound indicating that any one was awake anywhere around. Once again Augie cursed his wretched luck. Here he was, no telling how near Leah's home, with no way of finding her before morning. He would have preferred riding on in the box car from which he had dropped a few hours earlier to this miserable waiting and aimless wandering.

From the Los Angeles freight yards Augie had tramped down to Watts and thence found his way out to Mudtown, the Negro neighborhood on the edge of that suburb. He had come a great many miles to seek Leah, and he had actually been on his way a dozen years. Curiously, Fate had prolonged the intervals between the steps of his journey, and he had lingered on and on in the intervening cities — San Antonio, Austin, Waco, Santa Fe, Albuquerque, Tucson, and Phoenix. Sometimes the end had seemed far away, so far indeed that the hope of ever reaching it became dim. Yet each time it would finally rise up again like a young flame, and Augie would become restless and dissatisfied with his surroundings. Invariably, at such times, he caught the first west-bound freight train.

And at last he was in Mudtown. This section, before the blacks came, had evidently been a walnut grove. A few of the trees were still standing. Beneath them crude shacks had been built and vines — morning-glory, gourd, and honeysuckle — had promptly covered them, giving the whole neighborhood an aspect of savage wildness. Elsewhere shacks were built in clumps of castor-bean trees and thus almost completely hidden away.

The streets of Mudtown were three or four dusty wagon paths. In the moist grass along the edges cows were staked. Broken carts and useless wagons littered the front yards of the people, carts with turkeys and game chickens and guinea fowl roosting on the spokes of the wheels and wagons from the beds of which small dark mules were eating straw. Ducks were sleeping in the weeds, and there was on the air a suggestion of pigs and slime holes. Tiny hoot-owls were sitting bravely on fence posts while bats wavered overhead like shadows.

Augie got in the middle of the road and started back toward the railroad tracks again. A small dog crept from under a step and came yapping out at him. There were gnats in the air. Augie staggered on the rough road like a drunken man, stumbling in numerous chuckholes and bruising his shins. But he plodded steadily ahead.

In those days, fifteen or twenty years ago, Negroes were not plentiful in the far west. Least of all were they to be seen in the rural

parts. A few of them, to be sure, had come as early as the historical gold rush with the forty-niners, working in personal service.
Others had followed the conquest of the frontier. But the number
had remained small until the great transcontinental railway lines
established important terminals in Los Angeles and San Francisco.
Then the real migration began. First the railroad men, Pullman
porters and dining-car waiters, brought their families; hearing the
rumors of attractive working conditions, their friends followed. Still
the tendency was for them to remain in the larger centers and
particularly in the locality of the train yards.

The small group in Mudtown was exceptional. Here, removed
from the influences of white folks, they did not acquire the inhibi-
tions of their city brothers. Mudtown was like a tiny section of the
deep south literally transplanted. Throughout the warm summer
days old toothless men sat in front of the little grocery store on
boxes, chewing the stems of cob pipes, recalling the 'Mancipation,
the actual beginning of their race. Women cooked over fireplaces
in the yards and boiled their clothes in heavy iron kettles. There
were songs in the little frail houses and over the steaming pots.
Lilacs grew at every doorstep. In every house there was a guitar.

Augie, of course, was not interested in these features of the
place. He was seeking his sister Leah, returning home. Under a
shed at an unimportant railroad flag station, he found a crowd of
tramps sleeping on the ground. He looked at them a moment
scornfully, then went around to the back and rested his luggage.
He remembered the large bottle under his coat and took a long
drink. He was not sleepy.

"Come on up, Mistah Sun," he said. "Heah I is at de gates o'
home. Heah I is, waitin' for day to break. Like as not I done been
pas' Leah's door two o' t'ree times an' didn't know it. I'm gettin'
fidgety now. Come on up, Mistah Sun!"

Suddenly over the pulsing countryside the trumpeting of innumerable cocks tore the air. Somewhere a train whistled. Some
morning birds burst unexpectedly into singing. Augie felt a quick
excitement. His heart pounded against his ribs.

"It's comin' up," he exclaimed. "Day gonna break 'fo' you can
say 'Jack Robinson.' O Mistah Sun!"

Edmund Wilson

Aimee Semple McPherson was hardly the only evangelist to find fame in Los Angeles; throughout the 1920s and 1930s, the city was as notorious for its religious demagogues and faith healers as for the extravagant illusions of Hollywood. Among the most successful of these preachers was the Reverend Bob Shuler, whose congregation consisted largely of the people Louis Adamic called "the Folks"—midwestern farmers retired to Southern California, yet still longing for the fiery fundamentalism they'd left back home. Unlike McPherson, whom he detested, Shuler used his Trinity Methodist South Church as a political platform, railing against Jews and Catholics, and lashing out at any public policy or official he disagreed with. Edmund Wilson (1895–1972) portrays Shuler in the last days of his influence; not long after this article (later collected in *The American Earthquake*) appeared in 1931, the federal government withdrew his license to broadcast on radio station KGEF.

THE CITY OF OUR LADY
THE QUEEN OF THE ANGELS

From the heart of thriving Los Angeles rise the grooves of gorgeous business cathedrals: the blue Avocado Building, bawdy as the peacock's tail, with its frieze of cute little kewpids; the golden Lubrication Building, one of the glories of Southern California, which has just failed for $50,000,000; the regal and greenish Citrus Building, made throughout of the purest lime candy, which has gone a little sugary from the heat.

And there is Aimee McPherson's wonderful temple, where good-natured but thrilling native angels guard the big red radio-tower love-wand and see to it that not a tittle or vibration of their mistress's kind warm voice goes astray as it speeds to you in your sitting-room and tells you how sweet Jesus has been to her and all the marvelous things she has found in Him. There is Syd Grauman's Babylonian Garage, where Purr-Pull and Violet Ray gasolines ensure a maximum of road comfort and soothe the eye with a pretty color. There are little black-silver sandwich bars, functional *à la moderne* and fit to make Frank Lloyd Wright's heart go pit-a-pat in his boots. Nuestro Pueblo de Nuestra Señora la Reina de Los Angeles has more lovely girls serving peach-freezes and appetizing sandwich specials with little pieces of sweet pickle on the side than any other city in the world.

Now we motor agreeably and speedily through the beautiful residential boulevards. The residential people of Los Angeles are cultivated enervated people, lovers of mixturesque beauty—and they like to express their emotivation in homes that imaginatively symphonize their favorite historical films, their best-beloved movie actresses, their luckiest numerological combinations or their previous incarnations in old Greece, romantic Egypt, quaint Sussex or among the high priestesses of love in amoristic old India.

Here you will find a Pekinese pagoda made of fresh and crackly peanut brittle—there a snow-white marshmallow igloo—there a toothsome pink nougat in the Florentine manner, rich with embedded pecans. There rears a pocket-size replica of heraldic Warwick Castle—and there drowses a nausey old nance. A wee wonderful Swiss shilly-shally snuggles up beneath a bountiful bougainvillea which is by no means artificially colored; and a hot little hacienda, a regular *enchilada con queso*, with a roof made of rich red tomato sauce, hardly lifts her long-lashed lavender shades on the soul of old Spanish days.

Here and there handsome old flat houses of the early California frame-dwellers, or more imposing patrician mansions with scrolleries, cupolas and gigolos, give a conservative reminder of former fashions—while a big red brick Methodist church strikes a croak of coarse decorum. Yet not all the places of worship are sober—many cheery little odd-boxes, god-boxes, offer you a thousand assorted faiths and a thousand assorted flavors, from Theophistry to Christian Sirens. And in that rose garden, rapt in a trance, sits Buddha-like a roguey old Yogi, while pink clematis or purple clitoris rises or droops in rhythm to the movement of the mystic's fingers.

Those tall palms with their stiff tousled wigs are like Topsy, they just growed. And here we are in beautiful Beverley Hills—all flats, it is true, but what flats!—classy homes of real French filmsy-flamsy, coffee, toffee, chalky, cream, crome and bluff. Can't you just imagine Greta Garbo, lovely, alluring, aloof, slinking down the luxurious portico of that gay Riviera villa on the arm of a Mediterranean count! And hot little Clara Bow, who can romp with sailor boys like a *gamine*, serves tea with the grace of a *grande dame* in her chintzy classical palace which she has christened the Baths of Claraclara!

Leaving Hollywood itself behind, a bewilderment of fabricated features amazes us on either side: a blue will-o'-the-whimsy windmill and a trapper's cabin of plaster pine-logs that sells lime and lemon dope-flavored pop, a statue in papier-mâché of a woman in an old-fashioned sun-bonnet milking a cow with bright nickel teats, an ice-cream freezer in papier-mâché that deliciously glorifies ice cream and a big papier-mâché orange that seems to have gone bankrupt.

And you must visit the Hollywood zoo in its excitingly simulated bamboo-brake—where you can see a plaster lion, a rubber cobra, a mechanical crocodile, a gorilla with a colored boy inside and a new model of ball-bearing dinosaur that stands only eighteen inches high.

Surely that pretty little pink peppermint cabaña must be the home of dear Mickey and Minnie! And ye olde halffe-timberedde Pigglie Wigglie and ye Olde Gooffie Boofulle Shoppe—what fairy-tales these wonder-folks make true!

Here you may find real bargains in beach-lots of sand that is white as snow and lovebirds that will set you cooing—you can buy a swanky snooty chow puppy or a sunny walnut farm for a song! For a theme song, a Moorish sinagogue, a dream of dreams, a pitti-pitti palace, with bathrooms done in onyx Napoleonics and pornographic Pompeian red, with coverlimps in emerald and mauve sateen on the die-away divans for didoes, and a private slipping pool filled with green fountain-pen ink—a little bit blushful perhaps at selling itself to the pictures for $20,000 a year but happy as a real bribe and with all its prollems slobbed! And the Be-Happy-with-a-Home Realty Company is just a brokenne-downe olde picturesque cobwebby comfy shacke recalling the quaint olde toy-makers of Nuremberg who would plan you a little gingerbread cottage that the oil-trailers pass at high speed on their way up the macadam highway for about $9,000, including Paris-green blinds, a roof oh so lovingly poked in in spots, a weathervane shaped like a frolicsome seal and a view that takes in both the blue-blue sea where every little floozy wave croons, "Sunkist Caliphonia, here I come!" and the brown papier-mâché hills where every prospect appeases and the goofs hang like ripe fruit.

The Reverend Bob Shuler was born in a log cabin in the Blue Ridge. His people were mountain whites, all poor and most of them illiterate. As a boy, he worked with oxen in the fields. His clothes were made on a spinning-wheel by his mother out of flax grown behind the barn.

Bob's father had never got beyond the Second Reader, but he had always wanted to be a minister, and at thirty he studied for a degree at the Elm Creek Academy, while Mrs. Shuler took in boarders and Bob sold papers on the campus. They papered their new house, a two-room shack that had belonged to the Negro blacksmith, with the copies of the *Toledo Blade* and the *Cincinnati Post* that Bob hadn't been able to sell; and Bob read them all on the walls. He wanted to be a circuit-rider, too.

He tramped the railroads hunting jobs, cut wood behind backdoors for handouts, hoed corn, peddled stereoscopic views, worked at logging camps and finally taught in country schools. He worked his way through a Methodist college, and at seventeen he was licensed to preach.

He preached the Methodist gospel in the coal-mining towns of Virginia and Tennessee. At twenty-five, he married the only daughter of a family that had a big brick house with a big wheat plantation that was one of the show-places of the county. The next year he was transferred to Texas to take charge of a small circuit of churches and was paid a dollar a day, but the second year he was earning a thousand dollars.

He got to be more and more popular in Texas, but he was so fierce against the saloons and antagonized the liquor interests and the drinkers so that the bishop didn't know what to do with him. The people he attacked in his sermons used to get him into fist-fights outside, and somebody prosecuted him for libel. Then he was called to Trinity Church in Los Angeles.

Trinity Church, when Bob Shuler arrived, had only 900 members and was $70,000 in debt, and Bob Shuler has always believed that the bishop meant him to go down with the ship. But thirty days after he started in, the new pastor had raised $20,000. And in ten years the membership of Trinity had grown to 42,000, and the minister, through his genius for publicity, his evangelistic zeal and his passion for politics, had become one of the most powerful persons in Los Angeles.

Bob Shuler first made the front page with a sermon directed against some high-school girls who were reported to have had themselves photographed naked. This stimulated pious people to think about nude high-school girls and at once increased his following. Not long afterwards, he went to a charity bazaar; he won a ham in a raffle, and then took a chance on a wheel of fortune and had the man who ran it arrested for conducting a gambling game. Tipped off that if he would wait on a certain night at the door of a certain night club, he would see something that the public ought to know about, he caught the Los Angeles Chief of Police coming out with the wife and sister of a Mexican who was wanted for a crime.

All this went very big in Los Angeles, which has a solid Middle-Western foundation. Of the three million population of Southern California, at least half come from the Middle-Western farming states: Iowa leads with 400,000, but Illinois and Missouri are not far behind with 350,000 and 300,000. And Bob Shuler's appeal was perfectly gauged for these retired farmers and their families, who, finding themselves, after the War, unexpectedly rich from their wheat and corn, had come out to live in California bungalows and to bask in the monotonous sun, but for whom listening to sermons was one of their principal pastimes. Side by side with sporting oil-millionaires, an exotic California underworld and the celluloid romances of Hollywood, they were glad to get an intimate peek into the debauched goings-on of their neighbors, and at the same time be made to feel their own superior righteousness, and even—what was probably most gratifying of all—to have a hand in bringing the wicked to judgment.

Bob Shuler himself seemed one of them: he persisted in remaining rural. With his round head, humorous eyes and brown hair brushed boyishly across his forehead, his thick-set figure and cylindrical-looking arms that moved dynamically, as if all in one piece and with no trace of theatricality, his sudden alternations between rousing religious eloquence and the crackerbox vernacular of the backwoods, he seemed outspoken, homely and earnest, as well as exhilaratingly resourceful, indefatigable, engaging, magnetic. And he lived out at El Monte like a farmer, raising his own stock and vegetables. People who called him up on the phone might be greeted by Mrs. Shuler with, "You'll never guess what we've been doing! We've just killed a pig, and you ought to see my hands!"

"I came from the poorest of the poor," he would say. "I have been an underdog all my life, and my sympathies and efforts will always be on the side of the common people. . . . I must be forgiven for wanting this city run in the interests of the common people for the benefit of those who need protection and defense." He did not believe that "an honest officer would be active in enforcing the law against the defenseless and friendless while he closed his eyes to the lawlessness of the rich and powerful"; and he was "against the third degree, against special assessment of the poor, against confiscation of humble homes for public improvements." "I've found very few millionaires," he would say, "who didn't get their money in a manner that I doubted if God could own or bless." He was indignant in his intimations that his Baptist rival, Aimee McPherson, had diverted the money she raised on the pretext of pious purposes to her own luxurious living. When she had elicited, on one occasion, contributions for a monument for her husband's grave, Bob Shuler, several months afterwards, had photographs of the grave taken and would display them to his congregation, showing that there was nothing there but the original ignoble headstone.

It was true that he defended the power interests and was in the habit of going yachting with one of the big public-utility men; but he assured his congregation that this particular millionaire was "right with God."

Furthermore, he was a firm fundamentalist. Some years ago he fought a stout battle with a Congregational minister in Los Angeles, who accused Shuler of trying to "throttle progressivism" and attempted to dislodge him from the presidency of the ministerial union. Shuler stood fast: "If the old-time religion is not genuine," he declared, "then Christianity is bunk of the first water. No need to try to revamp it, to doctor and mend it, to repair and fix it up. If Jehovah is not God, then away with Christianity forever! It is unworthy of ordinary respect. It is a lie, a humbug, a cheat, a fraud! . . . For I am as certain as I live that either the old-time religion is genuine and worth a hundred cents on the dollar or else it is the very quintessence of rottenness and falsehood!" He triumphed; and Trinity Church "took her place as God's messenger and Christ's ambassador in a wicked city."

In Shuler's crusade against local corruption, his public lent him active support. First, an anonymous admirer in Pasadena supplied him with a private detective, who made it possible for him to delegate part of his labors of digging up scandals about public men; and then, when this assistant was mysteriously withdrawn, a big auto-supply man rallied to the pastor's rescue and set him up to a whole corps of spies.

But the climax of Bob Shuler's success came on Christmas, 1926. A woman called him up on the phone and said that she wanted to see him — she invited him to meet her in the Santa Monica Hotel. "Lady," was his immediate reply, "it would be as much as my life was worth to do it!" Since he had taken to exposing people, he had become apprehensive of being framed. But he checked on her and satisfied himself of her perfect respectability, discovered that she was a devout spinster, a Miss Glide who had made money in oil. He at last arranged to see her in the hotel lobby, with a male chaperon present. It turned out that she wanted to give him a Christmas present of a private radio station. He accepted; and thereafter his audience was multiplied to such an extent that he was able to play for Southern California the part of a veritable voice of God. Starting with 200,000 new hearers, he is said to have acquired 100,000 more every year — one of the largest religious audiences in the world.

KGEF was dedicated, in Shuler's own words, to "spreading the gospel and advancing civic betterment, and no modernist or evolutionist shall be allowed to speak over it." Two nights a week were consecrated to the advancement of civic betterment, and these soon came to outshine in public notice the purely religious part of the program. Bob Shuler was able to break a district attorney, a city prosecutor and another chief of police. The politicians began to play up to him — the newspapers and the juries came to fear him. No public official now was so powerful that the preacher had to respect him — no sin was too unseemly or too intimate for Shuler to search it out and to make it known to his public. He would reveal the rendezvous of Hollywood actors and actresses, the bootlegging of high-school students and public officials, the selling of birth-control devices by drug-stores, the attempts of the colored schoolteachers to flirt with the female white ones and the seduction of stenographers by millionaires. On one occasion, when a male schoolteacher had been hit and killed by a trolley while walking with a woman schoolteacher, he painted for his hungry audience the passion of their probable embraces, and suggested that the woman be tried for manslaughter for leading a married man to his death. It got to a point in Los Angeles where Bob Shuler's mere suspicions and hints were able to make courtrooms tremble: "Now I don't want to say anything against Judge Smith!" was his formula—"Judge Smith's sittin' up thar on that bench tryin' to be as fair as he can—but I will say that if I was Judge Smith, I wouldn't want people to think that a guilty man's money had saved him!"

It was impossible for the people the pastor attacked to retaliate by getting anything on him. "I have paid the price in clean living," he would say, "to be able to go on fighting the enemies I have made or may make in the future. One group of men did try to find something in my past life that they could use to stop me from fighting, but the investigator they sent on my trail came back and reported that he couldn't find a bug under any single chip in my past life. They can't find a scratch on my name if they hunt back to the cradle. I have never fooled with liquor, gambling, a woman or a dishonest deal. And they're never going to catch me in the situation Jacobson was found in because I never go to any woman's house in the course of my work as pastor of Trinity Church without taking a man along." Jacobson, a pious city-councilman who had obstructed the smooth functioning of the local machine, had, as everyone knew, been framed: a blonde had called at his office ostensibly to protest like Bob Shuler against the "special assessment of the poor," and had been found with him in her house under allegedly compromising circumstances by a party of detectives, reporters and simple amusement-seekers who had been summoned for the fun beforehand.

And that vast body of Middle-Western sentiment, marshaled and directed through the air, became one of the most formidable forces in Los Angeles. When the group known as the Julian oil

swindlers did some 40,000 investors out of some twenty million dollars, Bob Shuler was able not merely to arouse popular opinion
against the promoters and to facilitate the conviction of the District
Attorney for conspiracy to take a bribe by accusing him of participation in drinking parties and improper intimacy with the female
defendants, but even to cause the dismissal of a city prosecutor, the
morning after the latter had denounced Shuler over the radio for
the use of inflammatory language; and, when a crazed old man who
had lost his money shot a banker involved in the scandal and was
found to be carrying a copy of one of Shuler's pamphlets on the
"Julian Thieves," he immediately obtained the dismissal of the policeman who had told a reporter about it and raised an outcry in his
own vindication which caused the shooting to be forgotten.

There have been several attempts to "get" Shuler, but they have
so far proved ineffective. Twice he has been tried for criminal libel:
once for suggesting that the Mayor had acquired more money in
office than his salary accounted for, and once by the Knights of
Columbus, since he has always made war on the Catholics and has
written against them a pamphlet called *The Rise of Beastism*. And at
the time of the Pantages trials—when Mr. and Mrs. Pantages, the
theatrical magnates, had, by an unlucky coincidence, been indicted
at the same time for the crimes of, respectively, rape and killing a
man through drunken driving—Bob Shuler so hampered the im-
paneling of the jury by charges that the Pantages' money was being
used to fix it that the Los Angeles Bar Association finally had him
up for constructive contempt of court. He was fined and given fifteen days in jail; but this only had the effect of stimulating the loyalty of his followers. When released, he was enthusiastically welcomed both by the new Mayor, his own man, whose election he had
engineered, and by the District Attorney; and he was met outside by
a cheering throng who escorted him in triumph to his home. In the
meantime, they had raised the money to pay off the mortgage on his
church.

Some pressure has lately been brought on the Federal Radio
Commission to refuse him a new license, and, pending its final decision, he has been forced to be a little more discreet. But in the meantime, he has his own mayor and is for a season the real boss of Los
Angeles. At the election two years ago, he is said to have ruined by

vilification the chances of a dozen other possible candidates and to
have caused his adherents to vote for the present mayor, John C.
Porter, a dealer in secondhand automobile parts, an active worker
for the lay Church Brotherhood and a former member of the Ku
Klux Klan—whose principles Shuler has endorsed. Mayor Porter
has flabby hands and a long pale morose face. Though undoubtedly
a godly man, he is entirely uneducated and, except for once having
served as foreman of a grand jury, devoid of executive experience.
Since taking office as mayor, he has achieved international notoriety
by telegraphing King Alphonso of Spain, ousted by the revolution,
to come to the Los Angeles fiesta and "forget his troubles" there.

In Trinity Church, at any rate, radio license or no radio license,
an air of calm confidence reigns. They continue to fill the pews,
those dowdy and dry-faced women, those dowdy and pasty girls,
those old men with thin necks and sparse hairs, drooping forward
their small bald foreheads, drawing in their recessive chins—while
the Reverend Bob Shuler, with an American flag hanging down
from over his head, amid gargantuan baskets of chrysanthemums
which scent the Sunday-morning chill and underneath a dome
painted years ago with a cloudscape, now indistinct, in which, however, one bright electric bulb is intended to symbolize the Savior—
the Reverend Bob Shuler can still hold them with his every word.

In his loose brown suit, his flapping mottled tie and his greenish-
yellowish bone-rimmed glasses, he shifts from one gear to another
with an easy and expert hand. How tellingly, by a quite sudden
change of tone, he can come down face to face with his hearers—a
coarse-spoken and hearty old hillbilly talking frankly to neighbors
about everyday things! His sermon is a blast against make-up, and
he is explaining that, nevertheless, it is not the case that everything
artificial is bad: "I have a couple o' false teeth myself, and they make
me a lot o' trouble—I wish I didn't have to wear 'em! I have to take
'em out at night and put 'em back in again in the morning. But I've
got to wear 'em to chew—I wouldn't know what to do without 'em!"
And then, still candid and straight, with what seems a welling-up
of real feeling, he rises to dignity and eloquence: "When the spirit of
Christ enters in you, you don't need any false embellishment! Your
friends will see without that what's happened to ye—they won't
need to be told about it, they'll know by themselves about it, they

won't have any doubt about it—maybe ye won't say very much about it!"

It is Communion Sunday. The sermon over, the pastor announces that for those who stay there will be "a very beautiful service." He steps down from off the platform, and a young man in the orchestra comes forward and turns the microphone down to catch his words. He takes the sacrament first himself: "This is the body of Our Lord. . . ."

Dr. Gustav A. Briegleb, Bob Shuler's former lieutenant and present rival, is a graduate of Yale and a Presbyterian, and his congregation is recruited from a "better class" of people than Shuler's. Also evidently of Iowa and Missouri stock, they are better dressed and have fresher complexions. And Dr. Briegleb's fine new church, with its white walls and rough-hewn rafters, its furled American flag with a gleaming gold spike at the top, its choir in white gowns and only one basket of flowers on the platform, is a very much smarter affair than Bob Shuler's rather shabby temple.

Dr. Briegleb himself wears white flannel trousers and a semi-formal blue coat, with a handkerchief sticking out of the pocket. He does not pretend to be a man of the people like Shuler; and though, when active in the Ministerial Union at the time that Shuler was president, they battled side by side against "progressivism," and though, at the time of the Pantages' trials, Dr. Briegleb—for contempt of court—was fined twenty-five dollars when Shuler was fined seventy-five, he was often criticized by Shuler, even before their split, for his willingness to play up to the rich. When Dr. Briegleb had lent his support to the rich man's candidate for mayor rather than to the God-fearing Porter, Bob Shuler expressed himself as follows: "Dr. Briegleb thinks I'm stubborn and contrary, and that I constitutionally hate rich men and refuse even to go right if they want me to. On the other hand, I think Briegleb is one of the best fighters for the right who ever buckled on a sword. As I see it, his trouble is that the 'big boys' can feed him stuff."

Dr. Briegleb is, besides, a quite different type of man from the mountaineer Methodist preacher. With his stocky build, his grizzled hair and his frowning arrogant face, which is marked off by heavy lines in solidly molded sections, he suggests some Germanic divine

of the days of the Reformation. When he reads the lesson and announces the hymns, his broad a's and rolling r's impose themselves
as if with the authority of some sound theological seminary.

The first hymn on this Sunday evening is allowed to run its
modest course. Reverent Sunday voices invoke the divine calm:

> *Peace, peace, sweet peace,*
> *Wonderful peace from above!*
> *Peace, peace, sweet peace,*
> *Wonderful gift of God's love!*

But at the end of the first stanza of the second hymn, with its
lustier refrain of "Who could it be but Jesus?" their two-fisted pastor cracks down on them: "How many of you have never sung that
hymn before? Those that have never sung it hold up their hands!" A
certain number obey. "Those that have, hold up their hands!"—
"Why I've sung that hymn at Christian Endeavor ever since I was
a boy!" In a voice quite different from his seminary voice, a voice
domineering and brutal and appropriate to somebody's idea of a
powerful and hard-boiled business man, he tells them that they have
got to do better. But, in commanding them, he does not fail to temper his severity with humor: "It reminds me of the story about the
churches on the Yale campus. Over on one side of the campus, they
were singing, 'Will there be any stars in my crown?' and over on the
other side they were singing, 'No, not one!'" He makes the women
do a stanza by themselves, the men do a stanza by themselves, and
then both do a stanza together—and he tries to get them into the
spirit of the thing by a minstrel joke about men and women. A
strange thing happens to Dr. Briegleb's face every time he tells a
joke: his mouth, which is habitually tight and grim, partly opens in
a constrained gape. He is pausing for a laugh and trying to smile.
But the Doctor, though he has evidently applied himself to acquir-
ing the folksy technique of modern evangelism, will never be able to
make people laugh. The responses to his sallies are meager. Nevertheless, before starting his sermon, Dr. Briegleb speaks highly of
cheerfulness: he says that cheerfulness will help cure the depression.

But the sermon itself deals with a matter much closer to the
Doctor's heart. Last May, just before the municipal elections, a
young politician named Clark, who was a candidate for municipal

judge, shot and killed two other men in what was supposed to be a real-estate office on Sunset Boulevard. One of the men was a former saloonkeeper, who had risen to be boss of the Los Angeles underworld; the other, the owner of a local magazine, had evidently been one of his henchmen. When Clark was tried in August, he offered a plea of self-defense: he said that, in his campaign for the bench, he had pledged himself, if elected, to clean up Los Angeles, and that Crawford and Spencer had tried to kill him. Spencer had already talked to him over the telephone and warned him to lay off or "you will drive into your driveway some night and you will not get out of your car!" In the story told by Clark at the trial, Dr. Briegleb played a curious role. The pastor of St. Paul's Presbyterian Church had been on the friendliest terms with the murdered underworld boss. Crawford had come to the service one Sunday and had dropped a diamond ring, said to be worth $3,500, into the contribution box, and he had thereafter had himself baptized by Dr. Briegleb and had made further donations to the Faith, which had enabled Dr. Briegleb to build his new beautiful church, with its device, "A Church Where Sinners Are Welcome." This church contained a soundproof room, which was designed for a private radio station. With a radio station of his own, Dr. Briegleb was to achieve equality with his former colleague and captain, Bob Shuler. But at this point—before the station had actually been installed—Boss Crawford was shot by Clark.

Clark testified on the stand that he had approached Crawford before the election as to whether there was any chance of getting the influential Briegleb's support. Crawford had explained the situation as follows: "I have talked to Dr. Briegleb, but there is something big going to happen. Dr. Briegleb is going to have a radio, and I am back in the saddle, and next year is going to be the Olympic Games, one of the biggest years Los Angeles has ever seen, and I am going to run things the way they have never been run before." "And he had the sample ballots there," Clark went on to tell the court, "pink and blue sample ballots, and he said that Miss Fisher was going to typewrite a thousand of those, and that he would deliver those to friends of his and people he knew, and that each ballot that was delivered would guarantee from ten to fifty votes—also a clipping from one of the newspapers with a list of prospective grand jurors." Crawford had figured that about half the grand jury would be made up of his friends, and that, with these and the 75,000 or 100,000 votes that Briegleb was sure to bring him, he ought to be pretty safe. Clark had asked, "What about the district attorney's office?" Crawford had replied: "I was indicted for bribery, for bribing the Corporation Commissioner, and Buron Fitts dismissed it." "He said, 'Don't ask me any more questions about that. He won't say anything.'"

The boss had then, according to Clark, proposed that he should help them in frame-up of Chief of Police Steckel at a Santa Monica hotel. Clark, at this, had denounced them as follows: "You dirty lowdown skunks!—you were indicted for framing Councilman Jacobson some time ago, and now you join the church and profess to be a Christian, and you throw a big diamond in the plate! You dirty skunk, I am going out and I am going to tell the people from every platform that I get on and from every radio what happened in this room. You are two rats!" "With that, he [Crawford] said, 'No —— has ever talked to me that way!' and he pulled a gun out of his belt." The other man had pulled on Clark, too, but Clark had been quicker and had shot them both.

Clark's story was not generally believed by people who knew the personalities involved. It was assumed that the boss must have attempted to blackmail him: "There were three racketeers in that room!" it was said. But Clark was good-looking and young, and the jury, half of them women, would have acquitted him on the spot if it had not been for one stubborn old man, who—in defiance of his fair fellow jurymen, even with tears in their eyes—persisted in disbelieving the defendant's story. The forewoman, announcing mistrial, put on record the following statement: "I think he [Clark] is one of our noblest Americans. We believed every bit of his story of self-defense. We considered him a fine upstanding young man who told a straightforward story." (The old man who had disagreed later found a bomb under his house.)

Dr. Briegleb, who was Crawford's pastor and who was present at the boss's deathbed, takes, naturally, a different view, and he has spared no effort to make it prevail. One of the jurors originally chosen had turned out to be a trustee of St. Paul's Presbyterian Church, and he had had to be excused from duty when he admitted that he had been strongly influenced by his pastor's opinion of the case. Dr.

Briegleb appeared at the trial, but he was never called as a witness, and on this account he is openly furious. He announced last week his intention of preaching about the trial, since he was not allowed to testify at it, and tonight there are reporters in the congregation.

The text is from Acts V, 1–4, the fate of Ananias and Sapphira, and the application is that Clark was a liar.

When Dr. Briegleb gets on to the Clark defense, he entirely loses touch with that excellent seminary. He casts doubt upon the honesty of Clark's counsel, who, he says, had Clark's revolver cleaned before the trial; makes a damaging attack on Clark's character—if he was one of the noblest Americans, why was he kicked out of Annapolis?; insists that he himself was not trying to run away when, immediately after the shooting, he had gone up to his summer camp, but was merely in search of a little rest from a distressing experience and arduous labors; acts the rôle of a broken old man as he depicts the terrible grief of the godly parents of Clark, disgraced by the evil behavior—more especially by the *lies*—of their son. He denies that he had ever promised to deliver Crawford any votes, points out the absurdity of the accusation, remarks to the congregation that he supposes a good many of them don't vote at all—several members of his own family don't vote—declares that there was never any question of the radio's being installed to guarantee 100,000 votes for Crawford: it was for spreading the gospel of Jesus Christ. He wrings the hearts of his audience with an account of Crawford's deathbed and his late repentance, and insists that, though cartridges were found in Crawford's desk, he was positively not carrying a gun. He points out that he himself, Briegleb, had got Chief of Police Steckel his job, so how under Heaven could Crawford have wanted to frame Steckel? He strives to bring home to his audience the horror of telling and living a lie; and pounding the pulpit with his fist, he demands, "If religion isn't for sinners, what in God's name is it for?" Some of the women in the congregation are weeping.

Now and then in his sermon, Dr. Briegleb resorts to devices which surprise you even after you have become accustomed to his transitions from pompous to brutal. He occasionally resorts to a trick which is peculiar to singing evangelists' talks in the streets of Western towns and which is calculated to put a spell upon persons of simple intelligence: "And Peter said to Ananias—ah, 'Why hath Satan filled thine heart—ah, to lie to the Holy Ghost—ah?'" And, with an effect even more incongruous, he sometimes tries an imitation of Bob Shuler's folksy humor: "I called up the District Attorney from Arrowhead Lake and I told him how I felt about it—Ah wish Ah had muh money back!—it cost me $2.80, and Ah wish Ah had it back!" And from his frequent references to Shuler, his anxiety to associate himself with him and to show that they are both of the same mind, one can see how much he still looks instinctively to the authority of his old chief.

Poor Dr. Briegleb! When he accepted Crawford's diamond ring and was promised a private station and received his new underworld convert into the Presbyterian Church, Bob Shuler publicly declared that he would "as soon baptize a skunk as Charley Crawford!" and let Briegleb go his own way. And now Charley Crawford is dead, and Dr. Briegleb has still no station. He will never be quite clever enough to satisfy the whole of his ambition. He makes a point of being present on all public occasions, and he gives out long public statements to malign reporters who lead him on and then do not print what he says, while Bob Shuler can make the front page every time without putting himself out to go anywhere. Poor Dr. Briegleb! Some basic Germanic simplicity, Puritanical inflexibility, professional respectability, will always, one fears, prevent him from appealing to the public of Los Angeles as Aimee McPherson and Bob Shuler do. Shuler can still charm every heart with a whiff of the cow-manure from his heels. Aimee, in her jolly gaudy temple, enchants her enormous audience by her beaming inexhaustible sunshine and her friendly erotic voice. She writes them operas in which ancient oratorios and modern Italian opera are mingled with popular songs and tunes from musical comedies. She warms the hearts of the lonely by urging them, before they leave, to shake hands, in the auditorium, with at least three people whom they do not know. And she has recently excited them especially by her glamorous marriage in a plane to the young man who sings Pharaoh in her current opera and by subsequently having broadcast from the bridal chamber the kisses and cooings of the happy pair. They adore her and hand her their money. They feel good about their neighbor and themselves.

But poor Briegleb will never do this. However much he may labor to be racy like the Reverend Bob, to cultivate the tone of a sales manager giving pep-talks to tepid salesmen, though he may study the incantations of the humble Come-to-Christer and announce that "the worst harlot in this town can come to this church and be received!"—he will always be handicapped by his education and by his Calvinist conviction that religion is authoritative, rigorous and grim!

James M. Cain

For many Los Angeles transplants, moving to the city involves a certain ambivalence: it's as if in trying to make a home here one can't help but feel suspended between exile and return. Something of this floating quality seeps into James M. Cain's little-known essay "Paradise," published in March 1933 in *The American Mercury*. A former journalism professor at St. John's College in Annapolis, Maryland, and briefly managing editor of *The New Yorker*, Cain (1892–1977) came to Southern California in the early 1930s. His hard-boiled novels, such as *The Postman Always Rings Twice* (1934) and *Double Indemnity* (1938), led Edmund Wilson to characterize him as a "poet of the tabloid murder," and did much to establish the mythical landscape of what would become film noir. "Paradise" offers by contrast a more measured and even affectionate view.

PARADISE

I shall attempt, in this piece, an appraisal of the civilization of Southern California, but it occurs to me that before I begin I had better give you some idea what the place looks like. If you are like myself before I came here, you have formed, from Sunkist ads, newsreels, movie magazines, railroad folders, and so on, a somewhat false picture of it, and you will have to get rid of this before you can understand what I am trying to say.

Wash out, then, the "land of sunshine, fruit, and flowers": all these are here, but not with the lush, verdant fragrance that you have probably imagined. A celebrated movie comedian is credited with the remark that "the flowers don't smell and the women do," but in my observation nothing smells. Wash out the girl with the red cheeks peeping coyly from behind a spray of orange leaves. The girl is here, but the dry air has taken the red out of her cheeks; the orange trees are here, but they don't look that way: the whole picture has too much pep, life, and moisture in it.

Wash out the palm trees, half visible beyond the tap dancing platform. Palm trees are here, but they are all phonies, planted by people bemused with the notion of a sub-tropical climate, and they are so out of harmony with their surroundings that they hardly arrest your notice. Wash out the movie palazzos, so impressive in the photographs. They are here too, at any rate in a place called Beverly Hills, not far from Hollywood; but they are like the palm trees, so implausible in their surroundings that they take on the life-lessness of movie sets. Above all, wash out the cool green that seems to be the main feature of all illustrations got out by railroads. Wash that out and keep it out.

When you have got this far, you can begin quite starkly with a desert. As to what this desert looked like before it was touched by man you can get an idea by following it across the Mexican border into Lower California, where man is feeble and touches no more than he has to. On one side you can put an ocean, a placid oily-looking ocean that laps the sand with no sign of life on it except an occasional seal squirming through the swells, and almost no color. On the other side, some hundreds of miles inland, put some moun-tains. Between ocean and mountains, put some high hills that look as if they were spilled out carelessly with a gigantic sugar scoop, and between the hills, wide, flat valleys. Have both hills and valleys a gray, sunbaked tan; put a few tufts of dry grass on the hills and occasional clumps of stunted trees in the valleys, but see that the naked earth shows through everything that grows on it.

You are now ready for the handiwork of man. I suggest that you put it in with water-color, for if it blurs here and there, and lacks a very clear outline, that will be so much the better. The hills you can leave just as they were. In the valleys, in addition to the stunted clumps you already have, put in some trees: a few palms, eucalyp-tus, orange, fig, pomegranate, and other varieties that require little water. You might smear in some patches of green lawn, with hose sprinkling them: it will remind you that bringing water in by pipe-line is still the outstanding accomplishment of man in this region.

Now then, put in some houses. Most of them should be plain white stucco with red tile roofs, for the prevalent architecture is Spanish, although a mongrel Spanish that is corrupted by every style known on earth, and a few styles not hitherto known. But you can also let your fancy run at this point, and put in some structures *ad lib.*, just to exhibit your technique. If a filling-station occurs to you, a replica of the Taj Mahal, faithfully executed in lath and plaster, put that in. If you hit on a hot-dog stand in the shape of a hot dog, prone, with portholes for windows and a sign reading "Alligator Farm," put that in. Never mind why a hot-dog stand should have portholes for windows and a new line of alligators: we are concerned here with appearances, and will get to that part later.

If you think a blacksmith shop in the shape of a gilded tea-kettle would be an agreeable nifty, put that in; by the time you get it there it will be an Automobile Laundry, Cars Washed, 50¢, but leave it in anyhow. You might throw in a few structures in the shape of lemons, oranges, pagodas, igloos, windmills, mosques, and kangaroo heads, without bothering to inquire what they are doing there; if you must have signs on them, mark them "For Sale, Cheap." For the rest, long rows of wire poles, some advertising statuary done in *papier mâché*, and the usual bungalows and tract offices. It doesn't matter much, so you paint everything up gaudily and have it different from the place next door.

Now take your opus out in the noonday sun, tack it down on a board, and look at it. You will find that something has happened to it. In that dreadful glare, all the color you smeared on so lavishly has disappeared; your trees do not look like trees at all, but are inconsequential things reaching not .000001% of the distance to the heaven they aspire to; your green lawns are hardly visible, and the water that sprinkles them is but a misty mockery of water; your gay structures, for all their artistic incongruity, fail to apprise God of the joke: all that is left is the gray, sun-baked tan that you started with. Well, that is Southern California. The main thing to remember is the sunlight, and the immense expanse of sky and earth that it illuminates: it sucks the color out of everything that it touches, takes the green out of leaves and the sap out of twigs, makes human beings seem small and of no importance. Here there is no oppressive heat, you understand. The climate is approximately as represented: temperate in Summer, with cool evenings when you often light a fire; almost as temperate in Winter, except for the occasional night that makes you long for the steam heat of the East. It is simply that the sunlight gives everything the unmoving quality of things seen in a desert. And of course this is greatly aggravated by the similarity of the seasons, in itself. Nothing changes. Summer follows Winter without a Spring, Winter follows Summer without a Fall. The citrus trees flower and bear all at the same time: you never get a riot of blossoms as you do in Western Maryland when the apple-trees are in bloom, or a catharthis of stinking, primitive accomplishment, as you do in Delaware when the tomatoes go to the cannery. Here the oil wells flow right along, so do the orange trees, so does everything. It is terrifying.

You may suppose that here an addict of dark days is voicing an aversion to sunlight, and that I exaggerate the effect which the sun has on things, particularly on the appearance of the countryside. I don't think so, and I adduce one curious scrap of evidence to bolster my position. About halfway between Los Angeles and San Diego is a small beach colony, called Balboa. It lies on a lagoon that makes in from the ocean, an inlet perhaps half a mile wide and two or three miles long. This must be fairly deep, as it is a deep, indigo blue. Now this patch of blue is the only thing for miles, nay for hundreds of miles, that can compete with the sunlight, and nullify it, so that you see things as they really are. As a result, Balboa seems a riot of color, although it is nothing but a collection of ordinary beach cottages when you get into it. You stop your car when you come to it, feast your eyes on it, as an Arab might feast his eyes on an oasis; think foolishly of paintings depicting Italy and other romantic places.

I think that this circumstance, the fact that one patch of blue water can make such a difference in the appearance of the landscape, shows what really ails the look of this part of the country; gives a clue, too, to why the inhabitants are so indifferent to the really appalling atrocities that they have committed. Balboa, although not pretentious, is built in some sort of harmony, for with its setting the residents had an incentive to build something to go with it; but elsewhere, it makes no difference what people do, the result is the same. If they erect a beautiful house, as many of them have, the sun robs it of all force and life; if they erect a monstrosity, it passes unnoticed, is merely one more thing along the road.

There is no reward for æsthetic virtue here, no punishment for æsthetic crime; nothing but a vast cosmic indifference, and that is the one thing the human imagination cannot stand. It withers, or else, frantic to make itself felt, goes off into feverish and idiotic excursions that have neither reason, rhyme, nor point, and that even fail in their one, purpose, which is to attract notice.

II

Now, in spite of the foregoing, when you come to consider the life that is encountered here, you have to admit that there is a great deal to be said for it.

First, I would list the unfailing friendliness and courtesy of the people. It is a friendliness somewhat different from what you find elsewhere, for it does not as a rule include hospitality. The man who will take all sorts of trouble to direct you to some place you are trying to find does not ordinarily invite you into his house; it is not that he has any reason for keeping you out, it is merely that it does not occur to him to do it.

Hospitality, I think, comes when people have sent down roots; it goes with pride in a home, pride in ancestors that built the home, conscious identification with a particular soil. These people, in one way or another, are all exiles. They have come here recently, and their hearts are really in the places that they left. Thus, if they do not do as much visiting with each other as you see in other parts of the country, or the gossiping that goes with visiting, they do have the quick friendliness that exiles commonly show, and I must say it is most agreeable. You may encounter many things you do not like in California, but you will go a long way before you meet a churl.

With the friendliness and courtesy, I would bracket the excellent English that is spoken here. The Easterner, when he first hears it, is likely to mistake it for the glib chatter of habitual salesmanship. I think that is because the language you hear here, even from the most casual garage mechanic, is too articulate to seem plausible. For one accustomed to the bray of Eastern Virginia, or the gargle of Second Avenue New York, or the grunts of the West Virginia foothills, or the wim, wigor, and witality of Southern Pennsylvania, it is hard to believe that the common man can express himself coherently, unless he has learned the trick somehow by rote. So that when the common man out here addresses you in easy grammar, completes his sentences, shows familiarity with good manners, and in addition gives you a pleasant smile, you are likely to resent it,

and assume that he is parroting the radio, or the talkies, or else that
he has been under the tutelage of a high-pressure salesman somewhere, and supplied with a suitable line of gab. In other words, even
when you hear it you don't believe it; instead, you keep your ears
open for the "authentic" talk of the region, uncorrupted by influences tending to neutralize its flavor.

Well, I have listened to it for more than a year now, and I believe
it, and I think I am middling hard to fool about such things. The authentic talk of the region is simply good English, and you will hear it
wherever you go. The intonation is not what you may have supposed
from listening to Aimée over the radio. Aimée comes from Canada,
and her dreadful twang bears no relation to what is spoken here.

The actual accent, to my ear, has a somewhat pansy cast to it; it
produces on me the same effect as an Englishman's accent. It is
clipped, not as clipped as the New England accent, but a little
clipped; in addition, there is a faint musical undertone in it: they
"sing" it, which is probably why it affects me as an Englishman's
English, since he also sings his stuff, although in a different key.
Pronunciation is excellent. The populace seem to be on familiar
terms with most of the words in the language, and you rarely hear
that butchery of sonorous terms that is so common elsewhere.

With the good English goes an uncommonly high level of education. These people read, they know what is going on in the world,
even if they hold some strange ideas about it, of which more later.
And I might mention at this point a cleanliness hardly to be matched
elsewhere. Except for the few Mexican hovels in every town, there
is no squalor here, or dirt. The houses are very badly planned, but
two rooms in them are built with the best of skill, and polished with
the utmost care: the kitchen and the bathroom. There is no litter. As
in some European cities, where even on the most crowded Sunday
there is no scattering of lunch-wrappings in the parks, a homoge-
neous population takes pretty good care of its nest. And the sunshine, a blight in so many ways, may be due for credit here. It is a
sort of general disinfectant.

Next, I would list the things that require an effective communal
effort: schools, roads, gigantic water projects, recreation facilities,
and so on. The schools, in my opinion, are the best in the country.
I find three States ranked ahead of California, — Nevada, New York,

and Wyoming,—in the amount of money expended per unit of attendance, or population, or whatever it is that they measure by; but I say that money is not the only thing that counts in education. My brief for the California schools rests on the simple fact that our two children did terribly in the East, whereas here they do fine. They like school, learn their lessons, take an interest in what the school does; and so they get a great deal more out of their time than I got when I was their age. Also, they are treated with the utmost consideration, not only by their teachers, but by their colleagues in bondage.

This last is a great point with me, for they are foreigners (I am their stepfather, not their father), and I had been afraid they would run into the Ku Klux aspect of the American temperament when they got into American schools. They did run into it in New York: trust a foreigner who got here in 1930 to haze a foreigner who got here in 1931. But here they don't run into it, which gets me back to the friendliness of the people, probably one reason the schools do so well. For it makes no difference how much you spend on schools, if half your juice is wasted assimilating immigrants, as it is in New York, or fighting irregular attendance, as it is in rural sections of the East, or mopping up the swamps of illiteracy, as it is in the South, you are not going to have much of a school system. Here, the effort goes into the studies, the school paper, the sports, and the other things that children ought to be doing; there is a minimum of waste, particularly on "discipline," that infallible symptom of rasping gears. There seems to be hardly any disciplinary problem in California schools. When children enjoy being there, like their teachers, and do their work, why start the bastinado?

As to higher education, I can tell you nothing, as I have had no chance to study it. I would like it better if these various institutions weren't quite so wild about football; but it is only one man's opinion, so let it pass. I shall have to pass up the water projects too, as they have a Metropolitan Water District here whose workings I can't quite get the hang of, so that it would probably be better if I just flunked out. The main point, though, is that the water is here: it is piped into houses, lawns, fields, and orchards; it is the staff of life. I doubt if any other section of the country uses as much water as this one does, and these States, as you may have heard, are quick on the spigot.

The roads are superb. They run for miles in every direction, eight tracks wide where traffic is heavy, with illumination at night, beautiful curves and easy grades, no mean feat of construction when you consider that they never get very far without having to cross a range of mountainous hills. Of course, they are not primarily ornamental: this section, to a greater extent than any other, is dependent on the automobile, as forty years ago it was dependent on the horse. The distances are so vast, the waste of time so cruel if you go by bus or street car, that you must have your own transportation, and whether she needs greasing is literally a matter of greater moment than whether the roof leaks. Everybody has some kind of second- or third- or ninth-hand flivver; even the cook comes to work in her car. Of course, she can't cook when she gets there, but anyhow she arrives in style.

As you might expect, there is a great skill in everything that pertains to the automobile, that extends much further than the roads it runs on. No motor disease has been heard of that the local specialist can't cure, and at a reasonable price. Snagged top? A place that does nothing but fix tops. Crumpled fender? Another place that attends to fenders. Starter acting funny? Places everywhere that "reweld" starter teeth without removing flywheel. The markets, most of them, have smooth, flat parking areas in front of them, so you can drive right up and have the potatoes lifted into the back seat; there are lunch places that hook a tray on the side of your car, so that you can eat without so much as getting out. Of course, this gives me the colic, but it gives you an idea how far the thing goes.

Traffic control is perfect, with no endless tinkering with it as in the East; I think it moves through Los Angeles faster than through any other city on earth. This is the one section I ever heard of that did something about a place to park. Driving in New York is one long nightmare of finding a place to leave the car, as it is in most other American cities; here, there are parking places everywhere, run by brisk fellows in white smocks who whisk your car out of the way, hand you a ticket, and charge you from a nickel to twenty-five cents, depending on the location. What a load off your mind that is!

The recreation facilities are endless. Every town has its country club, or several of them, which will take in almost any presentable person who will pay the very moderate dues. But there are plenty of public places, either privately operated, or run by municipalities, where anybody can play for a small admission charge: golf courses, riding ranches, tennis courts, and so on, many of the last being free, as they are maintained by the towns chiefly for children. Plenty of them, you understand: no calling up two days in advance to reserve a court for one hour in the afternoon.

For my part, what I take most delight in is the swimming pools. Anywhere you go you can have a swim: a clean swim, a pleasant swim, a swim run by people who really know their stuff. Think what this means. In all of New York City, except for three or four hotels that have pools, and one or two small places uptown, there is not one place where the six million can get wet without going to Coney, Brighton, of some other dreadful beach. The city maintains "bath-houses," where worthy widows of dead policemen dispense towel and soap for three cents; but they are intended primarily to provide bums with a bath, and only one of them has a pool, a small, horrible affair that I should certainly hate to fall into.

But here all you have to do is drive up, plunk down a coin, get towel, soap, and suit, if you haven't brought one, and dive off. You can be sure the suit has been steamed and properly dried before you got it. No dirt, no noise, no slopping around a filthy dressing-room where uncouth voices yell "Hey locker!" I swam all last Summer in a high-school pool. It was the best I was ever in: the charge was fifteen cents. One curious thing about it may interest you. As it was a public pool, it took in just an ordinary run of people, about half children, half grown-ups; all clean, well-behaved, and dressed in gay suits, but just average people. Yet out of all the thousands I saw there, not five appeared during the whole Summer who could really swim. Down at the Ambassador, in Los Angeles, and at Agua Caliente, in Mexico, the idle sons of the rich dive, float, and crawl with the finest grace; but even so simple a trick, apparently, is beyond the idle sons of the poor.

III

Now I come to the tough part of my piece. If the foregoing is true, as it certainly is, and much more of the same that I could put in if I had space, why is it, you may well ask, that I don't break out into a decent hymn of praise at once, instead of making my bass a sour note under the twittering treble?

I wish I could, but I can't. The thing simply won't add up. When I take off the first shoe at night, and wonder what I have to show for the day, I usually know that I have nothing to show for it. I can't take a schoolhouse to bed with me, or a State road, or a swimming pool; some can, and if you can you had better come here at once, as this is the place you were born for. But not I. To me, life takes on a dreadful vacuity here, and I am going to have a hard time indicting it. Frankly, I don't know exactly what it is that I miss. But if you will bear with me while I grope a little, I shall try to get it down on paper.

Let us take a fresh start, a long way off, in a place that everybody can agree on: Paris. It may seem unfair to choose a city that had its beginnings in Roman times, and compare it with a section which in its present phase is hardly fifteen years old, but let it pass: an unfair comparison is precisely what I want. What is it, now, that charms me about Paris, that gives me what I don't find here? The so-called "culture"? The yodelling of the current Violetta at the Opera, or the pirouetting of her agile assistants, as they sway and whirl to thunderous applause and then sink lightly back into their wheelchairs? The actresses along the boulevards? The paintings in the art store windows? The symphony concerts?

Nay, none of these. If I want a Violetta, I should have heard the last one in Los Angeles, probably the best in the business; when I want hoofing, I can see better hoofers in Hollywood than in Paris, and the same goes for actresses; when I want paintings, I can see the best in the world in Pasadena; when I want symphonies, I can hear excellent performances in the Hollywood Bowl, and under pleasanter circumstances than in a stinking hall in Paris.

No, what I like is a jumble of the tangible and the intangible, of beauty and ugliness, that somehow sets me a-tingle: the sinister proximity of big things, and the smokestacks on hinges, pulled down as the boats go under the bridges; the glimpse of a medieval street, the way a boy chants *"Matin, le Temps, Echo de Paris!"*; the glow of lights behind the awnings as the gathering dark brings out the lettering, the captain in the Café de la Paix who looks like Otto Kahn; the patina on the arch and the Étoile, the salesman who says he has *les Camel, les Chesterfield, et les Licky Streak*; the bronze statues in the park behind the Louvre, the fake artist painting the wrong bridge down by the river; the great façade of Notre Dame, the shiny faced nuns hawking souvenirs beneath it; the fish market, and the discovery that they tie a lobster's claws here, instead of pegging them, as we do, and an ancient peasant, bending beneath a rack that fits him with the terrible precision of a polished yoke on the neck of oxen; the meal I had in the Avenue Victor Hugo, the meal I had in the Rue de la Pepiniere, the meal I had in the Rue Royale, the meal I had—wherever it was. In other words, a perpetual invitation to explore, to linger, to enjoy.

I think this beckoning jumble, in great or small degree, is the essence of the appeal which any place has for you, and that if it isn't there, you are going to be most unhappy about it, even if at first you don't quite know what ails you. Well, it is what this place lacks. You can drive for miles, and the one thing you can be sure of is that you are not going to be rewarded by so much as one little scrap, one little unexpected bit, one hint of charm, that you can sit down with for a moment, and, as I have said, take to bed with you that night. Of course, the place does have a history, and there are many fine relics of the Spanish occupation, all preserved with an admirable regard for what is due them. But they, after all, are a closed chapter. The one now being written somehow never manages to be delightful, produces nothing but an endless succession of Rabbit Fryers, 50¢; Eggs, Guaranteed Fresh, 23¢ Doz.; Canary Birds, 50¢, Also Baby Chix, Just Hatched; Car Mart, All Makes Used Cars, Lowest Prices; Orange Drink, 5¢; Eat; Drink Goat Milk for Health, Drive Right In; Pet Cemetery 300 Yds., Turn to Right; Finest English Walnuts, 15¢ Lb.; $100 Down Buys This Lot, Improvements Installed, No Assessments; Eat; Scotty Kennels, 100 Yds.; Pure Muscat Grapejuice, 35¢ Gal., We Deliver; Eat.

I have got so that if I go out for an afternoon's drive, I usually wind up at Goebel's Lion Farm, smoking a cigarette with Bert Parks, the chief attendant. God in Heaven, a cat is something to look at! I have followed all the doings out there faithfully, from the birth of the leopard cubs to the unfortunate fate of Jiggs when he strayed into a cage with two she-lions and got frightfully chewed up. I learned with great interest what happened when Paramount sent a star out there to have his picture taken feeding Caesar, as a bit of publicity for a forthcoming picture. Instead of biting the meat Caesar bit the actor. First time I knew a lion liked ham.

Eat. That is the measure, alas, of the cookery of the region. You can go from Santa Barbara to the border, and you will not strike one place where you can get a really distinguished meal. There are, to be sure, the various Biltmores, and in Los Angeles the Ambassador, a restaurant called the Victor Hugo, a hotel called the Town House, and Bernstein's sea-food place. All of them have their points, and the Town House, I must say, really knows how to put a meal together. But they suffer from two circumstances. The first is that they can't sell liquor. If you want food *and* drink at the same meal, you have to go to a speak, and a California speak is so bad that there is nothing to say about it. The other is that they really have nothing to make a distinguished meal with. Meats are obtainable here, and vegetables, the best you can get anywhere; but when it comes to fish, and particularly shellfish, those indispensable embellishments that transform eating into dining, they are simply not to be had. Brother, God hath laid a curse on this Pacific Ocean, and decreed that nothing that comes out of it shall be fit to eat; and anybody who tells you different has simply never fished in another ocean.

The oysters are frightful. They serve what they call Eastern oysters, which means oysters that have been transplanted from the East to Puget Sound or some such place, and taken after they are grown. They are pale, watery, and fishy. Then they serve the native oyster, known as the Olympia, or Olympic—there seems to be some difference of opinion on the point. These are small, dark, and mussel-like in appearance. The taste is quite beyond the power of words to convey: I had to exercise all of my 90 hp. will to get down enough to call it a test. If you can imagine a blend of fish, seaweed, copper, and pot-washings, all smelling like low tide on a mud-flat, you will have some faint notion of what an Olympia oyster is like.

The crab is an ocean crab, smooth, without spines, and singularly coarse and tasteless. As a rule they serve it as cracked crab, which means that they steam it, chill it, and cut it up quite nicely, with the shell cracked so you can pick out the meat with an oyster fork. I think it would be better if they didn't let the ice come in contact with the crab, and thereby suck out the salt, but I hope they don't begin taking pains with it, just to please me. Any way they served it, I wouldn't like it. The only good crab I ever had out here was the other night, at a little party in Beverly Hills. It was in a salad, and I at once sought out my hostess.

"I've got to know more about this," I said. "I'm just writing a piece saying the crabs out here are lousy."

"I don't think so," she said. "I've had good crab in the Brown Derby, lots of times."

"Never mind the Brown Derby," I said. "I've got to be reliable and accurate about this thing, and what I want to know is: Where did you *get* this crab?"

"Well if you've got to know," she said, "that's canned crab, but I don't know why you had to be so inquisitive."

In other words, it was good old Crisfield blue-claw, and maybe it didn't taste good!

The lobster is that crustacean known in the East as a crayfish and in France as a *langouste*, and it's not much, any way you take it. It has eight big legs, but no giant claws, so that there is no claw meat. The fat and coral are inedible, and there is hardly any shoulder meat. The gigantic tail, when steamed and served cold, is white and of even texture, but tasteless. Broiling doesn't help any. The tail muscle of a *langouste*, when broiled, splits off into pieces, like a rope that has been unravelled, so that it is disagreeable to eat, and has no more taste than it had before.

But the prize monster of these parts is called an abalone. The abalone, if pulled out of the North Sea, would be a *coquille*, and if pulled out of Long Island Sound would be a scallop; but as it is, it is pulled out of the Pacific, which makes it different. The shell is large, some six or eight inches across, and fluted like a scallop shell, very pretty. The thing itself is a lump of muscle about the size of a small lemon, and so tough that if you tried to cut it, it would jump off the plate and hit the lady at the next table in the eye. So they operate on it with a hammer to soften it up a bit. How many outfielders they have to post, to field it home when it jumps off the block, I don't know; but when they get through with it, it is a sort of Childs pancake, and this they dip in batter and fry. You can have it. I got half of one down once: what an experience that was!

There are barracuda, salmon, halibut, swordfish, and tarpon, but I personally don't regard them very highly. Swordfish, I suppose, is as good as it is said to be; but for my part, when they begin serving fish in steaks, it doesn't seem like fish any more. The medium-size fish, like shad and bass, which go so well after the soup, don't seem to taste right: perhaps the trouble is in the cookery. The only fish I can say much for out here are the sand-dab, which looks like a small English sole and tastes like perch; the grunion, a near-smelt that is against the law for some reason, and that you have to get bootleg, and the trout. The trout all seem to come from Noah Beery's trout farm, on the road to the Mohave Desert. They are pretty good, anyhow at the Town House, where they know how to make a *meunière* sauce.

IV

Now then, if there are no smells to caress my nose, and no sights to delight my eye, and no food to tickle my mouth, this gets us down pretty much to what we laughingly call my intellect. God knows I am not particular here, not anything like as particular as I am about oysters. I don't ask for talk about Proust, or familiarity with the cosmic ray theory, or acute critical appraisal of the latest Japanese painter; I can take such stuff or leave it alone, and I usually feel better when I am off it. But I do ask—what shall I say? Something that pricks my imagination a little, gives me some sort of lift, makes me feel that that day I heard something. And I am the sort that is as likely to get this from the common man as his more erudite cousin, the high-brow.

But what do I get? Nothing. For when a gentleman appears at my door, orange peeler in hand, bows gracefully at my halting invitation to come in, removes his hat with the utmost aplomb, enters, sits down easily, and explains in accents that would do credit to a Harvard man that this particular article is manufactured by the O'Peelo Company, and bears the signed guarantee of that firm, handsomely engraved with one extra blade all for ten cents—when that happens, it is hard for me to escape the reflection that what this wight has his mind on is an orange peeler.

Now, right there, I think, I finally get into words my main squawk against this section: the piddling occupations to which the people dedicate their lives. Bear in mind my disclaimer of high-brow leanings, which is honest, and the earthy nature of the intellectual fodder that I ask. I am greatly stimulated by a trapper boy in a West Virginia coal-mine, or a puddler in a Pennsylvania steel-mill, or a hand on a Nebraska corn-farm. These people, although they usually talk a dreadful jargon, are frequently morons, and sometimes anything but admirable personally, all take part in vast human dramas, and I find it impossible to disregard the stature which their occupations confer on them. If they are prosperous, it is big news; if they are hungry, it is tragic; and no matter what their condition is, they share some of the electric importance of the stages they tread.

But what electric importance can be felt in a peddler of orange peelers? Or of a dozen ripe avocados, just plucked that morning? Or a confector of Bar-B-Q? Or the proprietor of a goldfish farm? Or a breeder of rabbit fryers? They give me no kick at all. They give themselves no kick. The whole place is overrun with nutty religions, which are merely the effort of these people to inject some sort of point into their lives; if not on earth, then in the stars, in numbers, in vibrations, or whatever their fancy hits on. They are not, as I have hinted, and as I shall show more clearly in a moment, inferior people. Rather the other way around. But they suffer from the cruel feebleness of the play which the economy of the region compels them to take part in.

If it were only possible to create for them a suitable play artificially, as it is possible to fashion a play for childhood, where libraries, schoolhouses, athletic fields, and a few leagues and debating clubs are all that is needed to set things humming—the thing would have been done long ago. But with grown-ups it is not as simple as that. The yarn has to be there. There can be no build-up, as they say in the movies, for the main situation; it cannot be evoked at will, and it cannot be faked. If the voltage cannot be felt, the whole piece falls flat, and it will throw off no jumble of delightful sparks, of the kind we were talking about in connection with Paris.

They not only give themselves no kick, but they have developed, out of the things they do, a curious slant on life, particularly on Labor, which you have no doubt read about and probably misunderstood. For these occupations are not only piddling, but also fly-by-night; none of them seem to pay, and it is unusual to find a man who is doing the same thing now as he did last year. If he has a poultry farm, a few months ago he fixed flats and a few months before that had a news-stand.

This makes for the most incredible incompetence at those routine things that you have always taken for granted. The paper-hanger takes five days to do a job that a good man would finish in one; the restaurant has its lights so placed that your head casts a shadow on your plate, making it impossible to see your food; a house, well-designed otherwise, has one corner of the living-room gouged out to let in a trick stairway, the result being that you cannot lay a rug; the salesman has a persuasive line of talk about the merits of the article, and then has to look on the icebox door to find out the price; the telephone clerk reports that somebody called, but hasn't taken his number so you can call back; the waiter clamps a fork over the spoon when he serves peas, in the elegant manner of an Italian serving asparagus, not noticing that when it is peas he is serving, and not asparagus, this makes them bounce all over the table like shot; the bookstore is sorry, sir, but would have to know the publisher before it could order that book for you, apparently not knowing that the United States Index, which is lying open on the counter, was invented specifically to solve this problem; the apartment-house has it drawers built exactly three inches too short to hold a shirt; the movie impresario wires frantically to New York for a certain writer, only to discover that for a year he has had the varlet on his own lot.

You may think I overstate the case, in a strained effort to be comical. I assure you I do not. It is not only my observation. It is the observation of every Easterner who comes out here: I have talked with dozens of them on the subject, and all of them make the same report, most of them with much fancier illustrations than those I have given.

Now, this kind of thing, together with the state of affairs that lies back of it, has bred a fear of good, honest, well-paid craftsmanship that is at the bottom of the very genuine anti-union sentiment that you find here. This sentiment, no doubt, had its origin in the disturbances that led to the dynamiting of the Los Angeles *Times* office some years ago, and Big Business certainly had a hand in that fight.

But Big Business, so far as I have had a chance to observe it, is pretty sensible now. The core of the anti-union feeling here these days is not so much Big Business as Little Labor; and how this works out I can best show by quoting a man I talked with shortly after I came here.

"This is how it is," he said. "Your dirt farmer from Iowa, or wherever it is, gets here with a little pile, just about enough to keep him, and at first, after freezing his face in those blizzards for forty years, it's great. He has a swell time, sees the Mt. Wilson Observatory, the Pacific Ocean, the millionaires' houses in Pasadena, the Huntington Museum, and Hollywood; he's never seen anything like that before, and he loves it. But then what? There ain't no more. After six months he's so sick of doing nothing that he'll take fifteen dollars a week, or ten dollars a week, or three dollars a week; or he'll start any kind of cock-eyed business, he'll do *anything*, just to keep busy. And boy, maybe you think that baby can't hate union labor! Because union labor, anyhow the way he figures it, means that pretty soon he's out of a job, and there's *nothing* for him to do but water the grass."

That sums it up very simply, and it certainly takes the wind out of your indignation, makes all your fine theories about collective bargaining seem as silly as your theories about civil rights seem in Mexico. For indignation, particularly in this controversy, rests on some sort of sporting sympathy for the under-dog; but when you find out that the under-dog has a couple of mice under *him* yet, in great danger of being mashed flat, what are you going to do? Begin feeling sorry for the mice, I suppose. There they are, and they certainly confuse the issue quite thoroughly. Just the same, I greatly prefer a dog-fight to a mouse-fight; and the fact that these are worthy mice, down there through no fault of their own, doesn't relieve their doings of a certain what-of-it quality that I find very hard to get excited about.

What I would like to see here, to make an end of my carping, would be a vast increase in what might be called economic vitality. The whole place would be pepped up, I think, by big, slashing industries, industries that bind men together, make them feel their competence as workmen, fill them with the vanity that demands adequate recompense; industries that afford an afflatus of the ego that is requited only by fine food and drink; industries that produce pep, bustle, enjoyment of life. They are really what throw off the jumble of sparks, cover a country with things that appeal to the imagination. But so far there are not anything like enough of them.

Some, you understand. Oil production is enormous: I must say that a trip through the well forests, for all their dreadful reek, hands you something. Movie production is also important: I believe oil and movies account for nearly 25% of the revenues of the place from the outside. Furniture, Hollywood garments, and various other manufactures are growing. But still, not enough of these to go around. The typical Southern Californian is still the Middle Westerner who was a crack sidewalk contractor in Sioux City, and a punk rabbit breeder here. Nobody told him that many Southern California streets don't have sidewalks: no walking done, you know. So he is out of luck. So his talents are wasted. So it is not his fault. But he is terribly dull company.

A word about the nutty religions. They don't cut anything like as much ice as you might think from reading about them. They are here, and practically everybody polices his discourse with "pass on," instead of "die:" he can't be quite sure what cult you may belong to. Even so, they are more like pastimes than the religions you are probably accustomed to. People find in them a relief from boredom, give them the zealous attention that a fad might command elsewhere; but they change off pretty easily from one to the other, and apparently don't care about them very deeply.

Aimée doesn't seem to cut any ice at all. The newspapers treat her with the amiable levity that New York reserves for the Metropolitan Opera House, and I personally have never met a Californian who has even seen her. I am an object of curiosity, in fact, when I let it be known that I have seen her, and a great disappointment when I have to admit that this was before she reduced and changed the color of her hair.

V

I wish now to do a little speculating about the future of this place. From what I have said, you may think it is pretty dark, but I wouldn't bet on it; there are a number of favorable factors, and I should like to check them over briefly.

First, let me emphasize again the distinctly superior human material that is on hand. Circumstances, particularly the fact that at the moment there are no very stimulating things for them to do, may have condemned these people to the kind of activity I was describing a moment ago, but they are capable of bucking stiffer winds, and when stiffer winds begin to blow they will acquit themselves impressively. I remind you that a selective process has affected the settlement here that has not gone on in many other American localities. In general, I think it can be said that most sections of the United States were first populated by failures. They are usually referred to as "pioneers," but that euphemism doesn't dispose of the fact that they were doing very badly where they were, and pulled up stakes to see if they couldn't do better somewhere else.

But that hasn't been the case here. Making all allowance for the automobile tramp and others of his kind who have come here, the person who has unpacked and stayed usually has had a pile. Sometimes it has been a big pile, for a great deal of wealth is visible: I hope I haven't given you the idea that everybody here is just one jump ahead of the sheriff. Oftener it has been a little pile, but anyhow it has been some kind of pile. The typical settler here has made what some walk of life regards as a success, and is here to enjoy the climate; that means that he is a person of some substance. Whatever he does after he gets here, the original ability is there; it is transmitted to his children, and it is something to be reckoned with.

Next, I shall surprise you by citing as a favorable factor the Los Angeles Chamber of Commerce, which with various affiliated organizations pretty much controls the commercial development of the region. It seems to me that the economic situation out here has forced it, perhaps unconsciously, to acquire a profounder notion of its responsibilities than you will find in most organizations of its kind. The average American chamber of commerce, in my experience with it, is a noisy, tiresome, and exceedingly childish booster affair, with no maturer idea of its function than to bring as many factories to town as possible, in order that merchants will have more customers, realtors more prospects for their lots, and property more benefit from the unearned increment. That, and a running wrangle with the Interstate Commerce Commission, carried on by the traffic department, over some freight differential enjoyed by a nearby city, is about the extent of its activity. As to whether the factories are desirable, as to whether abolishment of the differential would throw several railroads into bankruptcy, they seldom give a thought; and sometimes, as when one Eastern city proudly announced the advent of a soap factory that had stunk so badly it was run out of another city, you wonder whether they are quite bright.

But here the basic situation is different, and you can see what it is from the phrase you hear so often around the Los Angeles chamber: "We know we can't go on selling climate forever. People have got to have something to do after they get here." In other words, the boom is over. People fell for the climate all right, and bought lots, and settled down. But piles, whether big or little, have a distressing tendency to melt, so that the section faces the necessity of becoming an economic unit that can run under its own steam, piles or no piles. To that exceedingly difficult problem, which is after all the problem I have been stating in a roundabout way, the Los Angeles Chamber of Commerce is addressing itself with a sobriety which I must confess impresses me.

It is not content to get a new factory, although it has got plenty of these in the last few years. It has been forced to do what most Chambers of Commerce do not do: undertake an exhaustive study of the possibilities of the region, that takes into account the needs of the population as a whole, and that is much broader in its scope than the leather-bound "presentation" got up for some particular manufacturer.

Now, if this profounder attitude is real, and not something that I thought I detected and didn't, you would expect it to give some tangible evidence of its presence, something you could put your finger on and say, "There, that's what I mean." And so, in fact, you find it. The offices are quiet and run with swift efficiency. There are no signs telling you to "Smile, Damn You, Smile." There is an atmosphere not unlike what you associate with the research departments of a big university, with the difference that this research has a purpose, a smell of dealing with live, important things, that most university research plainly lacks.

And there is something that I pay a great deal of attention to when I try to estimate a man's integrity, which is a healthy respect for a fact. It amounts almost to a religion in this place. You hear frequently the rueful admission that "we've got a reputation to live down, all right": they seem terrified lest old mistakes will be repeated and come home to roost. So that you are no sooner handed a table of figures than you get the footnote: "Now listen: This is not any of our hooey. This comes right out of the United States Census Reports, and you can bank on it to the last decimal point." Well, I buy that. I am a sucker for the man who is worried about the last decimal point.

In other words, out of the Gethsemane of its woe these last few years, this Los Angeles Chamber of Commerce bids fair to emerge as what a chamber of commerce ought to be, and so seldom is. It is very powerful, much more so than the chambers of commerce you are probably accustomed to. It is a sort of government outside the government, bearing about the same relation to the body politic as the Communist party does in Russia. (I suppose I put that in out of pure malice.) And, like the Communist party in Russia, it is most intolerant of all schemes for monkeying with the gears. Radicalism of any kind is anathema to it. I suspect that the big fellows enrolled in it are not anything like so hot on this subject as they are thought to be; but big fellows are not the only ones it must satisfy: the very fact that it has a large membership, has to study the problems of even the littlest fellows, and is the repository of a highly concentrated leadership, has forced it in this matter to go along with the crowd.

This, I must say, I find deplorable. I never feel that a city is really in the Big Time unless it has soap boxers damning the government in the parks, and parades that occasionally result in cracked heads. Why I regard such things as cosmopolitan I don't know, but I do. Yet it would be foolish to maintain that I miss them out here as much as I would if they were absent, say, in New York. Again like Russia, this section is not ready for that kind of thing yet. You have to get the gears turning before you can throw left-handed monkey wrenches into them. And, of course, the basic realities take some of the sting out, too.

The one basic reality that can dignify Red goings-on is hunger, and there is very little of it here. Ten cents will buy an incredible amount of food, and hardly anybody lacks ten cents; if somebody does lack it, the genuinely humane treatment he gets here alters somewhat the circumstance that he can't put up a general squawk. What I am trying to say is that the air, the sun, the lay of the land, the feel of what is going on here, make the inalienable right of man to talk, wrangle, and fight himself out of his daily bread seem somewhat beside the point; that may be what other sections have their mind on, but not this one. It has its mind on something else, and it is only sensible to judge it by what it is trying to do, and not by what you think it ought to be trying to do.

Which brings me to my final point, which is the idea held by everybody here that some sort of destiny awaits the place. Of recent years, the implications of a destiny have bemused me greatly; and I believe that one of the troubles of the United States as a whole is that it no longer has one. In the beginning, its destiny was to reduce a continent, and that destiny, as long as it lasted, made everything hum; transformed the most shiftless bacon-and-beaner into a pioneer, placed an epic frame around our wars, gave the most trivial episode the stature of history. But the continent has been reduced, alas, so that destiny has blown up.

Now what? If you know, you are a wiser man than I am. We have a great deal of running around about it, visionaries providing us with a lot of pat destinies: one set trying to make us the most cultured nation on earth, and demanding that we pile novel on top of symphony on top of skyscraper until we claim our place in the æsthetic sun; another set trying to make us the most moral nation on earth, piling Prohibition laws on top of cigarette laws on top of anti-Evolution laws on top of blue laws; another set trying to make us the most prosperous nation on earth, piling tariffs on top of R.F.C.'s on top of apostrophes to the Forgotten Man. But all these stars, unfortunately, begin to look a great deal like fish-scales, and where we are actually headed, if anywhere, it is pretty hard, for me at least, to see.

So that when you come to a place that not only thinks it has a destiny, but knows it has a destiny, you cannot but be arrested.

Where this place is headed is to be the leader in commerce, art, citrus production, music, rabbit breeding, oil production, furniture manufacture, walnut growing, literature, olive bottling, short- and long-distance hauling, clay modelling, æsthetic criticism, fish export, canary-bird culture, playwrighting, shipping, cinematic creativeness, and drawing-room manners. In short, it is going to be a paradise on earth. And, with such vaulting ambitions, it might pull off something: you can't tell. It is keenly aware of the Orient, and also of Mexico; streams are meeting here that ought to churn up some exciting whirlpools. I, personally, even if the first act hasn't been so hot, am not going to walk out on the show. One thing it *is* going to be, within the twelve-month, is the wine center of the New World. I guess you think I'm going to walk out on that, do you? That will make a lot of things different.

No, I stay. The climate suits me fine.

William Faulkner

There is a story, perhaps apocryphal, that when William Faulkner (1897–1962) was working at MGM in the 1930s, he asked his supervisor late one day if he could take his work home with him. After the request was okayed, Faulkner proceeded to take his work home—to Oxford, Mississippi. Despite his many protracted stays, mostly devoted to working on such Howard Hawks productions as *The Road to Glory*, *To Have and Have Not*, and *The Big Sleep*, Faulkner's feelings about Hollywood are summed up in a 1945 letter: "I don't like this damn place any better than I ever did. That is one comfort: at least I cant be any sicker tomorrow for Mississippi than I was yesterday." Many writers have lamented the tribulations and debilitating temptations of the screenwriting life, but few could resist the urge to incorporate Hollywood into their own work. Faulkner, by contrast, used a California setting once only. "Golden Land," published in 1935, distills his misgivings into an archetypal tale of insidious corruption.

GOLDEN LAND

If he had been thirty, he would not have needed the two aspirin tablets and the half glass of raw gin before he could bear the shower's needling on his body and steady his hands to shave. But then when he had been thirty neither could he have afforded to drink as much each evening as he now drank; certainly he would not have done it in the company of the men and the women in which, at forty-eight, he did each evening, even though knowing during the very final hours filled with the breaking of glass and the shrill cries of drunken women above the drums and saxophones—the hours during which he carried a little better than his weight both in the amount of liquor consumed and in the number and sum of checks paid—that six or eight hours later he would rouse from what had not been sleep at all but instead that dreamless stupefaction of alcohol out of which last night's turgid and licensed uproar would die, as though without any interval for rest or recuperation, into the familiar shape of his bedroom—the bed's foot silhouetted by the morning light which entered the bougainvillaea-bound windows beyond

which his painful and almost unbearable eyes could see the view
which might be called the monument to almost twenty-five years of
industry and desire, of shrewdness and luck and even fortitude—
the opposite canyonflank dotted with the white villas halfhidden
in imported olive groves or friezed by the sombre spaced columns
of cypress like the façades of eastern temples, whose owners'
names and faces and even voices were glib and familiar in back
corners of the United States and of America and of the world where
those of Einstein and Rousseau and Esculapius had never sounded.

He didn't waken sick. He never wakened ill nor became ill from
drinking, not only because he had drunk too long and too steadily
for that, but because he was too tough even after the thirty soft
years; he came from too tough stock on that day thirty-four years
ago when at fourteen he had fled, on the brakebeam of a westbound
freight, the little lost Nebraska town named for, permeated with, his
father's history and existence—a town to be sure, but only in the
sense that any shadow is larger than the object which casts it. It was
still frontier even as he remembered it at five and six—the projected
and increased shadow of a small outpost of sodroofed dugouts on
the immense desolation of the plains where his father, Ira Ewing
too, had been first to essay to wring wheat during the six days
between those when, outdoors in spring and summer and in the
fetid halfdark of a snowbound dugout in the winter and fall, he
preached. The second Ira Ewing had come a long way since then,
from that barren and treeless village which he had fled by a night
freight to where he now lay in a hundred-thousand-dollar house,
waiting until he knew that he could rise and go to the bath and put
the two aspirin tablets into his mouth. They—his mother and
father—had tried to explain it to him—something about fortitude,
the will to endure. At fourteen he could neither answer them with
logic and reason nor explain what he wanted: he could only flee.
Nor was he fleeing his father's harshness and wrath. He was fleeing
the scene itself—the treeless immensity in the lost center of which
he seemed to see the sum of his father's and mother's dead youth
and bartered lives as a tiny forlorn spot which nature permitted to
green into brief and niggard wheat for a season's moment before
blotting it all with the primal and invincible snow as though (not
even promise, not even threat) in grim and almost playful augury of

the final doom of all life. And it was not even this that he was fleeing because he was not fleeing: it was only that absence, removal,
was the only argument which fourteen knew how to employ against
adults with any hope of success. He spent the next ten years half
tramp half casual laborer as he drifted down the Pacific Coast to
Los Angeles; at thirty he was married, to a Los Angeles girl, daughter of a carpenter, and father of a son and a daughter and with a
foothold in real estate; at forty-eight he spent fifty thousand dollars
a year, owning a business which he had built up unaided and preserved intact through nineteen-twenty-nine; he had given to his
children luxuries and advantages which his own father not only
could not have conceived in fact but would have condemned completely in theory—as it proved, as the paper which the Filipino
chauffeur, who each morning carried him into the house and undressed him and put him to bed, had removed from the pocket of
his topcoat and laid on the reading table proved, with reason. On
the death of his father twenty years ago he had returned to
Nebraska, for the first time, and fetched his mother back with him,
and she was now established in a home of her own only the less
sumptuous because she refused (with a kind of abashed and
thoughtful unshakability which he did not remark) anything finer
or more elaborate. It was the house in which they had all lived
at first, though he and his wife and children had moved within the
year. Three years ago they had moved again, into the house where
he now waked in a select residential section of Beverley Hills, but
not once in the nineteen years had he failed to stop (not even during the last five, when to move at all in the mornings required a terrific drain on that character or strength which the elder Ira had
bequeathed him, which had enabled the other Ira to pause on the
Nebraska plain and dig a hole for his wife to bear children in while
he planted wheat) on his way to the office (twenty miles out of his
way to the office) and spend ten minutes with her. She lived in as
complete physical ease and peace as he could devise. He had arranged her affairs so that she did not even need to bother with
money, cash, in order to live; he had arranged credit for her with a
neighboring market and butcher so that the Japanese gardener who
came each day to water and tend the flowers could do her shopping
for her; she never even saw the bills. And the only reason she had no

servant was that even at seventy she apparently clung stubbornly to the old habit of doing her own cooking and housework. So it would seem that he had been right. Perhaps there were times when, lying in bed like this and waiting for the will to rise and take the aspirin and the gin (mornings perhaps following evenings when he had drunk more than ordinarily and when even the six or seven hours of oblivion had not been sufficient to enable him to distinguish between reality and illusion) something of the old strong harsh Campbellite blood which the elder Ira must have bequeathed him might have caused him to see or feel or imagine his father looking down from somewhere upon him, the prodigal, and what he had accomplished. If this were so, then surely the elder Ira, looking down for the last two mornings upon the two tabloid papers which the Filipino removed from his master's topcoat and laid on the reading table, might have taken advantage of that old blood and taken his revenge, not just for that afternoon thirty-four years ago but for the entire thirty-four years.

When he gathered himself, his will, his body, at last and rose from the bed he struck the paper so that it fell to the floor and lay open at his feet, but he did not look at it. He just stood so, tall, in silk pajamas, thin where his father had been gaunt with the years of hard work and unceasing struggle with the unpredictable and implacable earth (even now, despite the life which he had led, he had very little paunch) looking at nothing while at his feet the black headline flared above the row of five or six tabloid photographs from which his daughter alternately stared back or flaunted long pale shins: APRIL LALEAR BARES ORGY SECRETS. When he moved at last he stepped on the paper, walking on his bare feet into the bath; now it was his trembling and jerking hands that he watched as he shook the two tablets onto the glass shelf and set the tumbler into the rack and unstoppered the gin bottle and braced his knuckles against the wall in order to pour into the tumbler. But he did not look at the paper, not even when, shaved, he re-entered the bedroom and went to the bed beside which his slippers sat and shoved the paper aside with his foot in order to step into them. Perhaps, doubtless, he did not need to. The trial was but entering its third tabloidal day now, and so for two days his daughter's face had sprung out at him, hard, blonde and inscrutable, from every paper he opened; doubtless he had never forgot her while he slept even, that he had waked into thinking about remembering her as he had waked into the dying drunken uproar of the evening eight hours behind him without any interval between for rest or forgetting.

Nevertheless as, dressed, in a burnt orange turtleneck sweater beneath his gray flannels, he descended the Spanish staircase, he was outwardly calm and possessed. The delicate iron balustrade and the marble steps coiled down to the tilefloored and barnlike living room beyond which he could hear his wife and son talking on the breakfast terrace. The son's name was Voyd. He and his wife had named the two children by what might have been called mutual contemptuous armistice—his wife called the boy Voyd, for what reason he never knew; he in his turn named the girl (the child whose woman's face had met him from every paper he touched for two days now beneath or above the name, April Lalear) Samantha, after his own mother. He could hear them talking—the wife between whom and himself there had been nothing save civility, and not always a great deal of that, for ten years now; and the son who one afternoon two years ago had been delivered at the door drunk and insensible by a car whose occupants he did not see and, it devolving upon him to undress the son and put him to bed, whom he discovered to be wearing, in place of underclothes, a woman's brassière and step-ins. A few minutes later, hearing the blows perhaps, Voyd's mother ran in and found her husband beating the still unconscious son with a series of towels which a servant was steeping in rotation in a basin of ice-water. He was beating the son hard, with grim and deliberate fury. Whether he was trying to sober the son up or was merely beating him, possibly he himself did not know. His wife though jumped to the latter conclusion. In his raging disillusionment he tried to tell her about the woman's garments but she refused to listen; she assailed him in turn with virago fury. Since that day the son had contrived to see his father only in his mother's presence (which neither the son nor the mother found very difficult, by the way) and at which times the son treated his father with a blend of cringing spite and vindictive insolence half a cat's and half a woman's.

He emerged onto the terrace; the voices ceased. The sun, strained by the vague high soft almost nebulous California haze, fell upon the terrace with a kind of treacherous unbrightness. The terrace, the sundrenched terra cotta tiles, butted into a rough and savage shear of canyonwall bare yet without dust, on or against which a solid mat of flowers bloomed in fierce lush myriad-colored paradox as though in place of being rooted into and drawing from the soil they lived upon air alone and had been merely leaned intact against the sustenanceless lavawall by someone who would later return and take them away. The son, Voyd, apparently naked save for a pair of straw-colored shorts, his body brown with sun and scented faintly by the depilatory which he used on arms, chest and legs, lay in a wicker chair, his feet in straw beach shoes, an open newspaper across his brown legs. The paper was the highest class one of the city, yet there was a black headline across half of it too, and even without pausing, without even being aware that he had looked, Ira saw there too the name which he recognized. He went on to his place; the Filipino who put him to bed each night, in a white service jacket now, drew his chair. Beside the glass of orange juice and the waiting cup lay a neat pile of mail topped by a telegram. He sat down and took up the telegram; he had not glanced at his wife until she spoke:

"Mrs. Ewing telephoned. She says for you to stop in there on your way to town."

He stopped; his hands opening the telegram stopped. Still blinking a little against the sun he looked at the face opposite him across the table—the smooth dead makeup, the thin lips and the thin nostrils and the pale blue unforgiving eyes, the meticulous platinum hair which looked as though it had been transferred to her skull with a brush from a book of silver leaf such as window painters use. "What?" he said. "Telephoned? Here?"

"Why not? Have I ever objected to any of your women telephoning you here?"

The unopened telegram crumpled suddenly in his hand. "You know what I mean," he said harshly. "She never telephoned me in her life. She don't have to. Not that message. When have I ever failed to go by there on my way to town?"

"How do I know?" she said. "Or are you the same model son you have been a husband and seem to be a father?" Her voice was not shrill yet, nor even very loud, and none could have told how fast her breathing was because she sat so still, rigid beneath the impeccable and unbelievable hair, looking at him with that pale and outraged unforgiveness. They both looked at each other across the luxurious table—the two people who at one time twenty years ago would have turned as immediately and naturally and unthinkingly to one another in trouble, who even ten years ago might have done so.

"You know what I mean," he said, harshly again, holding himself too against the trembling which he doubtless believed was from last night's drinking, from the spent alcohol. "She don't read papers. She never even sees one. Did you send it to her?"

"I?" she said. "Send what?"

"Damnation!" he cried. "A paper! Did you send it to her? Don't lie to me."

"What if I did?" she cried. "Who is she, that she must not know about it? Who is she, that you should shield her from knowing it? Did you make any effort to keep me from knowing it? Did you make any effort to keep it from happening? Why didn't you think about that all those years while you were too drunk, too besotted with drink, to know or notice or care what Samantha was—"

"Miss April Lalear of the cinema, if you please," Voyd said. They paid no attention to him; they glared at one another across the table.

"Ah," he said, quiet and rigid, his lips scarcely moving. "So I am to blame for this too, am I? I made my daughter a bitch, did I? Maybe you will tell me next that I made my son a f—"

"Stop!" she cried. She was panting now; they glared at one another across the suave table, across the five feet of irrevocable division.

"Now, now," Voyd said. "Don't interfere with the girl's career. After all these years, when at last she seems to have found a part that she can—" He ceased; his father had turned and was looking at him. Voyd lay in his chair, looking at his father with that veiled insolence that was almost feminine. Suddenly it became completely feminine; with a muffled halfscream he swung his legs out to spring up and flee but it was too late; Ira stood above him, gripping him not by the throat but by the face with one hand, so that Voyd's mouth puckered and slobbered in his father's hard, shaking hand. Then the mother sprang forward and tried to break Ira's grip but he flung her away and then caught and held her, struggling too, with the other hand when she sprang in again.

"Go on," he said. "Say it." But Voyd could say nothing because of his father's hand gripping his jaws open, or more than likely because of terror. His body was free of the chair now, writhing and thrashing while he made his slobbering, moaning sound of terror while his father held him with one hand and held his screaming mother with the other one. Then Ira flung Voyd free, onto the terrace; Voyd rolled once and came onto his feet, crouching, retreating toward the French windows with one arm flung up before his face while he cursed his father. Then he was gone. Ira faced his wife, holding her quiet too at last, panting too, the skillful map of makeup standing into relief now like a paper mask trimmed smoothly and pasted onto her skull. He released her.

"You sot," she said. "You drunken sot. And yet you wonder why your children —"

"Yes," he said quietly. "All right. That's not the question. That's all done. The question is, what to do about it. My father would have known. He did it once." He spoke in a dry light pleasant voice: so much so that she stood, panting still but quiet, watching him. "I remember. I was about ten. We had rats in the barn. We tried everything. Terriers. Poison. Then one day father said, 'Come.' We went to the barn and stopped all the cracks, the holes. Then we set fire to it. What do you think of that?" Then she was gone too. He stood for a moment, blinking a little, his eyeballs beating faintly and steadily in his skull with the impact of the soft unchanging sunlight, the fierce innocent mass of the flowers. "Philip!" he called. The Filipino appeared, brownfaced, impassive, with a pot of hot coffee, and set it beside the empty cup and the icebedded glass of orange juice. "Get me a drink," Ira said. The Filipino glanced at him, then he became busy at the table, shifting the cup and setting the pot down and shifting the cup again while Ira watched him. "Did you hear me?" Ira said. The Filipino stood erect and looked at him.

"You told me not to give it to you until you had your orange juice and coffee."

"Will you or won't you get me a drink?" Ira shouted.

"Very good, sir," the Filipino said. He went out. Ira looked after him; this had happened before: he knew well that the brandy would not appear until he had finished the orange juice and the coffee, though just where the Filipino lurked to watch him he never knew. He sat again and opened the crumpled telegram and read it, the glass of orange juice in the other hand. It was from his secretary: MADE SETUP BEFORE I BROKE STORY LAST NIGHT STOP THIRTY PER-CENT FRONT PAGE STOP MADE APPOINTMENT FOR YOU COURT-HOUSE THIS P.M. STOP WILL YOU COME TO OFFICE OR CALL ME. He read the telegram again, the glass of orange juice still poised. Then he put both down and rose and went and lifted the paper from the terrace where Voyd had flung it, and read the half headline: LALEAR WOMAN DAUGHTER OF PROMINENT LOCAL FAMILY. Admits Real Name Is Samantha Ewing, Daughter of Ira Ewing, Local Realtor. He read it quietly; he said quietly, aloud:

"It was that Jap that showed her the paper. It was that damned gardener." He returned to the table. After a while the Filipino came, with the brandy-and-soda, and wearing now a jacket of bright imitation tweed, telling him that the car was ready.

II

His mother lived in Glendale; it was the house which he had taken when he married and later bought, in which his son and daughter had been born—a bungalow in a cul-de-sac of pepper trees and flowering shrubs and vines which the Japanese tended, backed into a barren foothill combed and curried into a cypress-and-marble cemetery dramatic as a stage set and topped by an electric sign in red bulbs which, in the San Fernando valley fog, glared in broad sourceless ruby as though just beyond the crest lay not heaven but hell. The length of his sports model car in which the Filipino sat reading a paper dwarfed it. But she would have no other, just as she would have neither servant, car, nor telephone—a gaunt spare slightly stooped woman upon whom even California and ease had put no flesh, sitting in one of the chairs which she had insisted on bringing all the way from Nebraska. At first she had been content to allow the Nebraska furniture to remain in storage, since it had not been needed (when Ira moved his wife and family out of the house and into the second one, the intermediate one, they had bought new furniture too, leaving the first house furnished complete for his mother) but one day, he could not recall just when, he discovered that she had taken the one chair out of storage and was using it in the house. Later, after he began to sense that quality of unrest in her, he had suggested that she let him clear the house of its present furniture and take all of hers out of storage but she declined, apparently preferring or desiring to leave the Nebraska furniture where it was. Sitting so, a knitted shawl about her shoulders, she looked less like she lived in or belonged to the house, the room, than the son with his beach burn and his faintly theatrical gray temples and his bright expensive suavely antiphonal garments did. She had changed hardly at all in the thirty-four years; she and the older Ira Ewing too, as the son remembered him, who, dead, had suffered as little of alteration as while he had been alive. As the sod Nebraska outpost had grown into a village and then into a town, his father's aura alone had increased, growing into the proportions of a giant who at some irrevocable yet recent time had engaged barehanded in some titanic struggle with the pitiless earth and endured and in a sense conquered—it too, like the town, a shadow out of all proportion to the gaunt gnarled figure of the actual man. And the actual woman too as the son remembered them back in that time. Two people who drank air and who required to eat and sleep as he did and who had brought him into the world, yet were strangers as though of another race, who stood side by side in an irrevocable loneliness as though strayed from another planet, not as husband and wife but as blood brother and sister, even twins, of the same travail because they had gained a strange peace through fortitude and the will and strength to endure.

"Tell me again what it is," she said. "I'll try to understand."

"So it was Kazimura that showed you the damned paper," he said. She didn't answer this; she was not looking at him.

"You tell me she has been in the pictures before, for two years. That that was why she had to change her name, that they all have to change their names."

"Yes. They call them extra parts. For about two years, God knows why."

"And then you tell me that this—that all this was so she could get into the pictures—"

He started to speak, then he caught himself back out of some quick impatience, some impatience perhaps of grief or despair or at least rage, holding his voice, his tone, quiet: "I said that that was one possible reason. All I know is that the man has something to do with pictures, giving out the parts. And that the police caught him and Samantha and the other girl in an apartment with the doors all locked and that Samantha and the other woman were naked. They say that he was naked too and he says he was not. He says in the trial that he was framed—tricked; that they were trying to black-mail him into giving them parts in a picture; that they fooled him into coming there and arranged for the police to break in just after they had taken off their clothes; that one of them made a signal from the window. Maybe so. Or maybe they were all just having a good time and were innocently caught." Unmoving, rigid, his face broke, wrung with faint bitter smiling as though with indomitable and impassive suffering, or maybe just smiling, just rage. Still his mother did not look at him.

"But you told me she was already in the pictures. That that was why she had to change her—"

"I said, extra parts," he said. He had to catch himself again, out of his jangled and outraged nerves, back from the fierce fury of the impatience. "Can't you understand that you don't get into the pictures just by changing your name? and that you don't even stay there when you get in? that you can't even stay there by being female? that they come here in droves on every train—girls younger and prettier than Samantha and who will do anything to get into the pictures? So will she, apparently; but who know or are willing to learn to do more things than even she seems to have thought of? But let's don't talk about it. She has made her bed; all I can do is to help her up: I can't wash the sheets. Nobody can. I must go, anyway; I'm late." He rose, looking down at her. "They said you telephoned me this morning. Is this what it was?"

"No," she said. Now she looked up at him; now her gnarled hands began to pick faintly at one another. "You offered me a ser-vant once."

"Yes. I thought fifteen years ago that you ought to have one. Have you changed your mind? Do you want me to—"

Now she stopped looking at him again, though her hands did not cease. "That was fifteen years ago. It would have cost at least five hundred dollars a year. That would be—"

He laughed, short and harsh. "I'd like to see the Los Angeles servant you could get for five hundred dollars a year. But what—" He stopped laughing, looking down at her.

"That would be at least five thousand dollars," she said.

He looked down at her. After a while he said, "Are you asking me again for money?" She didn't answer nor move, her hands picking slowly and quietly at one another. "Ah," he said. "You want to go away. You want to run from it. So do I!" he cried, before he could catch himself this time; "so do I! But you did not choose me when you elected a child; neither did I choose my two. But I shall have to bear them and you will have to bear all of us. There is no help for it." He caught himself now, panting, quieting himself by will as when he would rise from bed, though his voice was still harsh: "Where would you go? Where would you hide from it?"

"Home," she said.

"Home?" he repeated; he repeated in a kind of amazement: "home?" before he understood. "You would go back there? with those winters, that snow and all? Why, you wouldn't live to see the first Christmas: don't you know that?" She didn't move nor look up at him. "Nonsense," he said. "This will blow over. In a month there will be two others and nobody except us will even remember it. And you don't need money. You have been asking me for money for years, but you don't need it. I had to worry about money so much at one time myself that I swore that the least I could do was to arrange your affairs so you would never even have to look at the stuff. I must go; there is something at the office today. I'll see you tomorrow."

It was already one o'clock. "Courthouse," he told the Filipino, settling back into the car. "My God, I want a drink." He rode with his eyes closed against the sun; the secretary had already sprung onto the runningboard before he realized that they had reached the courthouse. The secretary, bareheaded too, wore a jacket of authentic tweed; his turtleneck sweater was dead black, his hair was black too, varnished smooth to his skull; he spread before Ira a dummy newspaper page laid out to embrace the blank space for the photograph beneath the caption: APRIL LALEAR'S FATHER. Beneath the space was the legend: IRA EWING, PRESIDENT OF THE EWING REALTY CO., — WILSHIRE BOULEVARD, BEVERLY HILLS.

"Is thirty percent all you could get?" Ira said. The secretary was young; he glared at Ira for an instant in vague impatience fury.

"Jesus, thirty percent is thirty percent. They are going to print a thousand extra copies and use our mailing list. It will be spread all up and down the Coast and as far East as Reno. What do you want? We can't expect them to put under your picture, 'Turn to page fourteen for halfpage ad,' can we?" Ira sat again with his eyes closed, waiting for his head to stop.

"All right," he said. "Are they ready now?"

"All set. You will have to go inside. They insisted it be inside, so everybody that sees it will know it is the courthouse."

"All right," Ira said. He got out; with his eyes half closed and the secretary at his elbow he mounted the steps and entered the courthouse. The reporter and the photographer were waiting but he did not see them yet; he was aware only of being enclosed in a gaping crowd which he knew would be mostly women, hearing the secretary and a policeman clearing the way in the corridor outside the courtroom door.

"This is O.K.," the secretary said. Ira stopped; the darkness was easier on his eyes though he did not open them yet; he just stood, hearing the secretary and the policeman herding the women, the faces, back; someone took him by the arm and turned him; he stood obediently; the magnesium flashed and glared, striking against his painful eyeballs like blows; he had a vision of wan faces craned to look at him from either side of a narrow human lane; with his eyes shut tight now he turned, blundering until the reporter in charge spoke to him:

"Just a minute, chief. We better get another one just in case." This time his eyes were tightly closed; the magnesium flashed, washed over them; in the thin acrid smell of it he turned and with the secretary again at his elbow he moved blindly back and into the sunlight and into his car. He gave no order this time, he just said, "Get me a drink." He rode with his eyes closed again while the car cleared the downtown traffic and then began to move quiet, powerful and fast under him; he rode so for a long while before he felt the car swing into the palmbordered drive, slowing. It stopped; the doorman opened the door for him, speaking to him by name. The elevator boy called him by name too, stopping at the right floor without direction; he followed the corridor and knocked at a door and was fumbling for the key when the door opened upon a woman in a bathing suit beneath a loose beach cloak—a woman with treated hair also and brown eyes, who swung the door back for him to enter and then to behind him, looking at him with the quick bright faint serene smiling which only a woman nearing forty can give to a man to whom she is not married and from whom she has had no secrets physical and few mental over a long time of pleasant and absolute intimacy. She had been married though and divorced; she had a child, a daughter of fourteen, whom he was now keeping in boarding school. He looked at her, blinking, as she closed the door.

"You saw the papers," he said. She kissed him, not suddenly, without heat, in a continuation of the movement which closed the door, with a sort of warm envelopment; suddenly he cried, "I can't understand it! After all the advantages that . . . after all I tried to do for them—"

"Hush," she said. "Hush, now. Get into your trunks; I'll have a drink ready for you when you have changed. Will you eat some lunch if I have it sent up?"

"No. I don't want any lunch. —after all I have tried to give—"

"Hush, now. Get into your trunks while I fix you a drink. It's going to be swell at the beach." In the bedroom his bathing trunks and robe were laid out on the bed. He changed, hanging his suit in the closet where her clothes hung, where there hung already another suit of his and clothes for the evening. When he returned to the sitting room she had fixed the drink for him; she held the match to his cigarette and watched him sit down and take up the glass, watching him still with that serene impersonal smiling. Now he watched her slip off the cape and kneel at the cellarette, filling a silver flask, in the bathing costume of the moment, such as ten thousand wax female dummies wore in ten thousand shop windows that summer, such as a hundred thousand young girls wore on California beaches; he looked at her, kneeling—back, buttocks and flanks trim enough, even firm enough (so firm in fact as to be a little on the muscular side, what with unremitting and perhaps even rigorous care) but still those of forty. But I don't want a young girl, he thought. Would to God that all young girls, all young female flesh, were removed, blasted even, from the earth. He finished the drink before she had filled the flask.

"I want another one," he said.

"All right," she said. "As soon as we get to the beach."

"No. Now."

"Let's go on to the beach first. It's almost three o'clock. Won't that be better?"

"Just so you are not trying to tell me I can't have another drink now."

"Of course not," she said, slipping the flask into the cape's pocket and looking at him again with that warm, faint, inscrutable smiling. "I just want to have a dip before the water gets too cold." They went down to the car; the Filipino knew this too: he held the door for her to slip under the wheel, then he got himself into the back. The car moved on; she drove well. "Why not lean back and shut your eyes," she told Ira, "and rest until we get to the beach? Then we will have a dip and a drink."

"I don't want to rest," he said. "I'm all right." But he did close his eyes again and again the car ran powerful, smooth, and fast beneath him, performing its afternoon's jaunt over the incredible distances of which the city was composed; from time to time, had he looked, he could have seen the city in the bright soft vague hazy sunlight, random, scattered about the arid earth like so many gay scraps of paper blown without order, with its curious air of being rootless — of houses bright beautiful and gay, without basements or founda-tions, lightly attached to a few inches of light penetrable earth, lighter even than dust and laid lightly in turn upon the profound and primeval lava, which one good hard rain would wash forever from the sight and memory of man as a firehouse flushes down a gutter — that city of almost incalculable wealth whose queerly appropriate fate it is to be erected upon a few spools of a substance whose value is computed in billions and which may be completely destroyed in that second's instant of a careless match between the moment of striking and the moment when the striker might have sprung and stamped it out.

"You saw your mother today," she said. "Has she —"

"Yes." He didn't open his eyes. "That damned Jap gave it to her. She asked me for money again. I found out what she wants with it. She wants to run, to go back to Nebraska. I told her, so did I. . . . If she went back there, she would not live until Christmas. The first month of winter would kill her. Maybe it wouldn't even take winter to do it."

She still drove, she still watched the road, yet somehow she had contrived to become completely immobile. "So that's what it is," she said.

He did not open his eyes. "What what is?"

"The reason she has been after you all this time to give her money, cash. Why, even when you won't do it, every now and then she asks you again."

"What what . . ." He opened his eyes, looking at her profile; he sat up suddenly. "You mean, she's been wanting to go back there all the time? That all these years she has been asking me for money, that that was what she wanted with it?"

She glanced at him swiftly, then back to the road. "What else can it be? What else could she use money for?"

"Back there?" he said. "To those winters, that town, that way of living, where she's bound to know that the first winter would . . . You'd almost think she wanted to die, wouldn't you?"

"Hush," she said quickly. "Shhhhh. Don't say that. Don't say that about anybody." Already they could smell the sea; now they swung down toward it; the bright salt wind blew upon them, with the long-spaced sound of the rollers; now they could see it—the dark blue of water creaming into the blanched curve of beach dotted with bathers. "We won't go through the club," she said. "I'll park in here and we can go straight to the water." They left the Filipino in the car and descended to the beach. It was already crowded, bright and gay with movement. She chose a vacant space and spread her cape.

"Now that drink," he said.

"Have your dip first," she said. He looked at her. Then he slipped his robe off slowly; she took it and spread it beside her own; he looked down at her.

"Which is it? Will you always be too clever for me, or is it that every time I will always believe you again?"

She looked at him, bright, warm, fond and inscrutable. "Maybe both. Maybe neither. Have your dip; I will have the flask and a cigarette ready when you come out." When he came back from the water, wet, panting, his heart a little too hard and fast, she had the towel ready, and she lit the cigarette and uncapped the flask as he lay on the spread robes. She lay too, lifted to one elbow, smiling down at him, smoothing the water from his hair with the towel while he panted, waiting for his heart to slow and quiet. Steadily between them and the water, and as far up and down the beach as they could see, the bathers passed—young people, young men in trunks, and young girls in little more, with bronzed, unselfconscious bodies. Lying so, they seemed to him to walk along the rim of the world as though they and their kind alone inhabited it, and he with his forty-eight years were the forgotten last survivor of another race and kind, and they in turn precursors of a new race not yet seen on the earth: of men and women without age, beautiful as gods and goddesses, and with the minds of infants. He turned quickly and looked at the woman beside him—at the quiet face, the wise, smiling eyes, the grained skin and temples, the hairroots showing where the dye had grown out, the legs veined faint and blue and myriad beneath the skin. "You look better than any of them!" he cried. "You look better to me than any of them!"

III

The Japanese gardener, with his hat on, stood tapping on the glass and beckoning and grimacing until old Mrs. Ewing went out to him. He had the afternoon's paper with its black headline: LALEAR WOMAN CREATES SCENE IN COURTROOM. "You take," the Japanese said. "Read while I catch water." But she declined; she just stood in the soft halcyon sunlight, surrounded by the myriad and almost fierce blooming of flowers, and looked quietly at the headline without even taking the paper, and that was all.

"I guess I won't look at the paper today," she said. "Thank you just the same." She returned to the living room. Save for the chair, it was exactly as it had been when she first saw it that day when her son brought her into it and told her that it was now her home and that her daughter-in-law and her grandchildren were now her family. It had changed very little, and that which had altered was the part which her son knew nothing about, and that too had changed not at all in so long that she could not even remember now when she had added the last coin to the hoard. This was in a china vase on the mantel. She knew what was in it to the penny; nevertheless, she took it down and sat in the chair which she had brought all the way from Nebraska and emptied the coins and the worn timetable into her lap. The timetable was folded back at the page on which she had folded it the day she walked downtown to the ticket office and got it fifteen years ago, though that was so long ago now that the pencil circle about the name of the nearest junction point to Ewing, Nebraska, had faded away. But she did not need that either; she knew the distance to the exact halfmile, just as she knew the fare to the penny, and back in the early twenties when the railroads began to become worried and passenger fares began to drop, no broker ever watched the grain and utilities market any closer than she watched the railroad advertisements and quotations. Then at last the fares became stabilized with the fare back to Ewing thirteen dollars more than she had been able to save, and at a time when her source of income had ceased. This was the two grandchildren. When she entered the house that day twenty years ago and looked at the two babies for the first time, it was with diffidence and eagerness both. She would be dependent for the rest of her life, but she would give something in return for it. It was not that she would attempt to make another Ira and Samantha Ewing of them; she had made that mistake with her own son and had driven him from home. She was wiser now; she saw now that it was not the repetition of hardship: she would merely take what had been of value in hers and her husband's hard lives—that which they had learned through hardship and endurance of honor and courage and pride—and transmit it to the children without their having to suffer the hardship at all, the travail and the despairs. She had expected that there would be some friction between her and the young daughter-in-law, but she had believed that her son, the actual Ewing, would be her ally; she had even reconciled herself after a year to waiting, since the children were still but babies; she was not alarmed, since they were Ewings too: after she had looked that first searching time at the two puttysoft little faces feature by feature, she had said it was because they were babies yet and so looked like no one. So she was content to bide and wait; she did not even know that her son was planning to move until he told her that the other house was bought and that the present one was to be hers until she died. She watched them go; she said nothing; it was not to begin then. It did not begin for five years, during which she watched her son making money faster and faster and easier and easier, gaining with apparent contemptible and contemptuous ease that substance for which in niggard amounts her husband had striven while still clinging with undeviating incorruptibility to honor and dignity and pride, and spending it, squandering it, in the same way. By that time she had given up the son and she had long since learned that she and her daughter-in-law were irrevocable and implacable moral enemies. It was in the fifth year. One day in her son's home she saw the two children take money from their mother's purse lying on a table. The mother did not even know how much she had in the purse; when the grandmother told her about it she became angry and dared the older woman to put it to the test. The grandmother accused the children, who denied the whole affair with perfectly straight faces. That was the actual break between herself and her son's family; after that she saw the two children only when the son would bring them with him occasionally on his unfailing daily visits. She had a few broken dollars which she had brought from Nebraska and had kept intact for five years, since she had no need for money here; one day she planted one of the coins while the children were there, and when she went back to look, it was gone too. The next morning she tried to talk to her son about the children, remembering her experience with the daughter-in-law and approaching the matter indirectly, speaking generally of money. "Yes," the son said. "I'm making money. I'm making it fast while I can. I'm going to make a lot of it. I'm going to give my children luxuries and advantages that my father never dreamed a child might have."

"That's it," she said. "You make money too easy. This whole country is too easy for us Ewings. It may be all right for them that have been born here for generations; I don't know about that. But not for us."

"But these children were born here."

"Just one generation. The generation before that they were born in a sodroofed dugout on the Nebraska wheat frontier. And

the one before that in a log house in Missouri. And the one before
that in a Kentucky blockhouse with Indians around it. This world
has never been easy for Ewings. Maybe the Lord never intended it
to be."

"But it is from now on," he said; he spoke with a kind of triumph. "For you and me too. But mostly for them."

And that was all. When he was gone she sat quietly in the single
Nebraska chair which she had taken out of storage—the first chair
which the older Ira Ewing had bought for her after he built a house
and in which she had rocked the younger Ira to sleep before he
could walk, while the older Ira himself sat in the chair which he had
made out of a flour barrel, grim, quiet and incorruptible, taking his
earned twilight ease between a day and a day—telling herself quietly that that was all. Her next move was curiously direct; there was
something in it of the actual pioneer's opportunism, of taking immediate and cold advantage of Spartan circumstance; it was as though
for the first time in her life she was able to use something, anything,
which she had gained by bartering her youth and strong maturity
against the Nebraska immensity, and this not in order to live further
but in order to die; apparently she saw neither paradox in it nor dis-
honesty. She began to make candy and cake of the materials which
her son bought for her on credit, and to sell them to the two grandchildren for the coins which their father gave them or which they
perhaps purloined also from their mother's purse, hiding the coins
in the vase with the timetable, watching the niggard hoard grow.
But after a few years the children outgrew candy and cake, and then
she had watched railroad fares go down and down and then stop
thirteen dollars away. But she did not give up, even then. Her son
had tried to give her a servant years ago and she had refused; she
believed that when the time came, the right moment, he would not
refuse to give her at least thirteen dollars of the money which she
had saved him. Then this had failed. "Maybe it wasn't the right
time," she thought. "Maybe I tried it too quick. I was surprised into
it," she told herself, looking down at the heap of small coins in her
lap. "Or maybe he was surprised into saying No. Maybe when he
has had time . . . " She roused; she put the coins back into the vase
and set it on the mantel again, looking at the clock as she did so. It
was just four, two hours yet until time to start supper. The sun was

high; she could see the water from the sprinkler flashing and glinting in it as she went to the window. It was still high, still afternoon;
the mountains stood serene and drab against it; the city, the land,
lay sprawled and myriad beneath it—the land, the earth which
spawned a thousand new faiths, nostrums and cures each year but
no disease to even disprove them on—beneath the golden days
unmarred by rain or weather, the changeless monotonous beautiful
days without end countless out of the halcyon past and endless into
the halcyon future.

"I will stay here and live forever," she said to herself.

M . F . K . Fisher

The rapid development of Los Angeles, which threatened to turn everything in its path into a suburb or an amusement park, swallowed up a good
many smaller communities that in retrospect look like lost paradises. By
the time M.F.K. Fisher (1908–1992) wrote the pieces collected here, the
places she describes—a sleepy beach, a mountain landscape—were
already remnants of an earlier time. Fisher, the most revered of American
food writers, grew up in Whittier, and began writing in the early 1930s.
"Pacific Village," her first published piece, appeared in *Westways*, the magazine of the Automobile Club of Southern California, in 1935; "A Thing
Shared" is from her 1943 collection, *The Gastronomical Me*.

PACIFIC VILLAGE

OLAS is a coast village, beautifully located. Artists and pseudo-
artists flock to it, and people in hurrying autos go more slowly
along the smooth State highway past its hills sloped up behind and
the coves and curving beaches along its edge. And Olas itself, the
village, is far from ugly—if you know where to look. It has many
most desirable qualities, social, political, commercial—if you know
how to choose.

And Olas is on the spot, for those who have long known it as a
quiet, lovely place and want it to remain so, and those who feel in its
present restless state a promise of prosperity and prominence as a
booming beach resort, are lined up grim and hateful on either side
of a wall of bitter prejudice.

Santa Catalina lies west from Olas on the sea-line, with San
Clemente its shadow southward. A hard, broad road, neat and
empty of character as a dairy lunchroom, strings the village. Out of
Olas to the north it hurries toward Los Angeles, and south, down
the coast, curves less straightly to San Diego and the dimming pleasures of Mexican border freedom. Inland, roads lead from Olas
through the endless tawny rollings of round hills, through orange
valleys to the mountains.

Near Olas, the coast line is erratically lovely. It is the kind that inspires nine out of ten visitors interviewed by the weekly news sheet to reminisce of the Riviera, Italian or French. They usually speak of the blue sky, the yellow sand, and the foam-sprayed cliffs of any correct postcard, comparing them more or less hazily with the sky, the sand, and the cliffs of Olas. And they are more or less right.

There are people, though, who feel that if a place is a place, with a personality strong and clear, comparisons are as unnecessary as they are annoying. There are people, many of them, who feel that Olas is such a place.

Some of them, artists, old settlers, young enthusiasts for life in the raw with no hate and no golf-clubs, want to keep it just as it is — or, even more desirable, as it used to be: quiet, so unknown that Saturday and Sunday were like Tuesday, beaches empty, rocks and cliffs free for uninterrupted sketching of any kind.

Olas' other lovers, just as sincerely, want to exploit to the bursting point its strong and attractive character. They want to develop it, to lure more people to it, so that all the houses may be full. Then more roads will be built into the silent hills, more houses sown on more lots, and more businesses will flourish on the bustling streets of what will soon change from village to town.

Olas itself is very sensitive to this inner struggle. There is restlessness in the air, and a kind of bewilderment. Change bubbles and fumes like yeast in a warm beer-crock. Overnight the face of the village changes.

Streets are being smoothed and straightened. Old eucalyptus trees are uprooted to make way for curbings. "Desecration!" the artists shriek. "Necessity," sooth the progressives, and plant more trees in much more orderly rows.

Hills are chopped and scarred into level roads, and the old guard moans in pain. "Ah, but we must take out dangerous curves," the developers explain, and as a palliative, "See how we are planting groups of ornamental shrubs, and neat rows of ice-plant on the banks."

In the meantime, the outlines of the village are intact. Hills behind and around, sea before, it lies small and pleasant in a little hollow, with houses clustered north and south along the coast. The streets are not quite straight. Fine trees shade some of them.

The buildings are small and for the most part extremely ugly, possessing the one architectural virtue of unadornment.

The upper end of the village proper, with the housing and amusement of impecunious weekenders its main excuse, is plainly hideous. It is Olas' more interesting half. A tent city, many umbrella and hot-dog concessions, a movie house, and a squat dance-hall make patterns vivid and noisy.

Strange here are the two municipal halls to Beauty and Science, the art gallery and a California college's marine laboratory. One, knowingly built like an electric power-plant, houses monthly collections of bilge and occasional greatness. The other, strangely suggestive of a ratty old Louisiana mansion, fills every summer with earnest biology majors and peculiar smells.

Toward the south, the other half of the village pulls discreetly away. Its tent city is a bulky hotel or two. Its hash-houses become restaurants whose food, if no better, is served with less clatter and more pomp. Its ships of abalone shell souvenirs and leather pillows stamped "X the Beach Beautiful" suddenly change to "antique" shops. They are equally cluttered, but here the prices are higher, the variety is infinite, and the wares range from raffia beach sandals to jade — real jade — opium pipes. There are Chinese, Mexican, Florentine and Persian stores. And there are a myriad "Gifte Shoppes." Most of them, like their humbler competitors at the other end of Olas, are promisingly crowded on weekends, and quite deserted in between.

The weekly visitors are, of course, divided like the village topography into two main camps. To the first goes the usual army of clerks from banks and stores, college professors, movie extras, and various types of professional weekenders. They are in Olas to get away from noise and business, or to make noise, or to do business. They live inexpensively in a part of the village that makes enough money from their two days' occupancy to send its proprietors to Palm Springs or Lake Arrowhead for the other five.

The other army that swarms into Olas on Fridays and Saturdays heads straight for the synthetic luxury of the hotels and restaurants to the south. It comes in bigger cars. It has fatter paunches and purses. It is made up of bank presidents and college trustees, movie magnates of the first and second rank in white turtleneck sweaters, fussy old ladies in conservative town-cars. And, as in the other army, there are many professional weekenders. And business flourishes.

For two days the beaches teem with people. Back roads have their full share of puffing bicyclists, and the dusty bridle-paths more than theirs of riders trying to make tired rented nags prance like polo ponies. The dance-hall sags and shudders and every hole-in-the-wall sends up a cheery reek of popcorn and hamburger. Drugstores outdo their own versatility. Motorcycle officers herd people handsomely across the car-lined streets.

Monday morning is like dawn on another planet. The hordes have fled. Six or seven cars are parked sheepishly in the quiet streets. A few people walk about. At eleven, after the morning mail is distributed at the post office, the villagers do their marketing. There is a mild stir. A few go to the sand in the afternoon. At five, mail again collects small gossiping crowds. At night, a quiet shuffling about sends various groups to rehearsals, the movie, the chamber of commerce, the bridge clubs. Olas is normal again, living that life so completely unsuspected by the people who come and go each weekend.

Socially this seven-days-a-week-Olas is very complex. Two main divisions separate it roughly into the artistic and the progressive elements, but that is a crude simplification. Each element has its interweaving intricacies, with all the bad and most of the good qualities of a small-town society long and firmly established.

Old settlers, in Olas since its cow-pathian days, take quite for granted their positions as social and political arbiters. They would be politely incredulous if by some shock they were made conscious of the affectionate mockery which surrounds them. They live smugly, simply. Reminiscence flows in mild flood from them, monotonously interesting.

They speak of the old road, the true Camino Real, that wound like snail-silver along the cliffs. Indians once camped by it, and gave fish to the ambling padres. There are gardens now whose gray soil prickles with the thin bones of their bass and corbina—gardens and gas stations.

Then there were the old ranches, five or six of them back in the hills. The cowboys would sweep down the canyons in the fall of the year, and gather on the beach at Olas for three-day drunks. They sang wildly. Their children still race seaward, still sing, but oftener.

Then the days of the old postoffice with its high steps easy for sitting—ah me!—and the little newspaper! Didn't that old Dutchman write it, set it up, print it, sell it all himself? And the artists! Real ones they were, not pretty boys who just love color! Well, those were the days, the good days.

And the old settlers shake their heads, lonesomely. All about them is bustle and confusion. They hear nothing but wind in the groves of tall trees long levelled to the earth.

Theatre groups breed plays like maggots. They inter-hate ferociously. Two and three shows open on one night, ethics and economics are swept aside, clandestine throat-cutting springs gleefully into the light. Whole casts are shanghaied. The result is amusing and valuable. Directors of unusual ability, in their burning hope and hate, drag powers of beautiful, almost great acting from local lifeguards and waitresses and unemployed professors. Butchers and service-station flunkeys design fine sets and do most artful lightings.

There are writers in Olas—too many to count. Some have made a steady sum for years from pulp magazines; a few have sold to publishers novels that people wouldn't buy, or have seen lone stories starred in minor anthologies. One or two have written best-sellers. But most of Olas' "authors" rank among the permanently unpublished. Their publics are small: wives, friends, awed offspring. They write for the chosen few, quite happy. They gossip glibly among themselves of agents and markets and pulps and slickies. And sometimes they discuss Letters.

Somewhere between this group and the theatre enthusiasts lies a strange band of stragglers from both: the Talkers. Where do they sleep, where eat? With an uncanny knowledge of when to appear, they crop up from nowhere at picnics and parties and informal meetings. At the first lull in sound, they pounce. And the evening is theirs. Art, politics, abalone fishing, sex, Tahiti, California wines: information fills the air, like a rushing of winds. The Talkers are pests. Oddly enough, they are for the most part charming pests.

And it is these muse-fed villagers and these old settlers who lead the artist faction in Olas. It is they who cry "Down with billboards! Away with publicity! Out with subdividers and go-getters!" And they are very bitter. "Olas has been ruined, prostituted," they howl. "Her trees are felled, her hills pitted—give us back our old Olas!" And they stay in Olas and bring their friends, who usually stay too.

And all, artists and old settlers and the indeterminate stragglers of many professions, are equally unaware of the amused tolerance with which they are treated by the other half of the village. Misunderstanding is mutual, perhaps, but where the artists dismiss with scornful ravings the dull bourgeois of Olas, the latter view with a kind of embarrassed enjoyment the incomprehensible antics of their enemies.

They live the ordered existence of good citizens of any small town on the earth. Their pleasures are cautiously licentious, their business dealings honestly corrupt. They support, with some prodding, a Red Cross and a municipal church.

Clubs thrive in their circles. There are several different varieties of women's organizations: junior, senior, garden, parent-teacher, sewing. The men have rival luncheon clubs with all the usual backslappings and buttons and good ostentatious charities. The children of the club-goers go to clubs: puppy clubs, doll clubs. And bridge clubs knit the whole faction into a nightly knot of systems and four-sided animosities.

Frequent elections exercise all the political muscles of the various groups, and real estate salesmen, garagists, and chain-store managers stalk past each other on the street with an axes-at-twenty-paces-look which changes at the next primaries and then shifts again.

And all these people, these reactionary progressives, these bank employees and owners of drug stores and gifte-shoppes and eating places—why do they want Olas to thrive and grow fat? It is very natural. They want to grow fat with her, to thrive that their children may thrive.

Real estate dealers need water in distant subdivisions. They cut holes in the hills for pipes. Then they sell lots and make money and build more houses to rent to more people. And those people buy food and bathing caps and Chinese lanterns. And billboards bring people, and so does publicity in the city papers and on the air.

To the progressives it is a natural, a logical thing to want Olas to be bigger and noisier and more popular. They are patient enough with the grumbling, sneering artists, and, most ironically, use them as part of their publicity program. "Olas, Famous Artists' Colony," the billboards blurb, and "Visit Olas, Artist Haunt." At the New Year's Parade in a near neighbor, a great palette of roses represents the village, with hired Hollywood beauties dressed in transparent smocks and berets to represent Art. And at the annual fiesta, the esthetic high-note is reached when all the storekeepers and mechanics and beer-drawers don orange-and-green tam-o-shanters and flowing ties. They too represent Art.

So the two sides live together in the little village. One could not well exist without the other. Each fights with the tactics of righteous sincerity: each fights dirty.

And while shouts and sneers and low groans gather like warring birds in the air, Olas lies still in the creases of the ocean-slipping hills, one bead strung with many like it on the long coast road. It is rather uncomfortable. It aches at times. Rheumatism or growing pains?

P.S. Meanwhile—meanwhile the real artists, those men and women whose pictures of Olas will perhaps still be looked at in a hundred years, continue to paint. They are few—as always. They are unconscious of any village strife. All the high talk of Art, all the politics and scandal, all the hullabaloo of growth and change, is to them as unimportant and as natural as a sea-gull's dropping on a clean canvas. They paint as they did those years gone, trees and rocks and an old mission in a garden. And three hundred years from now—

A THING SHARED

Now you can drive from Los Angeles to my Great-Aunt Maggie's ranch on the other side of the mountains in a couple of hours or so, but the first time I went there it took most of a day.

Now the roads are worthy of even the All-Year-Round Club's boasts, but twenty-five years ago, in the September before people thought peace had come again, you could hardly call them roads at all. Down near the city they were oiled, all right, but as you went farther into the hills toward the wild desert around Palmdale, they turned into rough dirt. Finally they were two wheel-marks skittering every which way through the Joshua trees.

It was very exciting: the first time my little round brown sister Anne and I had ever been away from home. Father drove us up from home with Mother in the Ford, so that she could help some cousins can fruit.

We carried beer for the parents (it exploded in the heat), and water for the car and Anne and me. We had four blowouts, but that was lucky, Father said as he patched the tires philosophically in the hot sun; he'd expected twice as many on such a long hard trip.

The ranch was wonderful, with wartime crews of old men and loud-voiced boys picking the peaches and early pears all day, and singing and rowing at night in the bunkhouses. We couldn't go near them or near the pen in the middle of a green alfalfa field where a new prize bull, black as thunder, pawed at the pale sand.

We spent most of our time in a stream under the cottonwoods, or with Old Mary the cook, watching her make butter in a great churn between her mountainous knees. She slapped it into pats, and put them down in the stream where it ran hurriedly through the darkness of the butter-house.

She put stone jars of cream there, too, and wire baskets of eggs and lettuces, and when she drew them up, like netted fish, she would shake the cold water onto us and laugh almost as much as we did.

Then Father had to go back to work. It was decided that Mother would stay at the ranch and help put up more fruit, and Anne and I would go home with him. That was as exciting as leaving it had been, to be alone with Father for the first time.

He says now that he was scared daft at the thought of it, even though our grandmother was at home as always to watch over us. He says he actually shook as he drove away from the ranch, with us like two suddenly strange small monsters on the hot seat beside him.

Probably he made small talk. I don't remember. And he didn't drink any beer, sensing that it would be improper before two unchaperoned young ladies.

We were out of the desert and into deep winding canyons before the sun went down. The road was a little smoother, following streambeds under the live oaks that grow in all the gentle creases of the dry tawny hills of that part of California. We came to a shack where there was water for sale, and a table under the dark wide trees.

Father told me to take Anne down the dry streambed a little way. That made me feel delightfully grown-up. When we came back we held our hands under the water faucet and dried them on our panties, which Mother would never have let us do.

Then we sat on a rough bench at the table, the three of us in the deep green twilight, and had one of the nicest suppers I have ever eaten.

The strange thing about it is that all three of us have told other people that same thing, without ever talking of it among ourselves until lately. Father says that all his nervousness went away, and he saw us for the first time as two little brown humans who were fun. Anne and I both felt a subtle excitement at being alone for the first time with the only man in the world we loved.

(We loved Mother too, completely, but we were finding out, as Father was too, that it is good for parents and for children to be alone now and then with one another . . . the man alone or the woman, to sound new notes in the mysterious music of parenthood and childhood.)

That night I not only saw my Father for the first time as a person. I saw the golden hills and the live oaks as clearly as I have ever seen them since; and I saw the dimples in my little sister's fat hands in a way that still moves me because of that first time; and I saw food as something beautiful to be shared with people instead of as a thrice-daily necessity.

I forget what we ate, except for the end of the meal. It was a big round peach pie, still warm from Old Mary's oven and the ride over the desert. It was deep, with lots of juice, and bursting with ripe peaches picked that noon. Royal Albertas, Father said they were. The crust was the most perfect I have ever tasted, except perhaps once upstairs at Simpson's in London, on a hot plum tart.

And there was a quart Mason jar, the old-fashioned bluish kind like Mexican glass, full of cream. It was still cold, probably because we all knew the stream it had lain in, Old Mary's stream.

Father cut the pie in three pieces and put them on white soup plates in front of us, and then spooned out the thick cream. We ate with spoons too, blissful after the forks we were learning to use with Mother.

And we ate the whole pie, and all the cream . . . we can't remember if we gave any to the shadowy old man who sold water . . . and then drove on sleepily toward Los Angeles, and none of us said anything about it for many years, but it was one of the best meals we ever ate.

Perhaps that is because it was the first conscious one, for me at least; but the fact that we remember it with such queer clarity must mean that it had other reasons for being important. I suppose that happens at least once to every human. I hope so.

Now the hills are cut through with superhighways, and I can't say whether we sat that night in Mint Canyon or Bouquet, and the three of us are in some ways even more than twenty-five years older than we were then. And still the warm round peach pie and the cool yellow cream we ate together that August night live in our hearts' palates, succulent, secret, delicious.

Cedric Belfrage

On the night of March 12, 1928, in San Francisquito Canyon near Saugus, north of Los Angeles, the newly operational St. Francis Dam collapsed, sending a tidal wave of water pouring through the Santa Clara River Valley. By the time the torrent drained into the Pacific Ocean near Ventura, more than 400 people were dead and 1200 homes destroyed. The disaster is still considered by some the greatest American civil engineering failure of the 20th century, and it forever damaged the reputation of the dam's designer, William Mulholland, chief engineer of the Los Angeles Bureau of Water Works. In this excerpt from *Promised Land* (1938), a novel that incorporates a considerable swath of Los Angeles history, Cedric Belfrage (1904–1990) recounts the disaster and traces its connection to the Owens Valley water wars, in which Mulholland was also a key player. Belfrage, a prolific British-born writer and left-wing political journalist long resident in Los Angeles until he was deported in 1955, was editor of *The National Guardian*.

from

PROMISED LAND

1924

Ever since the four-day picnic, Old Si had had a thought growing in his head: To follow the aqueduct and find the Owens River gold that had been taken from him, that had been the centre and bloodstream of his life. You could steal a river but you couldn't kill it or hide it: no, sir, not the Owens River.

Where once the river had tumbled and gurgled past Old Si's ranch, there hadn't for a long time been anything but a dry watercourse between the twin rows of willows and reeds through which the breeze blew mockingly. The watercourse wound on down the valley to the lake, which was mostly dry salt-caked flats now. The *Betsy Baker*, which used to whistle as it puffed across the lake, had long since been beached by the receding waters, had lain for a while drunkenly on her side and had been broken up. Old Si had gradually sold off his cattle as the great greenness, which he and his father and David had made out of the desert, returned to desert again.

The only time the river ever put in an appearance outside Old Si's door now was when, in the flood-time, more water came down than the Los Angeles aqueduct could hold. Then it came swooshing down the old stream just to remind Old Si of the way it used to be. He would go and wander by the hour up and down the bank, oblivious of the hundreds of mosquitoes buzzing around, letting the sound of the water seep into him as though his brain were the throat of a thirsty man.

At the point between Big Pine and Independence where Los Angeles had diverted the river, the road ran along the far western side of the valley, and the river ran on the other side. The aqueduct intake could be reached down a little side road crossing the valley. Most of the Owens Valley people had been there. The Los Angeles men were scared of their grim faces when they approached. All night a guard sat in a tower beside the intake, with a great blinding searchlight from a Hollywood movie studio, so powerful that it picked out cars on the road two miles away. Old Si had not been there, but he knew just what had been done with his river. It flowed for a while down the open canal only a few yards from the old river-bed. Then it was led across the valley into a great concrete ditch hugging the lower western slopes. At one point the ditch, swinging eastward with an escarpment of the mountain, almost hung over the road. There was a spillway here for emergency control of excessive water. Finally the water started on its way to San Fernando Valley through the great pipe which could be seen winding away over the mountains.

It was at the spillway that the picnic took place. It was a fine picnic while it lasted, which was four days. Not all the population of Owens Valley turned out for it. There were those who, already set on retiring or leaving the district, had voluntarily sold out and were grateful for the chance that brought them higher prices for their land than they could normally have expected. The Los Angeles aqueduct had been operating over ten years. The city was in the market for all the land in the valley, and was offering good prices as values went in such a place. But many ranchers would not sell, either for plain sentimental reasons, or not knowing where else they could go to farm under familiar conditions, or because they resented the trickery and intimidation used against them. Above or below the aqueduct intake, all were in the same beached boat. The city wanted not some of the water, but all. It wasn't satisfied with the river, but dug wells, all over the valley to get the sub-surface water too. Its armed men had torn out the dams in tributaries of the river which diverted water into irrigation canals. They had dynamited holes in their own aqueduct wall. The holes were easily repaired; the credit of the valley ranchers, not so easily. The ranchers were drawn together by a deep, spontaneous craving for justice. They saw the fruits of their toil being stolen from them. It all culminated in a picnic. The people of the valley picnicked around the spillway for four days.

But first, because it is pleasant to picnic to the sound of a waterfall, they opened the spillway. Children played games by the rushing torrent and the grown people chatted in little excited groups. Old Si went every day and sat on the ground looking at the waterfall, laughing till the tears ran down his creased old cheeks. He thought of all the miles and miles of huge piping and canal and tunnel which it had taken all those thousands of men years to build across the mountains and the desert—all dry now, because the people of Owens Valley wanted the water to make pleasant music for their picnic.

The Sheriff came to take the picnickers' names, which were given proudly. Now and again Los Angeles officials would come up in groups, address the picnickers and ask them to go home. The picnickers laughed. The young men laughed quietly, standing with their feet firm on the ground around the spillway, their arms crossed on their chests. The little children laughed shrilly and bolder ones suggested that the officials should find themselves a block and run around it. But the one who laughed loudest and longest was Old Si.

But of course the picnic couldn't last for ever. On the fourth day the city had sent emissaries to say that, if everyone would return home peacefully, there would be a full investigation of their grievances.

There had already been investigations by the city. They were fine except that Owens Valley residents had been excluded from giving evidence. Sworn testimony had been taken that three times as much Owens River water had been supplied to San Fernando Valley ranches as to the City of Los Angeles. It had been asserted and not denied that Mulholland himself, who built the aqueduct, owned some of the San Fernando Valley land which the aqueduct has boosted nine figures in value. It was for this that the taxpayers of Los Angeles had spent $25,000,000.

But despite all this, some of the picnickers clung to the hope that truth and the City Fathers of Los Angeles might not be for ever strangers. The picnic came to an end. The people went home to their desiccated, decrepit ranches. Once again the river proceeded on its long westward journey. While hopes for the investigation faded, dynamitings of the aqueduct increased. Armies of detectives and strong-arm men came into the valley. Cars were stopped on the roads. Fights were frequent and a kind of martial law existed. The people of Los Angeles read in their newspapers that the grasping, illiterate, un-American people of Owens Valley had gone berserk but that the forces of progress and civilization had the situation under control.

It was pure sentiment on Si's part that he hadn't sold out years before. River or no river, his ranching days were over. He had a few thousand dollars to show for them. He was an old man, nearly into his eighties, although an unusually active one. The cross at Lone Pine commemorating his wife, whose fertility was the fertility of the valley soil with the river on it, was covered deep in moss. David and another son and a daughter were dead. The other son and three daughters were living in Canada and in the eastern states, all of them in cities. There had been suggestions that Old Si should sell out and go east to end his days. But the idea of leaving California was to him unthinkable. The loneliness of life in the decaying ranch-house, with only a couple of Indians for company, was not so great as would be the loneliness of life in some city of the east.

But soon after the four-day picnic, Old Si had a surprise visit from his grandson, Don. He hadn't seen Don since the boy left the valley in 1907 with David. He took a fancy to him.

It seemed to Don that living thus alone with his memories, seeing his life work slowly undone by the man-made drought, had already begun to soften Old Si's brain. He'd always been eccentric about the river, talked of it as "gold". Now he talked as if it were a living creature: almost as if it were a beautiful young wife who had been snatched from him. He was too old to possess the wife any more now. But she was his, he had the right to her society and companionship. So Don, whose efforts to make Old Si quit the valley and come to live in Los Angeles had till then been fruitless, tried a new tack.

"If you came to live near Uncle Ed's place in Hollywood," he said to Old Si, jokingly, "you'd have your river right beside you." The river was like a stolen wife to Old Si, Don reflected. So surely he'd rather be near the wife herself, captive though she was, than live with the bed she used to lie in.

"How's that?" asked Old Si.

"Well, the latest dam built by this bird Mulholland to store the Owens River water after it comes from the San Fernando reservoirs is half a mile from Uncle Ed's, in Weid Canyon right above the middle of Hollywood. From what people say, the dam wasn't necessary, any more than it was necessary to take the whole Owens River from where God put it. They've already laid out more dams than two Owens Rivers could fill. But they just like to build dams, and the majority of the taxpayers are too busy to bother about it. They say that one fellow, who paid $2,000 to get expert opinions on the necessity for the Hollywood dam, took it to Mulholland and all he got in reply was, 'I've decided to build a dam there'. Then this fellow asked him if he could to build a dam that could withstand any earthquake. Mulholland went up like an exploding balloon and said he could. Not that there's any chance of an earthquake in Hollywood. Tell you what I think: Mulholland built that dam specially so you could come and live in Hollywood and have your relations and your river to keep you company."

Old Si was amused by the way Don talked; he liked the independent way the boy's mind seemed to work. He didn't think much of the idea of living in Los Angeles. He'd probably go crazy in a week of city life. But here was a fine chance to make a reality of his whim: to follow his river along the aqueduct, and see for himself how it was doing. He knew that, though his river was in bondage, it was still working far across the mountains, fertilizing desert soil and making the earth bring forth its bounty.

So when Don headed out of the Owens Valley for Los Angeles, Old Si rode with him.

Old Si had never visited the city before. He had heard about it, and nothing he had heard made him want to go. His instinct had always been to be suspicious of anything coming from a city. What had happened in the valley had sharpened the edge of that scepticism and added fear, the kind of fear a man has for a rattlesnake. Don saw at once that the idea of Si living in the city was absurd. It seemed as if the old man couldn't breathe properly until, on the second day, Don drove him out to San Fernando Valley.

In the city the old fellow clung in a pathetic way to the handle of the car door. But the moment they got out into the open country again his whole body relaxed. They drove first to the reservoirs where the Owens River aqueduct ended. The water lay there placidly in great grey-blue sheets on which a fierce sun beat down.

It was a lonely spot where Old Si's raped wife, his old friend, his gold, was imprisoned. For a long time they sat in the stationary car and Old Si looked at the water lying there.

The sun was beginning to relax westward when Don started the car again and drove in the direction of San Francisquito Canyon. They left the main highway beyond Saugus and drove in a swirl of dust across the desert. Skirting a range of hills and diving through a little pass they came to the bare, splendid majesty of the canyon.

"This is where they're building the next dam," Don said. "Up at the top of this canyon."

A few adobe houses could be seen dotted about. In the distance, on the floor of the canyon, a herd of cows and some horses grazed. It was very quiet. A warm evening breeze stirred the chaparral. The mountains framing the scene faded into empurpled haze where the sun was setting.

Don was conscious of Si's stillness. Glancing sideways he caught something in the old man's eyes which he vaguely remembered from many years ago. Si was gazing at a little creek of water which ran down the middle of the canyon floor. They drove on up the twisting gradient for a couple of miles and rounded an escarpment. Ahead, overalled men moved among a great litter of machinery and dusty lorries and cement bags. The men were knocking off work for the day and strolling in twos and threes toward the huts which were scattered about — evidently their quarters during the dam building. Don brought the car to a halt where they could see the beginning of the dam's foundations.

"That's where they're going to keep your gold," he laughed.

Si had a good look and blew down his nose. One of the workmen came by the car and Don engaged him in conversation. "She'll
have 200 feet of water behind there," the workman told them.
"Make a lake four miles back from here. There'll be a powerhouse
on top of her."

"See," Don said, "how generous the Los Angeles taxpayer is. He
spent twenty-five millions for the aqueduct, and now a few more
millions for the dam, and then he hands it over to a private power
company to make blue-sky profits selling him the electricity."

They drove back down to where the houses were. There was a
community of Navajo Indians there, fine husky fellows with some
soft-eyed squaws and a few sparrow-like papooses hopping about.
Old Si got out and chatted with some of the Indians. They said
there were several hundred people altogether living in the canyon,
whites and Mexicans and Indians. The Indians had only recently
arrived. They had been brought by Harry Carey, the movie actor
and rancher, who had a big place himself in the canyon and was
trying to reconstruct a western trading-post as of the old days.

Old Si didn't want to leave. He got on well with the Indians and
felt more at home than he'd done in years. One of them said that this
was the first place where gold had been discovered in California,
away back in the 'thirties.

It wasn't at all the same, it was artificial in a way, and yet this
settlement in the canyon reminded Si of Owens Valley as it had
been during his early years. That was funny, considering that it was
just there, 250 miles away from Owens Valley, that it had been
decided to imprison Si's stolen river.

They lingered till long after dark. It was past midnight when
they got back to Los Angeles. Old Si did not seem to be tired at all
by the long day's outing. Don said good night to him and the old
man's eyes were gleaming like stars.

Old Si returned next day to Owens Valley. The day after that he
notified the Los Angeles land-purchasing agent that he was ready to
sell his property.

When he left Owens Valley for the last time, his two Indians
came with him. They headed for Los Angeles but they did not come
as far as the city. Before Saugus they turned off the highway to San
Francisquito Canyon. And there Old Si and his two Indians built a
small adobe house.

The creek ran down past Old Si's new place. It was only a trickle compared with what his lost river had been. Si liked to wander up and down listening to it tinkle as it ran down. But better he liked to get himself a ride on one of the lorries up to where the dam was slowly rearing its great pyramided wall. He lounged about up there, joking with the workmen or just looking at the dam. He looked at it and laughed, chewing on his pipe. That was where his river would soon be imprisoned. It would have come a long way, but so would he, and there they would be together again, he and his river.

Raymond Chandler

The emergence of a distinctly Los Angeles literary tone was the unlikely achievement of Raymond Chandler (1888–1959), a writer who was born in Chicago and raised in England, and who never lost his ambivalence either about Los Angeles or about the pulp crime genre that he refined into unmistakable art in a score of short stories and seven novels. Chandler first arrived in Southern California in 1912, and eventually established himself as an executive in the oil business, his business career rising and falling with the boom-and-bust of the 1920s. After being fired for alcoholism, he reinvented himself at the age of 45 as a contributor to *Black Mask* and *Dime Detective*, where his novella "Red Wind" first appeared in 1938. It captures the quintessential mix of heart, toughness, and aphoristic brilliance that marks Chandler's treatment of Los Angeles, which he described as "a big hard-boiled city with no more personality than a paper cup," and later, as if to modify the earlier statement, as "no worse than others, a city rich and vigorous and full of pride, a city lost and beaten and full of emptiness."

RED WIND

There was a desert wind blowing that night. It was one of those hot dry Santa Anas that come down through the mountain passes and curl your hair and make your nerves jump and your skin itch. On nights like that every booze party ends in a fight. Meek little wives feel the edge of the carving knife and study their husbands' necks. Anything can happen. You can even get a full glass of beer at a cocktail lounge.

I was getting one in a flossy new place across the street from the apartment house where I lived. It had been open about a week and it wasn't doing any business. The kid behind the bar was in his early twenties and looked as if he had never had a drink in his life.

There was only one other customer, a souse on a bar stool with his back to the door. He had a pile of dimes stacked neatly in front of him, about two dollars' worth. He was drinking straight rye in small glasses and he was all by himself in a world of his own.

I sat farther along the bar and got my glass of beer and said: "You sure cut the clouds off them, buddy. I will say that for you."

"We just opened up," the kid said. "We got to build up trade. Been in before, haven't you, mister?"

"Uh-huh."

"Live around here?"

"In the Berglund Apartments across the street," I said. "And the name is John Dalmas."

"Thanks, mister. Mine's Lew Petrolle." He leaned close to me across the polished dark bar. "Know that guy?"

"No."

"He ought to go home, kind of. I ought to call a taxi and send him home. He's doing his next week's drinking too soon."

"A night like this," I said. "Let him alone."

"It's not good for him," the kid said, scowling at me.

"Rye!" the drunk croaked, without looking up. He snapped his fingers so as not to disturb his piles of dimes by banging on the bar.

The kid looked at me and shrugged. "Should I?"

"Whose stomach is it? Not mine."

The kid poured him another straight rye and I think he doctored it with water down behind the bar because when he came up with it he looked as guilty as if he'd kicked his grandmother. The drunk paid no attention. He lifted two dimes off his pile with the exact care of a crack surgeon operating on a brain tumor.

The kid came back and put more beer in my glass. Outside the wind howled. Every once in a while it blew the stained-glass swing-door open a few inches. It was a heavy door.

The kid said: "I don't like drunks in the first place and in the second place I don't like them getting drunk in here, and in the third place I don't like them in the first place."

"Warner Brothers could use that," I said.

"They did."

Just then we had another customer. A car squeaked to a stop outside and the swinging door came open. A fellow came in who looked a little in a hurry. He held the door and ranged the place quickly with flat, shiny, dark eyes. He was well set up, dark, good-looking in a narrow-faced, tight-lipped way. His clothes were dark and a white handkerchief peeped coyly from his pocket and he looked cool as well as under a tension of some sort. I guessed it was the hot wind. I felt a bit the same myself only not cool.

He looked at the drunk's back. The drunk was playing checkers with his empty glasses. The new customer looked at me, then he looked along the line of half-booths at the other side of the place. They were all empty. He came on in—down past where the drunk sat swaying and muttering to himself—and spoke to the bar kid.

"Seen a lady in here, buddy? Tall, pretty, brown hair, in a print bolero jacket over a blue crepe silk dress. Wearing a wide-brimmed straw hat with a velvet band." He had a tight voice I didn't like.

"No, sir. Nobody like that's been in," the bar kid said.

"Thanks. Straight Scotch. Make it fast, will you?"

The kid gave it to him and the fellow paid and put the drink down in a gulp and started to go out. He took three or four steps and stopped, facing the drunk. The drunk was grinning. He swept a gun from somewhere so fast that it was just a blur coming out. He held it steady and he didn't look any drunker than I was. The tall dark guy stood quite still and then his head jerked back a little and then he was still again.

A car tore by outside. The drunk's gun was a .22 target automatic, with a large front sight. It made a couple of hard snaps and a little smoke curled—very little.

"So long, Waldo," the drunk said.

Then he put the gun on the barman and me.

The dark guy took a week to fall down. He stumbled, caught himself, waved one arm, stumbled again. His hat fell off, and then he hit the floor with his face. After he hit it he might have been poured concrete for all the fuss he made.

The drunk slid down off the stool and scooped his dimes into a pocket and slid towards the door. He turned sideways, holding the gun across his body. I didn't have a gun. I hadn't thought I needed one to buy a glass of beer. The kid behind the bar didn't move or make the slightest sound.

The drunk felt the door lightly with his shoulder, keeping his eyes on us, then pushed through it backwards. When it was wide a hard gust of air slammed in and lifted the hair of the man on the floor. The drunk said: "Poor Waldo. I bet I made his nose bleed."

The door swung shut. I started to rush it—from long practice in doing the wrong thing. In this case it didn't matter. The car outside let out a roar and when I got onto the sidewalk it was flicking a red smear of tail-light around the nearby corner. I got its license number the way I got my first million.

There were people and cars up and down the block as usual. Nobody acted as if a gun had gone off. The wind was making enough noise to make the hard quick rap of .22 ammunition sound like a slammed door, even if anyone heard it. I went back into the cocktail bar.

The kid hadn't moved, even yet. He just stood with his hands flat on the bar, leaning over a little and looking down at the dark guy's back. The dark guy hadn't moved either. I bent down and felt his neck artery. He wouldn't move—ever.

The kid's face had as much expression as a cut of round steak and was about the same color. His eyes were more angry than shocked.

I lit a cigarette and blew smoke at the ceiling and said shortly: "Get on the phone."

"Maybe he's not dead," the kid said.

"When they use a .22 that means they don't make mistakes. Where's the phone?"

"I don't have one. I got enough expenses without that. Boy, can I kick eight hundred bucks in the face!"

"You own this place?"

"I did till this happened."

He pulled his white coat off and his apron and came around the inner end of the bar. "I'm locking the door," he said, taking keys out.

He went out, swung the door to and jiggled the lock from the outside until the bolt clicked into place. I bent down and rolled Waldo over. At first I couldn't even see where the shots went in. Then I could. A couple of tiny holes in his coat, over his heart. There was a little blood on his shirt.

The drunk was everything you could ask—as a killer.

The prowl-car boys came in about eight minutes. The kid, Lew Petrolle, was back behind the bar by then. He had his white coat on again and he was counting the money in the register and putting it in his pocket and making notes in a little book.

I sat at the edge of one of the half-booths and smoked cigarettes and watched Waldo's face get deader and deader. I wondered who the girl in the print coat was, why Waldo had left the engine of his car running outside, why he was in a hurry, whether the drunk had been waiting for him or just happened to be there.

The prowl-car boys came in perspiring. They were the usual large size and one of them had a flower stuck under his cap and his cap on a bit crooked. When he saw the dead man he got rid of the flower and leaned down to feel Waldo's pulse.

"Seems to be dead," he said, and rolled him around a little more. "Oh yeah, I see where they went in. Nice clean work. You two see him get it?"

I said yes. The kid behind the bar said nothing. I told them about it, that the killer seemed to have left in Waldo's car.

The cop yanked Waldo's wallet out, went through it rapidly and whistled. "Plenty jack and no driver's license." He put the wallet away. "O.K., we didn't touch him, see? Just a chance we could find did he have a car and put it on the air."

"The hell you didn't touch him," Lew Petrolle said.

The cop gave him one of these looks. "O.K., pal," he said softly. "We touched him."

The kid picked up a clean highball glass and began to polish it. He polished it all the rest of the time we were there.

In another minute a homicide fast-wagon sirened up and screeched to a stop outside the door and four men came in, two dicks, a photographer and a laboratory man. I didn't know either of the dicks. You can be in the detecting business a long time and not know all the men on a big city force.

One of them was a short, smooth, dark, quiet, smiling man, with curly black hair and soft intelligent eyes. The other was big, raw-boned, long-jawed, with a veined nose and glassy eyes. He looked like a heavy drinker. He looked tough, but he looked as if he thought he was a little tougher than he was. He shooed me into the last booth against the wall and his partner got the kid up front and the bluecoats went out. The fingerprint man and photographer set about their work.

A medical examiner came, stayed just long enough to get sore because there was no phone for him to call the morgue wagon.

The short dick emptied Waldo's pockets and then emptied his wallet and dumped everything into a large handkerchief on a booth table. I saw a lot of currency, keys, cigarettes, another handkerchief, very little else.

The big dick pushed me back into the end of the half-booth. "Give," he said. "I'm Copernik, Detective-Lieutenant."

I put my wallet in front of him. He looked at it, went through it, tossed it back, made a note in a book.

"John Dalmas, huh? A shamus. You here on business?"

"Drinking business," I said. "I live just across the street in the Berglund."

"Know this kid up front?"

"I've been in here once since he opened up."

"See anything funny about him now?"

"No."

"Takes it too light for a young fellow, don't he? Never mind answering. Just tell the story."

I told it—three times. Once for him to get the outline, once for him to get the details and once for him to see if I had it too pat. At the end he said: "This dame interests me. And the killer called the guy Waldo, yet didn't seem to be anyways sure he would be in. I mean, if Waldo wasn't sure the dame would be here, nobody could be sure Waldo would be here."

"That's pretty deep," I said.

He studied me. I wasn't smiling. "Sounds like a grudge job, don't it? Don't sound planned. No getaway except by accident. A guy don't leave his car unlocked much in this town. And the killer works in front of two good witnesses. I don't like that."

"I don't like being a witness," I said. "The pay's too low."

He grinned. His teeth had a freckled look. "Was the killer drunk really?"

"With that shooting? No."

"Me too. Well, it's a simple job. The guy will have a record and he's left plenty prints. Even if we don't have his mug here we'll make him in hours. He had something on Waldo, but he wasn't meeting Waldo tonight. Waldo just dropped in to ask about a dame he had a date with and had missed connections on. It's a hot night and this wind would kill a girl's face. She'd be apt to drop in somewhere to wait. So the killer feeds Waldo two in the right place and scrams and don't worry about you boys at all. It's that simple."

"Yeah," I said.

"It's so simple it stinks," Copernik said.

He took his felt hat off and tousled up his ratty blond hair and leaned his head on his hands. He had a long mean horse face. He got a handkerchief out and mopped it, and the back of his neck and the back of his hands. He got a comb out and combed his hair—he looked worse with it combed—and put his hat back on.

"I was just thinking," I said.

"Yeah? What?"

"This Waldo knew just how the girl was dressed. So he must already have been with her tonight."

"So what? Maybe he had to go to the can. And when he came back she's gone. Maybe she changed her mind about him."

"That's right," I said.

But that wasn't what I was thinking at all. I was thinking that Waldo had described the girl's clothes in a way the ordinary man wouldn't know how to describe them. Printed bolero jacket over blue crepe silk dress. I didn't even know what a bolero jacket was. And I might have said blue dress or even blue silk dress, but never blue crepe silk dress.

After a while two men came with a basket. Lew Petrolle was still polishing his glass and talking to the short dark dick.

We all went down to headquarters.

Lew Petrolle was all right when they checked on him. His father had a grape ranch near Antioch in Contra Costa County. He had given Lew a thousand dollars to go into business and Lew had opened the cocktail bar, neon sign and all, on eight hundred flat.

They let him go and told him to keep the bar closed until they were sure they didn't want to do any more printing. He shook hands all around and grinned and said he guessed the killing would be good for business after all, because nobody believed a newspaper account of anything and people would come to him for the story and buy drinks while he was telling it.

"There's a guy won't ever do any worrying," Copernik said, when he was gone. "Over anybody else."

"Poor Waldo," I said. "The prints any good?"

"Kind of smudged," Copernik said sourly. "But we'll get a classi-fication and teletype it to Washington some time tonight. If it don't click, you'll be in for a day on the steel picture-racks downstairs."

I shook hands with him and his partner, whose name was Ybarra, and left. They didn't know who Waldo was yet either. Nothing in his pockets told.

2

I got back to my street about 9 P.M. I looked up and down the block before I went into the Berglund. The cocktail bar was farther down on the other side, dark, with a nose or two against the glass, but no real crowd. People had seen the law and the morgue wagon, but they didn't know what had happened. Except the boys playing pinball games in the drugstore on the corner. They know every-thing, except how to hold a job.

The wind was still blowing, oven-hot, swirling dust and torn paper up against the walls.

I went into the lobby of the apartment house and rode the auto-matic elevator up to the fourth floor. I unwound the doors and stepped out and there was a tall girl standing there waiting for the car.

She had brown wavy hair under a wide-brimmed straw hat with a velvet band and loose bow. She had wide blue eyes and eyelashes that didn't quite reach her chin. She wore a blue dress that might have been crepe silk, simple in lines but not missing any curves. Over it she wore what might have been a print bolero jacket.

I said: "Is that a bolero jacket?"

She gave me a distant glance and made a motion as if to brush a cobweb out of the way.

"Yes. Would you mind—I'm rather in a hurry. I'd like——"

I didn't move. I blocked her off from the elevator. We stared at each other and she flushed very slowly.

"Better not go out on the street in those clothes," I said.

"Why, how dare you——"

The elevator clanked and started down again. I didn't know what she was going to say. Her voice lacked the edgy twang of a beer-parlor frill. It had a soft light sound, like spring rain.

"It's not a make," I said. "You're in trouble. If they come to this floor in the elevator, you have just that much time to get off the hall. First take off the hat and jacket—and snap it up!"

She didn't move. Her face seemed to whiten a little behind the not-too-heavy make-up.

"Cops," I said, "are looking for you. In those clothes. Give me the chance and I'll tell you why."

She turned her head swiftly and looked back along the corridor. With her looks I didn't blame her for trying one more bluff.

"You're impertinent, whoever you are. I'm Mrs. Leroy in Apartment Thirty-one. I can assure you——"

"That you're on the wrong floor," I said. "This is the fourth." The elevator had stopped down below. The sound of doors being wrenched open came up the shaft.

"Off!" I rapped. "Now!"

She switched her hat off and slipped out of the bolero jacket, fast. I grabbed them and wadded them into a mess under my arm. I took her elbow and turned her and we were going down the hall.

"I live in Forty-two. The front one across from yours, just a floor up. Take your choice. Once again—I'm not on the make."

She smoothed her hair with that quick gesture, like a bird preening itself. Ten thousand years of practice behind it.

"Mine," she said, and tucked her bag under her arm and strode down the hall fast. The elevator stopped at the floor below. She stopped when it stopped. She turned and faced me.

"The stairs are back by the elevator shaft," I said gently.

"I don't have an apartment," she said.

"I didn't think you had."

"Are they searching for me?"

"Yes, but they won't start gouging the block stone by stone before tomorrow. And then only if they don't make Waldo."

She stared at me. "Waldo?"

"Oh, you don't know Waldo," I said.

She shook her head slowly. The elevator started down in the shaft again. Panic flicked in her blue eyes like a ripple on water.

"No," she said breathlessly, "but take me out of this hall."

We were almost at my door. I jammed the key in and shook the lock around and heaved the door inward. I reached in far enough to switch lights on. She went in past me like a wave. Sandalwood floated on the air, very faint.

I shut the door, threw my hat into a chair and watched her stroll over to a card table on which I had a chess problem set out that I couldn't solve. Once inside, with the door locked, her panic had left her.

"So you're a chess-player," she said, in that guarded tone, as if she had come to look at my etchings. I wished she had.

We both stood still then and listened to the distant clang of elevator doors and then steps—going the other way.

I grinned, but with strain, not pleasure, went out into the kitchenette and started to fumble with a couple of glasses and then realized I still had her hat and bolero jacket under my arm. I went into the dressing-room behind the wall bed and stuffed them into a drawer, went back out to the kitchenette, dug out some extra fine Scotch and made a couple of high-balls.

When I went in with the drinks she had a gun in her hand. It was a small automatic with a pearl grip. It jumped up at me and her eyes were full of horror.

I stopped, with a glass in each hand, and said: "Maybe this hot wind has got you crazy too. I'm a private detective. I'll prove it if you let me."

She nodded slightly and her face was white. I went over slowly and put a glass down beside her, and went back and set mine down and got a card out that had no bent corners. She was sitting down, smoothing one blue knee with her left hand, and holding the gun on the other. I put the card down beside her drink and sat with mine.

"Never let a guy get that close to you," I said. "Not if you mean business. And your safety catch is on."

She flashed her eyes down, shivered, and put the gun back in her bag. She drank half the drink without stopping, put the glass down hard and picked the card up.

"I don't give many people that liquor," I said. "I can't afford to."

Her lips curled. "I supposed you would want money."

"Huh?"

She didn't say anything. Her hand was close to her bag again.

"Don't forget the safety catch," I said. Her hand stopped. I went on: "This fellow I called Waldo is quite tall, say five-eleven, slim, dark, brown eyes with a lot of glitter. Nose and mouth too thin. Dark suit, white handkerchief showing, and in a hurry to find you. Am I getting anywhere?"

She took her glass again. "So that's Waldo," she said. "Well, what about him?" Her voice seemed to have a slight liquor edge now.

"Well, a funny thing. There's a cocktail bar across the street . . . Say, where have you been all evening?"

"Sitting in my car," she said coldly, "most of the time."

"Didn't you see a fuss across the street up the block?"

Her eyes tried to say no and missed. Her lips said: "I knew there was some kind of disturbance. I saw policemen and red searchlights. I supposed someone had been hurt."

"Someone was. And this Waldo was looking for you before that. In the cocktail bar. He described you and your clothes."

Her eyes were set like rivets now and had the same amount of expression. Her mouth began to tremble and kept on trembling.

"I was in there," I said, "talking to the kid that runs it. There was nobody in there but a drunk on a stool and the kid and myself. The drunk wasn't paying any attention to anything. Then Waldo came in and asked about you and we said no, we hadn't seen you and he started to leave."

I sipped my drink. I like an effect as well as the next fellow. Her eyes ate me.

"Just started to leave. Then this drunk that wasn't paying any attention to anyone called him Waldo and took a gun out. He shot him twice—" I snapped my fingers twice—"like that. Dead."

She fooled me. She laughed in my face. "So my husband hired you to spy on me," she said. "I might have known the whole thing was an act. You and your Waldo."

I gawked at her.

"I never thought of him as jealous," she snapped. "Not of a man who had been our chauffeur anyhow. A little about Stan, of course —that's natural. But Joseph Choate——"

I made motions in the air. "Lady, one of us has this book open at the wrong page," I grunted. "I don't know anybody named Stan or Joseph Choate. So help me, I didn't even know you had a chauffeur. People around here don't run to them. As for husbands—yeah, we do have a husband once in a while. Not often enough."

She shook her head slowly and her hand stayed near her bag and her blue eyes had glitters in them.

"Not good enough, Mr. Dalmas. No, not nearly good enough. I know you private detectives. You're all rotten. You tricked me into your apartment, if it is your apartment. More likely it's the apartment of some horrible man who will swear anything for a few dollars. Now you're trying to scare me. So you can blackmail me — as well as get money from my husband. All right," she said breathlessly, "how much do I have to pay?"

I put my empty glass aside and leaned back. "Pardon me if I light a cigarette," I said. "My nerves are frayed."

I lit it while she watched me grimly, no fear — or not enough fear for any real guilt to be under it. "So Joseph Choate is his name," I said. "The guy that killed him in the cocktail bar called him Waldo."

She smiled a bit disgustedly, but almost tolerantly. "Don't stall. How much?"

"Why were you trying to meet this Joseph Choate?"

"I was going to buy something he stole from me, of course. Something I happen to value. Something that's valuable in the ordinary way too. It cost fifteen thousand dollars. The man I loved gave it to me. He's dead. There! He's dead! He died in a burning plane. Now, go back and tell my husband that, you slimy little rat!"

"Hey, I weigh a hundred and ninety stripped," I yelled.

"You're still slimy," she yelled back. "And don't bother about telling my husband. I'll tell him myself. He probably knows anyway."

I grinned. "That's smart. Just what was I supposed to find out?"

She grabbed her glass and finished what was left of her drink. "So he thinks I'm meeting Joseph," she sneered. "Well, I was. But not to make love. Not with a chauffeur. Not with a bum I picked off the front step and gave a job to. I don't have to dig down that far, if I want to play around."

"Lady," I said, "you don't indeed."

"Now I'm going," she said. "You just try and stop me." She snatched the pearl-handled gun out of her bag.

I grinned and kept on grinning. I didn't move.

"Why you nasty little string of nothing," she stormed. "How do I know you're a private detective at all? You might be a crook. This card you gave me doesn't mean anything. Anybody can have cards printed."

"Sure," I said. "And I suppose I'm smart enough to live here two years because you were going to move in today so I could blackmail you for not meeting a man named Joseph Choate who was bumped off across the street under the name of Waldo. Have you got the money to buy this something that cost fifteen grand?"

"Oh! You think you'll hold me up, I suppose!"

"Oh!" I mimicked her, "I'm a stick-up artist now, am I? Lady, will you please either put that gun away or take the safety catch off? It hurts my professional feelings to see a nice gun made a monkey of that way."

"You're a full portion of what I don't like," she said. "Get out of my way."

I didn't move. She didn't move. We were both sitting down — and not even close to each other.

"Let me in on one secret before you go," I pleaded. "What in hell did you take the apartment down on the floor below for? Just to meet a guy down on the street?"

"Stop being silly," she snapped. "I didn't. I lied. It's his apartment."

"Joseph Choate's?"

She nodded sharply.

"Does my description of Waldo sound like Joseph Choate?"

She nodded sharply again.

"All right. That's one fact learned at last. Don't you realize Waldo described your clothes before he was shot — when he was looking for you — that the description was passed on to the police — that the police don't know who Waldo is — and are looking for somebody in those clothes to help tell them? Don't you get that much?"

The gun suddenly started to shake in her hand. She looked down at it, sort of vacantly, slowly put it back in her bag.

"I'm a fool," she whispered, "to be even talking to you." She stared at me for a long time, then pulled in a deep breath. "He told me where he was staying. He didn't seem afraid. I guess black-mailers are like that. He was to meet me on the street, but I was late. It was full of police when I got here. So I went back and sat in my car for a while. Then I came up to Joseph's apartment and knocked.

Then I went back to my car and waited again. I came up here three times in all. The last time I walked up a flight to take the elevator. I had already been seen twice on the third floor. I met you. That's all."

"You said something about a husband," I grunted. "Where is he?"

"He's at a meeting."

"Oh, a meeting," I said nastily.

"My husband's a very important man. He has lots of meetings. He's a hydro-electric engineer. He's been all over the world. I'd have you know——"

"Skip it," I said. "I'll take him to lunch some day and have him tell me himself. Whatever Joseph had on you is dead stock now. Like Joseph."

She believed it at last. I hadn't thought she ever would somehow. "He's really dead?" she whispered. "Really?"

"He's dead," I said. "Dead, dead, dead. Lady, he's dead."

Her face fell apart like a bride's piecrust. Her mouth wasn't large, but I could have got my fist into it at that moment. In the silence the elevator stopped at my floor.

"Scream," I rapped, "and I'll give you two black eyes."

It didn't sound nice, but it worked. It jarred her out of it. Her mouth shut like a trap.

I heard steps coming down the hall. We all have hunches. I put my finger to my lips. She didn't move now. Her face had a frozen look. Her big blue eyes were as black as the shadows below them. The hot wind boomed against the shut windows. Windows have to be shut when a Santa Ana blows, heat or no heat.

The steps that came down the hall were the casual ordinary steps of one man. But they stopped outside my door, and somebody knocked.

I pointed to the dressing-room behind the wall bed. She stood up without a sound, her bag clenched against her side. I pointed again, to her glass. She lifted it swiftly, slid across the carpet, through the door, drew the door quietly shut after her.

I didn't know just what I was going to all this trouble for.

The knocking sounded again. The backs of my hands were wet. I creaked my chair and stood up and made a loud yawning sound. Then I went over and opened the door—without a gun. That was a mistake.

3

I didn't know him at first. Perhaps for the opposite reason Waldo hadn't seemed to know him. He'd had a hat on all the time over at the cocktail bar and he didn't have one on now. His hair ended completely and exactly where his hat would start. Above that line was hard white sweatless skin almost as glaring as scar tissue. He wasn't just twenty years older. He was a different man.

But I knew the gun he was holding, the .22 target automatic with the big front sight. And I knew his eyes. Bright, brittle, shallow eyes like the eyes of a lizard.

He was alone. He put the gun against my face very lightly and said between his teeth: "Yeah, me. Let's go on in."

I backed in just far enough and stopped. Just the way he would want me to, so he could shut the door without moving much. I knew from his eyes that he would want me to do just that.

I wasn't scared. I was paralyzed.

When he had the door shut he backed me some more, slowly, until there was something against the back of my legs. His eyes looked into mine.

"That's a card table," he said. "Some goon here plays chess. You?"

I swallowed. "I don't exactly play it. I just fool around."

"That means two," he said with a kind of hoarse softness, as if some cop had hit him across the windpipe with a blackjack once, in a third-degree session.

"It's a problem," I said. "Not a game. Look at the pieces."

"I wouldn't know."

"Well, I'm alone," I said, and my voice shook just enough.

"It don't make any difference," he said. "I'm washed up anyway. Some nose puts the but on me tomorrow, next week, what the hell? I just didn't like your map, pal. And that smug-faced pansy in the barcoat that played left tackle for Fordham or something. To hell with guys like you guys."

I didn't speak or move. The big front sight raked my cheek lightly, almost caressingly. The man smiled.

"It's kind of good business too," he said. "Just in case. An old con like me don't make good prints—not even when he's lit. And if I don't make good prints all I got against me is two witnesses. The hell with it. You're slammin' off, pal. I guess you know that."

"What did Waldo do to you?" I tried to make it sound as if I wanted to know, instead of just not wanting to shake too hard.

"Stooled on a bank job in Michigan and got me four years. Got himself a nolle prosse. Four years in Michigan ain't no summer cruise. They make you be good in them lifer states."

"How'd you know he'd come in there?" I croaked.

"I didn't. Oh yeah, I was lookin' for him. I was wanting to see him all right. I got a flash of him on the street night before last but I lost him. Up to then I wasn't lookin' for him. Then I was. A cute guy, Waldo. How is he?"

"Dead," I said.

"I'm still good," he chuckled. "Drunk or sober. Well, that don't make no doughnuts for me now. They make me downtown yet?"

I didn't answer him quick enough. He jabbed the gun into my throat and I choked and almost grabbed for it by instinct.

"Naw," he cautioned me softly. "Naw. You ain't that dumb."

I put my hands back, down at my sides, open, the palms towards him. He would want them that way. He hadn't touched me, except with the gun. He didn't seem to care whether I might have one too. He wouldn't—if he just meant the one thing.

He didn't seem to care very much about anything, coming back on that block. Perhaps the hot wind did something to him. It was booming against my shut windows like the surf under a pier.

"They got prints," I said. "I don't know how good."

"They'll be good enough—but not for teletype work. Take 'em airmail time to Washington and back to check 'em right. Tell me why I come here, pal."

"You heard the kid and me talking in the bar. I told him my name, where I lived."

"That's how, pal. I said why." He smiled at me. It was a lousy smile to be the last one you might see.

"Skip it," I said. "The hangman won't ask you to guess why he's there."

"Say, you're tough at that. After you, I visit that kid. I tailed him home from headquarters, but I figure you're the guy to put the bee on first. I tail him home from the city hall, in the rent car Waldo had. From headquarters, pal. Them funny dicks. You can sit in their laps and they don't know you. Start runnin' for a street car and they open up with machine guns and bump two pedestrians, a hacker asleep in his cab, and an old scrubwoman on the second floor workin' a mop. And they miss the guy they're after. Them funny lousy dicks."

He twisted the gun muzzle in my neck. His eyes looked madder than before.

"I got time," he said. "Waldo's rent car don't get a report right away. And they don't make Waldo very soon. I know Waldo. Smart he was. A smooth boy, Waldo."

"I'm going to vomit," I said, "if you don't take that gun out of my throat."

He smiled and moved the gun down to my heart. "This about right? Say when."

I must have spoken louder than I meant to. The door of the dressing-room by the wall bed showed a crack of darkness. Then an inch. Then four inches. I saw eyes, but I didn't look at them. I stared hard into the baldheaded man's eyes. Very hard. I didn't want him to take his eyes off mine.

"Scared?" he asked softly.

I leaned against his gun and began to shake. I thought he would enjoy seeing me shake. The girl came out through the door. She had her gun in her hand again. I was sorry as hell for her. She'd try to make the door—or scream. Either way it would be curtains—for both of us.

"Well, don't take all night about it," I bleated. My voice sounded far away, like a voice on a radio, on the other side of a street.

"I like this, pal," he smiled. "I'm like that."

The girl floated in the air, somewhere behind him. Nothing was ever more soundless than the way she moved. It wouldn't do any good, though. He wouldn't fool around with her at all. I had known him all my life but I had been looking into his eyes for only five minutes.

"Suppose, I yell," I said.

"Yeah. Suppose you yell. Go ahead and yell," he said, with his killer's smile.

She didn't go near the door. She was right behind him.

"Well—here's where I yell," I said.

As if that was the cue she jabbed the little gun hard into his short ribs, without a single sound.

He had to react. It was like a knee reflex. His mouth snapped open and both his arms jumped out from his sides and he arched his back just a little. The gun was pointing at my right eye.

I sank and kneed him with all my strength, in the groin.

His chin came down and I hit it. I hit it as if I was driving the last spike on the first transcontinental railroad. I can still feel it when I flex my knuckles.

His gun raked the side of my face but it didn't go off. He was already limp. He writhed down gasping, his left side against the floor. I kicked his right shoulder—hard. The gun jumped away from him, skidded on the carpet, under a chair. I heard the chessmen tinkling on the floor behind me somewhere.

The girl stood over him, looking down. Then her wide dark horrified eyes came up and fastened on mine.

"That buys me," I said. "Anything I have is yours—now and forever."

She didn't hear me. Her eyes were strained open so hard that the whites showed under the vivid blue iris. She backed quickly to the door with her little gun up, felt behind her for the knob and twisted it. She pulled the door open and slipped out.

The door shut.

She was bareheaded and without her bolero jacket.

She had only the gun, and the safety catch on that was still set so that she couldn't fire it.

It was silent in the room then, in spite of the wind. Then I heard him gasping on the floor. His face had a greenish pallor. I moved behind him and pawed him for more guns, and didn't find any. I got a pair of store cuffs out of my desk and pulled his arms in front of him and snapped them on his wrists. They would hold if he didn't shake them too hard.

His eyes measured me for a coffin, in spite of their suffering. He lay in the middle of the floor, still on his left side, a twisted, wizened, bald-headed little guy with drawn-back lips and teeth spotted with cheap silver fillings. His mouth looked like a black pit and his breath came in little waves, choked, stopped, came on again, limping.

"I'm sorry, guy," I grunted. "What could I do?"

That—to this sort of killer.

I went into the dressing room and opened the drawer of the chest. Her hat and jacket lay there on my shirts. I put them underneath, at the back, and smoothed the shirts over them. Then I went out to the kitchenette and poured a stiff jolt of whiskey and put it down and stood a moment listening to the hot wind howl against the window glass. A garage door banged, and a power-line wire with too much play between the insulators thumped the side of the building with a sound like somebody beating a carpet.

The drink worked on me. I went back into the living-room and opened a window. The guy on the floor hadn't smelled her sandalwood, but somebody else might.

I shut the window again, wiped the palms of my hands and used the phone to dial headquarters.

Copernik was still there. His smart-aleck voice said: "Yeah? Dalmas? Don't tell me. I bet you got an idea."

"Make that killer yet?"

"We're not saying, Dalmas. Sorry as all hell and so on. You know how it is."

"O.K. I don't care who he is. Just come and get him off the floor of my apartment."

"Holy ——!" Then his voice hushed and went down low. "Wait a minute, now. Wait a minute." A long way off I seemed to hear a door shut. Then his voice again. "Shoot," he said softly.

"Handcuffed," I said. "All yours. I had to knee him, but he'll be all right. He came here to eliminate a witness."

Another pause. The voice was full of honey. "Now listen, boy, who else is in this with you?"

"Who else? Nobody. Just me."

"Keep it that way, boy. All quiet. O.K.?"

"Think I want all the bums in the neighborhood in here sightseeing?"

"Take it easy, boy. Easy. Just sit tight and sit still. I'm practically there. No touch nothing. Get me?"

"Yeah." I gave him the address and apartment number again to save him time.

I could see his big bony face glisten. I got the .22 target gun from under the chair and sat holding it until feet hit the hallway outside my door and knuckles did a quiet tattoo on the door panel.

Copernik was alone. He filled the doorway quickly, pushed me back into the room with a tight grin and shut the door. He stood with his back to it, his hand under the left side of his coat. A big hard bony man with flat cruel eyes.

He lowered them slowly and looked at the man on the floor. The lad's neck was twitching a little. His eyes moved in short stabs — sick eyes.

"Sure it's the guy?" Copernik's voice was hoarse.

"Positive. Where's Ybarra?"

"Oh, he was busy." He didn't look at me when he said that. "Those your cuffs?"

"Yeah."

"Key."

I tossed it to him. He went down swiftly on one knee beside the killer and took my cuffs off his wrists, tossed them to one side. He got his own off his hip, twisted the bald man's hands behind him and snapped the cuffs on.

"All right, you——" the killer said tonelessly.

Copernik grinned and balled his fist and hit the handcuffed man in the mouth a terrific blow. His head snapped back almost enough to break his neck. Blood dribbled from the lower corner of his mouth.

"Get a towel," Copernik ordered.

I got a hand towel and gave it to him. He stuffed it between the handcuffed man's teeth, viciously, stood up and rubbed his bony fingers through his ratty blond hair.

"All right. Tell it."

I told it — leaving the girl out completely. It sounded a little funny. Copernik watched me, said nothing. He rubbed the side of his veined nose. Then he got his comb out and worked on his hair just as he had done earlier in the evening, in the cocktail bar.

I went over and gave him the gun. He looked at it casually, dropped it into his side pocket. His eyes had something in them and his face moved in a hard bright grin.

I bent down and began picking up my chessmen and dropping them into the box. I put the box on the mantel, straightened out a leg of the card table, played around for a while. All the time Copernik watched me. I wanted him to think something out.

At last he came out with it. "This guy uses a twenty-two," he said. "He uses it because he's good enough to get by with that much gun. That means he's good. He knocks at your door, pokes that gat in your belly, walks you back into the room, says he's here to close your mouth for keeps—and yet you take him. You not having any gun. You take him alone. You're kind of good yourself, pal."

"Listen," I said, and looked at the floor. I picked up another chessman and twisted it between my fingers. "I was doing a chess problem," I said. "Trying to forget things."

"You got something on your mind, pal," Copernik said softly. "You wouldn't try to fool an old copper, would you, boy?"

"It's a swell pinch and I'm giving it to you," I said. "What the hell more do you want?"

The man on the floor made a vague sound behind the towel. His bald head glistened with sweat.

"What's the matter, pal? You been up to something?" Copernik almost whispered.

I looked at him quickly, looked away again. "All right," I said. "You know damn well I couldn't take him alone. He had the gun on me and he shoots where he looks."

Copernik closed one eye and squinted at me amiably with the other. "Go on, pal. I kind of thought of that too."

I shuffled around a little more, to make it look good. I said slowly: "There was a kid here who pulled a job over in Boyle Heights, a heist job, and didn't take. A two-bit service station stickup. I know his family. He's not really bad. He was here trying to beg train money off me. When the knock came he sneaked in— there."

I pointed at the wall bed and the door beside. Copernik's head swiveled slowly, swiveled back. His eyes winked again. "And this kid had a gun," he said.

I nodded. "And he got behind him. That takes guts, Copernik. You've got to give the kid a break. You've got to let him stay out of it."

"Tag out for this kid?" Copernik asked softly.

"Not yet, he says. He's scared there will be."

Copernik smiled. "I'm a homicide man," he said. "What you have done, pal?"

I pointed down at the gagged and handcuffed man on the floor. "You took him, didn't you?" I said gently.

Copernik kept on smiling. A big whitish tongue came out and massaged his thick lower lip. "How'd I do it?" he whispered.

"Get the slugs out of Waldo?"

"Sure. Long twenty-twos. One smashed on a rib, one good."

"You're a careful guy. You don't miss any angles. You don't know anything about me. You dropped in on me to see what guns I had."

Copernik got up and went down on one knee again beside the killer. "Can you hear me, guy?" he asked with his face close to the face of the man on the floor.

The man made some vague sound. Copernik stood up and yawned. "Who the hell cares what he says? Go on, pal."

"You wouldn't expect to find I had anything, but you wanted to look around my place. And while you were mousing around in there"—I pointed to the dressing room—"and me not saying anything, being a little sore, maybe, a knock came on the door. So he came in. So after a while you sneaked out and took him."

"Ah." Copernik grinned widely, with as many teeth as a horse. "You're on, pal. I socked him and I kneed him and I took him. You didn't have no gun and the guy swiveled on me pretty sharp and I left-hooked him down the backstairs. O.K.?"

"O.K.," I said.

"You'll tell it like that downtown?"

"Yeah," I said.

"I'll protect you, pal. Treat me right and I'll always play ball. Forget about that kid. Let me know if he needs a break."

He came over and held out his hand. I shook it. It was as clammy as a dead fish. Clammy hands and the people who own them make me sick.

"There's just one thing," I said. "This partner of yours—Ybarra. Won't he be a bit sore you didn't bring him along on this?"

Copernik tousled his hair and wiped his hatband with a large yellowish silk handkerchief.

"That guinea?" he sneered. "To hell with him!" He came close to me and breathed in my face. "No mistakes, pal—about that story of ours."

His breath was bad. It would be.

4

There were just five of us in the chief-of-detectives' office when Copernik laid it before them. A stenographer, the chief, Copernik, myself, Ybarra. Ybarra sat on a chair tilted against the side wall. His hat was down over his eyes but their softness loomed underneath, and the small still smile hung at the corners of the cleancut Latin lips. He didn't look directly at Copernik. Copernik didn't look at him at all.

Outside in the corridor there had been photos of Copernik shaking hands with me, Copernik with his hat on straight and his gun in his hand and a stern, purposeful look on his face.

They said they knew who Waldo was, but they wouldn't tell me. I didn't believe they knew, because the chief-of-detectives had a morgue photo of Waldo on his desk. A beautiful job, his hair combed, his tie straight, the light hitting his eyes just right to make them glisten. Nobody would have known it was a photo of a dead man with two bullet holes in his heart. He looked like a dance-hall sheik making up his mind whether to take the blonde or the redhead.

It was about midnight when I got home. The apartment-house door was locked and while I was fumbling for my keys a low voice spoke to me out of the darkness.

All it said was: "Please!" but I knew it. I turned and looked at a dark Cadillac coupe parked just off the loading zone. It had no lights. Light from the street touched the brightness of a woman's eyes.

I went over there. "You're a darn fool," I said.

She said: "Get in."

I climbed in and she started the car and drove it a block and a half along Franklin and turned down Kingsley Drive. The hot wind still burned and blustered. A radio lilted from an open, sheltered, side window of an apartment house. There were a lot of parked cars but she found a vacant space behind a small brand-new Packard cabriolet that had the dealer's sticker on the windshield glass. After she'd jockeyed us up to the curb she leaned back in the corner with her gloved hands on the wheel.

She was all in black now, or dark brown, with a small foolish hat. I smelled the sandalwood in her perfume.

"I wasn't very nice to you, was I?" she said.

"All you did was save my life."

"What happened?"

"I called the law and fed a few lies to a cop I don't like and gave him all the credit for the pinch and that was that. That guy you took away from me was the man who killed Waldo."

"You mean—you didn't tell them about me?"

"Lady," I said again, "all you did was save my life. What else do you want done? I'm ready, willing, and I'll try to be able."

She didn't say anything, or move.

"Nobody learned who you are from me," I said. "Incidentally, I don't know myself."

"I'm Mrs. Frank C. Barsaly, Two-twelve Fremont Place. Olympia Two-four-five-nine-six. Is that what you wanted?"

"Thanks," I mumbled, and rolled a dry unlit cigarette around in my fingers. "Why did you come back?" Then I snapped the fingers of my left hand. "The hat and jacket," I said. "I'll go up and get them."

"It's more than that," she said. "I want my pearls."

I might have jumped a little. It seemed as if there had been enough without pearls.

A car tore by down the street going twice as fast as it should. A thin bitter cloud of dust lifted in the street lights and whirled and vanished. The girl ran the window up quickly against it.

"All right," I said. "Tell me about the pearls. We have had a murder and a mystery woman and a mad killer and a heroic rescue and a police detective framed into making a false report. Now we will have pearls. All right—feed it to me."

"I was to buy them for five thousand dollars. From the man you call Waldo and I call Joseph Choate. He should have had them."

"No pearls," I said. "I saw what came out of his pockets. A lot of money but no pearls."

"Could they be hidden in his apartment?"

"Yes," I said. "So far as I know he could have had them hidden anywhere in California except in his pockets. How's Mr. Barsaly this hot night?"

"He's still downtown at his meeting. Otherwise I couldn't have come."

"Well, you could have brought him," I said. "He could have sat in the rumble seat."

"Oh, I don't know," she said. "Frank weighs two hundred pounds and he's pretty solid. I don't think he would like to sit in the rumble seat, Mr. Dalmas."

"What the hell are we talking about, anyway?"

She didn't answer. Her gloved hands tapped lightly, provokingly on the rim of the slender wheel. I threw the unlit cigarette out the window, turned a little and took hold of her.

I was shaking when I let go of her. She pulled as far away from me as she could against the side of the car and rubbed the back of her glove against her mouth. I sat quite still.

We didn't speak for some time. Then she said very slowly: "I meant you to do that. But I wasn't always that way. It's only been since Stan Phillips was killed in his plane. If it hadn't been for that, I'd be Mrs. Phillips now. Stan gave me the pearls. They cost fifteen thousand dollars, he said once. White pearls, forty-one of them, the largest about a third of an inch across. I don't know how many grains. I never had them appraised or showed them to a jeweler, so I don't know those things. But I loved them on Stan's account. I loved Stan. The way you do just the one time. Can you understand?"

"What's your first name?" I asked.

"Lola."

"Go on talking, Lola." I got another dry cigarette out of my pocket and fumbled it between my fingers just to give them something to do.

"They had a simple silver clasp in the shape of a two-bladed propeller. There was one small diamond where the boss would be. That was because I told Frank they were store pearls I had bought myself. He didn't know the difference. It's not so easy to tell, I dare say. You see — Frank is pretty jealous."

In the darkness she came closer to me and her side touched my side. But I didn't move this time. The wind howled and the trees shook. I kept on rolling the cigarette around in my fingers.

"I suppose you've read that story," she said. "About the wife and the real pearls and her telling her husband —"

"I've read it," I said.

"I hired Joseph. My husband was in Argentina at the time. I was pretty lonely."

"*You* should be lonely," I said.

"Joseph and I went driving a good deal. Sometimes we had a drink or two together. But that's all. I don't go around —"

"You told him about the pearls," I snarled. "And when your two hundred pounds of beef came back from Argentina and kicked him out — he took the pearls, because he knew they were real. And then offered them back to you for five grand."

"Yes," she said simply. "Of course I didn't want to go to the police. And of course in the circumstance Joseph wasn't afraid of my knowing where he lived."

"Poor Waldo," I said. "I feel kind of sorry for him. It was a hell of a time to run into an old friend that had a down on you."

I struck a match on my shoe sole and lit the cigarette. The tobacco was so dry from the hot wind that it burned like grass. The girl sat quietly beside me, her hands on the wheel again.

"Hell with women — these fliers," I said. "And you're still in love with him, or think you are. Where did you keep the pearls?"

"In a Russian malachite jewelry box on my dressing-table. With some other costume jewelry. I had to, if I ever wanted to wear them."

"And they were worth fifteen grand. And you think Joseph might have hidden them in his apartment. Thirty-one, wasn't it?"

"Yes," she said. "I guess it's a lot to ask."

I opened the door and got out of the car. "I've been paid," I said. "I'll go look. The doors in my apartment house are not very obstinate. The cops will find out where Waldo lived when they publish his photo, but not tonight, I guess."

"It's awfully sweet of you," she said. "Shall I wait here?"

I stood with a foot on the running-board, leaning in, looking at her. I didn't answer her question. I just stood there looking in at the shine of her eyes. Then I shut the car door and walked up the street towards Franklin.

Even with the wind shriveling my face I could still smell the sandalwood in her hair. And feel her lips.

I unlocked the Berglund door, walked through the silent lobby to the elevator, and rode up to 3. Then I soft-footed along the silent corridor and peered down at the sill of Apartment 31. No light. I rapped—the old light, confidential tattoo of the bootlegger with the big smile and the extra-deep hip pockets. No answer. I took the piece of thick hard celluloid that pretended to be a window over the driver's license in my wallet, and eased it between the lock and the jamb, leaning hard on the knob, pushing it toward the hinges. The edge of the celluloid caught the slope of the spring lock and snapped it back with a small brittle sound, like an icicle breaking. The door yielded and I went into near darkness. Street light filtered in and touched a high spot here and there.

I shut the door and snapped the light on and just stood. There was a queer smell in the air. I made it in a moment—the smell of dark-cured tobacco. I prowled over to a smoking-stand by the window and looked down at four brown butts—Mexican or South American cigarettes.

Upstairs, on my floor, feet hit the carpet and somebody went into a bathroom. I heard the toilet flush. I went into the bathroom of Apartment 31. A little rubbish, nothing, no place to hide anything. The kitchenette was a longer job, but I only half searched. I knew there were no pearls in that apartment. I knew Waldo had been on his way out and that he was in a hurry and that something was riding him when he turned and took two bullets from an old friend.

I went back to the living-room and swung the wall bed and looked past its mirror side into the dressing-room for signs of still current occupancy. Swinging the bed farther I was no longer looking for pearls. I was looking at a man.

He was small, middle-aged, iron-gray at the temples, with a very dark skin, dressed in a fawn-colored suit with a wine-colored tie. His neat little brown hands hung limply down by his sides. His small feet, in pointed polished shoes, pointed almost at the floor.

He was hanging by a belt around his neck from the metal top of the bed. His tongue stuck out farther than I thought it possible for a tongue to stick out.

He swung a little and I didn't like that, so I pulled the bed down and he nestled quietly between the two clamped pillows. I didn't touch him yet. I didn't have to touch him to know that he would be cold as ice.

I went around him into the dressing-room and used my handkerchief on drawer-knobs. The place was stripped clean except for the light litter of a man living alone.

I came out of there and began on the man. No wallet. Waldo would have taken that and ditched it. A flat box of cigarettes, half full, stamped in gold: *"Louis Tapia y Cia, Calle de Paysand, 19, Montevideo."* Matches from the Spezzia Club. An under-arm holster of dark grained leather and in it a 9 millimeter Mauser.

The Mauser made him a professional, so I didn't feel so badly. But not a very good professional, or bare hands would not have finished him, with the Mauser—a gun you can blast through a wall with—undrawn in his shoulder holster.

I made a little sense of it, not much. Four of the brown cigarettes had been smoked, so there had been either waiting or discussion. Somewhere along the line Waldo had got the little man by the throat and held him in just the right way to make him pass out in a matter of seconds. The Mauser had been less useful to him than a toothpick. Then Waldo had hung him up by the strap, probably dead already. That would account for haste, for cleaning out the apartment, for Waldo's anxiety about the girl. It would account for the car left unlocked outside the cocktail bar.

That is, it would account for these things if Waldo had killed him, if this was really Waldo's apartment—if I wasn't just being kidded.

I examined some more pockets. In the left trouser one I found a gold penknife, some silver. In the left hip pocket a handkerchief, folded, scented. On the right hip another, unfolded but clean. In the right leg pocket four or five tissue handkerchiefs. A clean little guy. He didn't like to blow his nose on his handkerchief. Under these there was a small new keytainer holding four new keys—car keys.

Stamped in gold on the keytainer was: *Compliments of R. K. Vogelsang, Inc. "The Packard House."*

I put everything as I had found it, swung the bed back, used my handkerchief on knobs and other projections, and flat surfaces, killed the light and poked my nose out the door. The hall was empty. I went down to the street and around the corner to Kingsley Drive. The Cadillac hadn't moved.

I opened the car door and leaned on it. She didn't seem to have moved, either. It was hard to see any expression on her face. Hard to see anything but her eyes and chin, but not hard to smell the sandalwood.

"That perfume," I said, "would drive a deacon nuts . . . no pearls."

"Well—thanks for trying," she said in a low, soft, vibrant voice. "I guess I can stand it. Shall I . . . Do we . . . Or . . . ?"

"You go on home now," I said. "And whatever happens you never saw me before. Whatever happens. Just as you may never see me again."

"I'd hate—"

"Good luck, Lola." I shut the car door and stepped back.

The lights blazed on, the motor turned over. Against the wind at the corner the big coupe made a slow contemptuous turn and was gone. I stood there by the vacant space at the curb where it had been.

It was quite dark there now. Windows had become blanks in the apartment where the radio sounded. I stood looking at the back of a Packard cabriolet which seemed to be brand new. I had seen it before—before I went upstairs, in the same place, in front of Lola's car. Parked, dark, silent, with a blue sticker pasted to the right-hand corner of the shiny windshield.

And in my mind I was looking at something else, a set of brand-new car keys in a keytainer stamped, *"The Packard House,"* upstairs, in a dead man's pocket.

I went up to the front of the cabriolet and put a small pocket flash on the blue slip. It was the same dealer all right. Written in ink below his name and slogan was a name and address—*Eugenie Kolchenko, 5315 Arvieda Street, West Los Angeles.*

It was crazy. I went back up to Apartment 31, jimmied the door as I had done before, stepped in behind the wall bed and took the keytainer from the trousers pocket of the neat brown dangling corpse. I was back down on the street beside the cabriolet in five minutes. The keys fitted.

5

It was a small house, near a canyon rim out beyond Sawtelle, with a circle of writhing eucalyptus trees in front of it. Beyond that, on the other side of the street, one of those parties was going on where they come out and smash bottles on the sidewalk with a whoop like Yale making a touchdown against Princeton.

There was a wire fence at my number and some rose-trees, and a flagged walk and a garage that was wide open and had no car in it. There was no car in front of the house either. I rang the bell. There was a long wait, then the door opened rather suddenly.

I wasn't the man she had been expecting. I could see it in her glittering kohl-rimmed eyes. Then I couldn't see anything in them. She just stood and looked at me, a long, lean, hungry brunette, with rouged cheekbones, thick black hair parted in the middle, a mouth made for three-decker sandwiches, coral-and-gold pajamas, sandals—and gilded toenails. Under her ear lobes a couple of miniature temple bells gonged lightly in the breeze. She made a slow disdainful motion with a cigarette in a holder as long as a baseball bat.

"We-el, what ees it, little man? You want sometheeng? You are lost from the bee-ootiful party across the street, hein?"

"Ha, ha," I said. "Quite a party, isn't it? No. I just brought your car home. Lost it, didn't you?"

Across the street somebody had delirium tremens in the front yard and a mixed quartet tore what was left of the night into small strips and did what they could to make the strips miserable. While this was going on the exotic brunette didn't move more than one eyelash.

She wasn't beautiful, she wasn't even pretty, but she looked as if things would happen where she was.

"You have said what?" she got out, at last, in a voice as silky as a burnt crust of toast.

"Your car." I pointed over my shoulder and kept my eyes on her. She was the type that uses a knife.

The long cigarette holder dropped very slowly to her side and the cigarette fell out of it. I stamped it out, and that put me in the hall. She backed away from me and I shut the door.

The hall was like the long hall of a railroad flat. Lamps glowed pinkly in iron brackets. There was a bead curtain at the end, a tiger skin on the floor. The place went with her.

"You're Miss Kolchenko?" I asked, not getting any more action.

"Ye-es. I am Mees Kolchenko. What thee 'ell you want?"

She was looking at me now as if I had come to wash the windows, but at an inconvenient time.

I got a card out with my left hand, held it out to her. She read it in my hand, moving her head just enough. "A detective?" she breathed.

"Yeah."

She said something in a spitting language. Then in English: "Come in! Thees damn wind dry up my skeen like so much teessue paper."

"We're in," I said. "I just shut the door. Snap out of it, Nazimova. Who was he? The little guy?"

Beyond the bead curtain a man coughed. She jumped as if she had been stuck with an oyster fork. Then she tried to smile. It wasn't very successful.

"A reward," she said softly. "You weel wait 'ere? Ten dollars it is fair to pay, no?"

"No," I said.

I reached a finger towards her slowly and added: "He's dead."

She jumped about three feet and let out a yell.

A chair creaked harshly. Feet pounded beyond the bead curtain, a large hand plunged into view and snatched it aside, and a big hard-looking blond man was with us. He had a purple robe over his pajamas. His right hand held something in his robe pocket. He stood quite still as soon as he was through the curtain, his feet planted solidly, his jaw out, his colorless eyes like gray ice. He looked like a man who would be hard to take out on an off-tackle play.

"What's the matter, honey?" He had a solid, burring voice, with just the right sappy tone to belong to a guy who would go for a woman with gilded toenails.

"I came about Miss Kolchenko's car," I said.

"Well, you could take your hat off," he said. "Just for a light workout."

I took it off and apologized.

"O.K.," he said, and kept his right hand shoved down hard in the purple pocket. "So you came about Miss Kolchenko's car. Take it from there."

I pushed past the woman and went closer to him. She shrank back against the wall and flattened her palms against it. Camille in a high-school play. The long holder lay empty at her toes.

When I was six feet from the big man he said easily: "I can hear you from there. Just take it easy. I've got a gun in this pocket and I've had to learn to use one. Now about the car?"

"The man who borrowed it couldn't bring it," I said, and pushed the card I was still holding towards his face. He barely glanced at it. He looked back at me.

"So what?" he said.

"Are you always this tough?" I asked, "or only when you have your pajamas on?"

"So why couldn't he bring it himself?" he asked. "And skip the mushy talk."

The dark woman made a stuffed sound at my elbow.

"It's all right, honeybunch," the man said. "I'll handle this. Go on in."

She slid past both of us and flicked through the bead curtain.

I waited a little while. The big man didn't move a muscle. He didn't look any more bothered than a toad in the sun.

"He couldn't bring it because somebody bumped him off," I said. "Let's see you handle that."

"Yeah?" he said. "Did you bring him with you to prove it?"

"No," I said. "But if you put your tie and crush hat on, I'll take you down and show you."

"Who the hell did you say you were, now?"

"I didn't say. I thought maybe you could read." I held the card at him some more.

"Oh, that's right," he said. "John Dalmas, Private Investigator. Well, well. So I should go with you to look at who, why?"

"Maybe he stole the car," I said.

The big man nodded. "That's a thought. Maybe he did. Who?"

"The little brown guy who had the keys to it in his pocket, and had it parked around the corner from the Berglund Apartments."

He thought that over, without any apparent embarrassment. "You've got something there," he said. "Not much. But a little. I guess this must be the night of the Police Smoker. So you're doing all their work for them."

"Huh?"

"The card says private detective to me," he said. "Have you got some cops outside that were too shy to come in?"

"No, I'm alone."

He grinned. The grin showed white ridges in his tanned skin. "So you find somebody dead and take some keys and find a car and come riding out here—all alone. No cops. Am I right?"

"Correct."

He sighed. "Let's go inside," he said. He yanked the bead curtain aside and made an opening for me to go through. "It might be you have an idea I ought to hear."

I went past him and he turned, keeping his heavy pocket towards me. I hadn't noticed until I got quite close that there were beads of sweat on his face. It might have been the hot wind, but I didn't think so.

We were in the living-room of the house.

We sat down and looked at each other across a dark floor, on which a few Navajo rugs and a few dark Turkish rugs made a decorating combination with some well-used overstuffed furniture. There was a fireplace, a small baby grand, a Chinese screen, a tall Chinese lantern on a teakwood pedestal, and gold net curtains against lattice windows. The windows to the south were open. A fruit tree with a whitewashed trunk whipped about outside the screen, adding its bit to the noise from across the street.

The big man eased back into a brocaded chair and put his slippered feet on a footstool. He kept his right hand where it had been since I met him—on his gun.

The brunette hung around in the shadows and a bottle gurgled and her temple bells gonged in her ears.

"It's all right, honeybunch," the man said. "It's all under control. Somebody bumped somebody off and this lad thinks we're interested. Just sit down and relax."

The girl tilted her head and poured half a tumbler of whiskey down her throat. She sighed, said, "Goddam," in a casual voice, and curled up on a davenport. It took all of the davenport. She had plenty of legs. Her gilded toenails winked at me from the shadowy corner where she kept herself quiet from then on.

I got a cigarette out without being shot at, lit it and went into my story. It wasn't all true, but some of it was. I told them about the Berglund Apartments and that I had lived there and that Waldo was living there in Apartment 31 on the floor below mine and that I had been keeping an eye on him for business reasons.

"Waldo what?" the blond man put in. "And what business reasons?"

"Mister," I said, "have you no secrets?" He reddened slightly.

I told him about the cocktail lounge across the street from the Berglund and what had happened there. I didn't tell him about the printed bolero jacket or the girl who had worn it. I left her out of the story altogether.

"It was an undercover job—from my angle," I said. "If you know what I mean." He reddened again, bit his teeth. I went on: "I got back from the city hall without telling anybody I knew Waldo. In due time, when I decided they couldn't find out where he lived that night, I took the liberty of examining his apartment."

"Looking for what?" the big man said thickly.

"For some letters. I might mention in passing there was nothing there at all—except a dead man. Strangled and hanging by a belt to the top of the wall bed—well out of sight. A small man, about forty-five, Mexican or South American, well-dressed in a fawn-colored—"

"That's enough," the big man said. "I'll bite, Dalmas. Was it a blackmail job you were on?"

"Yeah. The funny part was this little brown man had plenty of gun under his arm."

"He wouldn't have five hundred bucks in twenties in his pocket, of course? Or are you saying?"

"He wouldn't. But Waldo had over seven hundred in currency when he was killed in the cocktail bar."

"Looks like I underrated this Waldo," the big man said calmly. "He took my guy and his payoff money, gun and all. Waldo have a gun?"

"Not on him."

"Get us a drink, honeybunch," the big man said. "Yes, I certainly did sell this Waldo person shorter than a bargain-counter shirt."

The brunette unwound her legs and made two drinks with soda and ice. She took herself another gill without trimmings, wound herself back on the davenport. Her big glittering black eyes watched me solemnly.

"Well, here's how," the big man said, lifting his glass in salute. "I haven't murdered anybody, but I've got a divorce suit on my hands from now on. You haven't murdered anybody, the way you tell it, but you laid an egg down at police headquarters. What the hell! Life's a lot of trouble, any way you look at it. I've still got honeybunch, here. She's a white Russian I met in Shanghai. She's safe as a vault and she looks as if she would cut your throat for a nickel. That's what I like about her. You get the glamor without the risk."

"You talk damn foolish," the girl spit at him.

"You look O.K. to me," the big man went on ignoring her. "That is, for a keyhole peeper. Is there an out?"

"Yeah. But it will cost a little money."

"I expected that. How much?"

"Say another five hundred."

"Goddam, thees hot wind make me dry like the ashes of love," the Russian girl said bitterly.

"Five hundred might do," the blond man said. "What do I get for it?"

"If I swing it—you get left out of the story. If I don't—you don't pay."

He thought it over. His face looked lined and tired now. The small beads of sweat twinkled in his short blond hair.

"This murder will make you talk," he grumbled. "The second one, I mean. And I don't have what I was going to buy. And if it's a hush, I'd rather buy it direct."

"Who was the little brown man?" I asked.

"Name's Leon Valesanos, a Uruguayan. Another of my importations. I'm in a business that takes me a lot of places. He was working in the Spezzia Club in Chiseltown—you know, the strip of Sunset next to Beverly Hills. Working on roulette, I think. I gave him the five hundred to go down to this—this Waldo—and buy back some bills for stuff Miss Kolchenko had charged to my account and delivered here. That wasn't bright, was it? I had them in my brief case and this Waldo got a chance to steal them. What's your hunch about what happened?"

I sipped my drink and looked at him down my nose. "Your Uruguayan pal probably talked cut and Waldo didn't listen good. Then the little guy thought maybe that Mauser might help his argument—and Waldo was too quick for him. I wouldn't say Waldo was a killer—not by intention. A blackmailer seldom is. Maybe he lost his temper and maybe he just held on to the little guy's neck too long. Then he had to take it on the lam. But he had another date, with more money coming up. And he worked the neighborhood looking for the party. And accidentally he ran into a pal who was hostile enough and drunk enough to blow him down."

"There's a hell of a lot of coincidence in all this business," the big man said.

"It's the hot wind," I grinned. "Everybody's screwy tonight."

"For the five hundred you guarantee nothing? If I don't get my cover-up, you don't get your dough. Is that it?"

"That's it," I said, smiling at him.

"Screwy is right," he said, and drained his highball. "I'm taking you up on it."

"There are just two things," I said softly, leaning forward in my chair. "Waldo had a getaway car parked outside the cocktail bar where he was killed, unlocked with the motor running. The killer took it. There's always the chance of a kickback from that direction. You see, all Waldo's stuff must have been in that car."

"Including my bills and your letters."

"Yeah. But the police are reasonable about things like that— unless you're good for a lot of publicity. If you're not, I think I can eat some stale dog downtown and get by. If you are—that's the second thing. What did you say your name was?"

The answer was a long time coming. When it came I didn't get as much kick out of it as I thought I would. All at once it was too logical.

"Frank C. Barsaly," he said.

After a while the Russian girl called me a taxi. When I left the party across the street was still doing all that a party could do. I noticed the walls of the house were still standing. That seemed a pity.

6

When I unlocked the glass entrance door of the Berglund I smelled policeman. I looked at my wrist watch. It was nearly 3 A.M. In the dark corner of the lobby a man dozed in a chair with a newspaper over his face. Large feet stretched out before him. A corner of the paper lifted an inch, dropped again. The man made no other movement.

I went on along the hall to the elevator and rode up to my floor. I soft-footed along the hallway, unlocked my door, pushed it wide and reached in for the light-switch.

A chain-switch tinkled and light glared from a standing-lamp by the easy chair, beyond the card table on which my chessmen were still scattered.

Copernik sat there with a stiff unpleasant grin on his face. The short dark man, Ybarra, sat across the room from him, on my left, silent, half-smiling as usual.

Copernik showed more of his big yellow horse teeth and said: "Hi. Long time no see. Been out with the girls?"

I shut the door and took my hat off and wiped the back of my neck slowly, over and over again. Copernik went on grinning. Ybarra looked at nothing with his soft dark eyes.

"Take a seat, pal," Copernik drawled. "Make yourself to home. We got pow-wow to make. Boy, do I hate this night sleuthing. Did you know you were all out of hooch?"

"I could have guessed it," I said. I leaned against the wall.

Copernik kept on grinning. "I always did hate private dicks," he said, "but I never had a chance to twist one like I got tonight."

He reached down lazily beside his chair and picked up a printed bolero jacket, tossed it on the card table. He reached down again and put a wide-brimmed hat beside it.

"I bet you look cuter than all hell with these on," he said.

I took hold of a straight chair, twisted it around and straddled it, leaned my folded arms on the chair and looked at Copernik.

He got up very slowly—with an elaborate slowness, walked across the room and stood in front of me smoothing his coat down. Then he lifted his open right hand and hit me across the face with it—hard. It stung but I didn't move.

Ybarra looked at the wall, looked at the floor, looked at nothing.

"Shame on you, pal," Copernik said lazily. "The way you was taking care of this nice exclusive merchandise. Wadded down behind your old shirts. You punk peepers always did make me sick."

He stood there over me for a moment. I didn't move or speak. I looked into his glazed drinker's eyes. He doubled a fist at his side, then shrugged and turned and went back to the chair.

"O.K.," he said. "The rest will keep. Where did you get these things?"

"They belong to a lady."

"Do tell. They belong to a lady. Ain't you the lighthearted ——! I'll tell you what lady they belong to. They belong to the lady a guy named Waldo asked about in a bar across the street—about two minutes before he got shot kind of dead. Or would that have slipped your mind?"

I didn't say anything.

"You was curious about her yourself," Copernik sneered on. "But you were smart, pal. You fooled me."

"That wouldn't make me smart," I said.

His face twisted suddenly and he started to get up. Ybarra laughed, suddenly and softly, almost under his breath. Copernik's eyes swung on him, hung there. Then he faced me again, blank-eyed.

"The guinea likes you," he said. "He thinks you're good."

The smile left Ybarra's face, but no expression took its place. No expression at all.

Copernik said: "You knew who the dame was all the time. You knew who Waldo was and where he lived. Right across the hall a floor below you. You knew this Waldo person had bumped a guy off and started to lam, only this broad came into his plans somewhere and he was anxious to meet up with her before he went away. Only he never got the chance. A heist guy from back East named Al Tessilore took care of that by taking care of Waldo. So you met the gal and hid her clothes and sent her on her way and kept your trap glued. That's the way guys like you make your beans. Am I right?"

"Yeah," I said. "Except that I only knew these things very recently. Who was Waldo?"

Copernik bared his teeth at me. Red spots burned high on his sallow cheeks. Ybarra, looking down at the floor, said very softly:

"Waldo Ratigan. We got him from Washington by teletype. He was a two-bit porch-climber with a few small terms on him. He drove a car in a bank stickup job in Detroit. He turned the gang in later and got a nolle prosse. One of the gang was this Al Tessilore. He hasn't talked a word, but we think the meeting across the street was purely accidental."

Ybarra spoke in the soft quiet modulated voice of a man for whom sounds have a meaning. I said: "Thanks, Ybarra. Can I smoke—or would Copernik kick it out of my mouth?"

Ybarra smiled suddenly. "You may smoke, sure," he said.

"The guinea likes you all right," Copernik jeered. "You never know what a guinea will like, do you?"

I lit a cigarette. Ybarra looked at Copernik and said very softly: "The word guinea—you overwork it. I don't like it so well applied to me."

"The hell with what you like, guinea."

Ybarra smiled a little more. "You are making a mistake," he said. He took a pocket nailfile out and began to use it, looking down.

Copernik blared: "I smelled something rotten on you from the start, Dalmas. So when we make these two mugs, Ybarra and me think we'll drift over and dabble a few more words with you. I bring one of Waldo's morgue photos—nice work, the light just right in his eyes, his tie all straight and a white handkerchief showing just right in his pocket. Nice work. So on the way up, just as a matter of routine, we rout out the manager here and let him lamp it. And he knows the guy. He's here as A. B. Hummel, Apartment Thirty-one. So we go in there and find a stiff. Then we go round and round with that. Nobody knows him yet, but he's got some swell finger bruises under that strap and I hear they fit Waldo's fingers very nicely."

"That's something," I said. "I thought maybe I murdered him."

Copernik stared at me for a long time. His face had stopped grinning and was just a hard brutal face now. "Yeah. We got something else even," he said. "We got Waldo's getaway car—and what Waldo had in it to take with him."

I blew cigarette smoke jerkily. The wind pounded the shut windows. The air in the room was foul.

"Oh we're bright boys," Copernik sneered. "We never figured you with that much guts. Take a look at this."

He plunged his bony hand into his coat pocket and drew something up slowly over the edge of the card table, drew it along the green top and left it there stretched out, gleaming. A string of white pearls with a clasp like a two-bladed propeller. They shimmered softly in the thick smoky air.

Lola Barsaly's pearls. The pearls the flier had given her. The guy who was dead, the guy she still loved.

I stared at them, but I didn't move. After a long moment Copernik said almost gravely: "Nice, ain't they? Would you feel like telling us a story about now, Mis-ter Dalmas?"

I stood up and pushed the chair from under me, walked slowly across the room and stood looking down at the pearls. The largest was perhaps a third of an inch across. They were pure white, iridescent, with a mellow softness. I lifted them slowly off the card table from beside her clothes. They felt heavy, smooth, fine.

"Nice," I said. "A lot of the trouble was about these. Yeah, I'll talk now. They must be worth a lot of money."

Ybarra laughed behind me. It was a very gentle laugh. "About a hundred dollars," he said. "They're good phonies—but they're phoney."

I lifted the pearls again. Copernik's glassy eyes gloated at me. "How do you tell?" I asked.

"I know pearls," Ybarra said. "These are good stuff, the kind women very often have made on purpose, as a kind of insurance. But they are slick like glass. Real pearls are gritty between the edges of the teeth. Try."

I put two or three of them between my teeth and moved my teeth back and forth, then sideways. Not quite biting them. The beads were hard and slick.

"Yes. They are very good," Ybarra said. "Several even have little waves and flat spots, as real pearls might have."

"Would they cost fifteen grand—if they were real?" I asked.

"Si. Probably. That's hard to say. It depends on a lot of things."

"This Waldo wasn't so bad," I said.

Copernik stood up quickly, but I didn't see him swing. I was still looking down at the pearls. His fist caught me on the side of the face, against the molars. I tasted blood at once. I staggered back and made it look like a worse blow than it was.

"Sit down and talk, you ——!" Copernik almost whispered.

I sat down and used a handkerchief to pat my cheek. I licked at the cut inside my mouth. Then I got up again and went over and picked up the cigarette he had knocked out of my mouth. I crushed it out in a tray and sat down again.

Ybarra filed at his nails and held one up against the lamp. There were beads of sweat on Copernik's eyebrows, at the inner ends.

"You found the beads in Waldo's car," I said, looking at Ybarra. "Find any papers?"

He shook his head without looking up.

"I'd believe *you*," I said. "Here it is. I never saw Waldo until he stepped into the cocktail bar tonight and asked about the girl. I knew nothing I didn't tell. When I got home and stepped out of the elevator this girl, in the printed bolero jacket and the wide hat and the blue silk crepe dress—all as he had described them—was waiting for the elevator, here, on my floor. And she looked like a nice girl."

Copernik laughed jeeringly. It didn't make any difference to me. I had him cold. All he had to do was know that. He was going to know it now, very soon.

"I knew what she was up against as a police witness," I said. "And I suspected there was something else to it. But I didn't suspect for a minute that there was anything wrong with her. She was just a nice girl in a jam—and she didn't even know she was in a jam. I got her in here. She pulled a gun on me. But she didn't mean to use it."

Copernik sat up very suddenly and he began to lick his lips. His face had a stony look now. A look like wet gray stone. He didn't make a sound.

"Waldo had been her chauffeur," I went on. "His name then was Joseph Choate. Her name is Mrs. Frank C. Barsaly. Her husband is a big hydro-electric engineer. Some guy gave her the pearls once and she told her husband they were just store pearls. Waldo got wise somehow there was a romance behind them and when Barsaly came home from South America and fired him, because he was too good-looking, he lifted the pearls."

Ybarra lifted his head suddenly and his teeth flashed. "You mean he didn't know they were phoney?"

"I thought he fenced the real ones and had imitations fixed up," I said.

Ybarra nodded. "It's possible."

"He lifted something else," I said. "Some stuff from Barsaly's briefcase that showed he was keeping a woman — out in Brentwood. He was blackmailing wife and husband both, without either knowing about the other. Get it so far?"

"I get it," Copernik said harshly, between his tight lips. His face was still wet gray stone. "Get the hell on with it."

"Waldo wasn't afraid of them," I said. "He didn't conceal where he lived. That was foolish, but it saved a lot of finagling, if he was willing to risk it. The girl came down here tonight with five grand to buy back her pearls. She never met Waldo. She came up here to look for him and walked up a floor before she went back down. A woman's idea of being cagey. So I met her. So I brought her in here. So she was in that dressing-room when Al Tessilore visited me to rub out a witness." I pointed to the dressing-room door. "So she came out with her little gun and stuck it in his back and saved my life," I said.

Copernik didn't move. There was something horrible in his face now. Ybarra slipped his nailfile into a small leather case and slowly tucked it into his pocket.

"Is that all?" he asked gently.

I nodded. "Except that she told me where Waldo's apartment was and I went in there and looked for the pearls. I found the dead man. In his pocket I found new car keys in a case from a Packard agency. And down on the street I found the Packard and took it to where it came from. Barsaly's kept woman. Barsaly had sent a friend from the Spezzia Club down to buy something and he had tried to buy it with his gun instead of the money Barsaly gave him. And Waldo beat him to the punch."

"Is that all?" Ybarra asked softly.

"That's all," I said, licking the torn place on the inside of my cheek.

Ybarra said slowly: "What do you want?"

Copernik's face convulsed and he slapped his long hard thigh. "This guy is good," he jeered. "He falls for a stray broad and breaks every law in the book and you ask him what does he want? I'll give him what he wants, guinea!"

Ybarra turned his head slowly and looked at him. "I don't think you will," he said. "I think you'll give him a clean bill of health and anything else he wants. He's giving you a lesson in police work."

Copernik didn't move or make a sound for a long minute. None of us moved. Then Copernik leaned forward and his coat fell open. The butt of his service gun looked out of its underarm holster.

"So what do you want?" he asked me.

"What's on the card table there. The jacket and hat and the phoney pearls. And some names kept away from the papers. Is that too much?"

"Yeah—it's too much," Copernik said almost gently. He swayed sideways and his gun jumped neatly into his hand. He rested his forearm on his thigh and pointed the gun at my stomach.

"I like better that you get a slug in the guts resisting arrest," he said. "I like that better, because of a report I made out on Al Tessilore's arrest and how I made the pinch. Because of some photos of me that are in the morning sheets going out about now. I like it better that you don't live long enough to laugh about that, baby."

My mouth felt suddenly hot and dry. Far off I heard the wind booming. It seemed like the sound of guns.

Ybarra moved his feet on the floor and said coldly: "You've got a couple of cases all solved, policeman. All you do for it is leave some junk here and keep some names from the papers. Which means from the D.A. If he gets them anyway, too bad for you."

Copernik said: "I like the other way." The blue gun in his hand was like a rock. "And God help you, if you don't back me up on it."

Ybarra said: "If the woman is brought out into the open, you'll be a liar on a police report and a chiseler on your own partner. In a week they won't even speak your name at headquarters. The taste of it would make them sick."

The hammer clicked back on Copernik's gun and I watched his big bony finger slide in farther around the trigger. The back of my neck was as wet as a dog's nose.

Ybarra stood up. The gun jumped at him. He said: "We'll see how yellow a guinea is. I'm telling you to put that gun up, Sam."

He started to move. He moved four even steps. Copernik was a man without a breath of movement, a stone man.

Ybarra took one more step and quite suddenly the gun began to shake.

Ybarra said evenly: "Put it up, Sam. If you keep your head everything lies the way it is. If you don't—you're gone."

He took one more step. Copernik's mouth opened wide and made a gasping sound and then he sagged in the chair as if he had been hit on the head. His eyelids drooped.

Ybarra jerked the gun out of his hand with a movement so quick it was no movement at all. He stepped back quickly, held the gun low at his side.

"It's the hot wind, Sam. Let's forget it," he said in the same even, almost dainty voice.

Copernik's shoulders sagged lower and he put his face in his hands. "O.K.," he said between his fingers.

Ybarra went softly across the room and opened the door. He looked at me with lazy, half-closed eyes. "I'd do a lot for a woman who saved my life, too," he said. "I'm eating this dish, but as a cop you can't expect me to like it."

I said: "The little man in the bed is called Leon Valesanos. He was a croupier at the Spezzia Club."

"Thanks," Ybarra said. "Let's go, Sam."

Copernik got up heavily and walked across the room and out of the open door and out of my sight. Ybarra stepped through the door after him and started to close it.

I said: "Wait a minute."

He turned his head slowly, his left hand on the door, the blue gun hanging down close to his right side.

"I'm not in this for money," I said. "The Barsalys live at Two-twelve Fremont Place. You can take the pearls to her. If Barsaly's name stays out of the paper, I get five C's. It goes to the Police Fund. I'm not so damn smart as you think. It just happened that way—and you had a heel for a partner."

Ybarra looked across the room at the pearls on the card table. His eyes glistened. "You take them," he said. "The five hundred's O.K. I think the fund has it coming."

He shut the door quietly and in a moment I heard the elevator doors clang.

7

I opened a window and stuck my head out into the wind and watched the squad car tool off down the block. The wind blew in hard and I let it blow. A picture fell off the wall and two chessmen rolled off the card table. The material of Lola Barsaly's bolero jacket lifted and shook.

I went out to the kitchenette and drank some Scotch and went back into the living-room and called her—late as it was.

She answered the phone herself, very quickly, with no sleep in her voice.

"Dalmas," I said. "O.K. your end?"

"Yes . . . yes," she said. "I'm alone."

"I found something," I said. "Or rather the police did. But your dark boy gypped you. I have a string of pearls. They're not real. He sold the real ones, I guess, and made you up a string of ringers, with your clasp."

She was silent for a long time. Then, a little faintly: "The police found them?"

"In Waldo's car. But they're not telling. We have a deal. Look at the papers in the morning and you'll be able to figure out why."

"There doesn't seem to be anything more to say," she said. "Can I have the clasp?"

"Yes. Can you meet me tomorrow at four in the Club Esquire bar?"

"You're rather sweet," she said in a dragged out voice. "I can. Frank is still at his meeting."

"Those meetings—they take it out of a guy," I said. We said good-bye.

I called a West Los Angeles number. He was still there, with the Russian girl.

"You can send me a check for five hundred in the morning," I told him. "Made out to the Police Fund, if you want to. Because that's where it's going."

Copernik made the third page of the morning papers with two photos and a nice half-column. The little brown man in Apartment 31 didn't make the paper at all. The Apartment House Association has a good lobby too.

I went out after breakfast and the wind was all gone. It was soft, cool, a little foggy. The sky was close and comfortable and gray. I rode down to the boulevard and picked out the best jewellry store on it and laid a string of pearls on a black velvet mat under a daylight-blue lamp. A man in a wing collar and striped trousers looked down at them languidly.

"How good?" I asked.

"I'm sorry, sir. We don't make appraisals. I can give you the name of an appraiser."

"Don't kid me," I said. "They're Dutch."

He focussed the light a little and leaned down and toyed with a few inches of the string.

"I want a string just like them, fitted to that clasp, and in a hurry," I added.

"How, like them?" He didn't look up. "And they're not Dutch. They're Bohemian."

"O.K., can you duplicate them?"

He shook his head and pushed the velvet pad away as if it soiled him. "In three months, perhaps. We don't blow glass like that in this country. If you wanted them matched—three months at least. And this house would not do that sort of thing at all."

"It must be swell to be that snooty," I said. I put a card under his black sleeve. "Give me a name that will—and not in three months— and maybe not exactly like them."

He shrugged, went away with the card, came back in five minutes and handed it back to me. There was something written on the back.

The old Levantine had a shop on Melrose, a junk shop with everything in the window from a folding baby carriage to a French horn, from a mother-of-pearl lorgnette in a faded plush case to one of those .44 Special Single Action Six-shooters they still make for Western peace officers whose grandfathers were tough.

The old Levantine wore a skull cap and two pairs of glasses and a full beard. He studied my pearls, shook his head sadly, and said: "For twenty dollars, almost so good. Not so good, you understand. Not so good glass."

"How like will they look?"

He spread his firm strong hands. "I am telling you the truth," he said. "They would not fool a baby."

"Make them up," I said. "With this clasp. And I want the others back too, of course."

"Yah. Two o'clock," he said.

Leon Valesanos, the little brown man from Uruguay, made the afternoon papers. He had been found hanging in an unnamed apartment. The police were investigating.

At four o'clock I walked into the long cool bar of the Club Esquire and prowled along the row of booths until I found one where a woman sat alone. She wore a hat like a shallow soup plate with a very wide edge, a brown tailor-made suit with a severe mannish shirt and tie.

I sat down beside her and slipped a parcel along the seat. "You don't open that," I said. "In fact you can slip it into the incinerator as is, if you want to."

She looked at me with dark tired eyes. Her fingers twisted a thin glass that smelled of peppermint. "Thanks." Her face was very pale.

I ordered a highball and the waiter went away. "Read the papers?"

"Yes."

"You understand now about this fellow Copernik who stole your act? That's why they won't change the story or bring you into it."

"It doesn't matter now," she said. "Thank you, all the same. Please—please, show them to me."

I pulled a string of pearls out of the loosely wrapped tissue paper in my pocket and slid them across to her. The silver propeller clasp winked in the light of the wall bracket. The little diamond winked. The pearls were as dull as white soap. They didn't even match in size.

"You were right," she said tonelessly. "They are not my pearls."

The waiter came with my drink and she put her bag on them deftly. When he was gone she fingered them slowly once more, dropped them into the bag and gave me a dry mirthless smile.

"As you said—I'll keep the clasp."

I said slowly: "You don't know anything about me. You saved my life last night and we had a moment, but it was just a moment. You still don't know anything about me. There's a detective downtown named Ybarra, a Mexican of the nice sort, who was on the job when the pearls were found in Waldo's suitcase. That's in case you would like to make sure—"

She said: "Don't be silly. It's all finished. It was a memory. I'm too young to nurse memories. It may be all for the best. I loved Stan Phillips—but he's gone—long gone."

I stared at her, didn't say anything.

She added quietly: "This morning my husband told me something I hadn't known. We are to separate. So I have very little to laugh about today."

"I'm sorry," I said lamely. "There's nothing to say. I may see you sometime. Maybe not. I don't move much in your circle. Good luck."

I stood up. We looked at each other for a moment. "You haven't touched your drink," she said.

"You drink it. That peppermint stuff will just make you sick."

I stood there a moment with a hand hard on the table.

"If anybody ever bothers you," I said, "let me know."

I went out of the bar without looking back at her, got into my car and drove west on Sunset and down all the way to the Coast Highway. Everywhere along the way gardens were full of withered and blackened leaves and flowers which the hot wind had burned.

But the ocean looked cool and languid and just the same as ever. I drove on almost to Malibu and then parked and went and sat on a big rock that was inside somebody's wire fence. It was about half-tide and coming in. The air smelled of kelp. I watched the water for a while and then I pulled a string of Bohemian glass imitation pearls out of my pocket and cut the knot at one end and slipped the pearls off one by one.

When I had them all loose in my left hand I held them like that for a while and thought. There wasn't really anything to think about. I was sure.

"To the memory of Mr. Stan Phillips," I said out loud. "Just another four-flusher."

I flipped her pearls out into the water one by one, at the floating seagulls.

They made little splashes and the seagulls rose off the water and swooped at the splashes.

John Fante

The year 1939 was a defining one for Los Angeles writing. Along with Raymond Chandler's *The Big Sleep* and Nathanael West's *The Day of the Locust*, it saw the publication of *Ask the Dust*, the second novel by John Fante (1909–1983) and a book whose reputation has, like those others, grown slowly but steadily over the years. What sets Fante apart is his celebration of the streets of downtown, its cafeterias and flophouses and dreamers, which came as something of a revelation; before him, no one had ever written about Southern California's nameless, faceless citizens with so much tenderness and love. Shortly after *Ask the Dust* appeared, Fante's family responsibilities—he had four children—led him to turn away from literature in favor of Hollywood, where he wrote screenplays for nearly three decades before returning to fiction in the last years of his life.

from

ASK THE DUST

One night I was sitting on the bed in my hotel room on Bunker Hill, down in the very middle of Los Angeles. It was an important night in my life, because I had to make a decision about the hotel. Either I paid up or I got out: that was what the note said, the note the landlady had put under my door. A great problem, deserving acute attention. I solved it by turning out the lights and going to bed.

In the morning I awoke, decided that I should do more physical exercise, and began at once. I did several bending exercises. Then I washed my teeth, tasted blood, saw pink on the toothbrush, remembered the advertisements, and decided to go out and get some coffee.

I went to the restaurant where I always went to the restaurant and I sat down on the stool before the long counter and ordered coffee. It tasted pretty much like coffee, but it wasn't worth the nickel. Sitting there I smoked a couple of cigarets, read the box scores of the American League games, scrupulously avoided the box scores of National League games, and noted with satisfaction that Joe DiMaggio was still a credit to the Italian people, because he was leading the league in batting.

A great hitter, that DiMaggio. I walked out of the restaurant, stood before an imaginary pitcher, and swatted a home run over the fence. Then I walked down the street toward Angel's Flight, wondering what I would do that day. But there was nothing to do, and so I decided to walk around the town.

I walked down Olive Street past a dirty yellow apartment house that was still wet like a blotter from last night's fog, and I thought of my friends Ethie and Carl, who were from Detroit and had lived there, and I remembered the night Carl hit Ethie because she was going to have a baby, and he didn't want a baby. But they had the baby and that's all there was to that. And I remembered the inside of that apartment, how it smelled of mice and dust, and the old women who sat in the lobby on hot afternoons, and the old woman with the pretty legs. Then there was the elevator man, a broken man from Milwaukee, who seemed to sneer every time you called your floor, as though you were such a fool for choosing that particular floor, the elevator man who always had a tray with sandwiches in the elevator, and a pulp magazine.

Then I went down the hill on Olive Street, past the horrible frame houses reeking with murder stories, and on down Olive to the Philharmonic Auditorium, and I remembered how I'd gone there with Helen to listen to the Don Cossack Choral Group, and how I got bored and we had a fight because of it, and I remembered what Helen wore that day—a white dress, and how it made me sing at the loins when I touched it. Oh that Helen—but not here.

And so I was down on Fifth and Olive, where the big street cars chewed your ears with their noise, and the smell of gasoline made the sight of the palm trees seem sad, and the black pavement still wet from the fog of the night before.

So now I was in front of the Biltmore Hotel, walking along the line of Yellow cabs, with all the cab drivers asleep except the driver near the main door, and I wondered about those fellows and their fund of information, and I remembered the time Ross and I got an address from one of them, how he leered salaciously and then took us to Temple Street, of all places, and whom did we see but two very unattractive ones, and Ross went all the way, but I sat in the parlor and played the phonograph and was scared and lonely.

I was passing the doorman of the Biltmore, and I hated him at once, with his yellow braids and six feet of height and all that dignity, and now a black automobile drove to the curb, and a man got out. He looked rich; and then a woman got out, and she was beautiful, her fur was silver fox, and she was a song across the sidewalk and inside the swinging doors, and I thought oh boy for a little of that, just a day and a night of that, and she was a dream as I walked along, her perfume still in the wet morning air.

Then a great deal of time passed as I stood in front of a pipe shop and looked, and the whole world faded except that window and I stood and smoked them all, and saw myself a great author with that natty Italian briar, and a cane, stepping out of a big black car, and she was there too, proud as hell of me, the lady in the silver fox fur. We registered and then we had cocktails and then we danced awhile, and then we had another cocktail and I recited some lines from Sanskrit, and the world was so wonderful, because every two minutes some gorgeous one gazed at me, the great author, and nothing would do but I had to autograph her menu, and the silver fox girl was very jealous.

Los Angeles, give me some of you! Los Angeles come to me the way I came to you, my feet over your streets, you pretty town I loved you so much, you sad flower in the sand, you pretty town.

A day and another day and the day before, and the library with the big boys in the shelves, old Dreiser, old Mencken, all the boys down there, and I went to see them, Hya Dreiser, Hya Mencken, Hya, hya: there's a place for me, too, and it begins with B, in the B shelf, Arturo Bandini, make way for Arturo Bandini, his slot for his book, and I sat at the table and just looked at the place where my book would be, right there close to Arnold Bennett; not much that Arnold Bennett, but I'd be there to sort of bolster up the B's, old Arturo Bandini, one of the boys, until some girl came along, some scent of perfume through the fiction room, some click of high heels to break up the monotony of my fame. Gala day, gala dream!

But the landlady, the white-haired landlady kept writing those notes: she was from Bridgeport, Connecticut, her husband had died and she was all alone in the world and she didn't trust anybody, she couldn't afford to, she told me so, and she told me I'd have to pay. It was mounting like the national debt, I'd have to pay or leave, every cent of it—five weeks overdue, twenty dollars, and if I didn't she'd hold my trunks; only I didn't have any trunks, I only had a suitcase and it was cardboard without even a strap, because the strap was around my belly holding up my pants, and that wasn't much of a job, because there wasn't much left of my pants.

"I just got a letter from my agent," I told her. "My agent in New York. He says I sold another one; he doesn't say where, but he says he's got one sold. So don't worry Mrs. Hargraves, don't you fret, I'll have it in a day or so."

But she couldn't believe a liar like me. It wasn't really a lie; it was a wish, not a lie, and maybe it wasn't even a wish, maybe it was a fact, and the only way to find out was watch the mailman, watch him closely, check his mail as he laid it on the desk in the lobby, ask him point blank if he had anything for Bandini. But I didn't have to ask after six months at that hotel. He saw me coming and he always nodded yes or no before I asked: no, three million times; yes, once.

One day a beautiful letter came. Oh, I got a lot of letters, but this was the only beautiful letter, and it came in the morning, and it said (he was talking about *The Little Dog Laughed*) he had read *The Little Dog Laughed* and liked it; he said, Mr. Bandini, if ever I saw a genius, you are it. His name was Leonardo, a great Italian critic, only he was not known as a critic, he was just a man in West Virginia, but he was great and he was a critic, and he died. He was dead when my airmail letter got to West Virginia, and his sister sent my letter back. She wrote a beautiful letter too, she was a pretty good critic too, telling me Leonardo had died of consumption but he was happy to the end, and one of the last things he did was sit up in bed and write me about *The Little Dog Laughed*: a dream out of life, but very important; Leonardo, dead now, a saint in heaven, equal to any apostle of the twelve.

Everybody in the hotel read *The Little Dog Laughed*, everybody: a story to make you die holding the page, and it wasn't about a dog, either: a clever story, screaming poetry. And the great editor, none but J. C. Hackmuth with his name signed like Chinese said in a letter: a great story and I'm proud to print it. Mrs. Hargraves read it and I was a different man in her eyes thereafter. I got to stay on in that hotel, not shoved out in the cold, only often it was in the heat, on account of *The Little Dog Laughed*. Mrs. Grainger in 345, a Christian Scientist (wonderful hips, but kinda old) from Battle Creek, Michigan, sitting in the lobby waiting to die, and *The Little Dog Laughed* brought her back to the earth, and that look in her eyes made me know it was right and I was right, but I was hoping she would ask about my finances, how I was getting along, and then I thought why not ask her to lend you a five spot, but I didn't and I walked away snapping my fingers in disgust.

The hotel was called the Alta Loma. It was built on a hillside in reverse, there on the crest of Bunker Hill, built against the decline of the hill, so that the main floor was on the level with the street but the tenth floor was downstairs ten levels. If you had room 862, you got in the elevator and went down eight floors, and if you wanted to go down in the truck room, you didn't go down but up to the attic, one floor above the main floor.

Oh for a Mexican girl! I used to think of her all the time, my Mexican girl. I didn't have one, but the streets were full of them, the Plaza and Chinatown were afire with them, and in my fashion they were mine, this one and that one, and some day when another check came it would be a fact. Meanwhile it was free and they were Aztec princesses and Mayan princesses, the peon girls in the Grand Central Market, in the Church of Our Lady, and I even went to Mass to look at them. That was sacrilegious conduct but it was better than not going to Mass at all, so that when I wrote home to Colorado to my mother I could write with truth. Dear Mother: I went to Mass last Sunday. Down in the Grand Central Market I bumped into the princesses accidentally on purpose. It gave me a chance to speak to them, and I smiled and said excuse me. Those beautiful girls, so happy when you acted like a gentleman and all of that, just to touch them and carry the memory of it back to my room, where dust gathered upon my typewriter and Pedro the mouse sat in his hole, his black eyes watching me through that time of dream and reverie.

Pedro the mouse, a good mouse but never domesticated, refusing to be petted or house-broken. I saw him the first time I walked into my room, and that was during my heyday, when *The Little Dog Laughed* was in the current August issue. It was five months ago, the day I got to town by bus from Colorado with a hundred and fifty dollars in my pocket and big plans in my head. I had a philosophy in

those days. I was a lover of man and beast alike, and Pedro was no
exception; but cheese got expensive, Pedro called all his friends, the
room swarmed with them, and I had to quit it and feed them bread.
They didn't like bread. I had spoiled them and they went elsewhere,
all but Pedro the ascetic who was content to eat the pages of an old
Gideon Bible.

Ah, that first day! Mrs. Hargraves opened the door to my room,
and there it was, with a red carpet on the floor, pictures of the English countryside on the walls, and a shower adjoining. The room was
down on the sixth floor, room 678, up near the front of the hill, so
that my window was on a level with the green hillside and there was
no need for a key, for the window was always open. Through that
window I saw my first palm tree, not six feet away, and sure enough
I thought of Palm Sunday and Egypt and Cleopatra, but the palm
was blackish at its branches, stained by carbon monoxide coming
out of the Third Street Tunnel, its crusted trunk choked with dust
and sand that blew in from the Mojave and Santa Ana deserts.

Dear Mother, I used to write home to Colorado, Dear Mother,
things are definitely looking up. A big editor was in town and I had
lunch with him and we have signed a contract for a number of short
stories, but I won't try to bore you with all the details, dear mother,
because I know you're not interested in writing, and I know Papa
isn't, but it levels down to a swell contract, only it doesn't begin for
a couple of months. So send me ten dollars, mother, send me five,
mother dear, because the editor (I'd tell you his name only I know
you're not interested in such things) is all set to start me out on the
biggest project he's got.

Dear Mother, and Dear Hackmuth, the great editor—they got
most of my mail, practically all of my mail. Old Hackmuth with his
scowl and his hair parted in the middle, great Hackmuth with a pen
like a sword, his picture was on my wall autographed with his signature that looked Chinese. Hya Hackmuth, I used to say, Jesus
how you can write! Then the lean days came, and Hackmuth got
big letters from me. My God, Mr. Hackmuth, something's wrong
with me: the old zip is gone and I can't write anymore. Do you
think, Mr. Hackmuth, that the climate here has anything to do with
it? Please advise. Do you think, Mr. Hackmuth, that I write as well
as William Faulkner? Please advise. Do you think, Mr. Hackmuth,

that sex has anything to do with it, because, Mr. Hackmuth, because, because, and I told Hackmuth everything. I told him about
the blonde girl I met in the park. I told him how I worked it, how
the blonde girl tumbled. I told him the whole story, only it wasn't
true, it was a crazy lie — but it was something. It was writing, keeping in touch with the great, and he always answered. Oh boy, he
was swell! He answered right off, a great man responding to the
problems of a man of talent. Nobody got that many letters from
Hackmuth, nobody but me, and I used to take them out and read
them over, and kiss them. I'd stand before Hackmuth's picture crying out of both eyes, telling him he picked a good one this time, a
great one, a Bandini, Arturo Bandini, me.

The lean days of determination. That was the word for it, determination: Arturo Bandini in front of his typewriter two full days in
succession, determined to succeed; but it didn't work, the longest
siege of hard and fast determination in his life, and not one line
done, only two words written over and over across the page, up and
down, the same words: palm tree, palm tree, palm tree, a battle to
the death between the palm tree and me, and the palm tree won: see
it out there swaying in the blue air, creaking sweetly in the blue air.
The palm tree won after two fighting days, and I crawled out the
window and sat at the foot of the tree. Time passed, a moment or
two, and I slept, little brown ants carousing in the hair on my legs.

Nathanael West

In his brief and singular career Nathanael West (1903–1940) wrote only four novels, which sank into obscurity after his sudden death in a car crash. It took decades for their brilliance and originality to register fully, but West is now recognized as one of the great wild talents of American fiction, a writer with a flair for grotesque black comedy and an alertness to the apocalyptic undercurrents of popular culture. Raised in Manhattan and educated at Brown University, West was employed as a hotel manager before going to Hollywood as a screenwriter, working mostly on such forgettable features as *Rhythm in the Clouds* and *Bachelor Girl.* His Southern California experiences formed the basis of his final novel, *The Day of the Locust* (1939), whose mood of desperate fantasy and simmering violence culminates in an unforgettable finale. The "Hollywood novel" has been a widely practiced genre, but it is safe to say that *The Day of the Locust* remains at or near the top of the list.

from

THE DAY OF THE LOCUST

Faye moved out of the San Berdoo the day after the funeral. Tod didn't know where she had gone and was getting up the courage to call Mrs. Jenning when he saw her from the window of his office. She was dressed in the costume of a Napoleonic vivandiere. By the time he got the window open, she had almost turned the corner of the building. He shouted for her to wait. She waved, but when he got downstairs she was gone.

From her dress, he was sure that she was working in the picture called "Waterloo." He asked a studio policeman where the company was shooting and was told on the back lot. He started toward it at once. A platoon of cuirassiers, big men mounted on gigantic horses, went by. He knew that they must be headed for the same set and followed them. They broke into a gallop and he was soon outdistanced.

The sun was very hot. His eyes and throat were choked with the dust thrown up by the horses' hooves and his head throbbed. The only bit of shade he could find was under an ocean liner made of

painted canvas with real life boats hanging from its davits. He stood
in its narrow shadow for a while, then went on toward a great forty-
foot papier mache sphinx that loomed up in the distance. He had to
cross a desert to reach it, a desert that was continually being made
larger by a fleet of trucks dumping white sand. He had gone only a
few feet when a man with a megaphone ordered him off.

He skirted the desert, making a wide turn to the right, and came
to a Western street with a plank sidewalk. On the porch of the
"Last Chance Saloon" was a rocking chair. He sat down on it and lit
a cigarette.

From there he could see a jungle compound with a water buffalo
tethered to the side of a conical grass hut. Every few seconds the
animal groaned musically. Suddenly an Arab charged by on a white
stallion. He shouted at the man, but got no answer. A little while
later he saw a truck with a load of snow and several malamute dogs.
He shouted again. The driver shouted something back, but didn't
stop.

Throwing away his cigarette, he went through the swinging
doors of the saloon. There was no back to the building and he found
himself in a Paris street. He followed it to its end, coming out in a
Romanesque courtyard. He heard voices a short distance away and
went toward them. On a lawn of fiber, a group of men and women
in riding costume were picnicking. They were eating cardboard
food in front of a cellophane waterfall. He started toward them to
ask his way, but was stopped by a man who scowled and held up a
sign — "Quiet, Please, We're Shooting." When Tod took another
step forward, the man shook his fist threateningly.

Next he came to a small pond with large celluloid swans floating on it. Across one end was a bridge with a sign that read, "To
Kamp Komfit." He crossed the bridge and followed a little path
that ended at a Greek temple dedicated to Eros. The god himself
lay face downward in a pile of old newspapers and bottles.

From the steps of the temple, he could see in the distance a road
lined with Lombardy poplars. It was the one on which he had lost
the cuirassiers. He pushed his way through a tangle of briars, old
flats and iron junk, skirting the skeleton of a Zeppelin, a bamboo
stockade, an adobe fort, the wooden horse of Troy, a flight of
baroque palace stairs that started in a bed of weeds and ended

against the branches of an oak, part of the Fourteenth Street elevated station, a Dutch windmill, the bones of a dinosaur, the upper half of the Merrimac, a corner of a Mayan temple, until he finally reached the road.

He was out of breath. He sat down under one of the poplars on a rock made of brown plaster and took off his jacket. There was a cool breeze blowing and he soon felt more comfortable.

He had lately begun to think not only of Goya and Daumier but also of certain Italian artists of the seventeenth and eighteenth centuries, of Salvator Rosa, Francesco Guardi and Monsu Desiderio, the painters of Decay and Mystery. Looking down hill now, he could see compositions that might have actually been arranged from the Calabrian work of Rosa. There were partially demolished buildings and broken monuments half hidden by great, tortured trees, whose exposed roots writhed dramatically in the arid ground, and by shrubs that carried, not flowers or berries, but armories of spikes, hooks and swords.

For Guardi and Desiderio there were bridges which bridged nothing, sculpture in trees, palaces that seemed of marble until a whole stone portico began to flap in the light breeze. And there were figures as well. A hundred yards from where Tod was sitting a man in a derby hat leaned drowsily against the gilded poop of a Venetian barque and peeled an apple. Still farther on, a charwoman on a stepladder was scrubbing with soap and water the face of a Buddha thirty feet high.

He left the road and climbed across the spine of the hill to look down on the other side. From there he could see a ten-acre field of cockleburs spotted with clumps of sunflowers and wild gum. In the center of the field was a gigantic pile of sets, flats and props. While he watched, a ten-ton truck added another load to it. This was the final dumping ground. He thought of Janvier's "Sargasso Sea." Just as that imaginary body of water was a history of civilization in the form of a marine junkyard, the studio lot was one in the form of a dream dump. A Sargasso of the imagination! And the dump grew continually, for there wasn't a dream afloat somewhere which wouldn't sooner or later turn up on it, having first been made photographic by plaster, canvas, lath and paint. Many boats sink and never reach the Sargasso, but no dream ever entirely disappears.

Somewhere it troubles some unfortunate person and some day, when that person has been sufficiently troubled, it will be reproduced on the lot.

When he saw a red glare in the sky and heard the rumble of cannon, he knew it must be Waterloo. From around a bend in the road trotted several cavalry regiments. They wore casques and chest armor of black cardboard and carried long horse pistols in their saddle holsters. They were Victor Hugo's soldiers. He had worked on some of the drawings for their uniforms himself, following carefully the descriptions in "Les Miserables."

He went in the direction they took. Before long he was passed by the men of Lefebvre-Desnouettes, followed by a regiment of gendarmes d'elite, several companies of chasseurs of the guard and a flying detachment of Rimbaud's lancers.

They must be moving up for the disastrous attack on La Haite Santee. He hadn't read the scenario and wondered if it had rained yesterday. Would Grouchy or Blucher arrive? Grotenstein, the producer, might have changed it.

The sound of cannon was becoming louder all the time and the red fan in the sky more intense. He could smell the sweet, pungent odor of blank powder. It might be over before he could get there. He started to run. When he topped a rise after a sharp bend in the road, he found a great plain below him covered with early nineteenth-century troops, wearing all the gay and elaborate uniforms that used to please him so much when he was a child and spent long hours looking at the soldiers in an old dictionary. At the far end of the field, he could see an enormous hump around which the English and their allies were gathered. It was Mont St. Jean and they were getting ready to defend it gallantly. It wasn't quite finished, however, and swarmed with grips, property men, set dressers, carpenters and painters.

Tod stood near a eucalyptus tree to watch, concealing himself behind a sign that read, "'Waterloo'—A Charles H. Grotenstein Production." Near by a youth in a carefully torn horse guard's uniform was being rehearsed in his lines by one of the assistant directors.

"Vive l'Empereur!" the young man shouted, then clutched his breast and fell forward dead. The assistant director was a hard man to please and made him do it over and over again.

In the center of the plain, the battle was going ahead briskly. Things looked tough for the British and their allies. The Prince of Orange commanding the center, Hill the right and Picton the left wing, were being pressed hard by the veteran French. The desperate and intrepid Prince was in an especially bad spot. Tod heard him cry hoarsely above the din of battle, shouting to the Hollande-Belgians, "Nassau! Brunswick! Never retreat!" Nevertheless, the retreat began. Hill, too, fell back. The French killed General Picton with a ball through the head and he returned to his dressing room. Alten was put to the sword and also retired. The colors of the Lunenberg battalion, borne by a prince of the family of Deux-Ponts, were captured by a famous child star in the uniform of a Parisian drummer boy. The Scotch Greys were destroyed and went to change into another uniform. Ponsonby's heavy dragoons were also cut to ribbons. Mr. Grotenstein would have a large bill to pay at the Western Costume Company.

Neither Napoleon nor Wellington was to be seen. In Wellington's absence, one of the assistant directors, a Mr. Crane, was in command of the allies. He reinforced his center with one of Chasse's brigades and one of Wincke's. He supported these with infantry from Brunswick, Welsh foot, Devon yeomanry and Hanoverian light horse with oblong leather caps and flowing plumes of horsehair.

For the French, a man in a checked cap ordered Milhaud's cuirassiers to carry Mont St. Jean. With their sabers in their teeth and their pistols in their hands, they charged. It was a fearful sight.

The man in the checked cap was making a fatal error. Mont St. Jean was unfinished. The paint was not yet dry and all the struts were not in place. Because of the thickness of the cannon smoke, he had failed to see that the hill was still being worked on by property men, grips and carpenters.

It was the classic mistake, Tod realized, the same one Napoleon had made. Then it had been wrong for a different reason. The Emperor had ordered the cuirassiers to charge Mont St. Jean not knowing that a deep ditch was hidden at its foot to trap his heavy cavalry. The result had been disaster for the French; the beginning of the end.

This time the same mistake had a different outcome. Waterloo, instead of being the end of the Grand Army, resulted in a draw.

Neither side won, and it would have to be fought over again the next day. Big losses, however, were sustained by the insurance company in workmen's compensation. The man in the checked cap was sent to the dog house by Mr. Grotenstein just as Napoleon was sent to St. Helena.

When the front rank of Milhaud's heavy division started up the slope of Mont St. Jean, the hill collapsed. The noise was terrific. Nails screamed with agony as they pulled out of joists. The sound of ripping canvas was like that of little children whimpering. Lath and scantling snapped as though they were brittle bones. The whole hill folded like an enormous umbrella and covered Napoleon's army with painted cloth.

It turned into a route. The victors of Bersina, Leipsic, Austerlitz, fled like schoolboys who had broken a pane of glass. "Sauve qui peut!" they cried, or, rather, "Scram!"

The armies of England and her allies were too deep in scenery to flee. They had to wait for the carpenters and ambulances to come up. The men of the gallant Seventy-Fifth Highlanders were lifted out of the wreck with block and tackle. They were carted off by the stretcher-bearers, still clinging bravely to their claymores.

Christopher Isherwood

By the eve of World War II, Southern California had become home to an astonishing variety of European artists in exile, some on the run from Nazism and fascism, others looking for a peaceful haven in a war-torn world. By the early 1940s, the expatriate community included Bertolt Brecht, Arnold Schoenberg, Theodor Adorno, Thomas and Klaus Mann, Franz Werfel and Alma Mahler, Aldous Huxley, and the screenwriters Berthold and Salka Viertel. In these entries from his copious and unfailingly frank diary, the British writer Christopher Isherwood (1904–1986)—who immigrated to the United States in 1939 with his friend W. H. Auden—provides a lively chronicle of his life in the company of L.A.'s multinational cultural elite during the war. Unlike many of his compatriots, Isherwood did not go home once peace returned to Europe; instead he remained in California, settling in Santa Monica, pursuing enlightenment as a disciple of the Vedanta teacher Swami Prabhavananda, remaining gainfully employed as a screenwriter (his scripts ranged from *The King's Thief* to *Barabbas*), and producing such novels as *Prater Violet* (1945) and *A Single Man* (1964).

from

DIARIES

May 1939

Toward evening, we came into downtown Los Angeles—perhaps the ugliest city on earth. It was a Saturday night, and the streets were swarming with drunks. We saw three sailors carrying a girl into a house, as though they were going to eat her alive. From the hotel, we telephoned Chris Wood. "How wonderful," he said, "to hear an effeminate British voice!"

Next day, we took a taxi into Hollywood. I was amazed at the size of the city, and at its lack of shape. There seemed no reason why it should ever stop. Miles and miles of little houses, wooden or stucco, under a technicolor sky. Miles of little gardens crowded with blossoms and flowering bushes; the architecture is dominated by the vegetation. A city without privacy, where neighbors share each other's lawns and look into each other's bedrooms. The whole place like a world's fair, quite new and already partly in ruins. The only permanent buildings are the schools and the churches. On the hill, giant letters spell "Hollywoodland," but this is only another advertisement. It is silly to say that Hollywood, or any other city, is "unreal." But what the arriving traveller first sees are merely advertisements for a city which doesn't exist.

We had arranged to meet Chris Wood at three o'clock, outside the Owl Drugstore, at the corner of Hollywood and Highland. (I mention the rendezvous because it seemed, at the time, as bizarre as Stanley's meeting with Livingstone, or a date made with one's maiden aunt outside the Potala in Lhasa.) We had an hour to spare, and we spent it finding an apartment.

We chose an apartment house called the Rose Garden, at the bottom of the steep hill on Franklin Avenue, between Cahuenga and Vine. It was a Spanish style building, with a courtyard full of trees and flowers. We had a big living room with a pull-down wall bed, a bathroom, a tiny dressing alcove and a kitchen—all furnished, for thirty-five dollars a month, with gas and light extra. Most of the tenants were small-time movie actors and ex-actors (if there is such a creature as a *live* ex-actor). The place was run by a family named Lundgren, who kept the radio on all day, shouting reports from the various racetracks. Its atmosphere was quite familiar to me: I'd seen a house exactly like it, in a movie about a girl from the Middle West who sets out to conquer Hollywood. It seemed just the right starting point for our adventures in this city.

November 1939

The biggest social event of that fall was an all-star picnic organized by the Huxleys at Tujunga Canyon. There were about thirty guests—Aldous, Maria, their doctor and his family, Bertrand Russell, his wife Peter and two or three stepchildren, Krishnamurti, Rajagopal and his wife Rosalind, Anita Loos, with friends, Salka Viertel and Berthold and Garbo.

I had seen Garbo already, at the Viertels', but we had only been together for a few minutes at a time. She was always full of secrets to be discussed in private with Salka, her closest confidante. She wore the famous straw gardening hat, with slacks, and a tiny patch of plaster between her eyebrows, to prevent wrinkles from forming. She was kittenish, in a rather embarrassing way; and her lack of makeup and general untidiness were obviously calculated. Just the same, I liked her and felt quite at ease in her company. She climbed the figtree in the Viertels' garden to get me some specially ripe figs. I remember how she referred to some business dealings with the studio, and said that one must always pretend to be a child when talking to the front office. She had her own kind of little-girl slyness.

Garbo had been lured to the picnic under false pretences. They had told her it would be a very quiet affair—just the Huxleys and Krishnamurti. Garbo was anxious to meet Krishnamurti. She was naturally drawn to prophets—genuine and otherwise. Salka said that she was very unhappy, restless and frightened. She wanted to be told the secret of eternal youth, the meaning of life—but quickly, in one lesson, before her butterfly attention wandered away again. Hence Stokowski, and Dr. Hauser's salads.

We picnicked on the stony riverbed, high up the canyon, where the road ends. It was a beautiful place, with forest precipices towering above us, not unlike a scene in the lower Alps. Garbo, of course, had her special diet with her in a basket. She and Krishnamurti were put next to each other, but they didn't speak much. I think they were both scared.

Krishnamurti was a slight, sallow little man with a scrubby chin and rather bloodshot eyes, whose face bore only faint traces of the extraordinary beauty he must have had as a boy. He was very quiet and modest, and never talked in ordinary company about philosophy or religion. He seemed fondest of animals and most at ease with children. Gerald complained that he got violently upset about trifles—like catching a train—and showed little sign of inward calm. Certainly, he didn't impress me as Prabhavananda did; but he had a kind of simple dignity which was very touching. And—there was no getting away from it—he had done what no other man alive today has done; he had refused to become a god.

After lunch, most of our party wandered a little further up the canyon, to a place where the forest rangers had built a high wire fence, right across the riverbed, with notices warning against trespass. (I think this was because a dam was under construction, to control the annual floods of the Los Angeles River.) Somebody said it looked like a barricade around a concentration camp. Anita Loos suggested that we should burrow under it, like escaping refugees.

It was a rather sinister joke, and the laughter was a bit forced, as several people began to dig, with their hands or pieces of rock. I remember Bertrand Russell holding forth to Aldous on some philosophical topic and digging as he talked, with the air of a father joining in a game to amuse the children. Only, in this case, he was both parent and child.

Inside a few minutes, there was quite a large, shallow pit. Most of us got into it and wriggled under the wire. It was funny to watch how, having done this, people became grown-ups again and strolled off in twos and threes, talking about the war. I don't know why they had taken all this trouble, for they paid no attention to the scenery. Berthold especially—that born city dweller—might just as well have been walking down Fifth Avenue.

I held back to the end of the procession, because I wanted to walk with Garbo. I had drunk a lot of beer at lunch, and knew no shame. I only wished my friends could see me. As we started out, Garbo said: "As long as we're on this side of fence, let's pretend we're two other people—quite, quite different." "You know," I announced solemnly, "I really wish you *weren't* Garbo. I like you. I think we could have been great friends." At this, Garbo let out a mocking, Mata Hari laugh: "But we *are* friends! You are my dear little brother. All of you are my dear little brothers." "Oh, shut up!" I exclaimed, enormously flattered.

I suppose everybody who meets Garbo dreams of saving her— either from herself, or from Metro-Goldwyn-Mayer, or from some friend or lover. And she always eludes them by going into an act. This is what has made her a universal figure. She is the woman whose life everyone wants to interfere with.

Just as we had finished our stroll and were returning to the wire fence by another path, we met a forest ranger who was cutting some wood. I could hardly believe my luck. What a situation! Of course, he would recognize her at once. Garbo evidently thought so, too, for she pulled down her wide hat brim. I fairly swelled with gallantry. When he asked us what the hell we were doing and took our names, I'd get in front of her and swear she was Miss Smith from Ocean Park, or maybe Mrs. Isherwood—and I'd give him my own address to let me know the amount of the fine. This, I thought, will really impress her.

The ranger looked us both over, quite pleasantly. Then he said: "Do you know what I'm doing here?"

"No," I answered. (This sounded like the build-up for some heavy sarcasm about our trespassing.)

"I'm killing two birds with one stone. This ground has to be cleared; so I'm cutting me some firewood for my cabin."

We passed on. Berthold, who had no straw hat and was nobody's dear little brother, met a different ranger and got his name taken, with severe rebukes for smoking cigarettes in a fire area. Later, he was fined.

December 23. I have decided to write this diary only during the periods when I am waiting for one or other of my friends to get ready. Nearly everybody I know habitually keeps me waiting. Today it was Berthold—for nearly two hours. I said to Frankie, the Filipino houseboy, "The only thing we learn in this life is waiting." "Yes, Mr. Isherwood," he answered, "we are all waiting for the last commencement."

Last night, Vernon and I went with Chris Wood to a big party at the Huxleys'. Their place is like a house in one of the Sherlock Holmes stories, where a murder will be committed. It stands back from the road, completely hidden—a large bungalow built and furnished in baroque-log-cabin style. It used to belong to a rich doctor, one of the founders of the Uplifters' Club, who gave huge parties here during the prohibition epoch. (The Uplifters' Club seems to have started as a sort of retreat for unfaithful, married business men. Now it is a mildly artistic, respectable colony—down in the canyon below the Huxleys' home.)

The walls are hung with semierotic, fetishist pictures of "cruel" ladies in boots, and with romantic photographs of nudes. The lighting is dim and sexually inviting—like an old-fashioned Berlin night spot. In fact, the living room was so dark that a lady—the first person I spoke to—said: "Will you please light my cigarette, so I can see your face?" This was Benita Hume, the actress, rather drunk. I liked her. She was hunting everywhere for Ronald Colman, her husband. He proved to be standing just behind her—the perfect tailor's dummy of a "man of a certain age," with gracefully grey temples, bright handsome dark eyes, an exquisitely discreet little moustache.

He seemed modest, gentle and kind—but now Aldous swam forward out of the warm gloom, like a great, blind deep-sea fish, to introduce me to his brother Julian, just arrived from England for a lecture tour. Julian disappointed me. I had expected him to be more human than Aldous, warmer, less pedantic. Actually, he seemed prim, severe and schoolmasterish, and Aldous, by contrast, appeared much more sympathetic. Julian was very much the official representative of England at war. Behind his sternness, I thought I could detect a certain puritanical sadism—a satisfaction that the lax peace-days were over, and that we'd all got to suffer. Perhaps I am being unjust to him. Perhaps he was only unhappy and tired. But I didn't like the triumphant ring in his voice as he declared that "everybody was agreed" that the Hitler menace had to be removed for ever—it suggested a pleasure in totalitarianism for its own sake, and woe to the dissenters. Somebody asked him if he had come to make propaganda for aid to Britain. No—he was absolutely opposed to propaganda: "We are opposed to it" (meaning the British Foreign Office). "We" actually hoped America wouldn't come into the war; because America's function was to help with economic reconstruction, afterwards. "One's got to make that clear to the people here."

Just to hear what he would reply, I asked him if he thought I should return home. No. If you had a job in the USA, and were earning American money, it was your duty to stay. Not for propaganda, but to represent "the British point of view." Nevertheless, Julian added, it would be a good thing to get into touch with the British in New York. They liked to have reports on the state of opinion in different parts of the country.

The British and French, he assured us, had no intention of attacking on the western front. If the Germans attacked, so much the better. He added that the war would produce an economic revolution in England. The small rentier class would disappear entirely. (Again the grim gleam of satisfaction.)

I turned from him in relief to George Cukor, who was gaily boasting that he had lost sixty pounds by dieting. Then Matthew Huxley took us out to drink champagne secretly in the kitchen. Maria is an absurdly bad hostess—she was so busy with her particular friends, Salka and Anita Loos, that she forgot to make introductions or produce the drinks. When it was finally time for us to leave, she was nowhere to be found.

Berthold, meanwhile, was going after Bertrand Russell, who had adopted Julian's phraseology: "I hear we sank a German submarine yesterday." Berthold's eye gleamed. "I am surprised," he said, with deadly courteousness, "to hear you say '*we*,' Lord Russell. In the last war, your '*I*' made history."

Then old Bob Flaherty, whom I haven't seen since London in 1934, wandered into the house by the wrong door, carrying his big stomach uneasily under his clothes, like something he had stolen. He is working on a U.S. Government film about land erosion. He talked to Julian, who at once became nicer, discussing the habits of gannets and basking sharks.

January 1, 1940

Garbo was at tea with us today. I think Peter is right when he says she's "a dumb cluck." She actually didn't know who Daladier was. If you watch her for a quarter of an hour, you see every one of her famous expressions. She repeats them, quite irrelevantly. There is the iron sternness of Ninotchka, the languorous open-lipped surrender of Camille, Mata Hari's wicked laugh, Christina's boyish toss of the head, Anna Christie's grimace of disgust. She is so amazingly beautiful, so noble, so naturally compelling and commanding, that her ridiculous artificiality, her downright silliness can't spoil the effect.

After tea, Garbo, Salka and Mercedes de Acosta (dressed in a kind of leather uniform) went out for a walk. I went with them as far as our house. They were going to the Uplifters', and I knew they'd have to return along Mesa Road. I kept a lookout, because I wanted Vernon to meet Garbo. When they finally appeared, I ran down the hill, explaining, quite unnecessarily, that I'd "happened" to see them go past. This didn't fool Garbo for a minute. She laughed, and said, with slightly sadistic amusement, "You were waiting for me, weren't you?" But she came back with me. Vernon, out of shyness, was very grand. When Garbo suggested we all three go on the beach, he declined, saying he was too busy.

Today, Garbo was playing the wayward little girl even more energetically than usual. Her dread of being recognized is coupled with a perverse desire to draw attention to herself. She stood on the fence, at the corner of Mabery Road, high above the shore, and theatrically extended her arms toward the sea. She waved at a good-looking boy who was passing. She threw her arms around my neck. She skipped along the beach, darting at the waves to gather foam in her hands. Several people recognized her—and soon our path was continually being crossed by casually strolling groups. But nobody tried to speak to her, and she didn't seem to care.

Specimens of conversation with Garbo:

> She (*taking my hand, and letting go of it again immediately*): We must not do that. This is New Year's Day. It might become a habit.
>
> Me (*politely*): Well, it would be a very good habit—as far as I'm concerned.
>
> She (*in her Hedda Gabler voice*): How can you say that? You do not know me at all. I do not know you. We might make a terrible mistake.
>
> Me (*gallant*): I'm willing to risk that.
>
> She (*raising tragic-ironic eyebrows*): Ah! You are a very *brave* young man!

As we were walking along the beach, she asked me how I had met Vernon. I told her.

> She: And when you came back to New York he was waiting for you? How *wonderful!* Nobody *ever* waited for *me!*
>
> Me (*not knowing the answer to this one*): Look at that bird diving under the wave. What kind is it?
>
> She (*the whimsical little girl*): A duck.
>
> Me: And those big birds flying over there?
>
> She: *Big* ducks.
>
> Me: They're pelicans.
>
> She: *No!* They are all ducks. And the people who live in that beautiful house—they, too, are ducks . . . You know, I am not surprised that people wait for you. You have a funny face.
>
> Me: Thank you.

She: Tell me, are you never sad? Never melancholic?

Me: I used to be sad, but I've given it up. (*etc. etc.*)

January 25. In the afternoon, I went to Chaplin's studio. Chaplin was in a talkative mood. He repeats himself, amplifies, contradicts. (Meltzer later imitated him saying: "The only thing I can say for myself is—I've never been melancholy. Never. Of course, everybody is melancholy around the age of twenty. When I was twenty-one, I was terribly melancholy. I was melancholy until I was thirty. Well, no—not exactly what you could call melancholy. I'm never melancholy, really . . . etc. etc.")

Today, he talked about the portrait painted of him by George Bergen, and its mysterious disappearance from the artist's studio, a few years ago. "Oh, it was a wonderful portrait. He painted me against a white wall, in a white silk jacket—a sort of a pyjama jacket. It was just a good straight portrait—none of that Van Dyck stuff—light and shadow." A day or two after it was finished, someone ripped it right out of its frame. The police searched everywhere, but they never found it.

Chaplin then got on to the subject of the Duke of Windsor, whom he met several times during a trip to Europe. Windsor was then the Prince of Wales. His first question was, "How old are you?" He wanted to know what Chaplin had done in the 1914 war —and when Chaplin told him, "Nothing," there was a frosty silence. Then Chaplin asked him how many uniforms he owned and how he knew which one to wear on any given occasion: did someone tell him? "No one," Windsor replied coldly, "ever tells me to do anything."

Nevertheless, he seems to have taken a great fancy to Chaplin and often asked him down to Fort Belvedere. Chaplin nearly committed a serious breach of etiquette by going into the lavatory when Windsor was already there. This is strictly against the rules.

Although Windsor had at once begun calling Chaplin "Charlie," Chaplin had stuck rigidly to the formal "Sir." He imitated himself saying demurely: "Oh, *no*, Sir! Oh, *yes*, Sir!" Behind all these anecdotes, there was the sparkle of guttersnipe impudence. One sees him in his classic role of debunker of official pomposity, always, everywhere. "How can they possibly go on with all that nonsense," he kept repeating.

Today, they were doing a scene outside on the lot. Hitler and Mussolini (Jack Oakie) are leaving the railway station. The crowd breaks through the police cordon. Madame Mussolini is pushed into it, and the dictators' car drives off without her. Meltzer says that the Hollywood extras are the most miserable, stupid, gutless crowd of people you could find anywhere in the world. The girls were all copies of famous filmstars—literal copies, made without the least imagination or individuality. The men were sullen, round shouldered, down-at-heel gum chewers. They showed not the slightest interest in Chaplin's instructions—but, when the shooting began, they put up a surprisingly convincing performance.

March 31

On Easter, a week ago, we drove out to Victorville and stopped the night at a dude ranch, the Yucca Loma. It lies right in the middle of a desert valley, looking toward high snow-covered mountains—a little colony of luxury dwellings, in ranchero-Mexican style, complete with stables, swimming pool and tennis court. The place is run by a Mrs. Behr, one of those art-corsairs of the desert, in bold gaudy clothes, who speak of their guests as "my little family." The guests were third-rate film notables, some nice college kids, with sound teeth, clear empty eyes and consciences, and a young man dying of TB who publishes a weekly newspaper supposed to be written by his dogs.

A terrible, shameful, almost insane attack of self-pity and despair. "I hate this place," I told Vernon, "I hate all Americans. I don't belong here. I shall have to go back to Europe." Poor Vernon was much distressed. And of course, I didn't mean what I said about the Americans or the ranch. I meant: I hate myself.

Actually, in my sane moments, I love this country. I love it just because I *don't* belong. Because I'm not involved in its traditions, not born under the curse of its history. I feel free here. I'm on my own. My life will be what I make of it.

I love the ocean, and the orange groves, and the desert, and the big mountains around Arrowhead, where the snow comes down to the shores of the lake and you see the eagles circling above. Nature is unfriendly, dangerous, utterly aloof. However hard I may try, I can't turn her into a stage set for my private drama. Thank God I can't. She refuses to become a part of my neurosis.

July 1940

A couple of days ago, on Sunset Boulevard, I picked up two youths who were thumbing a ride. One of them carried a radio. As soon as they were in the car, he asked me: "Say—when you stopped to pick us up, what did you think this was?" "I don't know," I said, "I didn't notice it particularly." "You didn't think it was a suitcase?" "Well—yes, I probably did. Why?" "You see?" The boy turned to his friend and grinned: evidently this decided some argument they had been having. "It's like this," the other boy explained to me: "If some folks notice you've got a suitcase with you, they won't stop—because they think maybe you might be carrying a gun in it." I pointed out that he might just as easily be carrying a gun in the pocket of his pants. The boy thought this over for a moment, quite seriously. "Yes," he said at last, "I guess you're right."

July 8. This morning, the embassy called on all British actors between eighteen and thirty-one to return to England.

Lunch with the Manns, at the new house they've leased for the summer on Rockingham. A big, half-empty place with an Italian garden and swimming pool. Klaus and I immediately got into an argument about the war. It seems that Wystan is being very cagey in New York—not telling anyone what he really thinks. I tried to explain my position and asked Klaus what he thought I should do. He said that I should "make a definite statement" in support of the Allies—since my silence is being misrepresented. Just a little statement; once or twice would be enough. I answered that, even if I believed this, I would hesitate to make propaganda, at a safe distance of six thousand miles, encouraging other people to get killed in my place. Klaus said I was being too "objective."

Of course, he added, he himself was a pacifist: he couldn't possibly kill anyone personally. But pacifism couldn't possibly be applied to every case: if you let the Nazis kill everyone, you allowed civilization to be destroyed. I quoted Aldous's argument, that civilization dies anyhow of blood poisoning the moment it takes up its enemies' weapons and exchanges crime for crime. Klaus replied that this view—that no war is always better than any war—seemed to him "merely cynical."

So we argued, each contradicting himself and slipping, as one always does, from one language to another—from the language of ethics to the language of politics, and back again. Klaus said that pacifism nowadays merely assists the work of the fifth column and the Nazis. That, I answered, is why I prefer to keep my mouth shut. Our talk was quite friendly, and I was glad, at any rate, to have had it out in the open.

At lunch were Thomas and Frau Mann. Despite their terrible anxiety over Heinrich and Golo (who were interned in France and may have been handed over to the Nazis) Thomas was urbane as ever. If the English saved democracy, he said, he would gladly tolerate all their faults, even the Oxford accent. He remembered how kind Galsworthy had been—lending the Manns his car while they were in London, and himself travelling by bus. Thomas told me how a sanatorium for consumptives in Colorado had invited him to visit them, adding as an inducement: "We have tried to make everything as much like *The Magic Mountain* as possible."

He looks wonderfully young for his age—perhaps because, as a boy, he was elderly and staid. With careful, deliberate gestures, he chooses a cigar, examines a cognac bottle, opens a furniture catalogue—giving each object his full, serious attention. Yet he isn't in the least pompous. He has great natural dignity. He is a true scholar, a gentlemanly householder, a gracefully ironic pillar of society—solid right through. He would be magnificent at his own trial. Indeed, he has been making his speech for the defence ever since he left Germany.

Klaus looks very tired. He is paler, fatter and has a bald patch like a tonsure on the crown of his head. He chain-smokes nervously. But, as always, there is something very attractive and even stimulating about him. He isn't a despairing loafer, like so many of the others. He's always on the alert, always working. He has energy and courage. He says he has started writing in English. He speaks very fluently nowadays.

September 23, 1942

Yesterday, the Swami drove down to visit us. The day passed off quite pleasantly, although there were some embarrassing silences. The Swami, as always, was very quiet and polite. We drove him up to Trabuco. "Iss smoking parmitted here?" he asked. It isn't. But he smoked.

How beautiful this house is! I feel as if I could never tire of being in it. It has a wonderful air of privacy—from the moment you enter the garden, with its high cypress hedges, bottlebrush trees and Cape honeysuckle. At first, you see only the tiled roof of the house, below you, on the very edge of the cliff. It comes gradually into view as you descend the steps, terrace by terrace, past the oleander bushes and the pomegranates and the orange and scarlet zinnias. On the balustrades of the garden stairs are two green Chinese dragons, and four elephants, two white and two green, with long crafty eyes. Gerald calls one pair of elephants "Apoplexy" and the other "Liver."

At the bottom of the steps is the patio, with a banana plant, a fish pool full of big goldfish and lotuses, an ugly blue and white Della Robbia plaque half-hidden by the ivy on the wall, and an outdoor fireplace with antique Spanish fire irons, within which a monster fern is growing. Behind the waxy white blossoms of a gardenia in a tub, a great glass screen shows you the terrace and the ocean: a blindingly illuminated picture which seems as unreal as back projection in a movie. The walls of the house are netted with quivering light. At the foot of the curving staircase to the balcony, there is a dwarf monkey puzzle in an Italian majolica pot, on which a sportsman is painted, out hunting with his gun and dogs. The balcony leads to Chris's and Gerald's bedrooms: there is an old ship's bell hanging above it, which is used to summon Gerald down to his meals. A corkscrew staircase, cut out of the rock, takes you from the patio to the bedroom in which I sleep. The steps are pitch-dark, even in the daytime: for some reason, they remind me of *Macbeth*. They would do as an air-raid shelter, if necessary. Chris keeps his musical boxes there.

The front of the house rises sheer above the cliff. The ocean is right at your feet, bubbling and creaming over huge lava reefs. The house stands on an outcrop of lava, which makes a firm foundation and enriches the soil of the vegetable garden. The air is so full of salt that very little can be gotten to grow on the terrace—only the cypress, and the aloes, like twisting green octopi with bloodstained tentacles, and an Australian tree with white blossoms and a flaky bark. The ironwork has rusted away to thin wires.

The day begins, usually, with thick fog—blowing up against the cliff face or standing out to sea in a dark wall. There are times when the ocean is clear, but grey and empty and unspeakably forlorn, with a single great gull flying across it—like the Spirit moving upon the face of the waters. Rarely, the sunshine comes early, lighting all the coast as far as Seal Rock, with fishing boats standing out white and far against the hard blue edge of the morning. The sun usually emerges around noon, and by teatime it has left the patio, and the seaward terrace is too hot to sit in. When the sun sets into a clear sea, with a low bar of cloud down along the horizon, its disk grows distorted, bulging and flattening into a glowing pyramid of red coal, without a top. Then, within half a minute, it slides away under the edge of the world, and suddenly the ocean seems enormous and cold, teeming with wrinkled waves, unutterably wet.

Tonight, the evening was grey, with sad steamy clouds and sharp gold gleams on the sea. The gulls winged past silently, just after sundown, northward. A small black dog ran out across the lawn of the villa on the headland with the striped garden umbrellas, and barked wildly, too late. Down below on the reef, on old grizzled gull was standing. He looked up at me, as I leaned over the terrace railing. "Don't trust that facile feeling of oneness," he warned me. "Oh yes—I know we're brothers—in a sense. But you wouldn't care for our life."

September 29

Went to the barber's. Whenever I've been out of town for some time, Hollywood Boulevard affects me with the most violent kind of depression. The bottles of Wildroot Tonic and Oil seemed scarcely to have the heart to keep up their pathetic pretence a moment longer. "We know we're not the best tonic," they sadly admitted. "We know we can't really stop your hair from falling out. We know it doesn't really matter about being well-groomed, or attracting girls, or making the grade, or selling your personality. We know you'll grow old and die, and others will be born, and new tonics will supersede us, with new slogans and old lies on the label." They despaired, already. And the tiled barber's shop, with MOVIE-LAND picked out in gold lettering on the arch above the basins, was like a tragic museum of stale, twenty-year-old glamor. And the gallantly lecherous customer in his fifties with a neat military moustache, who told dirty jokes to the barber and flirted with the manicurist— he despaired, behind his alert, smirking smile. And the manicurist glanced at herself in the mirror without enthusiasm: she was no longer quite fresh. Her voice was weary as she told the customer about her dog. What age was he? "Oh, he's ten years. He's *old*." These people, and the crowds in the street, and the trash in the shop windows, and the movie placards, and the advertisements warning you to get wise, get smart, get relaxed, get well, get sunburnt, get thrilled, get rich—and the newspapers with Japs fleeing and Stalingrad still unfallen—all these, silently or aloud, were yelling their despair because the "life" of *Life* magazine is deader than death, and there is nothing—no hope, no comfort, no refuge anywhere—but in the unthinkable, bottomless, horrible immensity of God.

When I tried to tell Peggy all this, she understood at once. "It's those *pitiful* little shops," she said. I'm spending the night at Alto Cedro, and shall go back to Laguna Beach tomorrow. This is Ben's birthday. He has a snare drum and Derek a clarinet.

Ben's beagle Cerberus has all the airs of a lapdog. He's like a son-in-law of whom Peggy and the rest of the family don't altogether approve. Peggy looked out of the window the other morning and saw Cerberus in the garden wistfully confronting a rabbit, with a look which seemed to say, "Oh dear—*why* can't we be friends?" He didn't attempt to chase it, and this shocked Peggy. Even in a pacifist household, the women like a man to be a man.

October 20. Denny is out of hospital and has gone to stay at the Beverly Hills Hotel. He has decided that he needs a little luxury to help his convalescence. I went down there today and swam in their pool. It is a USO Center, and servicemen are allowed in at certain hours. There was one very drunk sailor-boy who told us all that he was on leave and going to see his folks in Alabama. He whistled like a steam engine, out of tune, and did running dives into the pool, splashing everybody from head to foot. He was under the impression that he had a date with a movie star named Ellen, or maybe Helen, he wasn't certain; so he asked each girl in turn: "Hey, beautiful—what's your name?" A snooty-looking brunette who must have been sultry in the 1920s regarded him with extreme pain: she was reading Vivekananda's book on raja yoga. Denny claimed that she was a character from a Scott Fitzgerald novel who'd passed out during a wild party and slept for twenty years. Now she'd just woken up and thought this was all a horrible dream. Finally, the Alabama boy, who'd so far been tolerated with indulgent smiles, scandalized everybody by shouting to an old lady, crippled by arthritis: "Hey, beautiful—come on in! The water's fine!"

Still no word from the draft board. It's very odd. Can they possibly be considering my appeal? I try to keep my mind prepared for a call at any moment. But inevitably, after all this delay, a voice begins to whisper, "Who knows? Maybe they've forgotten you. Maybe you won't have to go."

Very hot weather. At night, the cicadas make a tremendous racket. One of them, which is nearly colorless, is as loud and shrill as a police whistle. A big brushfire in the hills above Malibu. The sun set right behind a ridge that was burning—lighting up the great crimson-purple cloud of smoke hanging in the airless sky. It looked like a volcano in eruption.

1943

February 4. Went down to Santa Monica in the morning and walked along the front. The cool winter sunshine. The big shabby hotels, now taken over by the navy. The reek of hamburgers, popcorn and pickles. The tumbledown bathhouses, smelling of old men, sweat and urine. "Muscle Beach," with the Mexican boys doing back flips. The great engines of amusement, standing idle. The pelicans and the human anglers. Goodbye. Goodbye. I shall see you often—but differently, I suppose.

Soldiers everywhere. The army will soon have absorbed all other types of life. Civilians will creep around the streets like clergymen, rare and queer.

August 18

Last night, because I was bored, I found myself doing what I would least have expected—hunting up Tennessee Williams. I located him, after some search, at a very squalid rooming house called The Palisades, at the other end of town—sitting typing a film story in a yatchting cap, amidst a litter of dirty coffee cups, crumpled bed linen and old newspapers. He seemed not in the least surprised to see me. In fact, his manner was that of the meditative sage to whose humble cabin the world-weary wanderer finally returns. He took it, with discreetly concealed amusement, as the most natural thing in the world that I should be having myself a holiday from the monastery. We had supper together on the pier and I drank quite a lot of beer and talked sex the entire evening. Tennessee is the most relaxed creature imaginable: he works till he's tired, eats when he feels like it, sleeps when he feels inclined. The autoglide has long since broken down, so Tennessee has stopped paying for it, and the dealer is suing him, and he doesn't give a damn. He also has a fight on with Metro. He probably won't stay here long.

August 20. Yesterday morning, I cycled to Malibu and back before breakfast: it was much further than I expected. In the evening Berthold took me to the Brechts'; [Hans] Eisler was there, too. I liked Brecht immediately. He has close-cropped hair, very deep-set eyes and a pale, scarred face: he dresses in loose grey clothes and felt slippers, like a convict prepared for electrocution. He's very lively, alert and nervous, with a high-pitched voice, not unlike Forster's. Frau Brecht, who's a Jewess, looks very strange; beautiful, in a way, and almost Chinese. She probably knows this, because she has smoothed her black hair back and tied it into a knot, and she wears the clothes of a Chinese peasant woman: a short jacket with a high collar and dark blue trousers. Eisler, the Red composer, is a little moon-faced man with peg teeth, short fat legs and a flat-backed head, who talks very rapidly in a loud unharmonious voice, with whirring wittiness. Stefan retired early to bed, with a deep bow: he had a chemistry test in the morning.

Spent most of today down on the beach with Tommy Viertel. He asks questions all the time—about politics, Buddhism, literature, everything—with his laborious, impeded articulation, listening very carefully and earnestly to my replies. I enjoy this, partly out of vanity, but also because I always like trying to state any problem in the simplest possible terms, and my frustrated schoolmaster instinct hasn't been indulged for a long time.

This evening, Berthold has been reading me poetry—Hölderlin, Brentano, and some of his own. It was very enjoyable—this time, I was the student, and I got Berthold to explain to me the difficult lines in "Heidelberg" and the three marvellous versions of "Dichtermut." We almost wept with excitement. It was like the old times— or as near as we can ever come to them now. For Berthold really does seem to be changed. He looks so much older, so furrowed and battered, and he is so desperately nervous. His preoccupation with the purely ephemeral aspect of this war—the opinions of commentators, the speeches of politicians, the exaggerations of journalists— sometimes seems just childish. I think he thinks of himself as a kind of prophet—it's the last pitiful bit of fancy dress in the depleted wardrobe of his egotism—and in this he is like most of his fellow refugees. They can't see how futile this role is. Even if they are right, occasionally—who cares? The war moves too fast. Prophecy is for peacetime. And they are seldom right: their judgment is shaken by their hope and their fear. They have nothing to contribute to the postwar world but the idea of mercy—they might be truly great in that, because they, as victims, have the right to forgive—but how many of them are capable of mercy? Berthold far more than most. But he's so unstable. A breath of emotion can set him raving.

September 20. Down to Santa Monica. Lunch with the Viertels. Supper with the Brechts. We talked about the adaptation of *The Duchess of Malfi* which Brecht has made for Elizabeth Bergner. Aside from some very ingenious rearrangements and cuts, Brecht's object has been to give Ferdinand a stronger motive for his persecution of the Duchess. Brecht says he must have been in love with her. In order to point this up, he has written in about a dozen lines of verse, in German; and these he wants translated into Elizabethan English. So he switches on all his charm, to woo me as a possible collaborator.

Until Berthold arrived. Then, fatally, we got on to the subject of Vedanta, and Brecht fairly blew his top. To him, it's all fascism and superstitious nonsense. Frau Brecht joined in—like a Salvation Army lass—calling on me to repent and remember my duty as a revolutionary writer. Berthold took my side—or rather, he apologized for my deviation, and tried to suggest that it was only temporary; that, in fact, I might be regarded as a sort of spy in the enemy's camp. If only—after two or three years—I'd write a book "showing up" mysticism once and for all, then my retirement would have been well worth while. All this was fairly funny, until they left me and got on to Huxley. Brecht said he was "verkauft"—had sold out. I was so angry that I nearly got up and left the house at once. I *did* leave very shortly afterwards.

Brecht is obviously sincere, in his way. But, humanly, he's no more worthy to criticize Aldous than I am to criticize Swami. He's just as arrant an individualist as I am, and pretty much of an opportunist, too. I asked him what he'd do if a local soviet committee of peasants didn't like his writing, and he answered that he'd talk them into liking it. In other words, he accepts the will of the majority as long as it's his will. I think it was extremely smart and realistic of him to align himself with the communists: they'll probably win out in Germany, anyway, and then he'll be on top. What I object to is his claim to be more *honest* than a man like Aldous, and his conviction that everyone who disagrees with him is getting a paycheck from the capitalist bosses.

Stefan, the ever-polite, sensed my rage and discreetly accompanied me to the bus stop. He would order my execution without flicking an eyelash, but, in contrast to his father, he has beautiful manners. . . .

April 13, 1944

Some Santa Monica notes: Early morning fog. The rocks of the breakwater, the pier, the dotted line of fishing boats in the harbor are very black and precise, but they only serve to heighten the immensity and mystery of the hazy ocean and sky. Like a statement about God.

Sign at Sam's hot-dog stand: "The California Bank does not serve food. Sam the Greek does not cash checks."

Early morning. A very black Negro driving a black truck at tremendous speed, like the last fragment of the night hurrying away before the rising sun.

I am reading a book about God in a coffee shop. The waitress thinks it's a crime story and asks, "Have you caught him yet?" I answer, "No—unfortunately."

The astonishing American talent for ignoring the radio. Denny has it. He turns it on full blast and then carries on a shouted conversation about some serious philosophical subject.

Some of our favorite catchphrases: "Famed in song and story." "All ghoul and a yard wide." "Quoi qu'il soit qu'il soit." (Dog French for "Be that as it may.") "As far as the eye can see." "Der sogenannte . . . . besteht aus zwei Teilen, und zwar, der Vorderteil und der Hinterteil." (This was supposed to parody a German professor lecturing.) "Dans la plus grande manière." (Dog French for "In the biggest way.") And all kinds of expressions borrowed and sometimes inverted from Gerald Heard: "Some of us who care a little less for this thing." "Appalling instantaneity," etc. etc.

Notice in Doc Law's Friendship Bar in the Canyon: "Dine in a nautical atmosphere. Open during blackouts and all clear. In case of direct hit we close immediately. Latitude 34.1. North. Longitude 118.30 West. Course straight ahead."

November 16. The sun is just going down into a sheeted calm of peacock blue and gold, with the islands all outlined in blue-black contours against a pure sky like a Japanese print. Tomorrow I leave for Laguna. Sad, because of the failure with Vernon. The bitterest part of it is that, if I'm not allowed to love him as a little brother, I find that, as an acquaintance, a casual house-companion, I rather dislike him. And yet I feel sorry and protective and hate to see him making things so hard for himself. I'm sure it's good for him to be here. He's painting quite a lot, and meditating (which is more than I am) and this place with its quietness and beauty is what he needs. The sun has touched the horizon. The land has grown suddenly very dark and densely wooded and still. Great winding trails of golden light on the water. Goodbye. Nothing now but the red horizon-glow. It's turning chilly. I must go in.

F. Scott Fitzgerald

F. Scott Fitzgerald (1895–1940) has become something of an archetype of the writer destroyed by Hollywood, the novelist squandering his talent in pursuit of the motion-picture industry's easy cash. While the image has some validity, it's also true that Fitzgerald never stopped writing fiction during his time in Southern California, from the Pat Hobby stories, with their O. Henryish vignettes of life inside the studio system, to *The Last Tycoon*, the ambitious novel (based on the life of producer Irving Thalberg) that he left unfinished at his death. "Last Kiss" is one such effort, a fairy tale of Hollywood never published during Fitzgerald's lifetime, and ultimately cannibalized for *The Last Tycoon*.

LAST KISS

It was a fine pure feeling to be on top. One was very sure that everything was for the best, that the lights shone upon fair ladies and brave men, that pianos dripped the right notes and that the young lips singing them spoke for happy hearts. All these beautiful faces, for instance, must be absolutely happy.

And then in a twilit rhumba, a face passed Jim's table that was not quite happy. It had gone before Jim decided this, but it remained fixed on his retina for some seconds thereafter. It belonged to a girl almost as tall as he was, with opaque brown eyes and cheeks as delicate as a Chinese tea-cup.

"There you go," said his hostess, following his glance. She sighed. "It happens in a second and I've tried for years."

Jim wanted to answer:

—But you've had your day—three husbands. How about me? Thirty-five and still trying to match every woman with a lost childhood love, still finding in all girls the similarities and not the differences.

The next time the lights were dim he wandered through the tables toward the entrance hall. Here and there friends hailed him—more than the usual number of course, because his contract as

251

a producer had been noticed in the *Hollywood Reporter* that morning, but Jim had made other steps up and he was used to that. It was a charity ball and by the bar ready to perform was the man who imitated wall paper and Bob Bordley with a sandwich board on his back which read:

AT TEN TONIGHT

IN THE HOLLYWOOD BOWL

SONJA HEINE

WILL SKATE ON

HOT SOUP

Nearby Jim saw the producer whom he was displacing tomorrow, having an unsuspecting drink with the agent who had contrived his ruin. Next to the agent was the girl whose face had seemed sad as she danced by in the rhumba.

"Oh, Jim," said the agent, "Pamela Knighton—your future star."

She turned to him with professional eagerness. What the agent's voice had said to her was: "Look alive! This *is* somebody."

"Pamela's joined my stable," said the agent. "I want her to change her name to Boots."

"I thought you said Toots," the girl laughed.

"Toots or Boots. It's the oo-oo sound. Cutie shoots Toots. Judge Hoots. No conviction possible. Pamela is English. Her real name is Sybil Higgins."

Jim felt the deposed producer looking at him with an infinite something in his eyes—not hatred, not jealousy but a profound and curious astonishment that asked "Why? Why? For God's sake, why?" More disturbed by this than by enmity, Jim surprised himself by asking the English girl to dance. As they faced each other on the floor he felt a rising exultation.

"Hollywood's a good place," he said, as if to forestall any criticism from her. "You'll like it. Most English girls do—they don't expect too much. I've had luck working with English girls."

"Are you a director?"

"I've been everything—from press agent on. I've just signed a producer's contract that begins tomorrow."

"I like it here," she said after a minute. "You can't help expecting things. But if they don't come I could always teach school again."

Jim leaned back and looked at her—the impression was of pink and silver frost. She was so far from a school marm, even a school marm in a Western, that he laughed. But again he saw that there was something sad and a little lost within the triangle formed by lips and eyes.

"Who are you with tonight?" he asked.

"Joe Becker," she answered naming the agent. "Myself and three other girls."

"Look—I have to go out for half an hour. To see a man—this is not phoney. Believe me. Will you come along for company and night air?"

She nodded.

On the way they passed his hostess who looked inscrutably at the girl and shook her head slightly at Jim. Out in the clear California night he liked his big new car for the first time, liked it better than driving himself. The streets through which they rolled were quiet at this hour and the limousine stole silently along the darkness. Miss Knighton waited for him to speak.

"What did you teach in school?" he asked.

"Sums. Two and two are five and all that."

"It's a long jump from that to Hollywood."

"It's a long story."

"It can't be very long—you're about eighteen."

"Twenty." Anxiously she asked: "Do you think that's too old?"

"Lord, no! It's a beautiful age. I know—I'm twenty-one myself and the arteries are only beginning to harden."

She looked at him gravely, estimating his age and keeping it to herself.

"I want to hear the long story," he said.

She sighed.

"Well, a lot of old men fell in love with me. Old, old men—I was an old man's darling."

"You mean old gaffers of twenty-two?"

"They were between sixty and seventy. This is all true. So I became a gold-digger and dug enough money out of them to come to New York. I walked into Twenty-one the first day and Joe Becker saw me."

"Then you've never been in pictures?" he asked.

"Oh yes—I had a test this morning."

Jim smiled.

"And you don't feel bad taking money from all those old men?" he inquired.

"Not really," she said, matter-of-fact. "They enjoyed giving it to me. Anyhow it wasn't really money. When they wanted to give me presents I'd send them to a jeweler I knew and afterwards I'd take the present back to the jeweler and get four fifths of the cash."

"Why, you little chiseller!"

"Yes," she admitted placidly. "Somebody told me how. I'm out for all I can get."

"Didn't they mind—the old men I mean—when you didn't wear their presents?"

"Oh, I'd wear them—once. Old men don't see very well, or remember. But that's why I haven't got any jewelry." She broke off. "I understand you can rent jewelry here."

Jim looked at her again and then laughed.

"I wouldn't bother about it. California's full of old men."

They had twisted into a residential district. As they turned a corner Jim picked up the speaking tube.

"Stop here." He turned to Pamela. "I have some dirty work to do."

He looked at his watch, got out and went up the street to a building with the names of several doctors on a sign. He went past the sign walking slowly, and presently a man came out of the building and followed him. In the darkness between two lamps Jim went close, handed him an envelope and spoke concisely. The man walked off in the opposite direction and Jim returned to the car.

"I'm having all the old men bumped off," he explained. "There's some things worse than death."

"Oh, I'm not free now," she assured him. "I'm engaged."

"Oh." After a minute he asked, "To an Englishman?"

"Well—naturally. Did you think—"She stopped herself but too late.

"Are we that uninteresting?" he asked.

"Oh, no." Her casual tone made it worse. And when she smiled, at the moment when an arc light shone in and dressed her beauty up to a white radiance, it was more annoying still.

"Now you tell *me* something," she said. "Tell me the mystery."

"Just money," he answered almost absently. "That little Greek doctor keeps telling a certain lady that her appendix is bad—we need her in a picture. So we bought him off. It's the last time I'll ever do anyone else's dirty work."

She frowned.

"Does she really need her appendix out?"

He shrugged.

"Probably not. At least that rat wouldn't know. He's her brother-in-law and he wants the money."

After a long time Pamela spoke judicially.

"An Englishman wouldn't do that."

"Some would," he said shortly, "—and some Americans wouldn't."

"An English gentleman wouldn't."

"Aren't you getting off on the wrong foot," he suggested, "if you're going to work here."

"Oh, I like Americans all right—the civilized ones."

From her look Jim took this to include him, but far from being appeased he had a sense of outrage.

"You're taking chances," he said. "In fact I don't see how you dared come out with me. I might have had feathers under my hat."

"You didn't bring a hat," she said placidly. "Besides Joe Becker said to. There might be something in it for me."

After all he was a producer and you didn't reach eminence by losing your temper—except on purpose.

"I'm *sure* there's something in it for you," he said, listening to a stealthy treacherous purr creep into his voice.

"Are you?" she demanded. "Do you think I'll stand out at all—or am I just one of the thousands."

"You stand out already," he continued on the same note. "Everyone at the dance was looking at you."

He wondered if this was even faintly true. Was it only he who had fancied some uniqueness?

"You're a new type," he went on. "A face like yours might give American pictures a—a more civilized tone."

This was his arrow—but to his vast surprise it glanced off.

"Oh, do you think so?" she cried. "Are you going to give me a chance?"

"Why certainly." It was hard to believe that the irony in his voice was missing its mark. "Except, of course, after tonight there'll be so much competition that—"

"Oh, I'd rather work for you," she declared; "I'll tell Joe Becker—"

"Don't tell him anything," he interrupted.

"Oh, I won't. I'll do just as you say."

Her eyes were wide and expectant. Disturbed, he felt that words were being put in his mouth or slipping from him unintended. That so much innocence and so much predatory toughness could go side by side behind this gentle English voice.

"You'd be wasted in bits," he began. "The thing is to get a fat part—" He broke off and began again, "You've got such a strong personality that—"

"Oh, don't!" He saw tears blinking in the corners of her eyes. "Let me just keep this to sleep on tonight. You call me in the morning—or when you need me."

The car came to rest at the strip of red carpet in front of the dance. Seeing Pamela, the crowd bulged forward grotesquely in the spilt glare of the drum lights. They held their autograph books at the ready, but failing to recognize her, they sighed back behind the ropes.

In the ballroom he danced her to Becker's table.

"I won't say a word," she whispered. From her evening case she took a card with the name of her hotel penciled on it. "If any other offers come I'll refuse them."

"Oh no," he said quickly.

"Oh yes." She smiled brightly at him and for an instant the feeling Jim had had on seeing her came back. There was an impression in her face, at least, of a rich warm sympathy, of youth and suffering side by side. He braced himself for a final quick slash to burst the scarcely created bubble.

"After a year or so—" he began. But the music and her voice overrode him.

"I'll wait for you to call. You're the—you're the most civilized American I've ever met."

She turned her back as if embarrassed by the magnificence of her compliment. Jim started back to his table—then seeing his hostess talking to someone across his empty chair, he turned obliquely away. The room, the evening had gone raucous—the blend of music and voices seemed inharmonious and accidental and his eyes covering the room saw only jealousies and hatreds—egos tapping like drum beats up to a fanfare. He was not above the battle as he had thought.

He started for the coat-room thinking of the note he would dispatch by waiter to his hostess: "You were dancing so I——" Then he found himself almost upon Pamela Knighton's table, and turning again he took another route toward the door.

II

A picture executive can do without creative intelligence but not without tact. Tact now absorbed Jim Leonard to the exclusion of everything else. Power should have pushed diplomacy into the background, leaving him free, but instead it intensified all his human relations—with the executives, with the directors, writers, actors and technical men assigned to his unit, with department heads, censors and "men from the East" besides. So the stalling off of one lone English girl, who had no weapon except the telephone and a little note that reached him from the entrance desk, should have been no problem at all.

Just passing by the studio and thought of you and of our ride. There have been some offers but I keep stalling Joe Becker. If I move I will let you know.

A city full of youth and hope spoke in it—in its two transparent lies, the brave falsity of its tone. It didn't matter to her—all the money and glory beyond the impregnable walls. She had just been passing by—just passing by.

That was after two weeks. In another week, Joe Becker dropped in to see him.

"About that little English girl, Pamela Knighton—remember? How'd she strike you?"

"Very nice."

"For some reason she didn't want me to talk to you." Joe looked out the window. "So I suppose you didn't get along so well that night."

"Sure we did."

"The girl's engaged, you see, to some guy in England."

"She told me that," said Jim, annoyed. "I didn't make any passes at her if that's what you're getting at."

"Don't worry—I understand those things. I just wanted to tell you something about her."

"Nobody else interested?"

"She's only been here a month. Everybody's got to start. I just want to tell you that when she came into Twenty-one that day the barflies dropped like—like flies. Let me tell you—in one minute she was the talk of Cafe Society."

"It must have been great," Jim said dryly.

"It was. And LaMarr was there that day too. Listen—Pam was all alone, and she had on English clothes I guess, nothing you'd look at twice—rabbit fur. But she shone through it like a diamond."

"Yeah?"

"Strong women wept into their vichysoisse. Elsa Maxwell—"

"Joe, this is a busy morning."

"Will you look at her test?"

"Tests are for make-up men," said Jim, impatiently. "I never believe a good test. And I always suspect a bad one."

"Got your own ideas, eh."

"About that. There've been a lot of bad guesses in projection rooms."

"Behind desks too," said Joe rising.

A second note came after another week.

When I phoned yesterday one secretary said you were away and one said you were in conference. If this is a run-around tell me. I'm not getting any younger. Twenty-one is staring me in the face—and you must have bumped off all the old men.

Her face had grown dim now. He remembered the delicate cheeks, the haunted eyes, as from a picture seen a long time ago. It was easy to dictate a letter that told of changed plans, of new casting, of difficulties which made it impossible. . . .

He didn't feel good about it but at least it was finished business. Having a sandwich in his neighborhood drugstore that night, he looked back at his month's work as good. He had reeked of tact. His unit functioned smoothly. The shades who controlled his destiny would soon see.

There were only a few people in the drugstore. Pamela Knighton was the girl at the magazine rack. She looked up at him, startled, over a copy of the *Illustrated London News*.

Knowing of the letter that lay for signature on his desk, Jim wished he could pretend not to see her. He turned slightly aside, held his breath, listened. But though she had seen him, nothing happened, and hating his Hollywood cowardice he turned again presently and lifted his hat.

"You're up late," he said.

Pamela searched his face momentarily.

"I live around the corner," she said. "I've just moved—I wrote you today."

"I live near here too."

She replaced the magazine in the rack. Jim's tact fled. He felt suddenly old and harassed and asked the wrong question.

"How do things go?"

"Oh very well," she said. "I'm in a play—a real play at the New Faces Theatre in Pasadena. For the experience."

"Oh, that's very wise."

"We open in two weeks. I was hoping you could come."

They walked out the door together and stood in the glow of the red neon sign. Across the autumn street newsboys were shouting the result of the night football.

"Which way?" she asked.

—The other way from you, he thought, but when she indicated her direction he walked with her. It was months since he had seen Sunset Boulevard, and the mention of Pasadena made him think of when he had first come to California ten years ago, something green and cool.

Pamela stopped before some tiny bungalows around a central court.

"Good night," she said. "Don't let it worry you if you can't help me. Joe has explained how things are, with the war and all. I know you wanted to."

He nodded solemnly—despising himself.

"Are you married?" she asked.

"No."

"Then kiss me goodnight."

As he hesitated she said, "I like to be kissed good night. I sleep better."

He put his arms around her shyly and bent down to her lips, just touching them — and thinking hard of the letter on his desk which he couldn't send now — and liking holding her.

"You see it's nothing," she said, "just friendly. Just good night."

On his way to the corner Jim said aloud, "Well, I'll be damned" and kept repeating the sinister prophecy to himself for some time after he was in bed.

III

On the third night of Pamela's play Jim went to Pasadena and bought a seat in the last row. He entered a tiny auditorium and was the first arrival except for fluttering ushers and voices chattering amid the hammers backstage. He considered a discreet retirement but was reassured by the arrival of a group of five, among them Joe Becker's chief assistant. The lights went out; a gong was beaten; to an audience of six the play began.

Jim watched Pamela; in front of him the party of five leaned together and whispered after her scenes. Was she good? He was sure of it. But with pictures drawing upon half the world for talent there was scarcely such a phenomenon as a "natural." There were only possibilities — and luck. He was luck. He was maybe this girl's luck — if he felt that her pull at his insides was universal. Stars were no longer created by one man's casual desire as in the silent days, but stock girls were, tests were, chances were. When the last curtain dropped, domestically as a Venetian blind, he went backstage by the simple process of walking through a door on the side. She was waiting for him.

"I was hoping you wouldn't come tonight," she said. "We've flopped. But the first night it was full and I looked for you."

"You were fine," he said shyly.

"Oh no. You should have seen me then."

"I saw enough," he said. "I can give you a little part. Will you come to the studio tomorrow?"

He watched her expression. Out of her eyes, out of the curve of her mouth gleamed a sudden and overwhelming pity.

"Oh," she said. "Oh, I'm terribly sorry. Joe brought some people over and next day I signed up with Bernie Wise."

"You did?"

"I knew you wanted me and at first I didn't realize you were just a sort of supervisor. I thought you had more power—" She broke off and assured him hastily, "Oh, I like you better *per*sonally. You're much more civilized than Bernie Wise."

He felt a stab of pain and protest. All right then, he was civilized.

"Can I drive you back to Hollywood?" he asked.

They rode through an October night soft as April. When they crossed a bridge, its walls topped with wire screens, he gestured toward it and she nodded.

"I know what it is," she said. "But how stupid! English people don't commit suicide when they don't get what they want."

"I know. They come to America."

She laughed and looked at him appraisingly. Oh, she could do something with him all right. She let her hand rest upon his.

"Kiss tonight?" he suggested after a while.

Pamela glanced at the chauffeur, insulated in his compartment.

"Kiss tonight," she said.

He flew East next day, looking for a young actress just like Pamela Knighton. He looked so hard that any eyes with an aspect of lovely melancholy, any bright English voice, predisposed him. It seemed rather a desperate matter that he should find some one exactly like this girl. Then when a telegram called him impatiently back to Hollywood, he found Pamela dumped in his lap.

"You got a second chance, Jim," said Joe Becker. "Don't miss it again."

"What was the matter over there?"

"They had no part for her. They're in a mess. So we tore up the contract."

Mike Harris, the studio head, investigated the matter. Why was a shrewd picture man like Bernie Wise willing to let her go?

"Bernie says she can't act," he reported to Jim. "And what's more she makes trouble. I keep thinking of Simone and those two Austrian girls."

"I've seen her act," insisted Jim. "And I've got a place for her. I don't even want to build her up yet. I want to spot her in this little part and let you see."

A week later Jim pushed open the padded door of Stage III and walked anxiously in. Extras in dress clothes turned toward him in the semi-darkness; eyes widened.

"Where's Bob Griffin?"

"In that bungalow with Miss Knighton."

They were sitting side by side on a couch in the glare of the make-up light, and from the resistance in Pamela's face Jim knew the trouble was serious.

"It's *no*thing," Bob insisted heartily. "We get along like a couple of kittens, don't we, Pam?"

"You smell of onions," said Pamela.

Griffin tried again.

"There's an English way and an American way. We're looking for the happy mean—that's all."

"There's a nice way and a silly way," Pamela said shortly. "I don't want to begin by looking like a fool."

"Leave us alone, will you, Bob?" Jim said.

"Sure. All the time in the world."

Jim had not seen her in this busy week of tests and fittings and rehearsals, and he thought now how little he knew about her and she of them.

"Bob seems to be in your hair," he said.

"He wants me to say things no sane person would say."

"All right—maybe so," he agreed. "Pamela, since you've been working here have you ever blown up in your lines?"

"Why—everybody does sometimes."

"Listen, Pamela—Bob Griffin gets almost ten times as much money as you do—for a particular reason. Not because he's the most brilliant director in Hollywood—he isn't—but because he never blows up in his lines."

"He's not an actor," she said puzzled.

"I mean his lines in real life. I picked him for this picture because once in a while I blow up. But not Bob. He signed a contract for an unholy amount of money—which he doesn't deserve, which nobody deserves. But he earns it because smoothness is the fourth dimension of this business and Bob has learned never to say the word 'I'. People of three times his talent—producers and troopers and directors—go down the sink because they can't learn that."

"I know I'm being lectured to," she said uncertainly. "But I don't seem to understand. An actress has her own personality—"

He nodded.

"And we pay her five times what she could get for it anywhere else—*if* she'll only keep it off the floor where it trips the rest of us up. You're tripping us all up, Pamela."

—I thought you were my friend, her eyes said.

He talked to her a few minutes more. Everything he said he believed with all his heart, but because he had twice kissed those lips he saw that it was support and protection they wanted from him. All he had done was to make her a little shocked that he was not on her side. Feeling rather baffled, and sorry for her loneliness he went to the door of the bungalow and called:

"Hey, Bob!"

Jim went about other business. He got back to his office to find Mike Harris waiting.

"Again that girl's making trouble."

"I've been over there."

"I mean in the last five minutes," cried Harris. "Since you left she's made trouble! Bob Griffin had to stop shooting for the day. He's on his way over."

Bob came in.

"There's one type you can't seem to get at—can't find what makes them that way."

There was a moment's silence. Mike Harris, upset by the situation, suspected that Jim was having an affair with the girl.

"Give me till tomorrow morning," said Jim. "I think I can find what's back of this."

Griffin hesitated but there was a personal appeal in Jim's eyes—an appeal to associations of a decade.

"All right, Jim," he agreed.

When they had gone Jim called Pamela's number. What he had almost expected happened but his heart sank none the less when a man's voice answered the phone.

IV

Excepting a trained nurse, an actress is the easiest prey for the unscrupulous male. Jim had learned that in the background of their troubles or their failures there was often some plausible confidence man, who asserted his masculinity by way of interference, midnight nagging, bad advice. The technique of the man was to belittle the woman's job and to question endlessly the motives and intelligence of those for whom she worked.

When Jim reached the bungalow hotel in Beverly Hills where Pamela had moved, it was after six. In the court a cold fountain plashed senselessly against the December fog and he heard Major Bowes' voice loud from three radios.

When the door of the apartment opened Jim stared. The man was old—a bent and withered Englishman with ruddy winter color dying in his face. He wore an old dressing gown and slippers and he asked Jim to sit down with an air of being at home. Pamela would be in shortly.

"Are you a relative?" Jim asked wonderingly.

"No, Pamela and I met here in Hollywood, strangers in a strange land. Are you employed in pictures, Mr.—— Mr.——"

"Leonard," said Jim. "Yes. At present I'm Pamela's boss."

A change came into the man's eyes—the watery blink became conspicuous, there was a stiffening of the old lids. The lips curled down and backward and Jim was gazing into an expression of utter malignanty. Then the features became old and bland again.

"I hope Pamela is being handled properly?"

"You've been in pictures?" Jim asked.

"Till my health broke down. But I am still on the rolls at Central Casting and I know everything about this business and the souls of those who own it—"

He broke off. The door opened and Pamela came in.

"Well hello," she said in surprise. "You've met? The Honorable Chauncey Ward—Mr. Leonard."

Her glowing beauty, borne in from outside like something snatched from wind and weather, made Jim breathless for a moment.

"I thought you told me my sins this afternoon," she said with a touch of defiance.

"I wanted to talk to you away from the studio."

"Don't accept a salary cut," the old man said. "That's an old trick."

"It's not that, Mr. Ward," said Pamela. "Mr. Leonard has been my friend up to now. But today the director tried to make a fool of me and Mr. Leonard backed him up."

"They all hang together," said Mr. Ward.

"I wonder—" began Jim. "Could I possibly talk to you alone."

"I trust Mr. Ward," said Pamela frowning. "He's been over here twenty-five years and he's practically my business manager."

Jim wondered from what deep loneliness this relationship had sprung.

"I hear there was more trouble on the set," he said.

"Trouble!" She was wide-eyed. "Griffin's assistant swore at me and I heard it. So I walked out. And if Griffin sent apologies by you I don't want them—our relation is going to be strictly business from now on."

"He didn't send apologies," said Jim uncomfortably. "He sent an ultimatum."

"An ultimatum!" she exclaimed. "I've got a contract, and you're his boss, aren't you?"

"To an extent," said Jim, "—but of course making pictures is a joint matter—"

"Then let me try another director."

"Fight for your rights," said Mr. Ward. "That's the only thing that impresses them."

"You're doing your best to wreck this girl," said Jim quietly.

"You can't frighten us," snapped Ward. "I've seen your type before."

Jim looked again at Pamela. There was exactly nothing he could do. Had they been in love, had it ever seemed the time to encourage the spark between them, he might have reached her now. But it was too late. He seemed to feel the swift wheels of the industry turning in the Hollywood darkness outside. He knew that when the studio opened tomorrow, Mike Harris would have new plans that did not include Pamela at all.

For a moment longer he hesitated. He was a well-liked man, still young, and with a wide approval. He could buck them about this girl, send her to a dramatic teacher. He could not bear to see her make such a mistake. On the other hand he was afraid that somewhere people had yielded to her too much, spoiled her for this sort of career.

"Hollywood isn't a very civilized place," said Pamela.

"It's a jungle," agreed Mr. Ward. "Full of prowling beasts of prey."

Jim rose.

"Well, this one will prowl out," he said. "Pam, I'm very sorry. Feeling like you do, I think you'd be wise to go back to England and get married."

For a moment a flicker of doubt was in her eyes. But her confidence, her young egotism, was greater than her judgment—she did not realize that this very minute was opportunity and she was losing it forever.

For she had lost it when Jim turned and went out. It was weeks before she knew how it happened. She received her salary for some months—Jim saw to that—but she did not set foot on that lot again. Nor on any other. She was placed quietly on that black list that is not written down but that functions at backgammon games after dinner, or on the way to the races. Men of influence stared at her with interest at restaurants here and there but all their inquiries about her reached the same dead end.

She never gave up during the following months—even long after Becker had lost interest and she was in want, and no longer seen in the places where people go to be looked at. It was not from grief or discouragement but only through commonplace circumstances that in June she died.

V

When Jim heard about it, it seemed incredible. He learned accidentally that she was in the hospital with pneumonia—he telephoned and found that she was dead. "Sybil Higgins, actress, English. Age 21."

She had given old Ward as the person to be informed and Jim managed to get him enough money to cover the funeral expenses, on the pretext that some old salary was still owing. Afraid that Ward might guess the source of the money he did not go to the funeral but a week later he drove out to the grave.

It was a long bright June day and he stayed there an hour. All over the city there were young people just breathing and being happy and it seemed senseless that the little English girl was not one of them. He kept on trying and trying to twist things about so that they would come out right for her but it was too late. That pink and silver frost had melted. He said good-by aloud and promised that he would come again.

Back at the studio he reserved a projection room and asked for her tests and for the bits of film that had been shot on her picture. He sat in a big leather chair in the darkness and pressed the button for it to begin.

In the test Pamela was dressed as he had seen her that first night at the dance. She looked very happy and he was glad she had had at least that much happiness. The reel of takes from the picture began and ran jerkily with the sound of Bob Griffin's voice off scene and with prop boys showing the number blocks for the takes. Then Jim started as the next-to-last one came up, and he saw her turn from the camera and whisper:

"I'd rather die than do it that way."

Jim got up and went back to his office where he opened the three notes he had from her and read them again.

. . . just passing by the studio and thought of you and of our ride.

—just passing by. During the spring she had called him twice on the phone, he knew, and he had wanted to see her. But he could do nothing for her and could not bear to tell her so.

"I am not very brave," Jim said to himself. Even now there was fear in his heart that this would haunt him like that memory of his youth, and he did not want to be unhappy.

Several days later he worked late in the dubbing room, and afterwards he dropped into his neighborhood drugstore for a sandwich. It was a warm night and there were many young people at the soda counter. He was paying his check when he became aware that a figure was standing by the magazine rack looking at him over the edge of a magazine. He stopped—he did not want to turn for a closer look only to find the resemblance at an end. Nor did he want to go away.

He heard the sound of a page turning and then out of the corner of his eye he saw the magazine cover, *The Illustrated London News*.

He felt no fear—he was thinking too quickly, too desperately. If this were real and he could snatch her back, start from there, from that night.

"Your change, Mr. Leonard."

"Thank you."

Still without looking he started for the door and then the magazine closed and dropped to a pile and he heard someone breathe close to his side. Newsboys were calling an extra across the street and after a moment he turned the wrong way, her way, and he heard her following—so plain that he slowed his pace with the sense that she had trouble keeping up with him.

In front of the apartment court he took her in his arms and drew her radiant beauty close.

"Kiss me goodnight," she said. "I like to be kissed goodnight. I sleep better."

—Then sleep, he thought as he turned away—sleep. I couldn't fix it. I tried to fix it. When you brought your beauty here I didn't want to throw it away, but I did somehow. There is nothing left for you now but sleep.

Charles Reznikoff

Charles Reznikoff (1894–1976) was a consummate New Yorker, a poet whose favorite activity was going for long walks, and his sequence "Autobiography: Hollywood" is fascinating for the way he seeks out those intervals of quietness and apparent stasis that he needs to sustain himself during a not altogether happy residence. Born and raised in Brooklyn, Reznikoff was, along with Louis Zukofsky and George Oppen, one of the Objectivist poets of the 1930s, a group whose work was not widely appreciated until they were rediscovered by younger poets in the 1960s. For many years Reznikoff published his own collections of poetry, printing them by hand on a press in his basement. His three-year stay in Los Angeles, from 1937 to 1940, was prompted by an invitation to work as a researcher for the producer Albert Lewin, a close friend. Reznikoff's discomfort with the Hollywood world is typified in a letter he wrote after attending a party where the guests included George Cukor and Alla Nazimova: "The party was all right, but I like walking better."

from

AUTOBIOGRAPHY: HOLLYWOOD

I like this secret walking
in the fog;
unseen, unheard,
among the bushes
thick with drops;
the solid path invisible
a rod away —
and only the narrow present is alive.

———

Shining on grass and flowers,
this is too wet for dew —
it is last night's rain;
yes, the bottom leaves of the bushes beside the walk

are still pasted to the asphalt.
The birds that merely cheeped at dawn
are whistling, chirping and twittering,
wherever I turn. Why then do I look askance
at this man
plodding along talking to himself?

———

In the picture,
a turbaned man and a woman are seated in a garden
in which — this very tree
with large white blossoms like tulips.
It is a long way from Persia to the Pacific,
and a long time from the Middle Ages;
yet both picture and blossoming tree
have lived through time and tide.

———

A clear morning
and another — yet another;
a meadow bright with dew;
blue hills
rising from a lake of mist;
single flowers
bright against a white-washed wall
and scattered
in the grass;
flowers in broad beds
beside the narrow walk;
look, soldiers of Ulysses,
your spears
have begun to flower, too!

———

Rainy Season

It has been raining for three days.
The faces of the giants
on the bill-boards
still smile;
but the gilt has been washed from the sky:
we see the iron world.

———

The cold wind and black fog and the noise of the sea.

———

An actress
powdered yellow for the camera—
daughter of the Greek princess buried in Mycenae
with a gold mask on her face. The hush
when into the restaurant crowded with faces
a star comes:
the painted lips are silent, the painted eyes turn.
The Mexican has finished playing;
he lifts his guitar and kisses it.

———

These gentlemen are great; they are paid
a dollar a minute. They will not answer
if you say, Good morning;
will neither smile nor nod—
if you are paid only a dollar or two
an hour. (Study
when to be silent, when to smile.)
The director who greets my employer loudly
and smiles broadly, reaching for his hand and back,
scowls and glares at my greeting. Now I understand

why he managed to give me only his fingers
when we were introduced. Why do you go to such trouble
to teach me that you are great?
I never doubted it until now.

———

I will not question the sunshine
that shines so pleasantly
on my face. I know the answer:
it will not last—for me.

Tomorrow it will rain, we say, and tomorrow is as clear as
    yesterday;
the mountains are green and yellow—clear of mist;
and the sea, free of fog, is bluer than ever.
But we do not believe this sunshine;
it will not last, we say darkly:
an earthquake will tumble a wall upon our heads
or a thorn scratch a finger and we shall die.

———

The cloudy afternoon is as pleasant
as silence. Who would think
one would ever have enough of sunshine?
A good epitaph, I suppose, would be
He liked the sunshine;
better still, *He liked to walk.*
And yet the dead, if it could speak, might say,
I had grown tired of walking,
yes, even of the sunshine.

Budd Schulberg

In "A Table at Ciro's," published in 1941, Budd Schulberg (b. 1914) sums up in a single story all the classic character types associated with Hollywood fiction: the overbearing producer, the starry-eyed ingenue, the scheming writer, or waiter, or assistant—all caught up in the machinations of a city forever on the make. In this fictional universe everyone is out for something: stardom, power, money, and usually a combination of the three. Schulberg had good reason to know that the fiction was not far from the reality. Raised in Hollywood—his father was one-time Paramount boss B. P. Schulberg— he made his name with the scathing *What Makes Sammy Run?* (1941). The book stirred up such strong feelings in the film establishment that Louis B. Mayer wanted him run out of town, a suggestion to which Schulberg's father is said to have responded, "For Christ's sake, Louie, he's the only novelist who ever came *from* Hollywood. Where the hell are you going to deport him, Catalina Island?" He fictionalized his ill-fated screenwriting collaboration with F. Scott Fitzgerald as *The Disenchanted* (1950), and recounted his Hollywood childhood in the memoir *Moving Pictures* (1981).

A TABLE AT CIRO'S

At half-past five Ciro's looks like a woman sitting before her dressing table just beginning to make up for the evening. The waiters are setting up the tables for the dinner trade, the cigarette and hat-check girls are changing from slacks to the abbreviated can-can costumes which are their work clothes, and an undiscovered Rosemary Clooney making her debut tonight is rehearsing. *Don't let the stars get in your eyes* . . .

A telephone rings and the operator, who is suffering from delusions of looking like Ava Gardner, answers, "Ci-ro's. A table for Mr. Nathan? For six. His usual table?" This was not what she had come to Hollywood for, to take reservations over the telephone, but even the small part she played in A.D. Nathan's plans for the evening brought her a little closer to the Hollywood that was like a mirage, always in sight but never within reach. For, like everyone else in Hollywood, the telephone operator at Ciro's had a dream. Once upon a time, ran

273

this one, there was a Famous Movie Producer (called Goldwyn, Zanuck or A.D. Nathan) and one evening this FMP was in Ciro's placing a million-dollar telephone call when he happened to catch a glimpse of her at the switchboard. "Young lady," he would say, "you are wasting your time at that switchboard. You may not realize it, but you *are* Naomi in my forthcoming farm epic, *Sow the Wild Oat!*"

Reluctantly the operator plugged out her dream and sent word of Nathan's reservation to André. André belonged to that great International Race, head waiters, whose flag is an unreadable menu and whose language is French with an accent. Head waiters are diplomats who happened to be born with silver spoons in their hands instead of their mouths. André would have been a typical head waiter. But he had been in Hollywood too long. Which meant that no matter how good a head waiter he was, he was no longer satisfied to be one. André wanted to be a screen writer. In fact, after working only three years, André had managed to finish a screen-play, entitled, surprisingly enough, *Confessions of a Hollywood Waiter.* He had written it all by himself, in English.

With casual deliberateness (hadn't Jimmy Starr called him the poor man's Adolphe Menjou?) André picked out a table one row removed from the dance floor for Mr. Nathan. The waiter, whose ringside table was A.D. Nathan's "usual," raised a protest not entirely motivated by sentiment. In Waiter's Local 67, A.D. Nathan's fame was based not so much on his pictures as on his tips. "Mr. Nathan will have to be satisfied with this table," André explained. "All the ringside tables are already reserved."

André had to smile at his own cleverness. A.D. Nathan did not know it yet, but from the beginning André had had him in mind as the producer of his scenario. A.D. seemed the logical contact because he remembered André as an ordinary waiter in Henry's back in the days before pictures could talk. But André knew he needed something stronger than nostalgia to bring himself to A.D.'s attention. Every Saturday night Nathan presided at the same table overlooking the floor. Tonight André would make him take a back seat. Nathan would threaten and grumble and André would flash his suave head-waiter smile and be *so sorry M'sieur Nathan, if there were only something I could do* . . . Then, at the opportune moment, just as the floor show was about to begin, André would discover that something could be done. And when Nathan would try to thank André with a crisp green bill for giving him the table André had been saving for him all evening. André's voice would take on an injured tone. *Merci beaucoup, M'sieur Nathan, thank you just the same, but André is glad to do a favor for an old friend.*

André thought of the scene in terms of a scenario. That was the dialogue, just roughed in, of course. Then the business of Nathan insisting on rewarding André for his efforts. And a close-up of André, shyly dropping his eyes as he tells M'sieur Nathan that if he really wants to reward André he could read *Confessions of a Hollywood Waiter* by André de Selco.

So that was André's dream and he dreamt it all the while he was fussing over last-minute details like a nervous hostess getting ready for a big party.

By the time Nathan's party arrived, the big room with the cyclamen drapes and pale-green walls of tufted satin was full of laughter, music, shop talk and an inner-circle intimacy that hung over the place like the smoke that rose from lipsticked cigarettes and expensive cigars. Everyone turned to stare at the newcomers, for Hollywood celebrities have a way of gaping at each other with the same wide-eyed curiosity as their supposedly less sophisticated brothers waiting for autographs outside.

Nathan entered with assurance, conscious of the way "There's A.D." was breathed through the room. His figure was slight but imposing, for he carried himself with the air of a man who was used to commanding authority. There was something ghostly about him, with his white hair and pale, clean, faintly pink skin, but his eyes were intensely alive, dark eyes that never softened, even when he smiled. As he followed André toward the dance floor, actors, agents, directors and fellow-producers were anxious to catch his eye. It was "Hello, A.D. How are you tonight, A.D.?," and he would acknowledge them with a word or a nod, knowing how to strike just the right balance between dignity and cordiality.

At his side was his wife, a tall brunette with sculpture-perfect features, hardened by a willful disposition. Some still remembered her as Lita Lawlor, who seemed on the verge of stardom not so many years ago. But she had sacrificed her screen career for love, or so the fan magazines had put it, though gossippers would have you believe that Lita was just swapping one career for another that promised somewhat more permanent security.

Accompanying the Nathans were a plain, middle-aged couple whom no one in Ciro's could identify, an undiscovered girl of seventeen who was beautiful in an undistinguished way, and Bruce Spencer, a young man whom Nathan was grooming as the next Robert Taylor. And grooming was just the word, for this male ingénue pranced and tossed his curly black mane like a horse on exhibition.

André led the party to the inferior table he had picked out for them.

"Wait a minute. André, this isn't my table," Nathan protested.

He frowned at André's silky explanations. He was in no mood to be crossed this evening. It seemed as if everything was out of sync today. First his three-thousand-dollar-a-week writer had turned in a dime-a-dozen script. Then he had decided that what he needed was an evening alone with something young and new like this Jenny Robbins, and instead here he was with his wife, that young ham of hers, and those Carterets he'd been ducking for months. And to top everything, there was that business in New York.

Impatiently Nathan beckoned the waiter. "A magnum of Cordon Rouge, 1935."

1935, Nathan thought. That was the year he almost lost his job. It was a funny thing. All these people hoping to be tossed a bone never thought of A.D. Nathan as a man with a job to hold. But that year, when the panic struck and the banks moved in, he had had to think fast to hold onto that big office and that long title. He wondered what would have become of him if he had lost out. He thought of some of the magic names of the past, like Colonel Selig and J.C. Blackburn, who could walk into Ciro's now without causing a head to turn. And he thought how frightening it would be to enter Ciro's without the salaaming reception he always complained about but would have felt lost without.

But he mustn't worry. His psychiatrist had told him not to worry. He looked across at Jenny with that incredibly young face, so pretty and soft, like a marmalade kitten, he thought. A little wearily, he raised his glass to her. He wondered what she was like, what she was thinking, whether she would. Then he looked at Mimi

Carteret. How old she and Lew had become. He could remember when they were the regulars at the Embassy Club and the Coconut Grove. Now their eyes were shining like tourists' because it had been such a long time since their last evening in Ciro's.

"Is the wine all right, Lew?" Nathan asked.

Lew Carteret looked up, his face flushed. "All right! I haven't had wine like this . . ." He paused to think. "In a long time," he said.

There was a silence, and Nathan felt embarrassed for him. He was glad when Mimi broke in with the anecdote about the time during Prohibition when they were leaving for Europe with their Western star, Tex Bradley, and Tex insisted on bringing his own Scotch along because he was afraid to trust those foreign bootleggers.

Nathan was only half-listening, though he joined in the laughter. When is Carteret going to put the bite on me for that job he wants?, he was thinking. And what will I have to give the little marmalade kitten? And though he could not divine André's plans, or guess how he figured in the dreams of the telephone operator who looked like Ava Gardner, he could not help feeling that Ciro's was a solar system in which he was the sun and around which all these satellites revolved.

"André," he beckoned, "will you please tell the operator I'm expecting a very important long-distance call?" An empty feeling of excitement rose inside him, but he fought it down. The dancers were swaying to a tango. Nathan saw Spencer and Lita, whirling like professionals, conscious of how well they looked together. He looked at Jenny, and he thought, with a twinge of weariness, of all the Jennys he had looked at this way. "Would you like to dance, my dear?"

He was an old man to Jenny, an old man she hardly knew, and it seemed to her that everybody in the room must be saying, "There goes A.D. with another one." But she tried to smile, tried to be having a terribly good time, thinking, If I want to be an actress, this is part of the job. And if I can't look as if I'm getting the thrill of my life out of dancing with this old fossil, what kind of an actress am I anyway?

Nathan could have told her what kind of an actress she was. He had expressed himself rather vividly on that subject after seeing her test that afternoon.

"Robbins stinks," he had told his assistants as the lights came on in the projection room. "She has a cute figure and a pretty face, but not unusual enough, and her acting is from Hollywood High School."

That's what he should have told her. But he needed to be surrounded by Jenny Robbinses. Even though the analyst had told him what that was, he went on tossing them just enough crumbs of encouragement to keep their hopes alive.

"Enjoying yourself, Jenny?" he said as he led her back to the table.

"Oh, I'm having an elegant time, Mr. Nathan," she said. She tried to say it with personality, her eyes bright and her smile fixed. She felt as if she were back on the set going through the ordeal of making that test again.

"After dancing a tango together, the least we could do is call each other by our first names," he said.

He tried to remember the first time he had used that line; on Betty Bronson he thought it was. But Jenny laughed as if he had said something terribly witty. She laughed with all her ambition if not with all her heart.

Her heart—or so she thought—had been left behind at 1441½ Orange Grove Avenue. That's where Bill Mason lived. Bill worked as a grip on Nathan's lot. The grip is the guy who does the dirty work on a movie set. Or, as Bill liked to explain it, "I'm the guy who carries the set on his back. I may not be the power behind the throne but I'm sure the power *under* it."

Jenny thought of the way she and Bill had planned to spend this evening, down at the Venice Amusement Pier. They usually had a pretty good time down there together Saturday nights. It was their night. Until A.D. Nathan had telephoned, in person.

"Oh, Mr. Nathan, how lovely of you to call! I do have an appointment, but . . ."

"I wish you could cancel it, dear," Nathan had said. "There's . . . there's something I'd like to talk to you about. I thought, over a drink at Ciro's . . ."

Jenny had never been to Ciro's, but she could describe every corner of it. It was her idea of what heaven must be like, with producers for gods and agents as their angels.

"Sorry to keep you waiting, Mac," Bill had called from the door a little later. "But that Old Bag" (referring to one of the screen's most glamorous personalities) "blew her lines in the big love scene fifteen straight times. I thought one of the juicers was going to drop a lamp on her." He looked at Jenny in the sequin dress, the pin-up model. "Hmmm, not bad. But a little fancy for roller-coasting, isn't it, honey?"

"Bill, I know I'm a monster," she had said, watching his face carefully, "but I've got to see Mr. Nathan tonight. I'd've given anything to get out of it, but, well, I don't want to sound dramatic but . . . my whole career may depend on it."

"Listen, Mac," Bill had said. "You may be kidding yourself, but you can't kid me. I was on the set when you made that test. If I'm ever going to be your husband I might as well begin right by telling you the truth. You were NG."

"I suppose you know more about acting than Mr. Nathan," she said, hating Bill, hating the Venice Pier, hating being nobody. "Mr. Nathan told me himself he wanted to keep my test to look at again."

"Are you sure it's the test he wants to keep?" Bill said.

Here in Ciro's the waiter was filling her glass again, and she was laughing at something funny and off-color that Bruce Spencer had just said. But she couldn't forget what she had done to Bill, how she had slapped him and handed back the ring, and how, like a scene from a bad B picture, they had parted forever.

For almost fifteen minutes Jenny had cried because Bill was a wonderful fellow and she was going to miss him. And then she had stopped crying and started making up her face for A.D. Nathan because she had read too many movie magazines. This is what makes a great actress, she thought, sorrow and sacrifice of your personal happiness, and she saw herself years later as a great star, running into Bill in Ciro's after he had become a famous cameraman. "Bill," she would say, "perhaps it is not too late. Each of us had to follow our own path until they crossed again."

"Oh, by the way, Lita," A.D. had told his wife when she came into his dressing room to find out if he had any plans for the evening, "there's a little actress I'd like to take along to Ciro's tonight. Trying to build her up. So we'll need an extra man."

"We might still be able to get hold of Bruce," Lita said. "He said something about being free when we left the club this afternoon."

Nathan knew they could get hold of Bruce. Lita and Bruce were giving the Hollywood wives something to talk about over their canasta these afternoons. Sometimes he dreamt of putting an end to it. But that meant killing two birds with bad publicity. And they were both his birds, his wife and his leading man.

"All right," he said, "I'll give Spence a ring. Might not be a bad idea for the Robbins girl to be seen with him."

Lita pecked him on the cheek. Bruce was dying to get that star-making part in *Wagons Westward*. This might be the evening to talk A.D. into it.

And then, since the four of them might look too obvious, Nathan had wanted an extra couple. He tried several, but it was too late to get anybody in demand, and that's how, at the last minute, he had happened to think of the Carterets.

When you talked about old-time directors you had to mention Lew Carteret in the same breath with D.W. Griffith and Mickey Neilan. Carteret and Nathan had been a famous combination until sound pictures and the jug had knocked Carteret out of the running. The last job he had had was a quickie Western more than a year ago. And a year in Hollywood is at least a decade anywhere else. A.D. had forgotten all about Carteret until he received a letter from him a few months ago, just a friendly letter, suggesting dinner some evening to cut up touches about old times. But A.D. knew those friendly dinners, knew he owed Carteret a debt he was reluctant to repay, and so, somehow, the letter had gone unanswered. But in spite of himself, his conscience had filed it away for further reference.

"I know who we'll get. The Lew Carterets. Been meaning to take them to dinner for months."

"Oh, God," Lita said, as she drew on a pair of long white gloves that set off her firm tanned arms, "why don't we get John Bunny and Flora Finch?"

"It might not be so bad," Nathan said, giving way to the sentimentality that thrives in his profession. "Mimi Carteret used to be a lot of fun."

"I can just imagine," said Lita. "I'll bet she does a mean Turkey Trot."

"Lew, do you think this means he's going to give you a chance again?" Mimi Carteret whispered as they walked off the dance floor together, "Easy on the wine, darling. We just can't let anything go wrong tonight."

"Don't worry, sweetheart," he answered. "I'm watching. I'm waiting for the right moment to talk to him."

Lita and Bruce were dancing again and Jenny was alone with A.D. at the table when the Carterets returned. It was the moment Jenny had been working toward. She could hardly wait to know what he thought of the test.

"I don't think it does you justice," Nathan was saying. "The cameraman didn't know how to light you at all. I think you have great possibilities."

Jenny smiled happily, the wine and encouragement going to her head, and Nathan reached over and patted her hand in what was meant to seem a fatherly gesture, though he lingered a moment too long. But Jenny hardly noticed, swept along in the dream.

Lew Carteret looked at his watch nervously. It was almost time for the floor show. There wouldn't be much chance to talk during the acts, and after that, the party would be over. He looked across at Mimi, trying to find the courage to put it up to A.D. If only A.D. would give him an opening. Lita and Bruce were watching too, wondering when to bring up *Wagons Westward*. And André, behind the head waiter's mask, was thinking, Only ten more minutes and I will be speaking to A.D. about my scenario.

"André," Nathan called, and the head waiter snapped to attention. "Are you sure there hasn't been a call for me?"

"No, m'sieur. I would call you right away, m'sieur."

Nathan frowned. "Well, make sure. It should have been here by now." He felt angry with himself for losing his patience. There was no reason to be so upset. This was just another long-distance call. He had talked to New York a thousand times before—about matters just as serious.

But when André came running with the message that New York was on the wire, he could not keep the old fear from knotting his stomach and he jostled the table in his anxiety to rise.

"You may take it in the second booth on the left, Mr. Nathan," said Ava Gardner, as she looked up from her switchboard with a prefabricated smile. But he merely brushed by her and slammed the door of the booth behind him. The telephone girl looked after him with the dream in her eyes. When he comes out I'll hafta think of something arresting to sayta him, she decided. God, wouldn't it be funny if he did notice me!

Five minutes later she heard the door of the booth sliding open and she looked up and smiled. "Was the connection clear, Mr. Nathan?"

That might do for a starter, she thought. But he didn't even look up. "Yes. I heard very well. Thank you," he said. He put half a dollar down and walked on. He felt heavy, heavy all over, his body too heavy for his legs to support and his eyes too heavy for the sockets to hold. He walked back to the table without seeing the people who tried to catch his glance.

"Everything all right?" his wife asked.

"Yes. Yes," he said. "Everything."

Was that his voice? It didn't sound like his voice. It sounded more like Lew Carteret's voice. Poor old Lew. Those were great old times when we ran World-Wide together. And that time I lost my shirt in the market and Lew loaned me 50 G's. Wonder what ever happened to Lew.

Then he realized this *was* Lew Carteret, and that he was listening to Lew's voice. "A.D., this has sure been a tonic for Mimi and me. I know we didn't come here to talk shop, but—well, you always used to have faith in me, and . . ."

"Sure, sure, Lew," A.D. said. "Here, you're one behind. Let me pour it. For old times."

He could feel an imperceptible trembling in his hand as he poured the wine.

Under the table a small, slender leg moved slowly, with a surreptitious life of its own, until it pressed meaningfully against his. Jenny had never slept with anybody except Bill. She was frightened, but not as frightened as she was of living the rest of her life in Hollywood as the wife of a grip in a bungalow court.

Bruce flipped open his cigarette case—the silver one that Lita had given him for his birthday—and lit a cigarette confidently. "By the way, A.D., Lita let me read the script on *Wagons*. That's a terrific part, that bank clerk who has to go west for his health and falls in with a gang of rustlers. Wonderfully written. Who's going to play it?"

"Any leading man in Hollywood except you," Nathan said.

Bruce looked undressed without his assurance. The silence was terrible.

Lita said, "But, A.D., that part was written for Bruce."

All the rest of his face seemed to be sagging, but Nathan's hard black eyes watched them with bitter amusement. "There isn't a part in the studio that's written for Bruce. The only thing that kept Bruce from being fired months ago was me. And now there's no longer me."

Lita looked up, really frightened now. "A.D. What do you mean?"

"I mean I'm out," he said. "Finished. Washed up. Through. Hudson called to say the Board voted to ask for my resignation."

"What are you going to do now?" she said.

He thought of the thing he had promised himself to do when his time came, drop out of sight, break it off clean. Hollywood had no use for anticlimaxes on or off the screen. But as he sat there he knew what would really happen. Move over, Colonel Selig and J.C. Blackburn, he thought. Make room for another ghost.

The floor show was just starting. The undiscovered Rosemary Clooney was putting everything she had into her number, and playing right to A.D.'s table. *Don't let the stars get in your eyes* . . .

And as she sang, André smiled in anticipation. So far everything had gone just as he had planned. And now the time had come to move A.D. up to that ringside table.

Bertolt Brecht

For Bertolt Brecht (1898–1956), the German poet and playwright who arrived at San Pedro harbor in July 1941, Los Angeles was the last leg of an escape journey from Nazi Germany, where the radical politics of such stage works as *The Threepenny Opera* (1928) and *The Rise and Fall of the City of Mahagonny* (1930) had made him a prime target. For six years Brecht endured what he facetiously called his "exile in paradise," lamenting the shallowness of Hollywood and the small-minded moralism of America, and failing to establish himself as a screenwriter. (His only credit was for Fritz Lang's *Hangmen Also Die,* an unhappy experience that confirmed Brecht's cynicism.) Despite his discontent—amply expressed in the poems and journal entries here—Brecht's California period was not unproductive; he wrote several plays, including *The Caucasian Chalk Circle,* and completed the English version of *Galileo* in a happy collaboration with Charles Laughton. The two of them worked together on a staging of the play at the Coronet Theater not long before Brecht finally left town in the wake of his 1947 questioning by the House Un-American Activities Committee.

Landscape of Exile

But even I, on the last boat
Saw the gaiety of the dawn in the rigging
And the grayish bodies of dolphins emerge
From the Japanese Sea.

The little horsecarts with gilt decorations
And the pink sleeves of the matrons
In the alleys of doomed Manila
The fugitive beheld with joy.

The oil derricks and the thirsty gardens of Los Angeles
And the ravines of California at evening and the fruit market
Did not leave the messenger of misfortune unmoved.

Hollywood Elegies

I

The village of Hollywood was planned according to the notion
People in these parts have of heaven. In these parts
They have come to the conclusion that God
Requiring a heaven and a hell, didn't need to
Plan two establishments but
Just the one: heaven. It
Serves the unprosperous, unsuccessful
As hell.

II

By the sea stand the oil derricks. Up the canyons
The gold prospectors' bones lie bleaching. Their sons
Built the dream factories of Hollywood.
The four cities
Are filled with the oily smell
Of films.

III

The city is named after the angels
And you meet angels on every hand.
They smell of oil and wear golden pessaries
And, with blue rings round their eyes
Feed the writers in their swimming pools every morning.

IV

Beneath the green pepper trees
The musicians play the whore, two by two
With the writers. Bach
Has written a Strumpet Voluntary. Dante wriggles
His shrivelled bottom.

V

The angels of Los Angeles
Are tired out with smiling. Desperately
Behind the fruit stalls of an evening
They buy little bottles
Containing sex odours.

VI

Above the four cities the fighter planes
Of the Defense Department circle at a great height
So that the stink of greed and poverty
Shall not reach them.

Californian Autumn

I

In my garden
Are nothing but evergreens. If I want to see autumn
I drive to my friend's country house in the hills. There
I can stand for five minutes and see a tree
Stripped of its foliage, and foliage stripped of its trunk.

II

I saw a big autumn leaf which the wind
Was driving along the road, and I thought; tricky
To reckon that leaf's future course.

The Democratic Judge

In Los Angeles, before the judge who examines people
Trying to become citizens of the United States
Came an Italian restaurant keeper. After grave preparations
Hindered, though, by his ignorance of the new language
In the test he replied to the question:
What is the 8th Amendment? falteringly:
1492. Since the law demands that applicants know the language
He was refused. Returning
After three months spent on further studies
Yet hindered still by ignorance of the new language
He was confronted this time with the question: Who was
The victorious general in the Civil War? His answer was:
1492. (Given amiably, in a loud voice). Sent away again

And returning a third time, he answered
A third question: For how long a term are our Presidents elected?
Once more with: 1492. Now
The judge, who liked the man, realised that he could not
Learn the new language, asked him
How he earned his living and was told: by hard work. And so
At his fourth appearance the judge gave him the question:
When
Was America discovered? And on the strength of his correctly
    answering
1492, he was granted his citizenship.

The Fishing-Tackle

In my room, on the whitewashed wall
Hangs a short bamboo stick bound with cord
With an iron hook designed
To snag fishing-nets from the water. The stick
Came from a second-hand store downtown. My son
Gave it to me for my birthday. It is worn.
In salt water the hook's rust has eaten through the binding.
These traces of use and of work
Lend great dignity to the stick. I
Like to think that this fishing-tackle
Was left behind by those Japanese fishermen
Whom they have now driven from the West Coast into camps
As suspect aliens; that it came into my hands
To keep me in mind of so many
Unsolved but not insoluble
Questions of humanity.

Garden in Progress

High above the Pacific coast, below it
The waves' gentle thunder and the rumble of oil tankers
Lies the actor's garden.
Giant eucalyptus trees shade the white house
Dusty relics of the former mission.
Nothing else recalls it, save perhaps the Indian
Granite snake's head that lies by the fountain
As if patiently waiting for
A number of civilisations to collapse.

And there was a Mexican sculpture of porous tufa
Set on a block of wood, portraying a child with malicious eyes
Which stood by the brick wall of the toolshed.

Lovely grey seat of Chinese design, facing
The toolshed. As you sit on it talking
You glance over your shoulder at the lemon hedge
With no effort.

The different parts repose or are suspended
In a secret equilibrium, yet never
Withdraw from the entranced gaze, nor does the masterly hand
Of the ever-present gardener allow complete uniformity
To any of the units: thus among the fuchsias
There may be a cactus. The seasons too
Continually order the view: first in one place then in another
The clumps flower and fade. A lifetime
Was too little to think all this up in. But
As the garden grew with the plan
So does the plan with the garden.

The powerful oak trees on the lordly lawn
Are plainly creatures of the imagination. Each year
The lord of the garden takes a sharp saw and
Shapes the branches anew.

Untended beyond the hedge, however, the grass runs riot
Around the vast tangle of wild roses. Zinnias and bright anemones
Hang over the slope. Ferns and scented broom
Shoot up around the chopped firewood.

In the corner under the fir trees
Against the wall you come on the fuchsias. Like immigrants
The lovely bushes stand unmindful of their origin
Amazing themselves with many a daring red
Their fuller blooms surrounding the small indigenous
Strong and delicate undergrowth of dwarf calycanthus.

There was also a garden within the garden
Under a Scotch fir, hence in the shade
Ten feet wide and twelve feet long
Which was as big as a park
With some moss and cyclamens
And two camelia bushes.

Nor did the lord of the garden take in only
His own plants and trees but also
The plants and trees of his neighbours; when told this
Smiling he admitted: I steal from all sides.
(But the bad things he hid
With his own plants and trees.)

Scattered around
Stood small bushes, one-night thoughts
Wherever one went, if one looked
One found living projects hidden.

Leading up to the house is a cloister-like alley of hibiscus
Planted so close that the walker
Has to bend them back, thus releasing
The full scent of their blooms.

In the cloister-like alley by the house, close to the lamp
Is planted the Arizona cactus, height of a man, which each year
Blooms for a single night, this year
To the thunder of guns from warships exercising
With white flowers as big as your fist and as delicate
As a Chinese actor.

Alas, the lovely garden, placed high above the coast
Is built on crumbling rock. Landslides
Drag parts of it into the depths without warning. Seemingly
There is not much time left in which to complete it.

from

JOURNALS

9 aug 41
i feel as if i had been exiled from our era, this is tahiti in the form of
a big city; at this very moment i am looking out on to a little garden
with a lawn, shrubs with red blossom, a palm tree and white garden
furniture, and a male voice is singing something sentimental to
piano accompaniment—it's not a wireless. they have nature here,
indeed, since everything is so artificial, they even have an exaggerated feeling for nature, which becomes alienated, from dieterle's
house you can see the san fernando valley; an incessant, brilliantly
illuminated stream of cars thunders through nature; but they tell
you that all the greenery is wrested from the desert by irrigation
systems. scratch the surface a little and the desert shows through:
stop paying the water bills and everything stops blooming. the
butchery 15,000 kilometres away, which is deciding our fate right
across europe at its broadest point, is only an echo in the hubbub of
the art-market here.

21 jan 42
odd, i can't breath in this climate. the air is totally odourless, morning and evening, in both house and garden. there are no seasons

here. it has been part of my morning routine to lean out of the window and breathe in fresh air; i have cut this out of my routine here. there is neither smoke nor the smell of grass to be had. the plants seem to me like the twigs we used to plant in the sand as children. after ten minutes their leaves were dangling limply. you keep wondering if they might cut off the water, even here, and what then? occasionally, especially in the car going to beverley hills, i get something like a whiff of landscape, which 'really' seems attractive; gentle lines of hills, lemon thickets, a californian oak, even one or other of the filling-stations can actually be rather amusing; but all this lies behind plate glass, and i involuntarily look at each hill or lemon tree for a little price tag. you look for these price tags on people too. — not being happy in my surroundings is not something i like, especially in these circumstances. i set great store by my status, the distinguished status of refugee, and it is quite unseemly to be so servile and keen to please refugees as the surroundings here are. but it is probably just the conditions of work that are making me impatient. custom here requires that you try to 'sell' everything, from a shrug of the shoulders to an idea, ie you have always to be on the look-out for a customer, so you are constantly either a buyer or a seller, you sell your piss, as it were, to the urinal. opportunism is regarded as the greatest virtue, politeness becomes cowardice.

25 mar 42

about 100,000 japanese (incl american citizens) are being evacuated from the coast here for military reasons. wonderful how humanity pulls through despite all these psychoses and panics. in the office where we too had to register as *enemy aliens* i saw an old japanese woman, half-blind, and not looking at all dangerous. she had her companion, a young girl, apologise to the people who were waiting that she was taking so much time to write. everybody smiled: the american officials were very polite. for the first time little people are buying their vegetables from the niseis (japanese born here) something they never did before because they did not think it hygienic; their markets are so empty. now a town is being built for tens of thousands. the military constantly stress that the escorts are only there in case americans molest them. the japanese can police themselves. an outcry in the correspondence columns of the times shows what the authorities have to contend with.

28 may 42

with lang, on the beach, thought about a hostage film (prompted by heydrich's execution in prague). there were two young people lying close together beside us under a big bath towel, the man on top of the woman at one point, with a child playing alongside. not far away stands a huge iron listening contraption with colossal wings which turns in an arc; a soldier sits behind it on a tractor seat, in shirt-sleeves, but in front of one or two little buildings there is a sentry with a gun in full kit. huge petrol tankers glide silently down the asphalt coast road, and you can hear heavy gunfire beyond the bay.

18 jun 42

one part of the little garden affords a dignified view, there you are surrounded by greenery, bushes and large-leaved fig-trees (the ath-letes among trees). if you place your chair right you don't see any of the tarted-up petty bourgeois villas with their depressing prettiness. only a little summer-house, one and a half metres square, meets the eye, but it is dilapidated and ennobled by decay.

Chester Himes

Chester Himes (1909–1984) wrote in his memoir *The Quality of Hurt* that the racism he found in L.A. "shattered" him, and that the place "hurt me racially as much as any city I have ever known—much more than any city I remember in the South." Born in Missouri into a middle-class family, Himes began publishing fiction while serving time in prison for armed robbery, and after his release was encouraged by writers including Louis Bromfield and Richard Wright. He went west in 1940 to find work in the movie business, but ended up in the San Pedro shipyards, an experience that inspired his first novel, *If He Hollers Let Him Go* (1945). Ultimately Himes settled in France, where he wrote his novels about the Harlem detectives Coffin Ed Johnson and Grave Digger Jones, including *Cotton Comes to Harlem* (1965) and *Blind Man with a Pistol* (1969).

from

IF HE HOLLERS LET HIM GO

I went out to the garage, threw up the door, backed half way out to the street on the starter, telling myself at the time I oughtn' to do it. I had a '42 Buick Roadmaster I'd bought four months ago, right after I'd gotten to be a leader man, and every time I got behind the wheel and looked down over the broad, flat, mile-long hood I thought about how the rich white folks out in Beverly couldn't even buy a new car now and got a certain satisfaction. I straightened out and dug off with a jerk, turned the corner at forty, pushed it on up in the stretch on Fifty-fourth between San Pedro and Avalon, with my nerves tightening, telling me to take it slow before I got into a battle royal with some cracker motorcycle cop, and my mind telling me to hell with them, I was a key man in a shipyard, as important as anybody now.

Homer and Conway were waiting in front of the drugstore at the corner of Fifty-fourth and Central.

"You're kinda tardy, playboy," Homer said, climbing in beside Conway.

I turned the corner into Central and started digging. "She wouldn't let me go," I said.

"You mean you had that last dollar left," Conway said.

I squeezed between a truck and an oncoming streetcar, almost brushing, and Homer said, "See that. Now he's tryna kill us. He don't mind dying hisself, but why he got to kill you and me too?"

"Just like that safety man said, gambling thirty seconds against thirty years," Conway said.

I pulled up in front of the hotel at Fifty-seventh and my other three riders climbed in the back.

"Is you ready to face the enemy, that's what I wanna know," Smitty said in his loud, grating voice, trying to be jolly. "Is you ready to meet the man, that's what I mean."

"Conway gonna show the man some teeth first thing," Pigmeat said. "That man done looked in Conway's mouth so much he know every time he have neck bones."

Before I started I turned to Pigmeat and said, "I own some parts of you, don't I, buddy?"

"Get over, goddamnit!" Johnson snarled at Smitty in the back seat and pushed him. "You want all the seat?"

"Don't call me no 'buddy,' man," Pigmeat said to me. "When I escaped from Mississippi I swore I'd lynch the first sonabitch that called me a 'buddy.'"

"There these niggers is fighting already," Homer said, shaking his head. "Whenever niggers gets together that's the first thing they gonna do."

Smitty squirmed over to give Johnson more room. "By God, here's a man wakes up evil every morning. Ain't just *some* mornings; this man wakes up evil *every* morning." He looked around at Johnson. "What's the matter with you, man, do your old lady beat you?"

Homer thought they were going to fight. He decided to be peacemaker. "Now you know how Johnson is," he said to Smitty. "That's just his way. You know he don't mean no harm."

As soon as Smitty found out somebody was holding him he began getting bad sure enough. "How do I know how he is?" he shouted. "Does he know how I is? Hell, everybody evil on Monday morning. I'm evil too. He ain't no eviler'n me."

"Shut up!" Conway yelled. "Bob's tryna say something." Then he turned to me. "Don't you know what a 'buddy' is, Bob? A 'buddy' drinks bilge water, eats crap, and runs rabbits. That's what a peckerwood means when he calls you 'buddy.'"

"I ain't kidding, fellow," I told Pigmeat.

He started scratching for his wallet. "Now that's a Senegalese for you," he complained. "Gonna put me out his car 'bout three lousy bucks. Whatcha gonna do with a fellow like that?" He passed me three ones.

"This is for last week," I said, taking them. "What about this week?"

"Aw, man, I'll give it to you Friday," he grumbled. "You raise more hell 'bout three lousy bucks——"

I mashed the starter and dug off without hearing the rest of it. At Slauson I turned east to Alameda, south again toward the harbor. Johnson had started beefing about the job, and now they all had it.

"How come it is we always got to get the hardest jobs?" Smitty asked. "If somebody'd take a crap on deck Kelly'd come and get our gang to clean it up."

"I been working in this yard two years—Bob'll tell you—and all I done yet is the jobs don't nobody else wanta do," Conway said. "I'm gonna quit this yard just as sure as I live and nothing don't happen and get me a job at Cal Ship."

"They don't want you over there neither," Pigmeat said.

"They don't even want a colored man to go to the school here any more," Homer put in. "Bessie ask Kelly the other day 'bout going to school—she been here three months now—and he told her they still filled up. And a peck come right after—I was standing right there—and he signed him up right away."

"You know they don't want no more nig—no more of us getting no mechanic's pay," Pigmeat said. "You know that in front. What she gotta do is keep on after him."

"If I ever make up my mind to quit," Johnson said, "he the first sonabitch I'm gonna whup. I'm gonna whup his ass till it ropes like okra."

Conway said, "I ain't gonna let you. He mine. I been saving that red-faced peckerwood too long to give 'im up now. I'm gonna whip 'im till he puke; then I'm gonna let 'im get through puking; then I'm gonna light in on him and whip 'im till he poot. . . ." He kept on as if it was getting good to him. "Then I'm gonna let 'im get through

pooting; then I'm gonna light in on 'im and whip 'im till he————"
They were all laughing now.

"You can't whip him until you get him," I called over my shoulder.

"You tell 'em, Bob," Smitty said. "We gonna see Kelly in a half hour, then we gonna see what Conway do."

"I ain't said I was gonna whip the man this morning," Conway backtracked. "I said when I *quit*—that's what I said."

The red light caught me at Manchester; and that made me warm. It never failed; every time I got in a hurry I got caught by every light. I pulled up in the outside lane, abreast a V-8 and an Olds, shifted back to first, and got set to take the lead. When the light turned green it caught a white couple in the middle of the street. The V-8 full of white guys dug off and they started to run for it; and the two white guys in the Olds blasted at them with the horn, making them jump like grasshoppers. But when they looked up and saw we were colored they just took their time, giving us a look of cold hatred.

I let out the clutch and stepped on the gas. Goddamn 'em, I'll grind 'em into the street, I thought. But just before I hit them something held me. I tamped the brake.

"What the hell!" Johnson snarled, picking himself up off the floor.

I sat there looking at the white couple until they had crossed the sidewalk, giving them stare for stare, hate for hate. Horns blasted me from behind, guys in the middle lanes looked at me as they passed; but all I could see was two rebbish pecks who didn't hate me no more than I hated them. Finally I went ahead, just missed sideswiping a new Packard Clipper. My arms were rubbery and my fingers numb; I was weak as if I'd been heaving sacks of cement all day in the sun.

After that everything got under my skin. I was coming up fast in the middle lane and some white guy in a Nash coupe cut out in front of me without signaling. I had to burn rubber to keep from taking off his fender; and the car behind me tapped my bumper. I didn't know whether he had looked in the rear-view mirror before he pulled out or not, but I knew if he had he could have seen we were a carful of colored—and that's the way I took it. I kept on his tail until I could pull up beside him, then I leaned out the window and shouted, "This ain't Alabama, you peckerwood son of a bitch. When you want to pull out of line, stick out your hand."

He gave me a quick glance, then looked straight ahead. After that he ignored me. That made me madder than if he'd talked back. I stuck with him clear out to Compton. A dozen times I had a chance to bump him into an oncoming truck. Then I began feeling virtuous and let him go.

But at the entrance to the Shell Refinery the white cop directing traffic caught sight of us and stopped me on a dime. The white workers crossing the street looked at the big new car full of black faces and gave off cold hostility. I gave them look for look.

"What's the matter with these pecks this morning?" Homer said. "Is everybody evil?"

By now it was a quarter of eight. It was twelve miles to the yard. I gritted my teeth and started digging again; I swore the next person who tried to stop me I'd run him down. But traffic on all harbor roads was heavy the whole day through, and during the change of shifts at the numerous refineries and shipyards it was mad, fast, and furious. Cars were strung out in both directions as far as you could see; drivers jockeyed for position. Shipyard workers are reckless drivers. Handling tons of steel all day long makes cars seem as small as scooters and flexible as cables. I had to fight and bluff for every foot. Although I knew they did everyone like that, I got to feeling that the white guys were trying to push me around. I got mad and started bulling.

It was a bright June morning. The sun was already high. If I'd been a white boy I might have enjoyed the scramble in the early morning sun, the tight competition for a twenty-foot lead on a thirty-mile highway. But to me it was racial. The huge industrial plants flanking the ribbon of road—shipyards, refineries, oil wells, steel mills, construction companies—the thousands of rushing workers, the low-hanging barrage balloons, the close hard roar of Diesel trucks and the distant drone of patrolling planes, the sharp, pungent smell of exhaust that used to send me driving clear across Ohio on a sunny summer morning, and the snow-capped mountains in the background, like picture post cards, didn't mean a thing to me. I didn't even see them; all I wanted in the world was to push my Buick Roadmaster over some peckerwood's face.

Time and again I cut in front of some fast-moving car, making rubber burn and brakes scream and drivers curse, hoping a paddy would bump my fender so I'd have an excuse to get out and clip him with my tire iron. My eyes felt red and sticky and my mouth tasted brown. I turned into the tightly patrolled harbor road, doing a defiant fifty.

Conway said at large, "Oh, Bob's got plenny money, got just too much money. He don't mind paying a fine."

Nobody answered him. By now we were all too evil to do much talking. We came into the stretch of shipyards—Consolidated, Bethlehem, Western Pipe and Steel—caught an open mile, and I went up to sixty. White guys looked at us queerly as we went by. We didn't get stopped but we didn't make it. It was five after eight when we pulled into the parking lot at Atlas Ship. I found a spot and parked and we scrambled out, nervous because we were late, and belligerent because we didn't want anybody to say anything about it.

The parking-lot attendant waited until I had finished locking the car, then came over and told me I had to move, I'd parked in the place reserved for company officials. I looked at him with a cold, dead fury, too spent even to hit him. I let my breath out slowly, got back into the car, and moved it. The other fellows had gone into the yard. I had to stop at Gate No. 2 to get a late card.

The gatekeeper said, "Jesus Christ, all you colored boys are late this morning."

A guard standing near by leered at me. "What'd y'all do las' night, boy? I bet y'all had a ball down on Central Avenue."

I started to tell him I was up all night with his mother, but I didn't feel up to the trouble. I punched my card without giving a sign that I had heard. Then I cut across the yard to the outfitting dock. We were working on a repair ship—it was called a floating dry dock—for the Navy. My gang was installing the ventilation in the shower compartment and the heads, as the toilets were called.

At the entrance to the dock the guard said, "Put out that cigarette, boy. What's the matter you colored boys can't never obey no rules?"

I tossed it over on the wooden craneway, still burning. He muttered something as he went over to step on it.

The white folks had sure brought their white to work with them that morning.

Carlos Bulosan

The grotesque netherworld described by the Filipino writer Carlos Bulosan (1911–1956) in his autobiography *America Is in the Heart* (1946) is one rarely encountered in the Los Angeles literature of the era. In this murky realm of sleazy dance halls, whiskey-soaked flophouses, and claustrophobic pool-rooms where cops discharge their pistols as if for sport, Bulosan fends off corruption as best he can and voices his outrage at the casual, horrific violence of the world that has claimed his brother Macario. Bulosan, a farmer's son who came to the U.S. in 1931, was the author of *Laughter of My Father* (1934) and *Letter from America* (1942), among other works. John Fante described him as "sartorially exquisite, always laughing through a face that masked tragedy. . . . He radiated kindness and goodness."

from

AMERICA IS IN THE HEART

I reached Los Angeles in the evening. An early autumn rain was falling. I waited in the station, looking among the passengers for Filipino faces. Then I went out and turned northward on Los Angeles Street, and suddenly familiar signs on barber shops and restaurants came to view. I felt as though I had discovered a new world. I entered a restaurant and heard the lonely sound of my dialect, the soft staccato sound of home. I knew at once that I would meet some people I had known in the Philippines.

I sat on one of the stools and waited. I saw three American girls come in with three Filipinos. I thought I knew one of the Filipinos, so I approached him and spoke in Ilocano. But he did not understand me; even when I spoke in Pangasinan, he did not understand me. He was of another tribe, possibly a Visayan.

"If you are looking for your brother," said the proprietor to me, "go to the dance hall. That is where you always find them."

I asked him to direct me. It was still early, but the girls were already arriving. They went hastily up the stairs and their perfume lingered after them. I stood outside for a long time watching through the door until the guard closed it.

Filipinos started going inside, putting their hands high above their heads so that the guard could search them for concealed weapons. The guard was a white man and he was very rough with them. I went to Main Street, turned to the north, and found the Mexican district. The sound of Spanish made me feel at home, and I mingled with the drunks and the jobless men. In the old plaza some men were debating a political issue; a shaggy old man was preaching to a motley crowd. And farther down the street, near Olvera Market, I saw little Mexican boys carrying shoeshine boxes. They were eating sunflower seeds and throwing the empty shells into each other's faces.

It was now getting late. The crowd in the street was dispersing. The bells in the church tower began to ring. I looked up and saw devotees coming out of the door. It was already ten o'clock and the night services were over. The haggard preacher in the plaza leaped from his perch and disappeared in the crowd. I sat on a wooden bench and put my cap over my face so that I could sleep in the glare of the street lamps.

Toward midnight a drunk came to my bench and lay down to sleep. I moved away from him, giving him enough space to be comfortable. Then a young Mexican whose voice sounded like a girl's sat beside me. He put his hand on my knee and started telling me about a place where we could get something to eat. I was hungry and cold, but I was afraid of him.

I walked away from him, watching the church across the street. When I was sure no one was looking, I rushed to the door and entered. The church was empty. I went to a comfortable corner and lay on the floor. I saw on old man with a white beard coming in the door, and I thought he saw me. But he went to the candles and blew them out one by one, then disappeared through a side door. It was like heaven, it was so warm and quiet and comfortable. I closed my eyes and went to sleep.

I was awakened in the morning by the merry peals of tiny bells. I ran across the room and through the door, bumping into many people who were arriving for the morning services. I walked in the crowded street toward the Filipino district. I felt as though a beast were tearing at the walls of my stomach. The pain nauseated me: I was hungry again.

I thought I saw my brother Macario in a streetcar. I jumped on with all the power of my legs, but I was wrong. I got out on the next block and started walking aimlessly. I began to wonder if my life would always be one long flight from fear. When had I landed in America? It seemed so long ago. I crossed the green lawn of the new City Hall.

I walked from Main Street to Vermont Avenue, three miles away. I returned to town by streetcar and went to First Street again. A Filipino poolroom was crowded, and I went inside to sit on a bench. The players were betting and once in a while they would give the table boy a dime. I waited until the men started coming in groups, because their day's work was done.

I was talking to a gambler when two police detectives darted into the place and shot a little Filipino in the back. The boy fell on his knees, face up, and expired. The players stopped for a moment, agitated, then resumed playing, their faces coloring with fear and revolt. The detectives called an ambulance, dumped the dead Filipino into the street, and left when an interne and his assistant arrived. They left hurriedly, untouched by their act, as though killing were a part of their day's work.

All at once I heard many tongues speaking excitedly. They did not know why the Filipino was shot. It seemed that the victim was new in the city. I was bewildered.

"Why was he shot?" I asked a man near me.

"They often shoot Pinoys like that," he said. "Without provocation. Sometimes when they have been drinking and they want to have fun, they come to our district and kick or beat the first Filipino they meet."

"Why don't you complain?" I asked.

"*Complain?*" he said. "Are you kidding? Why, when we complain it always turns out that *we* attacked them! And they become more vicious, I am telling you! That is why once in a while a Pinoy shoots a detective. You will see it one of these days."

"If they beat me I will kill them," I said.

The Filipino looked at me and walked away. As the crowd was beginning to disperse, I saw the familiar head of my brother Macario. He was entering the poolroom with a friend. I rushed to him and touched his hand. He could not believe that I was in America.

"Why didn't you write that you were coming?" he asked.

"I did not know I was coming, brother," I said. "Besides, I did not know your address. I knew that I would not stop traveling until I found you. You have grown older."

"I guess I have, all right," he said. Then suddenly he became quiet, as though he were remembering something. He looked at me and said, "Let's go to my hotel."

I noticed that he did not speak English the way he used to speak it in the Philippines. He spoke more rapidly now. As I walked beside him, I felt that he was afraid I would discover some horror that was crushing his life. He was undecided what to do when we reached Broadway Street, and stopped several times in deep thought. He had changed in many ways. He seemed in constant agitation, and he smoked one cigarette after another. His agitation became more frightening each minute.

"Why was the Filipino shot?" I asked, pretending not to notice his mental anguish.

"Someday you will understand, Carlos," he said.

Carlos! He had changed my name, too! Everything was changing. Why? And why all this secrecy about the death of one Filipino? Were the American people conspiring against us? I looked at my brother sidelong but said nothing. Suddenly I felt hungry and lonely and tired.

We turned to the north and came to a hotel near the Hall of Justice building. We took the slow elevator to the fifth floor. My brother knocked on a door and looked at me. There was a hunted look in his face. I heard many voices inside. A patter of feet, then the door opened. The strong smell of whisky brought tears to my eyes. It was so strong it almost choked me. I knew at once that there was party. I saw three American girls in evening gowns and ten Filipinos. I was amazed at their immaculate suits and shoes.

"Friends," my brother announced, "this is my kid brother — Carlos! He has just arrived from the Philippines."

"More than six months ago," I corrected him. "I went to Alaska first, then came down to Los Angeles. I think I like it here. I will buy a house here someday."

"Buy a house?" a man near me said, his face breaking into a smile. But when he noticed that my brother was looking hard at him, he suddenly changed his tone and offered me a glass. "Good, good!" he said. "Buy all the houses you want. And if you need a janitor—" He turned around to hide the cynical twist of his mouth.

Then they rushed to me. All at once several cocktail glasses were offered to me. The girls pulled me to the table, tilting a glass in my mouth. The Filipinos shouted to me to drink.

I looked at my brother, ashamed. "I don't drink," I said.

"Go on — drink!" a curly-haired boy prodded me. "Drink like hell. This is America. We all drink like hell. Go on, boy!"

He was only a boy, but he drank like a man. I watched him empty three glasses, one after the other. My brother came to me.

"This is a wedding party," he whispered.

"Who got married?" I asked, looking around.

"I think that one," he said, pointing to a woman. "That is the man. I think he is twenty years old."

"She is old enough to be his mother," I said.

"What is the difference?" the curly-haired boy said to me. "They know what they want, don't they?" He winked at me foolishly and emptied another glass.

I gripped the glass in my hand so hard that it nearly broke.

It was past midnight when the party was over. I thought some of the men would go home, but it was only Leon who announced that he was leaving. The bridal couple started undressing in the other room, and the other men came to the outer room with the two girls. The curly-haired boy switched off the lights and the men started grabbing the girls.

I could see the red glow of their cigarettes moving in the dark. The girls would protest for a while, cursing the men. Then they would quiet down and go to bed, laughing yolkily when they threw their gowns on the floor. My brother took my arm and told me to follow him. We walked silently through the hall and down the stairs. I heard the married woman squealing and laughing, and I was bewildered and afraid. I wanted my brother to explain everything to me.

The sky was overcast and the lights in the streets were out. Newsboys were shouting the morning papers. We walked for hours because it was hard to talk. We had not seen each other for years, and it was difficult to begin. We could only pick up fragments of our lives and handle them fearfully, as though the years had made us afraid to know ourselves. I was suddenly ashamed that I could not express the gentle feeling I had for my brother. Was this brutality changing me, too?

At dawn we walked back to the hotel. What I saw in the room would come back to me again and again. One of the girls was in the bed with two men. The other girl was on the couch with two other men. They were all nude. Six men were sleeping on the floor and three others were sprawled under the bed.

My brother motioned to me to undress, switching off the lights. I found a space near the closet, and I lay down hoping to sleep. My heart was pounding very fast. Leon came into the room with another girl. He cursed the sleeping forms and took the girl to the other room. They went to bed with the married couple.

I wanted to talk to my brother in the dark. But when I put my ear close to his mouth, I knew that he was already asleep. I could not sleep any more; my mind was wandering. I rolled over on my other side and tried to remember a prayer I used to recite when I was a little boy in Mangusmana.

A man named Nick was the first to wake up. He was making coffee in a big pot when I went to the kitchen. The girls were still in bed. My brother woke up suddenly and went to the bathroom. He was fully dressed when he came out.

"I'll look for a job today," he said.

"There is no use," Nick said. "I have been looking for a job for three months."

"I'll try, anyway," said my brother.

"Well, I hope some worker dies today," Nick said.

My brother looked at me. The girls woke up. They walked un-ashamedly in the room. The other men came to the kitchen and began drinking whisky again.

It was then that I learned their names. José, the curly-haired boy, was Nick's brother. They had both been going to college some months before, but the depression had deprived them of their jobs. Mariano, with the well-trimmed mustache, had been an agent for a clothing company that had failed. Victor and Manuel had worked in an apartment house in Hollywood. Luz, long out of a job, had come from the farm to live in the city. Gazamen was the life of the party: he was always singing and playing his portable phonograph. Leon was selling tickets in a dance hall: he was the only one who had a job. Alonzo was a college student, and had never worked as far as the other men knew. Ben was doing house work in Beverly Hills, but he seldom came home with money.

I found my brother Macario in a strange world. I could stand the poverty and hunger, but this desperate cynicism disturbed me. Were these Filipinos revolting against American society in this debased form? Was there no hope for them?

One night Leon, who was the sole mainstay of our company, came home with a bottle of bootleg whisky. He brought a girl with him. She was small and dark. Suddenly, in the middle of the night, the girl started screaming. We rushed to the other room, but it was too late. Leon was dead and cold. The girl cried loudly and hysterically. Mariano struck her with his fist, felling her. The blow was so hard it stunned her. It was not that he hated her; it was that this was the sad end of a little world that had revolved around a man who sold tickets in a dance hall.

Carey McWilliams

Carey McWilliams (1905–1980) came to Los Angeles in 1922 to attend USC Law School, and soon joined an emerging literary scene that included Louis Adamic, John Fante, and William Saroyan. Over the next 30 years he became one of the most distinctive and outspoken voices in the region, weighing in on everything from migrant farm labor to the proliferation of religious cults to the internment of Japanese-Americans during World War II. His many books include a landmark study, *Southern California Country: An Island on the Land* (1946), represented here by "The Growth of a Legend," an unsparing dissection of the "Ramona myth" that grew out of Helen Hunt Jackson's novel. In "Blood on the Pavements," a chapter from *North from Mexico: The Spanish-Speaking People of the United States* (1948), McWilliams examines the Zoot Suit Riots of 1943 to uncover official misrepresentation and public misperception. He did more than observe such issues: when nine Mexican-American teenagers were wrongly convicted in the Sleepy Lagoon murder case of 1942, McWilliams headed up the Sleepy Lagoon Defense Committee. In later years he relocated to New York, where he was the long-time editor of *The Nation*.

from

SOUTHERN CALIFORNIA COUNTRY: AN ISLAND ON THE LAND

Clear ring the silvery Mission bells
Their calls to vesper and to mass;
O'er vineyard slopes, thro' fruited dells,
The long processions pass.

The pale Franciscan lifts in air
The cross above the kneeling throng;
Their simple world how sweet with prayer,
With chant and matin song!

— Ina Coolbrith

The Growth of a Legend

Considering the long dark record of Indian mistreatment in Southern California, it is difficult to account for the curious legend that has developed in the region about the well-being of the natives under Mission rule. According to this legend, the Missions were havens of happiness and contentment for the Indians, places of song, laughter, good food, beautiful languor, and mystical adoration of the Christ. What is still more astonishing is the presence in the legend of an element of masochism, with the Americans, who manufactured the legend, taking upon themselves full responsibility for the criminal mistreatment of the Indian and completely exonerating the Franciscans. "In the old and happy days of Church domination and priestly rule," writes one Protestant historian, "there had been no 'Indian question.' That came only after American 'civilization' took from the red men their lands and gave them nothing in return."

Equally baffling, at first blush, is the intense preoccupation of Southern California with its Mission-Spanish past. Actually one of the principal charms of Southern California, as Farnsworth Crowder has pointed out, is that it is not overburdened with historical distractions. "As against any European country, certain parts of the United States and even neighboring Mexico," writes Mr. Crowder, "human culture has left relatively few marks, monuments and haunts over the vast virginal face of the state. Almost any square block of London is more drenched with flavors of the past than the whole of Los Angeles. The desert areas and valleys cannot evoke any such awareness of human antiquity and the genesis of great religions and civilizations as can the borderlands of the Mediterranean. No Wordsworths, no Caesars, no Pharaohs have made their homes here. The Californian simply cannot feed upon the fruits and signs of yesterday as can a Roman, a Parisian, an Oxonian." And yet this is precisely what he attempts to do. The newness of the land itself seems, in fact, to have compelled, to have demanded, the evocation of a mythology which could give people a sense of continuity in a region long characterized by rapid social dislocations. And of course it would be a tourist, a goggle-eyed umbrella-packing tourist, who first discovered the past of Southern California and peopled it with curious creatures of her own invention.

1. "H. H."

Some day the Los Angeles Chamber of Commerce should erect a great bronze statue of Helen Hunt Jackson at the entrance to Cajon

Pass. Beneath the statue should be inscribed no flowery dedication, but the simple inscription: "H. H.—In Gratitude." For little, plump, fair-skinned, blue-eyed Helen Hunt Jackson, "H. H." as she was known to every resident of Southern California, was almost solely responsible for the evocation of its Mission past, and it was she who catapulted the lowly Digger Indian of Southern California into the empyrean.

Born in Amherst on October 15, 1830, Helen Maria Fiske became a successful writer of trite romances and sentimental poems quite unlike those written by her friend and neighbor, Emily Dickinson. She was married in 1852 to Lieutenant Edward Bissell Hunt of the Coast Survey, who died a few years after the marriage. In later years, she married William Sharpless Jackson, a wealthy banker and railroad executive of Colorado Springs. It is rather ironic to note that Mrs. Jackson, who became one of the most ardent free-lance apologists for the Catholic Church in America, was a confirmed anti-Papist until she visited California. As might have been expected, she first became interested in Indians while attending a tea party in Boston. At this tea, she met Standing Bear and Bright Eyes, who were lecturing on the grievous wrongs suffered by the Poncas tribe. At the time of this meeting, Mrs. Jackson was forty-nine years of age, bubbling with enthusiasm, full of rhymes. Quick to catch the "aboriginal contagion," which had begun to spread among the writers of American romances, she immediately usurped the position of defender of the Poncas tribe and thereafter no more was heard of Standing Bear and Bright Eyes. In 1881 Harper's published her well-known work, *A Century of Dishonor*, which did much to arouse a new, although essentially spurious, interest in the American Indian.

In the spring of 1872, Mrs. Jackson had made a brief visit, as a tourist, to the northern part of California. Later she made three trips, as a tourist, to Southern California: in the winter of 1881–1882, the spring of 1883, and the winter, spring, and summer of 1884–1885. It scarcely needs to be emphasized that her knowledge of California, and of the Mission Indians, was essentially that of the tourist and casual visitor. Although she did prepare a valuable report on the Mission Indians, based on a field trip that she made with Abbot Kinney of Los Angeles, most of her material about Indians was second-hand and consisted, for the greater part, of odds and ends of gossip, folk tales, and Mission-inspired allegories of one kind or another.

She had originally been sent to Southern California by *Century* magazine to write some stories about the Missions, which, according to the illustrator who accompanied her, were to be "enveloped in the mystery and poetry of romance." In Southern California she became deliriously enamored of the Missions, then in a state of general disrepair and neglect, infested with countless swallows and pigeons, overrun by sheep and goats, and occasionally inhabited by stray dogs and wandering Indians. "In the sunny, delicious, winterless California air," these crumbling ruins, with their walled gardens and broken bells, their vast cemeteries and caved-in wells, exerted a potent romantic influence on Mrs. Jackson's highly susceptible nature. Out of these brief visits to Southern California came *Ramona*, the first novel written about the region, which became, after its publication in 1884, one of the most widely read American novels of the time. It was this novel which firmly established the Mission legend in Southern California.

When the book was first published, it provoked a storm of protest in the Southland. Egged on by various civic groups, the local critics denounced it as a tissue of falsehoods, a travesty on history, a damnable libel on Southern California. But the book was perfectly timed, providentially timed, to coincide with the great invasion of home-seekers and tourists to the region. As these hordes of winter tourists began to express a lively interest in visiting "Ramona's land," Southern California experienced an immediate change of attitude and, overnight, became passionately Ramona-conscious. Beginning about 1887, a Ramona promotion, of fantastic proportions, began to be organized in the region.

Picture postcards, by the tens of thousands, were published showing "the school attended by Ramona," "the original of Ramona," "the place where Ramona was married," and various shots of the "Ramona Country." Since the local chambers of commerce could not, or would not, agree upon the locale of the novel —one school of thought insisted that the Camulos rancho was the scene of the more poignant passages while still another school insisted that the Hacienda Guajome was the authentic locale—it was not long before the scenic postcards depicting the Ramona Country had come to embrace all of Southern California. In the 'eighties, the Southern Pacific tourist and excursion trains regularly stopped at Camulos, so that the wide-eyed Bostonians, guidebooks in hand, might detrain, visit the rancho, and bounce up and down on "the bed in which Ramona slept." Thousands of Ramona baskets, plaques, pincushions, pillows, and souvenirs of all sorts were sold in every curio shop in California. Few tourists left the region without having purchased a little replica of the "bells that rang when Ramona was married." To keep the tourist interest alive, local press agents for fifty years engaged in a synthetic controversy over the identities of the "originals" for the universally known characters in the novel. Some misguided Indian women began to take the promotion seriously and had themselves photographed—copyright reserved—as "the original Ramona." A bibliography of the newspaper stories, magazine articles, and pamphlets written about some aspect of the Ramona legend would fill a volume. Four husky volumes of Ramonana appeared in Southern California: *The Real Ramona* (1900), by D. A. Hufford; *Through Ramona's Country* (1908), the official, classic document, by George Wharton James; *Ramona's Homeland* (1914), by Margaret V. Allen; and *The True Story of Ramona* (1914), by C. C. Davis and W. A. Anderson.

From 1884 to date, the Los Angeles Public Library has purchased over a thousand copies of *Ramona*. Thirty years after publication, the same library had a constant waiting list for 105 circulating copies of the book. The sales to date total 601,636 copies, deriving from a Regular Edition, a Monterey Edition (in two volumes), a De Luxe Edition, a Pasadena Edition, a Tourist Edition, a Holiday Art Edition, and a Gift Edition. Hundreds of unoffending Southern California babies have been named Ramona. A townsite was named Ramona. And in San Diego thousands of people make a regular pilgrimage to "Ramona's Marriage Place," where the True Vow Keepers Clubs—made up of couples who have been married fifty years or longer—hold their annual picnics. The Native Daughters of the Golden West have named one of their "parlors," or lodges, after Ramona. The name Ramona appears in the corporate title of fifty or more businesses currently operating in Los Angeles. Two of Mrs. Jackson's articles for *Century*, "Father Junipero and His Work," and

"The Present Condition of the Mission Indians of Southern California," were for years required reading in the public schools of California. Reprints of Henry Sandham's illustrations for *Ramona* are
familiar items in Southern California homes, hotels, restaurants, and
places of business. In 1914 one of the Ramona historians truthfully
said that "Mrs. Jackson's name is familiar to almost every human
being in Southern California, from the little three-year-old tot, who
has her choice juvenile stories read to him, to the aged grandmother
who sheds tears of sympathy for Ramona." Two generations of
Southern California children could recite from memory the stanzas
from Ina Coolbrith's verses to Helen Hunt Jackson, often ornately
framed on the walls of Southern California homes:

> *There, with her dimpled, lifted hands,*
> *Parting the mustard's golden plumes,*
> *The dusky maid, Ramona, stands,*
> *Amid the sea of blooms.*
>
> *And Alessandro, type of all*
> *His broken tribe, for evermore*
> *An exile, hears the stranger call*
> *Within his father's door.*

Translated into all known languages, *Ramona* has also been dra-
matized. The play based on the novel was first presented at the
Mason Opera House in Los Angeles on February 27, 1905, the
dramatization having been written by Miss Virginia Calhoun and
General Johnstone Jones. Commenting upon Miss Calhoun's performance, in the role of Ramona, the Los Angeles *Times* reported
that "in the lighter parts she held a fascination that was tempered
with gentleness and playfulness. Her slender figure, graceful and
pliant as a willow, swayed with every light touch of feeling, and the
deeper tragic climaxes she met in a way to win tears from the eyes of
many." Over the years, three motion-picture versions of the novel
have appeared. In 1887, George Wharton James, who did much to
keep the Ramona promotion moving along, "tramped every foot of
the territory covered by Mrs. Jackson," interviewing the people she
had interviewed, photographing the scenes she had photographed,
and "sifting the evidence" she had collected. His thick tome on the

Ramona country is still a standard item in all Southern California libraries. For twenty-five years, the chambers of commerce of the Southland kept this fantastic promotion alive and flourishing. When interest seemed to be lagging, new stories were concocted. Thus on March 7, 1907, the Los Angeles *Times* featured, as a major news item, a story about "Condino, the newly discovered and only child of Ramona." In 1921 the enterprising Chamber of Commerce of Hemet, California, commissioned Garnet Holme to write a pageant about Ramona. Each year since 1921 the pageant has been produced in late April or early May in the heart of the Ramona country, by the Chamber of Commerce. At the last count, two hundred thousand people had witnessed the pageant.

The legendary quality of Mrs. Jackson's famous novel came about through the amazing way in which she made elegant pre-Raphaelite characters out of Ramona and "the half-breed Alessandro." Such Indians were surely never seen upon this earth. Furthermore, the story extolled the Franciscans in the most extravagant manner and placed the entire onus of the mistreatment of the Indians upon the noisy and vulgar gringos. At the same time, the sad plight of Ramona and Alessandro got curiously mixed up, in the telling, with the plight of the "fine old Spanish families." These fine old Spanish families, who were among the most flagrant exploiters of the Indian in Southern California, appeared in the novel as only slightly less considerate of his welfare than the Franciscans. Despite its legendary aspects, however, the Ramona version of the Indians of Southern California is now firmly implanted in the mythology of the region. It is this legend which largely accounts for the "sacred" as distinguished from the "profane" history of the Indian in Southern California.

It should be said to Mrs. Jackson's credit, however, that she did arouse a momentary flurry of interest in the Mission Indians. Her report on these Indians, which appeared in all editions of *A Century of Dishonor* after 1883, is still a valuable document. As a result of her work, Charles Fletcher Lummis founded the Sequoya League in Los Angeles in 1902, "to make better Indians," and, through the activities of the league, the three hundred Indians who were evicted from the Warner Ranch in 1901, were eventually relocated on lands purchased by the government. Aside from the relocation of these

Indians, however, nothing much came of Mrs. Jackson's work in Southern California, for the region accepted the charming Ramona, as a folk figure, but completely rejected the Indians still living in the area. A government report of 1920 indicated that 90% of the residents of the sections in which Indians still live in Southern California were wholly ignorant about their Indian neighbors and that deep local prejudice against them still prevailed.

At the sacred level, it is the half-breed Alessandro who best symbolizes the Indian heritage of Southern California. At the secular level, however, one must turn to the local annals to select more appropriate symbols. There is, for example, the character Polonia, an Indian of great stature and strength, whose eyes had been burned out of their sockets. Clad in a tattered blanket, this blind Indian was a familiar figure on the dusty streets of Los Angeles in the 'fifties and 'sixties. And there was Viejo Cholo, or Old Half-Breed, who wore a pair of linen pantaloons and used a sheet for a mantle. His cane was a broom handle; his lunch counter, the swill basket. Viejo Cholo was succeeded, as the principal Indian eccentric of Los Angeles, by another half-breed, Pinikahti. A tiny man, Pinikahti was only four feet in height. Badly pockmarked, he had a flat nose and stubby beard. He was generally attired, notes Harris Newmark, "in a well-worn straw hat, the top of which was missing, and his long, straight hair stuck out in clumps and snarls. A woolen undershirt and a pair of overalls completed his costume, while his toes, as a rule, protruded from his enormous boots." Playing Indian tunes on a flute made out of reeds from the bed of the Los Angeles River, Pinikahti used to dance in the streets of the town for pennies, nickels, and dimes, or a glass of aguardiente. Polonia, Viejo Cholo, and Pinikahti, these are the real symbols of the Indian heritage of Southern California.

2. REDISCOVERY OF THE MISSIONS

With the great Anglo invasion of Southern California after 1880, the Spanish background of the region was, for a time, almost wholly forgotten. "For many years," wrote Harry Carr, "the traditions of Los Angeles were junked by the scorn of the conquering gringos. When I was a school boy in Los Angeles, I never heard of Ortega or

Gaspar de Portola or Juan Bautista de Anza." And then with the publication of *Ramona*, the Spanish background began to be redis-covered, with the same false emphasis and from the same crass motives, that had characterized the rediscovery of the Indian. Both rediscoveries, that of the Indian and that of the Spaniard, occurred between 1883 and 1888, at precisely the period when the great real-estate promotion of Southern California was being organized.

In so far as the Spanish saga is concerned, it all began in 1888 when, as John A. Berger has written, "the romantic people of Southern California," under the leadership of Charles Fletcher Lummis, formed an Association for the Preservation of the Missions (which later became the Landmarks Club). With the gradual restoration of the Missions, a highly romantic conception of the Spanish period began to be cultivated, primarily for the benefit of the incoming tides of tourists, who were routed to the Missions much as they were routed to the mythical site of Ramona's birth-place. A flood of books began to appear about the Missions, with Mrs. Jackson's *Glimpses of California and the Missions* (1883) being the volume that inspired the whole movement. It was followed, after a few years, by George Wharton James's *In and Out of the Old Missions*, which, for a quarter of a century, was the "classic" in this field. My own guess would be that not a year has passed since 1900 without the publication of some new volume about the Missions. Not only has a library of books been written about the Missions, but each individual Mission has had its historians. Books have been written about the architecture of the Missions, about the Mis-sion bells, about the Franciscans (notably Father Junipero Serra, a popular saint in Southern California), and about the wholly syn-thetic Mission furniture. In fact, the Mission-Spanish background of the region has been so strongly emphasized that, as Max Miller has written, "The past is almost as scrambled as the present, and almost as indefinite . . . the whole thing got mixed up." With each new book about the Missions came a new set of etchings and some new paintings. In 1880, William Keith painted all of the Missions of California. He was followed by the artist Ford, of Santa Bar-bara, who, in 1890, completed his etchings of the Franciscan estab-lishments. Since 1890, the Missions have been painted by Jorgen-son, Edward Deakin, Alexander F. Harmer, William Sparks,

Gutzon Borglum, Elmer Wachtel, Minnie Tingle, and a host of other artists.

In 1902, Frank Miller, owner of the Glenwood Cottage Inn at Riverside, with funds provided by Henry Huntington, began to construct the famous Mission Inn. Designed by Myron Hunt, the Mission Inn was built wing by wing around the old adobe Glenwood Cottage, until the new structure covered an entire block. Once completed, the inn gave the initial fillip to Mission architecture, so called, and soon Missionesque and Moorish structures began to dot the Southern California landscape. It was here, in the Mission Inn, that John Steven McGroarty wrote the *Mission Play*, for which he was deservedly decorated by the Pope. The play had its premiere at San Gabriel on a warm spring evening, April 29, 1912, under the sponsorship of the Princess Lazarovic-Hrebrelanovic of Serbia, with a cast of "one hundred descendants of the Old Spanish families." On the opening night, "Queer chugging noises filled the air and the acrid smoke from burnt gasoline floated over the ancient Mission and the little adobes that nestled around it. It was the first big outpouring of automobiles that San Gabriel had ever had." The elite of Southern California turned out, en masse, for the premiere. The play, of course, was an enormous success. McGroarty boasted that it had been seen by 2,500,000 people, a world's record. During the sixteen consecutive seasons that it played at San Gabriel Mission, over 2,600 performances were recorded. Later the play was institutionalized, under official sponsorship, and became an enormous tourist attraction. A tourist who went to California and failed to see Catalina Island, Mt. Wilson, and the *Mission Play* was considered to have something wrong with his head. In recognition of his great services to Southern California, "Singing John," the songster of the green Verdugo hills, was made poet laureate of California on May 17, 1933. Needless to say, the play perpetuated the Helen Hunt Jackson version of the Indians, the Spanish Dons, and the Franciscans.

As a curious postscript to the growth of this amazing legend, it should be pointed out that the Catholic Church played virtually no role whatever in the Ramona-Mission revival in Southern California, which, from its inception, was a strictly Protestant promotion. As a matter of fact, Abbot Kinney, who took Mrs. Jackson through the Indian country in the 'eighties, later wrote that "the arch-bishops, bishops, and priests of those days were not, as a rule, much concerned about the condition of the Indians [theoretically still wards of the church] and the old Mission churches. Many of them were Catalans, who had little or no sympathy with the high ideals of the noble Franciscans. We actually found some of these priests, or those in higher authority, selling part of the lands that had originally been held by the Franciscans in trust for the Indians — not one foot of which belonged to the Church." With the exception of a few Irish priests, such as Father Joseph O'Keefe and Father John O'Sulli-van, the Catholic Church did not figure prominently in the move-ment to restore the Missions. Even today the expensively restored Missions, as J. Russell Smith has pointed out, are "little more than carefully preserved historical curiosities and penny-catchers." Since McGroarty was a converted Catholic, however, it can be said that through this faithful son the Church did exert considerable influ-ence on the formation of the Mission legend.

"Why is it," asked James L. Duff some years ago in the *Com-monweal*, "that such a distinctly non-Catholic city as Los Angeles should evince such a consistent emotional preoccupation with its Catholic past?" Scrutinizing the local directory, Mr. Duff reported that the word "mission" was to be found as part of the corporate name of over a hundred business enterprises in Los Angeles. He was also surprised to find that such expressions as, "in the days of the Dons," and "in the footsteps of the padres," had become commu-nity colloquialisms in Southern California. The dominantly Catholic city of San Francisco, with its Mission Dolores, has never been greatly interested in the Missions. The incongruity is only greater by reason of the fact that Los Angeles is not merely non-Catholic; it can scarcely be called a California city, except in a geographical sense. It is a "conglomeration" of newcomers and has always had the lowest percentage of native-born Californians of any city in the state. Paradoxically, the less Catholic a community is in Southern California, the more the Mission past has been emphasized. The incongruity, however, is never noticed. Not one of the numerous Pope-baiting fundamentalist pastors of Southern California has ever objected to this community-wide adoration of the Missions. "Here," writes Mr. Duff, "is a city that is almost militantly non-

Catholic, audaciously energetic, worshipping Progress, adulating the tinseled world of motion pictures, yet looking with dreaming eyes upon a day and a philosophy of life with which it has neither understanding nor communion, vaguely hoping that the emotion it is evoking is nostalgic."

Not only is Los Angeles a non-Catholic city, but, popular legend to the contrary, it is not a city of churches. Recently, the Los Angeles *Times* published an editorial under the caption: "What! No Church Bells?" The occasion was the May 13, 1945, celebration of V-E Day when, much to the astonishment of the *Times*, it was discovered that "church bells are exceedingly scarce in Los Angeles." At the present time, a movement is under way, sponsored by the *Times*, to bring church bells to Los Angeles, so that "thousands of residents of Los Angeles who formerly lived in Eastern and Mid-western states," may, "on the clear Sabbath mornings," be called to worship by the pealing of bells. "To hear that call again," comments the *Times*, "in their new home, would tend to keep them in touch with their childhood and with the simple, comforting faith with which childhood is blessed, but which sometimes is neglected and all but forgotten," particularly in Southern California.

With the rediscovery of the Catholic-Mission past, the same split occurred in the Spanish tradition of the region that had occurred in relation to its Indian background. Just as Ramona and Alessandro became the sacred symbols of the Indian past, so the Spanish Dons, rather than the Mexicano *paisanos*, became the sacred symbols of the Spanish past. A glance at almost any of the popular novels of Stewart Edward White will show, for example, how the romantic side of this tradition has been emphasized to the detriment—in fact, to the total neglect—of its realistic latter-day manifestations. Despite all the restorations, revivals, pageants, plays, paintings, museum collections, and laboriously gathered materials about this Spanish past, it was not until 1945 that a serious effort was launched to teach Spanish, as a language of the region, in the public schools.

Today there is scarcely a community in Southern California, however, that does not have its annual "Spanish Fiesta," of which the Santa Barbara fiesta is the most impressive. Attending one of the early Santa Barbara fiestas, Duncan Aikman reported that "every man, woman, and child who owed any allegiance to Santa Barbara was in costume. . . . Shoe salesmen and grocery clerks served you with a bit of scarlet braid on their trouser seams. Paunchy realtors and insurance solicitors full of mental mastery dashed about town in gaudy sashes. Deacons of the total immersion sects sported, at the least, a bit of crimson frill around their hat bands. High school boys scurried by, their heads gorgeously bound in scarfs and bandanas. . . . The very street-car conductors wore Spanish epaulettes and ear-rings and a look of grievance even more bitter than usual. Women wore mantillas and an apparently official uniform in the way of a waist of yellow, black and scarlet, so universally that you could tell the outland females by their native American costumes. The Mexican population dug up its old finery and musical instruments and paraded the sidewalks with the timid air of reasserting their importance after long abeyance." Once the fiesta is over, however, the Mexicans retreat to their *barrios*, the costumes are carefully put away for the balance of the year, and the grotesque Spanish spoken in the streets during the fiesta is heard no more. This particular attempt to revive the Mexican "Fiesta de la Primavera," like most similar attempts in Southern California, was first launched in the mid 'twenties, its immediate motivation in Santa Barbara being the popularly sensed need to inject a note of good cheer in the Santa Barbarans after the earthquake of 1924. The Santa Barbara fiesta is often highlighted by some extraordinary antic. Some years ago, for example, Cedric Gibbons and Dolores del Rio, of the motion-picture colony, dressed in fiesta costumes, astride their handsome Palominos, were the first couple to be married on horseback, a type of marriage ceremony now a regular feature of the fiesta.

About the most incongruous ceremonial revival of this sort in Southern California is the annual ride of the *Rancheros Visitadores*. This particular revival is based on the alleged practice of the rancheros, in former years, of making the round of the ranchos in the area, paying a visit to each in turn. "In May, 1930," to quote from the *Santa Barbara Guide*, "some sixty-five riders assembled for the first cavalcade. Golden Palominos and proud Arabian thoroughbreds, carrying silver-mounted tack, brushed stirrups with shaggy mustangs from the range. Emerging from the heavy gray mist of a reluctant day, they cantered with casual grace down the old familiar trails of the Santa Ynez, to converge in Santa Barbara. . . . Here, amid the tolling of bells, the tinkling of trappings, and the whinny-ing of horses, the brown-robed friars blessed them and bade them '*Vayan con dios.*' . . . This was the start of the first revival of the annual ride of the *Rancheros Visitadores.*"

Since this auspicious beginning, the affair has steadily increased in pomp and circumstance. Nowadays it is invariably reported in the Southern California press as a major social event of the year. A careful scrutiny of the names of these fancily dressed *visitadores* — these gaily costumed Rotarians — reveals that Leo Carrillo is about the only rider whose name carries a faint echo of the past and he is about as Mexican as the ceremony is Spanish. Ostensibly a gay affair, the annual ride represents a rather grim and desperate effort to escape from the bonds of a culture that neither satisfies nor pleases. Actually there is something rather pathetic about the spec-tacle of these frustrated business men cantering forth in search of *ersatz* week-end romance, evoking a past that never existed to cast some glamour on an equally unreal today.

All attempted revivals of Spanish folkways in Southern Cali-fornia are similarly ceremonial and ritualistic, a part of the sacred rather than the profane life of the region. The 3,279 Mexicans who live in Santa Barbara are doubtless more bewildered by these annual Spanish hijinks than any other group in the community. For here is a community that generously and lavishly supports the "Old Spanish Fiesta" — and the wealth of the *rancheros visitadores* is appar-ent for all to see — but which consistently rejects proposals to estab-lish a low-cost housing project for its Mexican residents. However, there is really nothing inconsistent about this attitude, for it merely reflects the manner in which the sacred aspects of the romantic past have been completely divorced from their secular connotations. The residents of Santa Barbara firmly believe, of course, that the Span-ish past is dead, extinct, vanished. In their thinking, the Mexicans living in Santa Barbara have no connection with this past. They just happen to be living in Santa Barbara. To be sure, many of them have names, such as Cota or Gutierrez, that should stir memories of the *dolce far niente* period. But these names are no longer important. They belong to the profane, and happily forgotten, side of the tradi-

tion. The sacred side of this tradition, as represented in the beautifully restored Mission, is worshipped by all alike without regard to
caste, class, or religious affiliation. The restored Mission is a much
better, a less embarrassing, symbol of the past than the Mexican
field worker or the ragamuffin *pachucos* of Los Angeles.

from

NORTH FROM MEXICO

Blood on the Pavements

On Thursday evening, June 3, 1943, the Alpine Club—made up
of youngsters of Mexican descent—held a meeting in a police
substation in Los Angeles. Usually these meetings were held in a
nearby public school but, since the school was closed, the boys had
accepted the invitation of a police captain to meet in the substation.
The principal business of the meeting, conducted in the presence of
the police captain, consisted in a discussion of how gang-strife could
best be avoided in the neighborhood. After the meeting had ad-
journed, the boys were taken in squad cars to the street corner nearest the neighborhood in which most of them lived. The squad cars
were scarcely out of sight, when the boys were assaulted, not by a
rival "gang" or "club," but by hoodlum elements in the neighborhood. Of one thing the boys were sure: their assailants were not of
Mexican descent.

Earlier the same evening a group of eleven sailors, on leave from
their station in Los Angeles, were walking along the 1700 block on
North Main Street in the center of one of the city's worst slum
areas. The surrounding neighborhood is predominantly Mexican.
On one side of the street the dirty brick front of a large brewery
hides from view a collection of ramshackle Mexican homes. The
other side of the street consists of a series of small bars, boarded-up
store fronts, and small shops. The area is well off the beaten paths
and few servicemen found their way this far north on Main Street.
As they were walking along the street, so they later stated, the
sailors were set upon by a gang of Mexican boys. One of the sailors

was badly hurt; the others suffered minor cuts and bruises. Accord-ing to their story, the sailors were outnumbered about three to one.

When the attack was reported to the nearest substation, the police adopted a curious attitude. Instead of attempting to find and arrest the assailants, fourteen policemen remained at the station after their regular duty was over for the night. Then, under the command of a detective lieutenant, the "Vengeance Squad," as they called themselves, set out "to clean up" the gang that had attacked the sailors. But—miracle of miracles!—when they arrived at the scene of the attack they could find no one to arrest—not a single Mexican—on their favorite charge of "suspicion of assault." In itself this curious inability to find anyone to arrest—so strikingly at variance with what usually happened on raids of this sort—raises an inference that a larger strategy was involved. For the raid accomplished nothing except to get the names of the raiding officers in the newspapers and to whip up the anger of the community against the Mexican popula-tion, which may, perhaps, have been the reason for the raid. . . .

Thus began the so-called "Zoot-Suit Race Riots" which were to last, in one form or another, for a week in Los Angeles.

1. THE TAXICAB BRIGADE

Taking the police raid as an official cue,—a signal for action,—about two hundred sailors decided to take the law into their own hands on the following night. Coming down into the center of Los Angeles from the Naval Armory in Chavez Ravine (near the "Chinatown" area), they hired a fleet of twenty taxicabs. Once as-sembled, the "task force" proceeded to cruise straight through the center of town en route to the east side of Los Angeles where the bulk of the Mexicans reside. Soon the sailors in the lead-car sighted a Mexican boy in a zoot-suit walking along the street. The "task force" immediately stopped and, in a few moments, the boy was lying on the pavement, badly beaten and bleeding. The sailors then piled back into the cabs and the caravan resumed its way until the next zoot-suiter was sighted, whereupon the same procedure was repeated. In these attacks, of course, the odds were pretty uneven: two hundred sailors to one Mexican boy. Four times this same treat-ment was meted out and four "gangsters,"—two seventeen-year-old youngsters, one nineteen, and one twenty-three, —were left lying on the pavements for the ambulances to pick up.

It is indeed curious that in a city like Los Angeles, which boasts that it has more police cars equipped with two-way radio than any other city in the world (Los Angeles *Times*, September 2, 1947), the police were apparently unable to intercept a caravan of twenty taxicabs, loaded with two hundred uniformed, yelling, bawdy sailors, as it cruised through the downtown and east-side sections of the city. At one point the police did happen to cross the trail of the caravan and the officers were apparently somewhat embarrassed over the meeting. For only nine of the sailors were taken into custody and the rest were permitted to continue on their merry way. No charges, however, were ever preferred against the nine.

Their evening's entertainment over, the sailors returned to the foot of Chavez Ravine. There they were met by the police and the Shore Patrol. The Shore Patrol took seventeen of the sailors into custody and sent the rest up to the ravine to the Naval Armory. The petty officer who had led the expedition, and who was not among those arrested, gave the police a frank statement of things to come. "We're out to do what the police have failed to do," he said; "we're going to clean up this situation. . . . Tonight [by then it was the morning of June fifth] the sailors may have the marines along" (I).

The next day the Los Angeles press pushed the war news from the front page as it proceeded to play up the pavement war in Los Angeles in screaming headlines. "Wild Night in L.A.—Sailor Zooter Clash" was the headline in the *Daily News*. "Sailor Task Force Hits L.A. Zooters" bellowed the *Herald-Express*. A suburban newspaper gleefully reported that "zoot-suited roughnecks fled to cover before a task force of twenty taxicabs." None of these stories, however, reported the slightest resistance, up to this point, on the part of the Mexicans.

True to their promise, the sailors were joined that night, June fifth, by scores of soldiers and marines. Squads of servicemen, arms linked, paraded through downtown Los Angeles four abreast, stopping anyone wearing zoot-suits and ordering these individuals to put away their "drapes" by the following night or suffer the consequences. Aside from a few half-hearted admonitions, the police made no effort whatever to interfere with these heralds of disorder.

However, twenty-seven Mexican boys, gathered on a street corner, were arrested and jailed that evening. While these boys were being booked "on suspicion" of various offenses, a mob of several hundred servicemen roamed the downtown section of a great city threatening members of the Mexican minority without hindrance or interference from the police, the Shore Patrol, or the Military Police.

On this same evening, a squad of sailors invaded a bar on the east side and carefully examined the clothes of the patrons. Two zoot-suit customers, drinking beer at a table, were peremptorily ordered to remove their clothes. One of them was beaten and his clothes were torn from his back when he refused to comply with the order. The other—they were both Mexicans—doffed his "drapes" which were promptly ripped to shreds. Similar occurrences in several parts of the city that evening were sufficiently alarming to have warranted some precautionary measures or to have justified an "out-of-bounds" order. All that the police officials did, however, was to call up some additional reserves and announce that any Mexicans involved in the rioting would be promptly arrested. That there had been no counterattacks by the Mexicans up to this point apparently did not enter into the police officers' appraisal of the situation. One thing must be said for the Los Angeles police: it is above all consistent. When it is wrong, it is consistently wrong; when it makes a mistake, it will be repeated.

By the night of June sixth the police had worked out a simple formula for action. Knowing that wherever the sailors went there would be trouble, the police simply followed the sailors at a conveniently spaced interval. Six carloads of sailors cruised down Brooklyn Avenue that evening. At Ramona Boulevard, they stopped and beat up eight teenage Mexicans. Failing to find any Mexican zoot-suiters in a bar on Indiana Street, they were so annoyed that they proceeded to wreck the establishment. In due course, the police made a leisurely appearance at the scene of the wreckage but could find no one to arrest. Carefully following the sailors, the police arrested eleven boys who had been beaten up on Carmelita Street; six more victims were arrested a few blocks further on, seven at Ford Boulevard, six at Gifford Street—and so on straight through the Mexican east-side settlements. Behind them came the police, stopping at the same street corners "to mop up" by arresting the injured victims of the mob. By morning, some forty-four Mexican boys, all severely beaten, were under arrest.

2. OPERATION "DIXIE"

The stage was now set for the really serious rioting of June seventh and eighth. Having featured the preliminary rioting as an offensive launched by sailors, soldiers, and marines, the press now whipped public opinion into a frenzy by dire warnings that Mexican zoot-suiters planned mass retaliations. To insure a riot, the precise street corners were named at which retaliatory action was expected and the time of the anticipated action was carefully specified. In effect these stories announced a riot and invited public participation. "Zooters Planning to Attack More Servicemen," headlined the *Daily News*; "Would jab broken bottlenecks in the faces of their victims. . . . Beating sailors' brains out with hammers also on the program." Concerned for the safety of the Army, the Navy, and the Marine Corps, the *Herald-Express* warned that "Zooters . . . would mass 500 strong."

By way of explaining the action of the police throughout the subsequent rioting, it should be pointed out that, in June, 1943, the police were on a bad spot. A man by the name of Beebe, arrested on a drunk charge, had been kicked to death in the Central Jail by police officers. Through the excellent work of an alert police commissioner, the case had finally been broken and, at the time of the riots, a police officer by the name of Compton Dixon was on trial in the courts. While charges of police brutality had been bandied about for years, this was the first time that a seemingly airtight case had been prepared. Shortly after the riots, a Hollywood police captain told a motion picture director that the police had touched off the riots "in order to give Dixie (Dixon) a break." By staging a fake demonstration of the alleged necessity for harsh police methods, it was hoped that the jury would acquit Dixon. As a matter of fact, the jury did disagree and on July 2, 1943, the charges against Dixon were dismissed.

On Monday evening, June seventh, thousands of *Angelenos*, in response to twelve hours' advance notice in the press, turned out for a mass lynching. Marching through the streets of downtown Los Angeles, a mob of several thousand soldiers, sailors, and civilians, proceeded to beat up every zoot-suiter they could find. Pushing its way into the important motion picture theaters, the mob ordered the management to turn on the house lights and then ranged up and down the aisles dragging Mexicans out of their seats. Street cars were halted while Mexicans, and some Filipinos and Negroes, were jerked out of their seats, pushed into the streets, and beaten with sadistic frenzy. If the victims wore zoot-suits, they were stripped of their clothing and left naked or half-naked on the streets, bleeding and bruised. Proceeding down Main Street from First to Twelfth, the mob stopped on the edge of the Negro district. Learning that the Negroes planned a warm reception for them, the mobsters turned back and marched through the Mexican east side spreading panic and terror.

Here is one of numerous eye-witness accounts written by Al Waxman, editor of *The Eastside Journal*:

> At Twelfth and Central I came upon a scene that will long live in my memory. Police were swinging clubs and servicemen were fighting with civilians. Wholesale arrests were being made by the officers.
>
> Four boys came out of a pool hall. They were wearing the zoot-suits that have become the symbol of a fighting flag. Police ordered them into arrest cars. One refused. He asked: "Why am I being arrested?" The police officer answered with three swift blows of the night-stick across the boy's head and he went down. As he sprawled, he was kicked in the face. Police had difficulty loading his body into the vehicle because he was one-legged and wore a wooden limb. Maybe the officer didn't know he was attacking a cripple.
>
> At the next corner a Mexican mother cried out, "Don't take my boy, he did nothing. He's only fifteen years old. Don't take him." She was struck across the jaw with a night-stick and almost dropped the two and a half year old baby that was clinging in her arms. . . .
>
> Rushing back to the east side to make sure that things were quiet here, I came upon a band of servicemen making a systematic tour of East First Street. They had just come out of a cocktail bar where four men were nursing bruises. Three autos loaded with Los Angeles policemen were on the scene but the soldiers were not molested. Farther down the street the men stopped a streetcar, forcing the motorman to open the door and proceeded to inspect the clothing of the

male passengers. "We're looking for zoot-suits to burn," they shouted. Again the police did not interfere. . . . Half a block away . . . I pleaded with the men of the local police substation to put a stop to these activities. "It is a matter for the military police," they said.

Throughout the night the Mexican communities were in the wildest possible turmoil. Scores of Mexican mothers were trying to locate their youngsters and several hundred Mexicans milled around each of the police substations and the Central Jail trying to get word of missing members of their families. Boys came into the police stations saying: "Charge me with vagrancy or anything, but don't send me out there!" pointing to the streets where other boys, as young as twelve and thirteen years of age, were being beaten and stripped of their clothes. From affidavits which I helped prepare at the time, I should say that not more than half of the victims were actually wearing zoot-suits. A Negro defense worker, wearing a defense-plant identification badge on his workclothes, was taken from a street car and one of his eyes was gouged out with a knife. Huge half-page photographs, showing Mexican boys stripped of their clothes, cowering on the pavements, often bleeding profusely, surrounded by jeering mobs of men and women, appeared in all the Los Angeles newspapers. As Al Waxman most truthfully reported, blood had been "spilled on the streets of the city."

At midnight on June seventh, the military authorities decided that the local police were completely unable or unwilling to handle the situation, despite the fact that a thousand reserve officers had been called up. The entire downtown area of Los Angeles was then declared "out of bounds" for military personnel. This order immediately slowed down the pace of the rioting. The moment the Military Police and Shore Patrol went into action, the rioting quieted down. On June eighth the city officials brought their heads up out of the sand, took a look around, and began issuing statements. The district attorney, Fred N. Howser, announced that the "situation is getting entirely out of hand," while Mayor Fletcher Bowron thought that "sooner or later it will blow over." The chief of police, taking a count of the Mexicans in jail, cheerfully proclaimed that "the situation has now cleared up." All agreed, however, that it was quite "a situation."

Unfortunately "the situation" had not cleared up; nor did it blow over. It began to spread to the suburbs where the rioting continued for two more days. When it finally stopped, the Eagle Rock *Advertiser* mournfully editorialized: "It is too bad the service-men were called off before they were able to complete the job. . . . Most of the citizens of the city have been delighted with what has been going on." County Supervisor Roger Jessup told the news-men: "All that is needed to end lawlessness is more of the same action as is being exercised by the servicemen!" While the district attorney of Ventura, an outlying county, jumped on the band-wagon with a statement to the effect that "zoot suits are an open indication of subversive character." This was also the opinion of the Los Angeles City Council which adopted a resolution making the wearing of zoot-suits a misdemeanor! On June eleventh, hun-dreds of handbills were distributed to students and posted on bul-letin boards in a high school attended by many Negroes and Mex-icans which read: "Big Sale. Second-Hand Zoot Suits. Slightly Damaged. Apply at Nearest U.S. Naval Station. While they last we have your Size."

3. WHEN THE DEVIL IS SICK . . .

Egging on the mob to attack Mexicans in the most indiscrimi-nate manner, the press developed a fine technique in reporting the riots. "44 Zooters Jailed in Attacks on Sailors" was the chief head-line in the *Daily News* of June seventh; "Zoot Suit Chiefs Girding for War on Navy" was the headline in the same paper on the following day. The moralistic tone of this reporting is illustrated by a smug headline in the Los Angeles *Times* of June seventh: "Zoot Suiters Learn Lesson in Fight with Servicemen." The riots, according to the same paper, were having "a cleansing effect." An editorial in the *Herald-Express* said that the riots "promise to rid the community of . . . those zoot-suited miscreants." While Mr. Manchester Boddy, in a signed editorial in the *Daily News* of June ninth excitedly announced that "the time for temporizing is past. . . . The time has come to serve notice that the City of Los Angeles will no longer be terrorized by a relatively small handful of morons parading as zoot suit hoodlums. To delay action *now* means to court disaster later on." As though there had been any "temporizing," in this sense, for the prior two years!

But once the Navy had declared the downtown section of Los Angeles "out of bounds," once the Mexican ambassador in Washington had addressed a formal inquiry to Secretary of State Hull, and once official Washington began to advise the local minions of the press of the utterly disastrous international effects of the riots, in short when the local press realized the consequences of its own lawless action, a great thunderous cry for "unity," and "peace," and "order" went forth. One after the other, the editors began to disclaim all responsibility for the riots which, two days before, had been hailed for their "salutary" and "cleansing" effect.

Thus on June eleventh the Los Angeles *Times*, in pious mood, wrote that,

> at the outset, zoot-suiters were limited to no specific race; they were Anglo-Saxon, Latin and Negro. The fact that later on their numbers seemed to be predominantly Latin was in itself no indictment of that race at all. No responsible person at any time condemned Latin-Americans as such.

Feeling a twinge of conscience, Mr. Boddy wrote that "only a ridiculously small percentage of the local Mexican population is involved in the so-called gang demonstrations. Every true Californian has an affection for his fellow citizens of Mexican ancestry that is as deep rooted as the Mexican culture that influences our way of living, our architecture, our music, our language, and even our food." This belated discovery of the Spanish-Mexican cultural heritage of California was, needless to say, rather ironic in view of the fact that the ink was not yet dry on Mr. Boddy's earlier editorial in which he had castigated the Mexican minority as "morons." To appreciate the ironic aspects of "the situation," the same news-papers that had been baiting Mexicans for nearly two years now began to extol them (2).

As might have been expected, this post-mortem mood of penitence and contrition survived just long enough for some of the international repercussions of the riots to quiet down. Within a year, the press and the police were back in the same old groove. On July 16, 1944, the Los Angeles *Times* gave front-page prominence to a curious story under the heading: "Youthful Gang Secrets Exposed." Indicating no source, identifying no spokesman, the story went on to say that "authorities of the Superior Court" had unearthed a dreadful "situation" among juvenile delinquents. Juveniles were using narcotics, marihuana, and smoking "reefers." Compelled to accept drug addiction, "unwilling neophytes" were dragooned into committing robberies and other crimes. Young girls were tatooed with various "secret cabalistic symbols" of gang membership. The high pompadours affected by the *cholitas*, it was said, were used to conceal knives and other "weapons." Two theories were advanced in the story by way of "explaining" the existence of these dangerous gangs: first, that "subversive groups" in Los Angeles had organized them; and, second, that "the gangs are the result of mollycoddling of racial groups." In view of the record, one is moved to inquire, what mollycoddling? by the police? by the juvenile authorities? by the courts? Backing up the news story, an editorial appeared in the *Times* on July eighteenth entitled: "It's Not a Nice Job But It Has To Be Done." Lashing out at "any maudlin and misguided sympathy for the 'poor juveniles,'" the editorial went on to say that "stern punishment is what is needed; stern and sure punishment. The police and the Sheriff's men *should be given every encouragement* to go after these young gangsters" (emphasis mine).

Coincident with the appearance of the foregoing news story and editorial, the Juvenile Court of Los Angeles entered a most remarkable order in its minutes on July 31, 1944. The order outlined a plan by which Mexican wards of the Juvenile Court, over sixteen years of age, might be turned over to the Atchison, Topeka, and Santa Fe Railroad for a type of contract-employment. A form of contract, between the parents of the youngsters and the railroad, was attached to the order. The contract provided that the ward was to work "as a track laborer" at 58½¢ per hour; that $1.03 per day was to be deducted for board, $2.50 per month for dues in a hospital association, and 10¢ a day for laundry. It was also provided that one-half of the pay was to be turned over to the probation officers to be held in trust for the ward. That this order was specifically aimed at *Mexican* juveniles is clearly shown by the circumstance that the court, prior to approving the arrangement, had first secured its approval by a committee of "representative" leaders of the Mexican-American community.

4. THE STRANGE CASE OF THE SILK PANTIES

All of this, one will say,—the Sleepy Lagoon case, the riots, etc.,—belongs to the past. But does it? On the morning of July 21, 1946, a thirteen-year-old Mexican boy, Eugene Chavez Monte-negro, Jr., was shot and killed by a deputy sheriff in Montebello Park on the east side of Los Angeles. The deputy sheriff later testi-fied that he had been called to the area by reports of a prowler. On arriving at the scene, he had stationed himself near a window of the house in question and had played his flashlight on the window. A little later, he testified, "a man" lifted the screen on the window, crawled out, and ran past him. When the "man" failed to halt on order, he had shot him in the back. At the coroner's inquest, the same deputy also testified that he had seen another officer remove a pair of "silk panties" from the dead boy's pocket and that the boy was armed with "a Boy Scout's knife."

While incidents of this kind have been common occurrences in Los Angeles for twenty years, in this case the officers had shot the wrong boy. For it turned out that young Montenegro was an honor student at St. Alphonsus parochial school; that his parents were a highly respectable middle-class couple; and that the neighbors, Anglo-Americans as well as Mexicans, all testified that the boy had an excellent reputation. Accepting the officers' version of the facts, it was still difficult to explain why they had made no effort to halt the boy, who was five feet three inches tall, when he ran directly past them within arms' reach. Before the hearings were over, the "silk panties" story was exposed as a complete fake. Despite a gal-lant fight waged by Mr. and Mrs. Montenegro to vindicate the reputation of their own son, nothing came of the investigation. "Raging Mother Attacks Deputy Who Slew Son" was the *Daily News* headline on the story of the investigation.

... On January 23, 1947, the attorney general of California ordered the removal of two police officers for the brutal beating of four Mexican nationals who, with eight hundred of their country-men, had been brought to Oxnard to harvest the crops.... On March 30, 1946, a private detective killed Tiofilo Pelagio, a Mexi-can national, in a café argument.... On the same day affidavits were presented to the authorities that confessions from four Mexi-

can boys, all minors, had been obtained by force and violence. . . .
Esther Armenta, sixteen years of age, complained to her mother
that she was being mistreated by Anglo-American classmates in a
Los Angeles junior high school. "They would spit on her," said Mrs.
Catalina Armenta, the mother, "and call her a 'dirty Mex.' Esther
would come home in tears and beg me to get her transferred." A few
weeks later the girl was in juvenile court charged with the use of
"bad language." She was then sent to the Ventura School for Girls,
a so-called "correctional" institution. When Mrs. Armenta finally
got permission to visit her daughter, in the presence of a matron, the
girl had "black and blue marks on her arm" and complained that she
had been whipped by one of the matrons. . . . On April 10, 1946,
Mrs. Michael Gonzales complained to the Federation of Spanish-
American Voters that her daughter had been placed in the Ventura
School without her knowledge or consent and that when she had
protested this action she had been threatened with deportation by
an official of the juvenile court. . . . On the basis of a stack of affidavits, the San Fernando Valley Council on Race Relations charged
on May 16, 1947, that the police had broken into Mexican homes
without search warrants; that they had beaten, threatened, and
intimidated Mexican juveniles; and that they were in the habit of
making "wholesale roundups and arrests of Mexican-American
boys without previous inquiry as to the arrested boys' connection —
if any — with the crime in question." . . . In 1946 a prominent official
of the Los Angeles schools told me that she had been horrified to
discover that, in the Belvedere district, Mexican-American girls,
stripped of their clothing, were forced to parade back and forth, in the
presence of other girls in the "gym," as a disciplinary measure. . . .*

5. THE POLITICS OF PREJUDICE

I reported the zoot-suit riots in Los Angeles for *PM* and *The New
Republic* and had a hand in some of the hectic events of that memorable week. Following the June seventh rioting, I chaired a meeting
of a hundred or more citizens at which an emergency committee

*For a detailed account of still another "incident," see *Justice for Salcido* by Guy
Endore, published by the Civil Rights Congress of Los Angeles, July, 1948.

was formed to bring about, if possible, a return to sanity in Los Angeles. That same evening we communicated with Attorney General Robert W. Kenny in San Francisco by telephone and urged him to induce Governor Earl Warren to appoint an official committee of inquiry. The next day the governor appointed a committee of five which included four names from a panel which I had submitted. The fifth member was the governor's own selection: Mr. Leo Carrillo. Mr. Carrillo, like the sheriff of Los Angeles, is a descendant of "an early California family." The committee immediately assembled in Los Angeles where Mr. Kenny presented to them a proposed report, with findings and recommendations, which I had prepared at his request. With some modifications, this report was adopted by the committee and submitted to the governor. Out of the work of our emergency committee there finally emerged, after a year of negotiation, the present-day Council of Civic Unity.

Praising the report of the governor's committee—which I had prepared—the Los Angeles *Times* devoted several harsh editorials to certain "reckless" individuals, myself included, who had suggested that "racial prejudice" might have had something to do with the riots! "When trouble arose," said the *Times* in an editorial of June 15, 1943, "through the depredations of the young gangs attired in zoot-suits, it was their weird dress and not their race which resulted in difficulties. That is a simple truth which no amount of propaganda will change." In the same editorial, the charges of unfairness which I had raised in connection with the Sleepy Lagoon case were branded as "distortions," "wild charges," and "inflammatory accusations" (charges later confirmed in minute detail by the District Court of Appeals).

When Mrs. Eleanor Roosevelt innocently remarked in her column that the zoot-suit riots were "in the nature of race riots," she was severely taken to task by the *Times* in an editorial of June eighteenth under the caption: "Mrs. Roosevelt Blindly Stirs Race Discord." Even the president of the Los Angeles Chamber of Commerce felt compelled to reply to Mrs. Roosevelt. "These so-called 'zoot-suit' riots," he said, "have never been and are not now in the nature of race riots. . . . At no time has the issue of race entered into consideration. . . . Instead of discriminating against Mexicans, California has always treated them with the utmost consideration" (3).

The zoot-suit riots in Los Angeles were the spark that touched off a chain-reaction of riots across the country in midsummer 1943. Similar "zoot-suit" disturbances were reported in San Diego on June ninth; in Philadelphia on June tenth; in Chicago on June fifteenth; and in Evansville, Indiana, on June twenty-seventh. Between June sixteenth and August first, large-scale race riots occurred in Beaumont, Texas, in Detroit, and in Harlem. The Detroit riots of June 20–21 were the most disastrous riots in a quarter of a century. The swift, crazy violence of the Harlem riot resulted, in a few hours' time, in property damage totalling nearly a million dollars. The rapid succession of these violent and destructive riots seriously interfered with the war effort and had the most adverse international repercussions. The spark that ignited these explosions occurred in *El Pueblo de Nuestra Señora La Reina de Los Angeles de Porciúncula,* founded by Felipe de Neve in 1781, settled by Mexican *pobladores.*

None of these disturbances had more serious international consequences than the zoot-suit riots. On April 20, 1943, President Roosevelt had held his historic meeting with President Camacho on the soil of Mexico. At the time the riots occurred, Mexico was our ally in the war against Germany, Italy, and Japan. Large-scale shipments of Mexican nationals had just begun to arrive in the United States to relieve the critical manpower shortage. "Our two countries," President Roosevelt had said, "owe their independence to the fact that your ancestors and mine held the same truths to be worth fighting for and dying for. Hidalgo and Juárez were men of the same stamp as Washington and Jefferson." President Camacho, replying to this toast, had said that "the negative memories" of the past were forgotten in the accord of today. And then in the largest city in the old Spanish borderland had come this explosion of hatred and prejudice against Spanish-speaking people.

In response to a request from the Mexican ambassador, Secretary of State Hull had asked Mayor Fletcher Bowron for an official explanation. With a perfectly straight face, the mayor replied that the riots were devoid of any element of prejudice against persons of Mexican descent! The same edition of the newspapers that carried this statement also carried another statement by the mayor under a headline which read: "Mayor Pledges 2-Fisted Action, No Wrist

Slap"—a reference to police action contemplated against the Mexican minority. On June ninth Mr. Churchill Murray, local representative of the coordinator of Inter-American Affairs, wired Mr. Rockefeller that the riots were "non-racial." "The frequency of Mexican names among the victims," he said, "was without actual significance." If all this were true, asked Dan G. Acosta in a letter to the Los Angeles press, "Why are we consistently called hoodlums? Why is mob action encouraged by the newspapers? Why did the city police stand around saying very nonchalantly that they could not intervene and even hurrahed the soldiers for their 'brave' action? Not until these questions are answered, will the Mexican population feel at ease."

What the riots did, of course, was to expose the rotten foundations upon which the City of Los Angeles had built a papier-mâché façade of "Inter-American Good Will" made up of fine-sounding Cinco de Mayo proclamations. During the riots, the press, the police, the officialdom, and the dominant control groups of Los Angeles were caught with the bombs of prejudice in their hands. One year before the riots occurred, they had been warned of the danger of an explosion. The riots were not an unexpected rupture in Anglo-Hispano relations but the logical end-product of a hundred years of neglect and discrimination.

The riots left a residue of resentment and hatred in the minds and hearts of thousands of young Mexican-Americans in Los Angeles. During the rioting, one Los Angeles newspaper had published a story to the effect that the *cholitas* and *pachucas* were merely cheap prostitutes, infected with venereal disease and addicted to the use of marihuana. Eighteen Mexican-American girls promptly replied in a letter which the metropolitan press refused to publish: "The girls in this meeting room consist of young girls who graduated from high school as honor students, of girls who are now working in defense plants because we want to help win the war, and of girls who have brothers, cousins, relatives and sweethearts in all branches of the American armed forces. We have not been able to have our side of the story told." The letter, with a picture of the girls, was published in Al Waxman's *Eastside Journal* on June 16, 1943. Still another group of Mexican-American girls,—real *pachucas* these,—bitterly protested the story in another letter which the metropolitan press did not publish. These girls insisted that they should be examined, as a group, by an officially appointed board of physicians so that they could prove that they were virgins. Long after the riots, I have seen Mexican-American boys pull creased and wrinkled newspaper clippings from their wallets and exhibit this slanderous story with the greatest indignation. Four years have now passed since the riots, but the blood has not yet been washed from the pavements of Los Angeles.

1. *Los Angeles Herald-Express*, June 5, 1943.
2. "Imported Mexican Workers Save Millions in Citrus Crops," reads a headline, *Los Angeles Times*, June 30, 1943.
3. *Los Angeles Times*, June 18, 1943.

Simone de Beauvoir

Simone de Beauvoir (1908–1986) spent four densely packed months exploring in early 1947. She was already famous enough to have *The New York Times Magazine* feature her in an article entitled "An Existentialist Looks at Americans." Her diary of the trip, *America Day by Day* (1948), has as much to say about her shifting states of consciousness as it does about the States: "I return to the movies. . . . I need black-and-white images like a drug." Opinionated and often critical of American politics and puritanical moral codes, Beauvoir nonetheless maintains a freshness of response that keeps her book alive as a kind of intellectual photograph album.

from

AMERICA DAY BY DAY

February 25

When I awoke yesterday morning, it was in an endless desert of pink stones. I spent the whole day in the bar with magnificent bay windows that allowed the desert to invade the train. In Albuquerque, the afternoon sun was burning-hot. On the platform, Indians with braids were selling rugs and little multicolored moccasins. In the garden of the beautiful Mexican-style hotel, tourists sitting in rocking chairs watched the train travelers, who watched them back. I knew I would return at leisure to these regions in a few weeks, so I felt no regret as I saw the great plateaus of flaming color and the Indian shacks disappear. It was still desert while I slept. But at dawn, when I pull back the curtain, the scenery has changed. A gray fog fills the damp prairies and the trees; in the distance the hills are a blur against a muggy sky. This is how I've entered California. The name is almost as magical as "New York." It's the land of streets paved with gold, of pioneers and cowboys. Through history and movies it's become a legendary country that, like all legends, belongs to my own past.

I'm burning with impatience. This time I'm not arriving as a tourist in a land where nothing is meant for me; I'm coming to see a woman friend who happens to be living in a land everyone says is

marvelous. It's perhaps even stranger to feel expected in an unknown place than to prepare yourself to disembark without help. I
don't know what awaits me, but someone knows. The sea, orange
juice, mountains, flowers, whiskeys—I'm not going to encounter
them and try to possess them; they will be given to me. Someone is
waiting for the right moment to present them to me as a gift. They
already are a gift; and in my heart I feel the anxiety and greed of
childhood Christmas Eves.

The fog lifts a little. I see long, shady avenues of palm trees and
quiet houses surrounded by fresh lawns. The train stops at a little
suburban station — Pasadena. For another half hour, we roll through
the outlying suburbs cut out of the shapeless countryside, and the
train goes underground. Los Angeles. A black employee unfolds
three folding steps, which connect the train car to the ground. I am
on the deserted platform, then in a corridor, and finally in the hall
where N. [Nathalie ("Natasha") Sorokine Moffatt, a close friend] is
waiting for me.

A year ago N. married a GI [Ivan Moffatt], who is now a
scriptwriter in Hollywood. When she came to join him, they hadn't a
penny between them, and I. was earning very little money. N. was
expecting a baby. Thanks to the credit system they practice here, they
could rent a kind of barn and transform it into a livable house and
also buy a car, something absolutely necessary in this city of vast distances. Now I.'s situation has improved, but his salary is almost
entirely consigned to paying off his debts. Besides, a law requires
parents to take their children to the doctor once a week during their
first year; this is very costly. It's hard to balance the budget every
month. I know all that and also that I.'s car is red. So I am utterly
astonished to see a little yellow car standing in front of the station. N.
tells me, "It's ours. I. bought it last week just so we could drive
around." "Nothing simpler," adds N., "since you buy without paying!" Obviously. But I'm stunned by such ease. Los Angeles also
stuns me. This city is unlike any other. Below me, the downtown
looks just like the downtowns of Rochester, Buffalo, and Cleveland,
which themselves evoke New York's downtown and Chicago's Loop.
It's the tall buildings housing banks, stores, and movie theaters; the
monotonous checkerboard of streets and avenues. But then, all the
neighborhoods we drive through are either disorganized outlying

districts or huge developments where identical wooden houses multiply as far as the eye can see, each one surrounded by a little garden. The traffic is terrifying; the broad roadways are divided into six lanes, three in each direction, marked off by white lines, and you are allowed to pass to either the right or the left. You can turn to the right only from the right lane, to the left only from the left; this last maneuver is often prohibited, which complicates one's itinerary. At intersections the car that has arrived first has priority, a rule that provokes thousands of disputes. The experts manage marvelously, and the cars move along at a disquieting speed. N. must also go as fast, or the car will be rear-ended; I understand why she might be a little tense behind the wheel. She relaxes when we arrive at the hills, where the most elegant part of the city rises in tiers. Here the avenues thread their way between golf courses, gardens, and parks, which conceal luxurious residences. We make our way slowly through Beverly Hills, where the Hollywood stars live. We take a broad, almost rustic road bordered by fields and gardens, and the car stops in front of a hedge, which is cut through by a gravel drive. We've been traveling for one hour, often at more than forty miles per hour.

The house is at the back of a garden blooming with roses and bordered by tall eucalyptus trees; it's a wooden house with an outside staircase, and it doesn't look American. The ground floor is a huge studio belonging to a painter whose own wooden house stands in another corner of the garden. N. lives only on the upper floor. The rooms are nearly bare, furnished with beds and stools that N. and I. made with boards painted in bright colors. There are a few Indian rugs, a few beautiful Mexican objects, a cock in shiny metal, wax oranges. The bathroom is already installed, but there is no refrigerator—they expect to have one next year. From the terrace at the top of the stairs, beyond the indistinct vastness of the city, you glimpse the sea. At the back of the garden there are three horses that belong to rich neighbors. N. has taken the horses on as boarders; she also raised ducks, but a coyote climbed up from the depths of the canyon and ate them all. The mountains in the distance look wild: one feels that the most sophisticated city in the world is surrounded by indomitable nature. If human pressure were relaxed for even a moment, the wild animals and the giant grasses would soon reclaim possession of their domain.

After a short stop, we leave again in the little car. It's a damp, foggy day; the sky is gray—such days are rare in California. I understand how I. has helped us by buying this car: there's no subway in this city at ground level, the bus and tram routes are interminable, and taxis are rare and expensive. As for walking, that's out of the question; there's not a single pedestrian on these endless roadways. Those who don't have a car hitch rides at the street corners. Los Angeles is almost as big as the Côte d'Azur; in fact, it isn't a city at all but a collection of villages, residential neighborhoods, and encampments separated by woods and parks. Brentwood, Westwood, Beverly Hills, and Hollywood are each autonomous areas. The area closest to our house is Westwood, which is five or six miles away. It's a real "village," in the American sense of the word. It has its main street, stores, banks, and drugstores, and around this commercial center it has its residential neighborhoods. One peculiar aspect of Westwood is that because of its proximity to a university, the consumption and sale of alcohol are prohibited—there's no bar, no liquor store. You have to go as far as Brentwood if you want to buy a bottle of wine.

Hollywood, as everyone knows, is where the studios are. The stars live in Beverly Hills. To see their houses, you have to enter an artificial park humming with neither the muffled life of the countryside nor the feverish life of the city; the luxurious villas are surrounded by a false solitude. Avenues lined with garages and with flat-roofed boutiques, barely one-story high; a blue coastal road above the sea; vast camps of parked trailers, those caravans in which many homeless Americans live on the outskirts of towns; working-class sections filled with monotonous shacks—all this is spinning in my head. Along the roads, large billboards suggest, "To visit the houses of the stars, call the Smith Agency." The fog has dissipated. Against the hard blue of the sky, airplanes write advertising announcements in trailing white letters. In the sun, the dust, the noise, Los Angeles has the ugliness of a Parisian fair.

We lunch at the seaside at the counter of a restaurant-bar whose walls are lined with photographs of stars. At the end of the afternoon

I give a lecture, an activity that seems out of place today. At dusk we meet I. in a Hollywood bar. I am amazed to see him in civilian clothes. Perhaps because the soldiers wore the American uniform in such a nonmilitary fashion in Paris, it seemed to me like a form of national dress. When I arrived in New York, I was vaguely surprised to find men dressed in business suits. In the twilight the harshness of the city is softened. Hollywood Boulevard follows the contours of a hill; sitting at the bar, we look through a large bay window and see at our feet the spread of houses where the first lights are coming on. Little by little Los Angeles is transformed into a large, glittering lake. The window that frames the night and my friends' presence near me make this vision a performance meant for me. Los Angeles has prepared a triumphant welcome for me: all evening I am going to walk through a celebration given in my honor.

The back fins on I.'s big red car bear the traces of many misadventures: life is hard here for automobiles. It carries us toward the Mexican part of town. There are few blacks in Los Angeles; instead, there are many Mexicans, who are more or less despised, and sometimes boycotted, but for whom the whites feel no racial hatred. On the East Coast, California seems like an exotic land; in California, exoticism means Mexico, which is so close geographically and historically, since a hundred years ago this coast belonged to Mexico. We drive for half an hour, and when we stop, I'm dazzled by an extravagant riot of colors: it's the energy, the life, the gaiety of Spanish markets and Moroccan *souks*. The street is a large bazaar: small kiosks lit by candles are set up on the esplanade, where you can buy wonderful objects—yellow or red jackets embroidered with palm trees and birds, colorful dresses, cowboy boots decorated with red or green leather, sandals, dolls, pottery, rugs, fabrics, necklaces, and beaded bracelets. They sell miniature skulls and little jointed skeletons, favorite fetishes of a people in love with death. One of the most seductive novelties is a garland of pinecones and dried foliage painted in crude blue, yellow, and red; it's a decoration to be hung from the ceiling, and it has the rustic splendor of strings of onions and garlic, dried mushrooms, and hams hung from the wooden beams of French farmhouses. On both sides of the street, stores sell the same sparkling merchandise. Of all the shops, the most beautiful is the one where they make candles. It's a palace of colors. In a penetrating odor of wax and resin, enormous tapers rise up from the floor, hang from the ceiling, and decorate the walls. There are fat ones, thin ones, red ones, yellow ones, blue ones, green ones; they are decorated with hearts, tears, and scrolls. Scarlet wax pinecones, oranges, and pineapples sit in cut metal candleholders. And the wax boils in large vats. In the *souks* of Marrakech the dyers brew the same blue, yellow, and blood red dye in similar vats. But here the colors melting together are dangerous to touch; they burn. Once cooled, they form enormous pedestals, where they are jumbled together in a rococo confusion.

All the jumbled wonders of the bazaar have found their place in the restaurant we enter. The tables are lit by tapers for which the most amazing chandeliers have been devised: stuck in an empty bottle, the candles weep multicolored tears night after night, and the glass is drowned in the thickness of a rainbow formed by wax stalactites. These candleholders seem fashioned by the whim of some petrifying fountain, but also conceived by a slightly delirious mind —at once natural wonder and surrealist fantasy. The waiters and waitresses wear Mexican dress. We order some tequila, and the waiter hesitates: N. looks very young, and they cannot serve liquor to minors. She shows them her identity card. In any case, since adult consumption is unlimited, we could easily have tricked them, but this way she has the right to her own glass. I watch the Mexican dances and eat chili con carne, which takes the roof off my mouth. I drink the tequila, and I'm utterly dazed with pleasure. In New York I knew the keen joy of discovery; here, I receive gifts—it's another kind of happiness.

February 26

None of the Americans I knew in the East had ever set foot in California. When they have free time, they're more drawn to Europe, which is almost as close. And there are many people in this part of the country who have never seen New York. It's impossible to find the New York papers here, except in rare, specialized shops; everyone in Los Angeles reads the Los Angeles papers. All the states have their local press and a vivid sense of their own uniqueness. But California is, I'm told, the only state—along with Texas, perhaps— that thinks of itself as California before feeling it's part of the U.S.A.

Its attitude is explained by its history, its geographic situation, and especially its economic autonomy. If I think about New York or Chicago here, in Los Angeles, I have the impression of being altogether elsewhere and yet still part of the same world. Through its radio, its magazines, and its manufactured products, America is utterly present in each of its parts—but these are more or less strangers to one another. There is no direct communication between the different states, yet they all participate in the unity that transcends them. The result is a mixture of uniformity and regionalism that is often disconcerting.

N. takes me for another daylong tour through a Los Angeles that is both familiar and utterly unexpected. Near Westwood I see a veterans' hospital that is like a village unto itself. Here they rehabilitate the wounded, the amputees, the disturbed; they shelter the invalids and the incurables and provisionally lodge certain veterans who have not yet found either work or housing. There are living quarters, libraries, drugstores, and cafeterias, where the sale of alcohol is prohibited, of course. In front of the doors, men sit sadly warming themselves on benches in the sun, and others walk around looking bored.

We cross one suburb after another—nothing but suburbs. The city slips away like a phantom city. The streets thrown down any which way on the sides of hills, in the hollows of valleys, have been laid out at random as needed, without any general plan. We drive a long time before arriving at our destination—the "optimistic" cemetery called Forest Lawn Mortuary. It covers a vast hill where, as at Arlington, broad roads wind their way. It's a verdant park shaded by luxurious trees. Here and there on the damp lawns stands a flat plate with just a name. It looks like the dead are buried beneath the grass with rural simplicity, as in Corsican cemeteries: there's no monumental tomb, no mortuary chapel; one imagines simple wooden coffins ingenuously entrusted to the earth. We find an open grave with men gathered around it. We approach without qualms, since no one has accompanied the dead to his grave—it's not the custom in this cheerful land. In fact, the grass is merely a light crust covering a vast network of masonry. The graves are built of concrete; the coffin is lowered by a system of ropes and pulleys. The grave diggers are not gardeners but mechanics. And as for the grass that disguises the cement architecture, it comes in large strips that are rolled out like linoleum. It must be mass-produced somewhere. N. tells me that the coffins themselves are airtight so that worms cannot live in them; the bodies are mummified with greater or lesser perfection, depending on the cost of the plan. In any case, the insides have been removed, the faces made-up and painted; they are on view for a day or two to relatives and friends in the funeral home. At the top of the hill there is a panoramic view of Los Angeles, the sea, and the mountains behind. A chapel stands there, but the most astonishing monument is the "Book of David," a simulacrum of a book that is at least as tall as a man and open in the middle. On the open pages, written in large printed letters, one reads an inscription that says in effect, "How beautiful it is, from the height of this majestic cliff, to look down upon the city of the living and the city of the dead. This is one of the summits of the world. But what you do not see is that in the sides of this hill are the largest reservoirs of water in Los Angeles. They contain x gallons of water, and it is thanks to them that our lawns are always green. Such is the greatness of man!"

Again, suburbs, developments, and intersections, and here we are in Pasadena. Softly sloping avenues loll between orange trees and thickset palms. The big oil families live in these sumptuous homes; compared with the stars of Beverly Hills, they represent an old aristocracy. Suddenly we come out into wild nature; hairy vegetation covers the sides of a steep canyon, and stark mountains are outlined on the horizon. The little road jumps from one side to the other with turns so complicated that we get lost. Not a car, not a house, not a pedestrian—you'd think you were hours from civilization. We drive a long time without finding anyone to tell us which way to go.

I'm utterly astonished to see that the place where I'm supposed to give my lecture is a little house lost on the edge of the canyon. It looks like a hunting lodge. To get back to Westwood, we follow a broad drive where cars whiz by at deafening speed. From time to time, we're passed by one of those little cars called "hot rods," which young men make themselves from old models. They take off the frame, the bumper, the doors—anything that isn't absolutely necessary—and they attach an instrument to the engine that boosts its power and makes a terrible racket. The wild young people squeeze into it in bunches; their favorite sport is to jump from one lane to another, leaving all the other cars in the dust. It's a dangerous game that often causes accidents.

Back in town, I'm surprised by the number of pedestrians hitchhiking at the street corners. N. tells me that drivers no longer stop as readily as before. In America, the car is a familiar machine. Whereas in France one hesitates to entrust the wheel to a friend, here they even hand it over to strangers. Launched on the endless American roadways, a traveler used to welcome the company of someone who could relieve him; when they had a long way to go, they often advertised for a companion who knew how to drive. But in recent times so many drivers have been robbed or killed and so many cars have been stolen that people are now afraid. They're especially mistrustful in the evening. However, Americans are obliging, and these young men [who are hitchhiking] aren't risking much if a car breaks down—there are so many cars! Again this evening, the traffic is maddening. I admire the boldness and skill of those children, ten to fifteen years old, who hawk newspapers at the intersections, weaving between the cars, jumping onto the curbs.

This evening we're dining in a canyon that opens onto the sea and where a whole colony of artists or would-be artists lives. There are little cafés vaguely reminiscent of old Montparnasse, among them a charming café-restaurant. It has a kind of half-dome decorated with hangings in green, white, and red stripes with a semicircular bar in the middle and only five or six tables against the walls. The owner is a homosexual and sleeps with the cook; the cook makes the rules and accepts only clients he remembers. He serves us magnificent steaks dripping with the beautiful red blood that usually scares off puritanical Americans. Where shall we go from here? I. hesitates. He says that nights in Los Angeles are not much fun. Bars and nightclubs must close at midnight. It's a very moralistic town. Children don't have the right to walk around freely after nine in the evening. In many districts, alcohol is prohibited. No "burlesque" houses—the shows are censored. Besides, the recession is being felt here, as in New York, and the clubs are half-empty. Of course, the moralism in which Hollywood encases itself doesn't stop the papers from announcing some sensational new crime every day.

At the moment, Los Angeles is haunted by the ghost of Black Dahlia. Around a month ago, a beautiful young brunette called "Black Dahlia" was found dismembered in a vacant lot. Since then, two or three young women who live in the same neighborhood have been murdered in approximately the same way, and as in a cheap crime novel, a card was found near the cadaver with the words "Black Dahlia." That's what they now call the murderer himself. He hasn't been found. The interesting thing is that these crimes have provoked hysterical attacks of denunciation and self-accusation. Women have written or called the police to turn in unfaithful lovers; men have turned themselves in, recounting their crimes in great detail, and serious interrogations were needed to convince them of their innocence. They were released, and in the night the real Black Dahlia may lie in wait for a new victim. Women are afraid to walk alone after midnight. If they venture out, the next day many say they were followed, accosted, or even assaulted by a man who was surely the Black Dahlia—they give different descriptions. Each day, the local papers devote long columns to this story, which is also the main topic covered by *Time, Life,* and all the big magazines.

I think N. and I. decided to give me a taste of how sinister Los Angeles nights are, because they take me to Venice. This is a deserted seaside amusement park. No one is riding the carousels, no one is laughing in the fun house. The streets are brightly lit but deserted. Among the satin cushions and dolls, the vendors look like they are keeping a vigil over the dead. In hopes of cheering ourselves up, we climb onto the "Scenic Railway" [a roller coaster], but from below we hadn't gauged the terrifying turns. Carried into a ghastly vertical drop, N. and I close our eyes while a firm and sepulchral voice intones behind us, "Oh, boy, am I sorry we did this!"

As we drive back toward Westwood, the bars close one by one. And on the heels of the Black Dahlia, terror slips through the deserted streets.

February 27

The house is open day and night, and when we leave, no one thinks of locking up; I'm not even sure there are locks. In France, people always bolted the doors of houses in the country or suburbs when they left them. I love this trusting unconcern. Delivery people come in quite calmly and deposit the milk, bread, eggs, and bills on the kitchen table. To tell the truth, at N.'s house, there isn't much to steal. In general, though, the idea of theft is not an obsession in America. Objects are not sacred; they can always be replaced.

This morning I'm awakened at eight o'clock by a car stopping in front of the house. Someone climbs the stairs and pushes open the door; this morning visit intrigues me. When I get up, I meet a rather elegant young woman in the dining room, who greets me guardedly. This is the housekeeper. She, too, has a car; it would be impossible for her to earn a living if every hour of work were doubled by an hour in transit. Gasoline and auto maintenance cost nothing here. The purchase is on credit; it's to her advantage to save her time, which is worth around a dollar an hour.

Today I am going to visit the Hollywood studios. I. made a lunch date with us. We cruise along for a good fifteen minutes around Gower Street without finding any place to park the little yellow car. From time to time we see a free place: we rush over, but there's always a red line that means no parking. Opposite RKO Studios there's a parking lot reserved for employees; N. decides to try it, but the guard fiercely defends the little rectangle of asphalt where she manages to slip in. "It's my husband's car." "I. M.'s car is red," the guard protests. But in the end, he admits defeat.

We are invited to lunch by S. [George Stevens, cofounder of Liberty Films], the director I. works with. He has reserved a table at Lucy's, a restaurant situated between the three big studios: Warner, RKO, and Paramount. It would be impossible to get a table without this precaution; it's the fashionable spot where all the beautiful movie people congregate. The elegance of the patrons is rather flamboyant; the platinum blondes are dressed in soft pink and pale blue, and as in New York, they're decorated with feathers. Of course, they suffer here from the bane of all wealthy America — superabundance. Too much noise, too much perfume, too much heat, too much luxury. But after martinis — which are to martinis in Paris what the ideal circle is to circles drawn on a blackboard — the meal is delicious. S. has asked two scriptwriters to join us, a man and a woman who are friends of I. The work of these "writers" does not exactly correspond to that of the French scenario or dialogue writer. They work for the studio, where they spend eight hours a

day in an office. They must find ideas for films, either in their imagination or preferably in the latest published books, and sketch out
the structure of a script. They must also collaborate on the editing
and dialogue of films that are already in the works. All these are
thankless tasks, due to a division of labor so extreme that no one has
a hold on the complete work. They repeat to me that censorship has
become increasingly harsh in the past two years, which makes coming up with a subject more and more difficult. They think of making
a film from the latest Steinbeck book, *Wayward Bus,* but there's a
respectable young woman in it who sleeps with the driver, purely
for pleasure. It is impossible to include such an episode in a movie,
yet it's essential to the story. It will have to be replaced by a sentimental drama of the usual moral and touching sort, which would
distort the characters and remake the plot so drastically that nothing would be left of the original novel. They hesitate. They tell me
that they constantly find themselves hamstrung in this way. The
scripts are becoming increasingly stupid and monotonous, and the
public is beginning to notice. Being served their favorite dish day
after day, they are finally fed up with it. Hence the success, particularly in New York, of English and Italian films, and even French
films, which are poorly distributed and always distorted by arbitrary cuts. And Hollywood is in decline. Many films made in the
studios during the last ten years have never been sold. Apparently,
the directors lack the enthusiasm needed to undertake important
work. S., for example, who was once very successful, today limits
himself to routine work.

   S. is around forty-five years old, with a big, friendly face. He has
always lived in California, where he was born, and his father
worked in the movies, too. S. is as accomplished a man as anyone
could be; he's had stunning successes, he's had affairs with the most
beautiful stars in Hollywood, and he's got an enormous fortune. Yet
he is usually ill at ease in company and hardly speaks. Today he
seems relaxed. He loves N. and I., and the story of our evening in
Venice puts him in a good mood. He tells me emotionally how he
entered Paris several days after the Liberation. I can just imagine
him in uniform, under a helmet. As he describes his campaign, he
repeats earnestly several times: "It was a moment of truth." Yes. A
moment of truth; he's right to speak of it nostalgically.

We change the subject. We say that N. and I are going to take a car trip for several days through California. S. perks up. We are planning to go through Lone Pine, where he spent his childhood and where, ten years ago now, he made his greatest film [*Gunga Din*]. He hasn't been back since, although the place is only four hours from Los Angeles. It would be wonderful to go back. He suggests joining us there with I. and showing us the area. The date is set, and S. is as happy as a child. He has four cars, he's the master of his time and his life, and he has only a little work at the moment; why hasn't he ever done this four-hour trip he's so taken with? I have already noticed among several Americans this lack of initiative and inventiveness, but this case is the most surprising of all. I., who is half-English and who spent his youth in London, tells me that he was also stunned to learn how many Americans were entangled in their freedom. This trait is particularly striking in California, especially in Hollywood. S., who is bored at the studio from morning to night without much to do, knows no better diversion than alcohol. It's from a lack of imagination that so many Americans obstinately drink themselves into a stupor. Yet S. is intelligent, curious, full of overflowing vitality. He takes us to his office. His secretary brings us one of those tasteless coffees they drink here. She's blond, around forty years old, ravaged by drink. She's legendary at the studio because she often has terrible hangovers in the mornings. Since she lives on the other side of the valley, she telephones to declare with aplomb that she can't come because the valley is flooded. S. questions me with passionate interest about France, its intellectual life, its literature, its philosophy, and makes me promise that at Lone Pine I will give him a serious explanation of the Cartesian cogito.

The Hollywood studios don't seem so different from their French counterparts. To be sure, these are cities. But I'm beginning to get the idea: a college, a hospital, a warehouse—here, right away, it's a city. In a large hall they're in the process of taking publicity stills. Aspiring pinups in fanciful bras and panties show their sumptuous legs. They are photographed in the most complicated poses, perched precariously on the steps of stools and ladders, which will, of course, be invisible on the posters. They'll appear natural and relaxed. How exhausting it must be to produce one of those smiles, broadcasting in every direction that life is fun! It's a pitiful job that doesn't pay much. I see them shoot an interior scene; there are the same hesitations, the same delays as at Joinville or Épinay [French film lots]. And you encounter the same De Chirico-like miracles: a tree planted in the middle of a bedroom, a Louis Philippe dining room that's open to the sky. On the whole, this fairground of wonders exudes fatigue and boredom; everyone works indolently, without great ambition, not even financial. Outside in front of one of the gates, three men are sitting on folding chairs at the edge of the sidewalk: it is a cool day, and they are burning bits of wood to warm themselves. They stretch their hands toward the flames in the classic gesture of tramps. They are strikers. It's been three months since the carpenters have gone on strike for more pay; by now, it's a lost cause, and this symbolic picket line is heartbreaking.

Los Angeles is far from possessing the beauty of New York or the depth of Chicago, and I understand why some French people spoke to me about it with such distaste: without friends, I'd be lost. But it can be as enjoyable as a kaleidoscope—with a shake of the wrist, the pieces of colored glass give you the illusion of a new rosette. I surrender to this hall of mirrors. After visiting Mexico the day before yesterday, this evening I'm going to Hawaii. The French consul has invited me to dinner with N. and I. In the entrance hall there is an exhibition of Hawaiian jewelry, shell necklaces, leis, and softly colored seeds. I have never seen such an enchanting restaurant: it's as beautiful as the Palais des Mirages in the Musée Grevin. Greenhouses with luxuriant plants, aquariums, aviaries where birds colored like butterflies swoop, all bathed in a murky, submarine light. The tables are glass pedestals in which the gleaming ceiling is reflected; the prismatic pillars are faceted mirrors in which space is infinitely multiplied. We dine under a straw hut at the end of a lake, in a forest, in the middle of an enormous diamond. The waitresses' costumes are a modest version of Hawaiian dress. In cylindrical glasses, which hold nearly a pint, we are served zombies (cocktails made from seven kinds of rum poured on top of each other: the amber liquid is layered from dark brown to light yellow). The meal transports us, unexpectedly, to China. The dishes don't have that overly visual impact that often discourages the palate in America; instead, they look very appealing. And if French cooking is "thoughtful," as Colette says, this cuisine seems the fruit of a thousand years of meditation.

At midnight we are alone on top of a hill. We sit on the ground and smoke in silence. Los Angeles is beneath us, a huge, silent fairyland. The lights glitter as far as the eye can see. Between the red, green, and white clusters, big glowworms slither noiselessly. Now I am not taken in by the mirage: I know that these are merely street lamps along the avenues, neon signs, and headlights. But mirage or no mirage, the lights keep glittering; they, too, are a truth. And perhaps they are even more moving when they express nothing but the naked presence of men. Men live here, and so the earth revolves in the quiet of the night with this shining wound in its side.

Truman Capote

Christmas in Los Angeles might seem an oxymoron: how else reconcile snow and palm trees, Santa Claus and sunshine? The answer, suggests Truman Capote (1924–1984), is that, like much else in Southern California, Christmas is not what it appears to be. In this brief sketch, from his 1950 collection *Local Color*, Capote recalls a holiday visit to Hollywood not long after the war, and in the process weaves in some characteristically chatty observations about everything from the private manners of movie stars to the difficulties of shopping for fresh fruit.

HOLLYWOOD

Approaching Los Angeles, at least by air, is like, I should imagine, crossing the surface of the moon: prehistoric shapes, looming in stone ripples and corroded, leer upward, and paleozoic fish swim in the shadowy pools between desert mountains: burned and frozen, there is no living thing, only rock that was once a bird, bones that are sand, ferns turned to fiery stone. At last a welcoming fleet of clouds: we have crept between a sorcerer's passage, snow is on the mountains, yet flowers color the land, a summer sun juxtaposes December's winter sea, down, down, the plane splits through plumed, gold, incredible air. Oh, moaned Thelma, I can't stand it, she said, and poured a cascade of Chiclets into her mouth. Thelma had boarded the plane in Chicago; she was a young Negro girl, rather pretty, beautifully dressed, and it was the most wonderful thing that would ever happen to her, this trip to California. "I know it, it's going just to be grand. Three years I've been ushering at the Lola Theatre on State Street just to save the fare. My auntie tells the cards, and she said — Thelma, honey, head for Hollywood 'cause there's a job as private secretary to a movie actress just waiting for you. She didn't say what actress, though. I hope it's not Esther Williams. I don't like swimming much."

Later on she asked if I was trying for film work, and because the idea seemed to please her, I said yes. On the whole she was very encouraging, and assured me that as soon as she was established as a private secretary, thereby having access to the ears of the great, she would not forget me, would indeed give me every assistance.

At the airport I helped with her luggage, and eventually we shared a taxi. It came about then that she had no place specific to go, she simply wanted the driver to let her off in the "middle" of Hollywood. It was a long drive, and she sat all the way on the edge of the seat, unbearably watchful. But there was not so much to see as she'd imagined. "It don't look correct," she said finally, quite as if we'd been played a wretched trick, for here again, though in disguise, was the surface of the moon, the noplace of everywhere; but how very correct, after all, that here at continent's end we should find only a dumping ground for all that is most exploitedly American: oil pumps pounding like the heartbeat of demons, avenues of used-car lots, supermarkets, motels, the gee dad I never knew a Chevrolet gee dad gee mom gee whiz wham of publicity, the biggest, broadest, best, sprawled and helplessly etherized by immaculate sunshine and sound of sea and unearthly sweetness of flowers blooming in December.

During the drive the sky had grown ash-colored, and as we turned into the laundered sparkle of Wilshire Boulevard, Thelma, giving her delicate feathered hat a protective touch, grumbled at the possibility of rain. Not a chance, said the driver, just wind blowing in dust from the desert. These words were not out of his mouth before the palm trees shivered under a violent downpour. But Thelma had no place to go, except into the street, so we left her standing there, rain pulling her costume apart. When a traffic light stopped us at the corner, she ran up and stuck her head in the window. "Look here, honey, remember what I say, you get hungry or anything you just find where I'm at." Then, with a lovely smile, "And listen, honey, lotsa luck!"

December 3. Today, through the efforts of a mutual friend, Nora Parker, I was asked to lunch by the fabled Miss C. There is a fortress wall surrounding her place, and at the entrance gate we were more or less frisked by a guard who then telephoned ahead to announce our arrival. All this was very satisfying; it was nice to know that at least someone was living the way a famous actress should. At the door we were met by a red-faced, overly nourished child with a gooey pink ribbon trailing from her hair. "Mummy thinks I should entertain you till she comes down," she said apathetically, then led us into a large and, now that I think about it, preposterous room: it looked as though some rich old rascal had personally decorated himself a lavish hideaway: sly, low-slung couches, piles of lecherous velvet pillows and lamps with sinuous, undulating shapes. "Would you like to see Mummy's things?" said the little girl.

Her first exhibit was an illuminated bibelot cabinet. "This," she said, pointing to a bit of Chinese porcelain, "is Mummy's ancient vase she paid Gump's three thousand dollars for. And that's her gold cocktail shaker and gold cups. I forget how much they cost, an awful lot, maybe five thousand dollars. And you see that old teapot? You wouldn't believe what it's worth . . ."

It was a monstrous recital, and toward the end of it, Nora looking dazedly round the room for a change of topic, said, "Such lovely flowers. Are they from your own garden?"

"Heavens, no," replied the little girl disdainfully. "Mummy orders them every day from the most expensive florist in Beverly Hills."

"Oh?" said Nora, wincing. "And what is your favorite flower?"

"Orchids."

"Now really. I don't believe orchids could be your favorite flower. A little girl like you."

She thought a moment. "Well, as a matter of fact, they aren't. But Mummy says they are the most expensive."

Just then there was a rustling at the door; Miss C. skipped like a schoolgirl across the room: her famous face was without make-up; hairpins dangled loosely. She was wearing a very ordinary flannel housecoat. "Nora, darling," she called, her arms outstretched, "do forgive my being so long. I've been upstairs making the beds."

Yesterday, feeling greedy, I remembered ravishing displays of fruit outside a large emporium I'd driven admiringly past a number of times. Mammoth oranges, grapes big as ping-pong balls, apples piled in rosy pyramids. There is a sleight of hand about distances here, nothing is so near as you supposed, and it is not unusual to travel ten miles for a package of cigarettes. It was a two-mile walk before I even caught sight of the fruit store. The long counters were tilted so that from quite far away you could see the splendid wares, apples, pears. I reached for one of these extraordinary apples, but it seemed to be glued into its case. A salesgirl giggled. "Plaster," she said, and I laughed too, a little feverishly perhaps, then wearily followed her into the deeper regions of the store where I bought six small, rather mealy apples, and six small, rather mealy pears.

It is Christmas week. And it is evening now a long time. Below the window a lake of light bulbs electrifies the valley. From the haunting impermanence of their hilltop homes impermanent eyes are watching them, almost as if suddenly they might go out, like candles at last consumed.

Earlier today I took a bus all the way from Beverly Hills into downtown Los Angeles. The streets are strung with garlands, we passed a motorized sleigh that was spinning along spilling a wake of white cornflakes, at corners sweating woolly men rustle bells under the shade of prefabricated trees; carols, hurled from lamppost loudspeakers, pour their syrup on the air, and tinsel, twinkling in twenty-four-karat sunshine, hangs everywhere like swamp moss. It could not be more Christmas, or less so. I once knew a woman who imported a pink villa stone by stone from Italy and had it reconstructed on a demure Connecticut meadow: Christmas is as out of place in Hollywood as the villa was in Connecticut. And what is Christmas without children, on whom so much of the point depends? Last week I met a man who concluded a set of observations by saying, "And of course you know this is the childless city."

For five days I have been testing his remark, casually at first, now with morbid alarm; preposterous, I know, but since commencing this mysterious campaign I have seen less than half a dozen children. But first, a relevant point: a primary complaint here is overpopulation; old-guard natives tell me the terrain is bulging with "undesirable" elements, hordes of ex-soldiers, workers who moved here during the war, and those spiritual Okies, the young and footloose; yet walking around I sometimes have the feeling of one who awakened some eerie morning into a hushed, deserted world where overnight, like sailors aboard the *Marie Celeste,* all souls had disappeared. There is an air of Sunday vacancy; here where no one walks cars glide in a constant shiny silent stream, my shadow, moving down the stark white street, is like the one living element of a Chirico. It is not the comfortable silence felt in small American towns, though the physical atmosphere of stoops and yards and hedges is very often the same; the difference is that in real towns you can be pretty sure what sorts of people there are hiding beyond those numbered doors, but here, where all seems transient, ephemeral, there is no general pattern to the population, and nothing is intended — this street, that house, mushrooms of accident, and a crack in the wall, which might somewhere else have charm, only strikes an ugly note prophesying doom.

1. A teacher here recently gave a vocabulary test in which she asked her students to provide the antonym of *youth*. Over half the class answered *death*.

2. No stylish Hollywood home is thought quite sanitary without a brace of modern masters to brighten up the walls. One producer has what amounts to a small gallery; he refers to paintings merely as good investments. His wife is less modest: "Sure we know about art. We've been to Greece, haven't we? California is just like Greece. Exactly. You'd be surprised. Go over there and talk to my husband about Picasso; he can give you the real low-down."

The day I saw their famous collection I had a picture that I was taking to a framer, a small colored Klee lithograph. "Pleasant," said the producer's wife cautiously. "Paint it yourself?"

Waiting for a bus, I ran into P., of whom I am rather admiring. She has the sort of wit that excludes malice, and, what is more uncommon, she has managed thirty years of Hollywood with humor and dignity. Naturally, she is not very rich. At the moment she is living above a garage. It is interesting, because by local standards she is a failure, which along with age, is unforgivable; even so, success pays her homage, and her Sunday coffee sessions are quite luminously attended, for above that garage she contrives a momentary sense of security, and for all a feeling of having roots. She is an inexhaustible scrapbook, too, the time sequence of her conversation shifting, sliding, until, as she fixes you with her cornflower eyes,

Valentino passes lightly brushing your arm, the young Garbo hovers at the window, John Gilbert appears on the lawn, stands there like a twilight statue, the senior Fairbanks roars up the driveway, two mastiffs baying in the rumble seat.

P. offered to drive me home. We went by way of Santa Monica, in order that she could drop off a present for A., that sad, jittery lady who once, after the departure of her third husband, threw an Oscar into the ocean.

The thing about A. which most intrigued me was the way she applied make-up—such a brutally objective performance; cold-eyed, calculating, she wields her paints and powders altogether as if the face belongs to someone else, managing, in the process, to smooth away whatever time has given her.

As we were leaving, the maid came out to say that A.'s father would like to see us. We found him in a garden facing the ocean; a knotty, phlegmatic old man with blue-white hair and skin browner than iodine, he was slumped in a patch of sunshine, his eyes closed, no sound to disturb him but the slumbering slap of waves, the dozy singing of bees. Old people love California; they close their eyes, and the wind through the winter flowers says sleep, the sea says sleep: it is a preview of heaven. From daybreak to dark A.'s father follows the sun around his garden, and on rainy days he whiles away the time by making bracelets of beer-bottle caps. He gave each of us one of these bracelets, and in a voice that hardly carried through the honeyed, blowing air, said, "A merry Christmas, children."

Evelyn Waugh

Los Angeles has always loved its cemeteries, not least the gaudily splendid Forest Lawn Memorial Park, but outsiders like British satirist Evelyn Waugh (1903–1966) have sometimes found these burial grounds the ultimate symbol of L.A. extremism. Waugh skewered the Southern California death industry in his 1948 novel *The Loved One*, later filmed by Tony Richardson in the 1960s. This deft piece of reporting, originally published in *Life* in 1947, laid the groundwork for the novel's merciless burlesque.

DEATH IN HOLLYWOOD

In a thousand years or so, when the first archaeologists from beyond the date line unload their boat on the sands of Southern California, they will find much the same scene as confronted the Franciscan missionaries. A dry landscape will extend from the ocean to the mountains. Bel Air and Beverly Hills will lie naked save for scrub and cactus, all their flimsy multitude of architectural styles turned long ago to dust, while the horned toad and the turkey buzzard leave their faint imprint on the dunes that will drift on Sunset Boulevard.

For Los Angeles, when its brief history comes to an end, will fall swiftly and silently. Too far dispersed for effective bombardment, too unimportant strategically for the use of expensive atomic devices, it will be destroyed by drought. Its water comes 250 miles from the Owens River. A handful of parachutists or partisans anywhere along that vital aqueduct can make the coastal strip uninhabitable. Bones will whiten along the Santa Fe trail as the great recession struggles eastward. Nature will reassert herself and the seasons gently obliterate the vast, deserted suburb. Its history will pass from memory to legend until, centuries later, as we have supposed, the archaeologists prick their ears at the cryptic references in the texts of the 20th Century to a cult which once flourished on this forgotten strand; of the idol Oscar, sexless image of infertility; of the great Star Goddesses who were once noisily worshiped there in a Holy Wood.

Without the testimony of tombs the science of archaeology could barely exist, and it will be a commonplace among the scholars of 2947 that the great cultural decline of the 20th Century was first evident in the graveyard. The wish to furnish the dead with magnificent habitations, to make an enduring record of their virtues and victories, to honor them and edify their descendants, raised all the great monuments of antiquity, the Pyramids, the Taj Mahal, St. Peter's at Rome, and was the mainspring of all the visual arts. It died, mysteriously and suddenly, at the end of the 19th Century. England, once very rich in sepulchral statuary, commemorated her fallen soldiers of the First World War by a simple inscription in the floor of an Abbey built nine centuries earlier to shelter the remains of a Saxon king. Rich patrons of art, who in an earlier century would have spent the last decade of their lives in planning their own elaborate obsequies, deposed that their ashes should be broadcast from airplanes. The more practical Germans sent their corpses to the soap boiler. Only the primitive heathen of Russia observed a once universal tradition in their shrine to Lenin.

All this will be a commonplace in the schools of 2947. The discoveries therefore of the Holy Wood Archaeological Expedition will be revolutionary, for when they have excavated and catalogued and speculated hopelessly about the meaning of a temple designed in the shape of a Derby hat and a concrete pavement covered with diverse monopedic prints and have surveyed the featureless ruins of the great film studios, their steps will inevitably tend northward to what was once Glendale, and there they will encounter on a gentle slope among embosoming hills, mellowed but still firm-rooted as the rocks, something to confound all the accepted generalizations, a necropolis of the age of the Pharaohs created in the middle of the impious 20th Century, the vast structure of Forest Lawn Memorial-Park.

We can touch hands across the millennium with these discoverers, for it is in the same mood of incredulous awe that the visitors of our own age must approach this stupendous property. Visitors, indeed, flock there—in numbers approaching those that visit the Metropolitan Museum in New York—and with good reason, for there are many splendid collections of art elsewhere, but Forest Lawn is entirely unique. Behind the largest wrought-iron gates in

the world lie 300 acres of parkland judiciously planted with evergreen (for no plant which sheds its leaf has a place there). The
lawns, watered and drained by 80 miles of pipe, do not at first
betray their solemn purpose. Even the names given to their various
sections—Eventide, Babyland, Graceland, Inspiration Slope, Slum-
berland, Sweet Memories, Vesperland, Dawn of Tomorrow—and
none of them specifically suggestive of the graveyard. The visitor is
soothed by countless radios concealed about the vegetation which
ceaselessly discourse the *Indian Love Call* and other popular melodies
and the amplified twittering of caged birds. It is only when he leaves
the 7½ miles of paved roadway that he becomes aware of the thousands of little bronze plates which lie in the grass. Commenting on
this peculiarity in the *Art Guide of Forest Lawn with Interpretations*, Mr.
Bruce Barton, author of *What Can a Man Believe*, says, "The cemeteries of the world cry out men's utter hopelessness in the face of
death. Their symbols are pagan and pessimistic. . . . Here sorrow
sees no ghastly monuments, but only life and hope." The Christian
visitor might here remark that by far the commonest feature of
other graveyards is still the Cross, a symbol in which previous generations have found more Life and Hope than in the most elaborately watered evergreen shrub.

There are gardens and terraces and a huge range of buildings,
the most prominent of which is the rather Italian mausoleum. There
in marble-fronted tiers lie the coffins, gallery after gallery of them,
surrounded by statuary and stained glass. Each niche bears a
bronze plaque with the inmate's name, sometimes in magnified
counterfeit of his signature. Each has a pair of bronze vases which a
modest investment can keep perpetually replenished with fresh
flowers. Adjacent lies the columbarium where stand urns of ashes
from the crematory. There is the Tudor-style administration building, the mortuary (Tudor exterior, Georgian interior) and the more
functional crematory. All are designed to defy the operations of
time; they are in "Class A steel and concrete," proof against fire and
earthquake. The mausoleum alone, we are told, contains enough
steel and concrete for a 60-story office building and its foundations
penetrate 33 feet into solid rock.

The Memorial Court of Honor is the crowning achievement of
this group. "Beneath the rare marbles of its floor are crypts which

money cannot purchase, reserved as gifts of honored interment for Americans whose lives shall have been crowned with genius." There have so far been two recipients of this gift, Gutzon Borglum, the first sculptor in history to employ dynamite instead of the chisel, and Mrs. Carrie Jacobs Bond, author and composer of *The End of a Perfect Day*, at whose funeral this year, which cost $25,000, Dr. Hubert Eaton, the chairman of Forest Lawn, pronounced the solemn words: "By virtue of the authority vested in me by the Council of Regents . . . I do herewith pronounced Carrie Jacobs Bond an immortal of the Memorial Court of Honor."

There are already three nonsectarian churches, the Little Church of the Flowers, the Wee Kirk o' the Heather and the Church of the Recessional. The first is, with modifications, a replica of Stoke Poges church where Gray composed his *Elegy*; the second a reconstruction of the ruins of a chapel at Glencairn, Dumfriesshire, where Annie Laurie worshiped; the third, again with modifications, is a replica of the parish church of Rottingdean in Sussex where Rudyard Kipling is claimed by Dr. Eaton to have been inspired to write his poem, *Recessional*. The American visitor may well be surprised at the overwhelmingly British character of these places of worship in a state which has never enjoyed the blessings of British rule and is now inhabited by the most cosmopolitan people in the U.S. The British visitor is surprised also at the modifications.

It is odd to find a church dedicated to Kipling, whose religion was highly idiosyncratic. The building is used not only for funerals but for weddings and christenings. Its courtyard is used for betrothals; there is a stone ring, named by Dr. Eaton—the Ring of Aldyth, through which the young lovers are invited to clasp hands and swear fidelity to what Kipling described as "a rag and a bone and a hank of hair." Around the courtyard are incised the texts of *Recessional, If* and *When Earth's Last Picture Is Painted*. The interior of St. Margaret's Rottingdean is not particularly remarkable among the many ancient parish churches of England, but the architects of Forest Lawn have used their ingenuity to enliven it. One wall has been constructed of glass instead of stone and covered with potted plants and caged canaries; a chapel hidden in what is no doubt thought to be devotional half-darkness is illuminated by a spotlit painting of Bouguereau's, entitled *Song of the Angels*; in a kind of sacristy relics of the patron saint are exposed to veneration. They are not what ecclesiastics call "major relics"; some photographs by the Topical Press, a rifle score sheet signed by the poet, the photostatic copy of a letter to Sir Roderick Jones expressing Kipling's hope of attending a christening, a copy of Lady Jones's popular novel, *National Velvet,* an oleograph text from a nearby cottage, and so forth.

What will the archaeologists of 2947 make of all this and of the countless other rarities of the place? What webs of conjecture will be spun by the professors of Comparative Religion? We know with what confidence they define the intimate beliefs of remote ages. They flourished in the 19th Century. Then G. K. Chesterton, in a masterly book sadly neglected in Europe but honored in the U.S.A., *The Everlasting Man,* gently exposed their fatuity. But they will flourish again, for it is a brand of scholarship well suited to dreamy natures which are not troubled by the itch of precise thought. What will the professors of the future make of Forest Lawn? What do we make of it ourselves? Here is the thing, under our noses, a first-class anthropological puzzle of our own period and neighborhood. What does it mean?

Of course it is first self-evidently a successful commercial undertaking. The works of sculpture enhance the value of the grave sites; the unification in a single business of all the allied crafts of undertaking is practical and, I believe, unique. Secondly the park is a monument to local tradition. Europeans who measure those things by centuries err absurdly in supposing that American traditions, because they are a matter of decades, are the less powerful. They are a recent, swift and wiry growth.

The character of Southern California which everywhere strikes the tourist as unique came from its history. The territory was won by military conquest only a century ago, but the Spanish culture was obliterated and survives today only in ingenious reconstructions. The main immigrations took place within living memory and still continue. In 1930 it was calculated that of the million and a quarter inhabitants of Los Angeles a quarter of a million had arrived in the previous five years and only a third of the entire population could claim more than 15 years' standing, and this vast influx differs from all others in that it was the rich who came first. There was no pioneer period in which hungry and energetic young people won their living from the land. They did not come in covered wagons or in steerage bunks. Elderly wealthy people came in comfortable trains, bringing their money with them in order to enjoy it in the sunshine. There is now an industrial proletariat and a thriving criminal class, but the tradition of leisure is still apparent in the pathological sloth of the hotel servants and in the aimless, discursive coffee-house chatter which the film executives call "conferences."

It is not the leisure of Monte Carlo or Palm Beach where busy men go for a holiday. It is the leisure of those whose work is quite finished. Here on the ultimate sunset shore they lay themselves down, warm their old limbs and open their scaly eyes two or three times a day to browse on lettuce and avocado pears. They have forgotten the lands which gave them birth and the arts and trades which they once practiced. Here in profound oblivion you find men and women you supposed long dead, editors of defunct journals, playwrights and actresses your father spoke of, glorious stars of theaters long-ago demolished, novelists whose works line the shelves of requisitioned billiard rooms. They are gently spinning the cocoon which will cover their final transition. Death is the only event which can now disturb them, and priests of countless preposterous cults have gathered round to shade off that change until it becomes imperceptible. Old, old fancies are here retold as the "new" philosophy. Soon, they are assured, they will migrate into new bodies. Meanwhile Dr. Eaton is at hand to house the old one.

Dr. Eaton has set up his credo at the entrance. "I believe in a happy Eternal Life," he says. "I believe those of us left behind should be glad in the certain belief that those gone before have entered into that happier Life." This theme is repeated on Coleus Terrace: "Be happy because they for whom you mourn are happy— far happier than ever before." And again in Vesperland: ". . . Happy because Forest Lawn has eradicated the old customs of Death and depicts Life not Death."

The implication of these texts is clear. Forest Lawn has consciously turned its back on the "old customs of Death," the grim traditional alternatives of Heaven and Hell, and promises immediate eternal happiness for all its inmates. Similar claims are made for other holy places—the Ganges, Debra Libanos in Abyssinia, and others. Some of the simpler crusaders probably believed that they would go straight to heaven if they died in the Holy Land. But there is a catch in most of these dispensations, a sincere repentance, sometimes an arduous pilgrimage, sometimes a monastic rule in the closing years. Dr. Eaton is the first man to offer eternal salvation at an inclusive charge as part of his undertaking service.

There is a vital theological point on which Dr. Eaton gives no ex-cathedra definition. Does burial in Forest Lawn itself sanctify or is sanctity the necessary qualification for admission? Discrimination is exercised. There is no room for the Negro or the Chinese, however devout; avowed atheists are welcome but notorious ill-doers are not. Al Capone, for example, had he applied, would have been excluded although he died fortified by the last rites of his Church. Suicides, on the other hand, who in "the old customs of Death" would lie at a crossroads, impaled, come in considerable numbers and often, particularly in cases of hanging, present peculiar problems to the embalmer.

Embalming is so widely practiced in California that many believe it to be a legal obligation. At Forest Lawn the bodies lie in state, sometimes on sofas, sometimes in open coffins, in apartments furnished like those of a luxurious hotel and named Slumber Rooms. Here the bereaved see them for the last time, fresh from the final beauty parlor, looking rather smaller than in life and much more dandified. There is a hint of the bassinet about these coffins, with their linings of quilted and padded satin and their frilled silk pillows. There is more than a hint, indeed, throughout Forest Lawn that death is a form of infancy, a Wordsworthian return to innocence. "I am the Spirit of Forest Lawn," wrote K. C. Beaton in less than Wordsworthian phrase. "I speak in the language of the Duck Baby, happy childhood at play." We are very far here from the traditional conception of an adult soul naked at the judgment seat and a body turning to corruption. There is usually a marble skeleton lurking somewhere among the marble draperies and quartered escutcheons of the tombs of the high Renaissance; often you find, gruesomely portrayed, the corpse half decayed with marble worms writhing in the marble adipocere. These macaber achievements were done with a simple moral purpose—to remind a highly civilized people that beauty was skin deep and pomp was mortal. In those realistic times hell waited for the wicked and a long purgation for all but the saints, but heaven, if at last attained, was a place of perfect knowledge. In Forest Lawn, as the builder claims, these old values are reversed. The body does not decay; it lives on, more chic in death than ever before, in its indestructible Class A steel-and-concrete shelf; the soul goes straight from the Slumber Room to Paradise, where it enjoys an endless infancy—one of a great Caucasian nursery party where Knights of Pythias toddle on chubby, unsteady legs beside a Borglum whose baby fingers could never direct a pneumatic drill and a Carrie Jacobs Bond whose artless ditties are for the Duck Baby alone.

That, I think, is the message. To those of us too old-fashioned to listen respectfully, there is the hope of finding ourselves, one day beyond time, standing at the balustrade of heaven among the unrecognizably grownup denizens of Forest Lawn, and leaning there beside them, amicably gazing down on Southern California and sharing with them the huge joke of what the professors of anthropology will make of it all.

Octavio Paz

Although Octavio Paz's celebrated study of the Mexican character, *The Labyrinth of Solitude*, was not translated into English until 1961, it was originally published in 1950. The excerpt included here, his meditation on the archetypal figure of the Los Angeles *pachuco*, reflects a late 40s visit to California. At the time he wrote it, the Sleepy Lagoon case and the Zoot Suit Riots had recently given a sensationalized prominence to L.A.'s Mexican community. Paz (1914–1998) naturally enough is more interested in considering that community in relation to Mexican rather than U.S. culture. The author of more than 40 books of poetry and prose, Paz received the Nobel Prize for Literature in 1990.

from

THE LABYRINTH OF SOLITUDE

When I arrived in the United States I lived for a while in Los Angeles, a city inhabited by over a million persons of Mexican origin. At first sight, the visitor is surprised not only by the purity of the sky and the ugliness of the dispersed and ostentatious buildings, but also by the city's vaguely Mexican atmosphere, which cannot be captured in words or concepts. This Mexicanism—delight in decorations, carelessness and pomp, negligence, passion and reserve—floats in the air. I say "floats" because it never mixes or unites with the other world, the North American world based on precision and efficiency. It floats, without offering any opposition; it hovers, blown here and there by the wind, sometimes breaking up like a cloud, sometimes standing erect like a rising skyrocket. It creeps, it wrinkles, it expands and contracts; it sleeps or dreams; it is ragged but beautiful. It floats, never quite existing, never quite vanishing.

Something of the same sort characterizes the Mexicans you see in the streets. They have lived in the city for many years, wearing the same clothes and speaking the same language as the other inhabitants, and they feel ashamed of their origin; yet no one would mistake them for authentic North Americans. I refuse to believe that physical features are as important as is commonly thought. What distinguishes them, I think, is their furtive, restless air: they act like persons who are wearing disguises, who are afraid of a stranger's look because it could strip them and leave them stark naked. When you talk with them, you observe that their sensibilities are like a pendulum, but a pendulum that has lost its reason and swings violently and erratically back and forth. This spiritual condition, or lack of a spirit, has given birth to a type known as the *pachuco*. The *pachucos* are youths, for the most part of Mexican origin, who form gangs in Southern cities; they can be identified by their language and behavior as well as by the clothing they affect. They are instinctive rebels, and North American racism has vented its wrath on them more than once. But the *pachucos* do not attempt to vindicate their race or the nationality of their forebears. Their attitude reveals an obstinate, almost fanatical will-to-be, but this will affirms nothing specific except their determination—it is an ambiguous one, as we will see—not to be like those around them. The *pachuco* does not want to become a Mexican again; at the same time he does not want to blend into the life of North America. His whole being is sheer negative impulse, a tangle of contradictions, an enigma. Even his very name is enigmatic: *pachuco,* a word of uncertain derivation, saying nothing and saying everything. It is a strange word with no definite meaning; or, to be more exact, it is charged like all popular creations with a diversity of meanings. Whether we like it or not, these persons are Mexicans, are one of the extremes at which the Mexicans can arrive.

Since the *pachuco* cannot adapt himself to a civilization which, for its part, rejects him, he finds no answer to the hostility surrounding him except this angry affirmation of his personality.* Other groups react differently. The Negroes, for example, oppressed by racial intolerance, try to "pass" as whites and thus enter

---

*Many of the juvenile gangs that have formed in the United States in recent years are reminiscent of the post-war *pachucos*. It could not have been otherwise: North American society is closed to the outside world, and at the same time it is inwardly petrified. Life cannot penetrate it, and being rejected, squanders itself aimlessly on the outside. It is a marginal life, formless but hoping to discover its proper form.

society. They want to be like other people. The Mexicans have suffered a less violent rejection, but instead of attempting a problematical adjustment to society, the *pachuco* actually flaunts his differences. The purpose of his grotesque dandyism and anarchic behavior is not so much to point out the injustice and incapacity of a society that has failed to assimilate him as it is to demonstrate his personal will to remain different.

It is not important to examine the causes of this conflict, and even less so to ask whether or not it has a solution. There are minorities in many parts of the world who do not enjoy the same opportunities as the rest of the population. The important thing is this stubborn desire to be different, this anguished tension with which the lone Mexican—an orphan lacking both protectors and positive values—displays his differences. The *pachuco* has lost his whole inheritance: language, religion, customs, beliefs. He is left with only a body and a soul with which to confront the elements, defenseless against the stares of everyone. His disguise is a protection, but it also differentiates and isolates him: it both hides him and points him out.

His deliberately aesthetic clothing, whose significance is too obvious to require discussion, should not be mistaken for the outfit of a special group or sect. *Pachuquismo* is an open society, and this in a country full of cults and tribal costumes, all intended to satisfy the middle-class North American's desire to share in something more vital and solid than the abstract morality of the "American Way of Life." The clothing of the *pachuco* is not a uniform or a ritual attire. It is simply a fashion, and like all fashions it is based on novelty—the mother of death, as Leopardi said—and imitation.

Its novelty consists in its exaggeration. The *pachuco* carries fashion to its ultimate consequences and turns it into something aesthetic. One of the principles that rules in North American fashions is that clothing must be comfortable, and the *pachuco*, by changing ordinary apparel into art, makes it "impractical." Hence it negates the very principles of the model that inspired it. Hence its aggressiveness.

This rebelliousness is only an empty gesture, because it is an exaggeration of the models against which he is trying to rebel, rather than a return to the dress of his forebears or the creation of a new style of his own. Eccentrics usually emphasize their decision to break away from society—either to form new and more tightly closed groups or to assert their individuality—through their way of dressing. In the case of the *pachuco* there is an obvious ambiguity: his clothing spotlights and isolates him, but at the same time it pays homage to the society he is attempting to deny.

This duality is also expressed in another, perhaps profounder way: the *pachuco* is an impassive and sinister clown whose purpose is to cause terror instead of laughter. His sadistic attitude is allied with a desire for self-abasement which in my opinion constitutes the very foundation of his character: he knows that it is dangerous to stand out and that his behavior irritates society, but nevertheless he seeks and attracts persecution and scandal. It is the only way he can establish a more vital relationship with the society he is antagonizing. As a victim, he can occupy a place in the world that previously had ignored him; as a delinquent, he can become one of its wicked heroes.

I believe that the North American's irritation results from his seeing the *pachuco* as a mythological figure and therefore, in effect, a danger. His dangerousness lies in his singularity. Everyone agrees in finding something hybrid about him, something disturbing and fascinating. He is surrounded by an aura of ambivalent notions: his singularity seems to be nourished by powers that are alternately evil and beneficent. Some people credit him with unusual erotic prowess; others consider him perverted but still aggressive. He is a symbol of love and joy or of horror and loathing, an embodiment of liberty, of disorder, of the forbidden. He is someone who ought to be destroyed. He is also someone with whom any contact must be made in secret, in the darkness.

The *pachuco* is impassive and contemptuous, allowing all these contradictory impressions to accumulate around him until finally, with a certain painful satisfaction, he sees them explode into a tavern fight or a raid by the police or a riot. And then, in suffering persecution, he becomes his true self, his supremely naked self, as a pariah, a man who belongs nowhere. The circle that began with provocation has completed itself and he is ready now for redemption, for his entrance into the society that rejected him. He has been its sin and its scandal, but now that he is a victim it recognizes him at last for what he really is: its product, its son. At last he has found new parents.

The *pachuco* tries to enter North American society in secret and daring ways, but he impedes his own efforts. Having been cut off from his traditional culture, he asserts himself for a moment as a solitary and challenging figure. He denies both the society from which he originated and that of North America. When he thrusts himself outward, it is not to unite with what surrounds him but rather to defy it. This is a suicidal gesture, because the *pachuco* does not affirm or defend anything except his exasperated will-not-to-be. He is not divulging his most intimate feelings: he is revealing an ulcer, exhibiting a wound. A wound that is also a grotesque, capricious, barbaric adornment. A wound that laughs at itself and decks itself out for the hunt. The *pachuco* is the prey of society, but instead of hiding he adorns himself to attract the hunter's attention. Persecution redeems him and breaks his solitude: his salvation depends on his becoming part of the very society he appears to deny. Solitude and sin, communion and health become synonymous terms.*

*No doubt many aspects of the *pachuco* are lacking in this description. But I am convinced that his hybrid language and behavior reflect a physic oscillation between two irreducible worlds—the North American and the Mexican—which he vainly hopes to reconcile and conquer. He does not want to become either a Mexican or a Yankee. When I arrived in France in 1945, I was amazed to find that the young men and women of certain quarters, especially students and "artists," wore clothing reminiscent of that of the *pachucos* in southern California. Was this a quick, imaginative adaptation of what these young people, after years of isolation, thought was in fashion in North America? I questioned a number of people about it, and almost all of them told me it was a strictly French phenomenon that had come into existence at the end of the Occupation. Some even considered it a manifestation of the Resistance: its Baroque fantasy was a reply to the rigid order of the German. Although I do not exclude the possibility of a more or less indirect imitation, I think the similarity is remarkable and significant.

Ray Bradbury

As Simone de Beauvoir noted, people don't walk much in Los Angeles. To some extent, that has to do with the city's sprawl and its car culture, but at times it can feel as if there's a deep-rooted suspicion of anyone traveling on foot. Such a notion motivates Ray Bradbury's "The Pedestrian," which first appeared in the collection *The Golden Apples of the Sun* (1953). Although Bradbury (b. 1920) has rarely written directly about L.A., the city resides, metaphorically, at the heart of much of his work. *The Martian Chronicles*, for instance, has been seen as an allegory of how California changes people, while *Fahrenheit 451*, with its vast boulevards and its society in which books have been outlawed, conjures up the well-established image of Southern California as an anti-intellectual culture obsessed with speed and entertainment. In "The Pedestrian," the futuristic urban setting is generic, but the experience Bradbury describes is familiar to anyone who has taken a night-time stroll along the empty boulevards and side streets of Los Angeles, and wondered how, in a city of three million, he could be so alone.

THE PEDESTRIAN

To enter out into that silence that was the city at eight o'clock of a misty evening in November, to put your feet upon the buckling concrete walk, to step over grassy seams and make your way, hands in pockets, through the silences, that was what Mr. Leonard Mead most dearly loved to do. He would stand upon the corner of an intersection and peer down long moonlit avenues of sidewalk in four directions, deciding which way to go, but it really made no difference; he was alone in this world of 2052 A.D., or as good as alone, and with a final decision made, a path selected, he would stride off, sending patterns of frosty air before him like the smoke of cigar.

Sometimes he would walk for hours and miles and return only at midnight to his house. And on his way he would see the cottages and homes with their dark windows, and it was not unequal to walking through a graveyard where only the faintest glimmers of firefly light appeared in flickers behind the windows. Sudden gray phantoms seemed to manifest upon inner room walls where a curtain was still undrawn against the night, or there were whisperings and murmurs where a window in a tomb-like building was still open.

Mr. Leonard Mead would pause, cock his head, listen, look, and march on, his feet making no noise on the lumpy walk. For long ago he had wisely changed to sneakers when strolling at night, because the dogs in intermittent squads would parallel his journey with barkings if he wore hard heels, and lights might click on and faces appear and an entire street be startled by the passing of a lone figure, himself, in the early November evening.

On this particular evening he began his journey in a westerly direction, toward the hidden sea. There was a good crystal frost in the air; it cut the nose and made the lungs blaze like a Christmas tree inside; you could feel the cold light going on and off, all the branches filled with invisible snow. He listened to the faint push of his soft shoes through autumn leaves with satisfaction, and whistled a cold quiet whistle between his teeth, occasionally picking up a leaf as he passed, examining its skeletal pattern in the infrequent lamplights as he went on, smelling its rusty smell.

"Hello, in there," he whispered to every house on every side as he moved. "What's up tonight on Channel 4, Channel 7, Channel 9? Where are the cowboys rushing, and do I see the United States Cavalry over the next hill to the rescue?"

The street was silent and long and empty, with only his shadow moving like the shadow of a hawk in mid-country. If he closed his eyes and stood very still, frozen, he could imagine himself upon the center of a plain, a wintry, windless Arizona desert with no house in a thousand miles, and only dry river beds, the streets, for company.

"What is it now?" he asked the houses, noticing his wrist watch. "Eight-thirty P.M.? Time for a dozen assorted murders? A quiz? A revue? A comedian falling off the stage?"

Was that a murmur of laughter from within a moon-white house? He hesitated, but went on when nothing more happened. He stumbled over a particularly uneven section of sidewalk. The cement was vanishing under flowers and grass. In ten years of walking by night or day, for thousands of miles, he had never met another person walking, not one in all that time.

He came to a cloverleaf intersection which stood silent where two main highways crossed the town. During the day it was a thunderous surge of cars, the gas stations open, a great insect rustling and a ceaseless jockeying for position as the scarab-beetles, a faint incense puttering from their exhausts, skimmed homeward to the far directions. But now these highways, too, were like streams in a dry season, all stone and bed and moon radiance.

He turned back on a side street, circling around toward his home. He was within a block of his destination when the lone car turned a corner quite suddenly and flashed a fierce white cone of light upon him. He stood entranced, not unlike a night moth, stunned by the illumination, and then drawn toward it.

A metallic voice called to him:

"Stand still. Stay where you are! Don't move!"

He halted.

"Put up your hands!"

"But——" he said.

"Your hands up! Or we'll shoot!"

The police, of course, but what a rare, incredible thing; in a city of three million, there was only one police car left, wasn't that correct? Ever since a year ago, 2052, the election year, the force had been cut down from three cars to one. Crime was ebbing; there was no need now for the police, save for this one lone car wandering and wandering the empty streets.

"Your name?" said the police car in a metallic whisper. He couldn't see the men in it for the bright light in his eyes.

"Leonard Mead," he said.

"Speak up!"

"Leonard Mead!"

"Business or profession?"

"I guess you'd call me a writer."

"No profession," said the police car, as if talking to itself. The light held him fixed, like a museum specimen, needle thrust through chest.

"You might say that," said Mr. Mead. He hadn't written in years. Magazines and books didn't sell any more. Everything went on in the tomblike houses at night now, he thought, continuing his fancy. The tombs, ill-lit by television light, where the people sat like the dead, the gray or multicolored lights touching their faces, but never really touching them.

"No profession," said the phonograph voice, hissing. "What are you doing out?"

"Walking," said Leonard Mead.

"Walking!"

"Just walking," he said simply, but his face felt cold.

"Walking, just walking, walking?"

"Yes, sir."

"Walking where? For what?"

"Walking for air. Walking to see."

"Your address!"

"Eleven South Saint James Street."

"And there is air in your house, you have an air *conditioner,* Mr. Mead?"

"Yes."

"And you have a viewing screen in your house to see with?"

"No."

"No?" There was a crackling quiet that in itself was an accusation.

"Are you married, Mr. Mead?"

"No."

"Not married," said the police voice behind the fiery beam. The moon was high and clear among the stars and the houses were gray and silent.

"Nobody wanted me," said Leonard Mead with a smile.

"Don't speak unless you're spoken to!"

Leonard Mead waited in the cold night.

"Just *walking,* Mr. Mead?"

"Yes."

"But you haven't explained for what purpose."

"I explained; for air, and to see, and just to walk."

"Have you done this often?"

"Every night for years."

The police car sat in the center of the street with its radio throat faintly humming.

"Well, Mr. Mead," it said.

"Is that all?" he asked politely.

"Yes," said the voice. "Here." There was a sigh, a pop. The back door of the police car sprang wide. "Get in."

"Wait a minute, I haven't done anything!"

"Get in."

"I protest!"

"Mr. Mead."

He walked like a man suddenly drunk. As he passed the front window of the car he looked in. As he had expected, there was no one in the front seat, no one in the car at all.

"Get in."

He put his hand to the door and peered into the back seat, which was a little cell, a little black jail with bars. It smelled of riveted steel. It smelled of harsh antiseptic; it smelled too clean and hard and metallic. There was nothing soft there.

"Now if you had a wife to give you an alibi," said the iron voice. "But——"

"Where are you taking me?"

The car hesitated, or rather gave a faint whirring click, as if information, somewhere, was dropping card by punch-slotted card under electric eyes. "To the Psychiatric Center for Research on Regressive Tendencies."

He got in. The door shut with a soft thud. The police car rolled through the night avenues, flashing its dim lights ahead.

They passed one house on one street a moment later, one house in an entire city of houses that were dark, but this one particular house had all of its electric lights brightly lit, every window a loud yellow illumination, square and warm in the cool darkness.

"That's my house," said Leonard Mead.

No one answered him.

The car moved down the empty river-bed streets and off away, leaving the empty streets with the empty sidewalks, and no sound and no motion all the rest of the chill November night.

Tennessee Williams

During the summer of 1943, while living in a two-room apartment at 1647 Ocean Avenue in Santa Monica, Tennessee Williams (1911–1983) worked on the play that would catapult him into literary stardom, *The Glass Menagerie.* When he wasn't furiously writing he could gaze out his window to admire the "great powerful Narcissans" who disported at Muscle Beach. His delight in the affable hedonism of Santa Monica is plain from "The Mattress by the Tomato Patch," an autobiographical sketch published in his story collection *Hard Candy* (1954). What is less obvious is that like many of the drifters who gravitated to Santa Monica, Williams was at loose ends that summer, having just been fired from a screenwriting job at MGM. Assigned to work on a script for Lana Turner, Williams was struck from the beginning that screenwriting was "one of the funniest but most embarrassing things that ever happened to me. . . . I feel like an obstetrician required to successfully deliver a mastodon from a beaver."

THE MATTRESS BY THE TOMATO PATCH

My landlady, Olga Kedrova, has given me a bowl of ripe tomatoes from the patch that she lies next to, sunning herself in the great white and blue afternoons of California. These tomatoes are big as my fist, bloody red of color, and firm to the touch as a young swimmer's pectoral muscles.

I said, Why, Olga, my God, it would take me a month to eat that many tomatoes, but she said, Don't be a fool, you'll eat them like grapes, and that was almost how I ate them. It is now five o'clock of this resurrected day in the summer of 1943, a day which I am recording in the present tense although it is ten years past. Now there are only a couple of the big ripe tomatoes left in the pale-blue china bowl, but their sweetness and pride are undimmed, for their heart is not in the bowl which is their graveyard but in the patch that Olga lies next to, and the patch seems to be inexhaustible. It remains out there in the sun and the loam and in the consanguine presence of big Olga Kedrova. She rests beside the patch all afternoon on a raggedy mattress retired from service in one of her hotel bedrooms.

This resurrected day is a Saturday and all afternoon pairs of young lovers have wandered the streets of Santa Monica, searching for rooms to make love in. Each uniformed boy holds a small zipper bag and the sun-pinked-or-gilded arm of a pretty girl, and they seem to be moving in pools of translucent water. The girl waits at the foot of steps which the boy bounds up, at first eagerly, then anxiously, then with desperation, for Santa Monica is literally flooded with licensed and unlicensed couples in this summer of 1943. The couples are endless and their search is unflagging. By sundown and long after, even as late as two or three in the morning, the boy will bound up steps and the girl wait below, sometimes primly pretending not to hear the four-letter word he mutters after each disappointment, sometimes saying it for him when he resumes his dogged hold on her arm. Even as daybreak comes they'll still be searching and praying and cursing with bodies that ache from pent-up longing more than fatigue.

Terrible separations occur at daybreak. The docile girl finally loses faith or patience; she twists violently free of the hand that bruises her arm and dashes sobbing into an all-night café to phone for a cab. The boy hovers outside, gazing fiercely through fog and window, his now empty fist opening and closing on itself. She sits between two strangers, crouches over coffee, sobbing, sniffing, and maybe after a minute she goes back out to forgive him and rests in his arms without hope of anything private, or maybe she is relentless and waits for the cab to remove her from him forever, pretending not to see him outside the fogged window until he wanders away, drunk now, to look for more liquor, turning back now and then to glare at the hot yellow pane that shielded her from his fury. Son of a bitch of a four-letter word for a part of her woman's body is muttered again and again as he stumbles across the car tracks into Palisades Park, under royal palm trees as tall as five-story buildings and over the boom of white breakers and into mist. Long pencils of light still weave back and forth through the sky in search of enemy planes that never come over and nothing else seems to move. But you never can tell. Even at this white hour he might run into something that's better than nothing before the paddy-wagon picks him up or he falls onto one of those cots for service men only at some place like the Elks' Lodge.

Olga knows all this, but what can she do about it? Build more rooms single-handed? To look at Olga you'd almost believe that she could. She is the kind of woman whose weight should be computed not in pounds but in stones, for she has the look of a massive primitive sculpture. Her origin is the Middle East of Europe. She subscribes to the *Daily Worker*, copies of which she sometimes thrusts under my door with paragraphs boxed in red pencil, and she keeps hopefully handing me works by Engels and Veblen and Marx which I hold for a respectful interval and then hand back to her with the sort of vague comment that doesn't fool her a bit. She has now set me down as a hopelessly unregenerate prostitute of the capitalist class, but she calls me "Tennie" or "Villyums" with undiminished good humor and there is nothing at all that she doesn't tell me about herself and nothing about myself that she doesn't expect me to tell . . . When I first came to stay here, late in the spring, and it came out in our conversation that I was a writer at Metro's, she said, Ha ha, I know you studio people! She says things like this with an air of genial complicity which a lingering reserve in my nature at first inclined me to pretend not to understand. But as the summer wore on, my reserve dropped off, and at present I don't suppose we have one secret between us. Sometimes while we are talking, she will go in my bathroom and continue the conversation with the door wide open and her seated figure in full view, looking out at me with the cloudlessly candid eyes of a child who has not yet learned that some things are meant to be private.

This is a house full of beds and I strongly suspect that big Olga has lain in them all. These big old-fashioned brass or white iron beds are like the keyboard of a concert grand piano on which she is running up and down in a sort of continual arpeggio of lighthearted intrigues, and I can't much blame her when I look at her husband. It is sentimental to think that all sick people deserve our sympathy. Ernie is sick but I can't feel sorry for him. He is a thin, sour man whose chronic intestinal trouble was diagnosed eight years ago as cancer, but whose condition today is neither much worse nor better than when the diagnosis was made, a fact that confirms the landlady's contempt for all opinions that don't come through "The Party."

Ernie does the woman's work around the apartment-hotel, while Olga soaks up the sun on the high front steps or from the mattress by the tomato patch out back. From those front steps her lively but unastonished look can comprehend the whole fantasy of Santa Monica Beach, as far north as the "Gone with the Wind" mansion of former film star Molly Delancey and as far south as the equally idiotic but somewhat gayer design of the roller coasters at Venice, California.

Somehow it seems to me, because I like to think so, that this is the summer hotel, magically transplanted from the Crimean sea-coast, where Chekhov's melancholy writer, Trigorin, first made the acquaintance of Madame Arcadina, and where they spent their first weekend together, sadly and wisely within the quiet sound of the sea, a pair of middle-aged lovers who turn the lights off before they undress together, who read plays aloud to each other on heaps of cool pillows and sometimes find that the pressure of a hand before falling asleep is all that they really need to be sure they are resting together.

The Palisades is a big white wooden structure with galleries and gables and plenty of space around it. It stands directly over a munic-ipal playground known as "Muscle Beach." It is here that the acro-bats and tumblers work out in the afternoons, great powerful Nar-cissans who handle their weightless girls and daintier male partners with a sort of tender unconsciousness under the blare and activity of our wartime heavens.

While I am working at home, during my six-week lay-off-with-out-pay from the studio (a punishment for intransigence that pres-ages a short term of employment and forces me to push my play anxiously forward), it is a comfort now and then to notice Big Olga dreaming on the front steps or sprawled on that old mattress in back of the building.

I like to imagine how the mattress got out there . . .

This is how I see it.

On one of those diamond-bright mornings of early summer, Big Olga looms into an upstairs bedroom a soldier and his girl-friend have occupied for the week-end which has just passed. With non-chalant grunts, she looks at the cigarette stains and sniffs at the glasses on the bedside table. With only a token wrinkle or two of something too mild to be defined as disgust, she picks up the used contraceptives tossed under the bed, counts them and murmurs

"My God" as she drops them into the toilet and comes back out of the bathroom without having bothered to wash her hands at the sink. The boy and the girl have plainly enjoyed themselves and Olga is not the kind to resent their pleasure and she is philosophical about little damages to beds and tables incurred in a storm of love-making. Some day one of them will fall asleep or pass out in bed with a lighted cigarette and her summer hotel will burn down. She knows this will happen some day but till it happens, oh, well, why worry about it.

She goes back to the bed and jerks off the crumpled sheets to expose the mattress.

My God, she cries out, the condition this mattress is in!

Bad? says Ernie.

Completely ruined, she tells him.

Pigs, says Ernie.

But Olga is not unhappy.

Pigs, pigs, pigs, says Ernie with almost squealing repugnance, but Olga says, Aw, shut up! A bed is meant to make love on, so why blow your stack about it?

This shuts Ernie up, but inwardly he boils and becomes short-winded.

Ernie, says Olga, you take that end of the mattress.

She picks up the other.

Where does it go? asks Ernie.

The little man backs toward the door but Olga thinks differently of it. She gives an emphatic tug toward the gallery entrance. This way, she says roughly, and Ernie, who rarely presumes anymore to ask her a question, tags along with his end of the mattress dragging the carpet. She kicks the screen door open and with a joyous gasp she steps out into the morning above the ocean and beach. The white clocktower of downtown Santa Monica is looking out of the mist, and everything glistens. She sniffs like a dog at the morning, grins connivingly at it, and shouts, Around this way!

The mattress is lugged to the inland side of the gallery, and Ernie is still not aware of what she is up to.

Now let go, says Olga.

Ernie releases his end and staggers back to the scalloped white frame wall. He is broken and breathless, he sees pinwheels in the sky. But Olga is chuckling a little. While the pinwheels blinded him, Olga has somehow managed to gather both ends of the mattress into her arms and has rolled them together to make a great cylinder. Hmmm, she says to herself. She likes the feel of the mattress, exults in the weight of it on her. She stands there embracing the big inert thing in her arms and with the grip of her thighs. It leans against her, a big exhausted lover, a lover that she has pressed upon his back and straddled and belabored and richly survived. She leans back with the exhausted weight of the mattress resting on her, and she is chuckling and breathing deeply now that she feels her power no longer contested. Fifteen, twenty, twenty-five years are in her of life still, not depleted more than enough to make her calm and easy. Time is no problem to her. Hugging the mattress, she thinks of a wrestler named "Tiger" who comes and goes all summer, remembers a sailor named Ed who has spent some liberties with her, thinks of a Marine Sergeant, brought up in a Kansas orphanage, who calls her Mama, feels all the weight of them resting lightly on her as the weight of one bird with various hurrying wings, staying just long enough to satisfy her and not a moment longer. And so she grips the big mattress and loves the weight of it on her. Ah, she says to herself, ah, hmmm . . .

She sees royal palm trees and the white clocktower of downtown Santa Monica, and possibly says to herself, Well, I guess I'll have a hot barbecue and a cold beer for lunch at the Wop's stand on Muscle Beach and I'll see if Tiger is there, and if he isn't, I'll catch the five o'clock bus to L.A. and take in a good movie, and after that I'll walk over to Olivera Street and have some tamales with chili and two or three bottles of Carta Blanca and come back out to the beach on the nine o'clock bus. That will be after sundown, and three miles east of the beach, they turn the lights out in the bus (because of the wartime blackout), and Olga will have chosen a good seat-companion near the back of the bus, a sailor who's done two hitches and knows the scoop, so when the lights go out, her knees will divide and his will follow suit and the traveling dusk will hum with the gossamer wings of Eros. She'll nudge him when the bus slows toward the corner of Wilshire and Ocean. They'll get off there and wander hand-in-hand into the booming shadows of Palisades Park, which Olga knows like a favorite book never tired of. All along that

enormously tall cliff, under royal palms and over the Pacific, are little summer houses and trellised arbors with benches where sudden
acquaintances burst into prodigal flower.

All of these things, these prospects, too vivid to need any
thought, are in her nerves as she feels the weight of the mattress
between her breasts and thighs, and now she is ready to show the
extent of her power. She tightens the grip of her arms on the soft-
hard bulk and raises the mattress to the height of her shoulders.

Watch out, my God, says Ernie, you'll rupture yourself!

Not I! says Olga, I'll not rupture myself!

Ha ha, look here! she orders.

Her black eyes flash as she coils up her muscles.

One for the money, two for the show, three to get ready, and
four to GO!

Christ Almighty, says Ernie without much breath or conviction,
as the mattress sails, yes, almost literally sails above the rail of the
gallery and out into the glistening air of morning. Fountains of delicate cotton fiber spurt out of at least a thousand ruptures in its cover
the moment the wornout mattress plops to the ground.

Hmmm, says Olga.

The act has been richly completed. She grips the rail of the
gallery with her hands that have never yet been fastened on anything they could not overwhelm if they chose to. The big brass ban-
gles she has attached to her ears are jingling with silly but rapturous
applause, and Ernie is thinking again, as he has thought so often,
since death so thoughtlessly planted a slow seed in his body: How is
it possible that I ever lay with this woman, even so long ago as that
now is!

With an animal's sense of what goes on behind it, Olga knows
what her invalid husband feels when she exhibits her power, and
her back to him is neither friendly nor hostile. And if tonight he has
a cramp in the bowels that doubles him up, she'll help him to the
bathroom and sit yawning on the edge of the tub with a cigarette
and a Hollywood fan-magazine, while he sweats and groans on the
stool. She'll utter goodhumored "phews" and wave her cigarette at
the stench of his anguish, sometimes extending a hand to cup his
forehead. And if he bleeds and collapses, as he sometimes does,
she'll pick him up and carry him back to bed and fall asleep with his

hot fingers twitching in hers, doing it all as if God had told her to do it. There are two reasons: He is a mean and sick little beast that once mated with her and would have been left and forgotten a long time ago except for the now implausible circumstance that she bore two offspring by him—a daughter employed as "executive secretary to a big wheel at Warner's." (She has to stay at his place because he's a lush and needs her constant attention.) And this one, "My God, look at him." A blownup Kodachrome snapshot of a glistening wet golden youth on some unidentified beach that borders a jungle. He makes his nakedness decent by holding a mass of red flowers before his groin. Olga lifts the picture and gives it five kisses as fast as machine-gun fire, which leave rouge-stains on the glass, as bright as the blossoms the grinning boy covers his sex with.

So those are the circumstances she feels behind her in Ernie, and yet they cast no shadow over the present moment. What she is doing is what is usual with her, she's thinking in terms of comfort and satisfaction as she looks down at the prostrate bulk of the mattress. Her eyes are soaking up the possibilities of it. The past of the mattress was good. Olga would be the last to deny its goodness. It has lain beneath many summers of fornications in Olga's summer hotel. But the future of the mattress is going to be good, too. It is going to lie under Olga on afternoons of leisure and under the wonderful rocking-horse weather of Southern California.

That is what the veteran mattress has done for the past few summers. The rain and the sun have had their influence on it. Unable to dissolve and absorb it into themselves, the elements have invested it with their own traits. It is now all softness and odors of ocean and earth, and it is still lying next to the prodigal patch of tomatoes that make me think of a deck of green-backed cards in which everything but diamonds and hearts have been thrown into discard.

(What do you bid? demands the queen of hearts. But that is Olga, and Olga is bidding *forever!*)

On afternoons of leisure she lies out there on this overblown mattress of hers and her slow-breathing body is steamed and relaxed in a one-piece sarong-type garment that a Hollywood pinup girl would hardly dare to appear in. The cocker spaniel named Freckles is resting his chin on her belly. He looks like a butterscotch pudding with whipped cream on it. And these two indolent creatures drift in and out of attention to what takes place in Olga's summer hotel. The quarrels, the music, the wailing receipt of bad news, the joyful shouting, everything that goes on is known and accepted. Without even feeling anything so strong as contempt, their glances take in the activities of the husband having words with a tenant about a torn window shade or sand in a bathtub or wet tracks on the stairs. Nobody pays much attention to poor little Ernie. The Ernies of the world are treated that way. They butt their heads against the walls of their indignation until their dry little brains are shaken to bits. There he goes now, I can see him out this window, trotting along the upstairs gallery of the projecting back wing of the building with some linen to air, some bedclothes on which young bodies have taken their pleasure, for which he hates them. Ernie treats everyone with the polite fury of the impotent cuckold, and they treat Ernie in such an offhand manner it turns him around like a top till he runs down and stops. Sometimes while he complains, they walk right past him dripping the brine of the ocean along the stairs, which Ernie must get down on his hands and knees to wipe up. Pigs, pigs, is what he calls them, and of course he is right, but his fury is too indiscriminate to be useful. Olga is also capable of fury, but she reserves it for the true beast which she knows by sight, sound, and smell, and although she has no name for it, she knows it is the beast of mendacity in us, the beast that tells mean lies, and Olga is not to be confused and thrown off guard by smaller adversaries. Perhaps all adversaries are smaller than Olga, for she is almost as large as the afternoons she lies under.

And so it goes and no one resists the going.

The wonderful rocking-horse weather of California goes rocking over our heads and over the galleries of Olga's summer hotel. It goes rocking over the acrobats and their slim-bodied partners, over the young cadets at the school for flyers, over the ocean that catches the blaze of the moment, over the pier at Venice, over the roller coasters and over the vast beach-homes of the world's most successful kept women—not only over those persons and paraphernalia, but over all that is shared in the commonwealth of existence. It has rocked over me all summer, and over my afternoons at this green and white checkered table in the yellow gelatine flood of a burlesque show. It has gone rocking over accomplishments and defeats; it has covered it all and absorbed the wounds with the pleasures and made no discrimination. For nothing is quite so cavalier as this horse. The giant blue rocking-horse weather of Southern California is rocking and rocking with all the signs pointing forward. Its plumes are smoky blue ones the sky can't hold and so lets grandly go of . . .

And now I am through with another of these afternoons so I push the chair back from the table, littered with paper, and stretch my cramped spine till it crackles and rub my fingers gently over a dull pain in my chest, and think what a cheap little package this is that we have been given to live in, some rubbery kind of machine not meant to wear long, but somewhere in it is a mysterious tenant who knows and describes its being. Who is he and what is he up to? Shadow him, tap his wires, check his intimate associates, if he has any, for there is some occult purpose in his coming to stay here and all the time watching so anxiously out of the windows . . .

Now I am looking out of a window at Olga who has been sunning herself on that smoking-car joke of a mattress the whole live-long afternoon, while she ages at leisure and laps up life with the tongue of a female bull. The wrestler Tiger has taken the room next to mine, that's why she keeps looking this way, placidly alert for the gleam of a purple silk robe through his window curtains, letting her know of his return from the beach, and before he has hung the robe on a hook on the door, the door will open and close as softly as an eyelid and Olga will have disappeared from her mattress by the tomato patch. Once the cocker spaniel had the impudence to sniff and bark outside Tiger's door and he was let in and tossed right out the back window, and another time I heard Tiger muttering, Jesus, you fat old cow, but only a few moments later the noises that came through the wall made me think of the dying confessions of a walrus.

And so it goes and no one resists the going.

The perishability of the package she comes in has cast on Olga no shadow she can't laugh off. I look at her now, before the return of Tiger from Muscle Beach, and if no thought, no knowledge has yet taken form in the protean jelly-world of brain and nerves, if I am patient enough to wait a few moments longer, this landlady by Picasso may spring up from her mattress and come running into this room with a milky-blue china bowl full of reasons and explanations for all that exists.

Ross Macdonald

Ross Macdonald (1915–1983) took Raymond Chandler's model of the hardboiled detective novel and brought it into a different world: the postwar Southern California of sprawling suburbs, two-car garages, and private beach clubs "surrounded by a high wire fence topped with three barbed strands and masked with oleanders." Born Kenneth Millar in California of Canadian parents, and brought up in Ontario, Macdonald ultimately settled in Santa Barbara. He was at once native and outsider; like his detective hero Lew Archer, he was lovingly familiar with his adopted home without ever losing a sense of wariness about it. His peripatetic characters—fugitive children, forgotten parents, accidental criminals—change worlds and identities by driving from one neighborhood to another, with Los Angeles often the central hub of such transformations. In this episode from *The Barbarous Coast* (1956), Archer finds himself as usual prying at a false front to find the story buried underneath.

from

THE BARBAROUS COAST

Mrs. Campbell lived on a poor street of stucco and frame cottages half hidden by large, ancient oak trees. In their sun-flecked shadows, pre-school children played their killing games: Bang bang, you're dead; I'm not dead; you are so dead. A garbage truck on its rounds started a chorus of dogs barking in resentment at the theft of their masters' garbage.

Mrs. Campbell's cottage stood behind a flaked stucco wall in which a rusty gate stood permanently open. There was a new cardboard FOR SALE sign wired to the gate. In the courtyard, red geraniums had thrust up through a couple of stunted lime trees and converted them into red-flowering bushes which seemed to be burning in the sun. The thorned and brighter fire of a bougainvillæa vine surged up the front porch and the roof.

I stepped in under its cool shade and knocked on the screen door, which was tufted with cotton to ward off flies. A tiny barred window was set in the inner door. Its shutter snapped open, and an eye looked out at me. It was a blue eye, a little faded, surrounded with curled lashes and equipped with a voice like the sparrows' in the oak trees:

"Good morning, are you from Mr. Gregory?"

I mumbled something indistinguishable which might have been, yes, I was.

"Goodie, I've been expecting you." She unlocked the door and opened it wide. "Come in, Mr.—?"

"Archer," I said.

"I'm absotively delighted to see you, Mr. Archer."

She was a small, straight-bodied woman in a blue cotton dress too short and frilly for her age. This would be about fifty, though everything about her conspired to deny it. For an instant in the dim little box of a hallway, her bird voice and quick graces created the illusion that she was an adolescent blonde.

In the sunlit living-room, the illusion died. The dry cracks of experience showed around her eyes and mouth, and she couldn't smile them away. Her ash-blond boyish bob was fading into gray, and her neck was withering. I kind of liked her, though. She saw that. She wasn't stupid.

She ankled around the small living-room, lifting clean ashtrays and setting them down again. "Do have a chair, or would you prefer to stand up and look around? How nice of you to be interested in my little nest. Please notice the sea view, which is one of the little luxuries I have. Isn't it lovely?"

She posed her trim, small body, extended her arm toward the window and held it stiff and still, slightly bent up at the elbow, fingers apart. There was a view of the sea: a meager blue ribbon, tangled among the oak-tree branches.

"Very nice." But I was wondering what ghostly audience or dead daddy she was playing to. And how long she would go on taking me for a prospective buyer.

The room was crammed with dark old furniture made for a larger room, and for larger people: a carved refectory table flanked by high-backed Spanish chairs, an overstuffed red plush divan, thick red drapes on either side of the window. These made a cheerless contrast with the plaster walls and ceiling, which were dark green and mottled with stains from old leaks in the roof.

She caught me looking at the waterstains. "It won't happen again, I can guarantee you that. I had the roof repaired last fall, and, as a matter of fact, I've been saving up to redecorate this room. When all of a sudden my big move came up. I've had the most wondrous good luck, you know, or should I say my daughter has." She paused in a dramatic listening attitude, as if she were receiving a brief message in code on her back fillings. "But let me tell you over coffee. Poor man, you look quite peaked. I know what house-hunting is."

Her generosity disturbed me. I hated to accept anything from her under false pretenses. But before I could frame an answer she'd danced away through a swinging door to the kitchen. She came back with a breakfast tray on which a silver coffee set shone proudly, laid it on the table, and hovered over it. It was a pleasure to watch her pour. I complimented the coffeepot.

"Thank you very mooch, kind sir. It was one of my wedding presents, I've kept it all these years. I've held on to a lot of things, and now I'm glad I did, now that I'm moving back into the big house." She touched her lips with her fingertips and chuckled musically. "But of course you can't know what I'm talking about, unless Mr. Gregory told you."

"Mr. Gregory?"

"Mr. Gregory the realtor." She perched on the divan beside me, confidentially. "It's why I'm willing to sell without a cent of profit, as long as I get my equity out of this place. I'm moving out the first of the week, to go and live with my daughter. You see, my daughter is flying to Italy for a month or so, and she wants me to be in the big house, to look after it while she's gone. Which I'll be very happy to do, I can tell you."

"You're moving into a larger house?"

"Yes indeedy I am. I'm moving back into my own house, the one my girls were born in. You might not think it to look around you, unless you have an eye for good furniture, but I used to live in a grand big house in Beverly Hills." She nodded her head vigorously, as though I'd contradicted her. "I lost it—we lost it way back before the war when my husband left us. But now that clever daughter of mine has bought it back! And she's asked me to live with her!" She hugged her thin chest. "How she must love her little mother! Eh? Eh?"

"She certainly must," I said. "It sounds as if she's come into some money."

"Yes." She plucked at my sleeve. "I *told* her it would happen, if she kept faith and worked hard and made herself agreeable to people. I told the girls the very day we moved out that someday we'd move back. And, sure enough, it's happened, Hester's come in to all this uranium money."

"She found uranium?"

"Mr. Wallingford did. He was a Canadian mining tycoon. Hester married an older man, just as I did in my time. Unfortunately the poor man died before they'd been married a year. I never met him."

"What was his name?"

"George Wallingford," she said. "Hester draws a substantial monthly income from the estate. And then she's got her movie money, too. Everything seems to have broken for her at once."

I watched her closely, but could see no sign that she was lying consciously.

"What does she do in the movies?"

"Many things," she said with a wavy flip of her hand. "She dances and swims and dives—she was a professional diver—and of course she acts. Her *father* was an actor, back in the good old days. You've heard of Raymond Campbell?"

I nodded. The name belonged to a swashbuckling silent-movie star who had tried to make the transition to the talkies and been tripped by advancing years and a tenor voice. I could remember a time in the early twenties when Campbell's serials filled the Long Beach movie houses on Saturday afternoons. Me they had filled with inspiration: his Inspector Fate of Limehouse series had helped to make me a cop, for good or ill. And when the cops went sour, the memory of Inspector Fate had helped to pull me out of the Long Beach force.

She said: "You do remember Raymond, don't you? Did you know him personally?"

"Just on the screen. It's been a long time. What ever happened to him?"

"He died," she said, "he died of a broken heart, way back in the depression. He hadn't had a picture for years, his friends turned against him, he was terribly in debt. And so he died." Her eyes became glazed with tears, but she smiled bravely through them like one of Raymond Campbell's leading ladies. "I carried on the faith, however. I was an actress myself, before I subordinated my life to Raymond's, and I brought up my girls to follow in his footsteps, just as he would have wished. One of them, at least, has made the most of it."

"What does your other daughter do?"

"Rina? She's a psychiatric nurse, can you imagine? It's always been a wonder to me that two girls so close in age and looks could differ so in temperament. Rina actually doesn't *have* any temperament. With all the artistic training I gave her, she grew up just as cold and hard and practical as they come. Why, I'd drop dead with shock if Rina ever offered me a home. No!" she cried melodramatically. "Rina would rather spend her time with crazy people. Why would a pretty girl do a thing like that?"

"Maybe she wants to help them."

Mrs. Campbell looked blank. "She could have found a more feminine way. Hester brings real joy to others without demeaning herself."

A funny look must have crossed my face. She regarded me shrewdly, then snapped her eyelids wide and turned on her brights. "But I mustn't bore you with my family affairs. You came to look at the house. It's got just the three rooms, but it's *most* convenient, especially the kitchen."

"Don't bother with that, Mrs. Campbell. I've been imposing on your hospitality."

"Why, no you haven't. Not at all."

"I have, though. I'm a detective."

"A detective?" Her tiny fingers clawed at my arm and took hold. She said in a new voice, a full octave lower than her bird tones: "Has something happened to Hester?"

"Not that I know of. I'm simply looking for her."

"Is she in trouble?"

"She may be."

"I knew it. I've been so afraid that something would go wrong. Things never work out for us. Something goes wrong, always." She touched her face with her fingertips: it was like crumpled paper. "I'm in a damned hole," she said hoarsely. "I gave up my job on the strength of this, and I owe half the people in town. If Hester falls down on me now, I don't know what I'll do." She dropped her hands, and raised her chin. "Well, let's have the bad news. It is all a bunch of lies?"

"Is what a bunch of lies?"

"What I've been telling you, what she told me. About the movie contract and the trip to Italy and the rich husband who died. I had my doubts about it, you know—I'm not that much of a fool."

"Part of it may be true. Part of it isn't. Her husband isn't dead. He isn't old, and he isn't rich, and he wants her back. Which is where I come in."

"Is that all there is to it? No." Her eyes regarded me with hard suspicion. The shock had precipitated a second personality in her, and I wondered how much of the hardness belonged to her, and how much to hysteria. "You're holding out on me. You admitted she's in trouble."

"I said she may be. What makes you so sure?"

"You're a hard man to get information out of." She stood up in front of me, planting her fists on her insignificant hips and leaning forward like a bantam fighter. "Now don't try to give me the run-around, though God knows I'm used to it after thirty years in this town. Is she or isn't she in trouble?"

"I can't answer that, Mrs. Campbell. So far as I know, there's nothing against her. All I want to do is talk to her."

"On what subject?"

"The subject of going back to her husband."

"Why doesn't he talk to her himself?"

"He intends to. At the moment he's a little under the weather. And we've had a lot of trouble locating her."

"Who is he?"

"A young newspaperman from Toronto. Name's George Wall."

"George Wall," she said. "George Wallingford."

"Yes," I said, "it figures."

"What sort of a man is this George Wall?"

"I think he's a good one, or he will be when he grows up."

"Is he in love with her?"

"Very much. Maybe too much."

"And what you want from me is her address?"

"If you know it."

"I ought to know it. I lived there for nearly ten years. 14 Manor Crest Drive, Beverly Hills. But if that's all you wanted, why didn't you say so? You let me beat my gums and make a fool of myself. Why do that to me?"

"I'm sorry. It wasn't very nice. But this may be more than a run-away-wife case. You suggested yourself that Hester's in trouble."

"Trouble is what the word detective means to me."

"Has she been in trouble before?"

"We won't go into that."

"Have you been seeing much of her this winter?"

"Very little. I spent one weekend with her—the weekend before last."

"In the Beverly Hills house?"

"Yes. She'd just moved in, and she wanted my advice about redecorating some of the rooms. The people who had it before Hester didn't keep it up—not like the days when we had our Japanese couple." Her blue gaze strained across the decades, and returned to the present. "Anyway, we had a good time together, Hester and I. A wonderful weekend all by our lonesomes, chatting and tending to her clothes and pretending it was old times. And it ended up with Hester inviting me to move in the first of the year."

"That was nice of her."

"Wasn't it? I was so surprised and pleased. We hadn't been close at all for several years. I'd hardly seen her, as a matter of fact. And then, out of the blue, she asked me to come and live with her."

"Why do you think she did?"

The question seemed to appeal to her realistic side. She sat on the edge of her chair, in thinking position, her fingertips to her temple. "It's hard to say. Certainly not on account of my beautiful blue eyes. Of course, she's going to be away and she needs someone to stay in the house and look after it. I think she's been lonely, too."

"And frightened?"

"She didn't act frightened. Maybe she was. She wouldn't tell me if she was. My girls don't tell me anything." She inserted the knuckle of her right thumb between her teeth, and wrinkled her face like a baby monkey. "Will I still be able to move the first of the year? Do you think I will?"

"I wouldn't count on it."

"But the house must belong to her. She wouldn't spend all that money on redecorating. Mr. Archer—is that your name? Archer?—where is all the money coming from?"

"I have no idea," I said, though I had several.

Jack Kerouac

Los Angeles is just another stopover in the endless zigzagging journey that is Jack Kerouac's *On the Road* (1957), but his sketch of the city as a "huge desert encampment" has speed and humor and Kerouac's usual flair for prose melody. Kerouac (1922–1969) once fantasized about writing screenplays for big money, but his only (vicarious) brush with Hollywood came later, with the glossy MGM adaptation of his novel *The Subterraneans*. His own experience of Southern California was less glamorous, a drifter's quick tour of Sunset Boulevard, Central Avenue, and Arcadia.

from

ON THE ROAD

For the next fifteen days we were together for better or for worse. When we woke up we decided to hitchhike to New York together; she was going to be my girl in town. I envisioned wild complexities with Dean and Marylou and everybody—a season, a new season. First we had to work to earn enough money for the trip. Terry was all for starting at once with the twenty dollars I had left. I didn't like it. And, like a damn fool, I considered the problem for two days, as we read the want ads of wild LA papers I'd never seen before in my life, in cafeterias and bars, until my twenty dwindled to just over ten. We were very happy in our little hotel room. In the middle of the night I got up because I couldn't sleep, pulled the cover over baby's bare brown shoulder, and examined the LA night. What brutal, hot, siren-whining nights they are! Right across the street there was trouble. An old rickety rundown rooming house was the scene of some kind of tragedy. The cruiser was pulled up below and the cops were questioning an old man with gray hair. Sobbings came from within. I could hear everything, together with the hum of my hotel neon. I never felt sadder in my life. LA is the loneliest and most brutal of American cities; New York gets godawful cold in the winter but there's a feeling of wacky comradeship somewhere in some streets. LA is a jungle.

393

South Main Street, where Terry and I took strolls with hot dogs, was a fantastic carnival of lights and wildness. Booted cops frisked people on practically every corner. The beatest characters in the country swarmed on the sidewalks—all of it under those soft Southern California stars that are lost in the brown halo of the huge desert encampment LA really is. You could smell tea, weed, I mean marijuana, floating in the air, together with the chili beans and beer. That grand wild sound of bop floated from beer parlors; it mixed medleys with every kind of cowboy and boogie-woogie in the American night. Everybody looked like Hassel. Wild Negroes with bop caps and goatees came laughing by; then long-haired brokendown hipsters straight off Route 66 from New York; then old desert rats, carrying packs and heading for a park bench at the Plaza; then Methodist ministers with raveled sleeves, and an occasional Nature Boy saint in beard and sandals. I wanted to meet them all, talk to everybody, but Terry and I were too busy trying to get a buck together.

We went to Hollywood to try to work in the drugstore at Sunset and Vine. Now there was a corner! Great families off jalopies from the hinterlands stood around the sidewalk gaping for sight of some movie star, and the movie star never showed up. When a limousine passed they rushed eagerly to the curb and ducked to look: some character in dark glasses sat inside with a bejeweled blonde. "Don Ameche! Don Ameche!" "No, George Murphy! George Murphy!" They milled around, looking at one another. Handsome queer boys who had come to Hollywood to be cowboys walked around, wetting their eyebrows with hincty fingertip. The most beautiful little gone gals in the world cut by in slacks; they came to be starlets; they ended up in drive-ins. Terry and I tried to find work at the drive-ins. It was no soap anywhere. Hollywood Boulevard was a great, screaming frenzy of cars; there were minor accidents at least once a minute; everybody was rushing off toward the farthest palm—and beyond that was the desert and nothingness. Hollywood Sams stood in front of swank restaurants, arguing exactly the same way Broadway Sams argue at Jacob's Beach, New York, only here they wore light-weight suits and their talk was cornier. Tall, cadaverous preachers shuddered by. Fat screaming women ran across the boulevard to get in line for the quiz shows. I saw Jerry Colonna buying a car at Buick Motors; he was inside the vast plate-glass window, fingering his mustachio. Terry and I ate in a cafeteria downtown which was decorated to look like a grotto, with metal tits spurting everywhere and great impersonal stone buttockses belonging to deities and soapy Neptune. People ate lugubrious meals around the waterfalls, their faces green with marine sorrow. All the cops in LA looked like handsome gigolos; obviously they'd come to LA to make the movies. Everybody had come to make the movies, even me. Terry and I were finally reduced to trying to get jobs on South Main Street among the beat countermen and dishgirls who made no bones about their beatness, and even there it was no go. We still had ten dollars.

"Man, I'm going to get my clothes from Sis and we'll hitchhike to New York," said Terry. "Come on, man. Let's do it. 'If you can't boogie I know I'll show you how.'" That last part was a song of hers she kept singing. We hurried to her sister's house in the sliverous Mexican shacks somewhere beyond Alameda Avenue. I waited in a dark alley behind Mexican kitchens because her sister wasn't supposed to see me. Dogs ran by. There were little lamps illuminating the little rat alleys. I could hear Terry and her sister arguing in the soft, warm night. I was ready for anything.

Terry came out and led me by the hand to Central Avenue, which is the colored main drag of LA. And what a wild place it is, with chickenshacks barely big enough to house a jukebox, and the jukebox blowing nothing but blues, bop, and jump. We went up dirty tenement stairs and came to the room of Terry's friend Margarina, who owed Terry a skirt and a pair of shoes. Margarina was a lovely mulatto; her husband was black as spades and kindly. He went right out and bought a pint of whisky to host me proper. I tried to pay part of it, but he said no. They had two little children. The kids bounced on the bed; it was their play-place. They put their arms around me and looked at me with wonder. The wild humming night of Central Avenue—the night of Hamp's "Central Avenue Breakdown"—howled and boomed along outside. They were singing in the halls, singing from their windows, just hell be damned and look out. Terry got her clothes and we said good-by. We went down to a chickenshack and played records on the jukebox. A couple of Negro characters whispered in my ear about tea. One buck. I said

okay, bring it. The connection came in and motioned me to the cellar toilet, where I stood around dumbly as he said, "Pick up, man,
pick up."

"Pick up what?" I said.

He had my dollar already. He was afraid to point at the floor. It
was no floor, just basement. There lay something that looked like a
little brown turd. He was absurdly cautious. "Got to look out for
myself, things ain't cool this past week." I picked up the turd, which
was a brown-paper cigarette, and went back to Terry, and off we
went to the hotel room to get high. Nothing happened. It was Bull
Durham tobacco. I wished I was wiser with my money.

Terry and I had to decide absolutely and once and for all what to
do. We decided to hitch to New York with our remaining money.
She picked up five dollars from her sister that night. We had about
thirteen or less. So before the daily room rent was due again we
packed up and took off on a red car to Arcadia, California, where
Santa Anita racetrack is located under snow-capped mountains. It
was night. We were pointed toward the American continent. Holding hands, we walked several miles down the road to get out of the
populated district. It was a Saturday night. We stood under a road-
lamp, thumbing, when suddenly cars full of young kids roared by
with streamers flying. "Yaah! Yaah! we won! we won!" they all
shouted. Then they yoohooed us and got great glee out of seeing a
guy and a girl on the road. Dozens of such cars passed, full of young
faces and "throaty young voices," as the saying goes. I hated every
one of them. Who did they think they were, yaahing at somebody
on the road just because they were little high-school punks and their
parents carved the roast beef on Sunday afternoons? Who did they
think they were, making fun of a girl reduced to poor circumstances
with a man who wanted to belove? We were minding our own business. And we didn't get a blessed ride. We had to walk back to
town, and worst of all we needed coffee and had the misfortune of
going into the only place open, which was a high-school soda fountain, and all the kids were there and remembered us. Now they saw
that Terry was Mexican, a Pachuco wildcat; and that her boy was
worse than that.

With her pretty nose in the air she cut out of there and we wandered together in the dark up along the ditches of the highways. I

carried the bags. We were breathing fogs in the cold night air. I finally decided to hide from the world one more night with her, and the morning be damned. We went into a motel court and bought a comfortable little suite for about four dollars—shower, bathtowels, wall radio, and all. We held each other tight. We had long, serious talks and took baths and discussed things with the light on and then with the light out. Something was being proved, I was convincing her of something, which she accepted, and we concluded the pact in the dark, breathless, then pleased, like little lambs.

Lawrence Clark Powell

Despite the stereotype of Los Angeles as an artificial landscape, it may actually be the wildest, most natural of America's major cities, or at any rate the least urban in any traditional sense. Griffith Park, just northwest of downtown, is an oasis of wildlife and hiking trails, and the Pacific shore-line north of Santa Monica remains, in large part, craggy and windblown. In *"Ocian in View"* (the title is taken from the journals of Lewis and Clark), Lawrence Clark Powell (1906–2001) revels in the abundant splendor he discovered in "the Malibu" after he and his wife gave up their home in Westwood to rough it out along the coast. For many years head librarian at UCLA (the University's Powell Library is named after him), Powell was an early and passionate advocate for California's literary legacy.

from

"OCIAN IN VIEW"

My boyhood and youth were nourished by the San Gabriels and the San Bernardinos which together form the Sierra Madre range of Southern California. It was not until I went to work at UCLA, twenty years ago, and moved near to the campus that allegiance was transferred to the Santa Monicas, a less spectacular range which rises in Hollywood and extends fifty miles northwest to a marine ending at Point Mugu.

From living in Beverly Glen, I came to love the surrounding range of chaparral, oak, and sycamore. It was a good place for our sons to live as little boys, and now that they are grown to manhood, they find their subconscious minds full of memories of their mountain boyhood.

Although as I have already written, I discovered the western most part of the range in the poems of Madeleine Ruthven, it was not until a decade later in 1944 that I came actually to know this remote area. At war's end my friend Gordon Newell, the sculptor, and his wife Emelia acquired land on the north slope of the mountains, overlooking Seminole Hot Springs, and it served me as a kind of retreat from too much city. From driving and walking and talking to Newell, I came to know and to love his land and the sea of chaparral which enislanded it. The north slope of the Santa Monicas is green the year round from springs, one of which he had deepened and rock lined, so that it was an unfailing source of cold water, even in the dryest summer. Through the years I watched him quarry honey-colored flagstone, sift and sack oak leaf-mould, breed Nubian goats, keep bees, carve wood and cut stone, while his wife made delicate jewelry and airy mobiles, and their children grew and grew—in some ways a twentieth-century Theocritean idyll.

It takes time to assimilate the essences of a land. When after years of residence in Inyo County Mary Austin wrote *The Land of Little Rain*, her publishers wanted her to move around the country, writing similar books about the other places of residence. Her reply was that it would take her ten years in a locale to be able to evoke its spirit, as indeed she did later for Arizona-New Mexico in *The Land of Journeys' Ending*.

Thus although we moved to the Malibu, in the seaward lea of the Santa Monicas, as recently as 1955, I brought to the land years of slow growing knowledge and deepening love for this country "where the mountains meet the sea"; and I was ready to write about it, not as a stranger. In fact it was this long background of reading and seeing that motivated our move—that and the feeling we have always had for the seashore. Plus something else, instinctive, mysterious and right.

So it was a kind of magnetic homecoming, our move to the Malibu, and now our leisure time is divided between shoreline walks and mountain drives.

On that coast the seasons merge almost imperceptibly into each other. When the rainy season is regular, then it is easier to know the time of year. When drought comes, how is one to know summer and fall from winter and spring? by the stars to be sure, and the position of the sun—those heavenly clockworks that transcend earthly times of wet and dry.

In the late autumn the evening wears Vega like a blue white diamond. Arcturus has set long before the sun did. Capella comes up over the mountains, brightest of the northernmost stars, and toward midnight, when Sirius is well risen, there directly below it, just above the horizon, appears the sky's number two glitterer, the southern star Canopus, never rising high enough to get beyond the city's atmosphere, which lends it a baleful light.

The sun which in summer set behind the mountain has moved out to sea, dropping from sight at the point where San Nicolas Island lies, if we were high enough to see it. See it we did from the crest of the mountains, on one of the day's end drives which conclude our otherwise stay-at-home Sundays, lying between Santa Barbara Rock and the Santa Cruz-Anacapa conjunction, eighty miles out, dark whale on the blue sea, never to be seen from shoreline.

Living on the Malibu one can choose between many peaceful things to do—stay at home and read or write or garden and other chores, or just sit; or drive in the hills; or walk on the beach. There is choice too among the hill drives—whether it be up the Decker Road along Mulholland, and down the Arroyo Sequit to the sea again, or up Little Sycamore Canyon on the Yerba Buena Road, over Triunfo Pass with a view to Lake Sherwood, then down past the lake, through Hidden Valley, over the hills and down Long Grade Canyon to Camarillo and the coast highway; or west from Little Sycamore along narrow roads leading into cul-de-sacs, where one sees foxes and hawks, and water flowing out of rock-face—all of this within fifty miles of Los Angeles, unknown to the millions.

Last autumn, when the first of the two recent fires swept over the mountains from the valley, leaped the crest of Boney Ridge and devoured the forest of red shanks which graced that mountain's southern slope, we feared a long bareness for the burned flanks. Winter rains brought a myriad of flowers in places where the sun had not penetrated for years, and then in the spring we rejoiced to see rise from the base of the burned chaparral delicate new growth. The fire had not proved mortal, though ten years would be needed for the forest to recover.

Summer's flowers succeeded spring's pinks and blues and whites—orange monkey-flower, red gooseberry, and the purple sage, bee heaven on earth—while the arroyos became seco and sand choked the creek-mouths.

By summer the winter's creekwood had all been gathered, and the gleaning was again of plankwood cast up by the sea, that and shells and fragments to serve as gravel on the garden paths. All these years I had remembered the crushed abalone shells with which Una and Robin Jeffers gravelled their paths at Tor House, and now I began to strew our walks with shells and bones and jeweled bits from the seashore.

The Chumash who dwelled here were jewelry makers, and the Southwest Museum preserves examples of their necklaces of tideline treasures. Now I see why. The wash of water renders all things smooth, and after high tide recedes, one finds the beach strewn with beautiful fragments. Westward I walk, stooping, picking, filling the cloth bag I carry, until it becomes leaden and the way back weary. And when at last I empty it out on the path at home, the scattering iridescences and pearly bits — blue-black of mussel, flesh-pink of cowrie, purple of abalone — make a display Tiffany's should envy, and I am moved to acquire a polishing wheel, a cutter and a borer, a ball of cord, and become a necklace-maker. The abalone shells of this coast were prized by the Hopis far to the east, who ground them for dye tincture. These mollusca are rarely exposed by even the lowest tide, seeking the safety of deeper water, and even then skin-divers need powerful leverage to pry them loose, and woe to the man whose hand is caught. Freshly caught and sauteed in butter they are delicious, and their shells remain, forever beautiful.

Indians are buried everywhere from Mugu Lagoon to Malibu Creek. Every bulldozing operation brings their bones and artifacts to light, as one did just across Broad Beach Road from us — a dozen huddled skeletons, four or five hundred years old, taking no notice of their noisy resurrection. Our geranium garden, falling to Encinal Creek, is sure to be a burying ground, the diggers tell us. Mary Austin writes of the residue of personality that always haunts a place once inhabited by man. Jeffers' poetry is full of these hauntings. But I cannot say that I have encountered spirits here on the Malibu. Perhaps the diesels drive them away. I have no fear of them however. The Chumash were a gentle people, living on shell fish, roots, and acorn meal. We who are carnivorous may leave a different residue. Sometimes I wonder who will follow us here, and what they will make of our artifacts—books and discs and Scriptos, and less tangible, though perhaps more lasting, our love for this marine mountainscape called the Malibu.

Along the Malibu there has been a good aftermath of the storm, and the coast has been gathering manna. Mushrooms and other edible fungi rose overnight, and lived briefly in the light of day before consummating a buttery union in the skillet. Mustard greens likewise had a short life-span before they too yielded up on the stove. Last year's stalks were rooted out by the wind and piled like skeletons against the fences, to make room for the new growth now in its head-high yellow prime.

Mussels also are in season—no delicacy, true, but few meals are more satisfying than a mess of them, gathered at ebb tide in the twilight, then steamed open and dunked in lemon-butter, salty, sandy, tough little guys, tasting of kelpy iodine, an atavistic feast linking us with our predecessors on this coastal shelf, who gave names to many of the places, from Anacapa and Hueneme to Mugu, Malibu, and Topanga.

Now we know why they inhabited the lagoons at the creek-mouths, for when the rainy runoff swells these arroyo secos to savage streams, the rivers break their summer sandbars and run to the sea, bearing treasure to the tidelanders. We live on the cliff by the estuary of Encinal Creek, and at the height of the storm when we went down with shovels to divert ravenous runoffs, we saw the little watercourse, long barred from union with the ocean and held in stagnant continence, changed to a torrent, and raging out of the Santa Monicas to an eager consummation with the sea.

The Pacific was belying its name, roiled up for a mile off shore, wind-blown, coffee-colored, perilous to all but its native denizens— and I doubt they were pleased with the turmoil. We dwell on an open coast, with few shelters for small craft, and the shoreline is that seen by Cabrillo, Drake, Vancouver, and Dana, and in our day by the crews of purse-seiner, tuna-clipper, and tanker. The Catalina and Santa Barbara channel affords scant protection from south-westerlies, and the islands themselves are mostly steep and forbidding on both their lee and windward sides.

Life on the Malibu is richest at the creek-mouths, the Chumash knew; and so did we, after the storm was over and the runoff from the mountains washed upon the beaches. What a haul of firewood for the gleaning! We envy the Brents, whose open fireplace will take logs up to ten feet in length. Ours is only twenty inches wide, which means that sawing, chopping and splitting must follow gleaning and hauling.

It is years since the hills received such a scouring, yielding logs and stumps, burned roots, and rotting branches of oak, sycamore, red shanks and chamisal, much of it smashed to fireplace length in its fall down the streambeds, and sculptured into beautiful shapes.

The sea itself casts up wood, smoothed by wind and wave — empty packing-cases of water-chestnuts from Hong Kong and ammunition boxes from Navy vessels, flawed planks of pine, Douglas fir, oak and redwood, cast overboard from lumber schooners, flotsam, corks from fisherman's nets, an occasional Japanese glass float, battered lobster traps, and sundry jetsam not worth its salt.

The first step is to cache the wet wood and let it dry, before carrying it up the path to the cliff-top. If one posts his pile with a sign reading "Blest be he who leaves my logs; Curst be he who steals my sticks," he is certain to find it when he returns, and just half its weight.

The joy of gathering beachwood is matched by that of burning it, although an occasional twinge is felt, like eating one's pet rabbit, when a shaft of skin smooth chaparral is reduced to silvery ash. This wild wood's smoke has its own smells, different from those of domestic firewood — oak and walnut perfumey, eucalyptus acrid, orange bittersweet, and juniper like incense — and unless it has been submerged a long while, it does not burn with a blue flame. One twelve-foot length of 2 × 4 was difficult to identify. From its weight and grain and color I called it oak. When I began to saw it, I realized my error. The fragrance was like the interior of our clothes closet. Cedar! The smoke from its burning was even sweeter.

Characteristic of this coast is the offshore wind that blows after dark, very faintly, a mere breath of mountain air suspiring delicately toward the sea, bearing smells of sunwarmed brush and stream-bed with smoke from our chimney, ghosts of the beach-wood, drifting down over the dark sand and water, residue of fire, liberated energy, sweeter far than incense of cathedral.

Now winter's constellations are risen high, Sirius ruling the zenith and fiery Canopus, describing his short arc above the southern horizon. In the west the lighthouse opens like an eye, then closes, leaving the night darker than before. In the east, when it is very clear, the Point Vicente light can be seen on the Palos Verdes, and nearer, the light buoy off Point Dume. These smells and sights assure one that he can leave the world to the wakeful and seek his bed, with the final thought that another storm will find us in the wood business.

Gavin Lambert

The idea that Los Angeles is both a dead end and a kind of Eden permeates the city's culture. Nathanael West wrote in *The Day of the Locust*: "Where else should they go but California, the land of sunshine and oranges? Once there, they discover that sunshine isn't enough. They get tired of oranges, even of avocado pears and passion fruit. Nothing happens. They don't know what to do with their time." In his 1959 short story "The Slide Area," the English writer Gavin Lambert (b. 1924) explores a later phase of that sensibility, set against a beautifully evoked city of shifting and unreliable surfaces. A screenwriter, novelist, and biographer of Vivien Leigh and George Cukor among others, Lambert moved to L.A. in 1957 to work for director Nicholas Ray. He went on to write the cult novel *Inside Daisy Clover*, as well as the scripts for film adaptations of *Sons and Lovers*, *I Never Promised You a Rose Garden*, and *The Roman Spring of Mrs. Stone*.

THE SLIDE AREA

About this hour and season, four o'clock in the afternoon and early summer, I find myself looking out of the window and wondering why the world seems bright yet melancholy.

I am sitting in office 298 of a Hollywood film studio, working on a script and thinking that the film Cliff Harriston is going to make of it won't do either of us much good. This morning I noticed a truck parked outside one of the shooting stages. Scenery was being unloaded, the walls and furniture of a living-room carried into the empty stage where camera, lights and the high crane are already waiting. There is no stopping it now, I thought. Later, imagining the reality being hammered and painted and wheeled into shape over there, I looked at the pages on my desk and found them more unreal, more impossible than ever. Tomorrow there will be more arguments with executives. We shall plead our cause and discuss what is truth. I would like to start work on the novel I am hoping to write and pretend is already under way.

Office 298 is small and square and rather dim, because there are venetian blinds across the windows and heavy faded curtains that cannot be pulled back far enough. I have tried letting up the blinds, but the heat is unendurable. Better to be cool and slightly depressed. There is a desk with a telephone and typewriter and stack of paper, a tray full of finely-sharpened pencils and a calendar with leaves you are supposed to tear off each day. It doesn't seem worthwhile to tear off the leaves. Let time stand still or move back, it doesn't matter.

There used to be pictures hanging on the walls, coloured sketches for the sets of a recent production laid in ancient Rome. Another sketch was labelled *Costume for Mr. Victor Mature.* The designer had autographed them all with a grave flourish in the lower right-hand corner. I took them down my first day here and hid them behind the filing cabinet. No one will take them away, although I have asked the office cop several times and once in desperation left a note for the cleaners.

I glance at the cabinet and know they are *there.* About twice a week this obliges me to leave the office early. It always happens at the same time. From my swivel chair at the desk I face this cabinet and the door leading into the corridor; the dim light is strange and enervating, it reminds me of an unoccupied house swathed in blinds and dust-sheets. Swivelling, I look out of the window across the parking lot with its rows of shining two-toned saloons and convertibles, and the neat flower-beds dustily brilliant in puce and yellow. The sun is climbing down the sky. In another hour it will be cooler.

As I leave the building, the cop silently notes my early departure in his little book. He has already noted my late arrival this morning. A friendly ritual that we do not even bother to talk about.

Two men are staring at the newspaper rack near his desk. Both are plump and clean and perspiring, and wear white nylon shirts with sleeves rolled up. They have familiar anonymous executive faces.

For once a political event, though it was later found not to have taken place, occupies the front page headlines. With no kidnappings, aeroplane crashes or sex crimes blocked out in huge letters anywhere, I feel for a moment that something has gone wrong. So do the executives, as they gaze at each paper in turn and find no escape from REDS INVADE BURMA!

Their faces are solemn, sweat pours down. They scan the pages like people trying to find their bearings. Then, his eyes narrowing, one turns to the other. 'It says Bobo Rockefeller's got herself arrested.'

With sighs of relief they move on.

A white Lincoln shoots past, I glimpse a woman in a white sleeveless dress at the wheel, green silk scarf fluttering out of the window. She pulls up with a squall of brakes at a STOP sign, two feet from a weakly handsome young man in a beige tussore suit.

'Hi, Julie! Trying to kill me?'

She laughs loudly. 'Yeah, but I changed my mind.'

This is Julie Forbes, a famous star. She has been in pictures for thirty years and everyone is always saying how good she looks. The young man is an actor recently arrived from Broadway and placed under contract to the studio.

He leans charmingly on the window of the car. 'How about dinner this week?'

She shakes her head. 'I'm busy every night.'

'Next week?'

'Call me over the week-end and see how I'm fixed.'

He looks disappointed. She pats his hand. 'And pine for me, loved one.'

She drives away, scarf fluttering.

The studio is like a large country estate. Haphazardly ranged buildings are white and clean and look entirely uninhabited. What to do? I put a coin in the automatic Coca-Cola machine, the bottle slides out on a tray and I place it under the automatic opener. I don't like Coca-Cola much, but drink a little and pass the smiling Negro shoeblack at his stand.

'Hi, how are *you*?'

'I'm fine. How are *you*?'

Back lots with permanent exterior sets occupy most of the grounds. The residential street of white frame-houses with sprinklers on the front lawn, a nice replica of anywhere in the more modest stretches of Beverly Hills, has as much and perhaps more reality than the real thing. So has the small-town square: well stocked drugstore, a bank and a school, a church and an empty green. The windows of the bank are still shattered from a robbery scene staged there last month.

In the western town, the St. Louis Midland Express is always standing at the railway station. The Last Chance Saloon is empty except for silence and a few chairs broken and overturned from the last brawl. The main street turns a corner and is suddenly a footbridge across a dried-up stream. Beyond it lies something that began as a medieval French village and has been altered here and there to suit the centuries as a corner of Italy or Corsica. A rotted pulpit leans across the entrance to Our Lady of the Fields.

Further away the ground slopes up, then down again to an abandoned harbour town, slightly Dutch with its moored barges and rosebrick warehouses along the quayside. It is watched by an artificial canvas sky, shaped like an immense blue panoramic screen, bluer than the thing above my head. Spotlights are standing by, ready to reinforce the sun.

Then comes the point of no return. The great open air scene dock is like landscaped bric-à-brac. Derelict pioneer wagons left to flake and lurch in the dry grasses; a huddle of chipped classical pillars; an early ranch house with no glass in the windows and one wall missing and the stains of fire; an old stockade, a Chinese palace arch, a tall unhinged door fallen across a wheel, a rowing boat propped up against a castle watchtower, and a staircase winding to the sky.

Here it sleeps in the sun, this neglected litter of the past. Time and heat make their inroads a little more each day. A ruined secret world more real than practical avenues and boulevards, the only place you can be certain that ghosts walk.

What to do? In the parking lot, hidden among princely roadsters, stands my fog-grey seventy dollar 1947 Chevrolet with the battered front I refuse to have mended. As I drive out, the cop at the gate looks glad to see it go. Then he waves as a young actress and her massive grim-faced aunt edge quickly past me in a damask Cadillac embroidered from radiator cap to rear mudguard with mother-of-pearl.

It becomes a day for interesting cars. Stopping at a drugstore for cigarettes, I park behind a twenty-five-year-old Rolls-Royce that I know very well. A landaulette, painted silver and white, and the royal crest of the old Austro-Hungarian empire engraved on the doors. A young chauffeur sits at the wheel, chewing gum.

The drugstore is fairly empty, at the soda fountain a group of girls sip chocolate malts and a Filipino workman eats a hamburger. Everyone else is watching the Countess Osterberg-Steblechi, who pays no attention but very slowly revolves the paperbacked crime novels on their stands. It is the fate of the Countess to be stared at, and one cannot be surprised. She is like a balloon blown up into roughly human shape and ready to burst. All swollen and sagging contours except for her face; her beaky nose and sharp hooded eyes remind you of a falcon. She has hair that looks like a wig but is really her own dyed red, and wears a piece of garish linen printed all over with flowers and cornucopias like old-fashioned wallpaper.

Each time I see this great aristocratic wreck, I have the impression she has *got inside* her shoes, her dress, her hat if she wears one, by mistake. And she cannot get out. She is trapped, any movement could be fatal. She waddles dangerously up to me now, a paperbacked novel in one hand, a crocodile leather bag in the other.

'Dear child, have you read *The Case of the Black-Eyed Blonde*?' I shake my head as she holds up the book in front of me. 'How strange, nobody has. I looked at the first page and nearly fainted with excitement. Are you coming to tea with me Sunday?'

'I'd love to.'

She wheezes with pleasure, but the strain contracts her face. Now it looks like the moon after an explosion, the features are blasted fragments. 'There may be a kind of jumble sale, I hope to raise a few hundred dollars.'

'For what?' I ask, though I know the answer.

'For myself, of course, dear child. I wish I were not so heartrendingly poor.' She scratches her nose with a jewelled and freckled finger. 'Are you sure you haven't read *The Case of the Black Eyed Blonde*?'

'Absolutely.'

'Then I shall have to take it on trust. With an opening paragraph like that I think . . .' She breaks off vaguely, fumbling in her crocodile bag and giving the assistant a quarter.

The assistant says: 'Thirty-five cents, please.'

She takes an alarmed step backwards. 'You mean it's one of the expensive ones?'

'It's thirty-five cents.'

The Countess replaces the book in the Westerns rack. 'Much too expensive,' she says firmly, 'when no one knows if it's really good. I adore pulp literature but one must retain one's sense of values. Where is your selection of twenty-five cent crime novels, please?'

She is the widow of a distinguished European banker.

It is only a few miles' drive to the ocean, but before reaching it I shall be nowhere. Hard to describe the impression of unreality, because it is intangible; almost supernatural; something in the air. (The air . . . Last night on the weather telecast the commentator, mentioning electric storms near Palm Springs and heavy smog in Los Angeles, described the behaviour of the air as 'neurotic'. Of course. Like everything else the air must be imported and displaced, like the water driven along huge aqueducts from distant reservoirs, like the palm trees tilting above mortuary signs and laundromats along Sunset Boulevard.) Nothing belongs. Nothing belongs except the desert soil and the gruff eroded-looking mountains to the north. Because the earth is desert, its surface always has that terrible dusty brilliance. Sometimes it looks like the Riviera with a film of neglect over villas and gardens, a veil of fine invisible sand drawn across tropical colours. It is hard to be reminded of any single thing for long. The houses are real because they exist and people use them for eating and sleeping and making love, but they have no style of their own and look as if they've been imported from half a dozen different countries. They are imitation 'French Provincial' or 'new' Regency or Tudor or Spanish hacienda or Cape Cod, and except for a few crazy mansions seem to have sprung up overnight. The first settlers will be arriving tomorrow from parts unknown.

Los Angeles is not a city, but a series of suburban approaches to a city that never materializes. The noisy populous down-town section with its mixture of Americans and Mexicans, Negroes and Orientals, its glass and concrete new structures jostling fragile wooden slums, its heavy police force and ugly untidy look of sudden industrial growth, is a little like Casablanca. The older parts are exotic but tired, collapsing under the sleek thrust of commerce. There is a modest little Japanese quarter with movie houses, gift shops, *sukiyaki* signs, a steam bath and massage parlour and the Bank of Tokyo; a Chinatown pretty and synthetic as a planner's lifesize model; a Mexican quarter with a gaudy street market, sombreros and bullfighters' capes and scented candles always on display. There are oil derricks and power plants massed like geometrical forests, and a thin bitter smoke hangs in the air on a windless day.

No settlement can ever have grown more wastefully and swiftly. A century and a half ago pirates still raided this coast, were captured and hung in the village square, Indian slaves were dragging timber from the mountains to build first a jail and then a church. Invasion began with the Gold Rush, fishermen from the East and Scandinavia and Italy found the Pacific rich in salmon and tuna, even convicts arrived from Australia in stolen ships. Now Los Angeles is a welter of nearly five hundred square miles and four million people making aeroplanes and pumping oil, assembling automobiles and movies, processing food and petroleum, building quick framehouses that you can see being drawn along the streets at night by a truck and placed on a vacant lot like scenery for a movie set.

Along the main boulevards, between the office blocks, plots of untouched land are still for sale. On one of the plots, not long ago, the skeleton of a prehistoric animal was excavated. In the paleozoic past, before the land dried and crusted into desert, this was a quagmire under a hot sun, sloths and mastodons were trapped and dying there. Now the last victim has gone, the grave is cleared and the offices of a great insurance company can go up.

How to grasp something unfinished yet always remodelling itself, changing without a basis for change? So much visible impatience to be born, to grow, such wild tracts of space to be filled: difficult to settle in a comfortable unfinished desert. Because of the long confusing distances, the streets are empty of walking people, full of moving cars. Between where you are and where you are going to be is a no-man's-land. At night the neon signs glitter and the shop windows are lighted stages, but hardly anyone stops to look. A few people huddle at coffee stalls and hamburger bars. Those dark flat areas are parking lots, crammed solid.

I suppose that Europeans, accustomed to a world that changes more calmly and slowly, are not much interested any more in imitating its surface. It becomes more exciting to see appearances as a mask, a disguise or illusion that conceals an unexpected meaning. The theme of illusion and reality is very common in Europe. In America, illusion and reality are still often the same thing. The dream is the achievement, the achievement is the dream.

The ocean appears suddenly. You turn another hairpin bend and the land falls away and there is a long high view down Santa Monica Canyon to the pale Pacific waters. A clear day is not often. Sky and air are hazed now, diffusing the sun and dredging the ocean of its rightful blue. The Pacific is a sad blue-grey, and nearly always looks cold.

Each time I drive down here it feels like the end of the world. The geographical end. Shabby and uncared for, buildings lie around like nomads' tents in the desert. There is nowhere further to go, those pale waters stretch away to the blurred horizon and stretch away beyond it. There is no more land ever.

High lurching cliffs confront the ocean, and are just beginning to fall apart. Signs have been posted along the highway, DRIVE CAREFULLY and SLIDE AREA. Lumps of earth and stone fall down. The land is restless here, restless and sliding. Driving inland towards the mountains, it is the same: BEWARE OF ROCKS. The land is falling. Rocks fall down all over and the cliffs called Pacific Palisades are crumbling slowly down to the ocean. Who called them Palisades, I wonder? They cannot keep out the Pacific. There are mad eccentric houses above the Palisades, with turrets and castellations and tall Gothic windows, but no one wants to live in them any more in case the ground slides away.

It has slid again this afternoon. On one section of the highway a crowd has gathered. An ambulance stands by, winking red lights. A sheriff directs operations. From a great pile of mud and stones and sandy earth, the legs of old ladies are sticking out. Men with shovels are working to free the rest of their bodies. Objects are rescued first, a soiled table cloth and a thermos flask and what looks like a jumbo sandwich, long as a baby eel. Then an air cushion and more long sandwiches, and a picnic basket, and at last the three old ladies themselves. They are all right. They look shaken and angry, which is to be expected. A few minutes ago they had been sitting on the Palisades, in a pleasant little hollow free from the wind. The cloth was spread for a picnic. Miss Natalie O'Gorman laid out sandwiches on a plastic dish, her sister Clara unscrewed the thermos flask to pour out coffee, and their friend Willa North decided to blow up her air cushion.

Absolutely silent at first, the ground beneath them disappeared. The slide meant for a moment that there was no ground at all, it ceased to exist, and then as it gained momentum and scudded away like clouds breaking up in a gale, there was a light rumbling sound. The three ladies, Natalie O'Gorman with a sandwich in her hand, her sister with the flask and Willa North with her mouth pressed to the air cushion, went with the land and were practically submerged by it at the side of the highway below.

Now they are brushing their dresses with distracted motions and shaking little stones out of their bosoms and little clods out of their hair. Everyone is saying it is a miracle. Natalie O'Gorman would like to find her hat. Bones are felt and nothing is broken; they are scratched and bruised, that is all. 'We are all right,' they tell the crowd. 'Yes, we are quite all right.' Willa North says: 'I was taken completely by surprise!'

I drive on, past another SLIDE AREA sign. The beaches are still quite full. A group of tanned young men are wrestling and playing ball. Two girls watch them, eating hot dogs. An old Negro in a tattered blue suit walks by the edge of the ocean, a mongrel dog following him. Out to sea, someone is surfing. Stretching his arms, the muscular young lifeguard watches from his tower.

The southern end of Santa Monica, the ocean suburb, is not impeccable. Unlike the correct mechanized residential areas, Beverly

Hills, Westwood, Glendale, it is rather slatternly and interesting. Little wooden houses, their green and blue and yellow paint fading, slant above narrow streets. There are bins overflowing with garbage and trash. People walk in the streets, hang about on corners or outside bars where a juke-box is always playing. There is a pier, due to be condemned soon, with all the usual sideshows: hot dog, hamburger and ice-cream stands, and a submarine contraption that takes you under water and shows you an old disgruntled whale. The beach has fine dull sand and the water smells faintly rancid.

It is only five o'clock but the bar called The Place is quite full. *Mackie Messer* comes from the juke-box. An old man in a panama hat and dark glasses dances slowly with his cane. At the bar a tall drunk woman finishes her whisky and lights a cigarette from the stub of the one she has just finished. She has once been beautiful, but now her face has something ruined about it, as if she's been waiting too long, in vain, for the telephone to ring. She sees me, waves, runs unsteadily over, pulls at my arm and speaks in a fierce urgent whisper.

'She's dying!'

'Who?'

'Hank, my sister Hank.'

'What happened?'

She makes vague distracted movements with her hands. 'He shot her, darling, that's all I know. It doesn't matter. It's too late!' She pulls at my arm again. 'I call and call the hospital and they won't let me speak to her, and the nurse says not to worry in a way that means it's no use.' Tears are streaming down her face now. 'Hank's dying, darling, dying!'

I offer to phone the hospital.

'No use! They'll lie, it's a conspiracy of lies.'

'Let me try, Zeena.' I go to the telephone and put in a coin. She follows, muttering, 'hopeless . . .'

'St. Judith's.'

'I want some information about Miss Henrietta Nelson, please.'

A pause, a whispering, a clicking, and presently a new voice with a German accent comes on the line:

'St. Judith's.'

'I want some information about Miss Henrietta Nelson.'

'Who are you?'

'A friend of Miss Nelson.'

Another pause. Zeena clutches my elbow. 'You know they're all nuns? *Nuns!*'

I can hear footsteps approaching, then going away. The line crackles for a moment.

'Are you still there?'

'Yes.'

'Miss Henrietta Nelson is dead.'

'What?'

'Miss Nelson died shortly after four o'clock this afternoon.' The voice is merciless, pedantic, never shifting its level. 'We did not inform her sister as we did not care to break such news on the telephone. We asked her to arrive here and see us immediately, but her reply was not comprehensible. We received the impression she was not . . . sober. Last night we were obliged not to admit her to visit her sister as she arrived not . . . sober. Excuse me, but are you a responsible person?'

I hang up. Zeena is no longer there. The old man still dances with his cane.

The barman says: 'She just wandered out the way she does.'

She is not in the street outside. I get in my car, drive alongside the beach, which is almost deserted now. The sand looks grey, a fine white mist is dredging colour out of everything as the hazy sun slips down.

A figure walks uncertainly by the water's edge.

'Zeena,' I say as I come up to her, 'I'm afraid it's bad news.'

She has a weary look, throws her cigarette into the sea. 'Was it the German, darling? She's the worst.'

'They say Hank is dead.'

Zeena is very pale. A wave breaks, runs along the sand and wets her feet, she doesn't mind.

When the sun cools and everyone leaves the beach, only messages remain. Often there are dozens of them, traced with a stick or a finger in the sand. Zeena is looking at one now. JIMMY LOVES ELLA. And a little further away, MY NAME IS GRIFFIN.

She smiles, mutters 'I'll see you later,' and walks away.

She walks past I'M MAD ABOUT BOB, JOHNNY WAITED HERE and OH BILL I WANT TO MAKE YOU and a dead gull.

All this will be washed away tomorrow.

Dusk falls as I drive home. The mountains look black and farther away. The road winds uphill and there is a point where you can see Los Angeles sprawling away in the distance. Lights are coming on there now. Looking down on the straight intersecting lines of pink and yellow and green is like finding a vast abstract painting laid out on the earth. It has nothing at all to do with living. It is a bright winking mirage in the desert; you are afraid to look away in case it has vanished when you look back.

A mauve searchlight sweeps monotonously across the sky like a great silent pendulum.

When I get back to my apartment the telephone is ringing.

'Will you come immediately please?' The German nun from the hospital sounds a little breathless, but dry as ever. 'Miss Zeena Nelson refuses to go home. The police have asked all their questions and we give her a sedative, but she lies down in the waiting-room and refuses to go home. Come please.'

Unlike her voice, Sister Hertha seems plump and friendly. She wears a capacious white robe and a silver crucifix on a chain round her waist. When I ask her to tell me what happened, she looks surprised and straightens her rimless glasses, which have been a little askew. 'You know nothing?'

'Nothing. Except, something about a shooting.'

'That is so.' Sister Hertha lowers her voice. 'Last night a young man . . .' A nun passes with a tray of tea, Sister Hertha smiles and gives a little bow. 'Good evening, Sister!' She turns back to me. 'A young man in a red jacket came home with Miss Henrietta Nelson last night. He . . . eventually shot her through the head.' She fingers the crucifix at her stomach. 'A neighbour saw him leave, she saw his jacket but not his face. It appears Miss Nelson had many young friends. The police try to find if any of them wore a red jacket. Naturally.'

She leads me to the waiting-room, where Zeena lies back on a couch with her eyes closed. Sister Hertha coughs, and she looks up.

'Hello darling.'

'You still have no recollection of a young man in a red jacket?' asks the nun.

Zeena shakes her head. 'If he's been in The Place or any of the places, I must have seen him. But what does a person look like when he's crazy?'

Sister Hertha makes a sympathetic little noise with her teeth.

'Zeena, you mustn't stay here,' I tell her.

She gets up obediently. Sister Hertha gives an encouraging smile. 'I advise rest. A great deal of rest. Such situations are . . .' She wrinkles her nose, partly because she is searching for a word, partly because she has just noticed a pile of cigarette stubs on the floor near Zeena's feet. 'They are most disturbing,' she says, rattling her crucifix a little.

Zeena decides she wants to go home. We drive in silence, towards a full moon low in the sky. I feel that Sister Hertha has found the right word. There is a case like this quite often in the newspapers: SEX FIEND SLAYS GIRL. Tomorrow it will make a row of headlines on the studio rack.

'Turn the radio on, darling.' A moment later we are listening to Brahms. Zeena twists the knob, then drowses as somebody sings *Your Cheatin' Heart.*

Two months ago I passed a second-hand furniture store on the street along which we are now driving. There was an elegant little coffee table in the window. I went inside, found Zeena and Hank sitting on a broken-down antique couch with the stuffing split out, drinking canned beer. Probably I was the first customer they'd had for hours. The place was vague and untidy, like somewhere after an earthquake. 'This is really catching on,' Zeena said, trying to inter-est me in a heavy Victorian commode they'd sponged over with gold and white paint. I bought the coffee table. After that, I saw Zeena and Hank occasionally: in bars or on the beach. Once, coming out of an all-night movie theatre. This is how everybody met them. This is how I am with Zeena today, by accident.

She lives in Venice, near the furniture store. A mouldering unfinished little town along the coast beyond Santa Monica, it began fifty years ago as an imitation of the Italian city. Moonstruck, an industrialist from the Middle West decided to create a romantic resort on the dreary tidal flats. He built some florid villas, a copy of St. Mark's Square, a network of bridges, canals, lagoons, colonnades. The aged Sarah Bernhardt was imported to play *La Dame aux Camélias* on what is now a tawdry, neglected amusement pier. Hardly anyone went to see her. Hardly anyone hired a gondola for a trip along the mosquito-ridden flats. Then oil was struck, machinery converged upon the lagoons. A few bridges still remain, spanning dried up canals, with pumps and derricks stretching away beyond them. Drugstores, banks, service stations have settled in the empty spaces between colonnades, and the villas are apartment houses with rooms always vacant.

As we pass St. Mark's Square, I notice a group of young motor cyclists dressed in black, with tight belts and slanted caps, leaning against the colonnades. Pigeons cluster nearby, then disperse as the cyclists set off with a roar, speeding along the empty boulevard, past a neon sign announcing BEER, past the Bridge of Sighs and the derricks in silhouette.

The noise rouses Zeena. She blinks, looks out of the window and recognizes landmarks: a closed-up hotel with broken windows, a plot of waste land with an abandoned moonlit sign, BOATS FOR SALE. She murmurs: 'Why, I'm almost home!'

Lawrence Lipton

Abbot Kinney, the creator of L.A.'s Venice, was a more complex and accomplished person than one might glean from Lawrence Lipton's rather disparaging account. A U.S. Indian Commissioner who encouraged Helen Hunt Jackson in her exposure of the wrongs endured by California's Indians, a founder of public libraries, and a self-taught expert on forestry who campaigned for conservation, his career was marked by the kind of large-scale 19th-century ambition that led to the development of Venice. It is hardly surprising that Lipton (1898–1975), a self-appointed spokesman for the Beat scenes of the 1950s, should find little to praise in Kinney's grandiose undertaking. Yet in this excerpt from the first chapter of his widely read *The Holy Barbarians* (1959), a sort of tour guide to the avant-garde scene, he extracts a pulpish poetry from the spectacle of artists and hangers-on congregating among the ruins in the ramshackle beach community of Venice West.

from

SLUM BY THE SEA

It is Sunday in Venice. Not the Venice of the Piazza San Marco and memories of the Doges. Venice, California, the Venice of St. Mark's Hotel where the arched colonnades are of plaster, scaling off now and cracked by only a few decades of time, earthquake and decay. This is Venice by the Pacific, dreamed up by a man named Kinney at the turn of the century, a nineteenth-century Man of Vision, a vision as trite as a penny postal card. He went broke in heart and pocket trying to carry his Cook's Tour memories of the historic city on the Adriatic into the twentieth century.

The oil derricks came in and fouled up his canals, the Japanese moved in and set up gambling wheels and fan-tan games on the ocean front, and the imitation palaces of the Doges became flop joints. The Venice Pier Opera House, where Kinney dreamed of Nellie Melbas warbling arias and Italian tenors singing Neapolitan boat songs, went into history instead as the ballroom where Kid Ory first brought New Orleans jazz to the West Coast. And the

419

night air was filled, not with the songs of gondoliers, but with air-splitting screams from the roller coasters of the Venice Amusement Pier.

All that remains of Kinney's Folly are a few green-scum-covered canals, some yellowing photographs in the shop windows of old storekeepers who "remember when," and the PWA mural that decorates the Venice Post Office, in which the oil derricks are superimposed on the colonnades in a montage that is meant to be at once ironical and nostalgic. As for the Doges, the Doges of Venice are a gang whose teen-age members sometimes scribble the name on fences, smear it on shopwindows and even carve it into walls and bus seats, defacing private property and earning themselves the epithet of juvenile delinquents.

The sea-rotted Venice Amusement Park Pier has long ago been torn down, leaving a land's end, waterfront slum where there was once a fashionable resort, then a wide-open gambling town, then a wartime furlough spot for the sailors of the Pacific fleet and, till a few years ago, a bonanza for bingo operators.

Civic virtue, domiciled far away in hotel suites and suburban ranch houses, closed the bingo games. The luxury hotels along the beachfront promenade, too costly to tear down at present-day wrecking prices and not profitable enough to warrant proper upkeep and repair, stand like old derelicts, their plush and finery faded and patched. In their dim lobbies sit the pensioned-aged playing cards and waiting for the mailman to bring the next little brown envelope. Pension Row. Slum by the sea. Two, even three, one-story houses on a narrow lot, airless and lightless in a paradise of air and light. Night-blooming jasmine amidst the garbage cans.

To this area of Los Angeles, as to similar areas of other large cities, have come the rebellious, the nonconformist, the bohemian, the deviant among the youth. An unrentable store, with its show windows curtained or painted opaque, becomes a studio. A loft behind a lunchroom or over a liquor store becomes an ideal "pad" where you can keep your hi-fi going full volume at all hours of the night with no neighbors to complain. If you're a UCLA student shacking up with a girl friend, for love or just to save on the rent, you can find here a ramshackle three- or four-room cottage "in the back," preferably administered by a bank for some estate or by an agent for some absentee owner. As long as you are prompt with your rent payments no questions will be asked. As likely as not your neighbors will be Mexican-Americans who will not complain about your bongo drums as long as you do not complain about their three-families-in-a-four-room shack, seven-children-two-dog noise fests and their Saturday night all-night open-house drunk parties. If you can't sleep you're welcome to join them, but the chances are you won't because you'll be noising it up in your own pad, with your Chamber Jazz Quartet record offering poor decible competition to their television Hit Parade. Nobody is going to call the cops because they'll only drink up your liquor and make a pass at your women, and besides, they're too busy rounding up winos to clean up the drunk tank and the jail cells on Monday morning, taking the strain off the paid labor and saving the taxpayers' money.

The aged and the young. And the misfits. All the misfits of the world—the too fat and the too lean, the too tall and the too short, the jerk, the drip, the half-wit and the spastic, the harelip and the gimp. All the broken, the doomed, the drunk and the disillu-sioned—herding together for a little human warmth, where a one-room kitchenette is an apartment and the naked electric bulb hangs suspended from the ceiling like an exposed nerve.

Here, working couples with children find the run-down apart-ments and tumble-down shacks that the realtor has to offer. To them, too, it is Land's End. After being turned away in other parts of town with "No children, no pets," they stagger finally into Ocean Park and Venice, foot-sore or with an empty gas tank, ready to rent anything with four walls and a roof, even if the walls are paper-thin and the roof leaks and the toilet is stuffed up. "Wait till you see how I'll fix it up," says the wife with a tired little smile, and Dad has visions of puttering around Sunday morning with a paint brush and turning this time-rotted ruin into the American Dream Home of the magazine color pages.

The young who come here have no such dreams. The aged, liv-ing in the sealed-in loneliness of their television sets, will leave them alone. The working couples, fatigued after a night on the graveyard shift at nearby Douglas Aircraft, will nod over their beer and listen to the jukebox in the waterfront taverns. If books, painting or music, or all-night gab fests are more important to the young than the mop and dishrag, nobody will read them any lectures on neat-ness in a neighborhood where it is no crime to leave the beds unmade and two days' dishes in the sink. Nobody will turn to stare at beards and sandals or dirty Levi's on the beach where a stained sweat shirt or a leather jacket is practically formal dress.

Venice, U.S.A. Venice West, a horizontal, jerry-built slum by the sea, warm under a semitropical Pacific sun on a Sunday afternoon.

The doorbell rings. The regular week-end invasion has begun: all the impatient young-men-in-a-hurry, the lost, the seekers, the beat, the disaffiliated, the educated, diseducated, re-educated, in quest of a new vision; visitors from all over America passing through and stopping off to dig the Venice scene or come to hole in for a while in a Venice pad; young girls in flight from unendurable homes in other, fancier, parts of town, hiding their fears behind a mask of defiance, or trying to look "cool" or act "beat"; Hollywood writers dropping in to refresh their souls, hoping, perhaps, that some of the creative energy of dedicated artists will somehow rub off a little on them, maybe to do a little brain-picking, too, something they can turn into The Big Money; squares from Beverly Hills and San Fernando Valley ranch type houses looking for the shock of nonconformism, which is their own kind of "kick," or on the make for girls; newsmen and radio people on the prowl for "experience," or just plain hungry for a taste of intellectual honesty and artistic integrity, a kind of go-to-church-Sunday soul bath; ex-Communists with every kind of ideological hang-over coming to argue themselves out of something or into something or back to something; politicals, apoliticals, pacifists; interviewers coming to interview and interviewees coming to be interviewed; silent ones who come to sit and listen, to "dig" the talk and the jazz—and stay to eat, and listen some more and sit, just sit, till everybody else has gone and they can explode in a torrent of pent-up talk about themselves, their lives, their loves, their despairs, or make a quick touch; and always the parade of weekday office and factory workers, Sunday refugees from the rat race, panting for a little music and poetry in their lives, hoping to meet "the one" who will lift them out of the quiet desperation in which they move. And the poets . . . and the painters . . . and the camp followers of the Muse freeloading and tailchasing on the lower slopes of Parnassus. . . . The clowns, the make-believers, the self-deceivers—and the mad.

Norman Mailer

If John F. Kennedy was the celebrity candidate personified, a politician magnified and glamorized by television, then Norman Mailer (b. 1923) was the writer born to track the permutations and implications of that public spectacle. In this excerpt from his essay "Superman Comes to the Supermarket," collected in *The Presidential Papers* (1963), he follows Kennedy to Los Angeles to witness his nomination at the 1960 Democratic convention. Seeing both the Democratic party and Los Angeles itself as forms of show business, Mailer—who had already skewered Southern California in his 1955 novel *The Deer Park*—exuberantly seizes the chance to bring into the frame what the cameras don't usually show.

from

SUPERMAN COMES TO THE SUPERMARKET

"I was seeing Pershing Square, Los Angeles, now for the first time . . . the nervous fruithustlers darting in and out of the shadows, fugitives from Times Square, Market Street SF, the French Quarter—masculine hustlers looking for lonely fruits to score from, anything from the legendary $20 to a pad at night and breakfast in the morning and whatever you can clinch or clip; and the heat in their holy cop uniforms, holy because of the Almighty Stick and the Almightier Vagrancy Law; the scattered junkies, the small-time pushers, the queens, the sad panhandlers, the lonely, exiled nymphs haunting the entrance to the men's head, the fruits with the hungry eyes and the jingling coins; the tough teen-age chicks — 'dittybops' — making it with the lost hustlers . . . all amid the incongruous piped music and the flowers—twin fountains gushing rainbow colored: the world of Lonely America squeezed into Pershing Square, of the Cities of Terrible Night, downtown now trapped in the City of lost Angels . . . and the trees hang over it all like some type of apathetic fate."

—JOHN RECHY: *Big Table 3*

Seeing Los Angeles after ten years away, one realizes all over again that America is an unhappy contract between the East (that Faustian thrust of a most determined human will which reaches up and out above the eye into the skyscrapers of New

423

York) and those flat lands of compromise and mediocre self-expression, those endless half-pretty repetitive small towns of the Middle and the West, whose spirit is forever horizontal and whose marrow comes to rendezvous in the pastel monotonies of Los Angeles architecture.

So far as America has a history, one can see it in the severe heights of New York City, in the glare from the Pittsburgh mills, by the color in the brick of Louisburg Square, along the knotted greedy façades of the small mansions on Chicago's North Side, in Natchez' antebellum homes, the wrought-iron balconies off Bourbon Street, a captain's house in Nantucket, by the curve of Commercial Street in Provincetown. One can make a list; it is probably finite. What culture we have made and what history has collected to it can be found in those few hard examples of an architecture which came to its artistic term, was born, lived and so collected some history about it. Not all the roots of American life are uprooted, but almost all, and the spirit of the supermarket, that homogenous extension of stainless surfaces and psychoanalyzed people, packaged commodities and ranch homes, interchangeable, geographically unrecognizable, that essence of the new postwar Super-America is found nowhere so perfectly as in Los Angeles' ubiquitous acres. One gets the impression that people come to Los Angeles in order to divorce themselves from the past, here to live or try to live in the rootless pleasure world of an adult child. One knows that if the cities of the world were destroyed by a new war, the architecture of the rebuilding would create a landscape which looked, subject to specification of climate, exactly and entirely like the San Fernando Valley.

It is not that Los Angeles is altogether hideous, it is even by degrees pleasant, but for an Easterner there is never any salt in the wind; it is like Mexican cooking without chile, or Chinese egg rolls missing their mustard; as one travels through the endless repetitions of that city which is the capital of suburbia with its milky pinks, its washed-out oranges, its tainted lime-yellows of pastel on one pretty little architectural monstrosity after another, the colors not intense enough, the styles never pure, and never sufficiently impure to collide on the eye, one conceives the people who live here—they have come out to express themselves, Los Angeles is the home of self-expression, but the artists are middle-class and middling-minded; no passions will calcify here for years in the gloom to be revealed a decade later as the tessellations of a hard and fertile work, no, it is all open, promiscuous, borrowed, half bought, a city without iron, eschewing wood, a kingdom of stucco, the playground for mass men — one has the feeling it was built by television sets giving orders to men. And in this land of the pretty-pretty, the virility is in the barbarisms, the vulgarities, it is in the huge billboards, the screamers of the neon lighting, the shouting farm-utensil colors of the gas stations and the monster drugstores, it is in the swing of the sports cars, hot rods, convertibles, Los Angeles is a city to drive in, the boulevards are wide, the traffic is nervous and fast, the radio stations play bouncing, blooping, rippling tunes, one digs the pop in a pop tune, no one of character would make love by it but the sound is good for swinging a car, electronic guitars and Hawaiian harps.

So this is the town the Democrats came to, and with their unerring instinct (after being with them a week, one thinks of this party as a crazy, half-rich family, loaded with poor cousins, traveling always in caravans with Cadillacs and Okie Fords, Lincolns and quarter-horse mules, putting up every night in tents to hear the chamber quartet of Great Cousin Eleanor invaded by the Texas-twanging steel-stringing geetarists of Bubber Lyndon, carrying its own mean high-school principal, Doc Symington, chided for its manners by good Uncle Adlai, told the route of march by Navigator Jack, cut off every six months from the rich will of Uncle Jim Farley, never listening to the mechanic of the caravan, Bald Sam Rayburn, who assures them they'll all break down unless Cousin Bubber gets the concession on the garage; it's the Snopes family married to Henry James, with the labor unions thrown in like a Yankee dollar, and yet it's true, in tranquility one recollects them with affection, their instinct is good, crazy family good) and this instinct now led the caravan to pick the Biltmore Hotel in downtown Los Angeles for their family get-together and reunion.

The Biltmore is one of the ugliest hotels in the world. Patterned after the flat roofs of an Italian Renaissance palace, it is eighty-eight times as large, and one-millionth as valuable to the continuation of man, and it would be intolerable if it were not for the presence of Pershing Square, that square block of park with cactus and palm trees, the three-hundred-and-sixty-five-day-a-year convention of every junkie, pot-head, pusher, queen (but you have read that good writing already). For years Pershing Square has been one of the three or four places in America famous to homosexuals, famous not for its posh, the chic is round-heeled here, but because it is one of the avatars of the good old masturbatory sex, dirty with the crusted sugars of smut, dirty rooming houses around the corner where the score is made, dirty book and photograph stores down the street, old-fashioned out-of-the-Thirties burlesque houses, cruising bars, jukeboxes, movie houses; Pershing Square is the town plaza for all those lonely, respectable, small-town homosexuals who lead a family life, make children, and have the Philbrick psychology (How I Joined the Communist Party and Led Three Lives). Yes, it is the open-air convention hall for the small-town inverts who live like spies, and it sits in the center of Los Angeles, facing the Biltmore, that hotel which is a mausoleum, that Pentagon of traveling salesmen the Party chose to house the headquarters of the Convention.

So here came that family, cursed before it began by the thundering absence of Great-Uncle Truman, the delegates dispersed over a run of thirty miles and twenty-seven hotels: the Olympian Motor Hotel, the Ambassador, the Beverly Wilshire, the Santa Ynez Inn (where rumor has it the delegates from Louisiana had some midnight swim), the Mayan, the Commodore, the Mayfair, the Sheraton-West, the Huntington-Sheraton, the Green, the Hayward, the Gates, the Figueroa, the Statler Hilton, the Hollywood Knickerbocker — does one have to be a collector to list such names? — beauties all, with that up-from-the-farm Los Angeles décor, plate-glass windows, patio and terrace, foam-rubber mattress, pastel paints, all of them pretty as an ad in full-page color, all but the Biltmore where everybody gathered every day — the newsmen, the TV, radio, magazine, and foreign newspapermen, the delegates, the politicos, the tourists, the campaign managers, the runners, the flunkies, the cousins and aunts, the wives, the grandfathers, the eight-year-old girls, and the twenty-eight-year-old girls in the Kennedy costumes, red and white and blue, the Symingteeners, the Johnson Ladies, the Stevenson Ladies, everybody — and for three days before the convention and four days into it, everybody collected at the Biltmore, in the lobby, in the grill, in the Biltmore Bowl, in the elevators, along the corridors, three hundred deep always outside the Kennedy suite, milling everywhere, every dark-carpeted grey-brown hall of the hotel, but it was in the Gallery of the Biltmore where one first felt the mood which pervaded all proceedings until the convention was almost over, that heavy, thick, witless depression which was to dominate every move as the delegates wandered and gawked and paraded and set for a spell, there in the Gallery of the Biltmore, that huge depressing alley with its inimitable hotel color, that faded depth of chiaroscuro which unhappily has no depth, that brown which is not a brown, that grey which has no pearl in it, that color which can be described only as hotel-color because the beiges, the tans, the walnuts, the mahoganies, the dull blood rugs, the moaning yellows, the sick greens, the greys and all those dumb browns merge into that lack of color which is an over-large hotel at convention time, with all the small-towners wearing their set, starched faces, that look they get at carnival, all fever and suspicion, and proud to be there, eddying slowly back and forth in that high block-long tunnel of a room with its arched ceiling and square recesses filling every rib of the arch with art work, escutcheons and blazons and other art, pictures I think, I cannot even remember, there was such a hill of cigar smoke the eye had to travel on its way to the ceiling, and at one end there was galvanized-pipe scaffolding and workmen repairing some part of the ceiling, one of them touching up one of the endless squares of painted plaster in the arch, and another worker, passing by, yelled up to the one who was working on the ceiling: "Hey, Michelangelo!"

Randall Jarrell

In his poem "The Lost World," Randall Jarrell (1914–1965) evokes the Southern California of his boyhood with a mixture of discovery and regret. Born in Tennessee, Jarrell moved to L.A. as a toddler, then returned to the South with his mother after his parents divorced. In 1926 and 1927, he came back to Los Angeles for an extended visit with his grandparents, an experience that provided much of the raw material for this poem, reflecting a gentler side of a writer known for his powerful war poetry and sharp-edged satirical fiction.

THE LOST WORLD

I. Children's Arms

On my way home I pass a cameraman
On a platform on the bumper of a car
Inside which, rolling and plunging, a comedian
Is working; on one white lot I see a star
Stumble to her igloo through the howling gale
Of the wind machines. On Melrose a dinosaur
And pterodactyl, with their immense pale
Papier-mâché smiles, look over the fence
Of *The Lost World*.
                    Whispering to myself the tale
These shout—done with my schoolwork, I commence
My real life: my arsenal, my workshop
Opens, and in impotent omnipotence
I put on the helmet and the breastplate Pop
Cut out and soldered for me. Here is the shield
I sawed from beaver board and painted; here on top
The bow that only Odysseus can wield
And eleven vermilion-ringed, goose-feathered arrows.
(The twelfth was broken on the battlefield
When, searching among snap beans and potatoes,
I stepped on it.) Some dry weeds, a dead cane

428

Are my spears. The knife on the bureau's
My throwing-knife; the small unpainted biplane
Without wheels—that so often, helped by human hands,
Has taken off from, landed on, the counterpane—
Is my Spad.
                    O dead list, that misunderstands
And laughs at and lies about the new live wild
Loves it lists! that sets upright, in the sands
Of age in which nothing grows, where all our friends are old,
A few dried leaves marked THIS IS THE GREENWOOD—
O arms that arm, for a child's wars, the child!

And yet they are good, if anything is good,
Against his enemies . . . Across the seas
At the bottom of the world, where Childhood
Sits on its desert island with Achilles
And Pitamakan, the White Blackfoot:
In the black auditorium, my heart at ease,
I watch the furred castaways (the seniors put
A play on every spring) tame their wild beasts,
Erect their tree house. Chatting over their fruit,
Their coconuts, they relish their stately feasts.
The family's servant, their magnanimous
Master now, rules them by right. Nature's priests,
They worship at Nature's altar; when with decorous
Affection the Admirable Crichton
Kisses a girl like a big Wendy, all of us
Squirm or sit up in our seats . . . Undone
When an English sail is sighted, the prisoners
Escape from their Eden to the world: the real one
Where servants are servants, masters masters,
And no one's magnanimous. The lights go on
And we go off, robbed of our fruit, our furs—
The island that the children ran is gone.

The island sang to me: *Believe! Believe!*
And didn't I know a lady with a lion?
Each evening, as the sun sank, didn't I grieve

To leave *my* tree house for reality?
There was nothing there for me to disbelieve.
At peace among my weapons, I sit in my tree
And feel: *Friday night, then Saturday, then Sunday!*

I'm dreaming of a wolf, as Mama wakes me,
And a tall girl who is—outside it's gray,
I can't remember, I jump up and dress.
We eat in the lighted kitchen. And what is play
For me, for them is habit. Happiness
Is a quiet presence, breathless and familiar:
My grandfather and I sit there in oneness
As the Sunset bus, lit by the lavender
And rose of sunrise, takes us to the dark
Echoing cavern where Pop, a worker,
Works for our living. As he rules a mark,
A short square pencil in his short square hand,
On a great sheet of copper, I make some remark
He doesn't hear. In that hard maze—in that land
That grown men live in—in the world of work,
He measures, shears, solders; and I stand
Empty-handed, watching him. I wander into the murk
The naked light bulbs pierce: the workmen, making something,
Say something to the boy in his white shirt. I jerk
As the sparks fly at me. The man hammering
As acid hisses, and the solder turns to silver,
Seems to me a dwarf hammering out the Ring
In the world under the world. The hours blur;
Bored and not bored, I bend things out of lead.
I wash my smudged hands, as my grandfather
Washes his black ones, with their gritty soap: ahead,
Past their time clock, their pay window, is the blue
And gold and white of noon. The sooty thread
Up which the laborers feel their way into
Their wives and houses, is money; the fact of life,
The secret the grown-ups share, is what to do
To make money. The husband Adam, Eve his wife
Have learned how not to have to do without

Till Santa Claus brings them their Boy Scout knife—
Nor do they find things in dreams, carry a paper route,
Sell Christmas seals . . .
               Starting *his* Saturday, his Sunday,
Pop tells me what I love to hear about,
His boyhood in Shelbyville. I play
What he plays, hunt what he hunts, remember
What he remembers: it seems to me I could stay
In that dark forest, lit by one fading ember
Of his campfire, forever . . . But we're home.
I run in love to each familiar member
Of this little state, clustered about the Dome
Of St. Nicholas—this city in which my rabbit
Depends on me, and I on everyone—this first Rome
Of childhood, so absolute in every habit
That when we hear the world our jailor say:
"Tell me, art thou a Roman?" the time we inhabit
Drops from our shoulders, and we answer: "Yea.
I stand at Caesar's judgment seat, I appeal
Unto Caesar."
           I wash my hands, Pop gives his pay
Envelope to Mama; we sit down to our meal.
The phone rings: Mrs. Mercer wonders if I'd care
To go to the library. That would be ideal,
I say when Mama lets me. I comb my hair
And find the four books I have out: *The Food
Of the Gods* was best. Liking that world where
The children eat, and grow giant and good,
I swear as I've often sworn: "I'll never forget
What it's like, when *I've* grown up." A prelude
By Chopin, hammered note by note, like alphabet
Blocks, comes from next door. It's played with real feeling,
The feeling of being indoors practicing. "And yet
It's not as if—"a gray electric, stealing
To the curb on silent wheels, has come; and I
See on the back seat (sight more appealing
Than any human sight!) my own friend Lucky,
Half wolf, half police-dog. And he can play the piano—

Play that he does, that is — and jump so high
For a ball that he turns a somersault. "Hello,"
I say to the lady, and hug Lucky . . . In my
Talk with the world, in which it tells me what I know
And I tell it, "I know—"how strange that I
Know nothing, and yet it tells me what I know!—
I appreciate the animals, who stand by
Purring. Or else they sit and pant. It's so—
So *agreeable*. If only people purred and panted!
So, now, Lucky and I sit in our row,
Mrs. Mercer in hers. I take for granted
The tiller by which she steers, the yellow roses
In the bud vases, the whole enchanted
Drawing room of our progress. The glass encloses
As glass does, a womanish and childish
And doggish universe. We press our noses
To the glass and wish: the angel-and devilfish
Floating by on Vine, on Sunset, shut their eyes
And press their noses to their glass and wish.

II. A Night with Lions

When I was twelve we'd visit my aunt's friend
Who owned a lion, the Metro-Goldwyn-Mayer
Lion. I'd play with him, and he'd pretend
To play with me. I was the real player
But he'd trot back and forth inside his cage
Till he got bored. I put Tawny in the prayer
I didn't believe in, not at my age,
But said still; just as I did everything in fours
And gave to Something, on the average,
One cookie out of three. And by my quartz, my ores,
My wood with the bark on it, from the Petrified
Forest, I put his dewclaw . . .
                              Now the lion roars
His slow comfortable roars; I lie beside
My young, tall, brown aunt, out there in the past
Or future, and I sleepily confide

My dream-discovery: my breath comes fast
Whenever I see someone with your skin,
Hear someone with your voice. The lion's steadfast
Roar goes on in the darkness. I have been
Asleep a while when I remember: you
Are—you, and Tawny was the lion in—
In *Tarzan*. In *Tarzan!* Just as we used to,
I talk to you, you talk to me or pretend
To talk to me as grown-up people do,
Of *Jurgen* and Rupert Hughes, till in the end
I think as a child thinks: "You're my real friend."

III. A Street off Sunset

Sometimes as I drive by the factory
That manufactures, after so long, Vicks
VapoRub Ointment, there rises over me
A eucalyptus tree. I feel its stair-sticks
Impressed on my palms, my insteps, as I climb
To my tree house. The gray leaves make me mix
My coughing chest, anointed at bedtime,
With the smell of the sap trickling from the tan
Trunk, where the nails go in.
                                My lifetime
Got rid of, I sit in a dark blue sedan
Beside my great-grandmother, in Hollywood.
We pass a windmill, a pink sphinx, an Allbran
Billboard; thinking of Salâmmbo, Robin Hood,
The old prospector with his flapjack in the air,
I sit with my hands folded: I am good.

That night as I lie crossways in an armchair
Reading *Amazing Stories* (just as, long before,
I'd lie by my rich uncle's polar bear
On his domed library's reflecting floor
In the last year of the first World War, and see
A poor two-seater being attacked by four
Triplanes, on the cover of the *Literary*

Digest, and a Camel coming to its aid;
I'd feel the bear's fur warm and rough against me,
The colors of the afternoon would fade,
I'd reach into the bear's mouth and hold tight
To its front tooth and think, "I'm not afraid")
There off Sunset, in the lamplit starlight,
A scientist is getting ready to destroy
The world. "It's time for you to say good night,"
Mama tells me; I go on in breathless joy.
"Remember, tomorrow is a school day,"
Mama tells me; I go on in breathless joy.

At last I go to Mama in her gray
Silk, to Pop, to Dandeen in her black
Silk. I put my arms around them, they
Put their arms around me. Then I go back
To my bedroom; I read as I undress.
The scientist is ready to attack.
Mama calls, "Is your light out?" I call back, "Yes,"
And turn the light out. Forced out of life into
Bed, for a moment I lie comfortless
In the blank darkness; then as I always do,
I put on the earphones of the crystal set —
Each bed has its earphones — and the uneasy tissue
Of their far-off star-sound, of the blue-violet
Of space, surrounds the sweet voice from the Tabernacle
Of the Four-Square Gospel. A vague marionette,
Tall, auburn, holds her arms out, to unshackle
The bonds of sin, of sleep — as, next instant, the sun
Holds its arms out through the fig, the lemon tree,
In the back yard the clucking hens all cackle
As Mama brings their chicken feed. I see
My magazine. My magazine! Dressing for school,
I read how the good world wins its victory
Over that bad man. Books; book strap; jump the footstool
You made in Manual Training . . . Then we three
Sit down, and one says grace; and then, by rule,
By that habit that moves the stars, some coffee —

One spoonful—is poured out into my milk
And the milk, transubstantiated, is coffee.
And Mama's weekday wash-dress, Dandeen's soft black silk
Are ways that habit itself makes holy
Just as, on Sunday mornings, Wednesday nights, His will
Comes in their ways—of Church, of Prayer Meeting—to set free
The spirit from the flesh it questions.
                                        So,
So unquestioned, my own habit moves me
To and through and from school, like a domino,
Till, home, I wake to find that I am playing
Dominoes with Dandeen. Her old face is slow
In pleasure, slow in doubt, as she sits weighing
Strategies: patient, equable, and humble,
She hears what this last child of hers is saying
In pride or bewilderment; and she will grumble
Like a child or animal when, indifferent
To the reasons of my better self, I mumble:
"I'd better stop now—the rabbit . . ."
                                        I relent
And play her one more game. It *is* miraculous
To have a great-grandmother: I feel different
From others as, between moves, we discuss
The War Between the States. The cheerful troops
Ride up to our farmhouse, steal from us
The spoons, the horses—when their captain stoops
To Dandeen and puts Dandeen on his horse,
She cries . . . As I run by the chicken coops
With lettuce for my rabbit, real remorse
Hurts me, here, now: the little girl is crying
Because I didn't write. Because—
                                        of course,
I *was* a child, I missed them so. But justifying
Hurts too: if only I could play you one more game,
See you all one more time! I think of you dying
Forgiving me—or not, it is all the same
To the forgiven . . . My rabbit's glad to see me;
He scrambles to me, gives me little tame

Bites before he eats the lettuce. His furry
Long warm soft floppy ears, his crinkling nose
Are reassuring to a child. They guarantee,
As so much here does, that the child knows
Who takes care of him, whom he takes care of.

Mama comes out and takes in the clothes
From the clothesline. She looks with righteous love
At all of us, her spare face half a girl's.
She enters a chicken coop, and the hens shove
And flap and squawk, in fear; the whole flock whirls
Into the farthest corner. She chooses one,
Comes out, and wrings its neck. The body hurls
Itself out — lunging, reeling, it begins to run
Away from Something, to fly away from Something
In great flopping circles. Mama stands like a nun
In the center of each awful, anguished ring.
The thudding and scrambling go on, go on — then they fade,
I open my eyes, it's over . . . Could such a thing
Happen to anything? It could to a rabbit, I'm afraid;
It could to —
                    "Mama, you won't kill Reddy ever,
You won't ever, will you?" The farm woman tries to persuade
The little boy, her grandson, that she'd never
Kill the boy's rabbit, never even think of it.
He would like to believe her . . . And whenever
I see her, there in that dark infinite,
Standing like Judith, with the hen's head in her hand,
I explain it away, in vain — a hypocrite,
Like all who love.
                    Into the blue wonderland
Of Hollywood, the sun sinks, past the eucalyptus,
The sphinx, the windmill, and I watch and read and
Hold my story tight. And when the bus
Stops at the corner and Pop — Pop! — steps down
And I run out to meet him, a blurred nimbus,
Half-red, half-gold, enchants his sober brown
Face, his stooped shoulders, into the All-Father's.

He tells me about the work he's done downtown,
We sit there on the steps. My universe
Mended almost, I tell him about the scientist. I say,
"He couldn't really, could he, Pop?" My comforter's
Eyes light up, and he laughs. "No, that's just play,
Just make-believe," he says. The sky is gray,
We sit there, at the end of our good day.

Tom Wolfe

In the aftermath of the Second World War, a youth explosion began to transform Southern California, finding its most visible form in the "car culture" defined by hot rods, cruising, and rock 'n' roll. What to outsiders was a peculiar fad was to insiders a new form of art, and car customizers like George Barris and Big Daddy Roth, who lovingly rebuilt automobiles according to their inner visions, were master craftsmen who won both devoted teenage cult followings and admiration from artists such as Robert Irwin. In the early 1960s, Tom Wolfe (b. 1931) talked *Esquire* into sending him to California to write about the custom-car phenomenon. The result was "The Kandy-Kolored Tangerine-Flake Streamline Baby," which Wolfe and others have claimed as the starting point of the New Journalism. It became the title piece of Wolfe's first collection, published in 1965, a book whose stylistic reverberations are still being felt.

THE KANDY-KOLORED TANGERINE-FLAKE STREAMLINE BABY

The first good look I had at customized cars was at an event called a "Teen Fair," held in Burbank, a suburb of Los Angeles beyond Hollywood. This was a wild place to be taking a look at art objects—eventually, I should say, you have to reach the conclusion that these customized cars *are* art objects, at least if you use the standards applied in a civilized society. But I will get to that in a moment. Anyway, about noon you drive up to a place that looks like an outdoor amusement park, and there are three serious-looking kids, like the cafeteria committee in high school, taking tickets, but the scene inside is quite mad. Inside, two things hit you. The first is a huge platform a good seven feet off the ground with a hully-gully band—everything is electrified, the bass, the guitars, the saxophones—and then behind the band, on the platform, about two hundred kids are doing frantic dances called the hully-gully, the bird, and the shampoo. As I said, it's noontime. The dances the kids are doing are very jerky. The boys and girls don't touch, not even with their hands. They just ricochet around. Then you notice that all the girls are dressed exactly alike. They have bouffant hairdos —all of them—and slacks that are, well, skin-tight does not get the idea across; it's more the conformation than how tight the slacks are. It's as if some lecherous old tailor with a gluteus-maximus fixation designed them, striation by striation. About the time you've managed to focus on this, you notice that out in the middle of the park is a huge, perfectly round swimming pool; really rather enormous. And there is a Chris-Craft cabin cruiser in the pool, going around and around, sending up big waves, with more of these bouffant babies bunched in the back of it. In the water, suspended like plankton, are kids in Scuba-diving outfits; others are tooling around underwater, breathing through a snorkel. And all over the place are booths, put up by shoe companies and guitar companies and God knows who else, and there are kids dancing in all of them—dancing the bird, the hully-gully, and the shampoo—with the music of the hully-gully band piped all over the park through loudspeakers.

All this time, Tex Smith, from *Hot Rod Magazine*, who brought me over to the place, is trying to lead me to the customized-car exhibit—"Tom, I want you to see this car that Bill Cushenberry built, The Silhouette"—which is to say, here are two hundred kids ricocheting over a platform at high noon, and a speedy little boat barreling around and around and around in a round swimming pool, and I seem to be the only person who is distracted. The customized-car exhibit turns out to be the Ford Custom Car Caravan, which Ford is sending all over the country. At first, with the noise and peripheral motion and the inchoate leching you are liable to be doing, what with bouffant nymphets rocketing all over the place, these customized cars do not strike you as anything very special. Obviously they *are* very special, but the first thing you think of is the usual—you know, that the kids who own these cars are probably skinny little hoods who wear T shirts and carry their cigarette packs by winding them around in the T shirt up near the shoulder.

But after a while, I was glad I had seen the cars in this natural setting, which was, after all, a kind of Plato's Republic for teenagers. Because if you watched anything at this fair very long, you kept noticing the same thing. These kids are absolutely maniacal about form. They are practically religious about it. For example, the dancers: none of them ever smiled. They stared at each other's legs and feet, concentrating. The dances had no grace about them at all, they were more in the nature of a hoedown, but everybody was concentrating to do them exactly *right*. And the bouffant kids all had form, wild form, but form with rigid standards, one gathers. Even the boys. Their dress was prosaic—Levis, Slim Jims, sport shirts, T shirts, polo shirts—but the form was consistent: a stove-pipe silhouette. And they all had the same hairstyle: some wore it long, some short, but none of them had a part; all that hair was brushed back straight from the hairline. I went by one of the guitar booths, and there was a little kid in there, about thirteen, playing the hell out of an electric guitar. The kid was named Cranston something or other. He looked like he ought to be named Kermet or Herschel; all his genes were kind of horribly Okie. Cranston was playing away and a big crowd was watching. But Cranston was slouched back with his spine bent like a sapling up against a table, looking gloriously bored. At thirteen, this kid was being fanatically cool. They all were. They were all wonderful slaves to form. They have created their own style of life, and they are much more authoritarian about enforcing it than are adults. Not only that, but today these kids—especially in California—have *money*, which, needless to say, is why all these shoe merchants and guitar sellers and the Ford Motor Company were at a Teen Fair in the first place. I don't mind observing that it is this same combination—money plus slavish devotion to form—that accounts for Versailles or St. Mark's Square. Naturally, most of the artifacts that these kids' money-plus-form produce are of a pretty ghastly order. But so was most of the paraphernalia that developed in England during the Regency. I mean, most of it was on the order of starched cravats. A man could walk into Beau Brummel's house at 11 A.M., and here would come the butler with a tray of wilted linen. "These were some of our failures," he confides. But then Brummel comes downstairs wearing one perfect starched cravat. Like one perfect iris, the flower of Mayfair civilization. But the Regency period did see some tremendous formal architecture. And the kids' formal society has also brought at least one substantial thing to a formal development of a high order—the customized cars. I don't have to dwell on the point that cars mean more to these kids than architecture did in Europe's great formal century, say, 1750 to 1850. They are freedom, style, sex, power, motion, color—everything is right there.

Things have been going on in the development of the kids' formal attitude toward cars since 1945, things of great sophistication that adults have not been even remotely aware of, mainly because the kids are so inarticulate about it, especially the ones most hipped on the subject. They are not from the levels of society that produce children who write sensitive analytical prose at age seventeen, or if they do, they soon fall into the hands of English instructors who put them onto Hemingway or a lot of goddamn-and-hungry-breast writers. If they ever write about a highway again, it's a rain-slicked highway and the sound of the automobiles passing over it is like the sound of tearing silk, not that one household in ten thousand has heard the sound of tearing silk since 1945.

Anyway, we are back at the Teen Fair and I am talking to Tex Smith and to Don Beebe, a portly young guy with a white sport shirt and Cuban sunglasses. As they tell me about the Ford Custom Car Caravan, I can see that Ford has begun to comprehend this teen-age style of life and its potential. The way Ford appears to figure it is this: Thousands of kids are getting hold of cars and either hopping them up for speed or customizing them to some extent, usually a little of both. Before they get married they pour *all* their money into this. If Ford can get them hooked on Fords now, after the kids are married they'll buy new Fords. Even the kids who aren't full-time car nuts themselves will be influenced by which car is considered "boss." They use that word a lot, "boss." The kids used to consider Ford the hot car, but then, from 1955 to 1962, Chevrolet became the favorite. They had big engines and were easy to hop up, the styling was simple, and the kids could customize them easily. In 1959, and more so in 1960, Plymouth became a hot car, too. In 1961 and 1962, it was all Chevrolet and Plymouth. Now Ford is making a big push. A lot of the professional hot-rod and custom-car people, adults, will tell you that now Ford is the hot car, but you have to discount some of it, because Ford is laying money on everybody right and left, in one form or another. In the Custom Car Caravan, all the cars have been fashioned out of Ford bodies except the ones that are completely handmade, like the aforementioned Silhouette.

Anyway, Don Beebe is saying, over a loudspeaker, "I hate to break up that dancing, but let's have a little drag racing." He has a phonograph hooked up to the loudspeaker, and he puts on a record, produced by Riverside Records, of Drag-strip sounds, mainly dragsters blasting off and squealing from the starting line. Well, he doesn't really break up the dancing, but a hundred kids come over, when they hear the drag-strip sounds, to where Beebe has a slot racing stand. Slot racing is a model-train-type game in which two model drag racers, each about five inches long, powered by electricity, run down a model drag strip. Beebe takes a microphone and announces that Dick Dale, the singer, is here, and anybody who will race Dick at the slot-racing stand will get one of his records. Dick Dale is pretty popular among the kids out here because he sings a lot of "surfing" songs. The surfers—surfboard riders—are a cult much admired by all the kids. They have their own argot, with adjectives like "hang ten," meaning the best there is. They also go in for one particular brand of customizing: they take old wood-bodied station wagons, which they call "woodies," and fix them up for riding, sleeping and hauling surfing equipment for their weekends at the beach. The surfers also get a hell of a bang out of slot racing for some reason, so with Dick Dale slot racing at the Teen Fair, you have about three areas of the arcane teen world all rolled into one.

Dick Dale, rigged out in Byronic shirt and blue cashmere V-neck sweater and wraparound sunglasses, singer's mufti U.S.A., has one cord with a starter button, while a bouffant nymphet from Newport named Sherma, Sherma of the Capri pants, has the other one. Don Beebe flashes a starting light and Sherma lets out a cry, not a thrilled cry, just nerves, and a model 1963 Ford and a model dragster go running down the slot board, which is about chest high. The slot board is said to be one-twenty-fifth the actual size of a drag strip, which somehow reminds you of those incredible stamp-size pictures in the dictionary with the notation that this is one-hundredth the size of a real elephant. A hundred kids were packed in around the slot racers and did not find it incredible. That is, they were interested in who would win, Dick Dale or Sherma. I'm sure they had no trouble magnifying the slot racers twenty-five times to the size of the full-blown, esoteric world of hot rods and custom cars.

I met George Barris, one of the celebrities of the custom-car world, at the Teen Fair. Barris is the biggest name in customizing. He is a good example of a kid who grew up completely absorbed in this teen-age world of cars, who pursued the pure flame and its forms with such devotion that he emerged an artist. It was like Tiepolo emerging from the studios of Venice, where the rounded Grecian haunches of the murals on the Palladian domes hung in the atmosphere like clouds. Except that Barris emerged from the auto-body shops of Los Angeles

Barris invited me out to his studio—only he would never think of calling it that, he calls it Kustom City—at 10811 Riverside Drive in North Hollywood. If there is a river within a thousand miles of Riverside Drive, I saw no sign of it. It's like every place else out there: endless scorched boulevards lined with one-story stores, shops, bowling alleys, skating rinks, tacos drive-ins, all of them shaped not like rectangles but like trapezoids, from the way the roofs slant up from the back and the plate-glass fronts slant out as if they're going to pitch forward on the sidewalk and throw up. The signs are great, too. They all stand free on poles outside. They have horribly slick dog-legged shapes that I call boomerang modern. As for Kustom City—Barris grew up at the time when it was considered sharp to change all the C's to K's. He also sells Kandy Lac to paint cars Kandy Kolors with, and I know that sibilant C in City must have bothered the hell out of him at some point. It's interesting, I think, that he still calls the place Kustom City, and still sells Kandy Kolors, because he is an intelligent person. What it means is, he is absolutely untouched by the big amoeba god of Anglo-European sophistication that gets you in the East. You know how it is in the East. One day you notice that the boss's button-down shirt has this sweet percale roll to it, while your own was obviously slapped together by some mass-production graph keepers who are saving an eighth of inch of cloth per shirt, twelve inches per bolt or the like, and this starts eating at you.

Barris, whose family is Greek, is a solid little guy, five feet seven, thirty-seven years old, and he looks just like Picasso. When he's working, which is most of the time, he wears a heavy white T-style shirt, faded off-white pants cut full with pleats in the manner of Picasso walking along in the wind on a bluff at Rapallo, and crepe-sole slipper-style shoes, also off-white. Picasso, I should add, means nothing to Barris, although he knows who he is. It's just that to Barris and the customizers there is no one great universe of form and design called Art. Yet that's the universe he's in. He's not building cars, he's creating forms.

Barris starts taking me through Kustom City, and the place looks like any other body shop at first, but pretty soon you realize you're in a *gallery*. This place is full of cars such as you have never seen before. Half of them will never touch the road. They're put on trucks and trailers and carted all over the country to be exhibited at hot-rod and custom-car shows. They'll run, if it comes to that— they're full of big, powerful, hopped-up chrome-plated motors, because all that speed and power, and all that lovely apparatus, has tremendous emotional meaning to everybody in customizing. But it's like one of these Picasso or Miro rugs. You don't walk on the damn things. You hang them on the wall. It's the same thing with Barris' cars. In effect, they're sculpture.

For example, there is an incredible object he built called the XPAK-400 air car. The customizers love all that X jazz. It runs on a cushion of air, which is beside the point, because it's a pure piece of curvilinear abstract sculpture. If Brancusi is any good, then this thing belongs on a pedestal, too. There is not a straight line in it, and only one true circle, and those countless planes, and tremendous baroque fins, and yet all in all it's a rigid little piece of solid geometrical harmony. As a matter of fact, Brancusi and Barris both developed out of a design concept that we can call Streamlined Modern or Thirties Curvilinear—via utterly different roads, of course—and Barris and most other custom artists are carrying this idea of the abstract curve, which is very tough to handle, on and on and on at a time when your conventional designers—from architects to the guys who lay out magazines—are all Mondrian. Even the young Detroit car stylists are all Mondrian. Only the aircraft designers have done anything more with the Streamline, and they have only because they're forced to by physics, and so on. I want to return to that subject in a minute, but first I want to tell you about another car Barris was showing me.

This was stuck back in a storeroom. Barris wasn't interested in it any more since he did it nine years ago. But this car—this old car, as far as Barris was concerned—was like a dream prefiguration of a very hot sports car, the Quantum, that Saab has come out with this year after a couple of years of consultation with all sorts of aerodynamic experts and advance-guard designers. They're beautiful cars—Saab's and Barris'. They're the same body, practically—with this lovely topology rolling down over the tunneled headlights, with the whole hood curving down very low to the ground in front. I told Barris about the similarity, but he just shrugged; he is quite used to some manufacturer coming up with one of his cars five or six years later.

Anyway, Barris and I were walking around the side of Kustom City, through the parking lot, when I saw an Avanti, the new Studebaker sports model, very expensive. This one had paper mock-ups added to the front and the rear, and so I asked Barris about it. That wasn't much, he said; starting with the paper mock-ups, it brought the hood out a foot with a chic slope to it. He was doing the same sort of thing in the back to eliminate that kind of loaf-of-bread look. It really makes the car. Barris doesn't regard this as a very major project. It may end up in something like a kit you can buy, similar to the old Continental kits, to rig up front and back.

If Barris and the customizers hadn't been buried in the alien and suspect underworld of California youth, I don't think they would seem at all unusual by now. But they've had access to almost nothing but the hot-rod press. They're like Easter Islanders. Suddenly you come upon the astonishing objects, and then you have to figure out how they got there and why they're there.

If you study the work of Barris or Cushenberry, the aforementioned Silhouette, or Ed Roth or Darryl Starbird, can you beat that name?, I think you come up with a fragment of art history. Somewhere back in the thirties, designers, automobile designers among them, came up with the idea of the streamline. It sounded "functional," and on an airplane it is functional, but on a car it's not, unless you're making a Bonneville speed run. Actually, it's baroque. The streamline is baroque abstract or baroque modern or whatever you want to call it. Well, about the time the streamline got going—in the thirties, you may recall, we had curved buildings, like the showpieces later, at the World's Fair—in came the Bauhaus movement, which was blown-up Mondrian, really. Before you knew it, everything was Mondrian—the Kleenex box: Mondrian; the format of the cover of *Life* Magazine: Mondrian; those bled-to-the-edge photograph layouts in *Paris Match*: Mondrian. Even automobiles:

Mondrian. They call Detroit automobiles streamlined, but they're not. If you don't believe it, look down from an airplane at all the cars parked on a shopping-center apron, and except that all the colors are pastel instead of primary, what have you got? A Mondrian painting. The Mondrian principle, those straight edges, is very tight, very Apollonian. The streamline principle, which really has no function, which curves around and swoops and flows just for the thrill of it, is very free Dionysian. For reasons I don't have to labor over, the kids preferred the Dionysian. And since Detroit blew the thing, the Dionysian principle in cars was left to people in the teen-age netherworld, like George Barris.

Barris was living in Sacramento when he started customizing cars in 1940. As the plot develops, you have the old story of the creative child, the break from the mold of the parents, the garret struggle, the bohemian life, the first success, the accolade of the esoteric following, and finally the money starts pouring in. With this difference: We're out on old Easter Island, in the buried netherworld of teen-age Californians, and those objects, those cars, they have to do with the gods and the spirit and a lot of mystic stuff in the community.

Barris told me his folks were Greeks who owned a restaurant, and "they wanted me to be a restaurant man, like every other typical Greek, I guess," he said. But Barris, even at ten, was wild about cars, carving streamlined cars out of balsa wood. After a few years, he got a car of his own, a 1925 Buick, then a 1932 Ford. Barris established many of the formal conventions of customizing himself. Early in the game he had clients, other kids who paid him to customize their cars. In 1943 he moved to Los Angeles and landed in the middle of the tremendous teen-age culture that developed there during the war. Family life was dislocated, as the phrase goes, but the money was pouring in, and the kids began to work up their own style of life — as they've been doing ever since — and to establish those fanatic forms and conventions I was talking about earlier. Right at the heart of it, of course, was the automobile. Cars were hard to come by, what with the war, so the kids were raiding junkyards for parts, which led to custom-built cars, mostly roadsters by the very nature of it, and also to a lot of radical, hopped-up engines. All teen-age car nuts had elements of both in their work — customizing and hot-rodding, form and power — but tended to concentrate on one or the other. Barris—and Ed Roth later told me it was the same with him—naturally gravitated toward customizing. In high school, and later for a brief time at Sacramento College and the Los Angeles Art Center, he was taking what he described to me as mechanical drawing, shop, and free art.

I liked this term "free art." In Barris' world at the time, and now for that matter, there was no such thing as great big old fructuous Art. There was mechanical drawing and then there was free art, which did not mean that it was liberating in any way, but rather that it was footloose and free and not going anywhere in particular. The kind of art that appealed to Barris, and meant something to the people he hung around with, was the automobile.

Barris gets a wonderful reflective grin on his face when he starts talking about the old days—1944 to 1948. He was a hot-rodder when hot-rodders were hot-rodders, that's the kind of look he gets. They all do. The professional hot-rodders—such as the Petersen magazine syndicate (*Hot Rod Magazine* and many others) and the National Hot Rod Association—have gone to great lengths to obliterate the memory of the gamey hot-rod days, and they try to give everybody in the field transfusions of Halazone so that the public will look at the hot-rodders as nice boys with short-sleeved sport shirts just back from the laundry and a chemistry set, such an interesting hobby.

In point of fact, Barris told me, it was a lurid time. Everybody would meet in drive-ins, the most famous of them being the Piccadilly out near Sepulveda Boulevard. It was a hell of a show, all the weird-looking roadsters and custom cars, with very loud varoom-varoom motors. By this time Barris had a '36 Ford roadster with many exotic features.

"I had just come from Sacramento, and I wasn't supposed to know anything. I was a tourist, but my car was wilder than anything around. I remember one night this kid comes up with a roadster with no door handles. It looked real sharp, but he had to kick the door from the inside to open it. You should have seen the look on his face when he saw mine—I had the same thing, only with electric buttons."

The real action, though, was the drag racing, which was quite, but quite, illegal.

"We'd all be at the Piccadilly or some place, and guys would start challenging each other. You know, a guy goes up to another guy's car and looks it up and down like it has gangrene or something, and he says: 'You wanna *go?*' Or, if it was a real grudge match for some reason, he'd say, 'You wanna go for pink slips?' The registrations on the cars were pink; in other words, the winner got the other guy's car.

"Well, as soon as a few guys had challenged each other, everybody would ride out onto this stretch of Sepulveda Boulevard or the old divided highway, in Compton, and the guys would start dragging, one car on one side of the center line, the other car on the other. Go a quarter of a mile. It was wild. Some nights there'd be a thousand kids lining the road to watch, boys and girls, all sitting on the sides of their cars with the lights shining across the highway."

But George, what happened if some ordinary motorist happened to be coming down the highway at this point?

"Oh, we'd block off the highway at each end, and if some guy wanted to get through anyway, we'd tell him, 'Well, Mister, there are going to be two cars coming down both sides of the road pretty fast in a minute, and you can go through if you want to, but you'll just have to take your best shot.'

"They always turned around, of course, and after a while the cops would come. Then you *really* saw something. Everybody jumped in their cars and took off, in every direction. Some guys would head right across a field. Of course, all our cars were so hopped up, the cops could never catch anybody.

"Then one night we got raided at the Piccadilly. It was one Friday night. The cops came in and just started loading everybody in the wagons. I was sitting in a car with a cop who was off duty—he was a hot-rodder himself—or they would have picked me up, too. Saturday night everybody came back to the Piccadilly to talk about what happened the night before, and the cops came back again and picked up three hundred fifty that night. That pretty well ended the Piccadilly."

From the very moment he was on his own in Los Angeles, when he was about eighteen, Barris never did anything but customize cars. He never took any other kind of job. At first he worked in a body shop that took him on because so many kids were coming by wanting this and that done to their cars, and the boss really didn't know how to do it, because it was all esoteric teen-age stuff. Barris was making next to nothing at first, but he never remembers feeling hard up, nor does any kid out there today I talked to. They have a magic economy or something. Anyway, in 1945 Barris opened his own shop on Compton Avenue, in Los Angeles, doing nothing but customizing. There was that much demand for it. It was no sweat, he said; pretty soon he was making better than $100 a week.

Most of the work he was doing then was modifying Detroit cars—chopping and channeling. Chopping is lowering the top of the car, bringing it nearer to the hood line. Channeling is lowering the body itself down between the wheels. Also, they'd usually strip off all the chrome and the door handles and cover up the wheel openings in the back. At that time, the look the kids liked was to have the body lowered in the back and slightly jacked up in the front, although today it's just the opposite. The front windshield in those days was divided by a post, and so chopping the top gave the car a very sinister appearance. The front windshield always looked like a couple of narrow, slitty little eyes. And I think this, more than anything else, diverted everybody from what Barris and the others were really doing. Hot-rodders had a terrible reputation at that time, and no line was ever drawn between hot-rodders and custom-car owners, because, in truth, they were speed maniacs, too.

This was Barris' chopped-and-channeled Mercury period. Mercuries were his favorite. All the kids knew the Barris styling and he was getting a lot of business. What he was really doing, in a formal sense, was trying to achieve the kind of streamlining that Detroit, for all intents and purposes, had abandoned. When modified, some of the old Mercuries were more streamlined than any standard model that Detroit has put out to this day. Many of the coupes he modified had a very sleek slope to the back window that has been picked up just this year in the "fastback" look of the Rivieras, Sting Rays, and a few other cars.

At this point Barris and the other customizers didn't really have enough capital to do many completely original cars, but they were getting more and more radical in modifying Detroit cars. They were doing things Detroit didn't do until years later—tailfins, bubble-tops, twin headlights, concealed headlights, "Frenched" headlights, the low-slung body itself. They lifted some twenty designs from him alone. One, for example, is the way cars now have the exhaust pipes exit through the rear bumper or fender. Another is the bullet-shaped, or breast-shaped if you'd rather, front bumpers on the Cadillac.

Barris says "lifted," because some are exact down to the most minute details. Three years ago when he was in Detroit, Barris met a lot of car designers and, "I was amazed," he told me. "They could tell me about cars I built in 1945. They knew all about the four-door '48 Studebaker I restyled. I chopped the top and dropped the hood and it ended up a pretty good-looking car. And the bubbletop I built in 1954—they knew all about it. And all this time we thought they frowned on us."

Even today—dealing with movie stars and auto manufacturers and all sorts of people on the outside—I think Barris, and certainly the others, still feel psychologically a part of the alien teen-age netherworld in which they grew up. All that while they were carry-ing the torch for the Dionysian Streamline. They were America's modern baroque designers—and, oddly enough, "serious" designers, Anglo-European-steeped designers, are just coming around to it. Take Saarinen, especially in something like his T.W.A. terminal at Kennedy. The man in his last years came around to baroque modern.

It's interesting that the customizers, like sports-car fans, have always wanted cars minus most of the chrome—but for different ideals. The sports-car owner thinks chrome trim interferes with the "classic" look of his car. In other words, he wants to simplify the thing. The customizer thinks chrome interferes with something else —the luxurious baroque Streamline. The sports-car people snigger at tailfins. The customizers love them and, looked at from a baroque standard of beauty, they are really not so trashy at all. They are an inspiration, if you will, a wonderful fantasy extension of the curved line, and since the car in America is half fantasy anyway, a kind of baroque extension of the ego, you can build up a good argument for them.

Getting back to Easter Island, here were Barris and the others with their blowtorches and hard-rubber mallets, creating their ba-roque sculpture, cut off from the rest of the world and publicized almost solely via the teen-age grapevine. Barris was making a fairly good living, but others were starving at this thing. The pattern was always the same: a guy would open a body shop and take on enough hack collision work to pay the rent so that he could slam the door shut at 2 P.M. and get in there and do his custom jobs, and pretty soon the guy got so he couldn't even face *any* collision work. Dealing with all those crusty old arteriosclerotic bastards takes up all your *time*, man, and so they're trying to make a living doing nothing but custom work, and they are starving.

The situation is a lot like that today, except that customizing is beginning to be rationalized, in the sense Max Weber used that word. This rationalization, or efficient exploitation, began in the late forties when an $80-a-week movie writer named Robert Petersen noticed all the kids pouring money into cars in a little world they had created for themselves, and he decided to exploit it by starting *Hot Rod Magazine*, which clicked right away and led to a whole chain of hot-rod and custom-car magazines. Petersen, by the way, now has a pot of money and drives Maseratis and other high-status-level sports cars of the Apollonian sort, not the Dionysian custom kind. Which is kind of a shame, because he has the money to commission something really incredible.

Up to that time the only custom-car show in the country was a wild event Barris used to put on bereft of any sort of midwifery by forty-two-year-old promoters with Windsor-knot ties who usually run low-cost productions. This car show was utterly within the teen-age netherworld, with no advertising or coverage of any sort. It took place each spring—during the high-school Easter vacations—when all the kids, as they still do, would converge on the beach at Balboa for their beer-drinking-*Fasching* rites, or whatever the Germans call it. Barris would rent the parking lot of a service station on a corner for a week, and kids from all over California would come with their customized cars. First there would be a parade; the cars, about a hundred fifty of them, would drive all through the streets of Balboa, and the kids would line the sidewalks to watch them; then they'd drive back to the lot and park and be on exhibit for the week.

Barris still goes off to Balboa and places like that. He likes that scene. Last year at Pacific Ocean Park he noticed all these bouffant babies and got the idea of spraying all those great puffed-up dandelion heads with fluorescent water colors, the same Kandy Kolors he

uses on the cars. Barris took out an air gun, the girls all lined up and
gave him fifty cents per, and he sprayed them with these weird, brilliant color combinations all afternoon until he ran out of colors.
Each girl would go skipping and screaming away out onto the sidewalks and the beaches. Barris told me, "It was great that night to
take one of the rides, like the Bubble Ride, and look down and see
all those fluorescent colors. The kids were bopping [dancing] and
running around."

The Bubble is a ride that swings out over the ocean. It is supposed to be like a satellite in orbit.

"But the fellows sky-diving got the best look as they came down
by parachute."

In 1948 Petersen put on the first custom-car show in the Los
Angeles armory, and this brought customizing out into the open a
little. A wild-looking Buick Barris had remodeled was one of the
hits of the show, and he was on his way, too.

At some point in the fifties a lot of Hollywood people discovered
Barris and the customizers. It was somewhat the way the literary set
had discovered the puppeteer, Tony Sarg, during the thirties and
deified him in a very arty, in-groupy way, only I think in the case of
Hollywood and Barris there was something a lot more in-the-grain
about it. The people who end up in Hollywood are mostly Dionysian
sorts and they feel alien and resentful when confronted with the
Anglo-European ethos. They're a little slow to note the difference between topsides and sneakers, but they appreciate Cuban sunglasses.

In his showroom at Kustom City, down past the XPAK-400 air
car, Barris has a corner practically papered with photographs of
cars he has customized or handmade for Hollywood people: Harry
Karl, Jayne Mansfield, Elvis Presley, Liberace, and even celebrities
from the outside like Barry Goldwater (a Jaguar with a lot of air-
plane-style dials on the dashboard) and quite a few others. In fact,
he built most of the wild cars that show-business people come up
with for publicity purposes. He did the "diamond-dust" paint job on
the Bobby Darin Dream Car, which was designed and built by
Andy DiDia of Detroit. That car is an example, par excellence, of
baroque streamlining, by the way. It was badly panned when pictures of it were first published, mainly because it looked like Darin
was again forcing his ego on the world. But as baroque modern

sculpture — again, given the fantasy quotient in cars to begin with — it is pretty good stuff.

As the hot-rod and custom-car-show idea began catching on, and there are really quite a few big ones now, including one at the Coliseum up at Columbus Circle last year, it became like the culture boom in the other arts. The big names, particularly Barris and Roth but also Starbird, began to make a lot of money in the same thing Picasso has made a lot of money in: reproductions. Barris' creations are reproduced by AMT Models as model cars. Roth's are reproduced by Revel. The way people have taken to these models makes it clearer still that what we have here is no longer a car but a design object, an *objet*, as they say.

Of course, it's not an unencumbered art form like oil painting or most conventional modern sculpture. It carries a lot of mental baggage with it, plain old mechanical craftsmanship, the connotations of speed and power and the aforementioned mystique that the teenage netherworld brings to cars. What you have is something more like sculpture in the era of Benvenuto Cellini, when sculpture was always more tied up with religion and architecture. In a lot of other ways it's like the Renaissance, too. Young customizers have come to Barris' shop, for example, like apprentices coming to the feet of the master. Barris said there were eleven young guys in Los Angeles right now who had worked for him and then gone out on their own, and he doesn't seem to begrudge them that.

"But they take on too much work," he told me. "They want a name, fast, and they take on a lot of work, which they do for practically nothing, just to get a name. They're usually undercapitalized to begin with, and they take on too much work, and they can't deliver and they go bankrupt."

There's another side to this, too. You have the kid from the small town in the Midwest who's like the kid from Keokuk who wants to go to New York and live in the Village and be an artist and the like — he means, you know, things around home are but *hopelessly*, totally square; home and all that goes with it. Only the kid from the Midwest who wants to be a custom-car artist goes to Los Angeles to do it. He does pretty much the same thing. He lives a kind of suburban bohemian life and takes odd jobs and spends the rest of his time at the feet of somebody like Barris, working on cars.

I ran into a kid like that at Barris'. We were going through his place, back into his interiors—car interiors—department, and we came upon Ronny Camp. Ronny is twenty-two, but he looks about eighteen because he has teen-age posture. Ronny is, in fact, a bright and sensitive kid with an artistic eye, but at first glance he seems always to have his feet propped up on a table or something so you can't walk past, and you have to kind of bat them down, and he then screws up his mouth and withdraws his eyeballs to the optic chiasma and glares at you with his red sulk. That was the misleading first impression.

Ronny was crazy over automobiles and nobody in his hometown, Lafayette, Indiana, knew anything about customizing. So one day Ronny packs up and tells the folks, This is it, I'm striking out for hip territory, Los Angeles, where a customizing artist is an artist. He had no idea where he was going, you understand, all he knew was that he was going to Barris' shop and make it from there. So off he goes in his 1960 Chevrolet.

Ronny got a job at a service station and poured every spare cent into getting the car customized at Barris'. His car was right there while we were talking, a fact I was very aware of, because he never looked at me. He never took his eyes off that car. It's what is called semi-custom. Nothing has been done to it to give it a really sculptural quality, but a lot of streamlining details have been added. The main thing you notice is the color—tangerine flake. This paint—one of Barris' Kandy Kolor concoctions—makes the car look like it has been encrusted with chips of some kind of semi-precious ossified tangerine, all coated with a half-inch of clear lacquer. There used to be very scholarly and abstruse studies of color and color symbolism around the turn of the century, and theorists concluded that preferences for certain colors were closely associated with rebelliousness, and these are the very same colors many of the kids go for—purple, carnal yellow, various violets and lavenders and fuchsias and many other of these Kandy Kolors.

After he got his car fixed up, Ronny made a triumphal progress back home. He won the trophy in his class at the national hot-rod and custom-car show in Indianapolis, and he came tooling into Lafayette, Indiana, and down the main street in his tangerine-flake 1960 Chevrolet. It was like Ezra Pound going back to Hamilton,

New York, with his Bollingen plaque and saying, Here I am, Hamilton, New York. The way Ronny and Barris tell it, the homecoming was a big success—all the kids thought Ronny was all right, after all, and he made a big hit at home. I can't believe the part about home. I mean, I can't really believe Ronny made a hit with a tangerine-flake Chevrolet. But I like to conjecture about his parents. I don't know anything about them, really. All I know is, *I* would have had a hell of a lump in my throat if I had seen Ronny coming up to the front door in his tangerine-flake car, bursting so flush and vertical with triumph that no one would ever think of him as a child of the red sulk—Ronny, all the way back from California with his grail.

Along about 1957, Barris started hearing from the Detroit auto manufacturers.

"One day," he said, "I was working in the shop—we were over in Lynwood then—and Chuck Jordan from Cadillac walked in. He just walked in and said he was from Cadillac. I thought he meant the local agency. We had done this Cadillac for Liberace, the interior had his songs, all the notes, done in black and white Moroccan leather, and I thought he wanted to see something about that. But he said he was from the Cadillac styling center in Detroit and they were interested in our colors. Chuck—he's up there pretty good at Cadillac now, I think—said he had read some articles about our colors, so I mixed up some samples for him. I had developed a translucent paint, using six different ingredients, and it had a lot of brilliance and depth. That was what interested them. In this paint you look through a clear surface into the color, which is very brilliant. Anyway, this was the first time we had any idea they even knew who we were."

Since then Barris has made a lot of trips to Detroit. The auto companies, mainly GM and Ford, pump him for ideas about what the kids are going for. He tells them what's wrong with their cars, mainly that they aren't streamlined and sexy enough.

"But, as they told me, they have to design a car they can sell to the farmer in Kansas as well as the hot dog in Hollywood."

For that reason—the inevitable compromise—the customizers do not dream of working as stylists for the Detroit companies, although they deal with them more and more. It would be like Rene

Magritte or somebody going on the payroll of Continental Can to do great ideas of Western man. This is an old story in art, of course, genius vs. the organization. But the customizers don't think of corporate bureaucracy quite the way your conventional artist does, whether he be William Gropper or Larry Rivers, namely, as a lot of small-minded Babbitts, venal enemies of culture, etc. They just think of the big companies as part of that vast mass of *adult* America, sclerotic from years of just being too old, whose rules and ideas weigh down upon Youth like a vast, bloated sac. Both Barris and Roth have met Detroit's Young Stylists, and seem to look upon them as monks from another country. The Young Stylists are designers Detroit recruits from the art schools and sets up in a room with clay and styluses and tells to go to it—start carving models, dream cars, new ideas. Roth especially cannot conceive of anyone having any valid concepts about cars who hasn't come out of the teen-age netherworld. And maybe he's right. While the Young Stylists sit in a north-lit studio smoothing out little Mondrian solids, Barris and Roth carry on in the Dionysian loop-the-loop of streamlined baroque modern.

I've mentioned Ed Roth several times in the course of this without really telling you about him. And I want to, because he, more than any other of the customizers, has kept alive the spirit of alienation and rebellion that is so important to the teen-age ethos that customizing grew up in. He's also the most colorful, and the most intellectual, and the most capricious. Also the most cynical. He's the Salvador Dali of the movement—a surrealist in his designs, a showman by temperament, a prankster. Roth is really too bright to stay within the ethos, but he stays in it with a spirit of luxurious obstinacy. Any style of life is going to produce its celebrities if it sticks to its rigid standards, but in the East a talented guy would most likely be drawn into the Establishment in one way or another. That's not so inevitable in California.

I had been told that Roth was a surly guy who never bathed and was hard to get along with, but from the moment I first talked to him on the telephone he was an easy guy and very articulate. His studio—and he calls it a studio, by the way—is out in Maywood, on the other side of the city from North Hollywood, in what looked to me like a much older and more run-down section. When I walked

up, Roth was out on the apron of his place doing complicated drawings and lettering on somebody's ice-cream truck with an airbrush.
I knew right away it was Roth from pictures I had seen of him; he
has a beatnik-style beard. "Ed Roth?" I said. He said yeah and we
started talking and so forth. A little while later we were sitting in a
diner having a couple of sandwiches and Roth, who was wearing a
short-sleeved T shirt, pointed to this huge tattoo on his left arm that
says "Roth" in the lettering style with big serifs that he uses as his
signature. "I had that done a couple of years ago because guys keep
coming up to me saying, 'Are you Ed Roth?'"

Roth is a big, powerful guy, about six feet four, two hundred
seventy pounds, thirty-one years old. He has a constant sort of
court attendant named Dirty Doug, a skinny little guy who blew in
from out of nowhere, sort of like Ronny Camp over at Barris'. Dirty
Doug has a job sweeping up in a steel mill, but what he obviously
lives for is the work he does around Roth's. Roth seems to have a lot
of sympathy for the Ronny Camp–Dirty Doug syndrome and keeps
him around as a permanent fixture. At Roth's behest, apparently,
Dirty Doug has dropped his last name, Kinney, altogether, and
refers to himself as Dirty Doug—not Doug. The relationship between Roth and Dirty Doug—which is sort of Quixote and Sancho
Panza, Holmes and Watson, Lone Ranger and Tonto, Raffles and
Bunny—is part of the folklore of the hot-rod and custom-car kids.
It even crops up in the hot-rod comic books, which are an interesting phenomenon in themselves. Dirty Doug, in this folklore, is
every rejected outcast little kid in the alien netherworld, and Roth is
the understanding, if rather overly pranksterish, protective giant or
Robin Hood—you know, a good-bad giant, not part of the Establishment.

Dirty Doug drove up in one of his two Cadillacs one Saturday
afternoon while I was at Roth's, and he had just gone through
another experience of rejection. The police had hounded him out of
Newport. He has two Cadillacs, he said, because one is always in
the shop. Dirty Doug's cars, like most customizers', are always in
the process of becoming. The streaks of "primer" paint on the Cadillac he was driving at the time had led to his rejection in Newport.
He had driven to Newport for the weekend. "All the cops have to do
is see paint like that and already you're 'one of those hot-rodders,'"

he said. "They practically followed me down the street and gave me a ticket every twenty-five feet. I was going to stay the whole weekend, but I came on back."

At custom-car shows, kids are always asking Roth, "Where's Dirty Doug?", and if Dirty Doug couldn't make it for some reason, Roth will recruit any kid around who knows the pitch and install him as Dirty Doug, just to keep the fans happy.

Thus Roth protects the image of Dirty Doug even when the guy's not around, and I think it becomes a very important piece of mythology. The thing is, Roth is not buying the act of the National Hot Rod Association, which for its own reasons, not necessarily the kid's reasons, is trying to assimilate the hot-rod ethos into conventional America. It wants to make all the kids look like candidates for the Peace Corps or something.

The heart of the contretemps between the NHRA Establishment and Roth can be illustrated in their slightly different approach to drag racing on the streets. The Establishment tries to eliminate the practice altogether and restricts drag racing to certified drag strips and, furthermore, lets the people know about that. They encourage the hot-rod clubs to help out little old ladies whose cars are stuck in the snow and then hand them a card reading something like, "You have just been assisted by a member of the Blue Bolt Hot Rod Club, an organization of car enthusiasts dedicated to promoting safety on our highways."

Roth's motto is: "Hell, if a guy wants to go, let him *go*."

Roth's designs are utterly baroque. His air car—the Rotar—is not nearly as good a piece of design as Barris', but his beatnik Bandit is one of the great *objets* of customizing. It's a very Rabelaisian *tour de force*—a twenty-first century version of a '32 Ford hot-rod roadster. And Roth's new car, the Mysterion, which he was working on when I was out there, is another *tour de force*, this time in the hottest new concept in customizing, asymmetrical design. Asymmetrical design, I gather, has grown out of the fact that the driver sits on one side of the car, not in the middle, thereby giving a car an eccentric motif to begin with. In Roth's Mysterion—a bubbletop coupe powered by two 406-horsepower Thunderbird motors—a thick metal arm sweeps up to the left from the front bumper level, as from the six to the three on a clock, and at the top of it is an elliptical shape housing a bank of three headlights. No headlights on the right side at all; just a small clearance light to orient the oncoming driver. This big arm, by the way, comes up in a spherical geometrical arc, not a flat plane. Balancing this, as far as the design goes, is an arm that comes up over the back of the bubbletop on the right side, like from the nine to the twelve on a clock, also in a spherical arc, if you can picture all this. Anyway, this car takes the streamline and the abstract curve and baroque curvilinear one step further, and I wouldn't be surprised to see it inspiring Detroit designs in the years to come.

Roth is a brilliant designer, but as I was saying, his conduct and his attitude dilutes the Halazone with which the Establishment is trying to transfuse the whole field. For one thing, Roth, a rather thorough-going bohemian, kept turning up at the car shows in a T shirt. That was what he wore at the big National Show at the New York Coliseum, for example. Roth also insists on sleeping in a car or station wagon while on the road, even though he is making a lot of money now and could travel first class. Things came to a head early this year when Roth was out in Terre Haute, Indiana, for a show. At night Roth would just drive his car out in a cornfield, lie back on the front seat, stick his feet out the window and go to sleep. One morning some kid came by and saw him and took a picture while Roth was still sleeping and sent it to the model company Roth has a contract with, Revel, with a note saying, "Dear Sirs: Here is a picture of the man you say on your boxes is the King of the Customizers." The way Roth tells it, it must have been an extraordinarily good camera, because, he says with considerable pride, "There were a bunch of flies flying around my feet, and this picture showed all of them."

Revel asked Roth if he wouldn't sort of spruce up a little bit for the image and all that, and so Roth entered into a kind of reverse rebellion. He bought a full set of tails, silk hat, boiled shirt, cuff links, studs, the whole apparatus, for $215, also a monocle, and now he comes to all the shows like that. "I bow and kiss all the girls' hands," he told me. "The guys get pretty teed off about that, but what can they do? I'm being a perfect gentleman."

To keep things going at the shows, where he gets $1000 to $2000 per appearance—he's that much of a drawing card—Roth creates and builds one new car a year. This is the Dali pattern, too. Dali usually turns out one huge and (if that's possible any more) shocking painting each year or so and ships it on over to New York, where they install it in Carstairs or hire a hall if the thing is too big, and Dali books in at the St. Regis and appears on television wearing a rhinoceros horn on his forehead. The new car each year also keeps Roth's model-car deal going. But most of Roth's income right now is the heavy business he does in Weirdo and Monster shirts. Roth is very handy with the airbrush—has a very sure hand—and one day at a car show he got the idea of drawing a grotesque cartoon on some guy's sweat shirt with the airbrush, and that started the Weirdo shirts. The typical Weirdo shirt is in a vein of draftsmanship you might call Mad Magazine Bosch, very slickly done for something so grotesque, and will show a guy who looks like Frankenstein, the big square steam-shovel jaw and all, only he has a wacky leer on his face, at the wheel of a hot-rod roadster, and usually he has a round object up in the air in his right hand that looks like it is attached to the dash board by a cord. This, it turns out, is the gearshift. It doesn't look like a gearshift to me, but every kid knows immediately what it is.

"Kids *love* dragging a car," Roth told me. "I mean they really love it. And what they love the most is when they shift from low to second. They get so they can practically *feel* the r.p.m.'s. They can shift without hardly hitting the clutch at all."

These shirts always have a big caption, and usually something rebellious or at least alienated, something like "MOTHER IS WRONG" or "BORN TO LOSE."

"A teen-ager always has resentment to adult authority," Roth told me. "These shirts are like a tattoo, only it's a tattoo they can take off if they want to."

I gather Roth doesn't look back on his own childhood with any great relish. Apparently his father was pretty strict and never took any abiding interest in Roth's creative flights, which were mostly in the direction of cars, like Barris'.

"You've got to be real careful when you raise a kid," Roth told me several times. "You've got to spend time with him. If he's working on something, building something, you've got to work with him." Roth's early career was almost exactly like Barris', the hot rods, the drive-ins, the drag racing, the college (East Los Angeles Junior College and UCLA), taking mechanical drawing, the chopped and channeled '32 Ford (a big favorite with all the hot-rodders), purple paint, finally the first custom shop, one stall in a ten-stall body shop.

"They threw me out of there," Roth said, "because I painted a can of Lucky Lager beer on the wall with an airbrush. I mean, it was a perfect can of Lucky Lager beer, all the details, the highlights, the seals, the small print, the whole thing. Somehow this can of Lucky Lager beer really bugged the guy who owned the place. Here was this can of Lucky Lager beer on *his* wall."

The Establishment can't take this side of Roth, just as no Establishment could accommodate Dadaists for very long. Beatniks more easily than Dadaists. The trick has always been to absorb them somehow. So far Roth has resisted absorption.

"We were the real gangsters of the hot-rod field, " Roth said. "They keep telling us we have a rotten attitude. We have a different attitude, but that doesn't make us rotten."

Several times, though, Roth would chuckle over something, usually some particularly good gesture he had made, like the Lucky Lager, and say, "I am a real rotten guy."

Roth pointed out, with some insight, I think, that the kids have a revealing vocabulary. They use the words "rotten," "bad" and "tough" in a very fey, ironic way. Often a particularly baroque and sleek custom car will be called a "big, bad Merc" (for Mercury) or something like that. In this case "bad" means "good," but it also retains some of the original meaning of "bad." The kids know that to adults, like their own parents, this car is going to look sinister and somehow like an assault on their style of life. Which it is. It's rebellion, which the parents don't go for—"bad," which the kids *do* go for, "bad" meaning "good."

Roth said that Detroit is beginning to understand that there are just a hell of a lot of these bad kids in the United States and that they are growing up. "And they want a better car. They don't want an old man's car."

Roth has had pretty much the same experience as Barris with the motor companies. He has been taken to Detroit and feted and offered a job as a designer and a consultant. But he never took it seriously.

"I met a lot of the young designers," said Roth. "They were nice guys and they know a lot about design, but none of them has actually done a car. They're just up there working away on those clay models."

I think this was more than the craftsman's scorn of the designer who never actually does the work, like some of the conventional sculptors today who have never chiseled a piece of stone or cast anything. I think it was more that the young Detroit stylists came to the automobile strictly from art school and the abstract world of design—rather than via the teen-age mystique of the automobile and the teen-age ethos of rebellion. This status-group feeling is very important to Roth, and to Barris, for that matter, because it was only because of the existence of this status group—and this style of life—that custom-car sculpture developed at all.

With the Custom Car Caravan on the road—it has already reached Freedomland—the manufacturers may be well on the way to routinizing the charisma, as Max Weber used to say, which is to say, bringing the whole field into a nice, safe, vinyl-glamorous marketable ball of polyethylene. It's probably already happening. The customizers will end up like those poor bastards in Haiti, the artists, who got too much, too soon, from Selden Rodman and the other folk-doters on the subject of primitive genius, so they're all down there at this moment carving African masks out of mahogany— what I mean is, they never *had* an African mask in Haiti before Selden Rodman got there.

I think Roth has a premonition that something like that is liable to happen, although it will happen to him last, if at all. I couldn't help but get a kick out of what Roth told me about his new house. We had been talking about how much money he was making, and he told me how his taxable income was only about $6200 in 1959, but might hit $15,000 this year, maybe more, and he mentioned he was building a new house for his wife and five kids down at Newport, near the beach. I immediately asked him for details, hoping to hear about an utterly baroque piece of streamlined architecture.

"No, this is going to be my wife's house, the way she wants it, nothing way out; I mean, she has to do the home scene." He has also given her a huge white Cadillac, by the way, unadorned except for his signature—"Roth"—with those big serifs, on the side. I saw the thing, it's huge, and in the back seat were his children, very sweet-looking kids, all drawing away on drawing pads.

But I think Roth was a little embarrassed that he had disappointed me on the house, because he told me his idea of the perfect house—which turned out to be a kind of ironic parable:

"This house would have this big, round living room with a dome over it, you know? Right in the middle of the living room would be a huge television set on a swivel so you could turn it and see it from wherever you are in the room. And you have this huge easy chair for yourself, you know the kind that you can lean back to about ninety-three different positions and it vibrates and massages your back and all that, and this chair is on tracks, like a railroad yard.

"You can take one track into the kitchen, which just shoots off one side of the living room, and you can ride backward if you want to and watch the television all the time, and of course in the meantime you've pressed a lot of buttons so your TV dinner is cooking in the kitchen and all you have to do is go and take it out of the oven.

"Then you can roll right back into the living room, and if somebody rings the doorbell you don't move at all. You just press a button on this big automatic console you have by your chair and the front door opens, and you just yell for the guy to come in, and you can keep watching television.

"At night, if you want to go to bed, you take another track into the bedroom, which shoots off on another side, and you just kind of roll out of the chair into the sack. On the ceiling above your bed you have another TV set, so you can watch all night."

Roth is given, apparently, to spinning out long Jean Shepherd stories like this with a very straight face, and he told me all of this very seriously. I guess I didn't look like I was taking it very seriously, because he said, "I have a TV set over the bed in my house right now—you can ask my wife."

I met his wife, but I didn't ask her. The funny thing is, I did find myself taking the story seriously. To me it was a sort of parable of the Bad Guys, and the Custom Sculpture. The Bad Guys built themselves a little world and got onto something good and then the Establishment, all sorts of Establishments, began closing in, with a lot of cajolery, thievery and hypnosis, and in the end, thrown into a vinyl Petri dish, the only way left to tell the whole bunch of them where to head in was to draw them a huge asinine picture of themselves, which they were sure to like. After all, Roth's dream house is nothing more than his set of boiled shirt and tails expanded into a whole universe. And he is not really very hopeful about that either.

Jules Siegel

No pop group embodied Southern Californian youth culture more than the Beach Boys, whose odes to the surf and hot-rod scenes, fusing exquisite vocal harmonies inspired by the Four Freshmen with high-powered, state-of-the-art studio production techniques, dominated the music charts in the early 1960s. Their succession of hits ("Little Deuce Coupe," "I Get Around," and many others) owed everything to the creative brilliance and obsessive perfectionism of Brian Wilson. Wilson's temperament, however, was far removed from the self-satisfied hedonism proclaimed by "Fun, Fun, Fun," and he began to give free rein to more complex ambitions in the masterful *Pet Sounds* (1966) and "Good Vibrations" (1967). The follow-up was meant to be an album called *Smile*, but as Jules Siegel (b. 1935) reveals in this journalistic account, there were many factors—the drug culture of the late 1960s, the psychic intensities of the L.A. pop scene, and Brian Wilson's own insecurities—conspiring to bring about instead a debacle of extraordinary proportions. In his collection *Record*, Siegel notes that the piece was rejected by *The Saturday Evening Post* before it was published in the inaugural issue of *Cheetah* in October 1967.

GOODBYE SURFING, HELLO GOD!

It was just another day of greatness at Gold Star Recording Studios on Santa Monica Boulevard in Hollywood. In the morning four long-haired kids had knocked out two hours of sound for a record plugger who was trying to curry favor with a disk jockey friend of theirs in San Jose. Nobody knew it at the moment, but out of that two hours there were about three minutes that would hit the top of the charts in a few weeks, and the record plugger, the disk jockey and the kids would all be hailed as geniuses, but geniuses with a very small g.

Now, however, in the very same studio a Genius with a very large capital G was going to produce a hit. There was no doubt it would be a hit because this Genius was Brian Wilson. In four years of recording for Capitol Records, he and his group, the Beach Boys, had made surfing music a national craze, sold 16 million singles and earned gold records for 10 of their 12 albums.

Not only was Brian going to produce a hit, but also, one gathered, he was going to show everybody in the music business exactly where it was at; and where it was at, it seemed, was that Brian Wilson was not merely a Genius—which is to say a steady commercial success—but rather, like Bob Dylan and John Lennon, a GENIUS—which is to say a steady commercial success and hip besides.

Until now, though, there were not too many hip people who would have considered Brian Wilson and the Beach Boys hip, even though he had produced one very hip record, "Good Vibrations," which had sold more than a million copies, and a super-hip album, *Pet Sounds*, which didn't do very well at all—by previous Beach Boys sales standards. Among the hip people he was still on trial, and the question discussed earnestly among the recognized authorities on what is and what is not hip was whether or not Brian Wilson was hip, semi-hip or square.

But walking into the control room with the answers to all questions such as this was Brian Wilson himself, wearing a competition-stripe surfer's T-shirt, tight white duck pants, pale green bowling shoes and a red plastic toy fireman's helmet.

Everybody was wearing identical red plastic toy fireman's helmets. Brian's cousin and production assistant, Steve Korthoff was wearing one; his wife, Marilyn, and her sister, Diane Rovelle—Brian's secretary—were also wearing them, and so was a once-dignified writer from The Saturday Evening Post who had been following Brian around for two months.

Out in the studio, the musicians for the session were unpacking their instruments. In sport shirts and slacks, they looked like insurance salesmen and used-car dealers, except for one blonde female percussionist who might have been stamped out by a special machine that supplied plastic mannequin housewives for detergent commercials.

Controlled, a little bored after 20 years or so of nicely paid anonymity, these were the professionals of the popular music business, hired guns who did their job expertly and efficiently and then went home to the suburbs. If you wanted swing, they gave you swing.

A little movie-track lushness? Fine, here comes movie-track lushness. Now it's rock and roll? Perfect rock and roll, down the chute.

"Steve," Brian called out, "where are the rest of those fire hats? I want everybody to wear fire hats. We've really got to get into this thing." Out to the Rolls-Royce went Steve and within a few minutes all of the musicians were wearing fire hats, silly grins beginning to crack their professional dignity.

"All right, let's go," said Brian. Then, using a variety of techniques ranging from vocal demonstration to actually playing the instruments, he taught each musician his part. A gigantic fire howled out of the massive studio speakers in a pounding crash of pictorial music that summoned up visions of roaring, windstorm flames, falling timbers, mournful sirens and sweating firemen, building into a peak and crackling off into fading embers as a single drum turned into a collapsing wall and the fire-engine cellos dissolved and disappeared.

"When did he write this?" asked an astonished pop music producer who had wandered into the studio. "This is really fantastic! Man, this in unbelievable! How long has he been working on it?"

"About an hour," answered one of Brian's friends.

"I don't believe it. I just can't believe what I'm hearing," said the producer and fell into a stone glazed silence as the fire music began again.

For the next three hours, Brian Wilson recorded and re-recorded, take after take, changing the sound balance, adding echo, experimenting with a sound effects track of a real fire.

"Let me hear that again." "Drums, I think you're a little slow in that last part. Let's get right on it." "That was really good. Now, one more time, the whole thing." "All right, let me hear the cellos alone." "Great. Really great. Now let's *do it!*"

With 23 takes on tape and the entire operation responding to his touch like the black knobs on the control board, sweat glistening down his long, reddish hair onto his freckled face, the control room a litter of dead cigarette butts, Chicken Delight boxes, crumpled napkins, Coke bottles and all the accumulated trash of the physical end of the creative process, Brian stood at the board as the four speakers blasted the music into the room.

For the 24th time, the drum crashed and the sound effects crackle faded and stopped.

"Thank you, said Brian, into the control room mike. "Let me hear that back." Feet shifting, his body still, eyes closed, head moving seal-like to his music, he stood under the speakers and listened. "Let me hear that one more time." Again the fire roared. "Everybody come out and listen to this," Brian said to the musicians. They came into the control room and listened to what they had made.

"What do you think?" Brian asked.

"It's incredible, incredible," whispered one of the musicians, a man in his 50s, wearing a Hawaiian shirt and iridescent trousers and pointed black Italian shoes. "Absolutely incredible."

"Yeah," said Brian on the way home, an acetate trial copy or "dub" of the tape in his hands, the red plastic fire helmet still on his head. "Yeah, I'm going to call this 'Mrs. O'Leary's Fire' and I think it might just scare a whole lot of people."

As it turns out, however, Brian Wilson's magic fire music is not going to scare anybody — because nobody other than the few people who heard it in the studio will ever get to listen to it. A few days after the record was finished, a building across the street from the studio burned down and, according to Brian, there was also an unusually large number of fires in Los Angeles. Afraid that his music might in fact turn out to be magic fire music, Wilson destroyed the master.

"I don't have to do a big scary fire like that," he later said. "I can do a candle and it's still fire. That would have been a really bad vibration to let out on the world, that Chicago fire. The next one is going to be a candle."

A person who thinks of himself as understanding would probably interpret this episode as an example of perhaps too-excessive artistic perfectionism. One with psychiatric inclinations would hear all this stuff about someone who actually believed music could cause fires and start using words such as neurosis and maybe even psychosis. A true student of spoken hip, however, would say *hang-up*, which covers all of the above.

As far as Brian's pretensions toward hipness are concerned, no label could do him worse harm. In the hip world, there is a widespread idea that really hip people don't have hang-ups, which gives rise to the unspoken rule (unspoken because there is also the widespread idea that really hip people don't make *any* rules) that no one who wants to be thought of as hip ever reveals his hang-ups, except maybe to his guru, and in the strictest of privacy.

In any case, whatever his talent, Brian Wilson's attempt to win a hip following and reputation foundered for many months in an obsessive cycle of creation and destruction that threatened not only his career and his future but also his marriage, his friendships, his relationship with the Beach Boys and, some of his closest friends worried, his mind.

For a boy who used to be known in adolescence as a lover of sweets, the whole thing must have begun to taste very sour; yet, this particular phase of Brian's drive toward whatever his goal of supreme success might be began on a rising tide that at first looked as if it would carry him and the Beach Boys beyond the Beatles, who had started just about the same time they did, into the number-one position in the international pop music fame-and-power competition.

"About a year ago I had what I consider a very religious experience," Wilson told Los Angeles writer Tom Nolan in 1966. "I took LSD, a full dose of LSD, and later, another time, I took a smaller dose. And I learned a lot of things, like patience, understanding. I can't teach you or tell you what I learned from taking it, but I consider it a very religious experience."

A short time after his LSD experience, Wilson began work on the record that was to establish him right along with the Beatles as one of the most important innovators in modern popular music. It was called "Good Vibrations," and it took more than six months, 90 hours of tape and 11 complete versions before a three-minute-35-second final master tape satisfied him. Among the instruments on "Good Vibrations" was an electronic device called a theremin, which had its debut in the soundtrack of the movie *Spellbound*, back in the Forties. To some people, "Good Vibrations" was considerably crazier than Gregory Peck had been in the movie, but to others, Brian Wilson's new record, along with his somewhat earlier LP release, "Pet Sounds," marked the beginning of a new era in pop music.

"They've Found the New Sound at Last!" shrieked the headline over a London Sunday Express review as "Good Vibrations" hit the

English charts at number six and leaped to number one the following week. Within a few weeks, the Beach Boys had pushed the Beatles out of first place in England's New Musical Express' annual poll. In America, "Good Vibrations" sold nearly 400,000 copies in four days before reaching number one several weeks later and earning a gold record within another month when it hit the one-million sale mark.

In America, where there is none of the Beach Boys' California-mystique that adds a special touch of romance to their records and appearances in Europe and England, the news had not really reached all of the people whose opinion can turn popularity into fashionability. With the exception of a professor of show business (right, professor of show business; in California such a thing is not considered unusual) who turned up one night to interview Brian, and a few young writers (such as The Village Voice's Richard Goldstein, Paul Williams of Crawdaddy!, and Lawrence Dietz of New York Magazine) not too many opinion makers were prepared to accept the Beach Boys into the mainstream of the culture industry.

"Listen man," said San Francisco music critic Ralph Gleason who had only recently graduated from jazz into Bob Dylan and was apparently not yet ready for any more violent twists, "I recognize the L.A. hype when I hear it. I know all about the Beach Boys and I think I liked them better before, if only for sociological reasons, if you understand what I mean."

"As for the Beach Boys," an editor of The Saturday Evening Post chided his writer, who had filed the world's longest Western Union telegram of a story, "I want you to understand that as an individual you can feel that Brian Wilson is the greatest musician of our time, and maybe the greatest human being, but as a reporter you have got to maintain your objectivity."

"They want me to put him down," the writer complained. "That's their idea of objectivity—the put-down.

"It has to do with this idea that it's not hip to be sincere," he continued, "and they really want to be hip. What they don't understand is that last year hip was sardonic—camp, they called it. This year hip is sincere.

"When somebody as corny as Brian Wilson starts singing right out front about God and I start writing it—very *sincerely*, you understand—it puts them very uptight.

"I think it's because it reminds them of all those terribly sincere hymns and sermons they used to have to listen to in church when they were kinds in Iowa or Ohio.

"Who knows? Maybe they're right. I mean, who needs all this goddamn intense sincerity all the time?"

What all this meant, of course, was that everybody agreed that Brian Wilson and the Beach Boys were still too square. It would take more than "Good Vibrations" and *Pet Sounds* to erase three-and-a-half years of "Little Deuce Coupe"—a *lot* more if you counted in those J. C. Penney-style custom-tailored, kandy-striped sport shirts they insisted on wearing on stage.

Brian, however, had not yet heard the news, it appeared, and was steadily going about the business of trying to become hip. The Beach Boys, who have toured without him ever since he broke down during one particularly wearing trip, were now in England and Europe, phoning back daily reports of enthusiastic fan hysteria—screaming little girls tearing at their flesh, wild press conferences, private chats with the Rolling Stones. Washed in the heat of a kind of attention they had never received in the United States even at the height of their commercial success, three Beach Boys—Brian's brothers, Dennis and Carl, and his cousin, Mike Love—walked into a London Rolls-Royce showroom and bought four Phantom VII limousines, one for each of them and a fourth for Brian. Al Jardine and Bruce Johnston, the Beach Boys who are not corporate members of the Beach Boys' enterprises, sent their best regards and bought themselves some new clothing.

"I think this London thing has really helped," said Brian with satisfaction after he had made the color selection on his $32,000 toy—a ducal-burgundy lacquered status symbol ordinarily reserved for heads of state. "That's just what the boys needed, a little attention to jack up their confidence." Then, learning that he wouldn't be able to have his new car for three months, he went out and bought an interim Rolls-Royce for $20,000 from Mamas and Papas producer Lou Adler, taking possession of the automobile just in time to meet his group at the airport as they returned home.

"It's a great environment for conducting business," he explained as his friend and former road manager, Terry Sachen, hastily pressed into service as interim chauffeur for the interm Rolls-Royce, informally uniformed in his usual fringed deerskins and moccasins, drove the car through Hollywood and to one of Brian's favorite eating places, the Pioneer Chicken drive-in on Sunset Boulevard.

"This car is really out of sight," said Brian, filling up on fried shrimp in the basket. "Next time we go up to Capitol, I'm going to drive up in my Rolls-Royce limo. You've got to do those things with a little style. It's not just an ordinary visit that way—it's an arrival, right? Wow! That's really great—an *arrival*, in my limo. It'll blow their minds!"

Whether or not the interim Rolls-Royce actually ever blew the minds of the hard-nosed executives who run Capitol Records is something to speculate on, but no one in the record industry with a sense of history could have failed to note that this very same limousine had once belonged to John Lennon; and in the closing months of 1966, with the Beach Boys home in Los Angeles, Brian rode the "Good Vibrations" high, driving forward in bursts of enormous energy that seemed destined before long to earn him the throne of the international empire of pop music still ruled by John Lennon and the Beatles.

At the time, it looked as if the Beatles were ready to step down. Their summer concerts in America had been only moderately successful at best, compared to earlier years. There were ten thousand empty seats at Shea Stadium in New York and 11 lonely fans at the airport in Seattle. Mass media, underground press, music-industry trade papers and the fan magazines were filled with fears that the Beatles were finished, that the group was breaking up. Lennon was off acting in a movie; McCartney was walking around London alone, said to be carrying a giant torch for his sometime girl friend, Jane Asher; George Harrison was getting deeper and deeper into a mystical Indian thing under the instruction of sitar-master Ravi Shankar; and Ringo was collecting material for a Beatles museum.

In Los Angeles, Brian Wilson was riding around in the Rolls-Royce that had once belonged to John Lennon, pouring a deluge of new sounds onto miles of stereo tape in three different recording studios booked day and night for him in month-solid blocks, holding court nightly at his $240,000 Beverly Hills Babylonian-modern home, and, after guests left, sitting at his grand piano until dawn, writing new material.

The work in progress was an album called *Smile.* "I'm writing a teen-age symphony to God," Brian told dinner guests on an October evening. He then played for them the collection of black acetate trial records which lay piled on the floor of his red imitation-velvet wallpapered bedroom with its leopard-print bedspread. In the bathroom, above the wash basin, there was a plastic color picture of Jesus Christ with trick effect eyes that appeared to open and close when you moved your head. Sophisticate newcomers pointed it out to each other and laughed slyly, almost hoping to find a Keane painting among decorations ranging from Lava Lamps to a department-store rack of dozens of dolls, each still in its plastic bubble container, the whole display trembling like a space-age Christmas tree to the music flowing out into the living room.

Brian shuffled through the acetates, most of which were unlabeled, identifying each by subtle differences in the patterns of the grooves. He had played them so often he knew the special look of each record the way you know the key to your front door by the shape of its teeth. Most were instrumental tracks, cut while the Beach Boys were in Europe, and for these Brian supplied the vocal in a high sound that seemed to come out of his head rather than his throat as he somehow managed to create complicated four and five part harmonies with only his own voice.

"Rock, rock, Plymouth rock roll over," Brian sang. "Bicycle rider, see what you done done to the church of the native American Indian . . . Over and over the crow cries uncover the cornfields . . . Who ran the Iron Horse . . . Out in the farmyard the cook is chopping lumber; out in the barnyard the chickens do their number . . . Bicycle rider see what you done done . . ."

A panorama of American history filled the room as the music shifted from theme to theme; the tinkling harpsichord-sounds of the bicycle rider pushed sad Indian sounds across the continent; the Iron Horse pounded across the plains in a wide-open rolling rhythm that summoned up visions of the old West; civilized chickens bobbed up and down in a tiny ballet of comic barnyard melody; the inexorable bicycle music, cold and charming as an infinitely talented music box, reappeared and faded away.

Like medieval choirboys, the voices of the Beach Boys pealed out in wordless prayer from the last acetate, thirty seconds of chorale that reached upward to the vaulted stone ceilings of an empty cathedral lit by thousands of tiny votive candles melting at last into one small, pure pool that whispered a universal *amen* in a sigh without words.

Brian's private radio show was finished. In the dining room a candle-lit table with a dark blue cloth was set for ten persons. In the kitchen, Marilyn Wilson was trying to get the meal organized and served, aided and hindered by the chattering suggestions of the guests' wives and girl friends. When everyone was seated and waiting for the food, Brian tapped his knife idly on a white china plate.

"Listen to that," he said. "That's really great!" Everybody listened as Brian played the plate. "Come on, let's get something going here," he ordered. "Michael—do this. David—you do this." A plate-and-spoon musicale began to develop as each guest played a distinctly different technique, rhythm and melody under Brian's enthusiastic direction.

"That's absolutely unbelievable!" said Brian. "Isn't that unbelievable? That's so unbelievable I'm going to put it on the album. Michael, I want you to get a sound system up here tomorrow and I want everyone to be here tomorrow night. We're going to get this on tape."

Brian Wilson's plate-and-spoon musicale never did reach the public, but only because he forgot about it. Other sounds equally strange have found their way onto his records. On *Pet Sounds*, for example, on some tracks there is an odd, soft, hollow percussion effect that most musicians assume is some kind of electronically transmuted drum sound—a conga drum played with a stick perhaps, or an Indian tom-tom. Actually, it's drummer Hal Blaine playing the bottom of a plastic jug that once contained Sparklettes spring water. And, of course, at the end of the record there is the strangely affecting track of a train roaring through a lonely railroad crossing as a bell clangs and Brian's dogs, Banana, a beagle, and Louie, a dark brown weimaraner, bark after it.

More significant, perhaps, to those who that night heard the original instrumental tracks for both *Smile* and the Beach Boys new single, "Heroes and Villains," is that entire sequences of extra-ordinary power and beauty are missing in the finished version of the single, and will undoubtedly be missing as well from *Smile* —victims of Brian's obsessive tinkering and, more importantly, sacrifices to the same strange combination of superstitious fear and God-like conviction of his own power he displayed when he destroyed the fire music.

The night of the dining-table concerto, it was the God-like con-fidence Brian must have been feeling as he put his guests on his trip, but the fear was soon to take over. At his house that night, he had assembled a new set of players to introduce into his life game, each of whom was to perform a specific role in the grander game he was playing with the world.

Earlier in the summer, Brian had hired Van Dyke Parks, a super-sophisticated young songwriter and composer, to collaborate with him on the lyrics for *Smile*. With Van Dyke working for him, he had a fighting chance against John Lennon, whose literary skill and Liverpudlian wit had been one of the most important factors in making the Beatles the darlings of the hip intelligentsia.

With that flank covered, Brian was ready to deal with some of the other problems of trying to become hip, the most important of which was how was he going to get in touch with some really hip people. In effect, the dinner party at the house was his first hip social event, and the star of the evening, so far as Brian was concerned, was Van Dyke Parks' manager, David Anderle, who showed up with a whole group of very hip people.

Elegant, cool and impossibly cunning, Anderle was an artist who has somehow found himself in the record business as an execu-tive for MGM Records, where he had earned himself a reputation as a genius by purportedly thinking up the million-dollar movie-TV-record offer that briefly lured Bob Dylan to MGM from Columbia until everybody had a change of heart and Dylan decided to go back home to Columbia.

Anderle had skipped back and forth between painting and the record business, with mixed results in both. Right now he was doing a little personal management and thinking about painting a lot. His appeal to Brian was simple: everybody recognized David Anderle as one of the hippest people in Los Angeles. In fact, he was something like the mayor of hipness as far as some people were concerned. And not only that, he was a genius.

Within six weeks, he was working for the Beach Boys; everything that Brian wanted seemed at last to be in reach. Like a magic genie, David Anderle produced miracles for him. A new Beach Boys record company was set up, Brother Records, with David Anderle at its head and, simultaneously, the Beach Boys sued Capitol Records in a move to force a renegotiation of their contract with the company.

The house was full of underground press writers. Anderle's friend Michael Vosse was on the Brother Records payroll out scouting TV contracts and performing other odd jobs. Another of Anderle's friends was writing the story on Brian for The Saturday Evening Post and a film crew from CBS-TV was up at the house for a documentary to be narrated by Leonard Bernstein. The Beach Boys were having meetings once or twice a week with teams of experts briefing them on corporate policy, drawing complicated chalk patterns as they described the millions of dollars everyone was going to earn out of all this.

As 1967 opened it seemed as though Brian and the Beach Boys were assured of a new world of success; yet something was going wrong. As the corporate activity reached a peak of intensity, Brian was becoming less and less productive and more and more erratic. *Smile*, which was to have been released for the Christmas season, remained unfinished. "Heroes and Villains," which was virtually complete, remained in the can, as Brian kept working out new little pieces and then scrapping them.

Van Dyke Parks had left and come back and would leave again, tired of being constantly dominated by Brian. Marilyn Wilson was having headaches and Dennis Wilson was leaving his wife. Session after session was canceled. One night a studio full of violinists waited while Brian tried to decide whether or not the vibrations were friendly or hostile. The answer was hostile and the session was canceled, at a cost of some $3,000. Everything seemed to be going wrong. Even the Post story fell through.

Brian seemed to be filled with secret fear. One night at the house, it began to surface. Marilyn sat nervously painting her fingernails as Brian stalked up and down, his face tight and his eyes small and red.

"What's the matter, Brian? You're really strung out," a friend asked.

"Yeah, I'm really strung out. Look, I mean I really feel strange. A really strange thing happened to me tonight. Did you see this picture, *Seconds*?"

"No, but I know what it's about; I read the book."

"Look, come into the kitchen; I really have to talk about this." In the kitchen they sat down in the black and white houndstooth-check wallpapered dinette area. A striped window shade clashed with the checks and the whole room vibrated like some kind of op art painting. Ordinarily, Brian wouldn't sit for more than a minute in it, but now he seemed to be unaware of anything except what he wanted to say.

"I walked into that movie," he said in a tense, high-pitched voice, "and the first thing that happened was a voice from the screen said 'Hello, Mr. Wilson.' It completely blew my mind. You've got to admit that's pretty spooky, right?"

"Maybe."

"That's not all. Then the whole thing was there. I mean my whole life. Birth and death and rebirth. The whole thing. Even the beach was in it, a whole thing about the beach. It was my whole life right there on the screen."

"It's just a coincidence, man. What are you getting all excited about?"

"Well, what if it isn't a coincidence? What if it's real? You know there's mind gangsters these days. There could be mind gangsters, couldn't there? I mean look at Spector, he could be involved in it, couldn't he? He's going into films. How hard would it be for him to set up something like that?"

"Brian, Phil Spector is not about to make a million-dollar movie just to scare you. Come on, stop trying to be so dramatic."

"All right, all right. I was just a little bit nervous about it," Brian said, after some more back and forth about the possibility that Phil

Spector, the record producer, had somehow influenced the making of *Seconds* to disturb Brian Wilson's tranquillity. "I just had to get it out of my system. You can see where something like that could scare someone, can't you?"

They went into Brian's den, a small room papered in psychedelic orange, blue, yellow and red wall fabric with rounded corners. At the end of the room there was a juke box filled with Beach Boy singles and Phil Spector hits. Brian punched a button and Spector's "Be My Baby" began to pour out at top volume.

"Spector has always been a big thing with me, you know. I mean I heard that song three and a half years ago and I knew that it was between him and me. I knew exactly where he was at and now I've gone beyond him. You can understand how that movie might get someone upset under those circumstances, can't you?"

Brian sat down at his desk and began to draw a little diagram on a piece of printed stationery with his name at the top in the kind of large fat script printers of charitable dinner journals use when the customer asks for a hand-lettered look. With a felt-tipped pen, Brian drew a close approximation of a growth curve. "Spector started the whole thing," he said, dividing the curve into periods. "He was the first one to use the studio. But I've gone beyond him now. I'm doing the spiritual sound, a white spiritual sound. Religious music. Did you hear the Beatles album? Religious, right? That's the whole movement. That's where I'm going. It's going to scare a lot of people.

"Yeah," Brain said, hitting his fist on the desk with a slap that sent the parakeets in the large cage facing him squalling and whistling. "Yeah," he said and smiled for the first time all evening. "That's where I'm going and it's going to scare a lot of people when I get there."

As the year drew deeper into winter, Brian's rate of activity grew more and more frantic, but nothing seemed to be accomplished. He tore the house apart and half redecorated it. One section of the living room was filled with a full-sized Arabian tent and the dining room, where the grand piano stood, was filled with sand to a depth of a foot or so and draped with nursery curtains. He had had his windows stained gray and put a sauna bath in the bedroom. He battled with his father and complained that his brothers weren't trying hard enough. He accused Mike Love of making too much money.

One by one, he canceled out the friends he had collected, sometimes for the strangest reasons. An acquaintance of several months who thought he had become extremely close with Brian showed up at a record session and found a guard barring the door. Michael Vosse came out to explain.

"Hey man, this is really terrible," said Vosse, smiling under a broad-brimmed straw hat. "It's not you, it's your chick. Brian says she's a witch and she's messing with his brain so bad by ESP that he can't work. It's like the Spector thing. You know how he is. Say, I'm really sorry." A couple of months later, Vosse was gone. Then, in the late spring, Anderle left. The game was over.

Several months later, the last move in Brian's attempt to win the hip community was played out. On July 15th, the Beach Boys were scheduled to appear at the Monterey International Pop Music Festival, a kind of summit of rock music with the emphasis on love, flowers and youth. Although Brian was a member of the board of this nonprofit event, the Beach Boys canceled their commitment to perform. The official reason was that their negotiations with Capitol Records were at a crucial stage and they had to get "Heroes and Villains" out right away. The second official reason was that Carl, who had been arrested for refusing to report for induction into the Army (he was later cleared in court), was so upset that he wouldn't be able to sing.

Whatever the merit in these reasons, the real one may have been closer to something John Phillips of the Mamas and Papas and a Monterey board member suggested: "Brian was afraid that the hippies from San Francisco would think the Beach Boys were square and boo them."

But maybe Brian was right. "Those candy-striped shirts just wouldn't have made it at Monterey, man," said David Anderle.

Whatever the case, at the end of the summer, "Heroes and Villains" was released in sharply edited form and *Smile* was reported to be on its way. In the meantime, however, the Beatles had released *Sergeant Pepper's Lonely Hearts Club Band* and John Lennon was riding about London in a bright yellow Phantom VII Rolls-Royce painted with flowers on the sides and his zodiac symbol on the top.

In Life magazine, Paul McCartney came out openly for LSD and in the Haight-Ashbury district of San Francisco George Harrison walked through the streets blessing the hippies. Ringo was still collecting material for a Beatles museum. However good *Smile* might turn out to be, it seemed somehow that once more the Beatles had outdistanced the Beach Boys.

Back during that wonderful period in the fall of 1996 when everybody seemed to be his friend and plans were being laid for Brother Records and all kinds of fine things, Brian had gone on a brief visit to Michigan to hear a Beach Boys concert. The evening of his return, each of his friends and important acquaintances received a call asking everyone to please come to the airport to meet Brian, it was very important. When they gathered at the airport, Brian had a photographer on hand to take a series of group pictures. For a long time, a huge mounted blow-up of the best of the photographs hung on the living room wall, with some thirty people staring out — everyone from Van Dyke Parks and David Anderle to Michael Vosse and Terry Sachen. In the foreground was The Saturday Evening Post writer looking sourly out at the world.

The picture is no longer on Brian's wall and most of the people in it are no longer his friends. One by one each of them has either stepped out of the picture or been forced out of it. The whole cycle has returned to its beginning. Brian, who started out in Hawthorne, Calif., with his two brothers and a cousin, once more has surrounded himself with relatives. The house in Beverly Hills is empty. Brian and Marilyn are living in their new Spanish Mission estate in Bel-Air, cheek by jowl with the Mamas and Papas' Cass Elliott.

What remains, of course, is "Heroes and Villains." And there is also a spectacular peak, a song called "Surf's Up" that Brian recorded for the first time in December in Columbia Records Studio A for a CBS-TV pop music documentary. Earlier in the evening the film crew had covered a Beach Boys vocal session which had gone very badly. Now, at midnight, the Beach Boys had gone home and Brian was sitting in the back of his car, smoking a joint.

In the dark car, he breathed heavily, his hands in his lap, eyes staring nowhere.

"All right," he said at last. "Let's just sit here and see if we can get into something positive, but without any words. Let's just get into something quiet and positive on a nonverbal level." There was a long silence.

"OK, let's go," he said, and then, quickly, he was in the studio rehearsing, spotlighted in the center of the huge dark room, the cameramen moving about him invisibly outside the light.

"Let's do it," he announced, and the tape began to roll. In the control room no one moved. David Oppenheim, the TV producer, forty-ish, handsome, usually studiously detached and professional, lay on the floor, hands behind his head, eyes closed. For three minutes and 27 seconds, Wilson played with delicate intensity, speaking moodily through the piano. Then he was finished. Oppenheim, whose last documentary had been a study of Stravinsky, lay motionless.

"That's it," Wilson said as the tape continued to whirl. The mood broke. As if awakening from heavy sleep the people stirred and shook their heads.

"I'd like to hear that," Wilson said. As his music replayed, he sang the lyrics in a high, almost falsetto voice, the cameras on him every second.

"The diamond necklace played the pawn," Wilson sang. ". . . A blind class aristocracy, back through the opera glass you see the pit and the pendulum drawn.

"Columnated ruins domino," his voice reached upward; the piano faltered a set of falling chords.

In a slow series of impressionistic images the song moved to its ending:

> *I heard the word:*
> *Wonderful thing!*
> *A children's song!*

On the last word Brian's voice rose and fell, like the ending of that prayer chorale he had played so many months before.

"That's really special," someone said.

"Special, that's right," said Wilson quietly. "Van Dyke and I really kind of thought we had done something special when we finished that one." He went back into the studio, put on the earphones and sang the song again for his audience in the control room, for the revolving tape recorder and for the cameras which relentlessly followed as he struggled to make manifest what still only existed as a perfect, incommunicable sound in his head.

At home, as the black acetate dub turned on his bedroom hi-fi set, Wilson tried to explain the words.

"It's a man at a concert," he said. "All around him there's the audience, playing their roles, dressed up in fancy clothes, looking through opera glasses, but so far away from the drama, from life — 'Back through the opera glass you see the pit and the pendulum drawn.'

"The music begins to take over. 'Columnated ruins domino.' Empires, ideas, lives, institutions — everything has to fall, tumbling like dominoes.

"He begins to awaken to the music; sees the pretentiousness of everything. 'The music hall a costly bow.' Then even the music is gone, turned into a trumpeter swan, into what the music really is.

"'Canvas the town and brush the backdrop.' He's off in his vision, on a trip. Reality is gone; he's creating it like a dream. 'Dove-nested towers.' Europe, a long time ago. 'The laughs come hard in Auld Lang Syne.' The poor people in the cellar taverns, trying to make themselves happy by singing.

"Then there's the parties, the drinking, trying to forget the wars, the battles at sea. 'While at port a do or die.' Ships in the harbor, battling it out. A kind of Roman Empire thing.

"'A choke of grief.' At his own sorrow and the emptiness of his life, because he can't even cry for the suffering in the world, for his own suffering.

"And then, hope. 'Surf's up! . . . Come about hard and join the once and often spring you gave.' Go back to the kids, to the beach, to childhood.

"'I heard the word' — of God; 'Wonderful thing' — the joy of enlightenment, of seeing God. And what is it? 'A children's song!' And then there's the song itself; the song of children; the song of the universe rising and falling in wave after wave, the song of God, hiding the love from us, but always letting us find it again, like a mother singing to her children."

The record was over. Wilson went into the kitchen and squirted Reddi-Whip direct from the can into his mouth; made himself a chocolate Great Shake, and ate a couple of candy bars.

"Of course that's a very intellectual explanation," he said. "But maybe sometimes you have to do an intellectual thing. If they don't get the words, they'll get the music. You can get hung up in words, you know. Maybe they work; I don't know." He fidgeted with a tele-scope.

"This thing is so bad," he complained. "So Mickey Mouse. It just won't work smoothly. I was really freaked out on astronomy when I was a kid. Baseball, too. I guess I went through a lot of phases. A lot of changes, too. But you can really get into things through the stars. And swimming. A lot of swimming. It's physical; really Zen, right? The whole spiritual thing is very physical. Swim-ming really does it sometimes." He sprawled on the couch and con-tinued in a very small voice.

"So that's what I'm doing. Spiritual music."

"Brian," Marilyn called as she came into the room wearing a quilted bathrobe, "do you want me to get you anything, honey? I'm going to sleep."

"No, Mar," he answered, rising to kiss his wife goodnight. "You go on to bed. I want to work for a while."

"C'mon kids," Marilyn yelled to the dogs as she padded off to bed. "Time for bed. Louie! Banana! Come to bed. Goodnight, Brian. Goodnight, everybody."

Wilson paced. He went to the piano and began to play. His guests moved toward the door. From the piano, his feet shuffling in the sand, he called a perfunctory goodbye and continued to play, a melody beginning to take shape. Outside, the piano spoke from the house. Brian Wilson's guests stood for a moment, listening. As they got into their car, the melancholy piano moaned.

"Here's one that's really outasight from the fantabulous Beach Boys!" screamed a local early morning Top-40 DJ from the car radio on the way home, a little hysterical as usual, his voice drown-ing out the sobbing introduction to the song.

"We're sending this one out for Bob and Carol in Pomona. They've been going steady now for six months. Happy six months, kids, and dig! 'Good Vibrations!' *The Beach Boys! Outasight!*"

Joan Didion

The essays of Joan Didion (b. 1934) revolutionized the popular conception of Southern California when they first appeared in the 1960s, reimag-
ining the place in terms of distance, dissonance, as a landscape where the
standard social "narratives" don't apply. In each of these four pieces, she
traces a different aspect of this sense of disconnection, presenting L.A. as a
city on the edge, yet at the same time a place emblematic of modern America rather than an exotic coastal bloom. "Los Angeles Notebook" enlarges
on Raymond Chandler's description of the Santa Ana winds; "The Getty"
brings questions of taste into sharp focus; and in "Quiet Days in Malibu"
and "Fire Season" Didion explores Los Angeles from an elemental stand-
point, entertaining the paradox that Eden might contain the seeds of its
own destruction, that paradise and devastation might necessarily go hand
in hand. Of all the writers who have tried to make sense of the Southland,
none has internalized this vision quite so deeply as Joan Didion, whose
every word contains an undertone of prickly dread.

LOS ANGELES NOTEBOOK

There is something uneasy in the Los Angeles air this afternoon,
some unnatural stillness, some tension. What it means is that
tonight a Santa Ana will begin to blow, a hot wind from the northeast
whining down through the Cajon and San Gorgonio Passes, blowing
up sandstorms out along Route 66, drying the hills and the nerves to
the flash point. For a few days now we will see smoke back in the
canyons, and hear sirens in the night. I have neither heard nor read
that a Santa Ana is due, but I know it, and almost everyone I have
seen today knows it too. We know it because we feel it. The baby
frets. The maid sulks. I rekindle a waning argument with the telephone company, then cut my losses and lie down, given over to whatever it is in the air. To live with the Santa Ana is to accept, consciously
or unconsciously, a deeply mechanistic view of human behavior.

I recall being told, when I first moved to Los Angeles and was
living on an isolated beach, that the Indians would throw themselves into the sea when the bad wind blew. I could see why. The

Pacific turned ominously glossy during a Santa Ana period, and one woke in the night troubled not only by the peacocks screaming in the olive trees but by the eerie absence of surf. The heat was surreal. The sky had a yellow cast, the kind of light sometimes called "earthquake weather." My only neighbor would not come out of her house for days, and there were no lights at night, and her husband roamed the place with a machete. One day he would tell me that he had heard a trespasser, the next a rattlesnake.

"On nights like that," Raymond Chandler once wrote about the Santa Ana, "every booze party ends in a fight. Meek little wives feel the edge of the carving knife and study their husbands' necks. Anything can happen." That was the kind of wind it was. I did not know then that there was any basis for the effect it had on all of us, but it turns out to be another of those cases in which science bears out folk wisdom. The Santa Ana, which is named for one of the canyons it rushes through, is a *foehn* wind, like the *foehn* of Austria and Switzerland and the *hamsin* of Israel. There are a number of persistent malevolent winds, perhaps the best known of which are the mistral of France and the Mediterranean sirocco, but a *foehn* wind has distinct characteristics: it occurs on the leeward slope of a mountain range and, although the air begins as a cold mass, it is warmed as it comes down the mountain and appears finally as a hot dry wind. Whenever and wherever a *foehn* blows, doctors hear about headaches and nausea and allergies, about "nervousness," about "depression." In Los Angeles some teachers do not attempt to conduct formal classes during a Santa Ana, because the children become unmanageable. In Switzerland the suicide rate goes up during the *foehn*, and in the courts of some Swiss cantons the wind is considered a mitigating circumstance for crime. Surgeons are said to watch the wind, because blood does not clot normally during a *foehn*. A few years ago an Israeli physicist discovered that not only during such winds, but for the ten or twelve hours which precede them, the air carries an unusually high ratio of positive to negative ions. No one seems to know exactly why that should be; some talk about friction and others suggest solar disturbances. In any case the positive ions are there, and what an excess of positive ions does, in the simplest terms, is make people unhappy. One cannot get much more mechanistic than that.

Easterners commonly complain that there is no "weather" at all in Southern California, that the days and the seasons slip by relentlessly, numbingly bland. That is quite misleading. In fact the climate is characterized by infrequent but violent extremes: two periods of torrential subtropical rains which continue for weeks and wash out the hills and send subdivisions sliding toward the sea; about twenty scattered days a year of the Santa Ana, which, with its incendiary dryness, invariably means fire. At the first prediction of a Santa Ana, the Forest Service flies men and equipment from northern California into the southern forests, and the Los Angeles Fire Department cancels its ordinary non-firefighting routines. The Santa Ana caused Malibu to burn the way it did in 1956, and Bel Air in 1961, and Santa Barbara in 1964. In the winter of 1966–67 eleven men were killed fighting a Santa Ana fire that spread through the San Gabriel Mountains.

Just to watch the front-page news out of Los Angeles during a Santa Ana is to get very close to what it is about the place. The longest single Santa Ana period in recent years was in 1957, and it lasted not the usual three or four days but fourteen days, from November 21 until December 4. On the first day 25,000 acres of the San Gabriel Mountains were burning, with gusts reaching 100 miles an hour. In town, the wind reached Force 12, or hurricane force, on the Beaufort Scale; oil derricks were toppled and people ordered off the downtown streets to avoid injury from flying objects. On November 22 the fire in the San Gabriels was out of control. On November 24 six people were killed in automobile accidents, and by the end of the week the Los Angeles *Times* was keeping a box score of traffic deaths. On November 26 a prominent Pasadena attorney, depressed about money, shot and killed his wife, their two sons, and himself. On November 27 a South Gate divorcée, twenty-two, was murdered and thrown from a moving car. On November 30 the San Gabriel fire was still out of control, and the wind in town was blowing eighty miles an hour. On the first day of December four people died violently, and on the third the wind began to break.

It is hard for people who have not lived in Los Angeles to realize how radically the Santa Ana figures in the local imagination. The city burning is Los Angeles's deepest image of itself: Nathanael

West perceived that, in *The Day of the Locust*; and at the time of the 1965 Watts riots what struck the imagination most indelibly were the fires. For days one could drive the Harbor Freeway and see the city on fire, just as we had always known it would be in the end. Los Angeles weather is the weather of catastrophe, of apocalypse, and, just as the reliably long and bitter winters of New England determine the way life is lived there, so the violence and the unpredictability of the Santa Ana affect the entire quality of life in Los Angeles, accentuate its impermanence, its unreliability. The wind shows us how close to the edge we are.

2

"Here's why I'm on the beeper, Ron," said the telephone voice on the all-night radio show. "I just want to say that this *Sex for the Secretary* creature—whatever her name is—certainly isn't contributing anything to the morals in this country. It's pathetic. Statistics *show*."

"It's *Sex and the Office*, honey," the disc jockey said. "That's the title. By Helen Gurley Brown. Statistics show what?"

"I haven't got them right here at my fingertips, naturally. But they *show*."

"I'd be interested in hearing them. Be constructive, you Night Owls."

"All right, let's take *one* statistic," the voice said, truculent now. "Maybe I haven't read the book, but what's this business she recommends about *going out with married men for lunch*?"

So it went, from midnight until 5 a.m., interrupted by records and by occasional calls debating whether or not a rattlesnake can swim. Misinformation about rattlesnakes is a leitmotiv of the insomniac imagination in Los Angeles. Toward 2 a.m. a man from "out Tarzana way" called to protest. "The Night Owls who called earlier must have been thinking about, uh, *The Man in the Gray Flannel Suit* or some other book," he said, "because Helen's one of the few authors trying to tell us what's really going *on*. Hefner's another, and he's also controversial, working in, uh, another area."

An old man, after testifying that he "personally" had seen a swimming rattlesnake, in the Delta-Mendota Canal, urged "moderation" on the Helen Gurley Brown question. "We shouldn't get on the beeper to call things pornographic before we've read them," he complained, pronouncing it porn-ee-oh-graphic. "I say, get the book. Give it a chance." The original *provocateur* called back to agree that she would get the book. "And then I'll burn it," she added.

"Book burner, eh?" laughed the disc jockey good-naturedly.

"I wish they still burned witches," she hissed.

3

It is three o'clock on a Sunday afternoon and 105° and the air so thick with smog that the dusty palm trees loom up with a sudden and rather attractive mystery. I have been playing in the sprinklers with the baby and I get in the car and go to Ralph's Market on the corner of Sunset and Fuller wearing an old bikini bathing suit. That is not a very good thing to wear to the market but neither is it, at Ralph's on the corner of Sunset and Fuller, an unusual costume. Nonetheless a large woman in a cotton muumuu jams her cart into mine at the butcher counter. "*What a thing to wear to the market*," she says in a loud but strangled voice. Everyone looks the other way and I study a plastic package of rib lamb chops and she repeats it. She follows me all over the store, to the Junior Foods, to the Dairy Products, to the Mexican Delicacies, jamming my cart whenever she can. Her husband plucks at her sleeve. As I leave the check-out counter she raises her voice one last time: "*What a thing to wear to Ralph's*," she says.

4

A party at someone's house in Beverly Hills: a pink tent, two orchestras, a couple of French Communist directors in Cardin evening jackets, chili and hamburgers from Chasen's. The wife of an English actor sits at a table alone; she visits California rarely although her husband works here a good deal. An American who knows her slightly comes over to the table.

"Marvelous to see you here," he says.

"Is it," she says.

"How long have you been here?"

"Too long."

She takes a fresh drink from a passing waiter and smiles at her husband, who is dancing.

The American tries again. He mentions her husband.

"I hear he's marvelous in this picture."

She looks at the American for the first time. When she finally speaks she enunciates every word very clearly. "He . . . is . . . also . . . a . . . fag," she says pleasantly.

5

The oral history of Los Angeles is written in piano bars. "Moon River," the piano player always plays, and "Mountain Greenery." "There's a Small Hotel" and "This Is Not the First Time." People talk to each other, tell each other about their first wives and last husbands. "Stay funny," they tell each other, and "This is to die over." A construction man talks to an unemployed screenwriter who is celebrating, alone, his tenth wedding anniversary. The construction man is on a job in Montecito: "Up in Montecito," he says, "they got one square mile with 135 millionaires."

"Putrescence," the writer says.

"That's all you got to say about it?"

"Don't read me wrong, I think Santa Barbara's one of the most—Christ, *the* most—beautiful places in the world, but it's a beautiful place that contains a . . . *putrescence*. They just live on their putrescent millions."

"So give me putrescent."

"No, no," the writer says. "I just happen to think millionaires have some sort of lacking in their . . . in their elasticity."

A drunk requests "The Sweetheart of Sigma Chi." The piano player says he doesn't know it. "Where'd you learn to play the piano?" the drunk asks. "I got two degrees," the piano player says. "One in musical education." I go to a coin telephone and call a friend in New York. "Where are you?" he says. "In a piano bar in Encino," I say. "Why?" he says. "Why not," I say.

1965–1967

THE GETTY

The place might have been commissioned by The Magic Christian. Mysteriously and rather giddily splendid, hidden in a grove of sycamores just above the Pacific Coast Highway in Malibu, a commemoration of high culture so immediately productive of crowds and jammed traffic that it can now be approached by appointment only, the seventeen-million-dollar villa built by the late J. Paul Getty to house his antiquities and paintings and furniture manages to strike a peculiar nerve in almost everyone who sees it. From the beginning, the Getty was said to be vulgar. The Getty was said to be "Disney." The Getty was even said to be Jewish, if I did not misread the subtext in "like a Beverly Hills nouveau-riche dining room" (*Los Angeles Times*, January 6, 1974) and "gussied up like a Bel-Air dining room" (*New York Times*, May 28, 1974).

The Getty seems to stir up social discomforts at levels not easily plumbed. To mention this museum in the more enlightened of those very dining rooms it is said to resemble is to invite a kind of nervous derision, as if the place were a local hoax, a perverse and deliberate affront to the understated good taste and general class of everyone at the table. The Getty's intricately patterned marble floors and walls are "garish." The Getty's illusionistic portico murals are "back lot." The entire building, an informed improvisation on a villa buried by mud from Vesuvius in A.D. 79 and seen again only dimly during some eighteenth-century tunneling around Herculaneum, is ritually dismissed as "inauthentic," although what "authentic" could mean in this context is hard to say.

Something about the place embarrasses people. The collection itself is usually referred to as "that kind of thing," as in "not even the best of that kind of thing," or "absolutely top-drawer if you like that kind of thing," both of which translate "not our kind of thing." The Getty's damask-lined galleries of Renaissance and Baroque paintings are distinctly that kind of thing, there being little in the modern temperament that responds immediately to popes and libertine babies, and so are the Getty's rather unrelenting arrangements of French furniture. A Louis XV writing table tends to please the modern eye only if it has been demystified by a glass of field flowers and some silver-framed snapshots, as in a Horst photograph for *Vogue*.

Even the Getty's famous antiquities are pretty much that kind of thing, evoking as they do not their own period but the eighteenth- and nineteenth-century rage for antiquities. The sight of a Greek head depresses many people, strikes an unliberated chord, reminds them of books in their grandmother's parlor and of all they were supposed to learn and never did. This note of "learning" pervades the entire Getty collection. Even the handful of Impressionists acquired by Getty were recently removed from the public galleries, put away as irrelevant. The Getty collection is in certain ways unremittingly reproachful, and quite inaccessible to generations trained in the conviction that a museum is meant to be fun, with Calder mobiles and Barcelona chairs.

In short the Getty is a monument to "fine art," in the old-fashioned didactic sense, which is part of the problem people have with it. The place resists contemporary notions about what art is or should be or ever was. A museum is now supposed to kindle the untrained imagination, but this museum does not. A museum is now supposed to set the natural child in each of us free, but this museum does not. This was art acquired to teach a lesson, and there is also a lesson in the building which houses it: the Getty tells us that the past was perhaps different from the way we like to perceive it. Ancient marbles were not always attractively faded and worn. Ancient marbles once appeared just as they appear here: as strident, opulent evidence of imperial power and acquisition. Ancient murals were not always bleached and mellowed and "tasteful." Ancient murals once looked as they do here: as if dreamed by a Mafia don. Ancient fountains once worked, and drowned out that very silence we have come to expect and want from the past. Ancient bronze once gleamed ostentatiously. The old world was once discomfitingly new, or even nouveau, as people like to say about the Getty. (I have never been sure what the word "nouveau" can possibly mean in America, implying as it does that the speaker is gazing down six hundred years of rolled lawns.) At a time when all our public conventions remain rooted in a kind of knocked-down romanticism, when the celebration of natural man's capacity for moving onward and upward has become a kind of official tic, the Getty presents us with an illustrated lesson in classical doubt. The Getty advises us that not much changes. The Getty tells us that we were never any better than we are and will never be any better than we were, and in so doing makes a profoundly unpopular political statement.

The Getty's founder may or may not have had some such statement in mind. In a way he seems to have wanted only to do something no one else could or would do. In his posthumous book, *As I See It*, he advises us that he never wanted "one of those concrete-bunker-type structures that are the fad among museum architects." He refused to pay for any "tinted-glass-and-stainless-steel monstrosity." He assures us that he was "neither shaken nor surprised" when his villa was finished and "certain critics sniffed." He had "calculated the risks." He knew that he was flouting the "doctrinaire and elitist" views he believed endemic in "many Art World (or should I say Artsy-Craftsy?) quarters."

Doctrinaire and elitist. Artsy-craftsy. On the surface the Getty would appear to have been a case of he-knew-what-he-liked-and-he-built-it, a tax dodge from the rather louche world of the international rich, and yet the use of that word "elitist" strikes an interesting note. The man who built himself the Getty never saw it, although it opened a year and a half before his death. He seems to have liked the planning of it. He personally approved every paint sample. He is said to have taken immense pleasure in every letter received from anyone who visited the museum and liked it (such letters were immediately forwarded to him by the museum staff), but the idea of the place seems to have been enough, and the idea was this: here was a museum built not for those elitist critics but for "the public." Here was a museum that would be forever supported by its founder alone, a museum that need never depend on any city or state or federal funding, a place forever "open to the public and free of all charges."

As a matter of fact large numbers of people who do not ordinarily visit museums like the Getty a great deal, just as its founder knew they would. There is one of those peculiar social secrets at work here. On the whole "the critics" distrust great wealth, but "the public" does not. On the whole "the critics" subscribe to the romantic view of man's possibilities, but "the public" does not. In the end the Getty stands above the Pacific Coast Highway as one of those odd monuments, a palpable contract between the very rich and the people who distrust them least.

1977

QUIET DAYS IN MALIBU

In a way it seems the most idiosyncratic of beach communities, twenty-seven miles of coastline with no hotel, no passable restaurant, nothing to attract the traveler's dollar. It is not a resort. No one "vacations" or "holidays," as those words are conventionally understood, at Malibu. Its principal residential street, the Pacific Coast Highway, is quite literally a highway, California 1, which runs from the Mexican border to the Oregon line and brings Greyhound buses and refrigerated produce trucks and sixteen-wheel gasoline tankers hurtling past the front windows of houses frequently bought and sold for over a million dollars. The water off Malibu is neither as clear nor as tropically colored as the water off La Jolla. The beaches at Malibu are neither as white nor as a wide as the beach at Carmel. The hills are scrubby and barren, infested with bikers and rattlesnakes, scarred with cuts and old burns and new R.V. parks. For these and other reasons Malibu tends to astonish and disappoint those who have never before seen it, and yet its very name remains, in the imagination of people all over the world, a kind of shorthand for the easy life. I had not before 1971 and will probably not again live in a place with a Chevrolet named after it.

2

Dick Haddock, a family man, a man twenty-six years in the same line of work, a man who has on the telephone and in his office the crisp and easy manner of technological middle management, is in many respects the prototypical Southern California solid citizen. He lives in a San Fernando Valley subdivision near a freshwater marina and a good shopping plaza. His son is a high-school swimmer. His daughter is "into tennis." He drives thirty miles to and from work, puts in a forty-hour week, regularly takes courses to maintain his professional skills, keeps in shape and looks it. When he discusses his career he talks, in a kind of politely impersonal second person, about how "you would want like any other individual to advance yourself," about "improving your rating" and "being more of an asset to your department," about "really knowing your business." Dick Haddock's business for all these twenty-six years has been that of a professional lifeguard for the Los Angeles County Department of Beaches, and his office is a $190,000 lookout on Zuma Beach in northern Malibu.

It was Thanksgiving morning, 1975. A Santa Ana wind was just dying after blowing in off the Mojave for three weeks and setting 69,000 acres of Los Angeles County on fire. Squadrons of planes had been dropping chemicals on the fires to no effect. Querulous interviews with burned-out householders had become a fixed element of the six o'clock news. Smoke from the fires had that week stretched a hundred miles out over the Pacific and darkened the days and lit the nights and by Thanksgiving morning there was the sense all over Southern California of living in some grave solar dislocation. It was one of those weeks when Los Angeles seemed most perilously and breathtakingly itself, a cartoon of natural disaster, and it was a peculiar week in which to spend the day with Dick Haddock and the rest of the Zuma headquarters crew.

Actually I had wanted to meet the lifeguards ever since I moved to Malibu. I would drive past Zuma some cold winter mornings and see a few of them making their mandatory daily half-mile swims in open ocean. I would drive past Zuma some late foggy nights and see others moving around behind the lookout's lighted windows, the only other souls awake in all of northern Malibu. It seemed to me a curious, almost beatified career choice, electing to save those in peril upon the sea forty hours a week, and as the soot drifted down around the Zuma lookout on that Thanksgiving morning the laconic routines and paramilitary rankings of these civil servants in red trunks took on a devotionary and dreamlike inevitability. There was the "captain," John McFarlane, a man who had already taken his daily half-mile run and his daily half-mile swim and was putting on his glasses to catch up on a paperwork. Had the water been below 56 degrees he would have been allowed to swim in a wet suit, but the water was not below 56 degrees and so he had swum as usual in his red trunks. The water was 58 degrees. John McFarlane is 48. There was the "lieutenant," Dick Haddock, telling me about how each of the Department's 125 permanent lifeguards (there are also 600 part-time or "recurrent" lifeguards) learns crowd control at the Los Angeles County Sheriff's Academy, learns emergency driving techniques at the California Highway Patrol Academy, learns medical procedures at the U.S.C. Medical Center, and, besides running the daily half-mile and swimming the daily half-mile, does a monthly 500-meter paddle and a monthly pier jump. A "pier jump" is just what it sounds like, and its purpose is to gain practice around pilings in heavy surf.

There was as well the man out on patrol.

There were as well the "call-car personnel," two trained divers and cliff-climbers "ready to roll at any time" in what was always referred to as "a Code 3 vehicle with red light and siren," two men not rolling this Thanksgiving morning but sitting around the lookout, listening to the Los Angeles Rams beat the Detroit Lions on the radio, watching the gray horizon and waiting for a call.

No call came. The radios and the telephones crackled occasionally with reports from the other "operations" supervised by the Zuma crew: the "rescue-boat operation" at Paradise Cove, the "beach operations" at Leo Carillo, Nicholas, Point Dume, Corral, Malibu Surfrider, Malibu Lagoon, Las Tunas, Topanga North and Topanga South. Those happen to be the names of some Malibu public beaches but in the Zuma lookout that day the names took on the sound of battle stations during a doubtful cease-fire. All quiet at Leo. Situation normal at Surfrider.

The lifeguards seemed most comfortable when they were talking about "operations" and "situations," as in "a phone-watch situation" or "a riptide situation." They also talked easily about "functions," as in "the function of maintaining a secure position on the beach." Like other men at war they had charts, forms, logs, counts kept current to within twelve hours: *1405 surf rescues off Zuma between 12:01 A.M. January 1, 1975 and 11:59 P.M. Thanksgiving Eve 1975.* As well as: *36,120 prevention rescues, 872 first aids, 176 beach emergency calls, 12 resuscitations, 8 boat distress calls, 107 boat warnings, 438 lost-and-found children*, and *0 deaths*. Zero. No body count. When he had occasion to use the word "body" Dick Haddock would hesitate and glance away.

On the whole the lifeguards favored a diction as flat and finally poetic as that of Houston Control. Everything that morning was "real fine." The headquarters crew was "feeling good." The day was

"looking good." Malibu surf was "two feet and shape is poor."
Earlier that morning there had been a hundred or so surfers in the
water, a hundred or so of those bleached children of indeterminate
age and sex who bob off Zuma and appear to exist exclusively on
packaged beef jerky, but by ten they had all pocketed their Thanksgiving jerky and moved on to some better break. "It heats up, we
could use some more personnel," Dick Haddock said about noon,
assessing the empty guard towers. "That happened, we might move
on a decision to open Towers One and Eleven, I'd call and say we
need two recurrents at Zuma, plus I might put an extra man at Leo."

It did not heat up. Instead it began to rain, and on the radio the
morning N.F.L. game gave way to the afternoon N.F.L. game, and
after a while I drove with one of the call-car men to Paradise Cove,
where the rescue-boat crew needed a diver. They did not need a
diver to bring up a body, or a murder weapon, or a crate of stolen
ammo, or any of the things Department divers sometimes get their
names in the paper for bringing up. They needed a diver, with scuba
gear and a wet suit, because they had been removing the propeller
from the rescue boat and had dropped a metal part the size of a dime
in twenty feet of water. I had the distinct impression that they particularly needed a diver in a wet suit because nobody on the boat
crew wanted to go back in the water in his trunks to replace the propeller, but there seemed to be some tacit agreement that the lost part
was to be considered the point of the dive.

"I guess you know it's fifty-eight down there," the diver said.

"Don't need to tell me how cold it is," the boat lieutenant said.
His name was Leonard McKinley and he had "gone permanent" in
1942 and he was of an age to refer to Zuma as a "bathing" beach.
"After you find that little thing you could put the propeller back on
for us, you wanted. As long as you're in the water anyway? In your
suit?"

"I had a feeling you'd say that."

Leonard McKinley and I stood on the boat and watched the
diver disappear. In the morning soot from the fires had coated the
surface but now the wind was up and the soot was clouding the
water. Kelp fronds undulated on the surface. The boat rocked. The
radio sputtered with reports of a yacht named *Ursula* in distress.

"One of the other boats is going for it," Leonard McKinley said.

"We're not. Some days we just sit here like firemen. Other days, a day with rips, I been out ten hours straight. You get your big rips in the summer, swells coming up from Mexico. A Santa Ana, you get your capsized boats, we got one the other day, it was overdue out of Santa Monica, they were about drowned when we picked them up."

I tried to keep my eyes on the green-glass water but could not. I had been sick on boats in the Catalina Channel and in the Gulf of California and even in San Francisco Bay, and now I seemed to be getting sick on a boat still moored at the end of the Paradise Cove pier. The radio reported the *Ursula* under tow to Marina del Rey. I concentrated on the pilings.

"He gets the propeller on," Leonard McKinley said, "you want to go out?"

I said I thought not.

"You come back another day," Leonard McKinley said, and I said that I would, and although I have not gone back there is no day when I do not think of Leonard McKinley and Dick Haddock and what they are doing, what situations they face, what operations, what green-glass water. The water today is 56 degrees.

3

Amado Vazquez is a Mexican national who has lived in Los Angeles County as a resident alien since 1947. Like many Mexicans who have lived for a long time around Los Angeles he speaks of Mexico as "over there," remains more comfortable in Spanish than in English, and transmits, in his every movement, a kind of "different" propriety, a correctness, a cultural reserve. He is in no sense a Chicano. He is rather what California-born Mexicans sometimes call "Mexican-from-Mexico," pronounced as one word and used to suggest precisely that difference, that rectitude, that personal conservatism. He was born in Ahualulco, Jalisco. He was trained as a barber at the age of ten. Since the age of twenty-seven, when he came north to visit his brother and find new work for himself, he has married, fathered two children, and become, to the limited number of people who know and understand the rather special work he found for himself in California, a kind of legend. Amado Vazquez was, at the time I first met him, head grower at Arthur Freed

Orchids, a commercial nursery in Malibu founded by the late motion-picture producer Arthur Freed, and he is one of a handful of truly great orchid breeders in the world.

In the beginning I met Amado Vazquez not because I knew about orchids but because I liked greenhouses. All I knew about orchids was that back in a canyon near my house someone was growing them *in greenhouses.* All I knew about Amado Vazquez was that he was the man who would let me spend time alone in these greenhouses. To understand how extraordinary this seemed to me you would need to have craved the particular light and silence of greenhouses as I did: all my life I had been trying to spend time in one greenhouse or another, and all my life the person in charge of one greenhouse or another had been trying to hustle me out. When I was nine I would deliberately miss the school bus in order to walk home, because by walking I could pass a greenhouse. I recall being told at that particular greenhouse that the purchase of a nickel pansy did not entitle me to "spend the day," and at another that my breathing was "using up the air."

And yet back in this canyon near my house twenty-five years later were what seemed to me the most beautiful greenhouses in the world—the most aqueous filtered light, the softest tropical air, the most silent clouds of flowers—and the person in charge, Amado Vazquez, seemed willing to take only the most benign notice of my presence. He seemed to assume that I had my own reasons for being there. He would speak only to offer a nut he had just cracked, or a flower cut from a plant he was pruning. Occasionally Arthur Freed's brother Hugo, who was then running the business, would come into the greenhouse with real customers, serious men in dark suits who appeared to have just flown in from Taipei or Durban and who spoke in hushed voices, as if they had come to inspect medieval enamels, or uncut diamonds.

But then the buyers from Taipei or Durban would go into the office to make their deal and the silence in the greenhouse would again be total. The temperature was always 72 degrees. The humidity was always 60 per cent. Great arcs of white phalaenopsis trembled overhead. I learned the names of the crosses by studying labels there in the greenhouse, the exotic names whose value I did not then understand. *Amabilis* × *Rimestadiana* = *Elisabethae. Aphrodite* ×

Rimestadiana = *Gilles Gratiot*. *Amabilis* × *Gilles Gratiot* = *Katherine Siegwart* and *Katherine Siegwart* × *Elisabethae* = *Doris Doris* after Doris Duke. *Doris* which first flowered at Duke Farms in 1940. At least once each visit I would remember the nickel pansy and find Amado Vazquez and show him a plant I wanted to buy, but he would only smile and shake his head. "For breeding," he would say, or "not for sale today." And then he would lift the spray of flowers and show me some point I would not have noticed, some marginal difference in the substance of the petal or the shape of the blossom. "Very beautiful," he would say. "Very nice you like it." What he would not say was that these plants he was letting me handle, these plants "for breeding" or "not for sale today," were stud plants, and that the value of such a plant at Arthur Freed could range from ten thousand to more than three-quarters of a million dollars.

I suppose the day I realized this was the day I stopped using the Arthur Freed greenhouses as a place to eat my lunch, but I made a point of going up one day in 1976 to see Amado Vazquez and to talk to Marvin Saltzman, who took over the business in 1973 and is married to Arthur Freed's daughter Barbara. (As in *Phal. Barbara Freed Saltzman* "Jean McPherson," *Phal. Barbara Freed Saltzman* "Zuma Canyon," and *Phal Barbara Freed Saltzman* "Malibu Queen," three plants "not for sale today" at Arthur Freed.) It was peculiar talking to Marvin Saltzman because I had never before been in the office at Arthur Freed, never seen the walls lined with dulled silver awards, never seen the genealogical charts on the famous Freed hybrids, never known anything at all about the actual business of orchids.

"Frankly it's an expensive business to get into," Marvin Saltzman said. He was turning the pages of *Sander's List*, the standard orchid studbook, published every several years and showing the parentage of every hybrid registered with the Royal Horticultural Society, and he seemed oblivious to the primeval silence of the greenhouse beyond the office window. He had shown me how Amado Vazquez places the pollen from one plant into the ovary of a flower on another. He had explained that the best times to do this are at full moon and high tide, because phalaenopsis plants are more fertile then. He had explained that a phalaenopsis is more fertile at full moon because in nature it must be pollinated by a night-flying moth, and over sixty-five million years of evolution its period of highest fertility began to coincide with its period of highest visibility. He had explained that a phalaenopsis is more fertile at high tide because the moisture content of every plant responds to tidal movement. It was all an old story to Marvin Saltzman. I could not take my eyes from the window.

"You bring back five-thousand seedlings from the jungle and you wait three years for them to flower," Marvin Saltzman said. "You find two you like and you throw out the other four-thousand-nine-hundred-ninety-eight and you try to breed the two. Maybe the pollenization takes, eighty-five per cent of the time it doesn't. Say you're lucky, it takes, you'll still wait another four years before you see a flower. Meanwhile you've got a big capital investment. An Arthur Freed could take $400,000 a year from M.G.M. and put $100,000 of it into getting this place started, but not many people could. You see a lot of what we call backyard nurseries—people who have fifty or a hundred plants, maybe they have two they think are exceptional, they decide to breed them—but you talk about major nurseries, there are maybe only ten in the United States, another ten in Europe. That's about it. Twenty."

Twenty is also about how many head growers there are, which is part of what lends Amado Vazquez his legendary aspect, and after a while I left the office and went out to see him in the greenhouse. There in the greenhouse everything was operating as usual to approximate that particular level of a Malaysian rain forest—not on the ground but perhaps a hundred feet up—where epiphytic orchids grow wild. In the rain forest these orchids get broken by wind and rain. They get pollinated randomly and rarely by insects. Their seedlings are crushed by screaming monkeys and tree boas and the orchids live unseen and die young. There in the greenhouse nothing would break the orchids and they would be pollinated at full moon and high tide by Amado Vazquez, and their seedlings would be tended in a sterile box with sterile gloves and sterile tools by Amado Vazquez's wife, Maria, and the orchids would not seem to die at all. "We don't know how long they'll live," Marvin Saltzman told me. "They haven't been bred under protected conditions that long. The botanists estimate a hundred and fifty, two hundred years, but we don't know. All we know is that a plant a hundred years old will show no signs of senility."

It was very peaceful there in the greenhouse with Amado Vazquez and the plants that would outlive us both. "We grew in osmunda then," he said suddenly. Osmunda is a potting medium. Amado Vazquez talks exclusively in terms of how the orchids grow. He had been talking about the years when he first came to this country and got a job with his brother tending a private orchid collection in San Marino, and he had fallen silent. "I didn't know orchids then, now they're like my children. You wait for the first bloom like you wait for a baby to come. Sometimes you wait four years and it opens and it isn't what you expected, maybe your heart wants to break, but you love it. You never say, 'that one was prettier.' You just love them. My whole life is orchids."

And in fact it was. Amado Vazquez's wife, Maria (as in *Phal. Maria Vasquez* "Malibu," the spelling of Vazquez being mysteriously altered by everyone at Arthur Freed except the Vazquezes themselves), worked in the laboratory at Arthur Freed. His son, George (as in *Phal. George Vasquez* "Malibu"), was the sales manager at Arthur Freed. His daughter, Linda (as in *Phal. Linda Mia* "Innocence"), worked at Arthur Freed before her marriage. Amado Vazquez will often get up in the night to check a heater, adjust a light, hold a seed pod in his hand and try to sense if morning will be time enough to sow the seeds in the sterile flask. When Amado and Maria Vazquez go to Central or South America, they go to look for orchids. When Amado and Maria Vazquez went for the first time to Europe a few years ago, they looked for orchids. "I asked all over Madrid for orchids," Amado Vazquez recalled. "Finally they tell me about this one place. I go there, I knock. The woman finally lets me in. She agrees to let me see the orchids. She takes me into a house and . . ."

Amado Vazquez broke off, laughing.

"She has three orchids," he finally managed to say. "Three. One of them dead. All three from Oregon."

We were standing in a sea of orchids, an extravagance of orchids, and he had given me an armful of blossoms from his own cattleyas to take to my child, more blossoms maybe than in all of Madrid. It seemed to me that day that I had never talked to anyone so direct and unembarrassed about the things he loved. He had told me earlier that he had never become a United States citizen because he had an image in his mind which he knew to be false but could not shake: the image was that of standing before a judge and stamping on the flag of Mexico. "And I love my country," he had said. Amado Vazquez loved his country. Amado Vazquez loved his family. Amado Vazquez loved orchids. "You want to know how I feel about the plants," he said as I was leaving. "I'll tell you. I will die in orchids."

4

In the part of Malibu where I lived from January of 1971 until quite recently we all knew one another's cars, and watched for them on the highway and at the Trancas Market and at the Point Dume Gulf station. We exchanged information at the Trancas Market. We left packages and messages for one another at the Gulf station. We called one another in times of wind and fire and rain, we knew when one another's septic tanks needed pumping, we watched for ambulances on the highway and helicopters on the beach and worried about one another's dogs and horses and children and corral gates and Coastal Commission permits. An accident on the highway was likely to involve someone we knew. A rattlesnake in my driveway meant its mate in yours. A stranger's campfire on your beach meant fire on both our slopes.

In fact this was a way of life I had not expected to find in Malibu. When I first moved in 1971 from Hollywood to a house on the Pacific Coast Highway I had accepted the conventional notion that Malibu meant the easy life, had worried that we would be cut off from "the real world," by which I believe I meant daily exposure to the Sunset Strip. By the time we left Malibu, seven years later, I had come to see the spirit of the place as one of shared isolation and adversity, and I think now that I never loved the house on the Pacific Coast Highway more than on those many days when it was impossible to leave it, when fire or flood had in fact closed the highway. We moved to this house on the highway in the year of our daughter's fifth birthday. In the year of her twelfth it rained until the highway collapsed, and one of her friends drowned at Zuma Beach, a casualty of Quaaludes.

One morning during the fire season of 1978, some months after we had sold the house on the Pacific Coast Highway, a brush fire caught in Agoura, in the San Fernando Valley. Within two hours a Santa Ana wind had pushed this fire across 25,000 acres and thirteen miles to the coast, where it jumped the Pacific Coast Highway as a half-mile fire storm generating winds of 100 miles per hour and temperatures up to 2500 degrees Fahrenheit. Refugees huddled on Zuma Beach. Horses caught fire and were shot on the beach, birds exploded in the air. Houses did not explode but imploded, as in a nuclear strike. By the time this fire storm had passed 197 houses had vanished into ash, many of them houses which belonged or had belonged to people we knew. A few days after the highway reopened I drove out to Malibu to see Amado Vazquez, who had, some months before, bought from the Freed estate all the stock at Arthur Freed Orchids, and had been in the process of moving it a half-mile down the canyon to his own new nursery, Zuma Canyon Orchids. I found him in the main greenhouse at what had been Arthur Freed Orchids. The place was now a range not of orchids but of shattered glass and melted metal and the imploded shards of the thousands of chemical beakers that had held the Freed seedlings, the new crosses. "I lost three years," Amado Vazquez said, and for an instant I thought we would both cry. "You want today to see flowers," he said then, "we go down to the other place." I did not want that day to see flowers. After I said goodbye to Amado Vazquez my husband and daughter and I went to look at the house on the Pacific Coast Highway in which we had lived for seven years. The fire had come to within 125 feet of the property, then stopped or turned or been beaten back, it was hard to tell which. In any case it was no longer our house.

1976–1978

FIRE SEASON

"I've seen fire and I've seen rain," I recall James Taylor singing over and over on the news radio station between updates on the 1978 Mandeville and Kanan fires, both of which started on October 23 of that year and could be seen burning toward each other, systematically wiping out large parts of Malibu and Pacific

Palisades, from an upstairs window of my house in Brentwood. It was said that the Kanan fire was burning on a twenty-mile front and had already jumped the Pacific Coast Highway at Trancas Canyon. The stand in the Mandeville fire, it was said, would be made at Sunset Boulevard. I stood at the window and watched a house on a hill above Sunset implode, its oxygen sucked out by the force of the fire.

Some thirty-four thousand acres of Los Angeles County burned that week in 1978. More than eighty thousand acres had burned in 1968. Close to a hundred and thirty thousand acres had burned in 1970. Seventy-four-some thousand had burned in 1975, sixty-some thousand would burn in 1979. Forty-six thousand would burn in 1980, forty-five thousand in 1982. In the hills behind Malibu, where the moist air off the Pacific makes the brush grow fast, it takes about twelve years before a burn is ready to burn again. Inland, where the manzanita and sumac and chamise that make up the native brush in Southern California grow more slowly (the wild mustard that turns the hills a translucent yellow after rain is not native but exotic, introduced in the 1920s in an effort to reseed burns), regrowth takes from fifteen to twenty years. Since 1919, when the county began keeping records of its fires, some areas have burned eight times.

In other words there is nothing unusual about fires in Los Angeles, which is after all a desert city with only two distinct seasons, one beginning in January and lasting three or four months during which storms come in from the northern Pacific and it rains (often an inch every two or three hours, sometimes and in some places an inch a minute) and one lasting eight or nine months during which it burns, or gets ready to burn. Most years it is September or October before the Santa Ana winds start blowing down through the passes and the relative humidity drops to figures like 7 or 6 or 3 percent and the bougainvillea starts rattling in the driveway and people start watching the horizon for smoke and tuning in to another of those extreme local possibilities, in this case that of imminent devastation. What was unusual in 1989, after two years of drought and a third year of less than average rainfall, was that it was ready to burn while the June fogs still lay on the coastline. On the first of May that year, months earlier than ever before, the California Department of Forestry had declared the start of fire season and begun hiring extras crews. By the last week in June there had already been more than two thousand brush and forest fires in California. Three hundred and twenty of them were burning that week alone.

One morning early that summer I drove out the San Bernardino Freeway to the headquarters of the Los Angeles County Fire Department, which was responsible not only for coordinating fire fighting and reseeding operations throughout the county but for sending, under the California Master Mutual Aid agreement, both equipment and strike teams to fires around the state. Los Angeles County sent strike teams to fight the 116,000-acre Wheeler fire in Ventura County in 1985. (The logistics of these big fires are essentially military. Within twelve hours of the first reports on the Wheeler fire, which eventually burned for two weeks and involved three thousand fire fighters flown in from around the country, a camp had materialized, equipped with kitchen, sanitation, transportation and medical facilities, a communications network, a "situation trailer", a "what if" trailer for long-range contingency planning, and a "pool coordinator", to get off-duty crews to and from the houses of residents who had offered the use of their swimming pools. "We simply superimposed a city on top of the incident," a camp spokesman said at the time.) Los Angeles County sent strike teams to fight the 100,000-acre Las Pilitas fire in San Luis Obispo County the same year. It sent specially trained people to act as "overhead" on, or to run, the crews of military personnel brought in from all over the United States to fight the Yellowstone fires in 1988.

On the June morning in 1989 when I visited the headquarters building in East Los Angeles, it was already generally agreed that, as one of the men to whom I spoke put it, "we pretty much know we're going to see some fires this year", with no probable break until January or February. (There is usually some November rain in Los Angeles, often enough to allow crews to gain control of a fire already burning, but only rarely does November rain put enough moisture into the brush to offset the Santa Ana winds that blow until the end of December.) There had been unusually early Santa Ana conditions, a week of temperatures over one hundred. The measurable moisture in the brush, a measurement the Fire Department calls the "fuel stick", was in some areas already down to single digits. The daily "burn index", which rates the probability of fire on a scale running from 0 to 200, was that morning showing figures of 45 for the Los Angeles basin, 41 for what is called the "high country", 125 for the Antelope Valley, and, for the Santa Clarita Valley, 192.

Anyone who has spent fire season in Los Angeles knows some of its special language — knows, for example, the difference between a fire that has been "controlled" and a fire that has so far been merely "contained" (a "contained" fire has been surrounded, usually by a trench half as wide as the brush is high, but is still burning out of control within this line and may well jump it), knows the difference between "full" and "partial" control ("partial" control means, if the wind changes, no control at all), knows about "backfiring" and about "making the stand" and about the difference between a Red Flag Alert (there will probably be a fire today) and a Red Flag Warning (there will probably be a Red Flag Alert within three days).

Still, "burn index" was new to me, and one of the headquarters foresters, Paul Rippens, tried that morning to explain it. "Let's take the Antelope Valley, up around Palmdale, Lancaster," he said. "For today, temperature's going to be ninety-six, humidity's going to be seventeen percent, wind speed's going to be fifteen miles per hour, and the fuel stick is six, which is getting pretty low."

"Six burns very well," another forester, John Haggenmiller, said. "If the fuel stick's up around twelve, it's pretty hard to get it to burn. That's the range that you have. Anything under six and it's ready to burn very well."

"So you correlate all that, you get an Antelope Valley burn index today of one twenty-five, the adjective for which is 'high'," Paul Rippens continued. "The adjectives we use are 'low', 'moderate', 'high', 'very high', and 'extreme'. One twenty-five is 'high'. High probability of fire. We had a hundred-plus-acre fire out there yesterday, about a four-hour fire. Divide the burn index by ten and you get the average flame length. So a burn index of one twenty-five is going to give you a twelve-and-a half-foot flame length out there. If you've got a good fire burning, flame length has a lot to do with it."

"There's a possibility of a grass fire going through and not doing much damage at all," John Haggenmiller said. "Other cases, where the fuel has been allowed to build up — say you had a bug kill or a die-back, a lot of decadent fuel—you're going to get a flame length of thirty, forty feet. And it gets up into the crown of a tree and the whole thing goes down. That does a lot of damage."

Among the men to whom I spoke that morning there was a certain grudging admiration for what they called "the big hitters", the major fires, the ones people remember. "I'd say about ninety-five percent of our fires, we're able to hold down to under five acres," I was told by Captain Garry Oversby, who did community relations and education for the Fire Department. "It's the ones when we have extreme Santa Ana conditions, extreme weather—they get started, all we can do is try to hold the thing in check until the weather lays down a little bit for us. Times like that, we revert to what we call a defensive attack. Just basically go right along the edges of that fire until we can get a break. Reach a natural barrier. Or sometimes we make a stand several miles in advance of the fire—construct a line there, and then maybe set a backfire. Which will burn back toward the main fire and take out the vegetation, rob the main fire of its fuel."

They spoke of the way a true big hitter "moved", of the way it "pushed", of the way it could "spot", or throw embers and firebrands, a mile ahead of itself, rendering any kind of conventional firebreak useless; of the way a big hitter, once it got moving, would "outrun anybody". "You get the right weather conditions in Malibu, it's almost impossible to stop it," Paul Rippens said. He was talking about the fires that typically start somewhere in the brush off the Ventura Freeway and then burn twenty miles to the sea, the fires that roar over a ridge in a matter of seconds and make national news because they tend to take out, just before they hit the beach along Malibu, houses that belong to well-known people. Taking out houses is what the men at headquarters mean when they talk about "the urban interface".

"We can dump all our resources out there," Paul Rippens said, and he shrugged.

"You can pick up the flanks and channel it," John Haggenmiller said, "but until the wind stops or you run out of fuel, you can't do much else."

"You get into Malibu," Paul Rippens said, "you're looking at what we call two-story brush."

"You know the wind," John Haggenmiller said. "You're not going to change that phenomenon."

"You can dump everything you've got on that fire," Paul Rippens said. "It's still going to go to what we call the big blue break."

It occurred to me then that it had been eleven years since the October night in 1978 when I listened to James Taylor singing "Fire and Rain" between reports on how the Kanan fire had jumped the Pacific Coast Highway to go to the big blue break. On the twelve-year-average fire cycle that regulates life in Malibu, the Kanan burn, which happened to include a beach on which my husband and daughter and I had lived from 1971 until June of 1978, was coming due again. "Beautiful country burn again," I wrote in my notebook, a line from a Robinson Jeffers poem I remember at some point during every fire season, and I got up to leave.

A week or so later 3,700 acres burned in the hills west of the Antelope Valley. The flames reached sixty feet. The wind was gusting at forty miles an hour. There were 250 fire fighters on the ground, and they evacuated 1,500 residents, one of whom returned to find her house gone but managed to recover, according to the *Los Angeles Times*, "an undamaged American flag and a porcelain Nativity set handmade by her mother". A week after this Antelope Valley fire, 1,500 acres burned in the Puente Hills, above Whittier. The temperatures that day were in the high nineties, and the flames were as high as fifty feet. There were more than 970 fire fighters on the line. Two hundred and fifty families were evacuated. They took with them what people always take out of fires, mainly snapshots, mementos small enough to put in the car. "We won't have a stitch of clothing, but at least we'll have these," a woman about to leave the Puente Hills told the *Times* as she packed the snapshots into the trunk of her car.

People who live with fires think a great deal about what will happen "when", as the phrase goes in the instruction leaflets, "the fire comes". These leaflets, which are stuck up on refrigerator doors all over Los Angeles County, never say "if". When the fire comes there will be no water pressure. The roof one watered all the night before will go dry in seconds. Plastic trash cans must be filled with water and wet gunny-sacks kept at hand, for smothering the sparks that blow ahead of the fire. The garden hoses must be connected and left where they can be seen. The cars must be placed in the garage, headed out. Whatever one wants most to save must be placed in the cars. The lights must be left on, so that the house can be seen in the smoke. I remember my daughter's Malibu kindergarten sending home on the first day of the fall semester a detailed contingency plan, with alternative sites where, depending on the direction of the wind when the fire came, the children would be taken to wait for their parents. The last-ditch site was the naval air station at Point Mugu, twenty miles up the coast.

"Dry winds and dust, hair full of knots," our Malibu child wrote when asked, in the fourth grade, for an "autumn" poem. "Gardens are dead, animals not fed. . . . People mumble as leaves crumble, fire ashes tumble." The rhythm here is not one that many people outside Los Angeles seem to hear. In the *New York Times* this morning I read a piece in which the way people in Los Angeles "persist" in living with fire was described as "denial". "Denial" is a word from a different lyric altogether. This will have been only the second fire season over twenty-five years during which I did not have a house somewhere in Los Angeles County, and the second during which I did not keep the snapshots in a box near the door, ready to go when the first fire comes.

1989

Charles Bukowski

Born in Germany, Charles Bukowski (1920–1994) arrived in the United States at age three, and grew up in L.A. during the Depression, an experience that left its mark on his work. Working in relative obscurity for decades, Bukowski was an extraordinarily prolific writer whose poetry and fiction—most of it brought into print by the enterprising Santa Barbara publisher Black Sparrow—is a small-scale chronicle of the underside of Los Angeles, a city of drifters and the misbegotten. Either celebrated as a poet of the down-and-out or derided as two-dimensional and dissolute, Bukowski may be remembered finally for his gift at capturing, without sentiment or regret, the smallest and quietest of incidents, the everyday counterlife that runs parallel to the grandiosity of the public sphere.

waiting

hot summers in the mid-30's in Los Angeles
where every 3rd lot was vacant
and it was a short ride to the orange
groves—
if you had a car and the
gas.

hot summers in the mid-30's in Los Angeles
too young to be a man and too old to
be a boy.

hard times.
a neighbor tried to rob our
house, my father caught him
climbing through the
window,
held him there in the dark
on the floor:
"you rotten son of a
bitch!"

"Henry, Henry, let me go,
let me go!"

"you son of a bitch, I'll kill
you!"

my mother phoned the police.

another neighbor set his house on fire
in an attempt to collect the
insurance.
he was investigated and
jailed.

hot summers in the mid-30's in Los Angeles,
nothing to do, nowhere to go, listening to
the terrified talk of our parents
at night:
"what will we do? what will we
do?"

"god, I don't know . . ."

starving dogs in the alleys, skin taut
across ribs, hair falling out, tongues
out, such sad eyes, sadder than any sadness
on earth.

hot summers in the mid-30's in Los Angeles,
the men of the neighborhood were quiet
and the women were like pale
statues.

the parks full of socialists,
communists, anarchists, standing on the park
benches, orating, agitating
the sun came down through a clear sky and
the ocean was clean

and we were
neither men nor
boys.

we fed the dogs leftover pieces of dry hard
bread
which they ate gratefully,
eyes shining in
wonder,
tails waving at such
luck

as
World War II moved toward us,
even then, during those
hot summers in the mid-30's in Los Angeles.

b e t t i n g   o n   n o w

I am old enough to have died several
times and I almost have,
now I drive my car through the sun
and over the freeway and past
Watts and to the racetrack
where the parking lot attendants
and the betting clerks
throw garlands of flowers at
me.
I've reached the pause before the full
stop and they are celebrating
because it just seems proper.
what the hell.
the hair I've lost to chemo-
therapy is slowly growing
back but my feet are numb

and I must concentrate on my
balance.
old and battered, olden
matter,
I am still lucky with the
horses.
the consensus is that I
have a few seasons
left.
you would never believe
that I was once young
with a narrow razor face
and crazy eyes of
gloom.
no matter, I sit at my
table
joking with the waiters.
we know it's a fixed
game.
it's funny, Christ, look
at us:
sitting ducks.
"what are you having?"
asks my waiter.
"oh," I say and
read him something
from the menu.
"o.k.," he says
and walks away
between the earthquake,
the volcano and the
leopard.

THE DEATH OF THE FATHER

M y mother had died a year earlier. A week after my father's death I stood in his house alone. It was in Arcadia, and the nearest I had come to the house in some time was passing by on the freeway on my way to Santa Anita.

I was unknown to the neighbors. The funeral was over, and I walked to the sink, poured a glass of water, drank it, then went outside. Not knowing what else to do, I picked up the hose, turned on the water and began watering the shrubbery. Curtains drew back as I stood on the front lawn. Then they began coming out of their houses. A woman walked over from across the street.

"Are you Henry?" she asked me.

I told her that I was Henry.

"We knew your father for years."

Then her husband walked over. "We knew your mother too," he said.

I bent over and shut off the hose. "Won't you come in?" I asked. They introduced themselves as Tom and Nellie Miller and we went into the house.

"You look just like your father."

"Yes, so they tell me."

We sat and looked at each other.

"Oh," said the woman, "he had so *many* pictures. He must have liked pictures."

"Yes, he did, didn't he?"

"I just love that painting of the windmill in the sunset."

"You can have it."

"Oh, can I?"

The doorbell rang. It was the Gibsons. The Gibsons told me that they also had been neighbors of my father's for years.

"You look just like your father," said Mrs. Gibson.

"Henry has given us the painting of the windmill."

"That's nice. I *love* that painting of the blue horse."

"You can have it, Mrs. Gibson."

"Oh, you don't mean it?"

"Yes, it's all right."

The doorbell rang again and another couple came in. I left the door ajar. Soon a single man stuck his head inside. "I'm Doug Hudson. My wife's at the hairdresser's."

"Come in, Mr. Hudson."

Others arrived, mostly in pairs. They began to circulate through the house.

"Are you going to sell the place?"

"I think I will."

"It's a lovely neighborhood."

"I can see that."

"Oh, I just *love* this frame but I don't like the picture."

"Take the frame."

"But what should I do with the picture?"

"Throw it in the trash." I looked around. "If anybody sees a picture they like, please take it."

They did. Soon the walls were bare.

"Do you need these chairs?"

"No, not really."

Passersby were coming in from the street, and not even bothering to introduce themselves.

"How about the sofa?" someone asked in a very loud voice. "Do you want it?"

"I don't want the sofa," I said.

They took the sofa, then the breakfast nook table and chairs.

"You have a toaster here somewhere, don't you, Henry?"

They took the toaster.

"You don't need these dishes, do you?"

"No."

"And the silverware?"

"No."

"How about the coffee pot and the blender?"

"Take them."

One of the ladies opened a cupboard on the back porch. "What about all these preserved fruits? You'll never be able to eat all these."

"All right, everybody, take some. But try to divide them equally."

"Oh, I want the strawberries!"

"Oh, I want the figs!"

"Oh, I want the marmalade!"

People kept leaving and returning, bringing new people with them.

"Hey, here's a fifth of whiskey in the cupboard! Do you drink, Henry?"

"Leave the whiskey."

The house was getting crowded. The toilet flushed. Somebody knocked a glass from the sink and broke it.

"You better save this vacuum cleaner, Henry. You can use it for your apartment."

"All right, I'll keep it."

"He had some garden tools in the garage. How about the garden tools?"

"No, I better keep those."

"I'll give you $15 for the garden tools."

"O.K."

He gave me the $15 and I gave him the key to the garage. Soon you could hear him rolling the lawn mower across the street to his place.

"You shouldn't have given him all that equipment for $15, Henry. It was worth much more than that."

I didn't answer.

"How about the car? It's four years old."

"I think I'll keep the car."

"I'll give you $50 for it."

"I think I'll keep the car."

Somebody rolled up the rug in the front room. After that people began to lose interest. Soon there were only three or four left, then they were all gone. They left me the garden hose, the bed, the refrigerator and stove, and a roll of toilet paper.

I walked outside and locked the garage door. Two small boys came by on roller skates. They stopped as I was locking the garage doors.

"See that man?"

"Yes."

"His father died."

They skated on. I picked up the hose, turned the faucet on and began to water the roses.

Salka Viertel

For much of the 1930s and 1940s, the unofficial headquarters of Los Angeles's émigré arts community was the home where actress Salka Viertel (1889–1978) lived with her husband, Berthold, a director and writer who came to Southern California from Vienna in 1928 to collaborate with the German filmmaker F. W. Murnau. The Viertels intended to stay for only a few years, but by 1932 the uncertain political situation in Europe caused them to change their plans. In addition to hosting an intellectual open house that went on for decades, Salka enjoyed some success as a screenwriter, creating a number of vehicles for her friend Greta Garbo, including *Conquest*, *Anna Karenina*, and *Queen Christina*. In these excerpts from her 1969 memoir *The Kindness of Strangers*, Salka Viertel evokes her early years in California, culminating with America's entry into the Second World War.

from

THE KINDNESS OF STRANGERS

I expected California to be all sunshine and flowers but, just as we were robbed of the skyline view when we approached New York, so we found Los Angeles cold and overcast, with the sun, against which we had been so emphatically warned, invisible. While we were driving along Sunset Boulevard I noticed that there were no sidewalks in front of the uniform, clapboard houses and bungalows. An extraordinary fantasy was displayed in roof styling: some roofs were like mushrooms, many imitated Irish thatch and the shape of others was inspired by Hansel and Gretel's gingerbread house. Ice cream was sold in the gaping mouth of a huge frog, or inside a rabbit; a restaurant was called "The Brown Derby" and looked like one. The buses we passed offered SERVICE WITH A SMILE, and during our whole ride Berthold was busy writing in his notebook the slogans on stores, buildings and billboards:

"Hillside Homes of Happiness—your servants will enjoy working as you will enjoy living in an Outpost Home."

"Toilet seats shaped to conform to nature's laws."

"How easy it is to shave when you control hydrolysis."

"Less hair in the comb, more hair on your head."

"Don't fool yourself! Halitosis makes you unpopular."

"Teeth may shine like tinted pearls, still pyorrhea attacks four out of five."

To avoid the downtown traffic, our chauffeur did not drive through the city, which on the first fleeting glimpse was uninviting and ugly. JESUS SAVES, read a sign, towering over a large building, and Mr. Bing explained that this was Aimée Semple McPherson's Temple. We had never heard of Aimée Semple McPherson and wanted to know who she was. Our companions perked up and eagerly told us the gossip, and much of it appeared to be true, about the lady preacher. Aimée had brought romance and glamor to religion, joy to the poor, and her Temple rivaled the Roxy in showmanship. It sounded fascinating and we were determined to attend her services as soon as possible.

Our suite at the Roosevelt was almost identical with the one in our New York hotel, and just as overheated. There was a big bouquet of red roses for me and a case of whisky for Berthold, this time in the bathtub. The roses were from Murnau, the whisky a welcome from the studio.

"They must think we are alcoholics," I said to Bing.

He sighed: "In our profession one needs a drink rather often." I offered him one immediately.

Quite heavy, quite tall and still quite young, probably in his thirties, the son of German-Jewish immigrants, Bing had come to Hollywood as an actor. "I was a comedian," he said with a resigned smile. "I was not bad . . . not bad at all . . . I could be very funny."

After we were installed in our rooms he said good-bye, asking Berthold to call whenever he needed him and saying that he would report our arrvial to Mr. Murnau. In the car I had already noticed that when he mentioned Murnau he seemed to be terrified by his grandeur. It did not fail to irritate Berthold.

The telephone rang and I answered. It was Murnau, happy that we had arrived at last. I thanked him for the roses and said that Berthold was taking a shower and would call later.

"Just tell him I don't need him today. I am shooting tests," said Murnau. "Only wanted to say hello."

Berthold was furious when I gave him the message. Murnau's "I don't need him" was sheer Prussian arrogance. Although I explained that Murnau did not sound overbearing, the jarring note was a pre-lude to the many clashes in their odd friendship.

The German journalist Arnold Hoellriegel, who was also stay-ing in the Roosevelt, wanted us to have lunch with him. Coming downstairs we heard a cacophony of shrill voices as if from an enor-mous, excited poultry yard. The lobby was packed with women of whom the youngest could not have been less than seventy. About a hundred of them tottered around on high heels, in bright, flowered-chiffon dresses, orchid or gardenia corsages pinned to their bosoms. We wanted to know the purpose of the gathering but were told only that the ladies were Republicans. Hoellriegel's traveling companion and photographer, Max Goldschmidt, was not permitted to take pictures. After lunch Hoellriegel suggested that we take a look at the studios, but I pleaded that we drive first to the ocean.

The afternoon was gray and chilly, a mist hanging over Santa Monica. We drove along Pico Boulevard, a long, straight highway leading to the ocean. Again we saw shabby bungalows, occasional palm trees, gasoline stations, nurseries, markets and endless "lots for sale." Then the highway rose to a hilltop and we could see a bright, silvery glimmer, which changed into a wide strip of an iri-descent, mother-of-pearl hue. We passed a lovely cemetery shaded by trees, like those in the "old country." It was called Woodland. Turning right we stopped in front of a rambling hotel surrounded by an old, beautiful garden with enormous gum trees, sycamores and cypresses.

Having crossed the street and the well-kept lawn of an espla-nade, shaded by eucalyptus trees and tall palms, we found ourselves on the rim of a cliff. Below was a highway, with automobiles flitting by; beach houses and clubs turned their backs to the road and the glassed-in front porches faced the ocean. To our right was the little bay of Santa Monica Canyon, surrounded by hills covered with shrubs, trees, and scattered houses. On our left was a pier, whose wooden pillars reached far out into the ocean. We drove to its entrance. A gaudy, yellow building with a tower-like superstructure harbored a merry-go-round. It had the most magnificent, fierce horses, carved in wood and painted by a real artist. They looked like the steeds on the monuments of great generals. The loud orchestrion was playing old-fashioned music. At each end of the long pier were fishmarkets, between them ice cream stalls and little shops renting fishing rods and selling bait, dusty abalone shells, starfish, coral beads and chewing gum, and a shack where a Filipino lady in a sequined costume was telling fortunes. Men and women in sunbleached jeans, and of all ages, were fishing from the pier. Boats were tied up below and one could go sailing outside the little bay. Everything was so lovely and peaceful: the people on the pier and the merry-go-round and the swaying boats. I begged Berthold to let us live in Santa Monica.

When Berthold mentioned this in the studio, people were horrified: Santa Monica! Everybody who lived there became rheumatic, had chronic bronchitis and gout. "Then why would all the rich people have houses there?" I argued. I was told that those houses were air-conditioned and sound-proofed; their owners had the means to protect themselves from ocean air and the pounding surf. Only Herman Bing's objection made some sense: living in Santa Monica, Berthold would have to get up half an hour earlier to be on time at the studio. My vision of the mad daily rush made me resign myself to a house in Hollywood.

Emil and Gussy Jannings gave a party for us. Emil, a lusty character-actor, had the gross and expansive sense of humor one calls "Rabelaisian." His wife Gussy, blond and very chic, had once been a cabaret singer, a well-known *diseuse*, and had become a stoical, imperturbable, though sharp-tongued consort. Invited with us were Conrad Veidt, lanky and handsome, and short cigar-smoking Ernst Lubitsch, now a celebrated film maker, but who had not changed since our *Judith* days. Both had uninteresting pretty wives. A successful German director, Ludwig Berger, was also there. Paramount had signed him because of his European fame, but they did not know what to do with him. Max Reinhardt appeared after dinner, with young Raimund von Hoffmansthal, son of the Austrian poet. He said that he had fallen in love with California, which Jannings, who hardly knew it, detested.

All those who had been some time in Hollywood seemed starved for new faces and, as I soon discovered, irritated with the old.

The Jannings lived in a grand-style Hollywood mansion, which they rented from the millionaire Josef Schenk, one of "filmdom's pioneers." Situated in the center of Hollywood Boulevard, it had a large garden, swimming pool, tennis court, and a huge living room with a multitude of lamps. The diversity of lamps and especially the extraordinary shapes of the lampshades, struck me as a speciality of Hollywood interiors.

Throughout the evening the main topic of conversation was the catastrophic impact of the talking films upon the careers of foreign stars, until the exuberant entrance of the precocious "Mann children," Erika and Klaus, brightened the atmosphere. They had just arrived in Hollywood on their journey around the world. Very young and attractive, they were refreshingly irreverent and adventurous. They brought with them the atmosphere of Berlin's night life which electrified the party. It was very late when we left with them, discussing the evening on our way back to the hotel. Berthold was fascinated by Jannings's impersonation of "Jannings in real life," an amalgamation of his monstrous egotism with roles he had played: Harpagon, Henry VIII, with glimpses of the good-natured, straightforward *Deutscher Michel*. We agreed that it was a great performance; that Conny Veidt was most handsome and a darling; Lubitsch inscrutable but worth knowing better; and Ludwig Berger's fate a warning to European directors.

I had rented the least expensive house I could find. It was on Fairfax Avenue, near the hills of Laurel Canyon, unpretentious but pleasant.

As soon as we moved in I asked Bing to help me choose a car and teach me how to drive. Half an hour later we returned in a Buick. Berthold was doubtful that a good car could be bought so quickly. I sat behind the wheel, death-defying Bing next to me. Nonchalantly I released the brakes, shifted into first gear and drove around the block. At least one of our problems was solved.

Had Berthold had any sense of direction, had he been less absent-minded and more interested in mechanical things, and had he been able to remember the difference between the brake and the accelerator, he also would have learned to drive. Under the circumstances, it was lucky that he stalled the car as soon as he touched the gearshift. After smashing a bumper and tearing off two fenders, he conceded defeat and De Witt Fuller joined our household as chauffeur. Bing could now devote himself entirely to typing, translating Berthold's script and giving him English lessons. We also engaged

Emma, a Negro housekeeper, although Jannings threatened never to have a meal in our house. Now we were set, and certain that we would stay for a while in America.

———

The unconcerned sunbathers on the beach, their hairless bodies glistening and brown, the gigantic trucks rumbling on the highway, the supermarkets with their mountains of food, the studio with the oh-so-relaxed employees, the chatting extras pouring out from the stages at lunch time, the pompous executives marching to their "exclusive dining room" or to the barbershop, stopping to flirt with the endearing "young talent"—all these familiar scenes were a nerve-racking contrast to the war horror I constantly imagined. It did not help to tell myself that at least the bombings had ceased; what was life under Soviet rule like? The silence exasperated me. I also heard nothing from Vienna. All I knew was that my brother-in-law was staging operas in Buenos Aires; but had it been possible for Rose and the children to join him? I did not dare to cable her. Berthold had had reports that the German pogroms were nothing compared to the barbarism of the Austrian Nazis.

"Years of the Devil," my secretary Etta had written on the folder which contained the tragic letters from Austria, Prague and France. How well I remember the evening after the Molotov report came out, when Bertolt Brecht and a friend, Ruth Berlau, were sitting by the fireplace in my home and I said how guilty I felt because I had been spared. Next morning I found under my door a poem Brecht had written:

> *Ich weiss natürlich: einzig durch Glück*
> *Habe ich so viele Freunde überlebt. Aber heute Nacht im Traum*
> *Hörte ich diese Freunde von mir sagen: "Die Stärkeren überleben"*
> *Und ich hasste mich.*

It seemed inconceivable that with their many connections, with British and American friends (influential politicians and foreign correspondents), Camil and Irma Hoffmann, these two kindest and gentlest people, had to die in Auschwitz. Camil's last letter, in his precise, neat handwriting, thanked me for an affidavit I had got for his son Jan, and concluded: "We are staying here in Prague in an old house, having renounced a vacation trip because of the rainy summer. We cannot complain of boredom: thanks to the 'world theater' there is no lack of distraction."

Later I was told that while they were interned in Theresienstadt the Nazis, giving in to international pressure, offered to release Camil but not Irma. He rejected the perfidious offer and they were both shipped to Auschwitz.

Walter Hasenclever committed suicide in France, Ernst Toller in New York. Berthold had seen him three days before he killed himself:

> We had lunch together and he seemed so depressed that I hesitated to leave him. He told me about his insomnia and his utter hopelessness. I also had the impression that he needed money, but he denied it and now I read in the papers that he has left a substantial bank account. He was uncertain if he should go to England or stay in New York, and it was obvious that it was impossible for him to make any decision whatsoever. Nevertheless, I thought that he would conquer this depression. He showed such warmth towards me that I felt he had become more concerned for others and that in many ways he was beginning to find his true self. However, he no longer had the strength. In spite of his numerous contacts he was utterly alone and in spite of all his desperate activity people had lost confidence in him. One cannot stop thinking: if only he had not done it! But who can judge. . . .

This autumn of tears and anxiety brought also an unexpected joy. I had been reproaching Peter for spending more time on the tennis court than at his studies and one day he retorted, "How long can you support me?" I said: "Until you have a profession."

"All right, let's make a deal," he said. "If I get a job I won't have to study! If I don't, I'll go back to school."

"It's a deal."

Weeks went by and there was no indication whatever that Peter was looking for a job or playing less tennis, and I was confident that he would be enrolling at U.C.L.A. the next summer. Then, one evening, he appeared in tennis shorts, a racquet in his hand, and nonchalantly dropped a letter into my lap. It was from Harcourt and Brace, and said: "Dear Mr. Viertel: We are happy to inform you that your novel *The Canyon* has been accepted by us for publication." What's more, they offered him an advance. I was defeated.

The Canyon appeared in 1940, and critics unanimously expressed great hopes for the nineteen-year-old author. The book described a group of adventurous youngsters and adults, inhabitants of the Santa Monica Canyon, as it was when we first moved there. It was dedicated to "the foreign family up the street and to Anne." I never asked who Anne was.

After the war broke out, more Europeans moved into the Canyon. One of them was Christopher Isherwood, boyishly handsome, blue-eyed and, as Berthold had described him, with a great sense of humor. We saw a lot of each other as we also had friends in common: the Huxleys, Iris Tree, John Houseman, Klaus and Erika Mann. MGM signed him up to write screenplays, which he seemed to enjoy for a while. As the war went on he left to work with the Quakers. I felt that, at that time, he was going through great emotional strain.

Andrew, a thirteen-year-old refugee, son of Leonhard Frank (author of *Karl und Anna* and *Die Räuberbande*), joined our household. His parents were divorced. The mother, Lena, was in the East, struggling for a new existence, and until she could achieve it I offered to take care of Andrew. He was Tommy's age and extremely intelligent and lovable. Then Berthold's niece Susan, his sister Helene's daughter, arrived with an eight-month-old son. Her husband, St. John Mann, was an officer in the British Navy. As his duties took him far away from England, she and the baby came to stay with me. Of course Etta worried about the permanent overdrawing of my bank account, but admitted that there was nothing else we could do.

Ninotchka was in full production. Lubitsch came to my office every day, telling me what scenes they had shot and how wonderful Garbo was. And he maintained that considering his bitterness about the Stalin-Hitler pact, the film was not anti-Soviet. Piled up on my desk were novels and plays which the story department thought "excellent Garbo material."

I don't remember what provoked Gottfried and Sam Hoffenstein to urge me to take an agent, but they were convinced that Paul

Kohner would represent my interests better than myself. I had known Paul since our early days in Hollywood when he was a producer at Universal, and as our large household urgently demanded a greater income I said that I would be glad to have him as my agent. Paul agreed that I was underpaid: six hundred and fifty dollars a week was peanuts and I deserved twice as much. I was sending hundreds of dollars to Europe as well as large sums which, from time to time, unknown people with Jewish names, in Sweden or Switzerland, requested for my mother. It was impossible to investigate these demands; I refused to risk my mother's safety because someone might be taking advantage of me. (Later I found out that Mama and Dusko had received only a fraction of what I had sent.) Also Christmas was approaching and there was a long list of people I had to remember.

On the day Kohner was supposed to discuss my contract with Eddie Mannix I came home just as the telephone rang, and picked up the receiver. Steeling himself to firmness, the story editor informed me that he was taking me off the payroll. I remember that I said "thank you," although I still don't know why. Then he hung up.

As soon as I recovered from the shock, I phoned Kohner. He was flabbergasted. He said that Mannix had angrily refused to raise my salary, but that he should also fire me was quite unexpected. Gottfried came and reported that Mannix was furious that I had let an agent "barge in between us." After all, for seven years MGM had voluntarily increased my weekly check.

"She should see if Kohner can get her a better job," he shouted.

Bernie phoned and advised me to apologize to Mannix, but I refused. It was my right to be represented by an agent. Paul Kohner took up the challenge and said he would get me a job in another studio. It would take some time, as Christmas was so near. I had to be brave and optimistic. Roosevelt's reelection to a third term, with Henry Wallace as Vice President, was a comforting victory. For the first time in my life I voted and took an "active part in democratic procedure." My now twenty-one-year-old Hans, although pleased that Roosevelt had won, had voted for the Socialist Norman Thomas.

The work at the Reinhardt studio had taken Hans away from politics, but the murder of Trotsky in Mexico brought him, and me also subsequently, in contact with the young Trotskyites again. At first it appeared that Trotsky was only dangerously wounded and his adherents tried sending a famous Los Angeles brain surgeon to Mexico. They needed money and asked me if I could help. As I was already unable to pay my own expenses I thought of Ernst Lubitsch and Edward G. Robinson. Lubitsch had never said "no" when I asked him for money, and Robinson, who knew Trotsky personally from a visit to Mexico, had told me repeatedly how impressed he had been with the old man. Ernst gave me a hundred dollars in cash, Robinson a check for a hundred and fifty, made out in my name, and I added a hundred myself. But Trotsky died that same day and the distressed young people begged me to send the money to his widow. I am mentioning all this not because I want to give the impression of having been close to a historical event, but because my natural and human action was to have unforeseen consequences later, in the McCarthy era.

Worries and anxieties multiplied. In spite of the repeal of the embargo, Peter was sure that America would remain neutral and that he would never have a chance to fight the Nazis. "Your boys are not going to be sent into any foreign wars," Roosevelt promised American mothers. So Peter secretly tried to enlist in the Canadian RAF. He was rejected twice because his eyesight did not meet the requirements of the recruiting board. The third time he told me frankly that he was going to Vancouver and invited me to accompany him part of the way. It was June and we drove through the Yosemite Valley, along the Merced River swollen by hundreds of cascading waterfalls, its banks a jungle of fragrant wild lilac. This exuberant bloom could not dispell the visions of destruction and death into which my son was so eager to rush, just as life was offering him so much. I understood his decision but I did not want him to enlist in a "foreign" army; as a matter of fact, unheroic mother that I was, I did not want him to enlist in any army. I dreaded the thought of his being a pilot and my only hope was that my former house-keeper, Jessie's husband, was on the recruiting board. War or peace, the world is rather small when you think of it. Peter came home, as the only job offered him was in the coast defense artillery for which he had no taste; and for the time being I could breathe again.

To better my financial situation I was contemplating all kinds of moves. My favorite plan was to forget about the movies or stage and to open a restaurant either in Santa Monica or in Beverly Hills, but preferably in the Canyon. My friends praised the food in my house extravagantly and I had great success as a cook, but even the generous Ernst Lubitsch refused to finance me, saying: "You'll be feeding the whole town for nothing."

I thought of a hotdog stand which according to my sons, would be a "gold mine," or a goulash wagon on the beach; but all these plans provided only amusement at the dinner table and a lot of teasing from Gottfried, who prophesied that after a few weeks of punitive exile I would return, a prodigal daughter, to Eddie Mannix's open arms. Looking back I don't know whether it was lucky that Paul Kohner sold "my services" to Warner Brothers. For the moment it was a triumph and an enormous financial relief. Nevertheless in the long run the hotdog stand might have given us more permanent security. Anyway, I got an assignment which paid a thousand dollars a week. The mortgage on the house was taken care of, at least temporarily; and I could afford to raise the wage of the young refugee couple, Walter and Hedy Herlitschek, who kept house for us. (They changed their name to Herley as soon as they touched ground in the U.S.) Walter had been a salesman in a chic haberdashery shop in Vienna, Hedy a dressmaker; now she was a cook, Walter a "butler-chauffeur." Without bewailing their prosperous past, the majority of refugees grabbed any kind of work to provide for their families and the old and sick they had to leave behind and for whom the gates of the promised land would never open. It was easier for the women to get jobs, and many supported their men and children by catering at parties, and introducing the *Sachertorte* and *Apfelstrudel* to American palates. They washed, cleaned and sewed. As the defense industries were absorbing more and more workers and giving greater opportunities to Negroes, the demand for "domestics" benefited the refugees.

After the fall of Paris, the League of American Writers and the Emergency Rescue Committee took steps to save, at the last minute, the German intellectuals who had fled to the south of

France. With the help of Dorothy Thompson and Mrs. Roosevelt, Herman Budzislawski of the *Weltbuehne*, Schwarzschild, publisher of the *Tagebuch*, and the composer Hanns Eisler, received their visas; and the major studios hired, at a minimum salary of one hundred dollars a week, such renowned novelists as Heinrich Mann, Alfred Doeblin, Leonhardt Frank, Wilhelm Speyer, Alfred Neumann, and the journalists and critics Alfred Polgar, Walter Mehring, Jan Lustig and George Froeschel. Emil Ludwig, Franz Werfel and Lion Feuchtwanger rejected the offer, as their books were selling well in America. Hollywood could now boast of being the Parnassus of German literature, inasmuch as Thomas Mann had also become a resident of the Pacific Palisades. Alfred and Lisl Polgar had come from Lisbon and had been spared the ordeal which Heinrich Mann, his wife Nelly, the Werfels and Thomas Mann's son Golo went through crossing the Pyrenees on foot, the Gestapo close behind them.

It is unpardonable of me not to remember on what occasion I was introduced to Thomas Mann. It must have been at a meeting or banquet for some cause, most likely the Emergency Rescue Committee of which he and Dr. Kingdon, President of Newark University, were the chairmen. A slight man of medium height, he wore his hair parted on the side and a neat graying moustache under the jutting nose. He had the reserved politeness of a diplomat on official duty. His speeches, delivered in a careful, literary English, impressed the Americans, especially the younger generation, with their elevated intellectual content; and they were the pride of the refugee intelligentsia, anxious to preserve their cultural heritage. Frau Katja, his wife and the mother of his six children, accompanied him everywhere. Erika's beautifully-shaped head with the boyish haircut and dark eyes could sometimes be seen in the photos taken at banquets, meetings and lectures, but as a war correspondent she was rarely in the United States.

It was through Karl Kraus that Berthold met Heinrich Mann, one of the few contemporary writers whom Kraus appreciated. Mann's satirical masterpiece *Der Untertan* portrayed especially well the German subservience to militarism and nationalism. Later Heinrich Mann's pacifist-socialist convictions and his early awareness of Teutonic racism made him a great influence in the Popular

Front movement. In America, he was overshadowed by the fame of his brother. He was nearing seventy when, thanks to the Emergency Committee, he became a screenwriter at Warner Brothers. With his distinguished looks and the manners of a nineteenth-century *grand seigneur*, he appeared an odd figure in the Burbank studio. The German game: "Who is the greater writer, Heinrich or Thomas Mann?" continued to be played by the emigrants. Those inclined toward the left were for Heinrich, the more conservative for Thomas Mann.

At least thirty years younger than her husband, Nelly Mann was a voluptuous, blond, blue-eyed Teutonic beauty with red lips and sparkling teeth. Her sometimes ribald manner confirmed the rumor that she had been a barmaid in Hamburg. But even those she shocked had no doubts about her devotion to her husband. She drank secretly, slipping out to the bathroom or kitchen, coyly refusing the drinks offered at parties; then insisted on driving Heinrich home, to which he heroically consented.

Heinrich Mann's seventieth birthday was approaching and the "German writers in exile" felt that some notice should be taken of this event. Unfortunately, on the same day in March, 1941, Thomas Mann was to receive an Honorary Doctor's degree from the University of California in Berkeley. Immediately afterward he had a commitment for lectures, and would not return to Los Angeles until the end of April. After long diplomatic negotiations, the dinner had to be postponed until May. A major disagreement ensued as to whether it should take place in a restaurant or a private home. I called Berthold in New York and asked him whether I should not offer our house for the celebration. He was all for it. Lion Feuchtwanger and Liesl Frank were both delighted and promised to give me a list of guests, which had to be accepted by Nelly. She and Alma Mahler-Werfel were feuding and Nelly disapproved of everyone who was friendly with the Werfels. Finally the Feuchtwangers succeeded in arranging a truce and forty-five persons were invited. I set a long table in the living room; it could be removed quickly after the dinner was over. Decorated with flowers and candles it looked very festive.

Heinrich sat on my right and Thomas Mann on my left, Nelly was opposite us, towering over the very small Feuchtwanger on her right; on her left was Werfel. Everyone else was seated strictly

according to age and prominence. I had begged Berthold to send me
a telegram which would welcome Heinrich Mann, and I hoped to
get it before dinner. Good, faithful Toni Spuhler took over the
kitchen and managed very well, in spite of the many refugees who,
awed by the importance of the evening, had insisted on giving her a
hand, and also helping Walter and Hedy to serve. For them Heinrich and Thomas Mann, Alfred Neumann, Franz Werfel, Alfred
Polgar, Lion Feuchtwanger, Alfred Doeblin, Walter Mehring, Ludwig Marcuse, Bruno Frank represented the true Fatherland to
which in spite of Hitler they adhered, as they adhered to the German language.

We finished the soup and as the telegram had not arrived I made
a speech, which had the virtue of being very brief. Bruno Frank and
Feuchtwanger were to speak after the main course and I motioned
to Walter to go on serving but he discreetly pointed to Thomas
Mann, who had risen and was putting on his spectacles. Then, taking a sizeable manuscript out of the inner pocket of his tuxedo, he
began to read. I assumed it was at least fifteen pages long and I was
right, because many years later Thomas Mann mentioned this
speech in a letter to his son Klaus, offering it as an essay for the peri-
odical *Decision*. It was a magnificent tribute to the older brother, an
acknowledgement of Heinrich's prophetic political wisdom, his far-
sighted warnings to their unhappy country, and a superb evaluation
of his literary stature.

We hardly had time to drink Heinrich Mann's health before he
rose, also put on his glasses and also brought forth a thick manuscript. First he thanked me for the evening then, turning to his
brother, paid him high praise for his continuous fight against fascism. To that he added a meticulous literary analysis of Thomas
Mann's *oeuvre* in its relevance to the Third Reich. I no longer remember all the moving and profound thoughts expressed in both
speeches. It gave one some hope and comfort at a time when the
lights of freedom seemed extinguished in Europe, and everything
we had loved and valued buried in ruins. At the open door to the
pantry the "back entrance" guests were listening, crowding each
other and wiping their tears.

The roast beef was overdone and Toni was upset, but the guests
were elated and hungry and did not mind. Bruno Frank's and Lion

Feuchtwanger's speeches were brief and in a lighter vein. The dessert, my chocolate cake, a "speciality of the house," was served and disappeared rapidly. Toward the end of the dinner Martha Feuchtwanger spontaneously offered a toast, "To Nelly, who saved Heinrich Mann's life, practically carrying him in her arms on their rough trek through the Pyrenees. She supported him with her loving strength and gave courage to us all."

Nelly hid her face in her hands when we surrounded her to clink glasses and then, screaming with laughter, pointed to her red dress, which had burst open revealing her bosom in a lace bra.

Berthold's telegram was handed to me after we had left the table. I read it aloud and Heinrich Mann suggested that all the guests send a greeting to the absent host. While everyone gathered to sign his name, I said to Bruno Frank how touched I was by the wonderful homage the brothers had paid each other.

"Yes," said Bruno. "They write and read such ceremonial evaluations of each other, every ten years."

———

The German colony was divided into several groups, but Thomas Mann remained the representative, towering literary figure, his influence reaching as far as Washington, D.C. Bruno and Liesl Frank had been close to the Mann family for many years and the friendship continued in Hollywood. The Feuchtwangers, Franz and Alma Werfel, the Bruno Walters and Liesl Frank's famous mother, the musical comedy star Fritzi Massary, belonged to this circle, also the Dieterles. Then there was a devoted admiring group around Fritz Kortner.

The Polgars who did not belong to any group, spent their Sundays on Mabery Road. Max Reinhardt and Helene Thimig were preoccupied with the Workshop and the planning and preparing of its productions. They entertained rarely but these occasions were usually exceptionally pleasant. One evening I was invited with Sam Behrman, Franz Werfel and Alma, Mr. and Mrs. Erich Korngold and Gottfried. The Stravinskys came later, missing a marvelous dinner. They had never met Alma before. Remembering her position in the musical world, and forgetting Werfel, she rushed toward Stravinsky, announcing: "I am Alma Mahler." She was an imposing woman, still blond with large blue eyes and the old-fashioned charm of a Viennese beauty. The two great composers, Stravinsky and Schoenberg, avoided each other ostentatiously, and in fact only shortly before Schoenberg's death did they mutually acknowledge their importance. Later Stravinsky paid great homage to Schoenberg and to his music.

During his first years in Los Angeles, Schoenberg was teaching counterpoint at the University of California. His classes were crowded not only by students but also by jazz musicians of whom many also took private lessons from him. Edward used his summer vacations in Santa Monica to rehearse and prepare performances of Schoenberg's compositions, one of which, the "Pierrot Lunaire," took place in our living room, with Schoenberg conducting and the lovely Erika Wagner (Mrs. Fritz Stiedry in private life) speaking the text. All the literary and musical elite was present, among others three famous conductors: Bruno Walter, Otto Klemperer and Fritz Stiedry. The applause was not unanimous, but it was led by Thomas Mann, clapping his hands heartily while Bruno Walter whispered into his ear, obviously disapproving. That same winter Leopold Stokowski conducted Schoenberg's piano concerto in New York, with Edward as soloist. It was an almost unopposed success for everyone concerned.

The German invasion of Russia and the help America was sending to the Soviets had changed the attitude of the American Left, split during the Stalin-Hitler pact. In November, when the Germans had reached Sevastopol and Rostow, gloom settled on everyone. But in December the Soviets reconquered Rostow, relieving Moscow, and their offensive gave hope that the tide was turning. To this hope my mother and I clung persistently and desperately, praying for Dusko, Hania and Viktoria, and the millions of Slavic and Jewish people.

On one of the gray December afternoons I left the studio quite early and trying to fight my dismal dejection, I drove to the Santa Monica pier.

The clouds above the horizon had broken up and become purple, mauve, pink and silver-gray; the sun in their midst was like an enormous orange. I walked down the deserted pier, watching the orange ball disappear in the clouds, then suddenly come out blood-red and sink into the dark water. At the very end of the pier a young girl was sitting on the wooden planks, her legs in torn, faded jeans dangling through the railing. She wore a man's shirt, wide open, showing firm, round breasts. In one arm she held a fat baby which was sucking avidly; in her other hand a fishing rod, its line stretched far out in the water. She was watching the float with great concentration. I could not tear myself away from this sight of complete calm and satisfaction.

Next morning I took my mother for a drive in the open car along the Pacific and we listened to the Sunday concert from New York, which came over the radio. It was a combination of two of Mama's great pleasures. Arthur Rubinstein was just finishing the first movement of the Tchaikowsky Piano Concerto no. 1, when the broadcast was interrupted and the announcer said that early in the morning Japanese airplanes and submarines had attacked and sunk the American fleet in Pearl Harbor.

———

All the Japanese living in California were sent to concentration camps or, as they were politely called, "internment centers." Then Hitler declared war on the United States, and German refugees had to register as enemy aliens and to observe an 8 P.M. curfew. Thomas Mann and Albert Einstein appealed to the President: "The earliest and most far-sighted adversaries of the totalitarian governments, who have risked their lives by fighting and warning against forces of evil are now subjected to a humiliating treatment."

Strangely enough, there was no curfew in the East, where the "Bund" and the "Silver Shirts" had an impressively large membership of racists and pro-Nazis of German origin. In Hollywood most refugees goodnaturedly accepted the restriction of their liberty. They observed the blackouts and spent their evenings at home, convinced that a "fifth column" existed and caution was necessary. My former colleague from the Reinhardt theaters, Alexander Granch, used the time to write his moving memoirs. The younger men rushed to enlist in the army, which automatically made them American citizens.

Many of my friends, among them Annie von Bucovich, left Los Angeles to work at the Office of War Information. The Coordinator was our friend John Houseman, a producer at MGM.

I was visited several times by the FBI — strong, handsome young men, who would have served their country better in the Marines rather than in harassing the refugees. I specifically remember their inquiry about Annie:

"Is the lady a communist?"

"No, she is not."

"She is a Russian . . .?"

"She is neither a Russian nor a communist."

"She is anti-fascist?"

"Yes, she is."

The FBI man shook his head disapprovingly. "Oh, you people," he said with a deep sigh. "You are anti-fascist but I have never heard one of you say: I am anti-communist."

"Whom do you mean by 'you people'?" I asked belligerently. "The refugees? They were the first victims of the Nazi horror, the first enemies of the regime with which the U.S. is at war. And aren't the Russians our allies?" But I realized that my outburst was a waste of time and energy, so I assured him once more that Annie was not and had never been a communist and had never read a word of *Das Kapital*.

Reyner Banham

When the British architect and critic Reyner Banham (1922–1988) published *Los Angeles: The Architecture of Four Ecologies* in 1971, he shook up prevailing attitudes about L.A. as urban space. Where others had seen a sprawling mess of stucco and strip malls, he discerned a city in which ecology and technology interacted in unexpected fashion, and where the fluidity of the landscape became a metaphor for the constant reinvention of people's lives. Writers as diverse as Cees Nooteboom and John McPhee write sympathetically about Banham's insights elsewhere in this volume.

from

LOS ANGELES:
THE ARCHITECTURE OF FOUR ECOLOGIES

Like the film, the hamburger is a non-Californian invention that has achieved a kind of symbolic apotheosis in Los Angeles; symbolic, that is, of the way fantasy can lord it over function in Southern California. The purely functional hamburger, as delivered across the counter of say, the Gipsy Wagon on the UCLA campus, the Surf-boarder at Hermosa Beach or any McDonald's or Jack-in-the-Box outlet [1] anywhere, is a pretty well-balanced meal that he who runs (surfs, drives, studies) can eat with one hand; not only the ground beef but all the sauce, cheese, shredded lettuce, and other garnishes are firmly gripped between the two halves of the bun.

But the fantastic hamburger as served on a platter at a sit-down restaurant is something else again. Its component parts have been carefully opened up and separated out into an assemblage of functional and symbolic elements, or alternatively, a fantasia on functional themes. The two halves of the bun lie face up with the ground beef on one and, sometimes, the cheese on the other. Around and alongside on the platter are the lettuce leaves, gherkins, onion rings, fried potatoes, paper cups of relish or coleslaw, pineapple rings, and much more besides, because the invention of new varieties of hamburger is a major Angeleno culinary art. Assembled with proper

535

1. Jack-in-the-Box hamburger stand

care it can be a work of visual art as well; indeed, it must be considered as visual art first and foremost, since some components are present in too small a quantity generally to make a significant gustatory as opposed to visual contribution — for instance, the seemingly mandatory ring of red-dyed apple, which does a lot for the eye as a foil to the general greenery of the salads, but precious little for the palate.

The way in which the functional and symbolic parts of the hamburger platter have been discriminated, separated, and displayed is a fair analogue for the design of most of the buildings in which they are sold. No nonsense about integrated design, every part conceived in separated isolation and made the most of; the architecture of symbolic assemblage. But it was not always so; the earlier architecture of commercial fantasy of the city tended to yield primacy to a single symbolic form or *Gestalt* into which everything had to be fitted. The famous Brown Derby restaurant in the shape of a hat [2], the Cream Cans (in the shape of cream cans), the Hoot Hoot I Scream outlet (in the form of an owl, not an ice-cream) and the several Bonzo dogs that sold hot dogs in the twenties and thirties, repackaged their functional propositions in symbolic envelopes expressing a single, formal idea.

The building and the symbol are one and the same thing, and if this sounds like one of the approved aims of architecture as a fine art, then it can certainly be paralleled in the work of reputable art architects of the period and later — Henry Oliver's Spadina house of 1925, with its domestic functions re-packaged in a Hansel and Gretel image, or almost any Angeleno building where a single idea has been made dominant over everything else, most triumphantly, perhaps, in Lloyd Wright's Wayfarer's Chapel of 1949, which contrives to command respect both as architecture in the respectable sense of the word, and as Pop fantasy comparable to the wilder kind of gourmet-style restaurants.

Such symbolic packaging within a single conceptual form can impose strains even on a building with one function only to serve, let alone a multiplicity of functions, and there were always needs that drove fantasists in other directions. So Grauman's Chinese Theatre [3], the ultimate shrine of all the fantasy that was Hollywood, kept most of its fantastication as a garnish for the façade and

2. Brown Derby restaurant, Wilshire Boulevard, 1926

the pavilions flanking Meyer and Holler's generous forecourt, while the architecture underneath is plain bread-and-butter stuff like the buns of the hamburger. It is, indeed, a much less 'integrated design' than either of its two most celebrated fantastic contemporaries, both by Morgan Wall and Clements, the Assyrian-style Samson Rubber Company plant, and the recently demolished black-and-gold Rich-field Building [4] downtown. But one other properly appliquéed fantasy does survive from the twenties: the totally improbable Aztec Hotel in Monrovia [5]; intended by its designer to be Mayan rather than Aztec, it has his supposedly Mayan detailing stuck all over a relatively plain structure like piped icing on a pastry.

Fantasy is actually found only rarely in the planning of a build-ing, or the layout of adjoining clustered structures—even a much later fantasy such as the Bel Air hotel, laid out like a Spanish Colo-nial Revival village, finally proves to be a rational system of pedes-trian courts—the real fantasy there is the 'outdoor' fireplace under a tree in a rockery at the end of the dining-room. Fantasy of the ham-burger kind is all too often a compensation for the poverty of the

3. Grauman's Chinese Theatre, Hollywood, 1927, Meyer and Holler, architects

building behind or under it, or for the hard-nosed rationalism of the market economy, and this division between the rational, functional shell and the fantastic garnish has become more apparent as the years have passed. On Wilshire Boulevard, and over a time-span of a decade, the development can be seen in the two prime department stores. Bullock's-Wilshire [6] has an eye-catching tower that grows naturally out of the detailing and structural rhythms of what is below, an immensely professional piece of architecture by Parkinson and Parkinson in 1929; May Company at the end of Miracle Mile has its equally eye-catching gilt cylinder chopped back into the corner of a rectangular shopping-box [7] to which it is related only by physical attachment, Albert C. Martin in 1939 having turned in a piece of immensely professional store-planning, but not architecture in the earlier sense.

The next stage of the development can be seen, still on Wilshire, just across Fairfax Avenue from May Company; Johnies, which actually does sell hamburgers. Somewhere underneath the fantasy lurks a plain rectangular flat-roofed building [8], around which a purely notional butterfly roof has been sketched, but turned down front and back to give a sheltering form not unlike the nominal mansard roofs that give the name to the Gourmet Mansardic style

4. Richfield Building (demolished), downtown Los Angeles, 1928,
Morgan Walls and Clements, architects

of restaurant architecture. On the front this roof is garnished with
lettering, and the whole structure is flanked by entirely independent
signs, one merely lettered, the other humorously [*sic*] pictorial. And
a crowning non sequitur—an enormous sign which is part of the
structure but advertises something entirely different.

The lower down the scales of financial substance and cultural
pretensions one goes, the better sense it apparently makes (and has

5. Aztec Hotel, Monrovia, 1925, Robert Stacy-Judd, architect

made, visibly, for a couple of decades) to buy a plain standard building shell from Butler Buildings Corporation or a similar mass-producer and add symbolic garnish to the front, top, or other parts that show. It makes even better sense, of course, to acquire an existing disused building and impose your commercial personality on it with symbolic garnishes. But even if you are a major commercial operator with a chain of outlets, even a major oil company, it still makes financial sense to put up relatively simple single-storey boxes, and then make them tall enough to attract attention by piling up symbols and graphic art on top. So Jack-in-the-Box heaps storey heights of graphics and symbols on top of quite simple and unassumingly functional drive-by hamburger bars; or a big supermarket may even run up an entirely independent sign detached from any building, and make it a visually interesting

6. Bullock's-Wilshire, 1928, Parkinson and Parkinson, architects

structure in its own right, like the double-tapered lattice tower at Norwalk Square [9].

But having proposed this sliding scale of commercial frugality versus cultural or aesthetic status, I have to admit some major anomalies that spoil the graph—though this is fair enough in the realm of fantasy. Many banks, despite their manifest status as monuments to

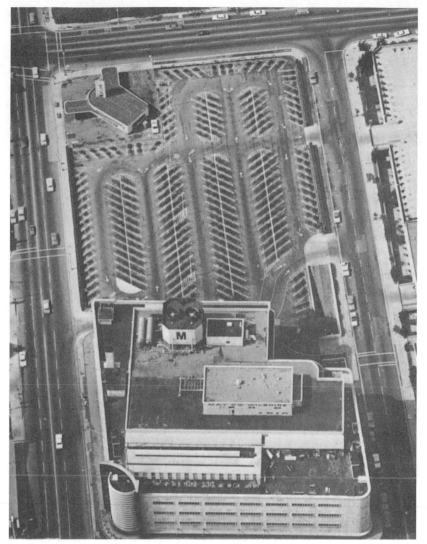

7. May Company, Miracle Mile, 1939, Albert C. Martin and Associates, architects

the most enduring cultural values of a frankly acquisitive way of life, make a strong pitch at the Pop commercial level. Sometimes — as with the notorious applied art work of the Ahmanson Banks — it is possible to suspect such a confusion of cultural intentions as to make further discussion pointless (though no less humorous), but there are a few bank buildings which are designed exactly by the rules discussed above. The best example is the Cabrillo Savings Bank building on the Pacific Coast Highway at Torrance, which has a three-storey-high arcaded porch *à la* Yamasaki (for which the local source would be Ed Stone's Perpetual Savings Banks) and clearly functioning as a symbol of superior cultural tone, but entirely separate from the single-storey bank building around which it is wrapped, a total discrimination between the functional and symbolic parts of the design.

The other and more interesting area of anomalies embraces the architecture of restaurants, where these have any pretensions above the level of burger bars or coffee shops. There is a fairly well-defined middle level of domestic affluence in Los Angeles whose presence can be identified by certain key adjectives used in advertising to signify the kind of pretension that is also common in the middle rank of restaurants. These are *Custom* ('custom view homes'), *Decorator* ('antiqued decorator bar-stools'), and *Gourmet* ('gourmet party dips'). Within its own field the last has such precise status, outranking *Delicatessen* by the same degree that *Delicatessen* outranks *grocery*, that it seems entirely appropriate to adopt *Gourmet* as the stylistic label for the more aspiring kind of restaurant architecture.

From the Brown Derby onwards, through the Velvet Turtle at Redondo Beach, and onwards into a plushly under-lit future of 'Total Meal Experience', restaurants have been the most intensely and completely designed buildings in the area—few, even, of the most expensive houses can have had so much detailed attention devoted to them inside and out, and some of Rudolph Schindler's most inventive and advanced design was inside the Sardi's he did in 1932. In their current incarnations, they tend to be dark, both in terms of levels of illumination and the colour of woodwork, floor-coverings (often tiles or brick) and other integral surfaces, much subdivided by pierced screens or theatrically focused on a massive open fire-hearth or two.

This kind of Gourmet/Decorator interior is common in other parts of the US, of course; the Los Angeles variant differs in its greater reliance on Spanish Colonial sources (including one or two genuine pre-1848 pieces of furniture if possible) but chiefly in being done with greater skill, resourcefulness, and conviction. The same is true of the gourmet exterior in its two chief local varieties. The

8. Johnies Wilshire, Miracle Mile, 1962

'Gracious Living' variant often recalls the kind of nineteenth-century architecture that Professor Hitchcock categorized as 'Second Empire and Cognate Modes' slightly compromised by Hudson River Bracketted. To the front of the standard lightweight rectangular building shell this style adds round-arched openings, thin pretty detailing such as balconies and the small, steeply pitched false roof-fronts that justify the stylistic epithet Gourmet Mansardic.

The 'Char-broiled Protein' variant, on the other hand, has its ultimate sources in the ranch-house style, locally modified by the influence of the Greene Brothers and Frank Lloyd Wright, and shaggy surfaces that have the same implications of masculinity as an unshaven chin; massive rough-tiled roofs pulled well down and well out beyond the building envelope, exposed and roughly finished timber within and without, supplemented by random rubble or field-stone for exposed structural columns and the open hearths which are, of course, fundamental to the whole style — even to the extent of being supplemented by purely symbolic fire-pits under metal hoods on the outside of the building in some examples. Planning variations within the style extend from the endlessly informal

9. Norwalk Square shopping center, Norwalk

to neatly balanced pairs of pavilions under 'mausoleum' roofs, Philadelphia-style, and the whole manner reaches one of its most notable local extremes in the so-called Polynesian restaurants.

In terms of geographical distribution, as well as stylistic pretensions, the Polynesians are everywhere from High-Gourmet 'Restaurant Row' next to Gallery Row on La Cienega Boulevard, to your local neighbourhood shopping centre. Epitomized by, say, the Tahitian Village in Bellflower [10], it exhibits a high, peaky roof pulled out across the side-walk in a long pointed gable that must owe more, ultimately, to Saarinen's Hockey Rink than to anything in the South Seas, and a profusion of carved wood and rough hewn surfaces (even the risers of the external steps have been distressed with a trowel before the cement was dry) buried in a positive green salad of impenetrable exotic evergreens.

A building as strikingly and lovably ridiculous as this represents well enough the way Los Angeles sums up a general phenomenon of US life; the convulsions in building style that follow when traditional cultural and social restraints have been overthrown and replaced by the preferences of a mobile, affluent, consumer-oriented society, in which 'cultural values' and ancient symbols are handled primarily as methods of claiming or establishing status. This process has probably gone further in, say, Las Vegas, yet it is in the context of Los Angeles that everyone seems to feel the strongest compulsion to discuss this fantasticating tendency.

And rightly so. Until Las Vegas became unashamedly middle-aged and the boring Beaux-Arts Caesars' Palace was built, its architecture was an extreme suburban variant of Los Angeles—Douglas Honnold, now a respected doyen of the architectural profession

10. Tahitian Village restaurant, Bellflower, 1965

11. Universal City film-lot

in Los Angeles, worked for Bugsy Siegel in the design of the Flamingo, the pioneer casino-hotel on the Strip. Las Vegas has been as much a marginal gloss on Los Angeles as was Brighton Pavilion on Regency London. More important, Los Angeles has seen in this century the greatest concentration of fantasy-production, as an industry and as an institution, in the history of Western man. In the guise of Hollywood, Los Angeles gave us the movies as we know them and stamped its image on the infant television industry. And stemming from the impetus given by Hollywood as well as other causes, Los Angeles is also the home of the most extravagant myths of private gratification and self-realization, institutionalized now in the doctrine of 'doing your own thing.'

Both Hollywood's marketable commercial fantasies, and those private ones which are above or below calculable monetary value, have left their marks on the Angel City, but Hollywood brought something that all other fantasists needed—technical skill and resources in converting fantastic ideas into physical realities. Since living flesh-and-blood actors and dancers had to walk through or prance upon Hollywood's fantasies, there was much that could not be accomplished with painted back-cloths or back-projections; much of Shangri-la had to be built in three dimensions, the spiral ramps of the production numbers of Busby Berkeley musical spectaculars had to support the weight of a hundred girls in silver top hats, and so on . . .

The movies were thus a peerless school for building fantasy as fact, and the facts often survived one movie to live again in another, and another and others still to come. Economy in using increasingly valuable acreage on studio-lots caused these fantastic facades and ancient architectures reproduced in plaster to be huddled together into what have become equally fantastic townscapes which not only survive as cities of romantic illusion [11], but have been elevated to the status of a kind of cultural monuments, which now form the basis for tourist excursions more flourishing than the traditional tours of film-stars' homes.

This business of showing the plant to visitors as a tourist attraction has spread beyond the movie industry, into such monuments of public relations as the Busch Gardens in the San Fernando Valley, where the real-life brewery is only one of the features shown, and back into the movie industry with Disneyland—the set for a film that was never ever going to be made except in the mind of the visitor. In creating this compact sequence of habitable fantasies, WED Enterprises seems to have transcended Hollywood, Los Angeles, Walt Disney's original talents and all other identifiable ingredients of this environmental phantasmagoria.

In terms of an experience one can walk or ride through, inhabit and enjoy, it is done with such consummate skill and such base cunning that one can only compare it to something completely outrageous, like the brothel in Genet's *Le Balcon*. It is an almost faultless organization for delivering, against cash, almost any type at all of environmental experience that human fancy, however inflamed, could ever devise [12a, b]. Here are pedestrian piazzas, seas, jungles, castles, outer space, Main Street, the old West, mountains, more than can be experienced in a single day's visit . . . and all embraced within some obvious ironies, as all institutionalized fantasies must be.

The greatest of these ironies has to do with transportation, and this underlies the brothel comparison. Set in the middle of a city obsessed with mobility, a city whose most characteristic festival is the

12a. The lake, Disneyland

Rose Parade in Pasadena, fantastically sculptured Pop inventions
entirely surfaced with live flowers rolling slowly down Colorado
Boulevard every New Year's Day—in this city Disneyland offers
illicit pleasures of mobility. Ensconced in a sea of giant parking-lots
in a city devoted to the automobile, it provides transportation that

does not exist outside—steam trains, monorails, people-movers, tram-trains, travelators, ropeways, not to mention pure transport fantasies such as simulated space-trips and submarine rides. Under-age children, too young for driver's licences, enjoy the licence of dri-ving on their own freeway system and adults can step off the pave-ment and mingle with the buses and trams on Main Street in a manner that would lead to sudden death or prosecution outside.

But more than this, the sheer concentration of different forms of mechanical movement means that Disneyland is almost the only place where East Coast town-planning snobs, determined that their cities shall never suffer the automotive 'fate' of Los Angeles, can bring their students or their city councillors to see how the alterna-tive might work in the flesh and metal—to this blatantly commercial fun-fair in the city they hate. And seeing how well it all worked, I began to understand the wisdom of Ray Bradbury in proposing that Walt Disney was the only man who could make rapid transit a suc-cess in Los Angeles. All the skill, cunning, salesmanship, and tech-nical proficiency are there.

They are also at diametrical variance with the special brand of 'innocence' that underlies the purely personal fantasies of Los

12b. Transportation fantasy, Disneyland

13a, b. Watts Towers, 1921–54, Simon Rodia, inventor

Angeles. Innocence is a word to use cautiously in this context, because it must be understood as not comprising either simplicity or ingenuousness. Deeply imbued with standard myths of the Natural Man and the Noble Savage, as in other parts of the US, this innocence grows and flourishes as an assumed right in the Southern

California sun, an ingenious and technically proficient cult of private and harmless gratifications that is symbolized by the surfer's secret smile of intense concentration and the immensely sophisticated and highly decorated plastic surf-board he needs to conduct his private communion with the sea.

This fantasy of innocence has one totally self-absorbed and perfected monument in Los Angeles, so apt, so true and so imaginative that it has gained the world-wide fame it undoubtedly deserves: Simon Rodia's clustered towers in Watts. Alone of the buildings of Los Angeles they are almost too well known to need description, tapering traceries of coloured pottery shards [13a, b] bedded in cement on frames of scrap steel and baling wire. They are unlike anything else in the world—especially unlike all the various prototypes that have been proposed for them by historians who have never seen them in physical fact. Their actual presence is testimony to a genuinely original creative spirit.

14. Home is where the (do-it-yourself) heart is

And in the thirty-three years of absorbed labour he devoted to their construction, and in his uninhibited ingenuity in exploiting the by-products of an affluent technology, and in his determination to 'do something big', and in his ability to walk away when they were finished in 1954, Rodia was very much at one with the surfers, hot-rodders, sky-divers, and scuba-divers who personify the tradition of private, mechanistic *satori*-seeking in California. But he was also at variance with the general body of fantastic architecture thereabouts.

15. Crenshaw Ford Agency, 1967

Architecture as a way of direct personal gratification like Rodia's rarely rises above the level of plaster-gnomery or home-is-where-the-heart-shaped-flower-bed-is [14]. The towers of Watts are as unique as they are proper in Los Angeles, for the going body of architectural fantasy is in the public, not private, domain, and constitutes almost the only public architecture in the city — public in the sense that it deals in symbolic meanings the populace at large can read. Both fantasy and public symbolism reached their apotheosis in the great commercial signs, in the style of design that Tom Wolfe acclaimed, in his own neologism, as 'electrographic architecture' — that is, a combination of artificial light and graphic art that can even comprise a whole building. Wolfe's chosen examples in Los Angeles are the Crenshaw Ford Agency [15] and the Crenshaw Mobil Station in which he sees, rightly, a move 'from mere lettering to whole structures designed primarily as pictures or representational sculpture'. Wild as these objects may appear, grotesque, ludicrous, stimulating or uplifting, they fit into an established local pattern of architectural invention that reaches deep into the city's history and style of life.

Historically, the tradition begins with the spires, not of Watts but of Westwood village: illuminated needles capping cinemas and even banks in order to be seen from Wilshire Boulevard, which is only a quarter of a mile away, but which was not (in the twenties, when Westwood was subdivided) zoned for commercial uses. And this tradition also crowns the city's life-style, not only in commercial signs, but also in one structure that is a public building in the conventional sense of the word, the only public building in the whole city that genuinely graces the scene and lifts the spirit (and sits in firm control of the whole basis of human existence in Los Angeles): the Water and Power Building [16] of 1964 by Albert C. Martin and Associates. In daylight it is a conventional rectangular office block closing the end of an uninspired civic vista and standing in an altogether ordinary pool full of the usual fountains, but at night it is transformed. Darkness hides the boredoms of the civic centre and from the flanking curves of the freeways one sees only this brilliant cube of diamond-cool light riding above the lesser lights of downtown. It is the only gesture of public architecture that matches the style and scale of the city.

16. Water and Power Building, Los Angeles Civic Centre, 1963, Albert
C. Martin and Associates, architects

Charles Mingus

The Central Avenue jazz scene that flourished in the 1940s produced one of its most brilliantly creative figures in the bassist and composer Charles Mingus (1922–1979), who fused complex harmonies and rhythms with open approaches to collective improvisation and produced a long string of masterpieces, including *Pithecanthropus Erectus* (1956), *Tijuana Moods* (1957), and *Blues and Roots* (1958). A passionate advocate for artists' rights, Mingus set up his own publishing and recording companies in the 1950s to protect his music, and developed the "Jazz Workshop," which offered young composers the opportunity to showcase their work. Born in Nogales, Arizona, he was raised in Watts. In the 1940s he toured with such legendary bandleaders as Kid Ory, Lionel Hampton, and Louis Armstrong, and played with Charlie Parker and Bud Powell. Notoriously volatile, Mingus once summed himself up in these terms: "In my music, I'm trying to play the truth of what I am. The reason it's difficult is because I'm changing all the time." In the following excerpts from his autobiography *Beneath the Underdog* (1971), he encounters Simon Rodia, the self-taught creator of the Watts Towers, and Buddy Collette, a dazzling multi-instrumentalist and key figure of West Coast jazz.

from

BENEATH THE UNDERDOG

At that time in Watts there was an Italian man, named Simon Rodia—though some people said his name was Sabatino Rodella, and his neighbors called him Sam. He had a regular job as a tile setter, but on weekends and at nighttime, under lights he strung up, he was building something strange and mysterious and he'd been working on it since before my boy was born. Nobody knew what it was or what it was for. Around his small frame house he had made a low wall shaped like a ship and inside it he was constructing what looked like three masts, all different heights, shaped like upside-down ice cream cones. First he would set up skeletons of metal and chicken wire, and plaster them over with concrete, then he'd cover that with fancy designs made of pieces of seashells and mirrors and things. He was always changing his ideas while he worked and tearing down what he wasn't satisfied with and starting over again, so pinnacles tall as a two-story building would rise up and disappear and rise again. What was there yesterday mightn't be there next time you looked, but then another lacy-looking tower would spring up in its place.

Tig Johnson and Cecil J. McNeeley used to gather sacks full of pretty rocks and broken bottles to take to Mr. Rodia, and my boy hung around with them watching him work while he waited for Gloria Scopes, one of his classmates who happened to live just across the street. Some people called her Charles's "girl," but he didn't feel that way about her—he was only stringing her along for something to do.

Mr. Rodia was usually cheerful and friendly while he worked, and sometimes, drinking that good red wine from a bottle, he rattled off about Amerigo Vespucci, Julius Caesar, Buffalo Bill and all kinds of things he read about in the old encyclopedia he had in his house, but most of the time it sounded to Charles like he was speaking a foreign language. My boy marveled at what he was doing and felt sorry for him when the local rowdies came around and taunted him and threw rocks and called him crazy, though Mr. Rodia didn't seem to pay them much mind. Years later when Charles was grown and went back to Watts he saw three fantastic spires standing there—the tallest was over a hundred feet high. By then Rodia had finally finished his work and given it all to a neighbor as a present and gone away, no one knew where.

———

During his seventeenth summer he shined shoes and walked at least fifteen to twenty miles a day with his shine box, weaving up one block and down the next all the way uptown to Compton City's main street boulevard or five miles to downtown Los Angeles and on some weekends fifty miles out to Santa Monica and back traveling on his Union roller skates. He disappeared from his usual hangouts and his friends didn't see much of him anymore.

He had a funny makeshift shine box that he'd found in the garage one day and he got some rags and brushes out of the house, fastened his belt to it for a shoulder strap, bought some shoe polish at the dime store and went walking out into the streets looking for business.

He was busy reading everything he could find in the library that went beyond his Christian Sunday School training—karma yoga, theosophy, reincarnation, Vedanta—and sitting on park benches he often became so engrossed in finding God that he forgot about shining shoes.

Sometimes down by the Million Dollar Theatre he'd see Eden Abez, a poet-mystic who wore long white robes and later wrote a song called "Nature Boy." They'd look at each other and speak with their minds in silent thought about the God of love and nod their heads and walk their separate ways.

This day as he leaned against a lamppost at the corner of One Hundred and Third Street and San Pedro reading a book and waiting for customers, a tall handsome young black man walked up to him and said, "Are you the kid that plays cello? Remember me? I'm Buddy Collette." He introduced the boys with him—Major Harrison, Charles Martin, Crosby Lewis and Ralph Bledsoe, who were all laughing and grinning though Charles failed to see anything funny.

"How'd you like to make bread and wear the sharpest clothes in the latest styles?" Buddy asked. "Look at yourself. You dress like a hobo."

"I don't dig clothes any more."

"How'd you like to have the finest chicks in town?"

Charles said he wouldn't mind that at all.

"All right, join the Union," Buddy said. My boy knew he didn't mean Local 47 of the A.F.M. The Union was a private Watts club that had started out collecting dues from shoeblacks, newsboys and soda jerks in return for providing "protection" against bullies and rowdies like Feisty and his crew. All the victim had to say was "I paid my Union dues" and he was safe. Lately the Union's interests had shifted to music and their private parties and social gatherings were causing plenty of gossip and speculation all over Watts.

"Go get yourself a bass and we'll put you in our Union swing band," Buddy told my boy. "We can use you."

"Get a *bass*?"

"That's right. You're black. You'll never make it in classical music no matter how good you are. You want to play, you gotta play a *Negro* instrument. You can't slap a cello, so you gotta learn to *slap that bass*, Charlie!"

Charles liked the way Buddy talked and admired his proud carriage and adult manner and extreme good looks so he went home and discussed it with his father, explaining he had a chance to make a lot of money if he traded his cello for a bass. His parents, as usual not really knowing but hoping for the best, agreed to help. Next day he and Daddy Mingus went down to Schirmer's on Broadway in midtown Los Angeles and turned in the cello for a brand-new German-made double bass and Daddy forked over one hundred and thirty dollars in addition.

Marc Norman

Broad and flat, with boundless park and beachside trailways and boule-vards that stretch for miles, Los Angeles ought to be a paradise for bicy-clists. Yet in his 1972 *Bike Riding in Los Angeles*, Marc Norman (b. 1941) imagines L.A.'s biking population as "outlaws ... caught like blinking mice between the steel laws of traffic and the iron laws of the universe." Norman went on to become a screenwriter and film producer, working on movies like *Oklahoma Crude* and *The Killer Elite*, and sharing screen credit with Tom Stoppard for the script of *Shakespeare in Love*.

from

BIKE RIDING IN LOS ANGELES

Old Neighborhood

One afternoon he's sitting in the living room with nothing to do, so he tells his wife he's going out for a ride, and he winds up, of all places, in his old neighborhood.

He has lots of old neighborhoods around the city, but this is the one where he spent the most time. Between Pico and Venice, and Hauser and Fairfax. It's just Los Angeles—it doesn't have a name of its own.

He's not surprised he winds up there—he's been meaning to do it for a while—but he is surprised it happens on this particular after-noon.

The streets are quiet and empty as he rides down them, just the way he remembers them from, what—fifteen years before. It's just as barren of trees and the lawns and houses are just as bleached. There are no voices, no shouts from the kitchens, no whoops from the halls, no radios on, no kids out in front damming the gutters with Popsicle sticks.

In fact, if he wants to be rigorous about it, there's no proof the houses are occupied at all. Oh, he knows they are—they always

were when he lived here, and there weren't any voices then either —
but they might not be; they might be simply a few streets of houses
waiting to be sold and moved, a field of them, like those clumps of
houses he's seen with ripped foundations, sitting on trailers at the
ends of freeways under construction, torn out of the right-of-way
and waiting to be auctioned off and hauled away, a regular used-
house lot. Maybe all the houses on this street have been abandoned — maybe somebody has come along and told the people: we'll
move you to where the land goes up and down and there are breezes
and the shouts of children, but you have to come now, right away,
with nothing but the clothes on your backs, and all his old neighbors have jumped at the chance, racing away and leaving everything, houses, cars, fences, garbage-cans, and barbecues.

No — there's somebody, behind the lifted corner of a venetian
blind, watching him from the house on the corner. When he looks
over, the blind drops.

So much for that theory.

All this barrenness bothers him, bothers him a lot, both as a
writer and as a child of the neighborhood.

As a writer, selfishly he supposes, but then this is supposed to be
his first-novel neighborhood. All the other writers he knows have
one — some special corner in a mad city, some great soup from which
they ladle all those wonderful laughing Italians and those charming
drunk Irish and the candy-store ethics and the strong widows and all
the lovers padding around in their socks with their shoes in their
hands, all those rich chunks of things that give his friends' novels
their tang and truth.

But he can't do that, not with the neighborhood allotted him.
There never were any Italians, any Irish — nobody ever sang, even
drank, as he recalls. If people suffered, they suffered indoors. At
night, husbands would screech into their driveways, run into the
house through the kitchen doors, and make no sound until morning.

Consommé. Bouillon, is what his old neighborhood was.

And even forgetting a first novel, it bothers him as a child of the
neighborhood because he'd like an old neighborhood to claim, one
simply to talk about, to remember. But he can't — he has no memory
of anything that ever happened in that neighborhood except what
he did by himself.

What a sad deprivation. He feels cheated, like an only child looking back and wondering why there were never any brothers and sisters.

And there on the street, the Bike Rider is struck by a sudden thought: Jesus, what if he's grown up bleak and bland and arid as the street?

It's a terrible thing to think, a horrible theory, but it has its power. It could explain a lot, this theory, throw light on a lot of the things inside him he hates or doesn't understand. It could explain some of those things that have lodged inside him without ever being invited. He can feel the theory spreading through him, the way he feels hot coffee spread.

But at this point, there's a response. The memory comes up with a quote from Louis Adamic concerning Los Angeles (*Laughing in the Jungle*, New York, 1932):

> . . . the native American came to Los Angeles with a conception of the good community, which was embodied in single-family houses, located on large lots, surrounded by landscaped lawns and isolated from business activities. Not for them multi-family dwellings, confined to narrow plots, separated by cluttered streets, and interspersed with commerce and industry. Their vision was epitomized by the residential suburb—spacious, affluent, clean, decent, permanent, predictable, and homogeneous—and violated by the great city—congested, impoverished, filthy, immoral, transient, uncertain, and heterogeneous.

Now the response does some spreading of its own. Yes, he thinks to himself, no wonder. If I am bland, there's a reason, he thinks. The people who came to Los Angeles, his own people, came for the blandness. They'd had it with their singing Italians, their drunken Irish, they'd had it up to here, and they'd fled from the East to the Sunny Southland (Shut-My-Mouthland!) and bought homes with thick stucco sides that kept the voices in and the noises out, and built patios with high walls to do the same with the visible patterns of their lives. They made their mark on the city, gave it its character—a huge, sprawling, but still a faceless, soundless, very private place.

The very thing he fears in himself was their goal—anonymity.

So here he is, on his new bike on his old street, with this terrible theory about why he is what he is. And a possible explanation. But the explanation seems forced, pushed and pulled around to make him feel better. He's not sure he wants to feel better. He's not sure he wants to let himself off so easily.

He figures nothing more will happen on this street this afternoon. He'll go home and let everything churn around inside for a few days and then see how he feels.

But in fact, it only takes the time to go a few blocks, up to Genesee, for him to embrace the explanation. He figures even if it isn't correct, it's a good thing to believe, because it makes what happened to him growing up in the old neighborhood seem part of a plan. And besides, if he lets himself off easily now, he might be able to get started on that little project he's been kicking around for a few weeks.

In his mind, he drafts a treaty with his old neighborhood. In return for its taking it easy on him, he vows to take it easy on his old neighborhood. Mutual nonaggression.

He vows to be kind to himself, as national policy.

Take it easy, he says to himself, and nudges himself on the shoulder and pats himself on the butt.

The Pollution Question

In parts of the San Gabriel valley, the smog is so fierce the people rub their eyes in pain and cry out. In Long Beach, smog coats the inside of the mouth like olive oil. Pasadena and Altadena often look like they're on fire, when seen from a distance during the summer. The smog backs up against the foothills to the north of these cities and settles, still and glowering.

But for most of the city, smog is more spiritual than tangible.

It's like what happened to his car's windshield once when he drove across Kansas. The morning was cool, but after an hour or so's drive, the heat came up and his windshield was coated with a thin brown wash of dust. By noon, there was a layer of pulverized dirt on top of the dust, actual clods, thrown back by the wheels of cars ahead of him. By four, the dirt had turned into sticky mud, mixed and stirred with the green blood of hundreds of splattered bugs. By six, he found himself straining to see through the last dim chinks in the dirt, and when he stopped for gas that evening, the man cleaned off his windshield with a putty knife.

Did this filth hurt him? Not directly. But it affected his opinion of Kansas.

Los Angeles being so big, it should be easy to get a grasp of the city, but it's not. Nobody's ever explained why, with all those people, there's no sense of a city, no feeling for a shared geographic experience.

One answer might be that the people in Los Angeles can't see each other.

This is not a frivolous statement.

The smog divides the city into three-mile chunks — on bad days, people can only see things under three miles away. Perhaps the mind, taught by the eye, gets the idea that all that exists is what it can see. Like the medieval peasant looking up at the mountains surrounding his valley and having only a dim interest in what goes on on the other side, perhaps the mind decides that its three-mile chunk is really the only one that counts, and all those other chunks off in the smog aren't worth worrying about.

This proposition could also explain the success of shopping centers. At the shopping center, they speak the chunk's language.

So does the smog hurt most of the people who live in Los Angeles?

No, but it affects their opinion of Los Angeles.

A few times a year, a wind comes up in the night — a hot east wind from the desert, a wet west wind from the ocean — and blows all the smog away.

Husbands walking out to the car the next morning stop, suddenly. Wives fling open their kitchen curtains. There, to the north are mountains, tall mountains, even snow-covered. It might be Denver.

And down at the beach, the water is a warm blue and the red roof tiles on the houses marching up the ravines from the beach burn in the clean sunlight. It might be Nice.

And all the trees are green, an intense green, with no mud in it. Like the trees in Paris.

And the thought runs through the city—maybe we are a city after all, maybe we could be a real city with our own cityness, like Denver or Nice or Paris. If only we could see ourselves so well more often.

"It's so *beautiful*," say the mothers in the park to each other.

"God, I wish they'd come out from New York on a day like this," say the men.

But during the next night, the wind dies, and by morning, the smog is back. The mountains and the tops of the trees are gone, and the men driving to work can see only three miles in any direction, as though every windshield has a built-in lamination of dust.

This is the actual, the men think. Yesterday was the fluke. The trees were probably spray-painted and the mountains were probably plaster things, only fifty feet high or so, hauled around on dollies.

Somebody was probably making a movie.

Los Angeles Dream Zones

In the 1890s, Edward Doheny dreamt of oil. He dug a well at the corner of Second and Glendale with a pick and shovel, and it produced. For a long time, people had suspected there was oil under their feet.

In a few years, there were wells everywhere.

The wells took over the city. Thousands of them to the west, a forest of them in Long Beach, all sucking, millions of kids at a great soda fountain, sucking strawberry oil. Pretty soon, the market was glutted—nobody needed so much oil. The wells kept pumping.

Just about the time things looked bad, along came the automobile to save everybody. Doheny became a millionaire.

When people say things always work out, this is the sort of thing they mean.

Today, most of the wells are gone, the pools are drying up, and the land is more valuable for apartment houses and stores. But there's a street named Doheny, running from Sunset south to Pico. And at the corner of Pico and Doheny, there's an oil well set behind attractive stone walls, padded for sound and painted sky-blue. It makes a better monument to Doheny than the street, because the well is still sucking.

Now here is Abbot Kinney, a cultured, genteel Easterner who has already made one dream come true. He has dreamt of creating a market for machine-made cigarettes. He calls them Sweet Caporals, and makes a bundle off them.

In 1900, he's in LA, and he takes a buggy ride out to Santa Monica, looking over the sand dunes south of town, at Timm's Cove. And he has another dream, this time a city of pleasure, a Venice transposed, with Moorish palaces, canals, gondolas, delicate bridges, elegant hotels. He will build his Venice-by-the-Sea and the rich will come, buy his land, erect their spreading summer homes. The city will grow and thrive, an All-American Cote d'Azur.

The name of Venice will become a watchword. Frank, I'll meet you at two by the lagoon in Venice and we'll sign the papers there, people will say. Guys will call their girlfriends: how'd you like me to tickle your poozle tonight in a real gondola rowed by a real Italian gondolier?

So he builds it. And the rich come.

But so do the oil wells, Doheny's wells, marching in from the east like the broomsticks in *The Sorcerer's Apprentice*, surrounding the town, besieging the placid lagoons and glittering canals. The rich hold their noses and flee inland. Abbot Kinney shakes his head and wonders what he did wrong.

Years later, the Bike Rider and his junior-high buddies ride their bikes down to Venice on summer Saturday afternoons, playing hide-and-seek among the few oil derricks left, kicking away the rusting no-trespassing signs, climbing ladders, whooping from the top. There's a small sad amusement park wedged in among the derricks and tarry pools, famous for its rollercoaster whose wheels actually lift off the tracks on a certain curve. The Bike Rider and his friends dare each other to go on it.

One day among the derricks, they discover a Venetian canal and a Venetian bridge. The canal is weed-lined and scummy—an old Ford sits in the middle of it, with only its roof showing. The bridge is crumbling—the steel reinforcing rods in the concrete have rusted through and send brown drips down its side. They gaze on it briefly, only a little curious, savages among the Easter Island statues.

They have no idea this is a major Los Angeles Dream Zone.

When the sun goes down, they're always too worn out to pedal home, so they hitch-hike, waiting like aristocrats for somebody with a pickup to come along so they can load their bikes in the back.

Cees Nooteboom

"A good part of any day in Los Angeles," Joan Didion wrote, "is spent driving, alone, through streets devoid of meaning to the driver, which is one reason the place exhilarates some people, and floods others with an amorphous unease." In his 1973 essay "Autopia," Dutch novelist and poet Cees Nooteboom (b. 1933) expresses equal measures of exhilaration and unease as he confronts a city that, to his amazement, has no center in the traditional sense. Few travel writers have captured the city's seductive fragmentation with such subtlety and concision.

AUTOPIA

You go to Los Angeles at your own risk. After all, if you're from Europe, you have a very definite idea of what a city is supposed to be—and that's San Francisco. As any American will tell you, San Francisco is the most European city in America. Make your visit to Los Angeles as brief as possible, they'll say. It's a desert of real estate, loosely woven and wrapped in yellow fog. You have to see it, but then you have to make a quick getaway.

In fact, this is not true. It is quite a shock to fly over Los Angeles after having crossed the entire continent—houses from horizon to horizon, blue shards of swimming pools, plenty of green in cabbage and lettuce tones. But mostly it's just houses, traversed by arteries that seem massive even from above, with traffic pushing along them. Still, it's not true. I stayed until my time was up, and I did not long for San Francisco.

Humanity, including its more sensitive members, falls into two groups: haters and lovers. On the first few pages of his magnificent book, *Los Angeles: The Architecture of Four Ecologies*,[1] Reyner Banham demonstrates this split clearly. "I know subjective opinions can vary," he quotes Adam Raphael from the *Guardian*, "but personally I reckon LA as the noisiest, the smelliest, the most uncomfortable and most uncivilised major city in the United States. In short a stinking sewer."[2]

But Banham also gives us Nathan Silver in the *New Statesman*: "On my first visit to Los Angeles I was conventionally prepared for almost anything except for what it really looked like — a quite beautiful place."[3]

And that's just how I experienced it. After the confusion of arrival (suitcases lost, later found), the confusion of ten-lane freeways on which people wove in and out of traffic, the blanket of heat after the austere Scottish weather on the northern coast of New England, I stayed inside for two days. I had taken a room in Beverly Hills and did not go out because of the myth prevalent here that you can't walk outside without the alibi of a dog. I was alone with the twenty-two eyes of the television set and a remote control in a severe draft of air-conditioning. Sometimes I would tiptoe down the stairs like a mouse to retrieve something out of the North Pole of the refrigerator. Perhaps it was autumn; in the mornings I heard the quiet gardener in my sleep, raking hard, dry, tropical leaves, but when I looked outside, the sun was standing over the swimming pool like a ball of fire, and high palm and eucalyptus trees stood motionless in the light.

On the third day, I ventured outside. I walked, which was crazy — not because it is dangerous but because it does not make sense. In a city with streets longer than fifty kilometers, the measure of one foot is absurd, and so is the use of one's feet as a means of transportation. But I did not know this yet, and I walked out the door with the idea of going to the city center. The street curved, and there were big houses on both sides, each with its own garden. In front of the houses stood big, silent cars. The street led to a larger, straight one with even bigger houses, bigger gardens, and bigger cars, but there was not a person in sight. It was silent, too. Every now and then one of those big machines would glide past me with creatures in human shape sitting inside, but there was no one on the street — no milkman, no cigar shop around the corner, only me with my steps, and a lot of them.

I don't know how long I walked along like that. After a while I came across a Hollywood billboard with an image that evoked visions of a seedy cinema back in Holland and black-and-white movies with Humphrey Bogart, but where I stood there was nothing but a very broad road with lawns in the middle and palm trees as high as cathedrals on either side. A black woman stood at the bus stop that curiously had appeared there, too. This was the first human being I had seen since I stepped outside, because you never know about those shadows in the cars.

"The city center?" I inquired. She looked at me as if I were crazy or, more accurately, as if there were a madman standing in front of her. "Walking?" she asked in disbelief. Then she disappeared onto a bus, and I set off in the direction I thought appropriate for the center of Los Angeles, not yet ready to take public transportation.

I wind up in the center of Beverly Hills. Jewelers, hotels, boutiques, and covert banks stand next to each other on scrubbed streets. I still hear myself walking. A black man in a Cardin suit is polishing shoes beneath an abstract work of art and discussing the Euro market (I think this image expresses it well). In my shock I go into a diner and order a hamburger. The only white member of the staff looks like somebody at the court of Philip II whose job it is to make sure all the missals are in place. Otherwise everyone is black, even the manager who waltzes his way to my table like a well-oiled athlete. A fragile film queen from the silent movie era is heading for her Rolls-Royce with a snug little dog pinned under her sticklike arm. Unfairness is the privilege of the impressionist writer: the unfairness of letting one image prevail over another; for me, Beverly Hills is that one faded star against the background of the Beverly Hills Hilton (and that against the background of the light sky), a star who sinks in her own Rolls-Royce, invisible once she is sitting inside.

Suddenly, as I am walking back, I imagine that there are people like this living in all these houses, gnawing on their celluloid pasts. I hear the chink of ice cubes in invisible martini glasses and see a Japanese gardener cutting a camellia, so I wade further through the warmth reflected by tropical gardens.

The next day I make another attempt. Still I do not dare to rent a car, afraid that I might get lost on the ten-lane freeways. I have bought a bus ticket with a transit map and want to learn from riding the bus how to "capture" the center, because, whatever my friends may say, I won't be dissuaded from the idea that Los Angeles must have one. They call it downtown and say it is nothing, not a "real" center, and they do not understand my obsession. Afterward I understand their inability to understand: the essence of Los Angeles lies in the fact that it hardly has a center. It is, if one can say this, a fluid, a "moving" city, not only a city that moves itself—breaks itself down, builds itself up again, displaces and regroups itself—but also a city in which movement, *freedom* of movement, is a strong premise of life.

I did not, of course, begin to think about cities only after being in Los Angeles, but until that moment I had always thought that a city had to be a drawing room, and that was that. But it's not that simple. Amsterdam is the city I like best, and Amsterdam is a drawing room. It is no Mediterranean, Spanish, or Arabian city in the sense that there is one meeting place to which everyone is drawn— an agora, a forum, a market. Amsterdammers look at each other in a drawing-roomy way in cafés or in front of the hazy backdrop of the canals, where the lamps behind the windowpanes give a drawing-roomy impression even to the outside. Coziness, safety are the essence. In the north, I do not need to seek the big, flashing moment in which one sees for the first time the Plaza Mayor in Salamanca or the Piazza San Marco in Venice, that sheer happiness of standing in the middle of the crowd and walking up and down the Ramblas in Barcelona for the first time.

Los Angeles has nothing to do with one or the other. It is totally different, and the difference is that Los Angeles means absolutely nothing if you don't have a car. This sounds fairly harsh, although I did not experience it that way. With their cars, Angelenos go places, they travel infinite numbers of kilometers in a world that continuously remains Los Angeles. Cars do not designate a lack of freedom but rather freedom itself; with their cars they reach houses, rich houses, poor houses, big, small, tropical wrecks, modernistic novelties, really great architecture, and ridiculous palaces, more toward the cool wind of the sea or more toward the arid breath of the desert but almost always standing free, built into space, not piled one atop another as in New York or Chicago.

Banham goes so far as to call this world "Autopia," a concept that goes very much against the grain of the spirit of our age. A week into my stay, however, I begin to see what he means. Now long back in my beloved drawing room by the North Sea, I see her in front of me again, mixed images of vulgarity and vitality, a world that conveys the feeling that it stretches to all sides around you but never looks down on you or presses you down, an "open" world that forms itself, however formless it may look, and which is experienced, in my case at least, as a unity despite its fragmented appearance.

The difficulty is that Los Angeles cannot be compared with anything else. To explain this, Banham uses a memorable image: "The city will never be fully understood by those who cannot move fluently through its diffuse urban texture. . . . So, like earlier generations of English intellectuals who taught themselves Italian in order to read Dante in the original, I learned to drive in order to read Los Angeles in the original."[4]

Well, I am still sitting in a bus on my way to the center. I drive across Sunset Boulevard, through Hollywood, and my heart beats more quickly; but Hollywood is only streets and houses and bus stops. Dean Martin does not get in, Doris Day does not get in, only people with tired big-city faces get in: black people, Chicanos, little old ladies who have lived through many catastrophes. The bus driver is a young black man with a Lumumba beard. He's getting a lesson. The system of tickets and fares, which have to be paid in exact change, seems quite complicated, and throughout the entire journey, each time he does something wrong, he is rapped on the knuckles by the head driver behind him.

They said they would tell me when I reached the center. I travel across the map and make little arrows and crosses for the day when I drive myself. Every now and then the road climbs, and I can see the crossings vanish in the faraway fog and smog without end. They just dissolve into a nonexistent distance, to the right and to the left. Every now and then a group of high buildings rises above everything else like a far, invincible Casbah.

Half an hour later I am standing on the plaza of the Music Center. These are not buildings *in* the city but elevated above the streets and freeways, a monument to higher things that merely tolerates people in and around it. A curious kind of monkey warder is walking in circles like a guardian of hell, and there is nothing further that invites me to come inside.

In the distance a fat, oily stream pulls the traffic via the Pasadena and the Hollywood Freeways, a six- or eight-lane snake pulling westward, the sun on the windshields, copper on its scales. I am free of everything. I find it hard to believe that the serpentine mass down there is caused by human beings whose being is an anecdote just as fragile as mine, because mine vanishes in this moment. I have, while I am clearly standing here, great difficulty believing in my presence. I harbor a great desire to vanish, to evaporate into the universe like a gas, or like nothing at all—but I will not. It irritates me that I will leave tracks behind.

This ecstasy quickly passes. I put on my tourist camouflage and set off for Chinatown, Little Tokyo, and the Mexican quarter— fragments of a Japanese, Chinese, Mexican cosmos, strange places where Americans can see that there are other worlds, as well, or where they can at least vaguely assume that this is so. The encroaching darkness cuts the most vulgar edges off tourism, and I am sitting on a bench next to an old Chinese man, holding a newspaper I cannot read (*The Young China*). I look at the pattern in the Suzie Wong faces of half-naked girls with compact little bodies (*Asian Beauty*), see a few men assemble in a yellowish structure around a rickety table with an American and a Taiwanese flag on it, the yellowed image of a generalissimo above them like an ancestral icon. I walk past innumerable bamboo sticks, painted eggs, jade dolls, fans, and other junk. My face is committed to film by at least one hundred American tourists, and I ask a Confucius under the dragon gate what he thinks of it, of America. "Don't be history," he says, and goes on meditating. Then he begins again: "Be history but don't be old."

Back on the bus, everything is much more beautiful. A breeze from Hawaii has chased away the smog; it smells of licorice, even in the middle of the city. The world lies around us like a lacquered box. The black driver makes a show out of it. Everyone who steps in knows him. If I had not watched so much television in Holland, I would say that there was a bond between him and his passengers.

"But that is because bus passengers in Los Angeles are all have-nots as well," says a sociologist friend of mine.

"Right, but I was told that it's precisely the poor whites and the other disenfranchised races who hate the blacks."

"It's not as simple as that," my friend says. "You don't see what you see. The nature of the Angelenos is tolerant; there are no hard racist excesses. There is only a totally indefensible economic policy that leads to joblessness, the forming of ghettos, despair, and the explosions that go with it, like the riots, or the uprising in Watts in 1965.

"Now it is silent in Watts, and it doesn't look as if anything is going to happen soon, either. But the reason for the uprising still has not been removed, despite the promises and the honeyed words. Unequal chances, economic discrimination, and rampant exploitation of black people by a new capitalism with no end in sight."

This is all true, all driving in a dark corner of this bus, a wounded corner in the souls of the passengers; only I can't see it now. The driver discusses a papaya recipe with a lady from a far-away country, and I see a balloon of dreaminess rising above her head; she would like to hijack the bus and kidnap the driver and light a little fire in bed with his round body, but he is already in a baseball discussion, then in a union row, then in a flirtation with a girl who would look like a Greek tragedienne, if she weren't sitting there knitting. Like this we glide forth, a soft sea of silent limousines around us, until we are in Hollywood.

A star every couple of yards! Fallen down, chiseled into the sidewalks in gold contours: Beniamino Gigli, Rudolph Valentino, Marlene Dietrich—people buried under the stones, dead and alive, some of them so long dead that I don't even know their names. Who was Mary Miles Minter and who John Miljan? I can hear somebody laugh, astonished at such stupidity. When my neck starts hurting from looking down, I see the rest of the world again and my feet do what time does: they wear down fame a foot further. At some point a long time hence, someone will wonder about the meaning of the gold coloring of these stones in the desert.

It is crowded on Sunset Boulevard. Short-cropped military young people are waiting for the sell; for people with other tastes there are also heavily painted boys in skirts and fluffy furs. Now and then one of the large cars stops, a short talk and the deal is done. Once I heard someone talk about the quantity of meat consumed in a large city: how many cows, pigs, chickens, and how many meadowsful that would be, and what a miracle it was that they were always ready for the table again when they were wanted; but what is that compared with the bodies that also have their needs, that want to be tied up, touched, stroked, liberated, beaten, and made love to?

When I enter "The Nudest Show in Town," there are about eleven men sitting in front of a long table, which looks more like a bar, plunged in deathly purple light. I sit next to them. Between us, on the table, an undernourished girl moves her naked body with inexpressible ennui to the rhythm of Slade. The purple light poisons the whiskey. I feel a sadness that does not stem from morality. Do I know that for certain? Yes.

Outside, it is becoming busier all the time. People sell books, copper figurines of movie stars; they hand out sadistic flyers, inviting others to attend mystical séances, explaining the universe by means of a stencil. I see a slim, lean, oh-so-beautiful Hell's Angel, wrapped in leather like a snake next to his oversexed bike, but when he turns around he is over seventy, a grin of malicious age under his black steel Nazi helmet, and behind him appears, as if directed by an evil genius, a real monster. It has to be a woman. She is sitting in a side-car, which she operates with her branchlike little arms and claws for fingers. There can't be many organs left in her body, which is no more than a shaky box, half a head askew on top of it, covered by a little beret.

The child standing next to me looks up from his cartoons pasted on a wall, gives a shriek of mortal terror, and jumps aside. I, older and much seedier, remain standing firmly on my feet, until the phantom has passed and I know that I didn't see anything, anywhere.

The evening begins to taste bitter. What? This is Hollywood? Where are the cowboys and the prairies, where are the armies of Cecil B. DeMille, where is the Rolls-Royce of the Marquise de la Falaise de Coudray, or Gloria Swanson and Gräfin Dombski, or

Pola Negri? And where is that dear, adorable face of Dr. Franken-stein's creature? Where is the make-believe?

Do I dare? I have that curious thing on my table, the finely lined map of Los Angeles, a route marked on it from Beverly Hills to Hol-lywood, from Hollywood to downtown L.A., from there to Watts, from Watts to Venice, from Venice to Santa Monica, from Santa Monica back to Beverly Hills. There must be no mistakes. If you get off the road in the wrong lane of a multiple exit, you can't get back on, and you can't stop to look at the map, so I glue a piece of paper to my windshield with the direction to take at each exit.

Then all of a sudden I'm sitting in a stream. I flow along, crawl out, stream back in again, needing to move at times across five lanes to get out again. At home it would never have worked, but here it does. Even on the very widest sections, the big cars pass by at a very measured speed, and nobody throws a wrench into the works if you panic all of a sudden because you see the sign EXIT NOW EXIT NOW that appears out of nowhere.

After a little while I begin to see what is happening around me, and here I fail as a chronicler because for me it is a film: *L'Amerique Insolite*, Godard, *Zabriskie Point*, *Play It as It Lays*, you name it. And here I do not mean film as movement but film as language because they are words and again words, flung at you from both sides: hamburger joints, gas stations, hotels, traffic information, churches praising God, words and names, names and words. And signs. And emblems. This begins as soon as you leave the freeways and you are driving on Sunset or Wilshire or Santa Monica Boulevard. It seems as if I were made from wet newspaper and the words had to be pressed into me with their strong colors and rudimentary messages: Gas! Eat! Sleep! Pray! Drink! Stop!

It may be something that passes if you are here longer, but on some street corners, at some hours, in some "settings," I have the irresistible feeling that I am acting in a movie, am an extra in a scene that somewhere means something entirely different. This may, of course, be nothing but a quirk of my own, but in France or in Italy I never feel this. I never feel like Maigret when I enter a *tabac*, never like Fellini when I watch a whitewashed transvestite push past me in a Rome nightclub.

The new generation, which flies to New York for five hundred guilders, will quickly dispense with those sentiments, but for me America obviously still has that quality of being larger than life, frightening and alluring, which belongs to not-being-part-of-reality, where everything has a different meaning from the one you can see and in which your own stroll toward a hamburger joint run by Mexicans on the edge of the black ghetto could be something other than what it really is: a tourist stepping out in the gas-filled air to eat a sandwich while a useless fluorescent light advertising Coca-Cola goes on and off in the much brighter light of day. I feel surrounded by that layer of "something else" that is just underneath reality and that might well be a film. Whatever it may be, it is not disagreeable, and I even walk differently, probably just above the subtitles.

I spend the entire day driving. It is cool inside the car. You can't go too fast, and the labyrinth is infinite. The radio is playing. I exchange neighborhood for neighborhood, sink and climb, look across the sea right to Japan and then no more. Black people in their Sunday clothes come out of churches, a whole herd of cars is standing somewhere with people eating inside, by a little ramp, being served by girls in white pinafores. I am nowhere alone, always a flood of other cars around me, the speed decreasing and swelling to the rhythm of the oh-so-slowly-changing stoplights.

It is quieter in Watts. Perhaps because it is Sunday, perhaps because of the obtrusive heat of midday, but I am driving through narrow, African American streets and there is nobody to be seen. The low, small wooden houses all have verandas with tiny gardens and large flowers in vivid colors.

Only later I come to larger streets with large, sparse, cubic and flat buildings full of seedy boutiques and angry graffiti. The great reconstruction still hasn't made itself felt. It is the obscene face of unveiled poverty, "the other America." Six months later I read that Nixon has decided, after his triumphal victory in Vietnam, to cut down on his internal redevelopment programs, of which Watts, of course, would have been the first in line.

A group of young black boys comes out of the Bright Star Church of God in Christ, dressed in crème caramel gowns with white hems, the radio says it is ninety-six degrees, the house at

10766 107th Street is protected by a Harris Steel fence, a colorless building is standing in a dump, "House of Uhuru" written on it, and the sound of Greek music by Jim Papadakis comes from an African American veranda. "Who is it?" asks a wall. "The Black Egyptians," answers the same wall. Then suddenly, from the sand-filled nothing on two sides of a dead rail track, I see strange, slim, high, open towers: the Watts Towers. The place that others visit on purpose just falls into my lap, a building without function, a cranky invention in stone, glass shards, steel, and shells, bottle bottoms, and pebbles, one of the miraculous buildings, built out of the shadow of one man's mind. For thirty-three years the Italian immigrant Simon Rodia worked on these towers alone, with his hands. When all was done and he was seventy-seven, he left his palace to a neighbor and vanished. His theory was that you have to be very good or very bad if you do not want to be forgotten, and now this cathedral of lace and concrete is standing in the middle of Watts; people are dwarfed beneath it, and it remembers the shadow of its maker.

Two hours later on the same day, when the air already has something of the dark of the impending evening, I stand in the same city by the grave of another shadow. The grave is a box, a stone drawer in a wall in between other, similar drawers in which the dead are lying, never to rise again. "Marilyn Monroe, 1926–1962." Nothing else is written there, but by the foot of the wall, another name veils a death just as dead. There are roses and other flowers, letters lying there, and objects, fragments of homesickness and pieces of fame. "Hello," the note begins, "I dreamt with you last night. Give my love to Venus if it's still real, Jeff." Another, trembling piece of paper: "You are still as close as always." Someone has hung a porcelain "Our Father" here, and next to it a card with the message "Every day in every way."

I stand between the other sniffers and dachshunds for a while, cannot suppress a necrophilic thought about underwear, listen to the porter by the fence who is rattling his keys and to the vengeful whispering of the dead, walk around the mausoleum in which the dust of the dead is stored in copper-colored urns in the shape of books, easier for God to read. James P. Beresford is lying there, an American flag made of paper is peeping out of a crack and is voting posthumously for Nixon. Next to it a double volume that the author has not yet finished: Peter I. Meremblum, 1890–1966, and Zinaida Abaza Meremblum, 1892–, to be filled in by the Great Author later, though the dummy is already there. Depressed by so much transitoriness, I leave this place of skulls and drive through the Hollywood of Scott Fitzgerald, Gary Cooper, Budd Schulberg, and Marilyn, home through an air of spider webs and discolored film.

1. Reyner Banham, *Los Angeles: The Architecture of Four Ecologies* (Harmondsworth, England: Penguin, 1971).
2. Banham, *Los Angeles* (note 1), 16, quoting Adam Raphael, originally published in *The Guardian*, 22 July 1968.
3. Banham, *Los Angeles* (note 1), 16, quoting Nathan Silver, originally published in *New Statesman*, 28 March 1969.
4. Banham, *Los Angeles* (note 1), 23.

Umberto Eco

When it opened in 1955 in Anaheim, Disneyland was a new kind of theme park, a wholly artificial dreamscape offering a succession of miniaturized fantasy worlds in a cozily protected environment. For Umberto Eco (b. 1932), a semiotician equally conversant with the works of St. Thomas Aquinas and Ian Fleming, Disneyland offers an almost too perfect occasion for uncovering the meanings embodied in a network of signs. A professor at the University of Bologna and the author of many volumes of theory, Eco is best known for his fiction, particularly his medieval mystery *The Name of the Rose* (1980). "The City of Robots" is from the title essay, first published in 1975, of his collection *Travels in Hyperreality*.

THE CITY OF ROBOTS

In Europe, when people want to be amused, they go to a "house" of amusement (whether a cinema, theater, or casino); sometimes a "park" is created, which may seem a "city," but only metaphorically. In the United States, on the contrary, as everyone knows, there exist amusement cities. Las Vegas is one example; it is focused on gambling and entertainment, its architecture is totally artificial, and it has been studied by Robert Venturi as a completely new phenomenon in city planning, a "message" city, entirely made up of signs, not a city like the others, which communicate in order to function, but rather a city that functions in order to communicate. But Las Vegas is still a "real" city, and in a recent essay on Las Vegas, Giovanni Brino showed how, though born as a place for gambling, it is gradually being transformed into a residential city, a place of business, industry, conventions. The theme of our trip—on the contrary—is the Absolute Fake; and therefore we are interested only in absolutely fake cities. Disneyland (California) and Disney World (Florida) are obviously the chief examples, but if they existed alone they would represent a negligible exception. The fact is that the United States is filled with cities that imitate a city, just as wax museums imitate painting and the Venetian palazzos or Pompeiian villas imitate architecture. In particular there are the "ghost towns," the Western cities of a century and more ago. Some are reasonably authentic, and the restoration or preservation has been carried out on an extant, "archeological" urban complex; but more interesting are those born from nothing, out of pure imitative determination. They are "the real thing."

There is an embarrassment of riches to choose from: You can have fragments of cities, as at Stone Mountain near Atlanta, where you take a trip on a nineteenth-century train, witness an Indian raid, and see sheriffs at work, against the background of a fake Mount Rushmore. The Six Guns Territory, in Silver Springs, also has train and sheriffs, a shoot-out in the streets and French can-can in the saloon. There is a series of ranchos and Mexican missions in Arizona; Tombstone with its OK Corral, Old Tucson, Legend City near Phoenix. There is the Old South Bar-b-Q Ranch at Clewison, Florida, and so on. If you venture beyond the myth of the West, you have cities like the Magic Mountain in Valencia, California, or Santa Claus Village, Polynesian gardens, pirate islands, Astroworlds like the one in Kirby, Texas, and the "wild" territories of the various Marinelands, as well as ecological cities, which we will discuss elsewhere.

There are also the ship imitations. In Florida, for example, between Tampa and St. Petersburg, you can board the *Bounty*, anchored at the edge of a Tahitian village, faithfully reconstructed according to the drawings preserved by the Royal Society in London, but with an eye also on the old film with Charles Laughton and Clark Gable. Many of the nautical instruments are of the period, some of the sailors are waxworks, one officer's shoes are those worn by the actor who played the part, the historical information on the various panels is credible, the voices that pervade the atmosphere come from the sound track of the movie. But we'll stick to the Western myth and take as a sample city the Knott's Berry Farm of Buena Park, Los Angeles.

Here the whole trick seems to be exposed; the surrounding city context and the iron fencing (as well as the admission ticket) warn us that we are entering not a real city but a toy city. But as we begin walking down the first streets, the studied illusion takes over. First of all, there is the realism of the reconstruction: the dusty stables, the sagging shops, the offices of the sheriff and the telegraph agent, the jail, the saloon are life size and executed with absolute fidelity; the old carriages are covered with dust, the Chinese laundry is dimly lit, all the buildings are more or less practical, and the shops are open, because Berry Farm, like Disneyland, blends the reality of trade with the play of fiction. And if the dry-goods store is fake nineteenth-century and the shopgirl is dressed like a John Ford heroine, the candies, the peanuts, the pseudo-Indian handicrafts are real and are sold for real dollars, just as the soft drinks, advertised with antique posters, are real, and the customer finds himself participating in the fantasy because of his own authenticity as a consumer; in other words, he is in the role of the cowboy or the gold-prospector who comes into town to be fleeced of all he has accumulated while out in the wilds.

Furthermore the levels of illusion are numerous, and this increases the hallucination—that is to say, the Chinese in the laundry or the prisoner in the jail are wax dummies, who exist, in realistic attitudes, in settings that are equally realistic, though you can't actually enter them; but you don't realize that the room in question is a glass display case, because it looks as if you could, if you chose, open the door or climb through the window; and then the next room, say, which is both the general store and the justice of the peace's office, looks like a display case but is actually practical, and the justice of the peace, with his black alpaca jacket and his pistols at his hips, is an actual person who sells you his merchandise. It should be added that extras walk about the streets and periodically stage a furious gun battle, and when you realize that the average American visitor is wearing blue jeans not very different from the cowboys', many of the visitors become confused with the extras, increasing the theatricality of the whole. For example, the village school, reconstructed with hyperrealistic detail, has behind the desk a schoolmarm wearing a bonnet and an ample checked skirt, but the children on the benches are little passing visitors, and I heard one tourist ask his wife if the children were real or "fake" (and you could sense his psychological readiness to consider them, at will, extras, dummies, or moving robots of the sort we will see in Disneyland).

Apparently ghost towns involve a different approach from that of wax museums or museums for copies of works of art. In the first nobody expects the wax Napoleon to be taken for real, but the hallucination serves to level the various historical periods and erase the distinction between historical reality and fantasy; in the case of the works of art what is culturally, if not psychologically, hallucinatory is the confusion between copy and original, and the fetishization of art as a sequence of famous subjects. In the ghost town, on the contrary, since the theatricality is explicit, the hallucination operates in making the visitors take part in the scene and thus become participants in that commercial fair that is apparently an element of the fiction but in fact represents the substantial aim of the whole imitative machine.

In an excellent essay on Disneyland as "degenerate utopia" ("a degenerate utopia is an ideology realized in the form of myth"), Louis Marin analyzed the structure of that nineteenth-century frontier city street that receives entering visitors and distributes them through the various sectors of the magic city. Disneyland's Main Street seems the first scene of the fiction whereas it is an extremely shrewd commercial reality. Main Street—like the whole city, for that matter—is presented as at once absolutely realistic and absolutely fantastic, and this is the advantage (in terms of artistic conception) of Disneyland over the other toy cities. The houses of Disneyland are full-size on the ground floor, and on a two-thirds scale on the floor above, so they give the impression of being inhabitable (and they are) but also of belonging to a fantastic past that we can grasp with our imagination. The Main Street façades are presented to us as toy houses and invite us to enter them, but their interior is always a disguised supermarket, where you buy obsessively, believing that you are still playing.

In this sense Disneyland is more hyperrealistic than the wax museum, precisely because the latter still tries to make us believe that what we are seeing reproduces reality absolutely, whereas Disneyland makes it clear that within its magic enclosure it is fantasy that is absolutely reproduced. The Palace of Living Arts presents its Venus de Milo as almost real, whereas Disneyland can permit itself to present its reconstructions as masterpieces of falsification, for

what it sells is, indeed, goods, but genuine merchandise, not reproductions. What is falsified is our will to buy, which we take as real,
and in this sense Disneyland is really the quintessence of consumer
ideology.

But once the "total fake" is admitted, in order to be enjoyed it
must seem totally real. So the Polynesian restaurant will have, in
addition to a fairly authentic menu, Tahitian waitresses in costume,
appropriate vegetation, rock walls with little cascades, and once you
are inside nothing must lead you to suspect that outside there is
anything but Polynesia. If, between two trees, there appears a
stretch of river that belongs to another sector, Adventureland, then
that section of stream is so designed that it would not be unrealistic
to see in Tahiti, beyond the garden hedge, a river like this. And if in
the wax museums wax is not flesh, in Disneyland, when rocks are
involved, they are rock, and water is water, and a baobab a baobab.
When there is a fake—hippopotamus, dinosaur, sea serpent—it is
not so much because it wouldn't be possible to have the real equivalent but because the public is meant to admire the perfection of the
fake and its obedience to the program. In this sense Disneyland not
only produces illusion, but—in confessing it—stimulates the desire
for it: A real crocodile can be found in the zoo, and as a rule it is
dozing or hiding, but Disneyland tells us that faked nature corre-
sponds much more to our daydream demands. When, in the space
of twenty-four hours, you go (as I did deliberately) from the fake
New Orleans of Disneyland to the real one, and from the wild river
of Adventureland to a trip on the Mississippi, where the captain of
the paddle-wheel steamer says it is possible to see alligators on the
banks of the river, and then you don't see any, you risk feeling
homesick for Disneyland, where the wild animals don't have to be
coaxed. Disneyland tells us that technology can give us more reality
than nature can.

In this sense I believe the most typical phenomenon of this universe is not the more famous Fantasyland—an amusing carousel of
fantastic journeys that take the visitor into the world of Peter Pan or
Snow White, a wondrous machine whose fascination and lucid
legitimacy it would be foolish to deny—but the Caribbean Pirates
and the Haunted Mansion. The pirate show lasts a quarter of an
hour (but you lose any sense of time, it could be ten minutes or

thirty); you enter a series of caves, carried in boats over the surface of the water, you see first abandoned treasures, a captain's skeleton in a sumptuous bed of moldy brocade, pendent cobwebs, bodies of executed men devoured by ravens, while the skeleton addresses menacing admonitions to you. Then you navigate an inlet, passing through the crossfire of a galleon and the cannon of a fort, while the chief corsair shouts taunting challenges at the beleaguered garrison; then, as if along a river, you go by an invaded city which is being sacked, with the rape of the women, theft of jewels, torture of the mayor; the city burns like a match, drunken pirates sprawled on piles of kegs sing obscene songs; some, completely out of their heads, shoot at the visitors; the scene degenerates, everything collapses in flames, slowly the last songs die away, you emerge into the sunlight. Everything you have seen was on human scale, the vault of the caves became confused with that of the sky, the boundary of this underground world was that of the universe and it was impossible to glimpse its limits. The pirates moved, danced, slept, popped their eyes, sniggered, drank — really. You realize that they are robots, but you remain dumbfounded by their verisimilitude. And, in fact, the "Audio-Animatronic" technique represented a great source of pride for Walt Disney, who had finally managed to achieve his own dream and reconstruct a fantasy world more real than reality, breaking down the wall of the second dimension, creating not a movie, which is illusion, but total theater, and not with anthropomorphized animals, but with human beings. In fact, Disney's robots are masterpieces of electronics; each was devised by observing the expressions of a real actor, then building models, then developing skeletons of absolute precision, authentic computers in human form, to be dressed in "flesh" and "skin" made by craftsmen, whose command of realism is incredible. Each robot obeys a program, can synchronize the movements of mouth and eyes with the words and sounds of the audio, repeating ad infinitum all day long his established part (a sentence, one or two gestures) and the visitor, caught off guard by the succession of events, obliged to see several things at once, to left and right and straight ahead, has no time to look back and observe that the robot he has just seen is already repeating his eternal scenario.

The "Audio-Animatronic" technique is used in many other parts of Disneyland and also enlivens a review of presidents of the United

States, but in the pirates' cave, more than anywhere else, it demonstrates all its miraculous efficacy. Humans could do no better, and would cost more, but the important thing is precisely the fact that these are not humans and we know they're not. The pleasure of imitation, as the ancients knew, is one of the most innate in the human spirit; but here we not only enjoy a perfect imitation, we also enjoy the conviction that imitation has reached its apex and afterwards reality will always be inferior to it.

Similar criteria underlie the journey through the cellars of the Haunted Mansion, which looks at first like a rundown country house, somewhere between Edgar Allan Poe and the cartoons of Charles Addams; but inside, it conceals the most complete array of witchcraft surprises that anyone could desire. You pass through an abandoned graveyard, where skeletal hands raise gravestones from below, you cross a hill enlivened by a witches' sabbath complete with spirits and beldams; then you move through a room with a table all laid and a group of transparent ghosts in nineteenth-century costume dancing while diaphanous guests, occasionally vanishing into thin air, enjoy the banquet of a barbaric sovereign. You are grazed by cobwebs, reflected in crystals on whose surface a greenish figure appears, behind your back; you encounter moving candelabra. . . . In no instance are these the cheap tricks of some tunnel of love; the involvement (always tempered by the humor of the inventions) is total. As in certain horror films, detachment is impossible; you are not witnessing another's horror, you are inside the horror through complete synesthesia; and if there is an earthquake the movie theater must also tremble.

I would say that these two attractions sum up the Disneyland philosophy more than the equally perfect models of the pirate ship, the river boat, and the sailing ship *Columbia*, all obviously in working order. And more than the Future section, with the science-fiction emotions it arouses (such as a flight to Mars experienced from inside a spacecraft, with all the effects of deceleration, loss of gravity, dizzying movement away from the earth, and so on). More than the models of rockets and atomic submarines, which prompted Marin to observe that whereas the fake Western cities, the fake New Orleans, the fake jungle provide life-size duplicates of organic but historical or fantastic events, these are reduced-scale models of mechanical realities of today, and so, where something is incredible, the full-scale model prevails, and where it is credible, the reduction serves to make it attractive to the imagination. The Pirates and the Ghosts sum up all Disneyland, at least from the point of view of our trip, because they transform the whole city into an immense robot, the final realization of the dreams of the eighteenth-century mechanics who gave life to the Writer of Neuchâtel and the Chess-playing Turk of Baron von Kempelen.

Disneyland's precision and coherence are to some extent disturbed by the ambitions of Disney World in Florida. Built later, Disney World is a hundred fifty times larger than Disneyland, and proudly presents itself not as a toy city but as the model of an urban agglomerate of the future. The structures that make up California's Disneyland form here only a marginal part of an immense complex of construction covering an area twice the size of Manhattan. The great monorail that takes you from the entrance to the Magic Kingdom (the Disneyland part proper) passes artificial bays and lagoons, a Swiss village, a Polynesian village, golf courses and tennis courts, an immense hotel: an area dedicated, in other words, to organized vacationing. So you reach the Magic Kingdom, your eyes already dazzled by so much science fiction that the sight of the high medieval castle (far more Gothic than Disneyland: a Strasbourg Cathedral, let's say, compared to a San Miniato) no longer stirs the imagination. Tomorrow, with its violence, has made the colors fade from the stories of Yesterday. In this respect Disneyland is much shrewder; it must be visited without anything to remind us of the future surrounding it. Marin has observed that, to enter it, the essential condition is to abandon your car in an endless parking lot and reach the boundary of the dream city by special little trains. And for a Californian, leaving his car means leaving his own humanity, consigning himself to another power, abandoning his own will.

An allegory of the consumer society, a place of absolute iconism, Disneyland is also a place of total passivity. Its visitors must agree to behave like its robots. Access to each attraction is regulated by a maze of metal railings which discourages any individual initiative. The number of visitors obviously sets the pace of the line; the officials of the dream, properly dressed in the uniforms suited to each specific attraction, not only admit the visitor to the threshold of the chosen sector, but, in successive phases, regulate his every move ("Now wait here please, go up now, sit down please, wait before standing up," always in a polite tone, impersonal, imperious, over the microphone). If the visitor pays this price, he can have not only "the real thing" but the abundance of the reconstructed truth. Like the Hearst Castle, Disneyland also has no transitional spaces; there is always something to see, the great voids of modern architecture and city planning are unknown here. If America is the country of the Guggenheim Museum or the new skyscrapers of Manhattan, then Disneyland is a curious exception and American intellectuals are quite right to refuse to go there. But if America is what we have seen in the course of our trip, then Disneyland is its Sistine Chapel, and the hyperrealists of the art galleries are only the timid voyeurs of an immense and continuous "found object."

David Hockney

David Hockney, whose pastel-hued paintings of swimming pools and hyperreal Polaroid collages capture the region's sharp light and ambiguously beautiful surfaces, has perhaps done more than any other artist to define Southern California's image. Born in 1937 in Bradford, England — "a soot-caked Victorian city," in the words of fellow expatriate Richard Rayner — Hockney first visited Los Angeles in 1963, and settled there the following year. He has long been at home in the Southland, with its sun and space and openness, qualities that resonate throughout his work. In this excerpt from his memoir *David Hockney by David Hockney* (1976) he describes his first encounter with the place.

from

DAVID HOCKNEY BY DAVID HOCKNEY

When I got to Los Angeles I didn't know a soul. People in New York said You're mad for going there if you don't know anybody and you can't drive. They said At least go to San Francisco if you want to go West. And I said No, no, it's Los Angeles I want to go to. So it was arranged; I was going to have an exhibition in New York, at Charles Alan's Gallery, and I said I'd paint the pictures in California. Charles said It's crazy, you know you won't even be able to leave the airport if you can't drive; it's madness. So he phoned up this guy who was a sculptor there, who showed in his gallery, called Oliver Andrews. He very kindly came to meet me at the airport and he drove me to a motel in Santa Monica and just dropped me. He gave me his phone number. I got into the motel, very thrilled; really, *really* thrilled, more than in New York the first time. I was so excited. I think it was partly a sexual fascination and attraction. I arrived in the evening. Of course I'd no transport but the motel was right by the bottom of Santa Monica Canyon, just where Christopher Isherwood lives. I didn't know him then and although I had his address I didn't know it was near there. I checked into this motel and walked on the beach and I was looking for the town; couldn't see it. And I saw some lights and I thought, that must be it. I walked two miles, and when I got there all it was was a big gas station, so brightly lit I'd thought it was the city. So I walked back and thought, what am I going to do? Next morning I phoned up Oliver and said I want to go into the town; I must buy a bicycle. And he said All right, I'll take you. It appeared the town was just at the back; I'd been looking the wrong way. He took me to buy a bicycle and he told me about an English writer there. I said You mean Christopher Isherwood? And he said Yes. He knew him. So I said I'd love to meet him.

I had read John Rechy's *City of Night*, which I thought was a marvellous picture of a certain kind of life in America. It was one of the first novels covering that kind of sleazy sexy hot night-life in Pershing Square. I looked on the map and saw that Wilshire Boulevard which begins by the sea in Santa Monica goes all the way to Pershing Square; all you have to do is stay on that boulevard. But of course, it's about eighteen miles, which I didn't realize. I started cycling. I got to Pershing Square and it was deserted; about nine in the evening, just got dark, not a soul there. I thought, where is everybody? I had a glass of beer and thought, it's going to take me an hour or more to get back; so I just cycled back and I thought, this just won't do, this bicycle is useless. I shall have to get a car somehow.

Then Oliver came to visit me next day and said How's the cycling going? And I said Well, I went to Pershing Square. Why did you go to Pershing Square? Nobody in Los Angeles ever goes to downtown Los Angeles, he said. I said I'll have to get a car. And he said I'll take you to the licence place and you can get a provisional licence and then you can drive round, practise a bit; it's easy, driving. I'd never driven before in my life. He showed me a bit of driving. He said All you do is put your foot here to go and your foot there to stop; automatic car, no gears; so I tried it out. We went up to the licence place and they said You fill out this form. And the form had questions on it like What is the top speed limit in California: 45 miles an hour, 65 miles an hour, 100 miles an hour. Well, you can guess, you don't have to be too smart or even to have read the highway code. And all the questions were like this. I just picked the answers using common sense. And they said You made four mistakes; that's allowed. Where's your vehicle? I said How do you mean, where's the vehicle? They said You take the driving test now, the practical bit; you passed the first part. I said Could I come back tomorrow? They said Come back this afternoon; you get three goes for your three dollars. If you fail you can come back. Oliver was amused that I'd inadvertently passed the first part of the test, and he showed me a bit, and then said You might as well have a go. And they gave me the licence.

I was thrilled but frightened. I thought, that's all you do and everybody's zipping about you? I went and bought a Ford Falcon in the afternoon, which cost about a thousand dollars; first car I'd ever had; and I was very scared driving it. I thought, I'll have to practise; and I just drove anywhere. I got on a freeway the second day and I daren't move off any of the lanes and I went all the way to San Bernardino on the freeway, sixty miles inland. I thought, I'll turn round here, if I can find where you get off. Then there's a sign: Las Vegas 200 miles. And I thought, wonderful, I'll practise in the desert, and I drove all the way to Las Vegas, and drove back at night.

The day after, I found a studio. Just drove down to Venice, this place for rent, little sign up. I said I'll take it; room overlooking the sea, not very big. Then I just rented a small apartment, very easy to find in Los Angeles. You just drive down the streets and there are notices saying $1\frac{1}{2}$ rooms to let; a very American way, I thought, half a room. I imagined the half-room being from the ceiling halfway down the walls. Within a week of arriving there in this strange big city, not knowing a soul, I'd passed the driving test, bought a car, driven to Las Vegas and won some money, got myself a studio, started painting, all in a week. And I thought, it's just how I imagined it would be.

I went into an art store and it was full of American equipment. I'd tried acrylic paint in England before and I hadn't liked it at all; texture, colours weren't so very good. But the American ones I liked. It was superior paint. And so I started to use it. It has one or two effects. For one thing you can work on one picture all the time because you never have to wait for it to dry, whereas you might work on two or three oil paintings at a time because it takes so long for the paint to dry.

I began to meet artists. In those days, all the galleries in Los Angeles were on one street in Hollywood. They were run by young people; they showed young artists. I didn't know the artists there at all; I was quite surprised. On a Monday evening the galleries were all open, and people parked their cars and walked up this street and looked in. It was very pleasant, and it was also a way for artists to meet each other socially each week. In a city like Los Angeles it's difficult to meet people accidentally. In Paris it's easy, but not in Los Angeles. At the top of the street there is that place called Barney's Beanerie; Ed Kienholz made a replica of it later. I went there to look around, and I talked, met, was introduced to people. There were a lot of young artists there about my age and there was a kind of small California pop art school, but I'd never heard of it. The only Californian artists I'd ever heard of before I went there were Richard Diebenkorn and David Park; they were from Northern California and painted in a slightly Bomberg way. Diebenkorn is a marvellous painter and a wonderful draughtsman; marvellous drawings always. He's always underplayed in America.

The very first picture I painted there was *Plastic Tree Plus City Hall* and the second was *California Art Collector*, and then *Ordinary Picture* which still has curtains.

After I'd been there a couple of months, Kasmin came out on his first visit to California, to see me and some collectors. I went with him to visit the collectors. I'd never seen houses like that. And the way they liked to show them off! They were mostly women — the husbands were out earning the money. They would show you the pictures, the garden, the house. So then I painted a picture, *California Art Collector*, in February 1964: it's a lady sitting in a garden with some art; there was a Turnbull sculpture. There was a lot of sculpture by Bill Turnbull; somebody'd been and sold them there a few years before. The picture is a complete invention. The only specific thing is the swimming pool, painted from an advertisement for swimming pools in the Sunday edition of the *Los Angeles Times*. The houses I had seen all had large comfortable chairs, fluffy carpets, striped paintings and pre-Columbian or primitive sculptures and recent (1964) three-dimensional work. As the climate and the openness of houses (large glass windows, patios, etc.) reminded me of Italy, I borrowed a few notions from Fra Angelico and Piero della Francesca.

I got into work straight away. By this time I had met Christopher Isherwood and we instantly got on. He was the first author I'd met that I really admired. I got to know him and Don Bachardy, whom he lives with, very well; they would invite me out, take me around to dinner; we had marvellous evenings together. Christopher is always interesting to talk to about anything and I loved it, really loved it. I don't know how it was that we hit it off, but we did. It wasn't only that we were English, but we were both from northern England. I remember Christopher later said Oh David, we've so much in common; we love California, we love American boys, and we're from the north of England. Of course Christopher's from the opposite side of the north of England: his family was quite rich, mine is working class.

I went to visit the place where *Physique Pictorial* was published in a very seedy area of downtown Los Angeles. It's run by a wonderful complete madman and he has this tacky swimming pool surrounded by Hollywood Greek plaster statues. It was marvellous! To me it had the air of Cavafy in the tackiness of things. Even Los Angeles reminded me of Cavafy; the hot climate's near enough to Alexandria, sensual; and this downtown area was sleazy, a bit dusty, very masculine—men always; women are just not part of that kind of life. I love downtown Los Angeles—marvellous gay bars full of mad Mexican queens, all tacky and everything. The *Physique Pictorial* people get men, boys, when they've just come out of the city gaol: Do you want to earn ten dollars? Take your clothes off, jump in the pool, that sort of thing. They're all a bit rough-looking, but the bodies are quite good. The faces are terrible, not pretty boys, really. I must admit I have a weakness for pretty boys; I prefer them to the big, butch, scabby ones. I was quite thrilled by the place, and I told the guy. I bought a lot of still photographs from him, which I still have.

Jan Morris

The pragmatic Los Angeles that Jan Morris (b. 1926) describes in "The Know-How City" is a far cry from the glitzy La-La Land of popular perception. Morris, whose books include *Conundrum* (1974), *Journeys* (1984), *Manhattan '45* (1987), and *Hong Kong: Xianggang* (1988), is one of the many visitors who in the 1970s were reevaluating Los Angeles in terms quite different from those of earlier satirists and detractors. This essay, originally published in *Rolling Stone* in 1976, was collected in *Destinations* (1980).

LOS ANGELES: THE KNOW-HOW CITY

Los Angeles is the city of Know-How. Remember "know-how"? It was one of the vogue words of the forties and fifties, now rather out of fashion. It reflected a whole climate and tone of American thought in the years of supreme American optimism. It stood for skill and experience indeed, but it also expressed the certainty that America's particular genius, the genius for applied logic, for systems, for devices, was inexorably the herald of progress.

As the English had thought in the 1840s, so the Americans thought a century later. They held the future in their hands and brains, and this time it *would* work. Their methods and inventions would usher not only America herself but all mankind into another golden age. Know-how would be America's great gift to history: know-how to rescue the poor from their poverty, to snatch the colored peoples from their ignominy, to convince the nations that the American way of free enterprise was the best and happiest way of all. Nothing was beyond know-how. Know-how was, if not actually the substance of God, at least a direct derivative.

One city in America, above all others, came to represent this enviable conviction. There has never been another town, and now there never will be, quite like El Pueblo de Nuestra Señora la Reina de Los Angeles de Porciúncula, Southern California, where the lost American faith in machines and materialism built its own astonishing monument.

596

Los Angeles, in the generic sense, was a long time coming. It is not a young city. Spaniards were here before the United States was founded, and I never get the feeling, as I wander around L.A.'s vast, amorphous mass, that it lies thinly on the ground. It is not like Johannesburg, for instance, where almost within living memory there was nothing whatsoever. Nor does it feel transient or flimsy, like some of those towns of the Middle West, which seem to have no foundations at all, but await the next tornado to sweep them away in a tumble of matchwood. In Los Angeles there are reminders of a long tradition. There is the very name of the city, and of its euphonious streets and suburbs—Alvarado, El Segundo, Pasadena, Cahuenga Boulevard. There is the pattern of its real estate, still recognizably descended from the Spanish and Mexican ranches of long ago. There is its exotic taste in architecture, its patios and its deep caves, its arcades, its courtyards. There are even a few actual buildings, heavily reconstructed but still authentic, which survive from the first Spanish pueblo—swarmed over by tourists now, but fitfully frequented too, I like to think, by the swaggering ghosts of their original caballeros.

A sense of age informs the very setting of L.A. From the air the city looks like some enormously exaggerated pueblo itself: flat, sprawling, rectilinearly intersected, dun colored, built of mud brick by some inconceivable race of primitives, and behind it the tawny mountains run away in a particularly primeval way, a lizardy, spiny way, their dry expanses relieved only by the flicker of white on a snow peak here and there, or the distant glimmer of a lake. In a huge amphitheater the city lies, accessible only by passes through the surrounding ridges, rather like a gigantic mining camp: and through the veil of its own artificial mist, suggestively whirled about and blended with the California sunshine, it looks across its golden beaches toward that most enigmatic of the oceans, the Pacific (never called the sea in Los Angeles, always "the ocean").

There is nothing Johnny-come-quick to this scene. Los Angeles is a complex merger of separate settlements, containing within its scrambled presence eighty different municipalities, and sprawling district by district, decade by decade, over its central plain and into its foothills. The witty Mr. David Clark, when he named his book *L.A. on Foot: A Free Afternoon*, was ironically emphasizing the amoebic

immensity of the place, territorially among the largest urban settlements in the world, and psychologically one of the most involved.
Though I would guess that nine-tenths of its buildings were erected
in the 20th century, still Los Angeles is, like some incurable disease,
a balefully organic phenomenon. Its streets are forever nibbling and
probing further into its perimeter hills, twisting like rising water
ever higher, ever deeper into their canyons, and sometimes bursting
through to the deserts beyond. If the city could be pried out of its
setting, one feels, it would be like a dried mat of some bacterial
mold, every bump, every corner exactly shaped to its landscape.

This is partly because the landscape itself is so individual, so
that unlike Chicago, say, or Paris, Los Angeles is inconceivable anywhere else. But it is also, I think, because this city genuinely springs
out of its own soil, possesses a true genius loci and forms a kind of
irreplaceable flash point: the point on the map where the intellectual, the physical and the historical forces of American history met
to produce—well, combustion, what else? Whatever happens to
L.A., it will always be the city of the automobile and the radio,
showbiz and the Brown Derby restaurant, the city where the American ideal of happiness by technique found its folk art in the ebul-
lience of Hollywood. It is essentially of the forties and the fifties,
and especially perhaps of the World War II years, when the American conviction acquired the force of a crusade, and sent its jeeps, its
technicians and its Betty Grables almost as sacred pledges across
the world. Los Angeles then was everyone's vision of the New
World; and so it must always remain, however it develops, a memorial to those particular times, as Florence means for everyone the
spirit of Renaissance, and Vienna speaks always of fin de siecle.

Across the car park from the remains of the original Spanish
pueblo, where the Mexican souvenir shops now huddle profitably
along Olvera Street, there stands Union Station. This was the last
great railway depot to be built in the United States, completed in
1939, and one of the most handsome. Cool, tall, elegant, and nowadays restfully unfrequented by trains, it has patios green with flowers and trees, shaded colonial-style arcades, and is rather the sort
of railway station a multibillionaire might devise, if he wanted one
at the bottom of the garden. In this it is very proper, for while

paying graceful respect to L.A.'s origins and pretensions, it honors too the first and fundamental quality of this city: organized, stylized movement.

It was not liberty that Los Angeles cherished in its prime, or at least not absolute liberty. A spiritual culture can be anarchical, a material culture must be disciplined. Implicit to the promise of technological fulfillment was the necessity of *system*, and L.A. soon became a firmly ordered place. The original Los Angeles public transport system, the electric trains and streetcars of the early 20th century, drew together the scattered settlements of the time, bringing them all into cityness.

When the car arrived the mesh was tightened, and L.A. built its incomparable freeways. These remain the city's grandest and most exciting artifacts. Snaky, sinuous, undulating, high on stilts or sunk in cuttings, they are like so many concrete tentacles, winding themselves around each block, each district, burrowing, evading, clambering, clasping every corner of the metropolis as if they are squeezing it all together to make the parts stick. They are inescapable, not just visually, but emotionally. They are always there, generally a few blocks away; they enter everyone's lives, and seem to dominate all arrangements.

To most strangers they suggest chaos, or at least purgatory, and there can certainly be more soothing notices than the one on the Santa Ana Freeway which announces MERGING BUSES AHEAD. There comes a moment, though, when something clicks in one's own mechanism, and suddenly one grasps the rhythm of the freeway system, masters its tribal or ritual forms, and discovers it to be not a disruptive element at all, but a kind of computer key to the use of Los Angeles. One is processed by the freeways. Elevated as they generally are above the flat and centerless expanse of the city, they provide a navigational aid, into which one locks oneself for guidance. Everything is clearer then. There are the mountains, to the north and east. There is the glimmering ocean. The civic landmarks of L.A., such as they are, display themselves conveniently for you, the pattern of the place unfolds until, properly briefed by the experience, the time comes for you to unlock from the system, undo your safety belt, and take the right-hand lane into the everyday life below.

The moment this first happened to me, Los Angeles happened too, and I glimpsed the real meaning of the city, and realized how firmly it had been disciplined by the rules of its own conviction.

Confusing, nevertheless, the Santa Ana with the San Diego Freeway, missing the exit at Bristol, mistaking Newport Avenue for Newport Boulevard, getting in the wrong lane at Victoria, miscounting the traffic lights on 22nd Street, an hour late exactly I arrived for lunch with the world's greatest authority on European naval history in the early 20th century.

Through apparent chaos to unmistakable authority. This was a not uncharacteristic Los Angeles experience. Expertise is the stock in trade of this metropolis, and behind the flash and the braggadocio, solid skills and scholarship prosper. There are craftsmen everywhere in L.A., craftsmen in electronics, in film-making, in literature, in social science, in advertising, in fashion. They say that in San Francisco there is less than meets the eye: in Los Angeles there is far more, for the reputation of the place makes no allowance for this corporate diligence and dexterity. Here Lockheed makes its aircraft. Here NASA makes its space shuttle orbiter. Here is UCLA, one of the most fertile universities in the Western world. Here the McCulloch Corporation has patented a device to pop the golf ball *out* of the hole, to save its owner stooping. This is no place for dilettantes. Even sport is assiduously, sometimes grimly, pursued: the tennis players of Beverly Hills joylessly strain toward perfection, the Malibu surfers seldom lark about, but take their pleasures with a showy dedication.

I went one morning to Burbank Studios to see them filming Neil Simon's macabre comedy, *Murder by Death.* This is one of those movies in which everyone is a star, and the set was cluttered with familiar figures. There was Truman Capote, described in the studio publicity as "acclaimed author and international celebrity," huddled with a young friend in a corner and wearing a wide-brimmed hat. There was Peter Falk, charmingly chatting with Elsa Lanchester. Alec Guinness looked truly gentlemanly, David Niven looked almost too elegant. Ray Stark the producer looked preternaturally successful, Robert Moore the director looked alarmingly gifted.

I am antipathetic to the famous, though, and I found that my eyes kept straying from these luminaries to the two sound technicians who, just off the set, sat nonchalantly over their equipment wearing headsets and reading the trade papers. One was called Jerry Jost, the other Bill Manooth, and they had both been in the business twenty years and more. How calm they looked, I thought, how sure of themselves, how easily aware of the fact that nobody in the whole world could do their job better than they could! They had seen the stars come and go, they had helped to make flops and winners, they had suffered every temperament, they had seen the film industry itself in boom and decline. Sometimes they looked up to exchange a pleasantry with a passer-by, sometimes they turned a page of the *Hollywood Reporter*: but they were always alert when the moment came, always watching their quivering instruments, always ready to mouth the magic word "Speed!"—which, with its assurance that they had got things right, gave the signal to that whole assembly, director, cameraman, actors, Capote and all, to proceed with their flamboyances.

For somewhere near the heart of the L.A. ethos there lies, unexpectedly, a layer of solid, old-fashioned, plain hard work. This is a city of hard workers. Out on the hills at Santa Monica, overlooking the Pacific Ocean, the writer Christopher Isherwood and the painter Don Bachardy share a house, sunlit and easygoing, with a view over the rooftops and shrubberies of the canyon. In such a place, with such occupants, in such warm and soothing sun, with the beach down the road and Hollywood up the freeway, it might seem a house for cultivated indolence, interminable wit around a swimming pool, long cool drinks with worldly neighbors before lunch. Not at all. "We are *working* people," Isherwood says, and so they literally are: each at his own end of the house, each with his art, the one surrounded by his books, the other by his brushes and pictures, carefully and skillfully they work through the day, friends and fellow laborers.

I very much like all this. It suggests to me, unexpectedly, the guild spirit of some medieval town, where the workers in iron or lace, the clockmakers and the armorers, competed to give their city the glory of their trades. All the mechanisms of Los Angeles are like apprentices to these matters: the robot lights and the TV cameras, the scudding helicopters, the laboring oil pumps bowed like slaves across the city, or the great telescopes of Mount Wilson, brooding among their conifers high above the city, which in the years before the Second World War more than doubled man's total knowledge of the physical universe.

It is true that this expertise is sometimes rather dated, but then L.A. is essentially a survivor of earlier times, and one is constantly plucked back to that simpler world of the forties, when values were surer than they are now, and the attainment of wealth or fame seemed the true gauge of contentment.

One citizen who honors those values still, in life as in principle, is Ed Davis, the celebrated police chief of Los Angeles. He is an inescapable figure there. I doubt if there is another police chief in the world better known among his citizenry. Powerful, controversial, dogmatic, his name entered almost every conversation I had about the city, and aroused powerful reactions everywhere. He was a pseudofascist reactionary. He was a great police chief. He was bigoted, unbalanced, hysterical. He was a staunch upholder of right and decency. He was a brute. He was a father figure. He ought to be shot. He ought to be President.

So I arranged to meet him, and arriving one sunny morning at police headquarters, familiar to everybody in Western civilization from a thousand prime times on TV—arriving in those hallowed halls, trodden before me by Sergeant Friday—arriving there reverent and docile ("Say," they told me, "there was a cop here from England only the other day—he was *dazzled* by the level of crime we have here")—dazzled then, by the historic ambiance, I proceeded to the *piano nobile*, where Davis was attended by his faithful middle-aged secretary Helen and by sundry lesser acolytes.

He was on the whole the most impressive man I met in L.A., but impressive in a faintly forlorn way. It is not that he really believes, as he once claimed, that hijackers should be publicly hanged at L.A. airport, or that he really harbors malice when he speaks of "raving faggots" or inveighs against illegitimate massage parlors: what dates him, and gives him a paradoxical poignancy, is his apparent belief that Order can somehow *cure* society's ills. He talked to me of crime in intellectual terms—"situation ethics," "symbiotic relationships," "the new morality," and he argued that even victimless crimes are like cancers on the body public: but he is really animated, I think, by an old-school, traditional faith in the redemptive power of discipline. He is a man of unchallenged technique, but like the technique of the automobile which has made L.A. what it is, it is the technique of an older America. It is not yet discredited—Ed Davis really has kept organized crime to a minimum in his city—but it is distinctly outmoded.

I thought him, for all his force and brilliance, rather a nostalgic figure, pining for the days of faith and family: and nostalgia too blurs the realities of Hollywood, the Versailles of Los Angeles, and peoples it forever with the royalty of another era, the Astaires, the Tracys, the Garbos, and nobles of even earlier vintage. Now as always the tourist buses circumnavigate the Homes of the Stars, and the touts peddle their street plans on Sunset Strip. Now as always Hollywood feeds upon narcissism, cosseted in sycophancy and sustained by snobbery. Scattered over the Hollywood Hills, and over the Santa Monica Mountains into the San Fernando Valley, the houses of the movie people stand sealed and suspicious in the morning, the only sounds the swishing of their sprinklers, the snarling of their guard dogs, or perhaps the labored breathing of their gardeners: and in their garages the cars are profligately stacked, Jag beside Merc, Rolls upstaging BMW. Hollywood prefers its own world to ours, loving and living, generation after generation, its own fairly tawdry legend.

I stayed in the middle of it all, and soon came to feel how period a piece it was. My hotel was the Chateau Marmont, a monument in itself, built in the French manner half a century ago, and directly overlooking Sunset Boulevard. Everyone in Hollywood knows the place. That's where Bogart proposed to Bacall, they say, that's where Garbo used to stay, Howard Hughes had a suite there, Boris Karloff loved it, Valentino preferred the penthouse. It is impregnated with showbiz, from the gigantic antiques in the downstairs lounge to the strains of the electronic organ from the pop group practicing in the garden bungalow: but what seems to the aficionado amusingly evocative seemed to me only a little threadbare, the ghostly thread of the stars did not make up for the lack of a dial telephone, and I often found myself pining for an honest downtown motel, where never a Gable raised his eyebrow, or a Garland threw a tantrum.

Every morning, too, I walked across the boulevard to have my breakfast at Schwab's, "The World's Most Famous Drugstore." Everyone knows Schwab's, too. Schwab's is where Lana Turner was discovered, sitting on a barstool. Hardly a Hollywood memoir is complete without a reference to Schwab's, and it is heavy with the old mystique. Elderly widows of émigré directors reminisce about Prague over their cornflakes. Young men in jerkins and expensive shoes ostentatiously read *Variety*, or greet each other with stagey endearments and expletives. Ever and again one hears across the hubbub, in the whining intonations peculiar to not very successful actors offstage, an exchange of critiques—"I love her, she's a fine, fine actress, but it just wasn't *her*"—"Well, but what can you expect with Philip directing, she needs *definite* direction"—"True, but shit, it just made me *puke*, the way she did that last scene. . . ." Nearly everyone seems to know nearly everyone else at Schwab's: I used to drink my coffee at the counter, until I found this instinct for intimacy too cloying for comfort, and took to sitting at a table with the divorced wife of a Mexican set designer who shared my enthusiasm for Abyssinian cats.

If fetish and nostalgia often make for vulgarity in L.A., they often make also for homeliness, in the English sense of the word—a community feeling, a domesticity. Even Hollywood is far less repulsive in its private aspects than in its public goings-on. This is largely because Los Angeles is a haven, to whose doors people have come from all over the world. It is a fraternity of refugees. Isherwood, showing me the view from his window one day, remembered the days when Stravinsky, Schönberg, Brecht and Aldous Huxley had all lived in the city out there. Hardly a day goes by without the death of some celebrated European resident, driven here long ago by war, ambition or persecution, and the British consul general told me that within his area there live more than 50,000 British subjects, some of whom fly Union Jacks from their roofs. San Francisco, up the coast, has an intimacy of a totally different kind, a hereditary or environmental closeness, bound up with the beauty of the place and the allure of its traditions. There is no such grace to the brotherhood of L.A. This is a charmless city really, humorless, often reactionary, a city without a gentry. Its comradeship lies only in a common sense of release or opportunity, tinged with a spice of holiday.

I used to buy my bread at Farmer's Market, a rambling enclave of stalls and tables off Wilshire Boulevard, and sitting over an orange juice afterward, nibbling bits off the end of my loaf, loved to watch the Angelenos go by. Often, of course, they were not Angelenos at all, but Japanese businessmen being shown around by bored local agents, or package tourists in wild sunglasses and kerchiefs, or bookish Europeans from UCLA deep in *Sociological Ratios in Southern California*. But there were always plenty of indigenes too, and they were instantly recognizable, not so much by their looks as by their posture, for they displayed all the somewhat impatient complacency of people who have discovered a Promised Land, and don't want to miss a minute of it. Though there are obviously lots of unhappy people in L.A., lots of dispossessed blacks, unemployed layabouts, junkies and nuts and winos and miscellaneous *bêtes noires* of Mr. Davis's department, still by and large this strikes me as a happy population—determinedly happy, perhaps. Nobody I met wanted to go back to New York or Detroit. With its Middle West squareness, its Manhattan bitterness, its imported touch of the European and its glorious Pacific sun, L.A. seems to please most people in the end—or for the moment.

In particular it provides a cheerful refuge for the jollier kind of American widow or divorcée, and many of these belatedly liberated souls frequent Farmer's Market. I often talked to them. There was a certain sameness to their appearance: in their bright blouses, leather jerkins, rather too tight slacks and rather too rakish sailor caps, bowed often by arthritis but resolutely vigorous of step, most of them looked more or less like Mr. Capote except, of course, for the layered makeup ineffectually disguising their cod-skin complexions. To their attitudes though there was a sprightly element of freedom. Briskly, gaily, talkatively they walked around the stalls, a pumpernickel loaf here, a bag of cashews there, and often they exchanged rather throaty comments with acquaintances about last night's movie or tomorrow's meeting of the Democratic party.

For such citizens L.A. offers an unexpected security, for its hard efficiency provides a bedrock, so to speak, upon which they can safely reconstruct their lives. It is nourished by the certainties they

were weaned upon, like the pre-eminence of gadgetry or the goodness of capitalism. For all its cosmopolitan excitement, to a far
greater degree than Chicago or San Francisco, let alone New York,
it is still a provincial American town. "Did you know," one Farmer's
Market lady asked me, supposing me, I imagine, to be a bit lost for
social satisfactions, "did you know that the telephone company
offers a free tour every day? My, that's a rewarding way of spending
an afternoon!"

More exotic refugees share an intenser camaraderie. Members
of the alternative society, for instance, seem to live rather in pha-
lanx, perhaps because Mr. Davis sees no moral necessity for them.
Southern California indeed has a long tradition of religious tolerance, sprouting cults, sects and rites like vivid fungi, and L.A. itself
welcomes eccentrics if they are rich and famous enough. Your honest dropout, though, your simple hash man, often finds the atmosphere inhospitable, and among the more poignant corners of the
metropolis is Venice, a struggling enclave of unorthodoxy on the
ocean south of Santa Monica. It is a forlorn kind of suburb anyway,
for it is the remains of a fin-de-siècle attempt to recreate the original
Venice, "Venice Italy," upon the Pacific coast. A few Renaissance
arcades remain, a Ruskinian window here and there, and there is a
hangdog system of canals which, with their low-built bridges, their
loitering ducks, their dog-messed paths, their smells of silt and dust
and their air of stagnant hush, really do contrive to preserve a truly
Venetian suggestion of decay. Here we seem to see a philosophy
with its back to the wall. It is like a caricature of itself, squeezed into
this ocean beachhead by the colossal pressures of Los Angeles, and
the society that frequents the place, too, suggests to me a culture on
the verge of dissolution.

On the other hand, aliens in the older sense, foreigners that is,
stand amazed still at the munificence of L.A. In some immigrant
cities—in Toronto, for example, perhaps the archetypical melting
pot of our time—your newcomer from Turkey or Sweden generally
views his new home cynically, simply as a place to make money. I do
not get this feeling with L.A.'s immigrants. They seem to see it still
as a place of hope and blessing. I went one night to one of those
Hollywood parades one used to see on newsreels long ago. Nothing

much had changed. The long motorcade crawled down Hollywood Boulevard in a welter of self-esteem, with drum majorettes and elephants and Scottish pipers and U.S. Marines and belly dancers and coveys of movie personalities in antique cars who stopped now and then to be interviewed by TV men — "Hey Bob, great to see you! How's everything? Isn't this a great parade?" "Sure is, Jim, fantastic, just great, and I wantya to meet my family, Jim, my wife Margie, this is my son Jason, my daughter Laureen!" "Great, fantastic, great to meet all you folks, nice talking with you, Bill." "Sure thing, Jim, sure is a great parade, fantastic. . . ." The echoes of the bands trumpeted across town, the belly dancers spangled their way past Grauman's Chinese Theater, and overhead the helicopters clanked and circled, playing their searchlights upon the junketings below.

I was touched by the crowd that watched this display, for I felt in it a truly innocent wonder. Its people came from everywhere. There were a few of my Market friends ("I forgot to mention this morning, dear, that the Municipal Cleansing Department offers a very interesting lecture tour Tuesday mornings"); but there were Mexicans, too, in bright ponchos with babies on their backs, and lots of Italians, and Hindus talking impeccable English, and Greeks talking Greek, and there was a Scotsman in a kilt looking maudlin when the pipers went by, and a man who looked like a Zulu chief, and a voluble family who seemed to be talking Finnish, or perhaps Basque, and there were thousands of that particular neo-American blend, of no particular color, no specific race, no exact dialect, the *Homo californii*; and though the cops strode up and down fiercely slapping their nightsticks against their thighs, still everybody seemed genuinely, guilelessly delighted to be participants in such an unmistakable Angeleno spectacle.

I stayed till the very end, and the last I saw of the parade were the winking red lights of the police cars which brought up the rear, blinking away slowly down the boulevard as the crowds flooded off the sidewalks to follow them.

Much of L.A.'s expertise is devoted to such display. The Goodyear dirigible loiters effortlessly over town (I could not get a ride in it, alas, the Goodyear PR person never having heard of

Rolling Stone). The freeways often seem to me to be as much show-manship as engineering. Sunset Strip, "the Billboard Center of the Western World," is one and a half miles of unremitting posters, 78 when I was there in the sixteen blocks between Crescent Heights and Doheny Drive: every day most of them seem to be changed, as one might replenish the drawing-room flowers, and marvelous is the professionalism by which the billboard men, with their slender cranes and their hefty trucks, bisect the torsos of rock singers, demolish romantic countrysides, split rodomontades or separate superlatives to hoist those tremendous announcements down in their several sections and trundle them away to oblivion or Las Vegas.

Yet Hollywood itself, its fact and its reputation, its studios and its publicity machine, is a family of sorts, not always very loving indeed, and frequently incestuous, but still bound by a common loyalty to its own legend. Its members often speak of it with true affection, especially if they are old. As the glamour of success fades, as the meaning of money blurs, so Hollywood memories acquire a mellower force, and elderly directors, dowager stars, speak of old Hollywood as others might remember happy school days, or Edwardian society. Age is paradoxically venerated in Hollywood, and one is told without pejoration that So-and-So is living in a home for aged actors, or assured with respect that Miss Estelle Winwood really *is* in her 93rd year. The new breed of entertainer often seems awkwardly anomalous, almost alienated, in this hierarchical community: which is why the Hyatt hotel on Sunset Boulevard, where the rock bravos tend to congregate, was long ago nicknamed the Continental Riot House.

Sometimes the camaraderie is oddly attractive. I went one day to a taping of the *Carol Burnett Show*, itself approaching institutional status after so many years on the screen, and found it an endearingly domestic occasion. Miss Burnett the star was married to Mr. Hamilton the executive producer, Miss Lawrence the ingenue brought her baby along. Everyone had known everyone else for years, and easily broke into a sort of family badinage: so that when somebody playfully pretended to sock somebody else on the jaw, even the sound effects man, somewhere out of sight, instantly contributed an impromptu *thunk*. Though it is currently the longest

running show on television, and one of the most consistently successful, it suggested to me a rehearsal for some unusually polished
but still folksy high school show, so that when Miss Burnett happened to tell me that she was dining that evening with Sir Alec
Guinness and Lord Olivier, I felt like saying "Lawsy me, Carol,
lucky old you. . . ."

At other times the bond can be sickly, or comic, or a bit morbid,
or even creepy. I went to a Democratic party meeting in Beverly
Hills which reminded me almost eerily, in its sense of inbred continuity, of the McCarthy era in Hollywood twenty years ago. There
were the very same writers and directors, I swear, whom we used to
see pale before the inquisitor's gaze; and there were their dauntless,
loyal wives, no longer in dirndls and home-weave blouses indeed,
but suitably beaded and denimed instead; and there was the same
curl of pipe smoke in the air, with the same progressive smiles, and
the same ladies went around getting signatures on petitions or prop-
agating similar liberal causes—"Can we persuade you to support
the Council for Universal Rights?"—"May I ask you to sign this
petition on behalf of the Coalition for Handgun Control?"—"You
do *know* about CDC, don't you, *so* important we feel"—until the
chairman called for silence, and there stepped handsomely to the
rostrum, just as he might have braved Senator McCarthy's furies
long ago, that young crusader of today's Los Angeles joustings, that
very antithesis of reaction, Jane Fonda's husband, whose name I
momentarily forget.

The Los Angeles ethos is intensely infectious, and transmutes
everything it touches. It can be great fun. The J. Paul Getty
Museum of Art, for instance, which is housed in a dazzling recreation of a Roman villa above the sea at Malibu, often excites the
scorn of critics and connoisseurs, but delights people of more
urbane taste. The Rolls-Royce motorcar, elsewhere in the world a
symbol of dignity and reserve, becomes in Los Angeles, where it
probably proliferates more than anywhere else, a young person's
runabout, to swish up the drive to the Beverly Hills Hotel, or weave
around the staid Cadillacs on the Palisades. Even the Californian
cultists are easily Los Angelized, when they venture from their com-
munes and mountain churches into the purlieus of the great city.

The flaming sign on the Santa Ana Freeway announcing the Amazing Prophecy Center does not look in the least out of place, and I was not at all surprised to learn that America's largest incense factory, Spiritual Sky Scented Products Inc., was the property of the Hare Krishna community (acronymically ISKCON — International Society for Krishna Consciousness).

I visited the factory, as a matter of fact, to see just how easily the mantra and the head knot would adapt to L.A.'s style of capitalism, and found that fusion had easily been achieved. The lady at the reception desk was dressed in full Indianified costume, and the company memo pads ended their list of practical alternatives (Take Action/See Me/Call Me/File) with the hardly less clear-cut spiritual injunction, clean across the bottom of the page in vaguely Oriental lettering, HARE KRISHNA, HARE KRISHNA, KRISHNA, KRISHNA, HARE, HARE/HARE RAMA, HARE RAMA, RAMA, RAMA, HARE, HARE. The plant manager was dressed more or less for Rotary, and told me that the Spiritual Sky line emphasized the incense America wants and loves — strawberry flavor especially: but when I pressed him on more spiritual matters, in no time at all he had pushed the *Wall Street Journal* aside and was enthusiastically explaining to me the principles of his Divine Master — rather wistfully, I thought, as though the management of Spiritual Sky was in the nature of a penance.

Just as often, though, the L.A. treatment only coarsens and degrades. It was no coincidence that so many of the Watergate acolytes were alumni of Los Angeles advertising agencies: the aerosol charm of John Dean, for instance, who entertained me most kindly to Dr. Peppers in his Laurel Canyon hideaway, blends very easily into the ambiance, and I suspect that Mr. Nixon himself, if ever he turned up in Farmer's Market, would be ecstatically welcomed. "Smartness," in the opportunist sense, the importance of image, the search for celebrity whatever its cause — all these are true L.A. characteristics, and are contagious. Many vegetarian restaurants, I am told, opening to a regular sacrament of organic ideals, soon degenerate into convenience foods, and even death of course becomes a packaged product up at Forest Lawn, where the Wee Kirk o' the Heather offers consolation in Time of Sorrow, and Companion Lawn Crypts provide the ultimate security of Reinforced Concrete. The TV game shows of Hollywood have evolved an entire language and ritual of falseness, from the stylized jumpings, handclappings and mock-bashfulness of the competitors to the palatial languor of the ravaged showgirls who act as ladies of the prize chamber.

For myself, I am left with an uneasy feeling even about Disneyland, where the most advanced technical resources, the most brilliant administrative systems, are used simply to animate a gigantic charade. The sham treads uncomfortably upon the heels of truth, and one begins to wonder whether a dummy castle from Snow White, a make-believe New Orleans restaurant, even a nonalcoholic mint julep, might not be as good, and as true, as the real thing. I found this inescapable illusion rather suffocating, and was revived, as I staggered from the King Arthur Carousel to the Casey Jr. Circus Train, through Tomorrowland to the Bear Country, only by the presence of the peripatetic bands, blues, brass or Mexican, who really were undeniably alive and irreplaceable by electronics even in L.A.

Saddest of all, for a visitor from over the water, is the spectacle of the liner *Queen Mary*, perhaps the most celebrated of all ocean steamships, which lies in the harbor of Long Beach in a condition of induced elation, as though she has been pumped full of stimulants. She has had the L.A. treatment with a vengeance. Her innards ripped out, her funnels replaced, part of her turned into a hotel, part into a museum, jazzed up, repainted, publicized, projected, she cost almost twice as much to turn into a tourist center as she cost to build as a ship, and has been losing money ever since. Would it not have been easier, the municipality is sometimes asked, to build a new one? It would, they gravely reply, but then it would have lacked *curiosity quotient*.

Curiosity quotient! It is arguably better than scrapping her, I suppose, but still I thought the experience of the *Queen Mary* infinitely depressing. How silly, the mock-nautical uniforms! How pitiful the spectacle of that lifeless bridge! How drear, the prospect of nuptials in the Wedding Chapel (*Promenade Deck: Wedding Coordinators and Ordained Minister*)! This was the pride of the Clyde when I was a child, this was the ship which, speeding through the wolf packs in the gray Atlantic, safely took half a million Americans to the liberation of Europe! Now she lies there tarted up and phony, the victim of a culture which, in the intoxicating mastery of its know-how, so often uses it ignobly.

And, unexpectedly, when I examine my feelings about this tremendous and always astonishing city, I find them inextricably shot through with regret. This is not, I think, a usual reaction to Los Angeles, and I am moved to it partly because I come from a temporarily discomfited civilization myself — "worrying the carcass of an old song," as the poet R. S. Thomas described us Welsh, "gnawing the bones of a dead culture."

Nobody driving down Wilshire Boulevard, say, or watching the surfers spring into the Pacific, could call the culture of L.A. dead. It is full of vitality still, full of fun and wealth. The refugees are still flocking to this haven beyond the deserts, the men of brilliance are still at work in labs and laboratories and studios from Malibu to Irvine. Almost every development of Western thought, from space research to comparative linguistics to Transcendental Lung Control, finds its niche, its expression and its encouragement somewhere in this metropolis. Surveyed in the morning from one of its mountain belvederes, Los Angeles really does look one of the classic cities, one of the archetypes. Its streets and houses and bridges and buildings seem to lie there *differently*, massed differently, differently integrated, sprouting here and there peculiarly with the clumps of their urban centers, and hung over already, as the sun rises over the deserts, with the particular chemical haze whose very name, smog, was a Los Angeles invention. Then it looks unmistakably a world city: and it will represent forever, I think, the apogee of urban, mechanical, scientific man, rational man perhaps, before the gods returned.

For it is past its prime already. It has lost the exuberant certainty that made it seem, even when I first knew it, unarguably the City of the Future, the City That Knew How. None of us Know now. The machine has lost its promise of emancipation, and if L.A. then seemed a talisman of fulfillment, now it is tinged with disillusion. Those terrific roads, those thousands of cars, the sheen of the jets screaming out of the airport, the magnificent efficiency of it all, the image building, the self-projection, the glamour, the fame — they were all false promises after all, and few of us see them now as the symptoms of redemption.

There is one monument in L.A. which hauntingly commemorates this failing faith. It is the queer cluster of pinnacles called the Watts Towers, and it stands in one of the shabbier parts of town, way out on 107th Street, beside the railway tracks. Simon Rodia, an Italian immigrant, built these arcane artifacts single-handedly, taking more than thirty years to do it. He made them of cement, stuck all over with bits of glass and pottery, strengthened by frames of scrap metal and wound about with curious studded spirals, rather like precipitous roller coasters. When he had built them he surrounded them with an irregular cement wall, like a row of tombstones, so that the whole ensemble has the air of a temple or shrine, rather Oriental in nature.

It is very dusty there, and all around are the unpretentious homes of black people, so that you might easily suppose yourself to be in some African railway town, in the Egyptian delta perhaps. Few cars go by. You can hear children playing, and dogs barking, and neighbors chatting across the way. It is like a simple country place, before technology arrived: and just as the Watts riots of the sixties were a protest against the failure of technique to give contentment to poor people, so the Watts Towers, years before their time, were a symbolic *cri du coeur* against the computer tyrannies to come.

Mr. Rodia was a prophet: and when he had built his towers he slipped away from Los Angeles once and for all, and went to live somewhere quite different.

John Rechy

For many years (as both Norman Mailer and David Hockney note else-where in this volume) the center of gay life in Los Angeles was Pershing Square, the city's oldest park and once one of the most notorious cruising spots in the United States. If Pershing Square had a poet laureate, it would be John Rechy (b. 1934), who came to public attention in 1963 with his first novel, *City of Night*, a frank look at the life of a gay hustler. This chapter of *The Sexual Outlaw* (1977), a book he describes as a "documentary," recalls a gay pride parade in Hollywood.

from

THE SEXUAL OUTLAW

The Gay Parade

It was Independence Day. Not only that, it was the 200th Fourth of July. In Los Angeles there would be as many parades, it seemed, as there are palmtrees hovering over this God-loved city. There would be the big parade down ritzy Wilshire Boulevard, but it would have to detour at Beverly Hills, which, snobbish even on the day of Democracy's birthday, had decreed its streets would not be clogged by rabble—and there would be local parades and cele-brations, WASP ones in Pasadena, black ones in Watts, Chicano ones in East L.A. And the gay parade.

The gay parade.

How curiously radical that still sounded. Even ten years ago, a cop might bust you for holding same-gender hands in public. It all *still* seemed too far out for many—hadn't the dinosauric *Los Angeles Herald-Examiner* lamented editorially the week before that so hor-rendous a time had arrived as would permit—on independence day!—a parade of perverts?

Of course the parade would be down Hollywood Boulevard. Where else but on the turf they've tried deviously with ordinances, openly with violence, to wrest from us year after year? Hollywood

Boulevard. Site of how many gay battles fought cruising and hustling, being chased away by the envious cops, and returning to cruise and hustle, on the same corner, your favorite? Our street, conquered with how many busts for loitering and soliciting and trespassing? how many charges of lewd conduct? how many citations for, even, jaywalking? Bought with how many cop interrogations and trips to jail to be hassled, questioned, booked, held, charged? Oh, yes, bought, and paid for, yes, in symbolic lavender bloodbaths, this beautiful ugly street, with its butch army-surplus store for workers' boots and muscle shirts; dandy shops for glitter concerts and times when you want to show your supertrim build; the store displaying the ubiquitous statue of David, in two groin sizes; this street with its cartoon-vamp-style shop featuring superb sequined clothes just right for a drag ball; this Boulevard with its outdoor food stands ingeniously right for loitering, cruising, soliciting, hustling, jaywalking-to, and lewd conduct.

Yes, we had fought dedicatedly and sometimes bitterly for this royal street, and now it was more symbolically ours than any other place in the world. And if they dig a cavern to replace it, we will cruise in it.

The day is warm, and there's the atmosphere of a fair. Thousands of gays on the Boulevard wait festively for the parade, or form informal "parades" along the sidewalks—dozens of homosexuals holding hands openly, some dressed in colorful regalia, some subdued; for some the less clothes the better, exhibiting tanned bodies proclaiming our unabashed sexuality. And ever-loving Lesbians, some butcher than even the butch muscled men, some femmer than the manikins in the Frederick's of Hollywood windows; yes, and the older gays—homosexuals, *please!*—are here, though not as many as one might hope for—not here, the older ones who still secretly cherish the ancient guilts, light symbolic nightly candles to Judy.

The cruising today is furious but not serious. Furious because perhaps ninety per cent—a solid majority, for once—of the thousands here are gay, not serious because, after all, we have come to see our very own independence day parade. Still, I hope an occasional couple will slip, or has slipped, behind a wall or between buildings to do it, and I myself feel the revolutionary temptation. But this is not really that kind of day.

The atmosphere veers toward euphoria, a euphoria that comes from pride in being open—even if your courage was bolstered only for this day and by the great numbers of us here. Well, what better day for this display than the Fourth? After all, we too were at the Boston Tea Party—one out of ten of us, or one out of six, depending on what Colonial Kinsey kept count.

I would not march in the parade. I wanted an overview, wanted to move, listen, see, absorb it all—and, besides, I don't really like "joining" anything. Walking down the festive street, I felt a crazy mixture of pride and apprehension. Apprehension because I couldn't help remember past gay parades—the tacky floats populated with withering bikinied boys throwing kisses to the clouds, moldy gay leaders riding in chauffeured limousine convertibles, flanked by a squad of marching acolytes. Oh, I had longed then for the ostensible unity and dignity of the civil-rights parades, everyone simply marching and singing, no floats, no limousines, Martin Luther King walking with the people.

God knows the first perceptible augury of this gay parade was grim. A gay gentleman renowed for his grindingly monstrous "taste" had days earlier arranged to register an elephant—an *elephant*—in a local hotel; one had to assume the elephant was gay. Television cameras had devoured the spectacle to spew it out later on their news screens, the elephant registering at the hotel to hail "Gay Pride Week" (proclaimed generously by the mayor, thank you, for gay accomplishments!). An elephant *and* gay pride. Yes'm, but *how*? Well, you see, you *see*, how can you take those fairies *seriously*?

Then absorbing the good atmosphere, tingling with fine vibrations—we were even being friendly to those we had no sexual interest in, we waved, smiled, said hello—I thought, So what if there is tackiness in the parade? Look at the Legion parades. Carefully, I explored my feelings, sensing a lurking demon; I found him, pushing me into that pitfall of all minorities, that we must not allow ourselves the freedom to be awful—and the implicit freedom to call whatever *is* awful "awful."

Here it comes!

The gay parade!

Even the most reactionary part of me needn't have feared. There was plenty of dignity, and, embarrassing to admit—man—I felt the itchy sentiment that signals real pride. Here you are, and here they are, and here we are. I remember Ma Joad's proud speech of the Okies' eventual triumph in "defeat." We keep coming, she said, because we're the people. (I didn't even let interfere with my mood the bitter knowledge that many of those very same Okies had unleashed mean red-neck children and even cops to pillage our sex-hunting grounds.)

Waving banners evoking some of our best moments, the gay contingents march in happy disarray, no regimentalized ranks for us, thanks. A group proclaims perhaps our finest day—the day of the Stonewall Inn riot. Students, young and happily defiant, chant, sing, hold hands, kiss. Even a contingent of straight supporters appears, predictably tiny but nevermind. Again the awareness occurs of what a radical happening this is within the context of only ten years ago. All those homosexuals, butch and femme, marching openly proclaiming:

> Two, four, six eight,
> Homosexuals are great!
> Three, five, seven, nine,
> Lesbians are really fine!

Not smashing poetry, no, but sweet to the ear this gorgeous summer afternoon.

Of course marchers cruised those on the sidewalks, and vice versa. Occasionally a group in the street would catch sight of someone particularly attractive on the sidelines, the word would pass, eyes would flank as if to a military eyes-right/left order, but happily. And wasn't that what it was all about? Freedom, freedom to be, do?

Oh, there was tackiness all right—and why not? I asked the pursuing demon. Tackiness may be an element—wayward but there, and harmless—of the gay sensibility. There's that fucking elephant again, followed by a small faction of "the society of enlightened enthusiasts" of said elephant-loving gentleman.

Fuck that—and ignore the fact of the gay leader on the goddamned convertible. Who cares when there's the beautiful, dazzling, simply fabulous, gorgeous, lavish, lovely, glamorous, scintillating, glittering, stunning Queen of the Long Beach Drag Ball and her princesses and she's seen you on the sidewalk and smiles and tells the princesses and blows a kiss at you *at the very same moment* that the bare-chested bodybuilder next to you is inching toward you while you inch, too, to touch thighs?

Faces grim, cops assigned to escort the parade grind their motorcycles in angry commentary. They roar the dark machines threateningly close to the often-bare tapping feet of the spectators on the curbs. The only allies of the cops here today are the bellowing jesuspeople, pitiful scraggy zombies who leapt easily from acid bummers into Bible hallucinations. They shout the curses inked on their placards: "Homosexuals are Damned." "Satan is the Homosexual god."

Everyone ignores them, as they ignore the cops.

And then a moment's epiphany: Defendants enmeshed in the iron spiderweb of courts and idiotic laws—busted during a notorious gay bathhouse raid—march along the street: a woman chained to a man, each flanked and handcuffed to a gay man in cop uniform—a chilling spectacle, a reminder to how many spectators of their own arrests? Then the group pauses, and the two gay men playing cops turn to each other and embrace lovingly, and kiss. The roar of the real-cops' motorcycles boomed like shots, the drivers—faces drained—had understood but resisted the message that would have cost them thousands of dollars on a psychiatrist's couch.

Then a touching group: A scattering of parents of gays.

A part of the parade, gay motorcyclists, real bikers, cut snappy figures on the street with their machines. The butchest, dieselest, lady-dude God ever made—tattoo on bulging biceps—matches them turn for turn.

Half a block more, and the parade will end. I felt a letdown. We had showed a part our numbers—and our colors—and everyone had felt, could not have helped but feel, the crackling energy, the electric charging pride. But now it will end. Along the block where the parade has already passed, others feeling the same urge to extend these bold moments rush impulsively into the street to join the parade.

Uncoiling the tight tension, four cops attack one man. One cop jumps him—mounts him—two other cops wrench his arms, another aims a bully club at his legs, three others rush in to join the rampage. (Later the man will be busted and charged with interference and resisting arrest, but a series of photographs recording the cop actions will clear him and pave the way for his suit charging violation of his rights.)

Other spectators attempt to join the parade.

Instantly the cops are on them. Joyous laughter roars into anger along the sidewalks. Then: Shots! No—just firecrackers. Waiting, ready, dozens of anxious cops storm the Boulevard. Red lights on squad cars spin dementedly. Sirens whine shrilly. The outraged cops are finally making their statement against the bewildering spectacle they witnessed—homosexuals openly parading, men kissing men, women kissing women, and "cops" kissing "cops." And so the cops pushed and shoved, just longing for a bashed head, a felled body—thrusting forward with their bully sticks held before them in transferred manhood, allowing no one to join the parade.

They march, clearing the street. A throng of gays flanks them. "Pigs, pigs! Fucking pigs! Pigs! Shit pigs! Pigs, pigs, pigs, pigs!"

The cops had blocked two streets, sealing off the parade route. It was the only gesture they could come up with to make their presence known, to reassert their hatred. Thirty cops on one side, thirty cops on the other. Sixty black-uniformed cops holding sixty wooden cocks protectively before them.

Now twenty-five squad cars invade the gay turf, this gay battleground.

Defiant gays mill before the lined cops. The remembered frustration of having to remain silent while cops hassled and insulted and threatened, cops secure because of their bully sticks, bully guns, bully chains—the bullying made possible because they know you can't answer back—it was that frustration that found its voice: "Huccome yawll standin there with yer cocks stickin up?" "Hey, why don't you suck a cock and then you won't have to hold that stick." "Don't you remember me?—you danced with me last night at—..."

Hands tightening on their sticks, the cops tensed perceptibly forward. What was happening? Weren't *they* the cops?—and L.A. cops, to boot! Nothing in their cop training—no, nothing in their *lives*—had prepared them for this. Gay men and women not afraid of them? Imagine! Gay men and women, and even an obviously straight woman, taunting *them*? Not only that, but questioning *their* masculinity. And it hurt. Oh, it hurt. After all, how much more clearly could they prove their masculinity? Hadn't they bashed the skulls of queers who resisted arrest, and even of those who didn't? How many handcuffs had they clicked smartly in raids on queer bars? And if the guy you said was groping the other guy wasn't really the right one, so what?—he probably groped or got groped yesterday. So nothing during those days of barracks intimacy, good days, buddy days, nothing in Police Academy had prepared them for this—not the showers, the recreation periods, the sweaty teams. Certainly nothing during the inspections by the chief of police, eyeing them from head to foot slowly—for flaws in their uniforms, of course—nothing had prepared them for *this*. Jesus-god, *they* were the cops, and *those* were the queers. Why then did it feel as if *they*—...? *What the fuck was happening here?*

So they held their bully clubs.

For a glaring moment seeing their drained faces, I felt—almost, almost, *almost*—a scent, almost a scent, of pity for them, those inheritors of the straight-world's hatred of homosexuals, a hatred exacerbating their self-doubts. But it wasn't even that simple. What myriad resentments, against the life they were forced to live, within their profession of paranoia, the locked boundaries of a cop's ugly world—what myriad resentments were aroused by the people whose worlds they could touch only as bullies? . . . But no. It was quickly drowned, that spark of pity for them, drowned in the memories of bashed heads and violence, in the graphic representation of their utmost lack of courage, the bully "courage" that depends on arbitrary authority, on a badge, only that; the greatest cowardice.

More sirens infected the air. Red lights flashed like popping bulbs.

Shirtless, lolling, a cluster of malehustlers gathered in tense good humor. Also heckling. Then a firecracker burst. Another. The cop sticks rose. Cops rushed the three hustlers. Handcuffs clicked tightly.

"Pigs, pigs, pigs, shit pigs, pigs!"

Barely inches away, I felt the inundating rage sweeping the street, and I had a vision of the inevitable gay apocalypse—of thousands of homosexuals rushing against the helmets and the sticks, the guns—thousands of gay men and women riding a tide of pent-up rage released at last. Abruptly that vision of apocalyptic violence stopped. Yes, that would be righteous — but was that indeed what the gay apocalpyse would be?

Perhaps. Yes, perhaps.

Suddenly I laughed aloud. But might it not be, instead, the ultimate, the liberating, public sex orgy?

"Please, please, gay brothers and sisters, please disperse, this is your gay monitor, walk to other corners. Please, leave the street, leave the street peacefully, this is your gay parade monitor, please let's avoid any violence."

Someone laughed bitterly. It was over.

For now.

John Gregory Dunne

For all the jokes and barbs that have been aimed at Los Angeles over the years, the city has developed a unique culture, argues John Gregory Dunne (b. 1932) in "Eureka!" Dunne writes with conviction about L.A.'s openness, its sense of space, its fostering of individual freedom and separateness. A native of Hartford, Connecticut, Dunne spent nearly a quarter century living in Los Angeles with his wife, Joan Didion, before their relocation to New York in 1988. His many books include the novel *True Confessions* (1977) and two unsparing insider's accounts of Hollywood, *The Studio* (1969) and *Monster* (1997).

EUREKA!

I moved to California on the fifth day of June 1964. I can be very specific about the date: I had to swear to it in a legal deposition, signed and witnessed and admitted into evidence in Civil Court, City of New York, in and for the County of New York, as an addendum in the case of *New York Telephone Company, Plaintiff*, vs. *John Gregory Dunne, Index No. 103886/1964*. The charge against me was nonpayment of a bill from New York Telephone in the amount of $54.09. The record of the proceeding, Index No. 103886/1964, noted that a subpoena had been issued ordering me to court to answer the charge, and a process server, fully cognizant, as the record shows, that his "statements are true under the penalties of perjury," swore under oath that he had served me with said subpoena on July 7, 1964, in person at my residence, 41 East 75th Street, City of New York, County of New York. The case of *New York Telephone Company, Plaintiff*, vs. *John Gregory Dunne* was heard on July 24, 1964, and in due course I was found guilty as charged, fined $5 plus $9 in court costs and $1.16 in interest on the unpaid bill, making the total default $69.25. A warrant was also issued for my arrest for failure to answer a court order, namely the subpoena allegedly served on July 7, 1964.

Sometime later that summer, the papers pertaining to Index No. 103886/1964, Civil Court, City of New York, in and for the County of New York, were forwarded to me at my new home in Portuguese Bend, California, a peninsula protruding into the Pacific Ocean on the southwestern tip of Los Angeles County. The equilibrium of my first western summer was upset. The sealed crates containing the records of my past were drawn from storage and opened. A check of my bank statements confirmed that the bill from New York Telephone had been paid on time, the evidence being a canceled check, No. 61, dated March 23, 1964, drawn in the amount of $54.09 on the Chase Manhattan Bank, Rockefeller Center Branch, and paid to the order of the plaintiff, the New York Telephone Company. Witnesses attested that I had not been out of Los Angeles County since my arrival on the fifth of June, making it difficult for the process server, whatever his affirmations that his statements were "true under the penalties of perjury," to have served me with a subpoena on the upper East Side of Manhattan on July 7. I engaged Carmine DeSapio's attorney and on his instructions sent this information to the president of the New York Telephone Company, copy as well to Mr. John McInerney, Clerk of the Civil Court, City of New York, in and for the County of New York. By return mail I received a letter from the president of New York Telephone apologizing for the unfortunate error, saying that the judgment had been vacated and that copies of the vacating order as well as his letter of apology had been put in my file. I was so warmed by this prompt recognition of corporate error that I immediately wrote back the president of New York Telephone, copies to Mr. Frederick Kappel, chairman of the board at AT&T, and to Mr. David Rockefeller at the Chase Bank, and told him to do something carnally improper to himself.

And so I was in California, on the lam, as it were, from the slam. Manifest Destiny, 1964. What was western expansion, after all, but a migration of malcontents and ne'er-do-wells, have-nots with no commitment to the stable society left behind, adventurers committed only to circumventing any society in their path. For eight years on the upper East Side of Manhattan, I had been a have-not and a malcontent. I dreamed of being an adventurer. When I was twenty-five, I had put up $100 to buy a piece of an antimony mine in Thailand. I was not sure what antimony was, but I saw myself in riding boots and a wide-brimmed hat in the jungles of Siam. There was a whisper of opium and there were women always called sloe-eyed, wearing *ao ∂ais* and practiced in the Oriental permutations of fellatio. The daydream, of course, was compensation for the reality I was then living. I was a traffic clerk in an industrial advertising agency, little more than a messenger in a Brooks Brothers suit and a white buttoned-down shirt and a striped tie, taking copy and lay-outs for industrial toilet fixtures to the client in the Bronx. At night I tried to write a novel titled *Not the Macedonian*. The first line of the novel—the only line I ever wrote—was "They called him Alexander the Great." Not, of course, the Macedonian. My Alexander was a movie director. In Hollywood. I had never met a movie director, I had never been in Hollywood. For that matter, I had never been west of Fort Carson, Colorado, where I had spent the last three months of a two-year stint as a peacetime Army draftee. Nor had I ever told anyone, least of all the girl I was then supposed to marry, that my fashionable address in New York's silk-stocking district was a rooming house, populated by men who had been beaten by the city. One roommate was a lawyer from South Carolina who had failed the New York Bar exam three times and was afraid to go home. Another was a drunk who had been out of work for eleven months. The owner-landlord of this townhouse between Madison and Park packed four people to a room, each at $56 a month, and day and night he prowled the corridors and stairwells looking for transgressions of his house rules. Once he threatened to evict me for tossing Q-Tips in the toilet, another time for violating the food pro-tocols. His kitchen was run on a nonprofit honor system; a price list was posted (2¢ for a saltine, 5¢ for a saltine with a dab of peanut butter, 7¢ for a saltine with peanut butter and jelly, etc.) and the tenant was expected to tot up his expenses on a file card. Snitches reported to the owner-landlord that I had been negligent in the accounting of my nightly inhalation of Hydrox and milk. My only defense was rapture of the snack. I threw myself on his mercy and was sentenced to permanent loss of kitchen privileges.

Each day I scoured the "Apartments to Share" column in the *Times* real-estate section, but it was not until a man in a green-flocked apartment on East Fifteenth Street told me there was only one bed in his flat that I realized the meaning of the phrase in the ads, "Must be compatible." I haunted the sleazy one-room employment agencies along Forty-second Street and up Broadway, looking for a better job. I felt that if I only broke through to $75 a week it would be the first step to the cover of *Time*. In the evenings I concocted resumés, listing jobs I had never held with references from people I had never met. The most elaborate fiction was the invention of a job on a daily newspaper in Colorado Springs. During my service at Fort Carson, I had noted that this paper did not give its reporters bylines and so I bought up enough back issues at the out-of-town newsstand on Times Square to create for myself an unbylined city room background. The employment agents were impressed. Except one, a man with rheumy eyes and dandruff flaking down on his shiny blue suit. Even now I sometimes awake with a start remembering that awful day when he told me he had checked out one of my *soi-disant* Colorado references, who reported that he had never heard of me.

I can say now what I dared not say then: I was a jerk.

In time, however, my nonexistent job on the city desk of the Colorado Springs newspaper helped me find employment with a trusting trade magazine, an opportunity that I later parlayed into a five-year sojourn on *Time*. There I learned discipline, met deadlines and became adept at dealing with the more evasive transitions, the elusive "but," the slippery "nevertheless," the chimerical "on the other hand." I also learned that the writer on a news magazine is essentially a carpenter, chipping, whittling, planing a field correspondent's ten-or twelve-page file down into a seventy-line story, in effect cutting a sofa into a bar stool; in the eyes of his editors, both are places to sit.

Since days in *Time*'s New York office are counted as enhancing one's world vision, I became, after three years, the magazine's Saigon watcher, even though I had never been there. In 1962, I persuaded my editors to pay my way to Indochina, my alleged sphere of expertise, where I fornicated for five weeks and in what now seems a constant postcoital daze floated to the nascent realization that the war beginning to metastasize in Vietnam was a malignant operation. It was a difficult induction to explain to my editors back in New York. A whore in Cholon did not seem much of a source, notwithstanding the brother she claimed was in Hanoi, from whom, in her text, she received periodic messages over an RFD route I suspected was not sanctioned by President Diem or Archbishop Thuc. It was just a feeling. I had the feeling when I monitored a conversation about Swiss bank accounts over drinks at the Cercle Sportif in Saigon, an abstract discussion punctuated by long silences, the simple question, "Do you favor Lausanne?" seeming to carry an absurd consignment of symbolic freight. I had the same feeling when I flew around the countryside for a few days with a four-star U.S. Army general from MACV. The bases he dropped in on reminded me of Fort Bliss or Fort Chaffee from my own Army days. The latrines were spotless, whitewashed stones lined the pathways between tents and the young volunteer American officers wore starched fatigues and spit-shined boots and their hair was clipped to the skull two inches over the ears. There were graphs and maps and overlays with grease pencil notations, and after every briefing there was coffee and optimism, but no American officer in whatever section we happened to be visiting could explain why the roads were not secure at night. Losing control of the roads at night was the nature of the war, the general said. He seemed to think this a reasonable explanation and stressed that the plans and procedures of his command were "viable"; I learned new and ambiguous meanings for the word "viable" during my short stay in Vietnam. A Turk nicknamed Cowboy had a less ambiguous expression. Cowboy was a former colonel in the Turkish air force who, after being declared redundant and forced into premature retirement, had signed on with the CIA for the Bay of Pigs. At $2,000 a month he was working off that contract in Vietnam, hedgehopping over the hills to avoid ground fire, summing up what was happening in the jungles below in two words: "All shit."

Cowboy carried no weight in the Time-Life Building. Briefed at the Pentagon, lunched at the White House, my editors saw the light at the end of the tunnel; they thought my sibylline meanderings the pornography of a malcontent. In the ensuing religious wars about Vietnam that rent *Time*, I sided with the doubters in the Saigon bureau and asked to be relieved of the Vietnam desk. My penance was reassignment to the Benelux portfolio, along with responsibility for the less doctrinaire capitals of Western Europe—a beat that encompassed by-elections in Liechtenstein, Scandinavian sexual mores and Common Market agricultural policy. "How small," I wrote, "is a small tomato?" I became sullen, a whisperer in the corridors. I did not get an expected raise, a short time later I married, a short time after that, still a malcontent, not yet a have, I quit my job. Ignorant of the impending posse from the New York Telephone Company, the adventurer routed himself to California.

Eureka, as the state motto has it: "I have found it."

I had found it.

2

What I found first was culture shock. Imagine: an Irish Catholic out of Hartford, Connecticut, two generations removed from steerage, with the political outlook of an alderman and social graces polished to a semigloss at the Hartford Golf Club. Imagine a traveler with this passport confronting that capitol south of the Tehachapis called El Pueblo de Nuestra Senora La Reina de Los Angeles. My wife was a fifth-generation Californian and was in a sense returning home (although her real home was the equally impenetrable flatland of the Central Valley), but to me it was a new world: *the* new world. I watched Los Angeles television, listened to Los Angeles radio, devoured Los Angeles newspapers trying to find the visa that would provide entry. "Go gargle razor blades," advised a local talk show host pleasantly; it was a benediction that seemed to set the tone of the place. Dawn televised live on the Sunset Strip: a minister of the Lord inquired of a stringy-haired nubile what she liked doing best in the world. An unequivocal answer: "Balling." Another channel, another preacher. This one ascribed the evils of the contemporary liberal ethic—my own contemporary liberal ethic, as modified in generations of smoke-filled rooms—to one "J. J. Russo." It was some time before I apprehended that the Italianate "J. J." was in fact Jean-Jacques Rousseau. In a newspaper I read of a man living on the rim of Death Valley who walked alone out into the desert, leaving behind a note that he wanted to "talk to God." God apparently talked back: the man was bitten by a rattlesnake and died.

Fundamentalism, the Deity, the elements—those familiar *aides-mémoire* that titillate the casual visitor to the western shore. I did not need a pony to find the immediate subtext of banality and vulgarity. It took a long time, however, to learn that the real lesson in each of those parables was to quite another point. Los Angeles is the least accessible and therefore the worst reported of American cities. It is not available to the walker in the city. There is no place where the natives gather. Distance obliterates unity and community. This inaccessibility means that the contemporary de Tocqueville on a layover between planes can define Los Angeles only in terms of his own culture shock. A negative moral value is attached to the taco stand, to the unnatural presence of palm trees at Christmas (although the climate of Los Angeles at Christmas exactly duplicates that of Bethlehem), even to the San Andreas fault. Whenever she thought of California, an editor at the *New York Times* once told me, she thought of Capri pants and plastic flowers. She is an intelligent woman and I do not think she meant to embrace the cliché with such absolute credulity; she would have been sincerely pained had I replied that whenever I thought of New York I thought of Halston and Bobby Zarem. (My most endearing memory of this woman is seeing her at a party in New York, as always meticulously pulled together, except that the side seam on her Pucci dress had parted. The parted seam was the sort of social detail that marked her own reportage, which had a feel for texture absent in her *a priori* invention of a California overrun with plastic greenery.) "I would love to see you play with the idea of California as the only true source of American culture," she wrote my wife and me, fellow conspirators, or so she thought, in her fantasy of the western experience. "I mean, what other state would have pearlized rainbow-colored plastic shells around its public telephones?"

Notice "plastic," that perfect trigger word, the one word that invariably identifies its user as culturally superior. When I arrived in California in 1964, the catch words and phrases meant to define the place were "smog" and "freeways" and "kook religions," which then spun off alliteratively into "kooky California cults." Still the emigré, I referred to my new country as "Lotusland"; it was a while before I realized that anyone who calls Los Angeles "Lotusland" is a functioning booby. In the years since 1964, only the words have changed. California is a land of "rapacious philodendron" and "squash yellow Datsuns," Marion Knox noted on the Op Ed page of the *New York Times*; seven months in the Los Angeles bureau of *Time* seemed to Ms. Knox an adventure in Oz. "Angel dust." "The 'in' dry cleaner." "Men in black bathing suits, glossy with Bain de Soleil." (Perhaps a tad of homophobia there, a residual nightmare of Harry's Bar in Bloomingdale's.) "The place of honor at . . . dinner parties," Ms. Knox reported, "is next to the hotshot realtor." I wonder idly whose dinner parties, wonder at what press party do you find the chic hairdresser and the hotshot realtor. I also think I have never read a more poignant illustration of Cecelia Brady's line in *The Last Tycoon*: "We don't go for strangers in Hollywood."

In *Esquire*, Richard Reeves spoke of "ideas with a California twist, or twisted California ideas—drinking vodka, est, credit cards, student revolts, political consultants, skateboards . . ." An absurd catalogue, venial sins, if sins they be at all, some not even Californian in origin. Ivy Lee had the Rockefeller ear before the term "political consultant" was invented, not to mention Edward Bernays and Benjamin Sonnenberg, who were plugged into the sockets of power when normalcy was still an idea to be cultivated. And what is est after all but a virus of psychiatry, a mutation of the search to find one's self, passed west from Vienna via Park Avenue, then carried back again, mutated, on the prevailing winds. (Stone-throwing in glass houses, this kind of exchange, a Ping-Pong game between midgets, est on one coast, Arica on the other, vodka drinking in California, Plato's Retreat in Manhattan, lacquered swimmers on the Malibu, their equally glossy brothers three time zones east in Cherry Grove.) The trigger words meant to define California become a litany, the litany a religion. The chief priests and pharisees attending the Los Angeles bureaus of Eastern publications keep the faith free from heresy. A year ago a reporter from *Time* telephoned my wife and said that the magazine was preparing a new cover story on California; he wondered if she had noticed any significant changes in the state since *Time*'s last California cover.

Still they come, these amateur anthropologists, the planes dis-
gorging them at LAX, their date books available for dinner with the
hotshot realtor. They are bent under the cargo of their preconceived
notions. "The only people who live in L.A. are those who can't make
it in New York," I once heard a young woman remark at dinner. She
was the associate producer of a rock-and-roll television special and
she was scarfing down chicken mole, chiles Jalapenos, guacamole,
sour cream, cilantro and tortillas. "You cook New York," she complimented her hostess. "Mexico, actually," her hostess replied
evenly, passing her a tortilla and watching her lather sour cream on
it as if it were jam. Another dinner party, this for an eastern publisher in town to visit a local author. There were ten at dinner, it was
late, we had all drunk too much. "Don't you miss New York?" the
publisher asked. "Books. Publishing. Politics. Talk." His tone was
sadly expansive. "Evenings like this."

The visitors have opinions, they cherish opinions, their opinions
ricochet around the room like tracer fire. The very expression of an
opinion seems to certify its worth. Socially acceptable opinion,
edged with the most sentimental kind of humanism, condescension
in drag. "Why can't you find the little guy doing a good job and give
him a pat on the back?" the managing editor of *Life* once asked my
wife. Little people, that population west of the Hudson, this
butcher, that baker, the candlestick maker, each with a heart as big
as all outdoors. Usually there is a scheme to enrich the life of this little person, this cultural dwarf, some effort to bring him closer to the
theater or the good new galleries. Mass transit, say. I remember one
evening when a writer whose expertise was in menopausal sexual
conduct insisted that mass transit was the only means of giving
southern California that sense of community she thought it so sadly
lacked. I did not say that I thought "community" was just another
ersatz humanistic cryptogram. Nor did I say that I considered mass
transit a punitive concept, an idea that runs counter to the fluidity
that is, for better or worse, the bedrock precept of southern California, a fluidity that is the antithesis of community. She would not
have heard me if I had said it, for one purpose of such promiscuous
opinionizing is to filter out the disagreeable, to confirm the humanistic consensus.

He who rejects the dictatorship of this consensus is said to lack "input." Actors out from New York tell me they miss the input, novelists with a step deal at Paramount, journalists trying to escape the eastern winter. I inquire often after input, because I am so often told that California (except for San Francisco) is deficient in it, as if it were a vitamin. Input is people, I am told. Ideas. Street life. I question more closely. Input is the pot-au-feu of urban community. I wonder how much input Faulkner had in Oxford, Mississippi, and it occurs to me that scarcity of input might be a benign deficiency. Not everyone agrees. After two weeks in California, the publisher of *New York* magazine told Dick Cavett at a party in New York, he felt "brain-damaged." Delphina Ratazzi was at that party, and Geraldo Rivera. And Truman Capote, Calvin Klein, Charlotte Ford, George Plimpton, Barbara Allen with Philip Niarchos, Kurt Vonnegut, Carrie Fisher with Desi Arnaz, Jr., Joan Hackett and Arnold Schwarzenegger. I do not have much faith in any input I might have picked up at that party.

3

California is not so much a state of the Union as it is an imagi-nation that seceded from our reality a long time ago. In leading the world in the transition from industrial to post-industrial society, California's culture became the first to shift from coal to oil, from steel to plastic, from hardware to software, from materialism to mysticism, from reality to fantasy. California became the first to discover that it was fantasy that led reality, not the other way around.

—WILLIAM IRWIN THOMPSON

Perhaps it is easiest to define Los Angeles by what it is not. Most emphatically it is not eastern. San Francisco is eastern, a creation of the gold rush, colonized by sea, Yankee architecture and Yankee attitudes boated around the Horn and grafted onto the bay. Any residual ribaldry in San Francisco is the legacy of that lust for yellow riches that attracted those early settlers in the first place. Small wonder Easterners feel comfortable there. They perceive an Atlantic clone; it does not threaten as does that space-age Fort Apache five hundred miles to the south.

Consider then the settling of southern California. It was—and in a real sense continues to be—the last western migration. It was a migration, however, divorced from the history not only of the West but of the rest of California as well, a migration that seemed to parody Frederick Jackson Turner and his theory on the significance of the frontier. In Turner's version, the way west was not for the judicious—overland, across a continent and its hard-scrabble history. Those who would amputate a past and hit the trail were not given to the idea of community. Dreamers or neurotics, they were individualists who shared an aversion to established values, to cohesion and stability. A hard man, Turner's western wayfarer, for a hard land.

The settlers of southern California traveled the same route across the Big Empty—but on an excursion ticket. By the mid-1880's, the frontier, as Turner noted, was for all intents and purposes closed, the continental span traced by a hatchwork of railroad lines. Where there were railroads, there was murderous competition, and when in 1886 the Santa Fe laid its track into southern California, it joined in battle with the Southern Pacific for the ultimate prize, the last terminal on the Pacific shore, a frontier of perpetual sunshine where the possibilities seemed as fertile as the land. The rate wars between the Santa Fe and the Southern Pacific denied sense. From the jumping-off points in the Missouri Valley, fares to southern California dropped from $125 to $100, and then in a maniacal frenzy of price-cutting to twelve, eight, six, four dollars. Finally on March 6, 1887, the price bottomed out at one dollar per passenger, one hundred copper pennies to racket down those trails blazed by the cattle drives and the Conestoga wagons, to cross that blank land darkened by the blood of the Indian wars.

What the railroads had essentially created in southern California was a frontier resort, a tumor on the western ethic. Bargain basement pioneers, every one a rebuke to Turner's hard man, flooded into southern California, 120,000 of them trained into Los Angeles alone by the Southern Pacific in 1887, the Santa Fe keeping pace with three and four trainloads a day. In such a melee, where personal histories were erased, the southland was an adventurer's nirvana. Land speculators preyed on the gullible, enticing them with oranges stuck into the branches of Joshua trees. But even when the land bubble burst, the newcomers stayed on, held captive by the sun, the prejudices and resentments of their abandoned life, the dreams and aspirations of their new one, cross-fertilizing in the luxuriant warmth.

And still they came, a generation on every trainload. If New York was the melting pot of Europe, Los Angeles was the melting pot of the United States. It was a bouillabaisse not to everyone's taste. "It is as if you tipped the United States up so all the commonplace people slid down there into southern California," was the way Frank Lloyd Wright put it. In *Southern California Country*, Carey McWilliams replied gently to Wright: "One of the reasons for this persistent impression of commonplaceness is, of course, that the newcomers have been stripped of their natural settings—their Vermont hills, their Kansas plains, their Iowa cornfields. Here their essential commonplaceness stands out garishly in the harsh illumination of the sun. Here every wart is revealed, every wrinkle underscored, every eccentricity emphasized."

Expansion, McWilliams noted, was the major business of southern California, the very reason for its existence. The volume and velocity of this migration set the tone of the place. From 1900 to 1940, the population of Los Angeles increased by nearly 1600 percent. Everyone was an alien, the newcomer was never an exile. In an immigrant place where the majority was nonindigenous, the idea of community could not flourish, since community by definition is built on the deposits of shared experience. The fact that the spectacular growth of Los Angeles exactly coincided with the automotive age further weakened the idea of community. Where older cities, radiating out from a core, were defined and limited both by transportation and geography, Los Angeles was the first city on wheels, its landscape in three directions unbroken by natural barriers that could give it coherence and definition, its mobility limited only by a tank of gas.

The newness of Los Angeles—it is, after all, scarcely older than the century—and the idea of mobility as a cultural determinant lent the place a bumptiousness that was as appealing to some as it was aggravating to others. In a word, southern California was different, and in the history of the land, what is different is seldom treasured. Exempt from the history of the West, the cut-rate carpetbaggers who settled in the southland could adopt the western ethic and reinterpret it for their own uses. The result is a refinement of that ad hoc populism that has characterized California politics in this century, an ingrained suspicion of order, the bureaucracy of order and the predators of order. It is a straight line from Hiram Johnson to Howard Jarvis, and when Jerry Brown intones, "Issues are the last refuge of scoundrels," he is speaking in the authentic voice of a state where skepticism about government is endemic.

This attitude toward politics, as well as southern California's particular and aggressive set toward the world, could be dismissed as a sunstroked curiosity as long as the region remained a provincial and distant colony, and so it did remain until World War II. Even with the steady infusion of people and ideas and capital, southern California had almost no industrial base until the war. There was plenty of technological know-how—Los Angeles was the first city in the country to be entirely lit by electricity—and even before the turn of the century there was a sense that the city's destiny did not lie in divine guidance from the Atlantic. "The Pacific is the ocean of the future," Henry Huntington said then. "Europe can supply her own wants. We shall supply the needs of Asia."

Cowboy talk: there was no industry to supply the needs of Asia. Agriculture dominated southern California (Los Angeles until 1920 was the nation's richest agricultural county) and the population boom had spawned an improvised ancillary economy of the most demeaning sort. It seemed a region of maids and clerks, of animal hospitals and car dealerships and roadside stands, of pool services and curbstone mediums. "Piddling occupations," James M. Cain wrote in 1933. "What electric importance can be felt in a peddler of orange peelers? Or a confector of Bar-B-Q? Or the proprietor of a goldfish farm? Or a breeder of rabbit fryers?" In this service economy, Hollywood was the ultimate service industry—it required no raw materials except celluloid, which cost little to ship either as raw stock or finished film—but its payroll was enormous and from 1920 to 1940 it gave southern California a simulated industrial base. In 1938 the movie industry ranked fourteenth among all American businesses in gross volume, eleventh in total assets.

And then came the war. The figures tell the story. In an eight-year period, 1940 to 1948, the federal government invested $1 billion in the construction of new industrial plants in California, and private industry kicked in $400 million more; industrial employment rose 75 percent; Los Angeles alone juggled $10 billion in war production contracts. These were just numbers, however, as ephemeral as any wartime figures. What was important was the technological scaffolding propping up the numbers. As Carey Mc-Williams points out in *The Great Exception*,* California "unlike other areas . . . did not *convert* to war production, for there was nothing much to 'convert'; what happened was that *new* industries and *new* plants were built overnight." "New" is a word that often takes on a suspect connotation when applied to California, but here were new plants untainted with the technological obsolescence afflicting so many older industries in the East. New processes using the new metals and new chemicals indigenous to California. New industries, such as aerospace and computers, which were mutually dependent, and in the case of aerospace particularly suited to the geography and climate of southern California, a place where hardware could be tested on the limitless wastes of the Mojave 365 days a year.

In effect the war allowed southern California to find a sense of itself. The self discovered was not particularly endearing. Think of Frederick Jackson Turner's hard man, glaze him with prosperity, put him in sunglasses and there you have it—a freeway Billy the Kid. There was an extravagance about the place, a lust for the new, and it was this lust that allowed southern California to capitalize on the technologies of the future, to turn its attention away from the rest of the nation, from the bedrock of history itself. The boom years made Los Angeles an independent money mart, no longer an economic supplicant, its vision west across the Pacific to Japan and Australia, toward those frontiers envisioned by Henry Huntington; look if you need proof at the Yellow Pages and those branch offices in Tokyo and Sydney. To some the lusts of southern California seemed to lead only to venereal disease. "Reality . . . was whatever people said it was," J. D. Lorenz wrote in *Jerry Brown: The Man on the White Horse*. "It was the fresh start, the self-fulfilling prophecy,

---

*It should be noted here that McWilliams's two books, *Southern California Country* and *The Great Exception*, are essential to any study of California. I think they are great books, not only because I am now and often have been in McWilliams's debt, but more importantly because they are cool and informative, history as literature in every sense.

the victory of mind over matter. In a land without roots, reality was image, image replaced roots, and if the image could be constructed quickly, like a fabricated house, it could also be torn down quickly." It is part of the fascination of southern California that it would enthusiastically agree with Lorenz's screed. Better the fresh start than roots choking with moral crab grass, better the fabricated house than the dry rot of cities, better mind over matter than a paralysis of will.

Prosperity stoked the natural bombast of the southern California frontier. Los Angeles, that upstart on the Pacific, looked back on the eastern littoral with a cool indifference that bordered on contempt. See what community got you, it seemed to say; what good are stability and cohesion if their legacy is the South Bronx? Economic independence, coupled with that western urge to be left alone, made southern California in some metaphoric sense a sovereign nation, Pacifica, as it were, with Los Angeles as its capital. And here is the other negative that defines Los Angeles: it no longer regards itself as a second city.

The history of nationhood is also largely the history of a nation's single city—that London, that Paris, that New York (with Washington as its outermost exurb) where politics, money and culture coalesce to shape a national idea. Every place else is Manchester or Marseilles. The claim of Los Angeles to be the coequal of New York could be dismissed as the braggadocio of a provincial metropolis except for one thing. Los Angeles had Hollywood, the dream factory that is both a manufacturer of a national idea and an interpreter of it. Hollywood—the most ridiculed and the most envied cultural outpost of the century. Think of it: technology as an art form, an art form, moreover, bankrolled and nurtured by men who, in Louis Sherwin's surpassing remark, "knew only one word of two syllables and that word was 'fillum.'" At times I admit a certain impatience with Hollywood and all its orthodoxies. I hear that film is "truth at twenty-four frames a second" and wonder if any art has ever had a credo of such transcendental crap. Try it this way: "truth at sixty words a minute." But that is a factor of age and taste. When I was an undergraduate, the trek of the ambitious and allegedly literate bachelor of arts was to the East; to be heard, one was published, and the headquarters of print was New York. Now that trek is a trickle. The status of image has usurped the status of type. The young graduates head west, their book bags laden with manuals on lenses and cutting, more conversant with Jewison than with Joyce, almost blissfully persuaded that a knowledge of *Dallas* and *San Francisco, Casablanca* and *Maracaibo* is a knowledge of the world at large.

It is this aspect of the Hollywood scene that eastern interpreters fasten upon. Zapping the vulgarity is less demanding than learning the grammar, the grammar of film, and by extension the grammar of Los Angeles, and of California itself. In the beginning, there was the vulgarity of the movie pioneers, many of whom were from Eastern Europe. No recounting of that era is complete without referring to those early movie moguls as former "furriers" or "rag merchants." It was an ethnic code, cryptological anti-Semitism. For furrier read Jew. No, not Jew: the Sulzbergers were Jews, and the Meyers; these unlettered rag-traders were nothing but ostentatious, parvenu sheenies, and there was always a good giggle in the Goldfish who changed his name to Goldwyn. I think of the Marxist critic who in the space of a few thousand words spoke about Josef von Sternberg, who "spurns as canard the rumor that he was born Joe Stern of Brooklyn"; about Mervyn Leroy, of whom "it is rumored that his real name is Lasky"; and about Lewis Milestone, "whose actual name is said to be Milstein."

It was easier to laugh than it was to examine the movie earthquake and its recurring aftershocks, easier to maintain that Los Angeles's indifference to the cultural heritage of the East was evidence of an indigenous lack of culture. But the lines had been drawn, the opinion media of the East versus the Western image media of movies and television, and the spoils were the hearts and minds of America. This country had always been defined by the East. Everything was good or bad to the extent that it did or did not coincide with the eastern norm; the making of cultural rules, the fact of being the nation's social and cultural arbiter, imbued confidence. The movies were a severe shock to that confidence, all the more so because those images up there on screen did not seem to have an apparent editorial bias. "The movies did not describe or explore America," Michael Wood wrote in *America in the Movies*. "They invented it, dreamed up an America all their own, and persuaded us to share the dream. We shared it happily, because the dream was true in its fashion—true to a variety of American desires—and because there weren't all that many other dreams around."

The opinion media and the image media—each has an invest-ment in its version of the American myth, each a stake in getting it wrong about the other. To the opinion media, southern California is the enemy camp, and their guerilla tactic is one of deflation. In their version, the quintessential native was born in Whittier and carries the middle name Milhous. Apostates and quislings are spokesmen: the refugee from Long Beach, now a practicing Manhattan intellec-tual, who reports that life in Los Angeles is the life of a turnip; the film director who curtsies to his critical constituency and says that if Solzhenitsyn lived in L.A., he would have a hot tub and be doing TM. Hatred of New York is seen as an epidemic. "What do you hate (or dislike) about New York City?" begins a letter from *New York* magazine. "We are asking a number of persons . . ." *Esquire* finds this hatred, and Woody Allen in *Annie Hall*. It is a kind of negative boost-erism that I find infinitely depressing. "As a well-known New York hater, you . . ." It was a correspondent from *Time* on the telephone. (*Time* again: its Los Angeles bureau is a Sun City for corporate remittance men.) I told the *Time* man that while I was gratified at being described as "well-known," I did not know how I had achieved the reputation of "New York hater." He admitted it was not from anything I had ever written. Nor anything I had said; we had never met. Nor anything he had heard secondhand. I persisted: how had I achieved that dubious reputation. "You live here," he said finally.

The call troubled me for a long time. If I had not thought much about New York's financial crisis (the actual reason for the call), I certainly took no pleasure in its plight (the assumption of my caller). It just never crossed my mind. And there it was, the canker, the painful sore of reciprocity: Los Angeles was indifferent to New York. It was the same indifference that for decades New York had shown, and was no longer showing, to the rest of the country.

4

The splendors and miseries of Los Angeles, the graces and grotesqueries, appear to me as unrepeatable as they are unprecedented. I share neither the optimism of those who see Los Angeles as the prototype of all future cities, nor the gloom of those who see it as the harbinger of universal urban doom. . . . It is immediately apparent that no city has ever been produced by such an extraordinary mixture of geography, climate, economics, demography, mechanics and culture; nor is it likely that an even remotely similar mixture will ever occur again.

REYNER BANHAM, *Los Angeles:*
The Architecture of Four Ecologies

"The freeway is forever" was the slogan of a local radio station the summer I arrived in California. Here was the perfect metaphor for that state of mind called Los Angeles, but its meaning eluded me for years. Singular not plural, *freeway* not *freeways*, the definite article implying that what was in question was more an idea than a road-way. Seen from the air at night, the freeway is like a river, alive, sinuous, a reticulated glow of headlights tracing the huge contours of a city seventy miles square. Surface streets mark off grids of economy and class, but the freeway is totally egalitarian, a populist notion that makes Los Angeles comprehensible and complete. Alhambra and Silver Lake, Beverly Hills and Bell Gardens, each an exit, each available. "The point about this huge city," observed Reyner Banham, "is that all its parts are equal and equally accessible from all other parts at once."

Driving the freeway induces a kind of narcosis. Speed is a virtue, and the speed of the place makes one obsessive, a gambler. The spirit is that of a city on the move, of people who have already moved here from somewhere else. Mobility is their common language; without it, or an appreciation of it, the visitor is an illiterate. The rear-view mirror reflects an instant city, its population trebled and retrebled in living memory. Its monuments are the artifacts of civil engineering, off-ramps and interchanges that sweep into concrete parabolas. There is no past, the city's hierarchy is jerry-built, there are few mistakes to repeat. The absence of past and structure is basic to the allure of Los Angeles. It deepens the sense of self-reliance, it fosters the idea of freedom, or at least the illusion of it. Freedom of movement most of all, freedom that liberates the dweller in this city from community chauvinism and neighborhood narcissism, allowing him to absorb the most lavish endowments his environment has to offer—sun and space.

The colonization of Los Angeles has reduced the concept of space to the level of jargon, to "my space" and "your space." Space is an idea. I do not think that anyone in the East truly understands the importance of this idea of space in the West. Fly west from the Atlantic seaboard, see the country open up below, there some lights, over there a town, on the horizon perhaps a city, in between massive, implacable emptiness. The importance of that emptiness is psychic. We have a sense out here, however specious, of being alone, of wanting, more importantly, to be left alone, of having our own space, a kingdom of self with a two-word motto: "Fuck Off." Fly east from the Pacific, conversely, and see the country as the Westerner sees it, urban sprawl mounting urban sprawl, a vast geographical gang-bang of incestuous blight, incestuous problems, incestuous ideas. People who vote Frank Rizzo and Abe Beame or Ed Koch into office have nothing to tell us. It is, of course, simple to say that both these views from the air are mirages, but even a mirage proceeds from some basic consciousness, some wish that seeks fulfillment. What, after all, is community? Space in the West, community in the East—these are the myths that sustain us.

When I think of Los Angeles now, after almost a decade and a half of living not only in it but with it, I sometimes feel an astonishment, an attachment that approaches joy. I am attached to the way palm trees float and recede down empty avenues, attached to the deceptive perspectives of the pale subtropical light. I am attached to the drydocks of San Pedro, near where I used to live, and to the refineries of Torrance, which at night resemble an extraterrestrial space station. I am attached to the particular curve of coastline as one leaves the tunnel at the end of the Santa Monica Freeway to drive north on the Pacific Coast Highway. I am attached equally to the glories of the place and to its flaws, its faults, its occasional revelations of psychic and physical slippage, its beauties and its betrayals.

It is the end of the line.
It is the last stop.
Eureka!
I love it.

1978

Art Pepper

Jazz in Los Angeles goes back a long way (Kid Ory moved out West and founded the city's first all-black jazz orchestra in the early 1920s), but its glory days were in the 1940s, when clubs like the Brown Bomber and Bird in a Basket opened on Central Avenue, the main boulevard of L.A.'s African-American community. Central Avenue attracted Charlie Parker, Art Tatum, Louis Armstrong, and other nationally known performers and provided a proving ground for such up-and-coming local musicians as Charles Mingus, Eric Dolphy, Dexter Gordon, and Teddy Edwards. Born in Gardena, alto saxophonist Art Pepper (1925–1982) began sitting in with Central Avenue groups while still in his teens and went on to play with the big bands of Stan Kenton and Shorty Rogers. His artistry blossomed on such classic albums as *Art Pepper Meets the Rhythm Section* (1957) and *Art Pepper + 11* (1959), but subsequently he spent years in and out of prison on drug charges. In the late 1970s Pepper re-emerged, making some of his finest recordings in the last few years of his life. His unblinking memoir *Straight Life* (1979) is a remarkable document of a difficult career.

from

STRAIGHT LIFE

When I was nine or ten I liked the big bands that I heard on the radio — Count Basie, Duke Ellington, Artie Shaw, Benny Goodman, Charlie Barnet. After I got my clarinet, I started buying their records. It became my goal to play Artie Shaw's part on "Concerto for Clarinet." Finally, after I'd been playing for a few years, Mr. Parry bought me the sheet music. I practiced all alone and with the record, and I was finally able to play it. It was a difficult piece.

Johnny Martizia was a guitar player; Jimmy Henson played trombone. I got together with them at their houses to play. Johnny would strum the guitar. He told me, "These are the chords to the blues, which all jazz emanates from. This is black music, from Africa, from the slave ships that came to America."

I liked what I heard, but I didn't know what chords were. Chords are the foundation for all music, the foundation jazz players improvise on. I said, "What shall I do?" He said, "Listen to the sounds I'm making on my guitar and play what you feel." He strummed the blues and I played things that felt nice and seemed to fit. We played and played, and slowly I began to play sounds that made sense and didn't clash with what he was doing. I asked him if he thought that I might have the right to play jazz. He said, "You're very fortunate. You have a gift." I wanted to become the greatest player in the world. I wanted to become a jazz musician.

I ran around with Johnny and his friends. We'd go into bars and ask if we could play. Sometimes they said yes. I was fourteen or fifteen. These guys took me down to Central Avenue, the black nightclub district, and asked if we could sit in. The people there were very encouraging.

I played clarinet in the school band in San Pedro but when I got to Fremont High I stopped playing in school and started working more jobs. I had been playing alto saxophone since I was twelve, and now I got a job playing alto with a trio at Victor McLaglen's. I began going by myself to Central Avenue. I met a lot of musicians there. I ran into a bass player, Joe Mondragon, who said he was going with Gus Arnheim in San Diego. He asked me if I wanted to go with the band. I was still going to school but I wasn't going regular. I went to San Diego and stayed for about three months.

Gus Arnheim was in a big ballroom down there. It was a very commercial band and I didn't fit in because there were no jazz solos to play—you just read music. It was good practice, but it got tiresome, so I left, came back, went to Central Avenue again, and ran into Dexter Gordon. He said that Lee Young was forming a band to go into the Club Alabam; they needed an alto player. I auditioned and I got the job. I think I auditioned at the colored union. They had a white union and a colored union. I had already joined the union when I lived in San Pedro.

This was in the early '40s and things were so different from the way they are now. Central Avenue was like Harlem was a long time ago. As soon as evening came people would be out on the streets, and most of the people were black, but nobody was going around in black leather jackets with naturals hating people. It was a beautiful time. It was a festive time. The women dressed up in frills and feathers and long earrings and hats with things hanging off them, fancy dresses with slits in the skirts, and they wore black silk stockings that were rolled, and wedgie shoes. Most of the men wore big, wide-brimmed hats and zoot suits with wide collars, small cuffs, and large knees, and their coats were real long with padded shoulders. They wore flashy ties with diamond stickpins; they wore lots of jewelry; and you could smell powder and perfume everywhere. And as you walked down the street you heard music coming out of everyplace. And everybody was happy. Everybody just loved everybody else, or if they didn't, I didn't know about it. Gerald Wiggins, the piano player, Slick Jones, the drummer, Dexter Gordon, and Charlie Mingus—we would just walk out in the street and pee off the curb. It was just cool. We'd light up a joint; we had Mota, which is moist and black, and we'd smoke pot right out in front of the club.

The dope thing hadn't evolved into what it is now, with all the police activity. I'd never heard of a narco, didn't know what the word meant. Nobody wanted to rat on anybody or plant their car with a joint or with some stuff. You didn't have to worry that the guy that asked you to go out and smoke a joint was a policeman or that the chick that wanted to take you over to her pad and ball you was trying to set you up for the cops. People just got high, and they had fun, and there were all kinds of places to go, and if you walked in with a horn everyone would shout. "Yeah! Great! Get it out of the case and blow some!" They didn't care if you played better than somebody else. Nobody was trying to cut anybody or take their job, so we'd get together and blow.

There was no black power. I was sixteen, seventeen years old, white, innocent, and I'd wander around all over the place, at all hours of the night, all night long, and never once was accosted. I was never threatened. I was never challenged to a fight. I was never called a honkie. And I never saw any violence at all except for an occasional fight over a woman or something like that. It was a whole different trip than it got be later on.

The club Alabam was the epitome of Central Avenue. It was right off Forty-second Street across from Ivy Anderson's Chicken Shack. There were a lot of other clubs, but the Club Alabam was really one of the old-time show-time places, a huge room with beautiful drapes and silks and sparklers and colored lights turning and flashing. The bandstand was plush and gorgeous with curtains that glistened. The waitresses were dressed in scanty costumes, and they were all smiling and wiggling and walking around, and everywhere you looked you saw teeth, people laughing, and everybody was decked out. It was a sea of opulence, big hats and white fluffy fur. And the cars out front were real long Cadillacs with little mudguards, little flappy little things, shiny things.

The band had two altos, two trumpets, a tenor, and a rhythm section. On the show was Avery Parrish. He was the one who wrote "After Hours" and made that famous, and when he played the whole place rocked with the music. There was Wynonie Harris, a real handsome guy, light skinned with glistening eyes and the processed hair, all shiny with every hair just perfectly in place. He had a good blues voice and just carried the audience away. The walls would start shaking; the people screaming and clapping. Every now and then they'd get up and start wiggling in the aisles next to their tables. Moke and Poke were on the bill, far-out comedians. When they came on they'd do this walking step, laughing, one right behind the other, moving in perfect synchronization. After their act they'd run into their dressing room, rip off their clothes, and throw on silk robes and come back and do this walk around the audience; every now and then, when they were walking, if the audience was really good, they'd have it so their joints would flop out of their robes, flopping in time, in perfect unison, and the chicks would go, "Ahhhhh!" And we'd just be shouting in the background, playing these real down-home blues. I'd go in there and play and get so caught up in the feeling that I never had a chance to think about anything bad that might be happening to me or to worry at all. It was such an open, such a free, such a beautifully right time.

There was a place on Vernon, right around the corner from the Club Alabam, called the Ritz Club. You went through a door into an empty storefront and walked through a curtain. You took bottles in, and they served mixes and food. The music started at two in the morning and went on all night. People would come and sit in: Jimmy Blanton, probably the greatest bass player that ever lived — he was so far ahead of any jazz musician on *any* instrument it was just ridiculous; Art Tatum came in; Louis Armstrong, Ben Webster, Coleman Hawkins, Roy Eldridge, Johnny Hodges, Lester Young.

You can imagine what a thrill it was to be in the same room with these people. I used to go sit in after my job at the Club Alabam and play with them. Then the management decided to hire a regular band at the Ritz Club so they'd always have somebody there to play when people came to sit in, and I was hired. That's when I started smoking pot; I was already drinking every night and taking pills.

I was hanging around with Dexter Gordon. We smoked pot and took Dexedrine tablets, and they had inhalers in those days that had little yellow strips of paper in them that said "poison," so we'd put these strips in our mouths, behind our teeth. They really got you roaring as an upper: your scalp would tingle, and you'd get chills all over, and then it would center in your head and start ringing around. You'd feel as if your whole head was lifting off. I was getting pretty crazy, and right about that time, I think, Dexter started using smack, heroin.

Dexter Gordon was an idol around Central Avenue. He was tall. He wore a wide-brimmed hat that made him seem like he was about seven feet tall. He had a stoop to his walk and wore long zoot suits, and he carried his tenor in a sack under his arm. He had these heavy-lidded eyes; he always looked loaded, always had a little half smile on his face. And everybody loved him. All the black cats and chicks would say, "Heeeeey, Dex!" you know, and pat him on the back, and bullshit with him. I used to stand around and marvel at the way they talked. Having really nothing to say, they were able to play these little verbal games back and forth. I envied it, but I was too self-conscious to do it. What I wouldn't give to just jump in and say those things. I could when I was joking to myself, raving to myself, in front of the mirror at home, but when it came time to do it with people I couldn't.

Lee Young was worried about me. I was so young. I think he felt he had an obligation to take care of me. Lee looked like the typical black musician of the '40s, the hep black man with the processed hair. He was light complected, very sharp, with diamond rings; he wore his clothes well; and he was a cat you'd figure could conduct himself in any situation. His brother was Lester Young, one of the greatest saxophone players that ever lived in this world. The most fantastic—equaled only fairly recently by John Coltrane. Better than Charlie Parker. In my humble opinion, better than Charlie

Parker, just marvelous, such beauty. And Lee, Lee played nice drums. He was capable but was in the shadow of his brother, and I think he felt that. He loved his brother and was very proud of him, but I don't see how he could help but feel sad that he couldn't have played with his brother and really set the world on fire.

Lee was very nice to me and thoughtful. To show you what kind of a person he was—I was playing my parts and nobody else would have worried about me. Why go out of their way to worry about a little white boy, you know? But Lee dug that I was hanging out with Dexter, and we were on that road, and he sat down with me. He said, "I've talked to Dexter, man, and he's got a way to go. There's cold awful dues he's got to pay and he's just going to have to pay 'em, I'm afraid. But you, man, why don't you—boy, I'd love to see you not have to pay those dues." I said, "No, I'm alright. I'm okay." He said, "Art, I really like you. I'd sure love to see you do right."

At that time Jimmy Lunceford's band lost Willie Smith, who had played lead alto with them for a long time. He went with Harry James. So Kurt Bradford, who had been with Benny Carter, went to Jimmy Lunceford, and Lee got me an audition with Benny. He tried to get me a job where he thought I'd be protected. I auditioned and I made the band.

Lawrence Weschler

A staff writer for *The New Yorker*, Lawrence Weschler (b. 1952) grew up in Southern California. He is the author of eight books, including *Mr. Wilson's Cabinet of Wonders* (1995), an elliptical study of Culver City's Museum of Jurassic Technology, and he is a two-time winner of the George Polk Award. In *Seeing Is Forgetting the Name of the Thing One Sees* (1982), Weschler profiles the artist Robert Irwin, one of the primary figures of the home-grown Light and Space Movement and, as this excerpt makes clear, a pure product of the Southern California scene. "L.A. Glows," published in *The New Yorker* in 1995, is a more recent excursus on the singular qualities of the city's light, flat and white and uninflected.

from

SEEING IS FORGETTING THE NAME OF THE THING ONE SEES

High School
(1943–46)

And then when I came back" — Robert Irwin was recalling some time he'd spent in Japan about ten years ago — "I'd taken one of those seventeen-hour flights from the Orient which really wipe you out. Anyway, I got home about midnight and went immediately to bed, thinking I'd probably sleep for two days. But I was so jazzed and hyper that I couldn't fall asleep. So I got in my car and put the top back and put my tape deck on and was just driving along in the middle of nowhere. Actually I first went over to Fatburger and bought a Coke from Jay, and then I set out cruising the freeways. I was driving over Mulholland Pass on the San Diego freeway, you know, middle of nowhere at about two o'clock in the morning, when I just got like these waves — literally, I mean I never had a feeling quite like it — just waves of well-being. Just tingling. It's like I really knew who I was, who I am. Not that you can't change it or what-ever. But that's who I am: that's my pleasure and that's my place in life. To ride around in a car in Los Angeles has become like one of my great pleasures. I'd almost rather be doing that than anything else I can think of."

Robert Irwin and I were sitting outside Mè & Mè, talking about him and his life. Mè & Mè is a falafel stand in the middle of the busiest section of Westwood, a fairly new stand, which means it has a fairly new Coke machine, which means it gives slightly better cola than some of its more established competitors. When they were new, Irwin used to frequent them—as it happened, the Coke fountain here was a bit past its prime, and for some days now Irwin had been restless (or as restless as he lets himself get), on the lookout for a new stand.

"In terms of just day-to-day life," he was continuing, "basically I can have a terrific time doing nothing. I'm quite at ease, and always on the plus side. I can come down here and sit on the corner, and, I mean, nothing's happening where I could say I'm having a hilarious time, but I'm feeling real good and the world's fine.

"I don't know how to explain it exactly. I guess I'm as confused by other people's insecurity as they are by my security. And my security is probably no more substantiated than their insecurity!"

Irwin is in his early fifties, but he gives the appearance of someone considerably younger, perhaps because he has something of a baby face—or, more precisely, a baby head, for his head is strikingly large, with soft benevolent features, and sits perched atop a comparatively thin neck, which in turn opens out onto a solid, almost hefty frame. There is a touch of elfin mischievousness in the delight that is usually transporting him, even in his serious moods. His forehead is high and broad, his hair thinning on top and greying to the sides. His body is still in very good shape; he downs a fistful of vitamins every morning and ritually jogs five miles in the afternoon.

I asked him if he had any notion what that sense of well-being grew out of, and without hesitation he replied, "High school. Or more generally, just the experience of growing up in southwest Los Angeles, which was a fairly unique experience—obviously turns out it must have been a *very* unique experience, because it produced a fairly interesting, rich activity. All of us at Ferus grew up basically with that same background." (He was referring to the extraordinary group of artists who ranged themselves around L.A.'s funky, pioneering, avant-garde Ferus Gallery during the late fifties and the early sixties). "For example, conversation was a continually running sarcasm; you never gave anybody a straight answer. You played games all the time, and where that comes from, I don't know. But, man, I can talk to somebody in Michigan, and I can spot a southern California person—West L.A. especially—in Europe or anywhere; I can spot them a mile away. We start a conversation, and it's like I've been talking to this person all my life, and I've never met him! There was just a whole free-wheeling attitude about the world, very footloose, and everybody in southwest Los Angeles had it. From the time you were fifteen, you were just an independent operator, and the world was your oyster. Maybe you didn't have that much, but the world was just always on the up side. And that's what that script is about, or at least I hope it's in there. It was just really a rich place to grow up."

For the past several years, Irwin has been living with Joan Tewkesbury, the celebrated scenarist whose credits include screenplays for Robert Altman's *Nashville* and *Thieves Like Us*. Partly at her instigation, Irwin composed *The Green and the White*, an unproduced screenplay about life at Los Angeles's Dorsey High School during the early forties (the school's team colors account for the title). This wistful memoir abounds with boisterous characters—Spider, Cannonball, Cat, Mole, Blinky, and others—but the protagonist Eddie Black ("his hair is a pompadour with a slight duck tail") is none other than Irwin himself. The screenplay's tone is raucously vital throughout, the incessant banter somehow simultaneously glib and heartfelt.

I asked Irwin if he'd be willing to take me on a drive around his old haunts, and he said, "Sure." The sun was shining, a warm breeze rustling through the high palm stalks—a perfect afternoon for a drive. We dispensed with our Cokes and headed back toward his house.

As we were walking the few blocks back into the Westwood hills, out of the bookshop-record-store-and-movie-house glut of the village, past fraternities and densely packed student apartments, then turning right onto a slightly less frantic sidestreet, Irwin continued speculating on his L.A. youth. "I mean, people talk about growing up Jewish in Brooklyn, know what I mean? And they always dwell on the dark side. I hear all of that, and I grant that it makes for good drama, makes good writing, and it makes good intellects, in a sense. Well, apparently this made for good artists, 'cause we didn't have nothing to do with all of that—no dark side, none of that struggle—everything was just a flow."

We just flowed into his carport and climbed into his car, a sleek, silver 1973 Cadillac Coupe de Ville, one of the few luxuries he allows himself within an otherwise Spartan life style. In one fluid motion, he selected a cassette from the box on the floor, popped it into the tape deck (Benny Goodman filled the car's interior), slid back the sunroof, slipped the key into the ignition and the car out of the driveway, and eased us into the midafternoon surge of L.A. traffic.

A few moments later we were barreling down the San Diego freeway, southbound, toward one of those amorphous undifferentiated communities that make up the mid–Los Angeles sprawl—not really a suburb, but not the central city either; not really poor, but by no means well-to-do. Bob spent his adolescence on the southeastern edge of Baldwin Hills, just north of Inglewood. (If you were to draw a line between the Hollywood Park Race Track to the south and the present site of the Los Angeles County Museum of Art to the north, Leimert Park, one of the main staging areas of Bob's youth, would constitute the midpoint.)

"I don't remember particularly much about my early childhood," Irwin was saying, "but it was never sad that I can think of. Kind of floating and suspended, maybe, but that's something I still do. The high school period I remember very well, however, and it was an unmitigated joy, even though it was in some ways minimal, because of my parents not having any money or anything. I had a job and worked the entire time, made all my own money. From the time I was very young, my mother had a lot to say about that sort of independence, which was nice for me. At age seven, I was selling *Liberty* magazine door to door, and within a few years I won this little award for being the magazine's top salesman in the county. To this day I'm a sucker for any kid along the street hawking flowers or newspapers or a shine. I had jobs in a movie theater, in coffee shops, at garages. During the summer I'd lifeguard up at Arrowhead or out on Catalina. All those jobs involved a lot of action, a lot of involvement. They were really part of my pleasure. And they were very important, because they gave me total independence from very early on. I never had to ask my parents for anything, and they never in a sense really stopped me from doing anything. They were real open to me in that sense."

As we threaded in and out of traffic, the warm air swirling about us, I flipped through the box of cassettes: Stan Kenton, Artie Shaw, Bing Crosby, Frank Sinatra, Count Basie, Al Hibbler, and Erskine Hawkins. "*That* of course was also a big part of those years," Bob volunteered, anticipating my question, "the incredible music and the dancing. In fact, dancing even became an important part of my financial picture.

"At first, when I was thirteen or so, I just had no sense of rhythm at all. But I taught myself to dance by using the doorknob in the living room as my partner, and I got to be a pretty good dancer, good enough so that I could contest-dance. For a period I was entering contests almost every night of the week. There was a whole circuit: Monday was the Jungle Club in Inglewood, Tuesday was the Dollhouse out in the Valley, Wednesday was in Compton, Thursday in Torrance, Friday in Huntington Park.

"You contest-danced with a partner, of course. So you always had one regular partner and a few maybe that you were building up. Because a good partner was crucial: she could make or break you. Interestingly, you weren't usually romantically involved with your dance partner. That was the thing about dancers, especially in terms of sex: got it all out dancing, that was their whole gig. It was just such a goddamned pleasure.

"Everybody at the school I went to, Dorsey, everybody was really into dancing. We used to dance at lunchtime and then after school. The big step at the time was called the Lindy, which was kind of like the New Yorker, only smoother. The key movement was the shoulder twist, where the girl came directly at you and then you spun each other around and she went on out. When you got it going real smooth, you could literally get to the point where you were almost floating off the ground, acting as counterweights for each other. It was absolutely like flying, just a natural high.

"At these contests there were maybe a half dozen regular couples who made the circuit, and they'd alternate winning, depending on who the judges were. You'd come out one couple at a time. You'd sort of be standing to the side, and they'd say, 'The next couple is

Bob Irwin and Ginger Snap,' or whatever, and you'd take her and throw her in the air, she'd come down, you'd come boogieing out on the side, and then you'd start your routine. And you could make a lot of money doing that. At my peak, I was bringing in upwards of a hundred a week!"

About ten minutes out of Westwood, we swung off the freeway onto Slauson, a wide boulevard that skirts the southern flank of the Baldwin Hills, and proceeded east about two miles.

"By the way, this here was the big drive-in," Bob indicated, turning off Slauson onto Overhill and then pulling into a parking lot. "Used to be called the Wich Stand—still is, I guess." In the broad daylight, the pink thrusting roof, the jagged stone pillars, the dusty palm trees flanking a garish, orange Union 76 signpost in the distance, the virtually empty asphalt lot: it seemed the most commonplace of Los Angeles vistas. But years ago, this had been the hub of teenage nightlife in the region. *The Green and the White* offers a vivid evocation: "A round drive-in set in the center with cars parked three and four deep radial around it: the show and pussy wagons with a few family irons. There is a parking area to the side where the more radical looking rods are neatly parked side by side with walk-around space. A lot of boys stand around eyeballing."

We negotiated a lazy arc around the lot, and just as we were about to ease back onto Overhill, Bob pointed toward one corner of the drive-in and commented offhandedly, "Over there's where I almost got shot once." He paused for effect.

"Yeah, I used to come over here after work most nights when I was working at one of the nearby garages. I'd come over for fries and a Coke, and . . . By the way, this used to be the race-strip right along here." (We were heading south on a wide stretch of Overhill, which indeed was beginning to take a decided downhill dip.) "For a while anyway, that is, until the cops succeeded in stopping us. That signal wasn't there.

"Anyway, I used to go there after work, all greasy and everything, and this real pretty girl started working there. Pretty soon I noticed that she was taking my car every time, and she started playing jokes, like putting roses on my tray, that kind of stuff. So we started having a kind of dialogue. I asked a couple of other drive-in ladies what the story was, and they said she'd just gotten married, so

I didn't make a run on her or anything. But one night she asked if I'd take her home, so I said okay. Had to wait till she got off at two A.M. and then drive her all the way out to Gardena, so I was kind of regretting it. But then she invited me to come in and—all this time I wasn't really thinking. But I went in, and the point is that we began to have this casual love affair. She was sensational, so all that was very great. She told me her husband was a real bad-ass and so forth and that they were getting divorced. He was a bandleader.

"Anyway, so one night I'm sitting in the drive-in with a friend of mine, and she comes up to the car and says, 'Don't say anything, my husband's in the very next car.'

"This, by the way, is Verdun, the street on which I lived in high school, and this here was my house—6221." We'd veered off Overhill down a very steep Sixty-third Street a few hundred yards to the corner of Verdun. The modest stucco house, slightly smaller than its neighbors, was perched atop a slight hill, the carport level with the street, the living room above it, a brick stair path leading up from the driveway to the front porch. The street was lined with trees, and we parked in the shade. Bob killed the engine—and Benny Goodman. "That window on the right was my bedroom. This house was one my parents got, I mean, my mother was the instigator of getting it. That was late in the depression, so it was a big stretch for them. Boy, it took every cent they had. They had to get $600 together for the down payment. But they made it, and then they lived here for a long time, only moved out about ten years back.

"But anyway, so this guy got out of his car, and he comes over to my car, and he says, 'I know everything. My wife told me everything,' and blah blah blah. I felt like a rat. 'I love her,' he says, and blah blah blah. I said, 'Listen, you know, I'll stay out of it,' because I never wanted to get involved in that sense anyway. So he said, 'God bless you,' which really made me nervous, because those kind of guys are very weird. So that was the end of that, I thought.

"Then I came in the drive-in one night like three months later, and there he was. He comes up to the car—he was real pissed off, just enraged—and he says that he wants to talk to me. So we walked over to the back of the drive-in, where I showed you. He pulls out a gun and sticks it right up against my forehead and hisses, 'You went all the way with her. She told me how you made her do it.' His eyes were bulging. All I said was, 'I never *made* her do anything.'

"By the way, that slope there was all ivy instead of lawn the way it is now. That was the bane of my existence, having to weed the ivy.

"Anyway, so he was shaking, nervous, sweating, and when I said that I never made her do anything, he broke down and started crying. He was leaning on my shoulder. At the time I didn't get scared, because I guess you just don't have time to put it all together. But he'd had four of Babe Pillsbury's boys in the back seat of that car with him. What he was originally going to do was just pull me off the side of the road and have them stomp me, which they could have done very well, because they were real bad-ass motherfuckers. But anyway, instead he broke down crying and everything, you know, 'God bless you' and all that again, and then he split. A few minutes afterwards I really got shook up, because he really had the gun and he had been dead serious thinking about using it. I mean, he really was shaking and all upset, and those kind of guys can do that sort of thing. So, anyway, that was a bizarre side tale."

He started up the engine again, Benny Goodman resurged, and we rolled out of the shade. We began climbing back toward Slauson, and the neighborhood steadily improved. "Over there's where I used to catch the bus before I had any car. See, our school was kind of schizophrenic. We were like 35 percent black; the blacks lived down in the flatlands, where we're heading now, and they had no money. (By the way, John Altoon, who later became one of the top Ferus artists, he lived down there, too, and also went to Dorsey, just a little bit ahead of me.) Then there were the kids who lived in the hills, and they had some money, although this was still the depression and nobody had much. But back there where I was living was 'over the hill,' so I always looked like I was coming from the hills, but actually I was from the other side of the tracks, too. I mean, one block further out and we'd have been in Inglewood.

"By the way, the whole stretch here we're driving now" (we had crossed Slauson and were continuing northeast on Angeles Vista, a wide, but lightly traveled thoroughfare flanked on either side by residential streets lined with incongruously tall palms), "this was the distance I'd run home each night after closing up the theater, where I was usher and then assistant manager. It was about a two-, three-mile run each night, leaving there at about one A.M. when the buses had ceased running and traffic was too light to hitchhike. The job was a pleasure, the run was wonderfully invigorating, and the next morning I always had to be up early for school."

I asked Bob about race relations at Dorsey High. "Well, maybe I'm a bad source for that, because, like the black thing, the feminist thing, those were just never issues with me. I never thought of women as being different or blacks as being lesser.

"For instance, girls. I used to chase girls—radically: every night was chasing girls. When I worked in the theater, I always had a girl stashed in the back row all the time I was an usher there. A girl was involved with everything I did. But I used to be amazed: I'd sit down with some of the guys, who were all doing this, just chasing anything that moved, and they'd all be talking about marrying virgins. I'd never particularly thought about it, but even at that time— I was fifteen, sixteen—I remember thinking, that's weird. They were going to marry virgins, and the chicks they were balling were all whores. I never thought like that. When a girl turned on to me, I never thought less of her, I always thought she was terrific, that she was doing something special for me. I mean, their attitude made no sense to me, it was just bare-ass backwards. For starters, it was self-defeating, because if you knock all the girls that put out, then if a chick's smart at all she don't put out. Any girls with any brains just don't put out to that kind of guy."

From the hills we had eased down to the flatlands and into the town center. We passed a skinny wedge of a park—crab grass, restrooms, asphalt, a dry fountain—across from which loomed an old art-deco-style movie house, now recast as a Jehovah's Witnesses Assembly Hall. The letters W-A-T-C-H-T-O-W-E-R streamed down its ornate tower.

"So this here's Leimert Park," Bob continued, "and it was kind of the center of our social life, this and the drive-in. Here's the theater I worked at for several years. Next door there was a little restaurant called Tip's, and I'd work there occasionally, too. That parking lot back there, which they shared, is where me and my buddies used to siphon gas out of unsuspecting vehicles. We'd take out the garbage and shift the hoses and cannisters. They were of course rationing in those days."

This was the first time the war had impinged on Bob's recollections. I wondered whether it had had any more significance for him then.

"Oh, no," Bob responded immediately. "We were just oblivious. We conducted ourselves like the war wasn't on in any way. Not having gas and all that was simply a challenge. I didn't have any older brothers, and come to think of it, none of my friends in that group did either. Maybe that was part of it. But basically we didn't pay any attention."

I asked him if the obliviousness of the local youth had bothered the older members of the community, whether he and his friends were criticized as irresponsible.

"I don't know. I mean, if I was oblivious to the war, I was certainly oblivious to any criticism!"

Irwin was thirteen at the time of the Japanese attack on Pearl Harbor, just graduating high school as the war ended. I asked him where he had been December 7, 1941.

"I don't know," he replied.

I asked him about the day the war ended.

"Haven't the slightest idea."

Hiroshima?

"Nope. *Hiroshima Mon Amour* was the story of a fairy tale."

I wondered if part of the reason he and his friends were having such a fiercely good time was because they all realized they were presently going to be shuttled off to the war.

"Oh, no," Bob dismissed the notion with a sweep of his hand. "Look. Look at it here. Look at how it is: calm, sunny, the palm trees. What is there to get all fucking upset about?" He laughed. "This is reality. In other words, the war was not reality. The war wasn't here. The war was someplace else. So any ideas you had about the war were all things you manufactured in your head from newspapers and that. To me, this was reality; this was my reality right here."

We had in the meantime swung out of the shopping district and were cruising along a pleasant residential street on our way back toward Baldwin Hills. "Right there is where one of my favorite girlfriends lived," he pointed, and then paused. "She was the champion. World Champion. She would get so knocked out, she would literally . . . I could hardly get her out of the car afterwards; she would be absolutely unable to walk. That was my introduction: she was my first real major sexual experience. So what I got was this total fantasy of what it was like, because she would literally pass out cold right in the middle of it. We'd be lying there in the back seat, and she'd be out, like 'bang!'"

How old were they?

"Sixteen. *Bang!* I mean, just out cold. No other girl has ever passed out on me since, you know. I used to have to walk her. . . . I'd park over in this alley and walk her up and down the block just to get her legs going so that she could walk into the house!"

Was that where one generally made out, in cars?

"Sure. The car was the key, the pivotal item in the whole ballgame. Everything was wrapped around the car. The car was your home away from home. And you put months and months into getting it just right. Everything was thought out in terms of who you were, how you saw yourself, what your identity was."

I asked him how his cars expressed his self, as opposed to how others expressed their owners.

"Well, first of all," he began, "there were three, maybe four categories. One was like 'go.' You built the thing—like the Cat and the Mole, they built things that were just rat-assed, but, boy, they went like a son of a bitch. The body could be almost falling off, you'd be sitting in an egg crate, but everything was in the engine, and *that* was very sanitary. Then there was 'go-and-show,' which was like a car that went real good but wasn't necessarily going to be in a class with the Cat and the Mole, but it would look fine. It was a question of taking a car that was a classic model and then just doing the few right things with it to accentuate why it was a classic model, building it up to absolutely cherry condition. Then there was 'show,' and then there were like 'pussy wagons,' which were strictly kind of like Chicano cars are now: lowered way down, everything exaggerated, blue lights under the fenders, Angora socks bobbing in the window, seats that tilt back, all that sort of bad taste, which has now achieved almost the level of a profession.

"Well, I was category two, go-and-show. Sort of a little bit of both. I mean, the car had to be real good, because it had to have an edge on it, but on the other hand, it had much more to do with its being an absolute classic model, with everything set up just right. I had a very hard time getting one in that condition, because they cost a lot of money, but that was my ambition."

How many cars had he worked his way through as an adolescent?

"Oh, not that many; about half a dozen. A little '32 roadster, a '34 five-window coupe. . . . The first car I wanted was a '32 B roadster. It was Fred Gledhill's car, and he was selling it. I didn't have enough money, and that was the only time I ever asked my father for some money. I asked him for $100, just as a loan, so I could make the down. And he wouldn't or couldn't loan it to me, I don't know which. That was the biggest disappointment of my life up till that point. It may be till this day the biggest disappointment. I don't think I ever had a bigger one. I mean, we won the war and what have you. . . ."

Several plotlines dovetail across the expanse of Irwin's screenplay, but perhaps the most involving concerns the loving devotion with which the protagonist, Bob's stand-in Eddie Black, nurses a beat-up '39 Ford back into "cherry" shape. Throughout the script, Eddie confers with his buddies prior to each decision.

CAT

Hey, Eddie-O, you got the '39 running?

EDDIE
[startled]

Huh? Oh, yeah. Yeah, it runs good, Cat. I've got it with me. After school I'm going over to get a set of mufflers.

CAT

Yeah, what kind?

[Mole walks up hearing Cat's conversation.]
MOLE

Get yourself a set of Sandys for a '39.

EDDIE

I was thinking of a set of 15-inch Porters.

CAT

Mole's right. Sandys have a real bark.

CANNONBALL
[approaching]

What's up, Eddie-O?

EDDIE

Got the '39 here. I'm getting a set of mufflers.

CANNONBALL

Oh, yeah. Hey, get some fine 18-inch Rileys with those down tips like I got on the '36.

EDDIE

Yeah, they're good.

MOLE

They got no bite.

CANNONBALL

They're real mellow.

CAT

They're for sneaking up on chicks.

EDDIE

I like when you back off the Porters. They have that nice deep throaty roll. No flat and no pop. Too much pop on Sandys.

And so forth. A few scenes later, the Porters installed, the car nearly completed, the script floats into a lyrical reminiscence of the late nights of a Southland youth.

The box office is closed. The theater is semi-dark waiting for the last show to be over. We see Black exiting. He says goodnight to the manager in a black tux. He exits toward us and turns left to his car which is parked almost in front of the theater. The '39 is looking very sharp now. It's sitting at just the right angle, lowered in the rear, the new chrome bright against the grey primer. The car is almost finished. Black sits for a moment letting the '39 idle and dialing the radio until he hits on a station, Bobby Sherwood's "Elks Parade."

He idles away from the curb. The car is driven with more than care. Each time he winds up just so before he shifts; then with a short rev of the engine between gears he gives the mufflers a slight rap. Once in a while, for no seeming reason, except pleasure, Eddie lets the '39 hang longer in first and second. Sometimes he snaps off the shift between the two, letting it back all the way down to a stop at the corner.

We follow Eddie through the now familiar neighborhood. He pauses in front of Susy Stewart's and Anna Grace's houses, each dark, and each time he raps the mufflers lightly.

We idle on to a main street. Crenshaw. It is wide and well lit. There is very little traffic. The radio is playing "I've Got A Crush on You," by Tommy Dorsey and Frank Sinatra. Black has a Coke and idles along. The lights pass in patterns.

We pass down Hollywood Boulevard, also well lit with no traffic. There are a few people walking.

Eddie idles through a drive-in. He does this twice and chips a little rubber as he leaves.

He heads for home. "Skylark" by Earl Hines and Billy Eckstine plays as he idles down the dark tree-lined street letting the mufflers back way down. He pulls into his driveway and the lights go out.

As we wheeled out of Baldwin Hills, back down many of the same streets Eddie Black had often cruised, Bob recalled that particular '39: "Well, I finally got that car finished. I had twenty coats of ruby-red maroon on the dash, and I had this great finish outside. The car was absolutely hunky-dory. Twenty coats of ruby-red maroon, let me tell you, to paint the dash: that means taking everything out, all the instruments and everything, painting it, building up these coats very slowly, spraying the lacquer. It was just a very exaggerated thing. So it took a lot of work, but I finally got it into that condition.

"That was just in time for Easter week in Balboa. Everybody'd go down to Balboa for Easter week. All the girls' sororities and clubs had their houses there, and we used to go down and hang out in various situations there. Maybe you'd do some work for them, but mostly you just played around and slept in your car or out on the beach. My friend Keith went with me one time, and we'd been sleeping on the beach, so we went over to the girls' house the next morning to shower and brush our teeth. I had a fairly good gig going, 'cause the car was in very cherry shape, which of course was very important to the whole scene."

Did girls really respond to the cars?

"Well, you at least thought they did. It gave you a sense of identity, and your identity was what you wanted it to be, sure. I don't know how much, but. . . .

"Anyway, so we'd gone over to this girls' house, and we were just shooting the breeze, and I asked if we could wash up, and they said sure. So I went in and showered, 'cause I had my stuff with me. Then Keith came in the bathroom, and I thought to myself, 'How the hell did he get his stuff?' 'cause his toothbrush and all were locked in the glove compartment. So I went down immediately and took a look. Instead of coming up and asking me for a key, Keith had just pried the glove compartment open with a screwdriver, which is unbelievable. I still can't believe it to this day. He'd broken the lock and also slipped the screwdriver and put this big gash across the dash right through my twenty coats of ruby-red maroon. Well, I just absolutely came on him. I mean, I just bounded up those stairs, blood in my eyes. He'd locked the door. The girls were yelling, 'Don't, don't!' I was tearing down the door, just kicking it in. And he, realizing that I was really going to tear him limb from limb, he leaped out of that second-story window, broke his ankle on the cement pavement, and still managed to scamper off. I didn't see him for another month after that. By that time I'd slowed down a bit, although I don't think I ever forgave him. Can *you* believe that? I can't."

We had come full circle back to Leimert Park and were idling by the crab grass. I asked Bob whether his work on cars, more than any particular art classes he subsequently took, might be seen as one origin of his artistic vocation. He concurred.

"Of course, what's going on in such situations is precisely an artistic activity. A lot of art critics, especially New York *Artforum* types, have a lot of trouble seeing the validity of such a contention. I once had a run-in with one of them about this—this was years later, in the middle of the Ferus period. This guy was out here, one of the head honchos, and he was upset—what was it?—oh, yeah—because Billy Al Bengston was racing motorcycles at the time. This critic just dismissed that out of hand as a superficial, suicidal self-indulgence. And I said you can't do that. We got going and ended up arguing about folk art. He was one of those Marxist critics who like to think they're real involved with the people, making great gestures and so forth, but they're hardly in the world at all. Anyway, he was talking about pot-making and weaving and everything, and my feeling was that that was all historical art but not folk art. As far as

I'm concerned, a folk art is when you take a utilitarian object, something you use every day, and you give it overlays of your own personality, what it is you feel and so forth. You enhance it with your
life. And a folk art in the current period of time would more appro-
priately be in the area of something like a motorcycle. I mean, a
motorcycle can be a lot more than just a machine that runs along;
it can be a whole description of a personality and an aesthetic.

"Anyway, so I looked in the paper, and I found this ad of a guy
who was selling a hot rod and a motorcycle. And I took the critic
out to this place. It was really fortunate, because it was exactly what
I wanted. We arrived at this place in the Valley, in the middle of
nowhere, and here's this kid: he's selling a hot rod and he's got
another he's working on. He's selling a '32 coupe, and he's got a '29
roadster in the garage. The '32 he was getting rid of was an absolute
cherry. But what was more interesting, and which I was able to
show this critic, was that here was this '29, absolutely dismantled, I
mean, completely apart, and the kid was making decisions about the
frame, whether or not he was going to cad plate certain bolts or
whether he was going to buff grind them, or whether he was just
going to leave them raw as they were. He was insulating and sound-
proofing the doors, all kinds of things that no one would ever know
or see unless they were truly a sophisticate in the area. But, I mean,
real aesthetic decisions, truly aesthetic decisions. Here was a fifteen-
year-old kid who wouldn't know art from schmart, but you couldn't
talk about a more real aesthetic activity than what he was doing,
how he was carefully weighing: what was the attitude of this whole
thing? What exactly? How should it look? What was the relationship in terms of its machinery, its social bearing, everything? I
mean, all these things were being weighed in terms of the aesthetics
of how the things should *look*. It was a perfect example.

"The critic simply denied it. Simply denied it: not important,
unreal, untrue, doesn't happen, doesn't exist. See, he comes from a
world in New York where the automobile . . . I mean, automobiles
are 'What? Automobile? Nothing.' Right? I mean, no awareness, no
sensitivity, no involvement. So he simply denied it: 'It doesn't exist.'
Like that: 'Not an issue.' Which we argued about a little on the way
back over the Sepulveda pass.

"I said, 'How can you deny it? You may not be interested, but how can you deny it? I mean, there it is, full blown, right in front of you, and it's obviously a folk art!'

"Anyway, he, 'No, no.'

"So I finally just stopped the car and made him get out. I just flat left him there by the road, man, and just drove off. Said, 'See you later, Max.'"

Bob was laughing uproariously by now, relishing the memory of the incident. Calming himself, he continued, "And that was basically the last conversation we two have ever had."

We started moving once again. "Well," Bob sighed, "I suppose all that's left to show you is the high school."

We cruised through a flat business district for several blocks. I observed that for all his tales of teenage life that afternoon, the school itself had cropped up only rarely in his recollections.

"Well," he explained, "from the tenth grade on I didn't even take a notebook. That shows how seriously I took school. If there was an assignment, I'd scribble it on some scrap of paper. School was essentially a place to go and meet. I went to school, and I went every day, because I really was having a good time: that's where all the action was."

Had any particular subjects interested him?

"Well, I took art classes, and I had art teacher who thought I was very talented; I guess I had a natural facility and it was easy. There were only two required classes that I ever took. My father definitely wanted me to take algebra, and my mother definitely wanted me to take Latin. I flunked them both, which shows you. My father really wanted me to take algebra, for the discipline. So I tried real hard, took it three times, beginning algebra, and flunked all three times."

"Did that matter at all to you, flunking classes?"

"Nope."

"Did it matter to your father?"

"Finally, I guess not."

We rounded a corner and confronted the school's sign, Dorsey High ("Registration, September 11—See you soon!"). Bob was pointing: "Over there, past the main entrance, there's like a large circle, which is where we all danced during lunch and after school. And over here"—we sidled round toward the playing field, where squadrons of green-and-white-jerseyed jocks (most of them black) were friskily sacking each other in the late afternoon sun—"this was the football field, scene of my many . . . whatever. I played end. We had a very good team, made the city finals. I was a good, solid participant, but hardly the star or anything."

I wondered how on earth Bob had time for all of this; it sounded like he had lived eighteen adolescences, rather than one. "Well," he explained, "we are talking about *three years* of high school," as if that explained anything. He went on to describe how he'd been a floater. "I wasn't really a member of any particular clique, although I floated between several. There were the guys who were into cars, others who were into girls, others into dancing, others into gambling—I just drifted between them, partaking of everything."

I asked him about the gambling. "Well, as you know, Hollywood Park Race Track is just a few miles back that way. And there was one group of guys—they hung out over at this pool hall on Adams—and they were into dressing up, wearing suits and pork pie hats, the whole dude routine. They were heavily into gambling, and I hovered around them. Starting around tenth grade, we began going to the ninth race each day, because after the eighth race they just opened the gates and let you in free (otherwise, we couldn't have gotten tickets, because we were still too young). But all day we'd be listening to the races, getting to know the horses, trying to pick 'em."

Was he making any money?

"Well, in the very beginning I wasn't making much. It was like two-dollar bets. I didn't really begin to make money gambling until I turned professional, which was years later. No, I'd win sometimes, lose sometimes. I don't know whether in the long run I came out ahead or behind, because I didn't keep track. If I came out behind, it was not very far behind, because (*a*) I could not afford to lose and (*b*) I never liked losing. I mean, losing is something I never took kindly to at all.

"It's funny. You know the theory about gamblers really being in it for the losing? Well, that's something that never entered my psyche. Losing, forgetting the money, just was no fun. To me, losing was not interesting. So if I'm losing, I don't play. That's why I never gamble in Las Vegas. I mean, I love to shoot craps. It's a great game, one of the great gambling games of all time, but basically you can't win. You're playing against the house, and it's strictly percentages, strictly mathematics. You can be a better gambler, have a few winning streaks, but basically you can't beat mathematics.

"You *can* beat other people, by playing better than they do. So any game where it's man-on-man, me-against-you, or me-against-the-crowd-at-the-race-track: that's my kind of gambling game. It's my skill and your skill, and if I'm better than you are, I'll beat you. Over the long run, you might beat me here, you might beat me there. In fact, in small nickel-and-dime games, I'd be inclined to let you win, but to play loosely enough so that it makes no difference, on the basis that you may eventually end up in a real game with me, at which point the investment will have proven worthwhile.

"But back in high school, this was still embryonic, just nickel-and-diming around. It was more just part of the pleasure."

The sun was low in the sky now, and we were meandering lazily toward it, back toward the freeway and home. Our conversation was drifting casually—curious associations. One thing led to another, gambling to . . . birth control. I asked Bob if kids in his circle worried much about pregnancy.

"Well, we thought about it," Bob reflected, "but not a hell of a lot. You did one thing or another. Sometimes you just kept your fingers crossed. It just depended what the occasion was, who you were with. Got very lucky, I guess. Just plain lucky. Joan sometimes talks about all the girls at her high school, how half of them got knocked up and had to get married before they even graduated. In my high school I don't remember anybody getting married . . . or knocked up. No abortions that I can remember. So sure, it was a concern, but not one that stopped you. Everybody was just lucky or something. We lived a sainted life or whatever you call it—a charmed life."

We had passed his junior high, and I asked him if that had been a similarly blessed time for him. He said not especially. "I have just a total blank in terms of memories before high school. Since that's come up a few times, I've wondered why. And part of it, I think, is that I never delve into it. I mean, people like Joan, with whom there are traumas in their youth, one thing about why there are traumas is that they dwell on them a little, they remember them and think back on them and use them as reference. I never think about that stuff at all, and I never go back. It's not so much a question of not having a memory as not having an interest in going back to think about those things. . . ."

L.A. GLOWS

The day of that infamous slow-motion Bronco chase—actually, it was already past sundown here in New York as I sat before the glowing TV in our darkening kitchen, transfixed by the unfurling stream of bob-and-wafting helicopter images, hot tears streaming down my cheeks—my eight-year-old daughter gazed for a while at the screen and then over at me, at which point, baffled and concerned, she inquired, "What's wrong, Daddy? Did you know that guy?"

"What guy?" I stammered, surfacing from my trance, momentarily disoriented. "Oh, no, no. I didn't know the guy. I don't give a damn about the guy. It's that *light!* That's the light I keep telling you girls about." You girls: her mother and her. That light: the late-afternoon light of Los Angeles—golden pink off the bay through the smog and onto the palm fronds. A light I've found myself pining for every day of the nearly two decades since I left Southern California.

Months passed, and on sporadic returns to L.A., for one project or another, I occasionally recounted my Bronco-chase experience, and everybody knew exactly what I was talking about. The light of the place is a subject that Angelenos are endlessly voluble about—only, it turns out, people bring all sorts of different associations to the subject.

For example, David Hockney maintains that the extravagant light of Los Angeles was one of the strongest lures drawing him to Southern California in the first place, more than thirty years ago— and, in fact, long before that. "As a child, growing up in Bradford, in the North of England, across the gothic gloom of those endless winters," he recalls, "I remember how my father used to take me along with him to see the Laurel and Hardy movies. And one of the things I noticed right away, long before I could even articulate it exactly, was how Stan and Ollie, bundled in their winter overcoats, were casting these wonderfully strong, crisp shadows. We never got shadows of any sort in winter. And already I knew that someday I wanted to settle in a place with winter shadows like that."

Robert Irwin, one of the presiding masters of L.A.'s Light and Space artistic movement of the late sixties and early seventies, and a native Angeleno, concurred that there's something extraordinary about the light of L.A., though he said that it was sometimes hard to characterize it exactly. "One of its most common features, however," he suggested, "is the haze that fractures the light, scattering it in such a way that on many days the world almost has *no* shadows. Broad daylight—and, in fact, lots and lots of light—and no shadows. Really peculiar, almost dreamlike. . . . I love walking down the street when the light gets all reverberant, bouncing around like that, and everything's just humming in your face."

A few days after my conversation with Irwin, I happened to be talking with John Bailey, the cinematographer, most recently of "As Good As It Gets," and he energetically confirmed Irwin's observation: "I have a sophisticated light meter, which in my work I'm always consulting. Most places in the world when it's overcast enough so that you get no shadows, the meter lets you know you have to set your aperture a stop to a stop and a half below full sun. Here in L.A. the same kind of diffuse light, no shadows—I could hardly believe the first time I encountered this—and my meter will read almost the same as for full sunlight. Other days, though, you'll be getting open sun, which, of course, here means open desert sun—a harshly contrasting light. After all, for all its human settlement, the Southland is still this freak of nature—a desert abutting the sea. And open desert light is very harsh—you get these deep, deep shadows."

I mentioned the Laurel and Hardy shadows of Hockney's youth. "Exactly," Bailey said. "Shadows and no shadows—that's the duality of L.A. light, isn't it? And how appropriate for a place where the sun rises in the desert and sets in the ocean."

Another day, I called Hal Zirin, out at Caltech—the man who founded and until recently ran the solar observatory up at Big Bear Lake. I suppose I was wondering how the sun itself looked in the light of L.A. "Ah, Southern California," Zirin responded, with improbable enthusiasm. "God's gift to astronomy!" I laughed, figuring he was joking. "Oh no," he assured me. "I'm completely serious. Mt. Wilson, Mt. Palomar, the Griffith Observatory, our solar observatory out at Big Bear . . . It's not for nothing that during the first two-thirds of this century a good three-quarters of the most significant discoveries in astronomy were made here in Southern California."

So wherefore was it?

"Well, it's all thanks to the incredible stability, the uncanny stillness, of the air around L.A. It goes back to that business people are always talking about—a desert thrusting up against the ocean, and, specifically, against the eastern shore of a northern ocean, with its cold, clockwise, southward-moving current. And the other crucial element in the mix is these high mountain ranges girdling the basin—so that what happens here is that ocean-cooled air drifts in over the coastal plain and gets trapped beneath the warmer desert air floating in over the mountains to the east. That's the famous thermal inversion, and the opposite of the usual arrangement, where warm surface air progressively cools as it rises. And the atmosphere below the inversion layer is incredibly stable. You must have noticed, for instance, how, if you're on a transcontinental jet coming in for a landing at LAX, once you pass over the mountains on your final approach, no matter how turbulent the flight may have been prior to that, suddenly the plane becomes completely silent and steady and still." (Actually, I had noticed and wondered about it.) "That's the stable air of L.A."

And why was such stability so important to astronomy?

"Well," Zirin explained, "have you noticed, for instance, how if you go out to the Arizona desert, say, it may be incredibly clear but the road off in the distance is shimmering? That's the heat rising in waves off the surface of the ground. On the other hand, go out to the Santa Monica palisade and gaze out over the cool water. It's completely clear and distinct, clean out to the horizon. The heat rising from the ground in most places—or, rather, the resultant interplay of pockets of hot and cold air, acting like distorting lenses in the atmosphere up above—is in turn what makes stars shimmer and twinkle in the night sky. A twinkling star can be very pretty and romantic, but twinkling is distortion, by definition, and if you're an astronomer you want your star—or, for that matter, your sun, if that's what you're looking at—to be distortion-free: solid as a rock. And that's what you get here. The stars don't twinkle in L.A."

And, it occurred to me, that might also account for the preternatural clarity of the encircling mountains, off in the distance—that hushed sense you sometimes get that you could just reach out and touch them—on those smog-free days, that is, when you're able to see them at all.

Angelenos tend to take perverse credit for the uncanny light of the place, as if they themselves were the ones who made it all happen; and, in fact, according to at least one way of looking at things, they may have a point. Someone told me that if it was air pollution I wanted to consider I should go talk to Glen Cass, at Caltech, a jovial, rotund, clear-eyed, and short-cropped professor of environmental engineering with a very specific interest in smog: he's obsessed with the effect of air pollution on visibility—in other words, exactly why it is that some afternoons he can go up on the roof of the Millikan Library there at Caltech, gaze out toward the San Gabriel Mountains, towering well over a mile high, less than five miles to the north, and not make out a thing through the bright, white (shadow-obliterating) atmospheric haze.

So, I asked Cass, what, exactly, was all that white stuff choking the view of his beloved mountains?

"Well, it turns out that there are all sorts of different sizes of particles floating in the air—from absolutely minuscule to relatively large and coarse," he explained. "Some of those—and especially the larger ones—simply get in the way of the line of vision between you and, say, that mountain over there. They blot out or defract the beams of reflected sunlight emanating from the mountain that would otherwise be conveying visual detail to your eyes. Contrary to what you might think, though, it's not so much the large, coarse particles that pose the biggest problem. Instead, it's those of a

specific intermediate size—about half a micrometre, to be exact—
that constitute the jokers in the deck when it comes to visibility.

"And the thing about particles of that size is that they happen to
have about the same diameter as the wavelength of natural sunlight.
So that, when the sunlight from over my shoulder, say, hits one of
those particles floating between me and the mountain that I'm trying to make out, the light bounces off the particle and right into my
eye. On some days there can be billions of such particles in the line
of sight between me and the mountain—each of them with the
mirrorlike potential to bounce white sunlight directly back into my
eye. It can get to be like having a billion tiny suns between you and
the thing you're trying to see. That's what the white stuff is. And
we have a technical term for it."

I hunkered down over my notebook, preparing to take down
complex technological dictation.

"We call it airlight."

The next morning, I happened to be jogging on the beach in
Santa Monica, heading north, in the direction of Malibu, as the sun
was rising behind me. The sky was already bright, though the sun
was still occluded behind a low-clinging fog bank over LAX. The
Malibu mountains up ahead were dark and clear and distinct, and
seemed as if freshly minted. Presently, the sun must have broken
out from behind the fog bank—I realized this because suddenly the
sand around me turned pale purplish pink and my own long shadow
shot out before me. I looked up at the mountains, and they were
gone: lost in the airlight.

Later, as I was describing the experience to a poet friend, Dennis Phillips, and trying to explain the business about the billion tiny
suns, he interrupted, correcting me. "No, no," he said. "You mean a
billion tiny moons."

Actually, the air-pollution situation in L.A. has been improving
markedly over the past fifteen years, as Cass is only too happy to
affirm. Nevertheless, the light seems more uncanny than ever—or,
rather, it may simply be reverting to its original splendor. What with
the thermal inversion, even as the smog has subsided a softer version of the airlight phenomenon has persisted—one noted by Carey
McWilliams, the poet laureate of California historians, who in 1946

recorded how, the region's aridity notwithstanding, "the charm of Southern California is largely to be found in the air and the light. Light and air are really one element: indivisible, mutually interacting, thoroughly interpenetrated."

I was recalling McWilliams's comments one morning while breakfasting with the architect Coy Howard, a true student of the light, and he concurred. "It's an incredibly loaded subject—this diaphanous soup we live in," he said. "It feels primeval—there's a sense of the undifferentiated, the nonhierarchical. It's not exactly a dramatic light. In fact, 'dramatic' is exactly what it's not. If anything, it's meditative. And there's something really peculiar about it. In places where you get a crisp, sharp light with deep, clean shadows—which we do get here sometimes—you get confronted with a strong contrasting duality: illumination and opacity. But when you have the kind of veiled light we get here more regularly you become aware of a sort of multiplicity—not illumination so much as luminosity. Southern California glows, not just all day but at night as well, and the opacity melts away into translucency, and even transparency."

I wasn't quite getting it, so Howard tried again.

"Things in the light here have a kind of threeness instead of the usual twoness. There's the thing—the object—and its shadow, but then a sense of reflection as well. You know how you can be walking along the beach, let's say, and you'll see a seagull walking along ahead of you, and a wave comes in, splashing its feet. At that moment, you'll see the bird, its shadow, and its reflection. Well, there's something about the environment here—the air, the atmosphere, the light—that makes *everything* shimmer like that. There's a kind of glowing thickness to the world—the diaphanous soup I was talking about—which, in turn, grounds a magic-meditative sense of presence."

The poet Paul Vangelisti knew exactly what Coy Howard was getting at when I related our conversation to him. In fact, he was blown away, for he claimed he'd been trying to frame almost that same point earlier that day, in the latest of a series of daily poems he'd been working on, based on the view across the neighboring arroyo from the window of his Echo Park studio, celebrating, in this instance:

. . . the pigeon flock
soaring and tumbling every noon
silver then white then sunlight
against the weight of air at the window.

"Coy Howard's associations run to seagulls," Vangelisti pointed out, "and mine run to pigeons — maybe not that surprising a convergence after all, since birds are the true citizens of light. But I know just what he means about the sense of threeness — silver then white then sunlight — and about the meditative, as opposed to the dramatic, quality of the light here."

The light is a constantly recurring theme among the poets of L.A., but I can think of few whose work is as light-saturated, as light-blasted, as Vangelisti's. He entitled his first collection, back in 1973, simply "Air."

"For one thing," he elaborated, "I think the light of L.A. is the whitest light I've ever seen, and the sky is one of the highest. You really notice it if you're playing baseball and you're in the outfield. You're always losing the ball in that high white sky. And then, too, there's a strange thing that happens with the sense of distance and of expanse. Because from here in Echo Park the ocean off in the distance is oceanic, but so is the intervening land, and indeed so is the sky. It's that even, undifferentiated, nonhierarchical quality Coy Howard is talking about. And a weird thing is how that light yields a simultaneous sense of distance and of flatness: things seem very sharp up close and far away, with nothing in between. And the uncanny result is that you lose yourself — somehow not outwardly but, rather, inwardly. Here the light draws you *inward*."

Anne Ayres, the gallery director at the Otis Institute, told me that some days the light of L.A. can drive her into a state of "egoless bliss." And John Bailey described to me his own occasional bouts with "rapture." But there were others I got in touch with who were having none of it.

"You're talking to the wrong guy," the director Peter Bogdanovich warned me when I reached him. "See, I'm a New Yorker, and though I've lived in L.A. for thirty years, I really haven't been that happy here the last fifteen. I miss seasons, and I hate the way the light of the place throws you into such a trance that you fail to realize how time is passing. It's like what Orson Welles once told me. 'The terrible thing about L.A.,' he said, 'is that you sit down, you're twenty-five, and when you get up you're sixty-two.'"

"But light is *over!*" Paul Schimmel, the chief curator at MOCA, the Museum of Contemporary Art, exclaimed when I broached my pet subject to him. "There hasn't been light in this city for more than ten years now." Schimmel was the creator of "Helter Skelter," a seminal show at MOCA, which endeavored to prove precisely that point back in 1992. On first arriving in L.A., in 1981, Schimmel had half expected to encounter some third- or fourth-generation version of the Light and Space orthodoxies that had come to be so closely identified with the L.A. art scene during the sixties and the early seventies—through the hegemony of masters ranging from Robert Irwin to Richard Diebenkorn. Instead, he found a younger generation of artists—exemplified by the likes of Mike Kelley and Nancy Rubins—who seemed to have rejected the light aesthetic entirely, opting instead for a decidedly darker, seedier, more grimly unsettling and dystopian view of the L.A. reality. "Partly," Schimmel speculated, "this was because by the late seventies and early eighties light in L.A. had been so academicized that it had really become little more than a commercial cliché. There was nowhere else to go with it. In part, too, long before a lot of other people, these artists were onto some of the bleak social transformations that were eroding the city itself. 'Helter Skelter' closed on a Sunday, and the worst riots in the city's history erupted the following Wednesday."

Of course, in its very title the "Helter Skelter" show acknowledged the fact that its countervision of the L.A. reality was itself rooted in a long countertradition—one that wended back from the Manson murders into the noir world of the great crime novelists and filmmakers of the thirties and forties. It's interesting how those noir novelists and filmmakers almost completely inoculated themselves against the blandishments of the light of L.A., in part by setting most of their scenes either at night or indoors—in fact, usually both. One of the distinct charms of such seventies reworkings of the genre as Polanski's "Chinatown" and, even more notably, Altman's "The Long Goodbye" was the way the filmmakers forced their hardened protagonists out into the light of day. (Altman's Marlowe spent the entire film in a perpetual squint, scuttling about like a naked crab summarily wrested from the dark, nestling comfort of its shell.)

Generally speaking, people I spoke with about the light of L.A. tended to fall on one side or the other. There were a few, however, whose responses were decidedly more nuanced.

One such was Don Waldie, whose remarkable book "Holy Days: A Suburban Memoir" I'd been reading on one of my flights out to Los Angeles. Born and raised in Lakewood (a sort of blue-collar West Coast Levittown, row upon row of near-identical frame-and-stucco tract houses laid out in a meticulously even grid just north of Long Beach), Waldie still lives in the community—indeed, in the very house—in which he was reared. In fact, his day job is public-information officer for Lakewood. Waldie doesn't drive, so he has to walk to and from City Hall each day—twenty-five minutes across an unvaryingly regular pattern of perpendicular zigs and zags. It was during such walks that he began composing—one at a time—the hauntingly lyrical, startlingly brief chapters that make up his book.

I resolved to include him in my survey, so as soon as I'd landed in L.A. I placed a call to Lakewood City Hall—he was out—and left a message on his machine. That evening, I got my own personal whiff of his method.

"Ah, yes," he said cheerfully when I reached him at home. "The light around here is quite remarkable, isn't it? In fact, I gave the matter some thought on my walk home this evening. And it seems to me, actually, that there are four—or, anyway, at least four—lights in L.A. To begin with, there's the cruel, actinic light of late July. Its glare cuts piteously through the general shabbiness of Los Angeles. Second comes the nostalgic, golden light of late October. It turns Los Angeles into El Dorado, a city of fool's gold. It's the light William Faulkner—in his story 'Golden Land'—called 'treacherous unbrightness.' It's the light the tourists come for—the light, to be more specific, of unearned nostalgia. Third, there's the gunmetal-gray light of the months between December and July. Summer in Los Angeles doesn't begin until mid-July. In the months before, the light can be as monotonous as Seattle's. Finally comes the light, clear as stone-dry champagne, after a full day of rain. Everything in this light is somehow simultaneously particularized and idealized: each perfect, specific, ideal little tract house, one beside the next. And that's the light that breaks hearts in L.A."

That and other lights. One evening, out on the palisade, I was watching the sunset in the company of a theatrical-lighting designer. Actually, we had our backs to the sea—the blush of sky and air and land is somehow even more glorious to the east in L.A. when the sun is setting. "Incredible," my designer friend marvelled, "the effects He gets with just one unit."

Incredible, too, the effects Vin Scully gets with just one unit—in his case, his voice. As the legendary radio announcer for the L.A. Dodgers, Scully has spent his life in that light, broadcasting the sunset itself between pitches night after night. (Indeed, it may be thanks to those broadcasts that many Angelenos, including me, first became truly sensitized to the light—and to the light of language as well.) When I reached him by phone, it didn't take much more than the word "light" to get him launched, rhapsodizing, for instance, about how "come late July, with the sun setting off third base, the air actually turns purple tinged with gold, an awesome sight to behold, the Master Painter at work once again, and, owing to the orientation of the stadium, out beyond center field, you're staring at the mountains, and mountains beyond mountains, indeed, the purple mountains' majesty spread out there for everyone to see. And on evenings like that it can get to be like a Frederic Remington or a Charles Russell painting, the dust billowing up from the passing cars on the freeway. If you squint your eyes and only let your imagination soar, it's as if a herd of wild horses were kicking by."

As I write, I'm back in New York, exiled from that light. Sixty years ago, it occurs to me, my maternal grandfather, the Austrian Jewish modernist composer Ernst Toch, found himself exiled into that light. He and my grandmother lived on the Franklin Street hill, at the very edge of Santa Monica and Brentwood, north of Wilshire, in a house facing out toward the Santa Monica Mountains. The view from their house, and particularly from the bay window of his composing studio, under the knotty branches of a spreading coral tree and out over the Brentwood Golf Course, was incredibly lovely, especially at the golden hour. (Come to think of it, maybe *that's* where I first became smitten with this thing about the light of Southern California.) Occasionally, my grandparents would entertain guests up there. They'd meander around the grounds and through the house and eventually into his studio, approaching his desk—wedged up against that magnificent bay window, with its enthralling light-filled view—and invariably somebody would crack wise, saying something along the lines of "Well, no wonder you can compose, with a view like that!"

At which point, invariably, my grandfather would respond, "Well, actually, no. When I compose, I have to close the curtains."

Robert Towne

Is there a more representative Los Angeles movie than Roman Polanski's 1974 detective drama *Chinatown*, with its film noir treatment of the story of the region's water wars? The brainchild of screenwriter Robert Towne (b. 1936), *Chinatown* is a sort of twisted creation myth that finds the city's roots in corruption and violence. Towne, a Southern California native, began his motion-picture career writing for B-picture maestro Roger Corman before graduating to screenplays such as *The Last Detail*, *Shampoo*, *Personal Best*, and *The Two Jakes*. Here he meditates on the tradition that inspired *Chinatown*, a tradition having less to do with Hollywood than with such literary forebears as Carey McWilliams and Raymond Chandler.

PREFACE AND POSTSCRIPT TO *CHINATOWN*

It was in Eugene, Oregon, in April of 1971 that I came across a public library copy of Carey McWilliams' *Southern California Country: An Island on the Land*—and with it the crime that formed the basis for "Chinatown."

It wasn't the compendium of facts in the chapter "Water! Water! Water!" or indeed in the entire book. It was that Carey McWilliams wrote about Southern California with sensibilities my eye, ear, and nose recognized. Along with Chandler he made me feel that he'd not only walked down the same streets and into the same arroyo—he smelled the eucalyptus, heard the humming of high tension wires, saw the same bleeding Madras landscapes—and so a sense of deja vu was underlined by a sense of jamais vu: no writers had ever spoken as strongly to me about my home.

The rapacious effects of a housing development in Deep Canyon nearby, and a photo essay called "Raymond Chandler's L.A." in the old *West* magazine provided, I think, the actual catalyst for the screenplay. The photos in *West*—a Plymouth convertible under an old streetlight in the rain outside Bullock's Wilshire, for example— reminded me there was still time to preserve much of the city's past on film, just as McWilliams had shown me that it was my past as well.*

When I returned to L.A. from Eugene, I began to work on "Chinatown" and began by searching for the story in the streets. I would take to driving around the city at night, thru Silverlake, Echo Park, down Temple, where the streetlamps were low and yellow and nippled and the palm trees were high with scrawny fronds like broken pinwheels, and now and then on top of one of the precipitous and sandy hillsides of corner lots high concrete retaining walls cracked and droopy ice plant could never quite hold the earth and clapboard in place and you could still see an oil derrick looking like a rusty praying mantis, trying to suck the last few barrels out of the dying crab grass in the backyard.

And if at five in the afternoon you happened to find yourself down by Union Station during a Santa Ana, you could feel the warm dry itch across your skin, look down the tracks to the mountains and sky and the pastels of lavender, salmon, and blue the color of painting from old tile-topped motels long since blown to rubble —you could still see the city McWilliams and Chandler wrote about and I remembered in those last moments before sunset. Usually these drives would end up at Tommy's where I would down Chilicheeseburgers and Pepsis and happily recall what I'd seen between burps, all the way home.

An old postcard from Riverside featuring a promenade of pepper trees would be thrust under my nose: suddenly I remembered walking back from school with their messy green shade overhead, tiny dry leaves and red-green bee-bees crunching on the cracked sidewalk the roots would have already raised and cracked beneath my feet. I was six years old but childhood is never a memory. You may grow up and cover up but now and then the blanket slips away, the child in you is naked and memories become new and frightening

---

*The development of the film starting with a dinner with Bob Evans at Dominick's where I told him I wouldn't do the screenplay for *Gatsby* because I was working on this thing called "Chinatown" and turned down his offer to finance the writing—only to take him up on it a month or so later in the same restaurant, from a cold-assed business point of view alone the only smart thing I ever did—through to my eventual conflict with Roman and enduring disappointment over the literal and ghoulishly bleak climax in "Chinatown" are not, of course, germane to the reason for the writing of it.

again—you get stung by a bee and breathlessly wait those first swelling milliseconds: is it going to end with exquisite pleasure or exquisite pain? Memories swell in the same way. When we first feel them in our skin there's that breathcatching moment before knowing whether we'll feel grief or joy. You only know that like childhood neither emotion is ever really left in the past.

So "Chinatown" for me was an acknowledgment that I lived with things I loved but could no longer see—even now if I drive Western around Lomita and Torrance I miss those stinky sloughs and their ratty cattails more than anyone would care to hear.

There are probably as many kinds of crimes as there are detective stories, as there are homicides and thefts as there are hatreds and fears in the human heart. Whatever the crime in "Chinatown," greed wasn't represented by money—land and water respectively did that. But I suppose the central crime of "Chinatown"—the wanton destruction of the past—wasn't a crime at all. Its perpetrators were far more likely to have Junior Highs or streets named after them than they were likely to go to jail. The truly murderous act in the movie was laying waste to land and to fragile communities as tho they were an incidental part of Noah Cross' grand vision—a vision about as grand and expansive as cancer. It was a rape worse than Cross could visit on his own daughter—hurting the land he inevitably hurt all children, affected where they'd live and what they'd see and even what they'd breathe. When a crime can no longer contain or content itself with the past and insists on visiting the future it's no longer a crime—it becomes a sin, and very difficult to punish.

The murdered Mulwray, who Cross had so outraged by making him a partner to his blasphemy, was posthumously honored for the very thing he loathed and for which he was murdered—like other public sins of far greater scope humanity is sometimes unable to punish, they are reduced to rewards.

But of course religious matters were far from my mind while I tried to figure out what Gittes should figure out. How about Cross' hankie-pankie? Should it be seen first with the land or with human life?

No script ever drove me nuttier, as I tried one way and another casually to reveal mountains of information about dams, orange groves, incest, elevator operators, etc. As in most states, it finally comes down to exile or death: my wife in her wisdom banished me and my growing shame to any island of choice—in this case the cheapest, closest and as it happened, most perfect, Catalina.

There in the fall of 1972, inside the flaking white and green trimmed dusty clapboard of Banning Lodge, perched between Cat Harbor and Isthmus Cove, I wrote the heart of "Chinatown"—with the aid and comfort of two friends, one who lived with me and one who visited me in banishment—Hira my dog and Edward Taylor, since college my Jiminy Crickett, Mycroft Holmes, and Edmund Wilson. Eddie would periodically drop out of the sky on a Catalina Seaplane, Hira would chase forty head of buffalo into the windsock waving at the shore line of Cat Harbor, just on a whim, and I would whine and wring my hands—and slowly discover my invisible collaborator on "Chinatown."

Go to the Isthmus sometime. It's not much. A skinny little strip separates the two harbors, as tho somebody with a clothespin pinched Catalina in half. From Isthmus pier to the windward sock just inside the Cat Harbor waterline, from harbor to harbor, leeward to windward, we'd walk down an eighth of a mile of dirt road with its brace of silver-dollar eucalyptus, and its rows of unevenly whitewashed stones looking like the dusty and loosened teeth of a yawning fossil. Hira of course could lope it in moments and still have leisure to stop, piss and generally have his way with a rock, tree, buffalo chip or even stray buffalo or two.

There are more buildings—huddled under high eucalyptus at a point that must be mid-way between the two coves is the California Yacht Club, its brick-red wooden slats velvety with dust and probably unchanged since the Union Army built it for barracks over a hundred and twenty-five years ago. Add some trailers, the Bombards' tiny ranch-style house with its sprig of bougainvillea, like celery in a Bloody Mary, the Jon Hall movie-set bar from the twenties expanded to a restaurant, and an adjacent marine accessories market (everything you always wanted for your Evinrude and more) and you've pretty much got it—except for the battered phone booths and public rest rooms and showers in landlord green, and except for something else, the air.

It was the air that brought me home or rather brought home to me, L.A. as it had been in 1940. One way and another it came to me with every fresh breath.

Like my struggling detective Gittes and my dog Hira I have always been to some extent led around by the nose. And, like them, stray scents in the air have more than once aroused my appetites, my curiosity, my memory. Smell, I think, is the most resonant sensibility we possess. A whiff of dry weed, cactus, and wet paint on an open porch, and in the split second the impulse makes its tiny synaptic leap it's liable to leap another forty years into the past, into another age, another country. Sometimes memory and passion, past and present commingle in a kind of exquisitely tortuous tangle: not long ago I stepped into an elevator, staring at nothing in particular. I was positively stung by the faintest trace of a certain perfume I hadn't encountered in years—it was like a gardenia someone had dried in the desert. Sand and brush seemed to have taken hold in the faded fragrance. I, as is my habit on such occasions, got dizzy and gripped the elevator rail at the back. As I did, I heard a voice without a blink in it at my shoulder. "Like it?" she said. I turned into a young woman's eyes. She was staring almost defiantly at me, as if she knew what I was thinking. I shot back as quick as I could— "Yeah." We looked at each other for another hostile moment til the elevator hit the lobby and we went our separate ways—whatever I'd done to her, she'd tossed me back about fifteen years, made me angry, excited and sad, and she knew it.

So, one way and another the Catalina air literally inspired me. It brought back my body—the way it was to taste, touch, smell, and see this city as a child. It made it clear enough to see the Milky Way at night, and it was quiet enough too. I remember sitting up on the hill with Hira, one particular dusk. We were hunched in front of a few strands of barbed wire just below my two-room barracks-type bungalow that hung on the Cat Harbor side of the hill, twenty or so crunchy steps along a gravel path below the main lodge. The windward breeze was no more than a whisper, breathy and teasing on the back of my neck. It fluttered thru Hira's white mop of a coat, thru the high mustard plant and weeds around us when—it must have been a hundred yards below, not far from that windsock—I actually heard the raven that spread its wings to set down, feather by feather with elegant deliberation, like a real sharp band leader staring in the mirror and shooting his cuffs.

I can't honestly say the air helped straighten out many plot points. But I can say there was never a moment where some errant breeze didn't bring me something that made me care, made me feel it was worth trying to straighten out the story, all the horrible melodramatic machinations that remove you farther from detectives and human life than any crossword puzzle.

It brought me back to saying, these things, dead and dying that still linger in the air, had more joy in them than I could have known, and this tepid, deft, adroit, dry breezy collaborator of mine, rustling thru weeds like a child wearing a sheet, this air was worth grieving over more than I ever supposed. There's no other word—"Chinatown" is a sort of eulogy for me.

It is a eulogy I'm afraid for things lost that would concern others about as much as a missing button or a dead mouse. Easterners, for example, have often tended to be a little snide about the tepid weather and negligible change in seasons—things I have loved perhaps the most about L.A. I've loved the first hint of October nipping thru the sunlight after school, New Year's Day, chilly and clear as crystal as tho someone put the sun in the freezer overnight, the February rains that came with Valentines and would flood intersections with muddy waters rushing around stalled cars, vacant lots in March that overnight sprouted thousands of sharp green spears you could pull and send with a clod of dark earth hurtling at another kid, little ponds of black polliwogs squiggling like animated commas—and then spring and summer with the smell of pepper trees mentholated more and more by eucalyptus, the green lots turning to straw leaving foxtails in your socks and smelling like hay in the morning, the Santa Anas progressively drying the city into sand and summer smells—and best of all then you could stand on the Palisades overlooking Portuguese Bend and have all the dry desert breeze at your back abruptly splashed with salt air from the sea crashing on the rocks and swirling tidepools a hundred feet below. Well—time, smog, and development have virtually obliterated these pastel sensations for pastel sensibilities like mine—but like most things I truly value, the weather, along with love and health, are more keenly missed by their absence than by any dramatic and pushy presence. In any case, I find the answer to the initial question properly ambiguous; as near as I can tell the motive for the screenplay of "Chinatown" came out of thin air.

"Chinatown" was in the theatres just eight years ago, but it seems like a lifetime. It is one lifetime — Hira died in my arms two weeks ago and he like the city belongs to my history — another one of those maddening things I love so much and can no longer see.

I look back on Paramount with almost embarrassing fondness — a courtly studio more likely to house a dashing Gene Kelly, a bouncy Debbie Reynolds, an ebullient Donald O'Connor than me and Bobby and Roman. Paramount eight years ago seemed much closer to a hoofer kicking up his heels and splashing his talent around in the rain, than what we were then or are now.

Edward Taylor, with that special curiosity, both kind and cunning and especially given to Irishmen, idiots, and saints, still holds my hand.

Bob Evans remains, in memory and in life, a standard for every kind of human generosity, and one I have yet to see matched in this town.

For the rest, I look out at the city and this exchange from "Chinatown" between Gittes and Yelburton occurs to me:

130   INTERIOR. DEPARTMENT OF WATER & POWER— YELBURTON & GITTES

> YELBURTON
> (*referring to bandage*)
> . . . my goodness, what happened to your nose?

> GITTES
> (*smiles*)
> I cut myself shaving.

> YELBURTON
> You ought to be more careful. That must really smart.

> GITTES
> Only when I breathe.

Carol Muske

In the quietly moving "August, Los Angeles, Lullaby" the city figures as a more or less benign backdrop to the unfolding of human intimacy. Born and raised in Minnesota, Carol Muske (b. 1945) moved to Southern California in 1983 and is the author of six volumes of poetry, including *Camouflage* (1975), *Red Trousseau* (1993), and *An Octave Above Thunder* (1997), and three novels (published under the name Carol Muske Dukes), as well as the memoir *Married to the Icepick Killer: A Poet in Hollywood* (2002).

AUGUST, LOS ANGELES, LULLABY

The pure amnesia of her face,
newborn. I looked so far
into her that, for a while,

the visual held no memory.
Little by little, I returned
to myself, waking to nurse

those first nights in that
familiar room where all
the objects had been altered

imperceptibly: the gardenia
blooming in the dark
in the scarred water glass,

near the phone my handwriting
illegible, the patterned lamp-
shade angled downward and away

from the long mirror where
I stood and looked at
the woman holding her child.

Her face kept dissolving
into expressions resembling
my own, but the child's was pure

figurative, resembling no one.
We floated together in the space
a lullaby makes, head to head,

half-sleeping. *Save it,*
my mother would say, meaning
just the opposite. She didn't

want to hear my evidence
against her terrible optimism
for me. And though, despite her,

I can redeem, in a pawnshop
sense, almost any bad moment
from my childhood, I see now

what she must have intended
for me. I felt it for *her*,
watching her as she slept,

watching her suck as she
dreamed of sucking, lightheaded
with thirst as my blood flowed

suddenly into tissue that
changed it to milk. No matter
that we were alone, there's a

texture that moves between me
and whatever might have injured
us then. Like the curtain's sheer

opacity, it remains drawn
over what view we have of dawn
here in this onetime desert,

now green and replenished,
its perfect climate
unthreatened in memory —

though outside, as usual,
the wind blew, the bough bent,
under the eaves, the hummingbird

touched once the bloodcolored hourglass,
the feeder, then was gone.

Wanda Coleman

If early Los Angeles writers were often exiles or visitors from somewhere else, sometime in the 1970s the balance began to shift toward the voices of writers who had grown up in the Southland. They had in common a sharp immediacy and an eye for the underside of the California dream. In "Angel Baby Blues," from her collection *Heavy Daughter Blues*, Wanda Coleman (b. 1946) offers her own take on the failed promises of Southern California. A prolific poet, fiction writer, and journalist, Coleman won the 1999 Lenore Marshall Poetry Prize for *Bathwater Wine*. Her book of poems *Mercurochrome* was a finalist for the 2001 National Book Award.

ANGEL BABY BLUES

they say if you fly high enough you will get your wings

one something keeps telling me i need to leave Los Angeles and i say i would if'n i could maybe it's smog addiction maybe it's ambition maybe it's civic pride maybe all of that maybe it's the other something telling me i'm gonna make it if i hang on long enough strong enough i'm going to make it or break it (*lose me lose your good thang*) and it's breakin' me not makin' it

double Scorpio under Leo what you got to high sign about? i gave the salami swami my astral statistics he refused to float me a loan did he foresee a felonious end? madness or death madness and death jonesed for get-over—*money money money* (i speak the lingo of liquor stores and laundromats)

maybe it's muleheadedness maybe it's memories/*let's go strollin'*

i remember before the freeways two and a half hours to Anaheim and the *see you later alligator* farm and me in strawberry polka dot chiffon grinning into the shutter box alongside the old Knotts injun chief wearing *Running Bear loved Little White Dove* leather and full headdress (do the pony like boni maroni) watching pink lemonade sunsets

687

i remember tacos hawked from vendor's wagons for 10¢ *habla Inglés* the Woodcraft Rangers *down among the dead men* failing tether-ball lime rickies riding the red car *The Mole People* the pie shop in Downey the 5th Street library Downtown goofing off at Dolphin's of Hollywood *do do the Watusi* hating John Wayne rooting for the chinks Japs Apaches cannibals and *The Duke of Earl*

    cruising Hollywood to Watts take Virgil to Beverly down Common-wealth to Wilshire to Hoover south to 23rd to Figueroa south to 54th east to Avalon south to 103rd—30 minutes as the soul flies

i remember chili Fritos interminable concrete blocks traversed on my way to and from Fremont and Washington highs *baby shake a tail feather* Slauson Village the Pharoahs the Businessmen bangs and ponytails discussing spin-the-bottle switch blades pillow fights razors monkey bites zip guns blind man's bluff between extremes of *Gidget* and *Blackboard Jungle* what it was really like to do reefer daddy cool swoopin' and low ridin' *there goes my baby movin' on down the line* and i couldn't get "upsies" to save my soles

    godzilla godzilla godzilla

i remember hip-huggers and pedal pushers the white teachers always put us in the back of the class till the white kids fled west *yo bettah get up and wail yo bettah move yo tail* we went from Ds to Bs last to first and the Mexican kids always held down their turf double-dare-yous rumbles drag races chicken-runs we held down ours except for me ("the professor") nobody mingled

    cruising Hollywood to East L.A. Santa Monica becomes Sunset becomes Macy south on Boyle hang a left at Whittier due east under 25 minutes burning rubber boogie

i remember Hunter (ol' H. K.) Hancock serenades between hot comb pressings "the Madison" *oopoopadoop* frying an egg on the side-walk on 114th in '58 sugartown endless summers the lassitude of puberty two-tone bobby-soxers oxford shoes the-nobody-told-her-about-periods hysteria the haunted eyes of the gangbanged girl *cherry cherry pop* how someone snidely said "she wanted it" and i wondered did trying to be cute mean you wanted it? i was square/afraid to want it even tho men and boys began to call me "big mama" *she come up like a rose . . . everybody knows*

i remember record hops doing the bop weirded out cuz Elvis

said he don't like chocolate drops drive-in movies cheeseburger pizza popcorn hot dog joy (havin' a fat attack) of futureless bliss between the extremes of *Fantasia* and *Psycho* first wave video crazy raved for *Flash Gordon Captain Midnight Mr. Lucky Perry Mason Peter Gunn The Pink Panther* mama how come black men don't get to be heroes? (*Cry the Beloved Country? The Defiant Ones?*) and where are the heroines who look like me? (*Anna Lucasta? Carmen Jones?*)

> cruising Hollywood to The Jungle take Wilton to Rodeo to Coliseum west to Buckingham hang a left at Santa Rosalia 15 minutes to get your biscuits fixed

i remember the city shut down the day President Kennedy was shot (i was busy terrorizing the girls gym with a potato bug when the news broke on Kathleen's portable) i remember curfew *who drinks the most us colored folks* tales about black boys brutalized by the heat found beat to death in dark alleys hung mysteriously in jail cells how *they* deny you equal opportunity how *they* don't want you livin' in their neighborhood

please please please

ain't this America? ain't this democracy? ain't this a city of angels? the entertainment capitol of the world? (better stay away from those Watts Niggers) *sixteen tons and what do you get* — burned baby burned

> cruising Hollywood to Playa Del Rey do Wilton south to Jefferson west becomes Sepulveda south make a right on Manchester be bleached and beached in 25 minutes

i remember that blond boy sneering at me in class laying down the tract: "if you're so smart why ain't you rich?" the pain of nobody going no place fast if not backwards so angry so eager to escape (*going to agogo*) to make it or break it get it get over get out get up get down get on with it do it or die in the effort *it hurts sooo baaaddd*

one something keeps telling me to quit call it splitsville *baby ooohhh baby boogaloo down Broadway* cuz nobody signals their intentions anymore and the stare down is as ugly in the 80s as it was in the 50s but i can't give it up or give up on it it's my birthplace it's my pride my price having paid my dues *forevah* paying dues hopin' to collect what's due me

> my wings

Mona Simpson

In "A Shopping Center Somewhere in the Valley," a chapter of her first novel *Anywhere But Here*, Mona Simpson (b. 1957) describes the struggle of an adolescent girl to avoid being overwhelmed by the chaos of her mother's life. The compellingly sketched setting is a suburban landscape that, if not unique to Los Angeles, certainly had its origins there. Although Simpson, who was born in Green Bay, Wisconsin, moved to Southern California with her mother at age thirteen, she stresses that her work is not directly autobiographical. She is the author of three subsequent novels: *The Good Father* (1992), *A Regular Guy* (1996), and *Off Keck Road* (2000).

from

ANYWHERE BUT HERE

A Shopping Center Somewhere in the Valley

We used to drive around at night, we didn't have anything else to do. We didn't like to be in our apartment. There weren't places we could sit and do things. If I read my homework on the bed, there wasn't anywhere for my mother to go. The sofa in the living room was old and uncomfortable. I didn't like both of us to be on the bed. So we drove around in the dark. We drove down Sunset and slowly through the quiet northern streets in Beverly Hills. Sometimes we parked and beamed the headlights over one lawn. Houses in Beverly Hills still amazed us.

After we sat for a while, peering out trying to see movement inside the frames of fuzzy, lighted windows far back on a lawn, my mother would sigh and turn on the ignition. "Someday," she'd say.

"Yeah. Right."

"I believe it. We'll have a house. And clothes. You'll have everything a teenage girl could want, Puss." She'd reach over and slap my thigh. I'd move closer to the door, stiffening. "I just have to meet the man and catch him. Should we stop and get an ice cream quick

690

before bed, for a little energy? Maybe it'll even get us up and working. That little sugar in our blood."

One night, we drove to Will Wright's, because my mother was dressed up. It was our favorite ice cream place. You could sit down in it. It was over-priced and old-fashioned, the garden circled with Christmas tree lights all year long. We sat outside in the courtyard at a small, wobbly table; I stuck a wad of gum under the metal base to even it. The round pink top was marble and the chair backs were lacy, heart-shaped wrought iron.

"You know, it's really something, when you think of it. Weather like this in March." That was one of the public things my mother said. When we were out, she only said things that could be overheard.

"Yeah, so."

She gave me a reproaching, corrective smile. "It's nice." She forced a laugh. "In Wisconsin now, you'd be freezing cold. You'd be in your bunny-fur coat."

Ice cream was my mother's favorite food, and in it she loved contrasts. Icy vanilla with scalding hot, hot fudge. Will Wright's served tiny sundaes: little silver dishes with a scoop of exquisite ice cream, flecked with black shavings of vanilla bean. The scoop was the size of a Ping-Pong ball. Two separate porcelain pitchers came with it: one of whole almonds, the other of hot fudge, which my mother spooned on, a bite at a time, to keep the maximum hot-cold contrast.

A tall man swaggered over to our table and, yanking a chair with him; turned it backwards and sat on it like a horse.

"Howdy, ladies," he said, extending his hand. "I was wondering if I could, uh, borrow a match."

"Honey, do you have a match?" If I had had a match, my mother would have killed me.

"Honey, I asked you a question."

"You know I don't."

She smiled at the man. "I'm terribly sorry. I'm afraid neither of us smoke." She rummaged in her handbag. "I sometimes carry them, for candles, but I don't seem to have any just now."

The man stayed. He didn't ask other people around us for matches and he didn't go back to his table in the corner.

"So, my name's Lonnie," he said. "Lonnie Tishman."

My mother stepped on my foot, hard, under the table.

"I'm Adele and this is my daughter, Ann."

"Your daughter? You two look just like sisters."

"Oh, no."

"You sure do. I said to my friend over there, I'll ask those two gals. They look like they'd be smokers."

"I'm twelve years old," I said. My mother kicked me, then pressed her shoe over my foot again, driving in the heel.

My mother and Lonnie Tishman were both moving. He stood up and turned his chair around and sat on it the regular way, then he crossed one leg over the other, like a woman's. He seemed rubbery, all joints. His top leg bounced off the other knee. His fingers drummed on the marble table top. My mother seemed to be in slow motion, her spoon abandoned on the saucer, her ice cream melting in a puddle, no hot-cold contrast anymore. She gradually realigned herself so everything, her legs, her shoulders, her hands, faced him.

I was the only one still. I'd learned when I was young to be very still and not move when I wanted something. I wanted Lonnie Tishman to leave. My knees pressed into each other. Later, I found tender bruises. But he stayed, breathing loudly. Lonnie was a mouth breather.

"So how are you gals tonight?"

"We're great, aren't we, Annie? We were just saying how we *love* this weather. We're new to LA and we really love it."

"Just got here? Where're you from?"   ·

"We're out of Bay City, Wisconsin."

Lonnie slapped his top knee, setting both legs jiggling.

"Golly. Wisconsin."

My mother looked down at the table and lifted the tips of her fingers.

"So, what are you two gals doing out here?"

"Well, I teach. I'm a speech therapist in the LA Public School System." There was something tiny about her pride. It killed me, I loved her. "And she's an actress," she said.

I stared down at my ice cream as if eating required all my concentration. They both looked at me hard, as if they were tracing me, drawing outlines on the sky.

Lonnie whistled through his teeth. "She's an actress." His chin fell down and the way his face turned, I could see, in his cheekbones, he was handsome.

"Mmhmm." It sounded like my mother could say more, but wouldn't. It was her imitation of modesty. Of course, there was nothing more to tell. I wasn't an actress. I only wanted to be.

"Whewee, a kid actress, huh? I knew a guy whose daughter was on TV. Little blond kid with the braids down the back. What was that show called. Her name's Linda, I think, or Lisa. Lisa Tannenbaum."

"Do you know her, Honey?"

That was harsh, like a twig snapped at my face. There wasn't any possible way I could have known Lisa Tannenbaum. "No," I said.

"Where do you gals live?" Lonnie pushed his chin close to my mother. He had short bristles on his face, which made me think of an electric field, things crackling, lightning on dry ground. I wished my mother would feel it, too, and pull away. It was something about men. When I was a child, I went to my cousin's house. I locked myself in the bathroom and looked at things. It was all different from ours. I felt something like electricity when I put their towels to my face. I thought it came from men, the smell of men. I imagined it had something to do with shaving.

"In Beverly Hills," my mother said quietly, dropping the words.

"Well, hey, what do you say, why don't we get together sometime."

"Sure," my mother said.

"Why don't you give me your phone number and I'll call you and we'll hook up?"

"We're 273-7672."

Lonnie took a pen from his shirt pocket and wrote our phone number on his wrist. He stood up, shoved the chair in towards the table, pulling the back to his leg. "Well, I'll be a-seeing ya," he said.

My mother put her hand over the bill. "Should we get going?" I'd finished my ice cream; my mother no longer seemed interested in hers. She quickly looked over her shoulder to see he was gone and then bent towards me, her face greedy with excitement.

"You know who that was, don't you?" There was something hard and individual about her face; her beauty was her beauty, her luck was her luck.

"No." I ground a stone under my shoe.

"Didn't you hear him say his name? That was Tishman: Lonnie Tishman. Haven't you seen those signs on Wilshire where they're building? That's all Tishman. They're everything. All the high rises. Those condominiums in Century City where we drove by, don't you remember? I said the top ones would be gorgeous. Who knows, I'll bet he'll give us one of them. He's all over. Believe me. *Ev-ery-where.*" There was something about the way she said it. I can't explain.

I knew I was supposed to be glad and excited; if I were excited, it would be like praise. She would shake her hair and bask. But I didn't believe her. He didn't look rich. Something about the way he rubbed his hands on his pants when he stood up.

"You know what this all means, don't you?"

"No."

My mother sighed, dragging her spoon in her coffee. "Boy, can you be dumb sometimes."

I was quiet, knowing I could be. I looked up at the sky and understood, without exactly thinking, that it was late on a school night again, eleven or twelve o'clock, and that I hadn't done my homework and I wouldn't do it. That tomorrow would be like other days, the hall of my school with old wooden doors, closing and closing, me coming up the stairs, alone and late. The sky was a dark blue, through the branches of the trees. The stars seemed very dim.

"You're going to make it, kiddo. Why do you think he came up to us?" My mother's voice curved; it was like a hook. She was scolding to get me back.

"He liked you, I suppose." I hated saying that. Her face lit up from her eyes.

"You think so?"

"I don know."

"Did you really think he liked me? Tell me, Ann."

"I guess."

"Well, he's going to put you on television." My mother clapped. From a lifetime of working with children, all my mother's emotions expressed themselves in claps.

"He's not an agent." I said that, but I could feel the beginning of something in her insistent, lilting voice. She worked with that voice, as hard as if she were building something both of us could see.

Sometimes, I felt my mother climbing up a long, long series of stairs, above what seemed true—my school, the hum of electric clocks behind closed wooden doors, my steps, late, the messy locker, my books, heavy and unlooked at, and I followed her up to the clear air. At the top, there was a sky, but when she pushed at it, it broke like so many sheets of colored tissue paper. She began to climb to the other side. I stood still below, next to her legs, but I could see air, feel the wind, from the other side.

"Oh, come on. Didn't you hear the way he said, he has a *friend* whose daughter is on TV? What do you think that meant? He was just testing you. That was his way of asking, do you really, really want it? You know, a lot of kids *say* they want to be on television, sure, but then when it comes right down to it, they don't have the commitment. Not really. We're different. We really do have it. This man's not the agent, but I'll bet his friend is, the one he was sitting with. I'll bet *he's* the agent and this Tishman's the producer. We'll just have to wait and see, but he has our number. I'll bet you land a TV show. And now it's all in the offing."

"When?"

I pulled closer to her and waited. She didn't have to build anymore or fight: we were there. Now, she could be slow. I needed every word. I moved close and watched her face, attentive, like a person holding a bowl, trying to catch single drops of rain.

She tilted her head for a moment, thinking. Her cheekbones seemed high, she looked thin, as if the bones in her face were very frail. When I was little, I'd once held a velvet-lined box with a glass cover, a perfect bird skeleton laid out inside. My grandmother had lifted the lid with her fingernail.

"I would say soon. Very soon."

It was all different now, where we were. I didn't snap or mope or sulk. I sat at the edge of my chair, leaning across the table to be near her. She was distracted, aloof—sure of me.

The night had the same blue perfect air as the inside of a bubble. I felt elated to touch the marble of the table under my hand. I slept that night easily, thoroughly pleased, the knowledge dissolving in me.

Lonnie Tishman called the next day. I answered the phone. I recognized his voice and for a moment I believed it was the call that would deliver me. A sound stage. Cameras. A voice would say, You have been chosen. You. But he just asked, "Your mom around?"

Then the usual came back. Brown doubts and suspicion. The wooden backs of doors.

"It's for you." I shoved the receiver away.

My mother, three feet to the left on the carpet, stood still in her tracks for a full minute. Then she walked the four steps to the night table, breathed in and picked up the phone. The mattress jiggled as she squirmed. She changed her legs, from the left to the right, on top. She laughed, but I could hear she was puzzled. She was trying, with her pauses and tones, to weld whatever he was saying into the shape of a normal date.

"Well, okay, I suppose. But actually, I don't cook very well." With one hand, she redistributed bobby pins in her hair. Her mouth was working. "Oh. Oh. Well, really, it's our kitchen. To tell the truth, I think I'd just as soon go out." This—a more aggressive statement than she liked to make to a man, especially at the beginning—was followed by an avalanche of helpless giggles. "Okay," she said, finally, bouncing her shoe off her toe. "We can do that."

She stood and clapped after she hung up the phone. "What do you know, Ann! We've got a date this Sunday night."

I stayed on the bed, doing nothing.

"Hey, Little Miss, you better paste a smile on that face, because this could just be your big break."

"Oh yeah. How's your date going to be my big break?"

She stuttered a second. Even speech therapists stutter. "He probably wants to check me out first and see if I'll really let you do all this. You know, a lot of mothers wouldn't cart their kids around to rehearsals and tryouts and to the studios. But I will. I really will. And that's probably what he wants to know."

We both got haircuts. My mother only let me get a trim, half an inch of split ends, so I was finished a long time before she was. I sat under the turned-off dryer and leafed through old movie magazines. I studied the dotted pictures of dark men. I thought it was possible I'd see a picture of my father.

"So this man wants to hide it," my mother said, to the woman teasing her hair. At the same time, she watched her curls fall around her face in the mirror. She tilted her head to the left. My mother held her face like a jewel, always moving a little to glance off another facet of light. "He doesn't want to know."

"Could be," the hairdresser said. "There's supposed to be one Tishman brother left and they say he's a little nuts."

"This is the man. I know it."

By the time we left, it was raining outside. My mother took my magazine and tented it over her head as we ran to the car.

"These people play down their money. Because they want you to like them for *them*. Lots of people are probably after him for his money. Sure. And this is his way of testing us." She nodded, preoccupied, as she warmed up the car. "Mmhmm. See, at first, I was upset, because he didn't want to go out to eat, and then when I kind of suggested it, you know, he wanted this Love's Bar-b-que, a really cheap place. No atmosphere or anything. Here, I thought, well, with all his money, he can take me somewhere a little better. But I can see now that he wants to find out if we really like him for *him*."

Again, the car screeched going down into the garage. "After all, we met him in the Beverly Hills Will Wright's. And anybody in there is somebody."

"What about us?" I said.

She shrugged. "You're right."

Sunday was the date. It was all we did. We woke up early, at six, when the alarm clock rang, for once. We cleaned, then shopped. We bought candy to put out in a bowl and things he could drink if he wanted to. In the afternoon, I sat on the bed, watching my mother dress. She'd already taken her bath. She moved around the small floor space in her bra and pantyhose, running from the closet back to the bathroom mirror.

I picked up a book to read, but every two minutes she interrupted, and I was glad to quit again. This was fun.

"Ann-honey, tell me something. Which way, up or down, what do you think? The hair, come on, concentrate a second. Down? Are you sure? Why?"

"Makes your neck look longer."

"It does, good. Are you sure?"

It occurred to me that my mother had never been alone. At home, she'd had Lolly, probably even before I was born. Lolly had always been there, bigger, quiet, sitting on the edge of some bed, watching my mother become shinier and shinier, enclosing more and more light in her body on a dull, late Saturday afternoon, getting ready to give herself, brilliant, to one man. For the first time ever, I felt sorry for Lolly. I remembered her scratchy plaid Bermuda shorts, her head bent, looking down at her big hands. At least I was younger. I could still be pretty myself someday.

I was asleep when they came home that night, but I heard the key work in the door and Lonnie's loud, raucous voice and her hushing him. And then I heard her giggles. That was the worst thing. I was awake then and I waited for it to stop. I wanted him to leave, so it would be quiet again. But he didn't. He never did. For the first time in that apartment, my mother didn't sleep with me in the bed. They opened the sofa; I heard the metal mattress frame scraping the floor.

"Shhh, you'll wake her."

"I forget you've got a child in here."

We'd never opened the sofa bed before. It must have been a dusty mess. The dark green vinyl sofa was a problem. At Christmas, we'd tried to drape it with a bolt of green felt, but it had looked wrong and you couldn't sit on it. We'd finally settled for cleaning it and draping a red mohair afghan over the back.

My mother stood a foot away from me, lifting sheets out of the closet. I held absolutely still. As a child, I'd dreamed of burglars coming in at night from the train. In the dream, I'd have to be still. Later, the burglar lined us up in the cellar. He was stealing our television and my mother blamed it on me. The burglar pointed a rifle at us and Benny saved everything by putting his finger in the hole at the end of the gun.

They must have been making the bed. It sounded like they dropped twenty shoes and tripped over each other each time. It seemed it would never be quiet.

"Shhh," my mother said and then giggled.

"Hell, I thought you said she was asleep."

"Well, she is, but she's a light sleeper."

Another shoe dropped. For what seemed like hours, layers and layers of time, I thought I heard something; the sheets moving, the metal of the bed. The sound of his mouth-breathing changed the whole air. I didn't want to close my eyes.

But I must have finally fallen asleep in the morning, because I missed the alarm. I put my hand over the buzzing clock, to stop the noise, but I didn't reset it. My mother woke up on her own and came and sat next to me on the bed. She moved her hand on the blanket, over my back.

"Get up, Honey. It's time to get ready for school. Upseedaisey. Really, Honey. It's time now."

"Is he still here?"

"He's sleeping."

I pulled the covers and bedspread around me, and walked into the closet. I put my jeans and T-shirt on there. My mother stepped in and grabbed my arm. There wasn't room for two. Our closet was small and full, with clothes on hangers and linens on the shelves.

"Ann, I didn't sleep with him," she whispered. "I mean, I slept with him, but I didn't. He didn't touch me, we just slept. I swear to God, Ann, that's all we did." She lifted her palm up like a child, scout's honor.

"I don't care what you did." I walked around him to the bathroom. There was almost nowhere to walk. Opened up, the sofa bed took the whole room.

My mother followed me to the sink. "Well, I care. And I didn't."

We were alone in the apartment, making my bed. My mother shook a pillow down into the pillowcase. We'd driven to a laundromat in Pacific Palisades. Of course, there were closer laundromats, but my mother had found this one and it was clean and there was a health food snack bar next door. The main thing was my mother didn't want to be seen in a laundromat. In Pacific Palisades, it was okay. We didn't know anybody there. And now that I had friends at school, I felt the same way. I didn't want them to see me doing wash. When we finished my bed, my mother opened the sofa and put sheets on. I didn't help her with that and she didn't ask me.

"The tingling is over. What can I say? That real excitement, the fantasizing—I just don't feel it anymore. So, let's just hope some money comes in on one of his deals so we get a little something. And soon."

Lonnie slept here every night now. We no longer pretended Lonnie was an agent or a producer. Now, it was supposed to be enough that he might have money and give us some, to help us out. And it was enough. We adjusted.

"What about all these buildings that say TISHMAN on the scaffolding? I saw another one today on the way to school. On Roxbury."

She sighed. "Could you come and help me here a second? Just tuck the other side." The sofa bed felt flimsy, metal springs and a three-inch mattress. Sometimes in the night I heard a crash when the metal legs buckled and collapsed. "This man wants to make it on his own. He doesn't want to just be the son of someone who made it big. But I think if one of his deals comes through, if this shopping center makes it, *then* he'll go back to his family and say, See, this is what I could do, alone."

"Are you sure it's even the same family? There're a lot of Tishmans in the phone book."

"Honey, I'm sure."

"How do you know? Did he tell you?"

"Ann, I just know. Okay? You just have to learn that I know some things you don't. Okay? I'm a grown-up."

"At least he could pay rent."

"Honey, he does pay rent. He pays rent on his own apartment in Hollywood."

We'd seen his building. It was dark red brick, old, set far away from the street. Once, after dinner, my mother had stopped there, outside his building, so he could run in and get clean clothes. While we were waiting for him in the car she pressed the button that locked our doors.

"He's never in it."

"Well, let's just cross our fingers and hope it comes through soon, okay, Honey? Because I need it too. Believe me. Believe me, I'm getting tired."

I dropped it.

I developed sores on my head; small red bumps with scabs. My mother thought it was either lice or some weird disease. She decided

I'd caught it from Lonnie. She called and made an appointment with a doctor in the Valley, an hour's drive away.

"You never know, people talk. Word gets around. Beverly Hills is really a very small community. And it's not the nicest thing to have, you know." My mother always worried that people would think we were unclean.

After school, we drove to the Valley. Sometimes, I really liked my mother. She drove easily, with one hand, as she pumped the gas with the toe of her high-heeled shoe. We looped on the freeway ramps smoothly. She talked to me and drove almost unconsciously on the six-lane highway with a freedom and confidence anyone at home in Bay City would have admired if they could have seen her. I remembered our first day in Los Angeles, how she'd clutched her whole body an inch away from the steering wheel. Her voice, when she told me to turn off the radio, fell stern and quiet. She'd been afraid for our lives. She'd driven on the right-hand side, almost on the gravel by the high aluminum fence. Her lips had moved and I thought she might have been praying. Now, she changed lanes and told me to look at the sun, just over a Coke sign on a dry hill. There were things to be proud of my mother for. I doubt she ever thought about it, how she'd learned to drive here.

She knew the Valley; she drove out to work every day. I didn't know much about her life without me. And my mother seemed shy and a little ashamed of what she did all day. Driving to the doctor, I asked her what she'd done at school. "Oh, nothing. You know. Just the usual," she said.

I imagined her in a room, plants on the windowsill, with tall boys and fat sloppy girls. With her they would all be timid. I imagined her standing close to them, holding their faces by the chin and looking in their eyes while she said the word. "Say thick. Th-th-th-thick." Their mouths wobbled crumbled sounds, trying to copy her lips.

We were speeding, my window cracked open, the sun a fuzzy line over the brown hills.

"There's my exit," she said, real joy in her voice, as if she were showing me the building where she worked.

The doctor didn't seem horrified by my head. My mother and I always felt calmed by doctors. They made us feel clean, like everyone else. He diagnosed the bumps as scabies, said I could have picked them up anywhere, probably in school, and matter-of-factly wrote out a prescription for Quell Lotion. He told us to wash my hair every day for eight days and put on the pink lotion afterwards. My mother nodded while he explained this, as if she were receiving critical and difficult instructions. That was all. He let us go. We bought the lotion downstairs in the pharmacy and then went for an early supper at the Van Nuys Hamburger Hamlet. We ordered big dinners and we each had dessert. It felt good to be alone, just the two of us.

We could have gone home after that and I could have washed my hair in our shower, but my mother panicked over anything having to do with uncleanliness, and when she panicked, spending money made her feel better, so she took me to her hairdresser. The hairdresser washed and blow-dried my hair so it looked thick and good, and then we had to ruin it, rubbing in the lotion, which made it greasy and rumpled.

"Ever hear from that Tishman fellow?" the hairdresser asked my mother.

"Mmmhmm, sometimes."

The next day she took me to a different beauty parlor.

After my last treatment, it was almost dark when we left the beauty shop. We drove to our apartment to pick up Lonnie, and then we drove farther out into the Valley than I'd ever been. We didn't have time for dinner because we were late. Lonnie had an appointment to meet someone for a business deal. He was supposed to be building a shopping center.

My mother drove and Lonnie sat in the front seat creating a chain reaction, hitting one hand on the other hand, which, in turn hit his knee. My mother let him play the radio while she drove. I was sitting up against the back door with a book open, trying to do my homework. I was trying to improve my life, do what I was supposed to do. My efforts to make myself better never went anywhere. I didn't really believe they would.

The land changed outside our car windows. It was brown and flat, the hills seemed lower, and buildings were small and scarce. It reminded me of little towns in the desert when we drove into California. We stopped at a light and a man in a cowboy hat crossed the road. There were no sidewalks, just highway and gravel on the sides. There were more trucks than cars on the road with us. Gray-brown tumbleweed dotted the hills above the shopping center, where my mother finally slowed the car.

There was a McDonald's in the shopping mall and Lonnie told my mother and me we should wait for him there. When we all got out of the car, he walked in the other direction, towards a bar, where he was supposed to meet his partner. He walked away, rubbing his hands on the front of his pants. We stood on the blacktop and my mother seemed distracted until she said, "Wait here a second, stay right here," and ran up to Lonnie, her purse hitting the side of her thigh as she ran. They weren't far away. "She can wait in the car. She'll study. Are you sure I shouldn't come along?"

I stood still, growing cold up from my feet.

"Hey, hey, comemeer a second, Woman. Let me give you a kiss before I go."

They stood there in the middle of the parking lot like two movie stars, her hair falling over her back and her stockinged heels rising up out of her shoes.

I looked the other way, at the window of a closed knitting store. I felt like I was nothing and I never would be. Then my mother came running back. She slapped her thigh when she stopped. "Come on. Let's hurry it up."

We sat against the inside glass wall of the McDonald's. There was a field on the other side of the highway, except for one gas station, nothing. My mother sipped coffee from a coated paper cup. We thought if we were going to sit here, we'd better buy something and we didn't want to spoil our appetites. My mother pointed on the glass.

"See, over there. That's where they're going to put the shopping center."

"Why?"

"What do you mean, why? So we can make some money, that's why. And buy a house, maybe. So I don't have to run myself ragged—"

"I mean, why there?"

"Oh, I don't know. They know where the best places are. This man is *the* expert on shopping centers. He's already made millions."

The sides of the highway were marked with glowing red circles on three-foot wooden stakes. It was just brown field on the other side, nothing, land that could have been anywhere. I didn't believe it. I couldn't believe Lonnie being in a bar down the mall with some guy would make a shopping center grow there.

I thought of something I hadn't remembered for a long time: the city I'd drawn under my grandmother's kitchen table with crayons. I'd planned houses and swimming pools, buses. I could easily draw for hours, working on one thing for my city. Now I looked outside and imagined the colored structures I'd drawn, huge and built, on the field across the street.

"But there's one already, across the highway. This one."

She sighed, tired and preoccupied. "I don't know, Honey. I'm not the expert. They are."

"What kind of people have business meetings at night, in the middle of nowhere, anyway?"

She didn't get mad. "Shhh, Honey. Just be quiet a minute. I've been working all day and I'm tired." She put her purse up on the plastic table top and unclasped it. "Here," she said, handing me a dollar. "Go get us french fries. But just a small because we don't want to spoil our appetites. If this meeting goes well, he'll take us out somewhere nice. We'll get you a good steak. Really, Honey."

We were still eating the french fries, not talking, when Lonnie came in, rubbing his palms on the front of his pants.

"Hiya," he said to my mother. He did that a lot, acted as if he was with just one person instead of two. He was wearing the same thing he wore every day. A velour pullover and a blue zip-up vinyl jacket.

I looked out the window at the dull field across the highway. Businessmen didn't look like this. Neither did millionaires.

Lonnie was nuzzling his flecked chin against my mother's neck. She hummed "mmmmm" with a noise that sounded vaguely electric.

"So, how's about a little supper?" he said.

"Okay. What do you feel like? Should we stay somewhere around here or head back towards home?" Then, she winked at me from over his shoulder.

"How's about here? I'd take a Big Mac and fries, how 'bout it. How 'bout it, Ann? Hamburger?"

"All right," my mother said, sliding back down onto the plastic chair.

There was an apology in her eyes as she turned and held her face in both hands, but she never would have said anything in front of Lonnie.

"Let's get it to go," Lonnie said, fidgeting at the counter.

My mother's car had changed. She never would have let me bring McDonald's into the cream-colored leather interior. But she let Lonnie. We ate on the way home, my mother asking me to hold her milkshake for her on the freeway.

"So what was the gist?" she was saying in the front seat. I had the ashtray in the back lifted and I was trying to read my homework by that little light.

"That's one proud man, I'll tell you," Lonnie said. He lowered his window so a whistle of air came in and he rested his elbow on the glass.

"So, do you think it'll go or not so much?"

"Hey," Lonnie said, beating his hand on his chest so the windbreaker made a rattling noise. My mother was driving, I held her milkshake, Lonnie's hands were free. "What kind of guy do you think I am, anyway? Course it'll go."

"Ann, you can hand me my malt now. Thank you."

I had my book propped as close to the ashtray as it would go. It stayed steady there as long as the car went straight on the freeway. I didn't look up until the book fell.

"This isn't our exit, Mom." We were past Beverly Hills. The streets where we were driving looked dark and unfamiliar.

"We're going to stop at Lonnie's apartment for a second."

Yellow lights shone from his building. My mother and I stayed in the car while he ran out to get a change of clothes. His apartment building looked very old. We had buildings like that in Wisconsin, the orphanage and paper mills along the river. Dark brick buildings, small windows, built in the last century.

"So what happened to our nice dinner?"

She turned the heat on. The doors were locked and the motor was still running. "Honey, I'm trying to get rid of him, too. Don't you think I'm scared? But let me do it slowly. I know how to manage this man."

Someone walked by on the sidewalk, a kid. My mother stiffened, clutching the wheel, watching him all the way away in the rearview mirror.

"I don't even like him anymore, believe me," she whispered. "I think he's on drugs. But he could hurt us, Ann. He's in with people who could really hurt us. Do you know what the Mafia is?"

"Some kind of straw?"

"No, no, that's raffia. Like we had at your birthday party the year with the piñata. That was fun, wasn't it?"

"I don know what it is then." The trees here scared me. Otherwise I would have lied. I didn't like admitting things I didn't know.

"Well, it's gangsters. Awful, awful people. Criminals, but whole gangs together. All over the country. They kill, they cheat, anything. And I think he's part of that. I'm worried for my life. And your life. This other man he met tonight could kill me."

Lonnie started across the lawn, holding his bag in front of him with both arms.

"What about the police?"

"The police can't stop them. Nothing can. So just let me take care of it, okay?"

I didn't say anything, I was too scared. When he came back into the car, with a wash of cold air and the sinister click of the locks after him, it was almost a relief. He was just Lonnie. He'd brought his clothes in a brown paper shopping bag, a white shirt on the top.

In bed that night, trying to sleep, I couldn't get warm. I thought of the shapes of my crayoned drawings, built, on a field of dull grass. I was scared to be in the same room with Lonnie.

We'd driven by Century City on the way home; a few floors stayed lit in the tall buildings. I thought that in offices there, in rooms with typewriters and metal desks, shopping centers were being planned. I believed and I didn't believe my mother. I was beginning to distrust her promises but I still believed her threats. I believed Lonnie was a criminal.

I barely slept that night. And in the morning, I got up when the alarm rang. Light was coming in through our faded Christmas green felt curtains, making delicate lacy patterns over the apartment. My mother and Lonnie were asleep in the middle of the room. Nothing looked so dangerous anymore. I bent down and shook my mother. For once, I wanted us all to be up on time.

"Why don't you get up already so we can eat some breakfast for a change."

"Shhh. He's sleeping. Five more minutes. Please, Hon."

"Fine, I don't care what you do." She turned over and pulled the blanket to her eye.

I took a shower and dressed. Then my mother got up. She stood by the bed, wearing nothing but Lonnie's T-shirt.

"You know, you're not the only person in the world," she said.

"So." I was buckling my shoes. I picked up my books. "I'm leaving."

"Just hold your horses. You have time. I'll be ready in a second. Sit down."

Lonnie was awake now, too. He looked tiny in his white jockey shorts, the leg holes stretched and bagging. He held his slacks out delicately as if he might trip stepping into them. His hair was a mess.

"I'm leaving," I said again.

"Just wait." My mother was yelling. "You'd think SHE's the only person in the world."

"I don't always have to wait for you just because you don't want to get up on time and eat breakfast and live like a normal person. I'm always waiting for you." I guess I was screaming, then.

"Oh, you, you—" My mother came at me, tripping over the huge sofa bed between us. She tripped and hit her knee, which made her madder. "I work, I slave, I run myself ragged, so SHE can live in Beverly Hills, so SHE can be a movie star, and what do I get? What do I get for thanks? A whole lot of guff from a stinky mouth."

"Who's a movie star," Lonnie said, one leg in his pants, one not.

"Thanks a lot."

"Hey." Lonnie lifted his hand in a grand gesture intended to silence us both. He looked at me, his face slack. "Your mother is a lovely woman," he said, his chin weaving slowly left and right, "you ought to treat her with respect."

My mother was still wearing nothing but the T-shirt, standing with her hands on her hips.

"I'm leaving."

Lonnie staggered up onto the bed, so he stood there, with his pants unzipped. "Hey," he said, loudly, raising his hand again. "Everyone quiet."

He didn't have a chance. Neither of us paid any attention.

"Oh, ohh, you lit-t—"

I was almost to the door when Lonnie jumped down and caught my arm, hard, twisting the skin. "Hey. Listen. I don't want to see you upset your mother like this." He looked back at her, she sat on the bed, crying now.

I twisted away. "Get your hands off me. Don't touch me. I'm leaving and I'm not coming back."

"You go ahead, you should. Go on and get lost. You don't deserve your mother. She's a lovely woman and you're nothing."

"Fuck you!"

My mother followed me to the door but I was already outside, down the sidewalk. She stepped for a moment onto the landing, wearing just the T-shirt, the toes of one foot on the other, shyly, shouting my name.

I kept walking. I heard the door slam and then I heard her shrill voice and Lonnie's low bellow. But they diminished as I walked, replaced by the small sounds of birds, slow tires, the first hammers on a construction site a few blocks away. The air felt kind, mild, windy as it touched my skin. I checked each of my pockets. I had everything I needed for a day. My hair was clean, just now beginning to lift a little as it dried, I had my books, money in my pocket. For once I had left early for school. The clean fronts of apartment houses, cars on the streets, the fountain at the corner of Wilshire and Little Santa Monica, all seemed indifferent and kind.

I'd been taught all my life or I knew somehow, I wasn't sure which, that you couldn't trust the kind faces of things, that the world was painted and behind the thin bright surface was darkness and the only place I was safe was home with my mother. But it seemed safer outside now, safer with indifference than care.

I decided I could go to Nibbler's. I had money, I had time. I could eat breakfast and then go to school. But my mother and the apartment had something on their side, a card to play against the bright, moving air: night. I had nowhere to go.

I kept walking. The air was cool on my skin, a leaf dropped on me—it tingled, the serrated sharpness of its edge like a scratch, then softness, a belly. I turned around. I kept expecting someone to stop me. But no one did and so I kept walking, now afraid to look back at the apartment.

Then I came to the street Nibbler's was on; it seemed large, a decision. I turned. Now if my mother or Lonnie left the apartment, I would be out of sight, gone. I was halfway there when I heard a car behind me that sounded like my mother's. I didn't have the nerve to turn around, because it seemed like something I'd made up, but I bit my lip and stood still. The tires sounded like ours. Then a Mustang pulled in front of me, forest green. My heart fell several inches lower.

I started walking again. I could hardly believe this was me. The noise of Wilshire Boulevard came closer. The day seemed to start in many places, like gears catching and moving, a huge machine. Beverly Hills was a city all of a sudden and I had six dollars and some change. I walked past the glass reflecting door of Nibbler's and stopped at Wilshire Boulevard in front of a purse shop. Then, somewhere behind me a car skidded and I heard heels and my mother was there, grabbing my arm, her fingernails biting my skin.

"Annie, Honey." She hugged me, her rib cage heaving, I felt her breasts move through her blouse. I just stood there and didn't say anything and then it was back to normal. "Let's go and park the car right and we'll have some breakfast at Nibbler's. He's gone, Honey. He's all packed. I told him he had to get out and he's gone. So it's just us again, thank God. I told him when he yelled at you like that, that was the end. No one, not anyone, can get between us." My mother's face seemed shallow and concave, like the inside of a pan.

"I'm hungry," I said. I started walking fast. Now I was thinking of time again, of not being late for school.

"Well, okay, wait a minute." She grabbed my arm. "We have to go a little slower. It's these damn heels." She lifted one foot and pushed something with her hand.

I felt the money in my pockets, the soft paper of the dollars. The buildings were just buildings again, what they seemed, familiar. The city looked beautiful and strong now, bright and silver, like a perfect train, drizzling light off its wheels as it moved. We could hear the fountain splashing behind our backs.

Lonnie was gone and we ate a big breakfast and I still had my money.

She paid.

Gary Snyder

The inspiration for the character of Japhy Ryder in Jack Kerouac's 1958 novel *The Dharma Bums*, Gary Snyder (b. 1930) has been a Zen Buddhist adept, a naturalist and environmental activist, a collector of indigenous native folk tales, and the Pulitzer Prize–winning author of sixteen volumes of poetry and prose. On April 8, 1956 (Buddha's birthday), Snyder began a long poem called *Mountains and Rivers Without End*, which he has described as "a sort of sutra—an extended poetic, philosophic, and mythic narrative" of North America; it was completed in 1996. "Night Song of the Los Angeles Basin," a section of that work, offers a sense of how nature and civilization encroach upon each other, a recurring theme in both Snyder's work and the literature of Los Angeles.

NIGHT SONG OF THE LOS ANGELES BASIN

Owl
calls,
pollen dust blows
Swirl of light strokes writhing
knot-tying light paths,

calligraphy of cars.

Los Angeles basin and hill slopes
Checkered with streetways. Floral loops
Of the freeway express and exchange.

Dragons of light in the dark
sweep going both ways
in the night city belly.
The passage of light end to end and rebound,
—ride drivers all heading somewhere—
etch in their traces to night's eye-mind

       calligraphy of cars.

Vole paths. Mouse trails worn in
On meadow grass;
Winding pocket-gopher tunnels,
Marmot lookout rocks.
Houses with green watered gardens
Slip under the ghost of the dry chaparral,

       Ghost
       shrine to the L.A. River.
       The *jinja* that never was there
       is there.
       Where the river debouches
       the place of the moment
       of trembling and gathering and giving
       so that lizards clap hands there
       —just lizards
       come pray, saying
       "please give us health and long life."

       A hawk,
       a mouse.

Slash of calligraphy of freeways of cars.

       Into the pools of the channelized river
       the Goddess in tall rain dress
       tosses a handful of meal.

       Gold bellies roil
       mouth-bubbles, frenzy of feeding,
       the common ones, the bright-colored rare ones
       show up, they tangle and tumble,

godlings ride by in Rolls Royce
wide-eyed in brokers' halls
lifted in hotels
being presented to, platters
of tidbit and wine,
snatch of fame,

churn and roil,

meal gone   the water subsides.

A mouse,
a hawk.

The calligraphy of lights on the night
freeways of Los Angeles

will long be remembered.

Owl
calls;
late-rising moon.

Carolyn See

Each of the city's neighborhoods—Echo Park, Hollywood Hills, West-wood, Topanga Canyon—has a distinct identity, and as you drive through town you can feel the changes. Carolyn See (b. 1934) expertly evokes that sensation in this excerpt from *Golden Days* (1987), a novel that culminates in a nuclear apocalypse. Born and raised in Los Angeles, See is the author of many books of fiction and nonfiction, including *Rhine Maidens* (1981), *Making History* (1991), and the family memoir *Dreaming: Hard Luck and Good Times in America* (1995). Of the city of her birth, she writes: "Los Angeles doesn't make raincoats and soup, it makes things like movies and bombs, which are good and bad dreams. It's the perfect place to write from."

from

GOLDEN DAYS

April–November 1980

Once, I remember, in an entirely different world, I interviewed that East Coast photographer who made a good living taking pictures of people as they jumped. He asked if he could take a picture of me, and I jumped! I put everything into it! I took a look outside of his white studio into the grimy New York streets below; I thought of how I'd jumped from a ratty house with a tired mom, past two husbands, one sad, one mad; hopscotched with kids and lovers and ended up—here? In *New York!* I sized up the directions of the room, tried to find east. I started out from there, ran a maximum of ten heavy steps, and jumped—not far, not far enough by a long shot—and came down hard.

The photographer winced. "Try it again," he said.

So I went back to the far corner, ran, defied gravity, jumped. This time I held up my arms, held up my chin, grinned. His camera clicked. "That's it."

"*That's it?*"

"You only have one jump in you," he said. (I found out later he said it to everybody.)

That wasn't fair. But maybe it was right. I began to notice—
I date it from that day, not that it was new material—most of us
have just one story in us; we live it and breathe it and think it and go
to it and from it and dance with it; we lie down with it, love it, hate
it, and that's our story.

About that time I noticed something else: There was a ratio involved here. Just as those poor woolly headed American nigras
only got seven-tenths of the vote (after the Civil War, if and when
they *got* the vote—I can't really remember), so, too, there was a
basic inequality in the country I grew up in and lived in. One man,
one story. For women, it generally took two or even three to make
one story. So that in shopping malls you sometimes saw two fat
women waddling along, casting sidelong glances at one another's
fat. Or two pretty girls outprettying each other. Two femmes fatales,
eyeing each other's seductions.

This is partly the story of Lorna Villanelle and me; two ladies
absolutely crazed with the secret thought that they were something
special. But if you think you aren't going to care about this story,
hold on. It's the most important story in the Western world!

Believe me.

Take this for a story. It's four in the afternoon: 1950 something.
A chunky thirteen-year-old walks home after school, kicking at
leaves with heavy shoes, up the buckling sidewalks of Micheltorena
Hill, in the parched and arid heart of Los Angeles. She dawdles, she
doesn't want to get there. Her father's gone, there's no joy here, or
ever, maybe. At 3:45 she drifts down through a small "Spanish"
patio and into a house that perches precariously on the side of this
hill—crackling with dried and golden rye grass—bangs the door,
clumps down the tiled hall to the sunken living room, where she
sees her mother crying. Her mother looks up, twists her tear-stained
linen handkerchief, and says, with all the vindictiveness a truly
heartbroken woman can muster, *"Must you always be so heavy?"*

The thirteen-year-old, her face flushed from the sun, the walk,
and pure shame, walks on tiptoe without speaking, past her mother
to the picture window, which faces diagonally west. She doesn't
think to look below, to the patio perfect for parties they'll never
give, but only *out*, out to the horizon where, past twenty miles of

miniature city, the ocean—thin strip—catches the afternoon sun, and blazes. Ah!

"*Don't* put your head on the window!" her mother snaps, and the girl lurches back as if the window burned, but her forehead mark, brain fingerprint, remains.

After the day of the clumsy jump I realized I wasn't built to live in New York. It was the greatest city in the world, but I couldn't get on its pretty side. I'll go further and say that after several short trips to Paris, Madrid, Rome, I realized that I'd been going in the wrong direction; the further east you got the further back in you were. By now I could look at my life as a series of sterling wrong choices: a marriage to an exquisitely handsome artist that had yielded up nothing more than a princess of a daughter, beautiful as the dawn —hence her fancy name, Aurora—and another marriage to an Australian on the make, who'd seen me as a meal ticket (poor deluded mate!), and that marriage had given me an emerald tomboy. Her dad, Dirk Langley (his name eventually to be spelled—incorrectly —on theater marquees in both hemispheres), wanted to call our baby "Denny," but I'd insisted on the sleepy and elegant French, Denise. . . . I'd majored in the wrong things in college, lived precariously in Manhattan's wrong sections. Now I wanted, so much, more than I can say, to get out.

And so, at the age of thirty-eight, I came back to L.A., I came back. I would live a gentle mimicry of my mother's story, alone with my two girls. I planned to earn my own money, and never to cry, and never to lay about with the cruel weapons of spite. I would take accounting courses. I would become a person who knew about riches, so that when people heard my name (when I became famous) they wouldn't hear "Edith Langley," who made two bad marriages and had to make her own way (or even, isn't she the *heavy* one who made the house shake when she came home from school?), but Edith Langley, whose name meant money, and money meant power.

Los Angeles, in 1980, was a different city from the one I'd left. I drove far out, to Santa Monica, found a bad motel, with two double beds and a television that worked. Then, after a day or two, I put

Aurora and Denise in the back seat of the old Porsche and went house hunting.

I drove with the kids one dreadful morning into the San Fernando Valley and felt that if there had to be a nuclear war, certainly it might do some good in this area. I drove through Topanga Canyon, fifteen miles from the Valley to the coast (like Switzerland after the A-bomb, some friend of mine had said years before), hands sweating on the steering wheel as I took the curves, and had to think that maybe I wasn't ready for the Canyon; maybe I just didn't have the nerve. I braked at the Pacific, knowing that Malibu was north and no way could I afford it yet. I turned south, looking for Venice . . . and headed—like a gerbil in a cage—back downtown.

They say L.A. is large, but they lie. It's true there are a zillion places no one in his right mind would like: Lakewood, Torrance, Brea, Compton, Carson, no one *real* lived there, any more than real people lived in those grey asphalt boxes that line the roads between New York's airport and its island. "Real" L.A. had its thick, coiled root downtown, and on the east, little underground rootlets; obscure Mexican restaurants. Then a thin stem, the Santa Monica freeway, heading due west and putting out greenery, places in this western desert where you'd love to live—if things went right.

I headed west again: Echo Park, old houses, fine artists in them. I didn't like the neighborhood; it was too close to where I'd started. Further west and to the right, the Hollywood Hills with the sign and all, and Aldous Huxley's widow tucked in just below the *H*. The *air* was still too thick for me. Sixty miles an hour and ten minutes later, there was Westwood to look at. A pretty town, safe, and rich, and if the kids wanted to go to UCLA, perfect for them. But the rents started at $800.

Hard to please? Got it from my mom. A charmer? Well, three lone souls out of four million might agree. I wanted the beach, so bad. I got back on the stem, ever closer to the great Pacific. So! North along the coast again, just for the ride, and something made me turn in again at steep, sparsely populated Topanga Canyon.

It was late in the day, maybe four o'clock, on an April afternoon. I'd driven through eastern sleet to get here, and "unseasonal" snow in the Rockies, and heat like a flat plate in the High Desert. But here, it was . . . perfect. April is the time for ceanothus in the

Canyon and great banks of bright blue I'd find out later were lupin. There was even, if you can believe it, a waterfall, a long silver string dropping casually off a high stone abutment. The trip inland started out shallow, against low hills. After a half-dozen tricky twists and turns we hit a half-mile straightaway, starting at the bottom of what seemed (that first time) like a thousand-foot-high cliff, and climbed steadily, hugging the northwest side of the canyon wall. My hands started sweating, slick on the wheel, and Aurora, my older daughter, lay down in back. "Tell me when it's over," she whispered.

But I've thought many times that, though I'd taken those early curves at a cautious twenty-five miles an hour, I resisted *even then* the temptation to speed up on the straightaway between the coast and the town, that piece of bad driving that forever separates the Canyon from the city dweller.

At the top of that half-mile run (which, I found out later, had to be rebuilt every five years as the rains washed it out) the road curled into three or four really spellbinding curves: How easy, I thought even then, to keep going straight when the road turned left, to arc out into *nothing* for one last carnival ride.

Ten minutes later I drew up, trembling, to a small stone building. We were in mountain country, for sure. Was this what I'd been looking for as I pressed my damp head against my mother's polished picture window? Do you think—*might* I have seen these fragrant cliffs from there?

"I'm going to throw up," Denise, my younger one, said. "I mean it. And I'm hungry!"

We stopped at a place called the Discovery Inn (Innkeeper, Marge Dehr). The inside smelled of dried flowers and old hamburger.

"What do *you* want?"

"Are you the hostess?"

"What if I am?"

"Could we . . ."

I remembered myself: tired, rasping voice, dirt brown hair frizzed out like that black woman's whose name I forget, my first diamonds—three-quarters of a carat (bought at what price!) jammed in my ears, eyeliner, dirt under my nails.

"We need a place to live."

"Don't you think it's a little fucking *late in the day*?"

"I thought . . ." I didn't know what I thought. "I just want to be sure that I get the kids back down before it gets dark . . ."

"The *kids* don't care! Sit down and eat. Order a Swinger. They're the best. Anyway, if you can't get *down* out of here, there's no point in coming *up*."

I couldn't argue with this logic. We ate, then groped our way back down the mountain to our crummy motel room. I watched the girls' faces as they watched television in one double bed; it's clear, or should be, that they were dearer to me than five hundred crates of diamond earrings in five hundred solid gold pick-up trucks.

The next morning we drove back up—those curves almost a snap by now—loving that pure *climb* into the sky and the feeling that once you got up there, in those mountains north of Santa Monica, you were safe; they couldn't get to you. (And later I learned that during Prohibition outlaws from all over California vamoosed to Topanga, because all the overlapping city limits that made up Los Angeles had left one lawless hole.)

In the cool morning air, with theatrical wisps of ground fog drifting up and over the harsh mountains from the Pacific, we rendezvoused at that ratty restaurant. Marge Dehr came slouching out, introduced us to a "realtor" who whisked up in a powder blue Ferrari. He drove us around all through the day, up one dizzying unpaved road after another. On one cliff you might see great grim stretches of that modern midden the San Fernando Valley, and on another rocky outcropping you might climb, creaking, out of that guy's cramped little cockroach of a car, walk ten steps down a dusty incline, and there see a sturdy *blue world*, a blue saddle shoe, light on top—that would be the sky—and on the bottom more dark blue than you could ever imagine in one place, the vast Pacific. Of course the houses with that dizzying prospect, mostly three-story, white stucco, and a million dollars apiece, were a little out of our range. But down in the strange dank hollows and washed-out deltas in the bowl of the canyon itself—an indentation of about five square miles, I'd guess, where clothing stores perched on creek banks and welfare mothers with sunny smiles watched their naked kids slushing in the mud—you could rent a trailer for thirty-five dollars a week.

As we drove, Aurora and Denise, usually impatient or droopy or long-suffering, began to get a dreamy look. The morning lengthened into hot, aromatic midday. "That's dodder, that orange stuff on the bushes," the house tout might say, and in the next breath he'd try out, "Of course a carpet like this is going to be unusual in the Canyon," or "You don't see a chandelier like this every day, up here." We even drove as far back west—down the canyon—to hit the "Gulch," a low, flat, damp place just across the highway from the ocean itself. Down in that low wash fifty people must have dumped their cars where the Topanga Creek seeped into swamp, and yards of trailing morning glories had turned each one of them into a blue mountain.

"D'rather go *up*," Denise said, slapping at mosquitoes.

"I think," I said to them, "I must have been to a party here once, years ago. I'm sure of it . . ."

But the man shrugged impatiently and, zipping us back up the steep slopes back to the dead center of this ever-better world, said, "Think we'll turn left into Old Canyon this time. Some people say this is the *tough* part. Some people say this is the *desert* part. Other people like it. *I* couldn't say." Then, glancing at me shrewdly as his jeweled and tan hands on the wheel expertly took these curves, shrouded on either side by beige stone and nothing else, "*This* road we're on is always the first to go out in winter when the rains come. Have to get out by horse through here. When the fires come, they take you out by helicopter. Most people stay though. Save their houses. Take a few trash cans, fill 'em with water, beat out the flames with rug scraps." Then, jerking his head, "Indians used to fish in the creek here. They used wild cucumber to float their nets . . ."

The house sat out on a wide raw crescent of cut and fill. That half-moon of dirt hung, just hung there in the air, over another one of those astonishing cliffs above nowhere. Across the chasm from what might be our "backyard" were stones the size of skyscrapers. Due east, a wilderness of bougainvillea and eucalyptus, sage, rosemary, mint, and a couple of blazing yellow acacias. We might have been in Australia with just a couple of aborigines for company, but instead we could hear Van Morrison, the Doors, windchimes, barking dogs. We smelled marijuana with the rosemary, and the house tout said, sizing us up, "If this section of the canyon caught fire, the city'd be high for a week. They *say*." And in the next breath talked about the wonderful elementary school.

Two stories, made out of fresh new cedar slats on the outside, California white-sheeted clapboard on the inside (no fireplace, a definite minus in the Canyon, where once every decade or so it had been known to snow great flakes), and all this only forty minutes away from downtown L.A.! There was no yard yet, this was a new place, just golden dust all around. Our neighbors "next door"—a shack a hundred yards up the grade—said later that we'd be living in rattlesnake heaven, but listen! Past where the bulldozers had rousted out those fiendish vipers, the *real* view started!

For years I had a picture of my daughters from that time, standing by a yucca taller than they were. They both had that dreamy look, the kind that used to make people in the city say that everybody up here was on drugs, but what it meant was that they were happy.

I'm not saying it was easy! God forbid. Do you think it's easy for a single mother who has "financial consultant" printed on her business cards to get credit in the greater Los Angeles area? My husbands found out I was back and put in some mean-spirited phone calls, the more so because I suggested they might like to kick in a little child support. And sweet spring rapidly turned into a summer so outrageously *fucking hot* that by some paradox it turned the inside of our new house a luminous black. We'd already found that the lady in the restaurant owned this rickety house and paid Mr. Slicko in his ill-gotten car something like a thirty percent commission to get it off her hands.

There came a day in early September, down in the old market at the Center of the Canyon, where, barefoot, I stood in line, holding my brown rice and hamburger, dreaming New York dreams, thinking, Oh, God, *another* wrong turn? I'd already gained maybe thirty pounds from smoking the days away with those guys next door and then putting together vast casseroles liberally seasoned with all that indigenous fragrant stuff. I stood in the dark store, sweating, fretting as always, that half my life was over but really, all my life was over, I'd *had* it, when over by the antique gumball machine that stood by the rusting screen door—pushed out over many years by how many heedless customers—I heard and saw two filthy little boys scrambling against each other on the sticky cement floor. "It's mine, assbite motherfucker, I saw it first!" "Shit if it is, stupid shit-head, I had it first and then I dropped it!"

Stolid and benumbed, I stood in line with other sweltering resi-dents as the two kids gouged each other's noses and eyes, pulled hair, for what I sadly supposed would be a gumball. They dove together, under the machine, and each came up with one end of a very distressed snake, who, until that moment had probably thought of himself as no more than three feet long. For an eternal moment they hauled in some frantic tug-of-war with the snake, who said a silent snake-*awk!* Until the man behind the register said, "Get out of here with that, willya?" and they disappeared out into the 120-degree heat. A sigh from behind me. It came from an artist with a national reputation, wearing shoulder-length hair left over from the sixties, bald pate slick with sweat. "Kind of makes you wonder, doesn't it?"

Only two months later, when November turned the air crisp, I was down in that same center, thin again, in a restaurant this time, drinking champagne for breakfast, picking at chicken livers and sour cream, when in this crowded, jovial, cozy place we heard a sound like a siren. A few of us went outside to see what was up, and there, in front of that same ratty grocery store, was a young man dressed all in white, doing a morning mantra. "Oooh," he sang, all on one note, "hooww beautiful is the Canyon in the morning!" He'd picked a note that made some of the parking-lot dogs crazy. One in particular danced about the guy, trying to put his paws around the singer's neck, howling happily on the same note. The singer had a girlfriend, or a devotée, who, since the singer definitely wasn't going either to stop or change his tune, undertook gently to shoo the dog back with a leafy branch. For minutes we stood out there, that Sun-day morning, the breath coming in steam from our smiling mouths, watching boy, girl, and dog, hearing that song. Then went back in to finish breakfast.

If you think finding the right place just happens, you've got another think.

Charles Willeford

Charles Willeford (1919–1988) is best known as the author of *Miami Blues* (1984), a ruefully comic variant on the classic private-eye novel that was made into a successful 1990 film. For nearly forty years before that, he worked in near obscurity, writing some of the strangest crime novels in the hardboiled canon, from such early, California-based works as *High Priest of California* (1953), whose sociopathic protagonist translates James Joyce's *Ulysses* in his spare time, *Pick-Up* (1954), *Wild Wives* (1956), and *The Woman Chaser* (1960), to the even more extreme *The Burnt Orange Heresy* (1971) and *Cockfighter* (1972). A twenty-year veteran of the U.S. Army, Willeford ended up teaching English and philosophy at Miami-Dade Junior College. In his posthumously published memoir *I Was Looking for a Street* (1988), Willeford gives us a typically downbeat, unsentimental account of his life as an orphan growing up in a working-class Los Angeles far removed from the city of glamorous daydreams.

from

I WAS LOOKING FOR A STREET

I don't think we were rich, or anything close to that, but we were well-to-do. We lived in a big two-story house in Topanga Canyon, which was still open country then, and everyone in the family was working except me. My grandmother, Mattie Sawyers, worked six days a week at the May Company in downtown Los Angeles, selling millinery in the French Room. My uncle Roy, Mattie's son, worked for Southwestern Bell, and he owned a new Model A Ford. My mother, Aileen, who had been widowed since my second birthday, had remarried, and her new husband, Joe Cassidy, owned a garage on Western Avenue. In addition to renting parking spaces, Joe did mechanical work at the garage, and he also held several points in a shock absorber he had helped invent. My mother, who had graduated from Boscobel College in Tennesse with a degree in music, taught piano, voice, and expression in our home in Topanga Canyon. So altogether, there was a good deal of money coming into that house every month.

We had a full-time Negro cook, and we ate big dinners at night—huge roasts, turkeys, chicken and dumplings, and I don't remember what all. Except for Joe Cassidy, who had moved to Los Angeles from New York City, Mattie, Mama, and Roy were from Greenville, Mississippi, so southern cooking predominated. Because I was the only child, and a boy at that, I was indulged. I liked Jell-O, for example, and regardless of the desserts the others had, I was always served Jell-O, usually the red kind with chopped bananas in it. I was also a finicky eater for a boy of seven, so each evening meal was preceded by a tablespoon of "Beef Wine & Iron" tonic, which was supposed to stimulate my appetite. I hated the taste of this tonic, but I rarely got out of taking it.

Joe Cassidy, who had married my mother—not me—didn't like me very much, but everyone else, including our cook, loved me. I had a bicycle, an Erector set, an electric train, toys of all kinds, and it was always summertime in Topanga, as I recall, because I didn't go to school. After breakfast, I rode my bike down the highway for about a mile and spent the morning in a public pool. I rode back for lunch, and afterward, when my mother's students came to the house for lessons, I played outside with the kids who were waiting for their turns at the piano. I giggled a lot during the voice and expression lessons, especially when some little girl would recite the "poor little worm" piece.

"Poor little worm," the girl would address the imaginary worm in her palm, "d'you wanna see God?" Then she would crush the worm in her hand, grinning with malice.

Every six weeks or so, Mama gave recitals in a rented church auditorium, with all of the parents of her students and their friends in the audience. I would sit in the back with Mattie, but Joe Cassidy and Uncle Roy didn't come to these student recitals.

When I was six, my mother had tried to give me piano lessons but I refused to take them. After two or three attempts, she gave up. She taught me how to sing two songs, however, "Freckles," and "Mighty Like A Rose," which I learned by heart. She accompanied me on the piano, and after I got these two songs perfected, including the hand and arm gestures, she curled my straight blond hair into tight little ringlets. I couldn't sit still, and the smell of the cooking hair made me cry. My hair was curled anyway, and I got a couple of painful scalp burns from the hot iron. A few bad days came then, but there weren't many of them. My mother didn't drive, so we had to take buses and streetcars, making several transfers, and then we waited—it seemed like hours—in movie studio waiting rooms. My turn would come, and I would sing my two songs to some indifferent man behind a desk while my mother accompanied me on the office upright. I wore a black velvet Lord Fauntleroy suit with short pants, a white waist (they weren't called shirts), a black string tie, white socks, and black patent-leather shoes. I was a pretty but sullen-mouthed kid, and nothing ever came from these auditions. I hated the curls, the long tiring bus and streetcar rides, the stuffy waiting rooms filled with shushed kids, and singing to strange men who almost always smoked smelly cigars while I sang my two songs. My mother was never discouraged, though. As she told Mattie, the fact that I was allowed to sing both songs, instead of being dismissed after the first, was a favorable sign of my talent.

But there were only four or five of these trips. My mother had tuberculosis and she was dying. She wasn't strong enough physically to keep taking me around to the studios on a regular basis, so the intervals between these auditions became longer, and eventually the trips stopped. My curls grew out, and my hair was straight again.

Every night when she came home from work, Mattie brought me a present—a pack of gum, a top, a toy boat for the bathtub, something. My uncle Roy read the funny papers to me after dinner, and then he always had to go out somewhere.

"Roy won't be happy," my mother said, "until he breaks every heart in Los Angeles."

Mattie just laughed. Roy was about twenty-six then, two years younger than Mama, and he had a lot of girl friends, although he never brought any of them to the house. He suspected that Mattie and Mama would never consider any girl he brought home good enough for him. He was a handsome, dapper man, and I never saw him without a suit and tie, even on Sunday mornings at breakfast.

Then, almost overnight it seemed, everything changed.

My mother had to enter a T.B. sanatorium in Anaheim. She had an operation, and one of her lungs was collapsed. A few weeks later she died there. After she died, Joe took half of the silverware (even though there was an Old English letter "W" intaglioed on each piece), sold his garage, and moved back to New York. We never saw or heard from Joe again. We had a parrot named Polly, and Roy taught the parrot to say, "Where's Joe?" But a few weeks later, Roy left, too.

The new dial system was coming in, and Roy was transferred temporarily to San Diego to teach people down there how to use it. He met a "hello girl" and married her. Mattie was very upset about this marriage because the girl was a Catholic, but because my mother had also become a Catholic to marry Joe Cassidy in the church, Mattie never said anything to me about it until long after Mama had died. Catholics, she explained, were compulsory breeders, and she hated the idea of Roy being tied down with a large family. And she was right. By the time I was twelve, Roy had three children, two girls and a boy. But by then his wife had ballooned to two hundred pounds, and they didn't have any more children.

After the breakup of our extended family, Mattie and I left the big house in Topanga Canyon, and she rented an apartment in the Figueroa Arms, at 41st Drive and Figueroa Avenue in southwest L.A. She could no longer afford a full-time cook or maid to look after me while she worked all day, so I was sent to the McKinley Industrial School for Boys in Van Nuys. I was eight years old, and for the first three days I was there I cried without stopping. The magic number, Mattie told me, was ten. When I was ten, she said, I would be able to look after myself after school, but for the next two years I would just have to tough it out at McKinley.

I adjusted to life at McKinley because I had to, and it wasn't a bad place to be; it was just that two years seemed like a long time. The school, as I was told, was supported in part by the Kiwanis Club, and the parents of the boys who were placed there paid a pro-rated fee, depending upon their income. Mattie paid fifty dollars a month, but there was a long waiting list, and it had taken "pull," she said, to get me into the school.

There were more than two hundred boys there, ranging in age from six to eighteen, and we were separated by age into dormitories in four different two-story brick buildings. There was a matron in charge of each age group, and I was in Founders, Junior, with eight-year-olds. We had our own wash room, with showers and toilet stalls, and a small study-room library in addition to the dormitory. There was a Book of Knowledge set in the study, a dictionary, a complete set of Tom Swift books, and several books by Horatio Alger, Junior, from the "Tattered Tom" series. After I read a couple of Alger's novels, I realized I had it very good at McKinley compared to the orphans in New York Alger was writing about. These bootblacks and newsboys were on their own, out in the cold, and slept in alleys at night. When they got into trouble, a judge would sentence them to thirty days on Blackwell's Island, where they did hard labor, and then they would be turned out into the streets again. Sometimes, by luck, one of them would rescue some girl by stopping a runaway horse, and be rewarded with a good job by the girl's father, but the rest of these boys, without luck, were still on the streets. There were no dates mentioned in these Alger novels, so I didn't make the distinction between the 1860s and the 1920s. I thought the books described current conditions. The boys who read Alger truly appreciated McKinley, so I imagine that's why there were several of these novels placed in every study room.

McKinley had two hundred and fifty acres of farmland, and the school was more or less self-sufficient for many of its needs. All kinds of vegetables were grown, and we had our own dairy and pasteurization plant. There was a bull, too, with a ring in his nose, rabbits, chickens, and goats. We ate very well in the dining room and surplus farm products were sold in Van Nuys. In addition to attending school (we had our own grammar school, but the older boys were bused into Van Nuys High School), every boy had a regular daily job of some kind. As we grew older, we were given more responsible jobs. I started out as a scraper. I scraped the garbage off the plates in the kitchen after each meal, and then handed the plates to another boy who took them over to the dishwashers. Two years later, by the time I left, I was a rabbit keeper, responsible for the feeding and watering of a hutch of long-haired rabbits. I also dropped the bucks in with the does for breeding, according to the schedule I was given, but another boy butchered and skinned the rabbits. I was glad I left McKinley before getting his job, which would have been my next task. The top job at McKinley was taking care of the cows, breeding them to the bull, milking them, and working in the pasteurization plant. This privileged work was reserved for boys sixteen and older, and was much sought after because they could go to the dairy any time the supervisor wasn't around and fuck the calves. When a boy graduated from high school, or turned eighteen, he had to leave McKinley, but there was only a handful of boys sixteen and older.

My grandmother visited me every Sunday, riding the streetcar to downtown L.A. and then transferring to the Pacific Electric train at the Hill Street station, which had a line out to Van Nuys and the valley. When she got off at the McKinley stop, she had almost a mile to walk to the main gate of the school. This was an all-day round-trip, including the hours she spent with me, and it was years before I realized what a sacrifice she made each week to come and see me on her only day off.

Once a month, however, I was allowed to go home for a weekend. I would leave the school on Friday afternoon after classes let out, and then ride the big red train through open country into downtown L.A. At the Hill Street station, I would walk slowly down Hill toward the May Company, and more often than not I would run into Mattie coming up the street toward the station. If she was late getting off work, or if I was a little early, I would wait for her outside the Eight Street employee exit. We would then eat dinner at Leighton's Cafeteria on Broadway. I almost always selected the same dinner: a breaded, fried pork chop; a cold artichoke with a saucer of mayonnaise; a wedge of watermelon or cantaloupe; and a piece of hot mince pie á la mode with vanilla ice cream. Inasmuch as Jell-O and junket were the desserts served most often at McKinley, I had lost my fondness for Jell-O and wanted a tastier dessert. I truly loved that basement cafeteria on Broadway, which I thought served the best food in the entire world.

After dinner we went to the movies. Usually we went to the Paramount Theater, which only showed Paramount pictures, because of the stage show between film showings. There was at least one headliner, someone like Pinky Tomlin or Bill "Bojangles" Robinson, and an M.C. who cracked jokes. I didn't always understand the jokes, but I laughed anyway. I rarely asked for an explanation, and was on my best behavior during my weekend visits, afraid that if I became a nuisance in some way my monthly weekends might stop.

When "Dixie" was played during the movie, and it often was, my grandmother would nudge me in the ribs. We then applauded throughout the song. Quite often, indeed, most often, we were the only people in the audience applauding, but when Mattie clapped, so did I. I never questioned her about it. I knew vaguely that "Dixie" and Mississippi were connected in some way, and that was enough for me. Later on, when Mattie told me stories about her life in Mississippi and Louisiana, and informed me that we came from "family," I gathered that we were superior to the Los Angeles "louts," and that we had to set some kind of an example for others. Because I was told so often as a child that I was superior I began to believe it, and although I know now (now that I am an old fart) that it wasn't altogether true, the belief has served me well throughout my life. It made me more tolerant of others, who didn't have my family background, and allowed me to accomplish a good many things I probably wouldn't have attempted otherwise. There is still no doubt in my mind that Mattie was a superior person. She was the most intelligent woman I have ever known, even though she was living then in what she called "reduced circumstances." As near as I can determine, she was about forty-five or -six when I entered McKinley, but she looked much younger. She was five feet tall, exactly, and she had a trim figure because she was on her feet all day. She had an abundance of pale blonde hair, dark blue eyes, and very white skin. Her fingers were arthritic, however, with red swollen knuckles, and she had bulging bunions on both big toes. Sometimes she would carve away at the bunions in the evenings with a razor blade. I couldn't bear to watch this procedure, even though she said it didn't hurt to slice off a few layers.

I remember her mostly in black because all of the salesladies at the May Company wore black dresses with detachable white cuffs and collars. Mattie had a closet full of black silk dresses, and she wore gold-rimmed glasses with a pince nez, glasses that were secured by a gold spring chain on a black shiny button pinned to her dress. These were reading glasses, but there were always two little dents in her nose where they pinched her. Mattie's skin was smooth and soft, and I would frequently touch her face with the tips of my fingers, and stroke her face just to feel the softness of her cheeks. She walked in a wobbling way she had been taught at a finishing school she had attended in Princeton, Kentucky, when she was a girl. She held her head and neck stiffly erect as though she were balancing a book on her head. Her feet, turned out at a forty-five degree angle, walked an imaginary straight line. To get the hang of the walk, they had actually balanced a book on their heads, she told me.

Mattie started to smoke Chesterfields after my mother died, and she was an awkward smoker. She was supposed to exercise her fingers, because of the arthritis, and she did this by playing solitaire, dealing one game after another. With both hands occupied with the cards, she would let a cigarette dangle from one corner of her mouth, squinting an eye against the smoke. The ash would get longer and longer, but she almost always remembered to knock off the ash before it fell. Her doctor told her that sauerkraut juice was good for arthritis, and she usually had a glass of iced sauerkraut juice on the table when she played different variations of solitaire. The grimaces she made when she took a sip made me laugh, and she would, of course, laugh, too. She had a soft southern accent, but most people thought that it was English—not southern—and many people would ask her, when they met her for the first time, if she came from England.

After the Friday night movie, we would take the "E" streetcar to Santa Barbara and Figueroa, walk the two blocks home, and get to bed by eleven or eleven-thirty.

When I awoke on Saturday mornings, around nine, she would be gone, already at work, and I would put up the beds. There were two large rooms in the apartment, a living room and a dining room. Both rooms had glass double doors, and the pull-down double beds were behind the doors, one in the living room and one in the dining room. The doors folded back, and the beds could be pulled down easily, but first we had to move the furniture to make room for them. The living room was furnished with a heavy overstuffed couch and matching mohair chair, and the carpet was an expensive Oriental. There were standing lamps with beaded fringes on the shades, and a large cabinet radio we called the "console." The dining room carpet was blue and green with a geometric pattern of darker blue lines that was supposed to be a Frank Lloyd Wright design. We still had the large mahogany dining table from the house in Topanga

Canyon, and the seven tall brocaded chairs that went with the table. Polly, however, when he got out of his cage from time to time, had torn strips of wood from the top of each chair. Mattie never said it was time to go to bed. She just said, "It's time to move the furniture."

I would make and put up the beds, move the furniture back into place, and then eat breakfast. Mattie had taught me how to fry eggs in bacon grease and how to use the toaster, and I always had a glass of milk with my breakfast. When we ate breakfast together and Mattie drank her morning coffee, I wanted coffee, too, but she said it would stunt my growth. I wasn't allowed to drink coffee until I was twelve years old.

At ten or ten-thirty I would catch the streetcar downtown. The May Company had a large rental library on the mezzanine, and outside the library there were soft leather chairs where a person could sit and read and look down on the main floor. I would check out two books on Mattie's library card and read on the mezzanine until noon, listening to the mysterious bell signals as they rang throughout the store. The store bells were a code, Mattie told me, but only the floor walkers were told what they meant. I read a lot of books on that mezzanine, beginning with the Tarzan and Mars novels by Edgar Rice Burroughs, and, later on, after I left McKinley and lived at home again, the racier novels of Viña Delmar, Donald Henderson Clarke, and Tiffany Thayer. The public libraries did not stock these authors, and if it hadn't been for the May Company rental library, I wouldn't have learned much of anything about sex, except, of course, for the usual misinformation I picked up from the other boys my age at McKinley. One thing I learned at McKinley: there were perverts in Los Angeles called "fruits," and they would do terrible things to a boy if they could catch a kid alone. But inasmuch as all fruits wore red neckties, they were easy to spot and avoid. I saw a good many of these fruits in downtown L.A., and I gave them a wide berth.

At noon I met Mattie in the May Company tea room. We ate tuna fish sandwiches with Coca Colas, and then she gave me a quarter before returning to the French Room.

After lunch I walked across the street to the Tower Theater and watched a double-feature. There was an orange juice stand on the corner of Eighth and Broadway, and you could drink all of the orange juice you wanted for a dime. But there was a trick to it, and I was cheated out of a dime several times until I finally caught on. The orange juice they pumped up was so astonishingly cold the first sip gave you a headache right between the eyes, and it was difficult to finish one glass, let alone two. The movie was a dime, too, and I usually spent my remaining nickel on a candy bar. I saw *One-Way Passage* with William Powell and Kay Francis in the Tower Theater, and the ending was so tragic it almost broke my heart. *One-Way Passage* is still my all-time favorite movie, but I have never risked seeing it again. I cried so hard when the movie ended the usher took me out to the lobby and gave me a glass of water.

At five-thirty I would go up to the French Room and, still carrying my books, would talk to the other salesladies in the millinery department while I waited for Mattie. These middle-aged ladies, all in black, all of them smiling, would make over me and kiss me and tell me how much I had grown since the last time they had seen me.

We would then ride the streetcar home, and Mattie would look at my books on the way. Sometimes she would ask if the books I had checked out were a little old for me, but she never censored my reading. I would finish the books before returning to McKinley on Sunday afternoon, and Mattie took the books back to the library on Monday, paying the three cents per day fee.

On the way home we would shop at Smith's Supermarket, at 45th Street and Figueroa. The supermarket was a new concept, and Smith's had been built without doors because it stayed open twenty-four hours a day. There was nothing else like it at the time, and people came from all over southwest Los Angeles to shop at Smith's. Mattie would then cook dinner while I listened to the radio and read in the living room. We always had a big dinner, and we used the good china and silverware. I would set the table, as she had taught me, including the salad and oyster forks, even though we had fairly simple meals. I liked pork chops, and chicken and dumplings, so we usually had one or the other; biscuits, which Mattie made from scratch; string beans or creamed peas; a small salad; and pound cake and ice cream for dessert. Neither one of us cared much for salads, but we always ate one before our main course because, as she said, we needed the "roughage." It was several years before I found out what she meant by "roughage."

On Saturday nights when I wasn't home, Mattie either went to a dance downtown with one of her lady friends, or she went back downtown to play auction bridge at a twentieth of a cent a point at a hotel on Spring Street. But when I was home for the weekend she stayed there with me. She would wash her hair, using Marchand's Golden Hair Rinse, curl it with an iron heated on the gas burner in the kitchen, and do other small chores she had put off during the week. Sometimes Marie Weller, Mattie's best friend, would come over. Marie had escaped from the May Company's French Room and had opened her own millinery store in Hollywood, which she called Maison Marie's. They would talk about hats, and rehash some of the arguments they had with Miss Gilbert, the tyrannical buyer at the May Company. They always referred to the buyer as Miss Gilbert, and I got the impression that this formidable woman, who went to Paris and New York on buying trips every year, was about eighty years old. Later on, when I finally met Miss Gilbert, I was astonished to discover that she was only about thirty-five, if that. Marie was interested in designing, and they talked interminably about hats. Mattie, of course, was an authority, and sometimes when we were out she would point out a woman and tell me how much the woman's hat had cost.

"There," she said, "is a five-dollar number. Common."

Things were either common or uncommon with Mattie. I learned gradually what was common and what was not. Common was something to be avoided, and good taste could be learned. Money had nothing to do with commonness because a person could be poor and still have good taste and good manners. A woman with manners always wore a hat and gloves on the street, and never smoked outside her home. Mattie never left the apartment, even for a dash across the street to the drugstore, without putting on her gloves and a hat. The lowest priced hats in the French Room were fifty dollars, and they were all "originals." Mattie got a commission on each hat she sold, as well as a salary. Mattie's hats were designed in the work room there, too, and when she saw one of her hats duplicated (the downtown Bullock's, she claimed, would steal the French Room ideas, and copy the hats in cheaper materials), she would either discard it or have it made over in the work room. Mattie had a lot of famous customers and one day, when she had stayed home from work with a cold, Norma Shearer, the movie actress, called her at home and asked how she was feeling. Mattie was pleased by the telephone call and told me that Miss Shearer was a "real lady," whereas some of the movie stars she waited on were "common as dirt." She also sold a hat to Mrs. Edgar Rice Burroughs, a large, overweight woman, and she told me about it because she knew how much I liked the Tarzan novels. But I was bewildered by this information at the time. I had thought that writers lived all alone in a room writing all the time, and it had never occurred to me that a writer would have a wife, children, and lead an outwardly normal life.

Mattie liked to sleep late on Sunday morning, but I was used to getting up early in the dormitory at McKinley. I would wake early and read until she got up at eleven, trying to finish my books so she could take them back to the store on Monday. I always told her I had finished them anyway, whether I had or not, because I didn't want her to keep them out for another month at three cents a day. As a consequence, I never learned how Viña Delmar's *Bad Girl* came out, but the title more or less gave it away. The heroine had to decide whether to sleep with her fiancé before they got married, and I am sure that she did, or the novel would have been called *Good Girl*.

When the time came to leave, around three-thirty, we always had the same argument. Mattie always wanted to ride the streetcar downtown with me to the P.E. station, but I didn't want her to go with me because she would just have to turn around and come back home again. At last she would compromise, and walk to Santa Barbara Avenue with me, and wait until I got on the streetcar. If I cried, she cried, too, so I learned how to hold it in until after I got on the streetcar. Parting was an ordeal for both of us, whether I left for McKinley from home, or whether she left McKinley after one of her Sunday visits. As a consequence, I learned later in life never to say good-bye to anyone. As an adult, I have never said good-bye. I have left wives and lovers, naturally, but I have always disappeared without a word. I am one of those men who leaves the house ostensibly to get a package of cigarettes, and is never heard from again. That way, it is easier on both parties. As long as a man leaves everything behind, including his money, possessions, and clothes, he will have no regrets when he begins a new life somewhere else.

When a boy is eight or nine years old, and an orphan, and all he has is a grandmother standing between him and his own demise, it is not unreasonable for this boy to think that this old lady of forty-five or -six will die before he sees her again. So each weekend, when I left Mattie at the corner, or when she left me at McKinley, I knew in my heart that she would die before I saw her again. For a boy of eight or nine, this kind of thinking is not irrational.

Rubén Martínez

An associate editor at Pacific News Service and a contributor to PBS's *Religion & Ethics Newsweekly*, Rubén Martínez (b. 1962) takes as "guiding light" a maxim of H. L. Mencken: "Comfort the afflicted, afflict the comfortable." He is the author of two books, *The Other Side* (1989), a collection of reportage, poems, and essays, and *Crossing Over: A Mexican Family on the Migrant Trail* (2001). In "Going Up in L.A.," first published in *LA Weekly* at a time when the city's gang violence was making headlines, Martínez describes a less explosive side of the gang experience, searching out the graffiti writers whose tags adorn the city streets like hieroglyphics, and probing the questions of identity that absorb them.

GOING UP IN L.A.

Los Angeles, April 1989

The stain on the old couch that sits in the empty lot has already turned brown, a dark flower spread out upon the grimy fabric. Although it's a school day and only 10:30 in the morning, about a dozen teenagers stand about, passing around a quart of Colt 45 Malt Liquor. Some of the faces show fear; others are hardened into stony stares. "We know who did it, but we're not going to tell you," says one of the younger boys. His hair is cropped stubby short, and he wears dark jeans and a plain T-shirt. "We're not going to spell it out, but you can pretty much guess what's going to happen tonight."

At approximately seven o'clock the previous evening, these kids had been seated on or standing around the couch. Among the group was Prime, a seventeen-year-old homeboy. They'd all been "kickin' it"—drinking and talking to the accompaniment of a ghettoblaster alternately pumping out hip-hop and oldies—when a car pulled up to the curb below, and two figures climbed up the hill in the darkness. "Where you from?" one of them yelled from a distance of about ten feet. A moment later, several rounds exploded from a shotgun and a .45. Prime and another boy fell in the hail of bullets, and lay bleeding on the couch.

We walk around to the side of one of the dilapidated stucco bungalows that crown the hill. A wall displays the local gang's roster — hundreds of names spraypainted in furious, spidery lettering. Someone points to the "R.I.P." section: more than a dozen names. "Rest In Power," mumbles one of the boys. Nobody is sure whether the next name to go up on the wall will be Prime's.

A few days earlier, Prime was sitting in his family's living room, which doubles as a bedroom, in a neighborhood not far from the empty lot. It is a crime-ridden area to be sure, dominated by one of the city's oldest Latino gangs. This is where Prime grew up, and where his two unemployed parents try to scrape by on welfare.

Although Prime admitted that he'd been "in the wrong place at the wrong time" on more than one occasion, he saw himself less as a gangster, more as a "writer" (as graffiti artists call themselves), one of the best-known among the city's thousands of young, spraycan-wielding "bombers."

Prime shook hands gingerly that day. His right hand still bore the chalky plaster stains from a cast that had been removed the day before, the bones in his right — and writing — hand having been broken in a fist fight.

As soon as I entered the room, he began to show off his canvases. After years of doing complex, colorful works on walls across the city, Prime had begun experimenting with acrylics, airbrush, oils, washes. It was Valentine's Day, and he'd done a piece for his girlfriend — a brightly colored Cupid surrounded by soft pink roses, with a dedication that read, "José and Nery, *por vida*." He pointed to a larger work dominated by grays, blacks and silvers, titled *Dazed and Confused*, an ambitious circular composition centered on a pair of dice that become a large syringe, then a huddled, shadowy figure and, finally, a large, wicked-looking skull.

Prime sat down on the sagging bed, the plaster wall behind him bulging with cracked paint. At the age of eight, he tells me, he snatched his sister's goldfleck hairspray and wrote "Little Joe, 18 Street" in the back yard. Soon afterward his initials were "up" in the neighborhood alleys.

"I never got really crazy," he told me. But as gang violence in the inner city increased dramatically in the mid-1980s, he was busted for various misdemeanors, including "vandalism" (i.e., spraypaint-ing), and he once almost did time for armed robbery. It wasn't until about 1984 that Prime graduated from gang-writing to more origi-nal and complex forms of graffiti. He developed a style that set him apart from other graffiti artists, working closely with several col-leagues in the K2S-STN ("Kill To Succeed-Second To None") crew, one of the first to appear on the city's Eastside.

By last Valentine's Day, Prime could look back on it all and vow that it was the art that really mattered in his life. And, as he brought out photo albums stuffed with color photographs of graffiti works he'd done over the years, he told me he'd enrolled in art classes at the East L.A. Occupational Center. He spoke to me of a future without drive-by shootings, overdoses or girls pregnant at fifteen. "I want to have a big lot when I grow older," he said, leaning forward, a small gold crucifix swinging in front of his dark blue sweatshirt. "It'll have big, long, movable walls. I'll put canvases up, and have kids and artists there, have it be like a big maze of art. Then, with the money I make in one day, I'll buy some more canvas and change the maze . . ."

By 1984, movies like *Wild Style, Beat Street* and *Breakin'* had apprised L.A. teenagers of the graffiti writing explosion that had taken place in the Bronx, where a complex, multicolored graffiti known as "wildstyle" had evolved in the late 1970s and early 1980s. Behind its New York counterparts by several years, L.A. created its own dis-tinct scene. In New York, most of the work had been painted onto the sides of subway cars. L.A.'s answer was to "bomb" the freeways.

L.A. writers had a rich history to draw upon. Graffiti had been around since the World War Two era Pachucos (the first style-con-scious Latino gangs, who incorporated Old English lettering into their "tags," or nicknames); the East L.A. mural artists of the sixties, with their close ties to Mexican muralism, were a local artistic and political institution. The city was ripe for a new public-art explosion.

The city's first graffiti "crew" was the L.A. Bomb Squad, whose membership consisted almost exclusively of Latino youths from the *barrios* of Pico-Union and East L.A. Soon, however, the movement spread west, south and north, to include teens from other impover-ished neighborhoods and from the middle-class suburbs as well.

And so the L.A. version of hip-hop graffiti was born. Many of the more aesthetically developed works (known as "pieces", short for "master-pieces") were done in hidden-away places like the Belmont Tunnel, an old, fenced-off trolley stop near Belmont High School. There were also more daring exploits. Simple tags and "throw-ups" (two-color tags) went up on buses, benches, sidewalks, street lights, stop signs, anywhere that was highly visible to the public. Competition as to who could top whom in originality and quantity was intense.

The glory days of the nascent L.A. scene came in 1984, when a youth club named Radio-Tron opened its doors. "It was a cultural center where people could go practice breaking and drawing," recalls Moda (the tag is Spanish for "fashion"), a founding member of the Bomb Squad. Housed in a building in the Westlake *barrio* near MacArthur Park, Radio-Tron was akin to an established artist's studio, a haven from the streets where writers always ran the risk of a bust. Soon, every inch of the site was covered with tags and pieces. "All the guys I knew were being thrown in jail or getting killed," says Primo D, also of the Bomb Squad. "Radio-Tron was an alternative."

The center's curriculum, according to founder and director Carmelo Alvarez, a longtime inner-city youth activist, included deejaying, scratch and rap, and "advanced graffiti." "I just took what they had and structured it." But the experiment didn't last long. Wrangles with the city (Alvarez balked when the Department of Parks and Recreation made a move to take over the center), as well as a Fire Marshall's citation (for storage of "hazardous chemicals"—acrosol cans), led to its being closed. "When Radio-Tron shut down, everybody started getting into the gang thing," says Primo D. "There was nothing else to do."

Not long after the Bomb Squad's tags and cartoonlike "characters" first appeared in the downtown area, a group of mostly middle-class Anglo Westside teens took note and founded WCA (West Coast Artists), soon the biggest crew in the city with an active membership of about thirty-five, plus a subsidiary crew (BC, or Beyond Control) of a dozen or so. Today, on any given weekend morning, you can see WCA at work, along with other Westside crews like

KSN (Kings Stop at Nothing), at one of their favorite spots, the Motor Yard in West Los Angeles.

Everything in the yard, including the rails, the ties, the torched wrecks of cars, has been tagged, pieced, bombed—as the writers say, "terrorized." The thousands of discarded spraycans testify to the countless generations of pieces that have gone up, one on top of another, on the half-mile stretch of concrete retaining wall that flanks the railroad tracks.

Carrying in dozens of Krylon spraycans in backpacks or milk crates, the crews usually arrive early in the day and work alongside the railroad tracks that run parallel to the Santa Monica freeway near National Boulevard. A box will invariably be blasting Eazy E's "Boys-N-the-Hood" or Boogie Down Production's "My Philosophy" as the writers, ranging in age from six to their early twenties, fish sketches out of their back pockets, the cans, press down customized nozzles ("fat tips" culled from small Testor's spraycans, which allow for a thicker, smoother line) and begin the sweeping rhythmic motions that trace the skeleton of a new piece.

Phoe of BC, a wiry, clean-cut teenager of Hawaiian-Filipino ancestry, is there one weekend, wearing a dark blue baseball cap embroidered with the name of his crew. His tag, he tells me, is an intentional misspelling of "foe," which, according to him, means "society's enemy." He works on a three-dimensional wildstyle piece that is typical of Westside work. The edges of the letters are sharp as shards of glass, but serif-like cuts and arrows make the composition virtually unreadable to the untrained eye.

"Writing is, like, a different community," says Phoe, yelling to be heard over the freeway roar that almost drowns out his high-pitched voice. "It's communication with other writers throughout the city." Wherever he goes ("even when I go out to dinner with my parents"), the tools of the trade—markers or spraycans—are at his disposal.

As with many Westside writers, Phoe's response to the city's anti-graffiti forces, or to those sympathetic adults who encourage him to professionalize his talent, is lackadaisical. "Yeah, yeah, yeah. They're telling me to go out and sign up for scholarships and art classes, and get paid for writing, and I'm, like, well, I don't really need the money because I work." Yet some WCA writers do take "legal" jobs now and then, pounding the streets in search of sympathetic business owners who'll pay them to paint storefront signs and the like. Risk, one of WCA's premier writers, recently did backgrounds for a Michael Jackson video.

Still, there's an allure to the "illegal" work. And, since most writers lack studio space, sites like the Motor Yard are indispensable. "They just don't understand," says Ash, another respected WCA writer. "We need this place to paint, or else we're going to bomb the streets more, straight up."

Although a few Westside writers are friendly with their Eastside counterparts, interaction between the two groups is limited. Indeed, the rivalry between WCA and K2S-STN dates back to the origins of the L.A. writing scene. Like breakdancers, writers "battle" each other. The spoils of victory may include several dozen spraycans, or the appropriation of a writer's tag.

As soon as WCA and K2S-STN each became aware of the other, the stage was set for the East-West battle, which took place at the Belmont Tunnel in 1985. WCA went up with the bigger production in their trademark flashy style, featuring a pastel-yellow/clover-green/pastel-aqua, black-outlined, white-highlighted, hot-pink-and-avocado-bordered piece by Risk. Next to it was a character by fellow writer Cooz, of a Japanese-animation-style buxom woman wearing shiny wraparound shield glasses, a cascade of auburn hair spilling over her shoulders.

K2S-STN countered with a shocker from Prime. Employing an abstract, futuristic style, he wrote his tag with an altered color scheme and composition: triangles and squares of hot pink, white, true blue and baby blue produced a new kind of three-dimensional effect. Next to it he drew a robot character he'd found in a comix mag.

Some West Coast writers congratulated Prime afterward in an apparent admission of defeat. By the next morning, however, all of the WCA productions, as well as a substantial part of Prime's, had been "dissed" (painted over) by unknown writers, and the bad blood began. To this day, some WCA writers maintain that Prime was the culprit, although he always denied the allegation.

There are substantial stylistic differences between East and West Los Angeles writers. WCA writers are sensitive to the charge that they are "biting" (the writer's term for plagiarism) New York styles. "We took the New York styles and made them into our own style," says Wisk, the crew's most prolific writer, a little defensively. Using thin letters with stylized swirls and blends of color accented with arrows and sparkles, West Coast's work often achieves a slick magazine look—the New York stamp is unmistakable. K2S-STN, on the other hand, while sometimes drawing on the same influences, produces more readable block- or bubblelike letters that echo old gang-writing styles updated with the wildstyle. The result is aesthetically analogous to the split between the Anglo and ethnic art worlds of the 1960s and 1970s—playful abstraction on the one hand, Socialist Realism–flavored work on the other.

But the stylistic differences between the two groups hide deeper tensions. The Eastside writers, who lay claim to being the original Los Angeles bombers, feel that WCA has received a disproportionate share of media attention, including articles in the *Los Angeles Times* that have largely ignored the Eastside writers in favor of Westsiders.

"It was only when white people started doing graffiti that they said it was art," Prime once said bitterly. "We were doing it before them, but [the media] were blaming us for vandalism." These sentiments are echoed by most Eastside writers, and their resentment is obviously both class- and race-based.

"Most of the West Coast writers are from middle-class families," says Moda of the original L.A. Bomb Squad. "On this side of town, you're faced with the gang problem and graffiti at the same time. It affects the writers from poor neighborhoods: because they have the distraction of gangs, they might not be able to pursue it all the way. Like Prime—he's stuck between gangs and graffiti."

Prime's father approaches the bed slowly. An oxygen mask all but hides the son's incipient beard and mustache. Dried blood is still encrusted on his forehead and temples. The father takes his son's bloody hand into his own, leans down and whispers something into his ear. Prime tries to speak, but the words are mumbled, delirious. His father lifts back the white sheet and peers at Prime's right arm, swathed in bandages. After two major operations, the doctors are finally willing to predict that Prime is going to make it.

Over the next few days, Prime's fellow writers will visit his bed-side in an endless procession. Among them is Duke, twenty years old, a native of Guatemala and a seven-year writing veteran of K2S-STN. Like Prime, Duke has been involved in gangsterism. When he heard the news about the shooting, his first impulse was "to go out and take care of shit," but he checked himself. "The art took me out of the trip," says Duke, who is dressed in his trademark smoke-gray jeans, his boyish face showing a spotty beard. "It helped me to look at this world in a more positive sense."

Initiated into gangs at an early age, Duke says his first spraycan escapade involved simple tagging. But after some heavy violence on the streets — he was once tied to a car bumper by rival gang mem-bers and dragged for two blocks — he decided to try to "clean up his act." When the first wave of graffiti art hit L.A., he began devoting more and more of his time to piecing.

"I wanted to kick back," Duke says of the early days of graffiti. At that time, when he was in tenth grade, "jungle football" clubs were sprouting up all over the inner city. The emphasis at first was on sports, but soon fights were breaking out between the rival groups. Then guns were brandished, and the club Duke had helped to organize quickly became one of the largest gangs in the Pico-Union area, a *barrio* that is home to over a quarter of a million cen-tral Americans.

Early one morning in October 1985, a shotgun blast tore Duke's stomach open as he was walking to school. The doctors later told him it was a miracle that he had survived. Then came family prob-lems and a difficult separation from his girlfriend. He gave up writ-ing for months and found himself at a crossroads, uncertain as to which path to follow. But today he's back in the writing scene, and serious about moving up from the streets to a "legal" career by painting storefront signs and doing everything he can to set up his own art studio at home.

Prime, like Duke, had begun to distance himself from the gang world before he was shot. "He wasn't the kind to go out and say, 'Let's take care of these dudes,'" says Duke after visiting Prime one day. "Thank God he's not gone. And I hope he never goes." Like Geo, who was shot for yelling out the wrong gang name when they asked him, "Where you from?" Or Sine who was stabbed when he tried to defend a younger kid from a gangster wielding a switch-blade. Or Risko, who died in a car that tumbled off a Harbor Free-way overpass as he and another friend fled from the police after a gang outing. All were writers associated with K2S-STN.

Veterans of the writing scene estimate that at any given time there are probably several hundred full-fledged writers at work in Los Angeles. But one must add to this figure the hundreds, perhaps thousands of teens who are bombing the city with single-color tags, the bane of the Rapid Transit District and other city agencies. "There are so many people into tagging, and that's what's messing it up for the people who do art," says Cash, a K2S-STN veteran. "Tags, all they do is destroy, make the city look ugly. The art beauti-fies the walls that have been tagged up."

On the other hand, there is no doubt that straight-out vandalism is part of the appeal, especially for the younger, or "toy," writers. On a recent Friday ("Ditching Day") morning, the Panic Zone, East L.A.'s best-known writing yard, was crawling with up-and-coming writers, most of them of junior high school age, and their crew names alone—KCC (Kids Committing Crime) and CIA (Criminals In Action)—tell the story. With a ravenous hunger for recognition, they announce their names: POSES, KORE, MICRO, MIST, ERGER, SED, SOEWHAT, DEVO, SKOE, DEES, STINGER, BEAST, DEFEAT, KINE, SETO. The selection of a tag is the all-important first step in establishing the writer's originality (hence the purposeful misspellings). Most of the tags deliberately cultivate either a dark, brooding image— DOOM, DREAD, DYE—or conjure a notion of hip-hop "badness"— REGENT, PRIME, SLICK.

The young writers at the Panic Zone are rabid taggers. "We all write on 'em all," proclaims one writer whose voice hasn't changed yet, pointing at the buses lined up at the Rapid Transit District maintenance yard, which lies only about fifty yards from the north-ernmost end of the Panic Zone. Why? "To get up, be known!" he says, and all the other writers nod eagerly.

Government agencies in Los Angeles County spend some $150 mil-lion annually in the war against graffiti. Sandblasters are available for heavy-duty "buffing" across the city, and a city-run warehouse doles out free paint to any citizen who asks for it. (30,000 gallons, enough to cover 6 million square feet of graffiti, have been given away since 1986.) A legal offensive is also in the works. Daniel Ramos, a.k.a. Chaka, probably the most prolific writer in the history of graffiti (some 10,000 tags up and down the state), was busted by the LAPD and the City Attorney threw the proverbial book at him. He languished in jail for months and was recently assigned to a special reformatory "boot camp." Anti-graffiti forces, springing from well-to-do and generally conservative home-owners' associations nationwide, have lobbied for special anti-graffiti legislation—a ban on the sale of spraycans, for example.

"We're really deterring them," says LAPD spokesperson William Medina, who coordinates a neighborhood cleanup effort in the Ra-mpart *barrio* area of L.A. For the LAPD, even the elaborate pieces that have gone up at the various "yards" around town are considered illegal. "We view it as graffiti," says Medina. "The only things we don't consider illegal are [city-] organized and approved murals."

Community meetings focusing on graffiti typically draw standing-room-only audiences. Responding to an increasingly vociferous public, Mayor Tom Bradley formed the Mayor's Committee for Graffiti Removal and Prevention. The chairman of the committee, Stuart Haines, is the owner of Textured Coatings of America, a profitable paint manufacturing company. "It's like a guy who works in a weapons manufacturing plant being named head of a task force to stop a war," said one supporter of graffiti art.

The adult response, then, has placed top priority on eradication and enforcement of anti-vandalism statutes. Only a pittance has been funnelled into public mural programs, which give youngsters the opportunity to refine their talents under the tutelage of established artists. "The real answer is to pass tougher laws to punish the graffiti artists who deface public property, along with the gang members who are identifying their turf," says Stuart Haines.

Among the adults searching for alternatives to this deadlock is Adolfo V. Nodal, the general manager of the city's Cultural Affairs Department and a longtime supporter of public arts, via endeavors like the MacArthur Arts Project, which featured art by local writers on the park's amphitheater. "Arresting kids and abatement through paint-outs is not the only way to do it," says Nodal. "It has to be an issue of implementing cultural programs for kids. We've been fighting a losing battle on this issue."

"We haven't looked at *why* they're painting," says Mary Trotter of the Vernon Central Merchants Association, which is sponsoring a graffiti art contest that offers a cash prize of $1,200, plus wall space donated by neighborhood businesses. "They want to communicate something to us, and we're not listening."

"Hollywood should understand," says independent filmmaker Gary Glaser, who produced a documentary on the L.A. writing scene called *Bombing L.A.* "This is hype town Number One. The kids can't get on television, so they tag."

Beneath the visor of a baseball cap that barely contains his shock of bushy red hair, the sea of parking lights is reflected in Wisk's glasses. It's about nine in the evening, and we are driving east on the Santa Monica Freeway.

One of the most famous taggers in town, Wisk is a founding member of WCA. His simple but undeniably attractive tag consists of a butterfly-like *W*. He numbers every one of them, as would an artist producing a limited edition of serigraphs. The *W*s are visible as far west as Venice Beach, north to the San Fernando Valley, south to Watts and east to Pomona. After two years of almost nightly "bombing" runs, Wisk broke the 2,000 mark this week.

Blowing bubbles and snapping his wad of chewing gum, Wisk directs me to exit the Santa Monica Freeway at Crenshaw Avenue, and we park near an overpass. He opens the door a crack and shakes each of his cans, pressing the nozzles a touch to make sure they're in working order.

"Ready?" asks Wisk. He pushes his glasses back up on his nose.

We walk, real cool and slow, across the overpass to a spot of fence already bent from previous bombing raids. We slow down, even walk in place until no more cars are passing by. After a glance left and right to make sure nobody's around, Wisk says, "Go!" and we hop over the fence.

Like soldiers on maneuvers, we run low alongside the freeway wall, Wisk shaking his can all the way. We zip past sooty ivy and sickly palm trees, the roar of traffic all around us. Wisk stops about two hundred yards down from the overpass, before a spot of wall clear of bushes and trees. "Stay low, dude! Look out for 5-0s and if you see one, yell out, 'Cops!'"

The can hisses as Wisk moves up and down, arcs around, outlining his throw-up in black. Then comes the fill-in, rapid back-and-forth motions with white or silver. *Ws* number 2021, 2022, 2023 are up in a matter of minutes.

"Everybody takes the freeways," says Wisk, pausing before beginning *W* number 2024. "Everybody, *everybody* and their mother sees this! This is like the subways in New York, except you move past it instead of having it move past you."

Wisk, getting greedy and perhaps a bit reckless, risks a bust by going up with *W* number 2025. He's already covered fifty yards. Whatever aerosol mist doesn't make it onto the wall rises up in a cloud that is gilded by the amber street lamp above us. Wisk notices me looking at the sight. "I love it!" he exclaims, satisfaction sweeping over his freckled face.

Later, driving back down the freeway, westbound, Wisk tells me, "Look at that shit that we did the other night," pointing excitedly to his and a fellow WCA writer's tags. "Look! *W, W, W, W, J-A, J-A, J-A*! Look at all them *W*s lined up, bro'! Boom! Boom! Boom! Boom! Boom!"

"We were just kickin' it up there, drinking beer," says Skept, his freckled face and light green eyes showing the strain of the days since Prime was shot. His usual gregarious demeanor is subdued. "We were sitting down on the couch. Then, *chk, chk, BOOM! BOOM! BOOM!*"

Skept (short for "Skeptical"), a Japanese-American who grew up in a mostly Latino *barrio*, is another veteran of K2S-STN. Like Duke and Prime, he's been leading a double life for years now, although he's long since left the old old hood and now lives in a comfortable downtown loft with his father, a well-known abstract expressionist. We walk into the ample, brightly lit studio. His father sits near the southernmost wall, smoking a pipe, poring over papers. Skept's room is at the northern end. We enter and he closes the door behind him, revealing a poster of the heavy metal group Iron Maiden.

He pops a Jungle Brothers rap tape into the player and brings out some photo albums. There's a piece by Prime, in his trademark color-patch style. And there's a photo of Geo standing before a piece, a shot taken not long before he died. He was a good-looking, slightly overweight Latino kid with a bright, adolescent smile. "Lots of friends have passed away in the last couple of years," says Skept, staring at the photo.

Then he shows me his recent work, "psychedelic" paintings on small art boards, pieces that "even my dad was surprised by." Multi-colored circles, squares and bubbles appear to float in a primordial miasma. He plans on doing such a piece soon, up on a wall, perhaps here, downtown.

The question that is running through my mind as we kick back and talk about writing is, Why did Skept have to go back to the neighborhood the night the shooting took place, knowing that there was a possibility of yet another drive-by killing?

Instead I ask, "You know what adults would tell you about all this, don't you?"

"'You shouldn't go, this and that.' My dad doesn't even know I was there when they shot him. I haven't even told anybody in my family about Prime. I didn't want to hear it. I already know what they'll say."

Skept will sometimes ensconce himself in the studio, drawing for days on end. Or he'll go out piecing at the yards. Then there'll be the urge to do a daring, illegal piece on the streets. Then he'll go back and "kick it" in the old gang neighborhood. "But the shooting," I remind him.

"It's happened so many times already, I'm getting used to it," he says, then pauses. "But—I don't know why—this time it seems so different. Maybe because I was there, I was so close . . ."

"You'll go back even though you know this might happen again?" I ask.

"Probably."

A few days earlier, I had accompanied Skept, who was un-shaven and had sleepless circles under his eyes, on a writing ex-cursion to the Belmont Tunnel. Several writers were out that day, but Skept wandered off by himself to an out-of-the-way spot in the shadow of the old trolleycar station. There, he did a quick throw-up. With a baby-blue outline and a dark gray fill-in, he wrote his crew's name. The fat, blocklike letters seemed to collapse upon each other, as though plummeting through the air. In gold he wrote the names of Geo and Sine. He knelt before the piece in silence for several minutes.

Prime is sitting up in bed, flanked by two *cholos* in dark glasses. He offers his left hand in greeting. The doctors, he says, have told him that he's doing all right, "so far." He's kind of worried about their emphasis on the "so far," but says he's already going stir-crazy. He wants to go home.

He reminisces about the writing binges of the early days, when he and Skept and Geo would "walk from the Beverly Center Mall all the way downtown, tagging up all the way." They'd go all night sometimes, catching a wink wherever they could rather than go home. At dawn, they'd search for an apartment building with a swimming pool for a makeshift bath, then warm up at a local laundromat.

Prime stops suddenly. A grimace of pain crosses his face, and his right shoulder twitches involuntarily. I ask him about his arm. "I don't know, ey. I don't know," he says, looking away.

On my way out of Prime's room, I run into Duke and Radio-Tron founder Carmelo Alvarez, who continues to work closely with many of the K2S-STN writers. Duke stays with me in the hallway, leaning against the yellow wall under the bad fluorescent lights. He's working on a storefront for a neighborhood residents' association, he tells me. And he's recently been talking with Frank Romero, the famous Chicano artist. "I tripped out when he said that I could work with him on a project," says Duke, flashing a quick grin. For now, everything's "fresh."

I recall a photo Duke once showed me of Prime. It was taken on the day they worked together on a big piece near Belmont High, not far from where Prime was shot. The photo was taken looking down from the top of the wall, showing Prime frozen in mid-stroke — his right arm raised, a look of tremendous concentration on his face.

The piece they worked on that day is the one Duke is proudest of. He drew his "Dream Lady," with a soft, sensuous aqua face and windborne orange hair. Prime contributed a Cerebus-like character,

K2S-STN's mascot, in baby blue, with touches of clover green and turquoise. The piece is long gone, but has been immortalized in Duke's photo album.

"If Prime comes out not being able to draw with his right hand, he'll do it with his left," Duke says with almost desperate conviction. "And if he comes out not being able to move his left hand, he'll do it with his feet."

It is difficult not to be impressed by Duke's determination. At the same time, I find myself doubting. Graffiti art is temporal, fragile. It has a lifespan of only a week or two before another writer goes over a piece, or the city buffs it out. How far can the kids really go with it? The New York gallery scene's fascination with street art only directly affected a few writers in the short time it lasted. And even if some do make it into the L.A. galleries, will their work lose its power in that context?

And what of the inner-city black hole that threatens to swallow all the colors and deny every escape route? One well-known Eastside writer was awarded a scholarship to a prestigious local art school, which he attended for three years. He's now doing time for murder. Art doesn't always save, but here's Duke before me, all enthusiasm and faith, and who's to say that he and Prime and Skept can't realize their dreams?

Later, Prime's visitors are walking out of the County together, past the emergency entrance, where two paramedic trucks and a sheriff's patrol car are parked. The sun has just set and high, dark gray clouds streak across the sky, creating a dark canvas. Duke stops and stares. He has caught something we hadn't noticed: a small, baby-blue aperture in the gray.

"It's like a gateway to a new world," he says.

John McPhee

L.A., the old joke goes, has four seasons: fire, flood, earthquake, and drought. In this excerpt from *The Control of Nature* (1989), John McPhee (b. 1931) describes a natural calamity that even the most disaster-savvy Angeleno might not anticipate. McPhee has written more than two dozen books of extraordinarily artful nonfiction, among them *The Pine Barrens* (1968), *The Curve of Binding Energy* (1974), *Looking for a Ship* (1990), and his Pulitzer Prize–winning *Annals of the Former World* (1998), which is virtually a geological history of North America.

from

THE CONTROL OF NATURE

In Los Angeles versus the San Gabriel Mountains, it is not always clear which side is losing. For example, the Genofiles, Bob and Jackie, can claim to have lost and won. They live on an acre of ground so high that they look across their pool and past the trunks of big pines at an aerial view over Glendale and across Los Angeles to the Pacific bays. The setting, in cool dry air, is serene and Mediterranean. It has not been everlastingly serene.

On a February night some years ago, the Genofiles were awakened by a crash of thunder—lightning striking the mountain front. Ordinarily, in their quiet neighborhood, only the creek beside them was likely to make much sound, dropping steeply out of Shields Canyon on its way to the Los Angeles River. The creek, like every component of all the river systems across the city from mountains to ocean, had not been left to nature. Its banks were concrete. Its bed was concrete. When boulders were running there, they sounded like a rolling freight. On a night like this, the boulders should have been running. The creek should have been a torrent. Its unnatural sound was unnaturally absent. There was, and had been, a lot of rain.

The Genofiles had two teen-age children, whose rooms were on the uphill side of the one-story house. The window in Scott's room looked straight up Pine Cone Road, a cul-de-sac, which, with hun-

dreds like it, defined the northern limit of the city, the confrontation
of the urban and the wild. Los Angeles is overmatched on one side
by the Pacific Ocean and on the other by very high mountains. With
respect to these principal boundaries, Los Angeles is done sprawling. The San Gabriels, in their state of tectonic youth, are rising as
rapidly as any range on earth. Their loose inimical slopes flout the
tolerance of the angle of repose. Rising straight up out of the mega-
lopolis, they stand ten thousand feet above the nearby sea, and they
are not kidding with this city. Shedding, spalling, self-destructing,
they are disintegrating at a rate that is also among the fastest in the
world. The phalanxed communities of Los Angeles have pushed
themselves hard against these mountains, an aggression that requires a deep defense budget to contend with the results. Kimberlee
Genofile called to her mother, who joined her in Scott's room as they
looked up the street. From its high turnaround, Pine Cone Road
plunges downhill like a ski run, bending left and then right and then
left and then right in steep christiania turns for half a mile above a
three-hundred-foot straightaway that aims directly at the Genofiles'
house. Not far below the turnaround, Shields Creek passes under
the street, and there a kink in its concrete profile had been plugged
by a six-foot boulder. Hence the silence of the creek. The water was
now spreading over the street. It descended in heavy sheets. As the
young Genofiles and their mother glimpsed it in the all but total
darkness, the scene was suddenly illuminated by a blue electrical
flash. In the blue light they saw a massive blackness, moving. It was
not a landslide, not a mudslide, not a rock avalanche; nor by any
means was it the front of a conventional flood. In Jackie's words, "It
was just one big black thing coming at us, rolling, rolling with a lot
of water in front of it, pushing the water, this big black thing. It was
just one big black hill coming toward us."

In geology, it would be known as a debris flow. Debris flows
amass in stream valleys and more or less resemble fresh concrete.
They consist of water mixed with a good deal of solid material, most
of which is above sand size. Some of it is Chevrolet size. Boulders
bigger than cars ride long distances in debris flows. Boulders
grouped like fish eggs pour downhill in debris flows. The dark
material coming toward the Genofiles was not only full of boulders;
it was so full of automobiles it was like bread dough mixed with

raisins. On its way down Pine Cone Road, it plucked up cars from driveways and the street. When it crashed into the Genofiles' house, the shattering of safety glass made terrific explosive sounds. A door burst open. Mud and boulders poured into the hall. We're going to go, Jackie thought. Oh, my God, what a hell of a way for the four of us to die together.

The parents' bedroom was on the far side of the house. Bob Genofile was in there kicking through white satin draperies at the panelled glass, smashing it to provide an outlet for water, when the three others ran in to join him. The walls of the house neither moved nor shook. As a general contractor, Bob had built dams, department stores, hospitals, six schools, seven churches, and this house. It was made of concrete block with steel reinforcement, sixteen inches on center. His wife had said it was stronger than any dam in California. His crew had called it "the fort." In those days, twenty years before, the Genofiles' acre was close by the edge of the mountain brush, but a developer had come along since then and knocked down thousands of trees and put Pine Cone Road up the slope. Now Bob Genofile was thinking, I hope the roof holds. I hope the roof is strong enough to hold. Debris was flowing over it. He told Scott to shut the bedroom door. No sooner was the door closed than it was battered down and fell into the room. Mud, rock, water poured in. It pushed everybody against the far wall. "Jump on the bed," Bob said. The bed began to rise. Kneeling on it—on a gold velvet spread—they could soon press their palms against the ceiling. The bed also moved toward the glass wall. The two teen-agers got off, to try to control the motion, and were pinned between the bed's brass railing and the wall. Boulders went up against the railing, pressed it into their legs, and held them fast. Bob dived into the muck to try to move the boulders, but he failed. The debris flow, entering through windows as well as doors, continued to rise. Escape was still possible for the parents but not for the children. The parents looked at each other and did not stir. Each reached for and held one of the children. Their mother felt suddenly resigned, sure that her son and daughter would die and she and her husband would quickly follow. The house became buried to the eaves. Boulders sat on the roof. Thirteen automobiles were packed around the building, including five in the pool. A din of rocks kept banging against them. The stuck horn of a buried car was blaring. The family in the darkness in their fixed tableau watched one another by the light of a directional signal, endlessly blinking. The house had filled up in six minutes, and the mud stopped rising near the children's chins.

Stories like that do not always have such happy endings. A man went outside to pick up his newspaper one morning, heard a sound, turned, and died of a heart attack as he saw his house crushed to pieces with his wife and two children inside. People have been buried alive in their beds. But such cases are infrequent. Debris flows generally are much less destructive of life than of property. People get out of the way.

If they try to escape by automobile, they have made an obvious but imperfect choice. Norman Reid backed his Pontiac into the street one January morning and was caught from behind by rock porridge. It embedded the car to the chrome strips. Fifty years of archival news photographs show cars of every vintage standing like hippos in chunky muck. The upper halves of their headlights peep above the surface. The late Roland Case Ross, an emeritus professor at California State University, told me of a day in the early thirties when he watched a couple rushing to escape by car. She got in first. While her husband was going around to get in his side, she got out and ran into the house for more silverware. When the car at last putt-putted downhill, a wall of debris was nudging the bumper. The debris stayed on the vehicle's heels all the way to Foothill Boulevard, where the car turned left.

Foothill Boulevard was U.S. Route 66—the western end of the rainbow. Through Glendora, Azusa, Pasadena, it paralleled the mountain front. It strung the metropolitan border towns. And it brought in emigrants to fill them up. The real-estate line of maximum advance now averages more than a mile above Foothill, but Foothill receives its share of rocks. A debris flow that passed through the Monrovia Nursery went on to Foothill and beyond. With its twenty million plants in twelve hundred varieties, Monrovia was the foremost container nursery in the world, and in its recovery has remained so. The debris flow went through the place picking up pots and cans. It got into a greenhouse two hundred feet long and smashed out the southern wall, taking bougainvillea and hibiscus with it. Arby's, below Foothill, blamed the nursery for damages, citing the hibiscus that had come with the rocks. Arby's sought compensation, but no one was buying beef that thin.

In the same storm, large tree trunks rode in the debris like javelins and broke through the sides of houses. Automobiles went in through picture windows. A debris flow hit the gym at Azusa Pacific College and knocked a large hole in the upslope wall. In the words of Cliff Hamlow, the basketball coach, "If we'd had students in there, it would have killed them. Someone said it sounded like the roar of a jet engine. It filled the gym up with mud, and with boulders two and three feet in diameter. It went out through the south doors and spread all over the football field and track. Chain-link fencing was sheared off—like it had been cut with a welder. The place looked like a war zone." Azusa Pacific College wins national championships in track, but Coach Hamlow's basketball team (12-18) can't get the boulders out of its game.

When a debris flow went through the Verdugo Hills Cemetery, which is up a couple of switchbacks on the mountain front, two of the central figures there, resting under impressive stones, were "Hiram F. Hatch, 1st Lieut. 6th Mich. Inf., December 24, 1843– October 12, 1922," and "Henry J. Hatch, Brigadier General, United States Army, April 28, 1869–December 31, 1931." The two Hatches held the hill while many of their comrades slid below. In all, thirty-five coffins came out of the cemetery and took off for lower ground. They went down Hillrose Street and were scattered over half a mile. One came to rest in the parking lot of a supermarket. Many were reburied by debris and, in various people's yards, were not immediately found. Three turned up in one yard. Don Sulots, who had moved into the fallout path two months before, said, "It sounded like thunder. By the time I made it to the front door and got it open, the muck was already three feet high. It's quite a way to start off life in a new home—mud, rocks, and bodies all around."

Most people along the mountain front are about as mindful of debris flows as those corpses were. Here today, gone tomorrow. Those who worry build barricades. They build things called deflection walls—a practice that raises legal antennae and, when the caroming debris breaks into the home of a neighbor, probes the wisdom of Robert Frost. At least one family has experienced so many debris flows coming through their back yard that they long ago installed overhead doors in the rear end of their built-in garage. To guide the flows, they put deflection walls in their back yard. Now when the boulders come they open both ends of their garage, and the debris goes through to the street.

Between Harrow Canyon and Englewild Canyon, a private street called Glencoe Heights teased the mountain front. Came a time of unprecedented rain, and the neighborhood grew ever more fearful—became in fact so infused with catastrophic anticipation that it sought the drastic sort of action that only a bulldozer could provide. A fire had swept the mountainsides, leaving them vulnerable, dark, and bare. Expecting floods of mud and rock, people had piled sandbags and built heavy wooden walls. Their anxiety was continuous for many months. "This threat is on your mind all the time," Gary Lukehart said. "Every time you leave the house, you stop and put up another sandbag, and you just hope everything will be all right when you get back." Lukehart was accustomed to losing in Los Angeles. In the 1957 Rose Bowl, he was Oregon State's quarterback. A private street could not call upon city or county for the use of heavy equipment, so in the dead of night, as steady rain was falling, a call was put in to John McCafferty—bulldozer for hire. McCafferty had a closeup knowledge of the dynamics of debris flows: he had worked the mountain front from San Dimas to Sierra Madre, which to him is Sarah Modri. ("In those canyons at night, you could hear them big boulders comin'. They sounded like thunder.") He arrived at Glencoe Heights within the hour and set about turning the middle of the street into the Grand Canal of Venice. His Cat was actually not a simple dozer but a 955 loader on tracks, with a two-and-a-quarter-yard bucket seven feet wide. Cutting water mains, gas mains, and sewers, he made a ditch that eventually extended five hundred feet and was deep enough to take in three thousand tons of debris. After working for five hours, he happened to be by John Caufield's place ("It had quit rainin', it looked like the worst was over") when Caufield came out and said, "Mac, you sure have saved my bacon."

McCafferty continues, "All of a sudden, we looked up at the mountains—it's not too far from his house to the mountains, maybe a hundred and fifty feet—and we could just see it all comin'. It seemed the whole mountain had come loose. It flowed like cement." In the ditch, he put the Cat in reverse and backed away from the oncoming debris. He backed three hundred feet. He went up one side of the ditch and was about halfway out of it when the mud and boulders caught the Cat and covered it over the hood. In the cab, the mud pushed against McCafferty's legs. At the same time, debris broke into Caufield's house through the front door and the dining-room window, and in five minutes filled it to the eaves.

Other houses were destroyed as well. A garage left the neighborhood with a car in it. One house was buried twice. (After McCafferty dug it out, it was covered again.) His ditch, however, was effective, and saved many places on slightly higher ground, among them Gary Lukehart's and the home of John Marcellino, the chief executive officer of Mackinac Island Fudge. McCafferty was promised a lifetime supply of fudge. He was on the scene for several days, and in one span worked twenty-four hours without a break. The people of the street brought him chocolate milkshakes. He had left his lowbed parked around the corner. When at last he returned to it and prepared to go home, he discovered that a cop had given him a ticket.

A metropolis that exists in a semidesert, imports water three hundred miles, has inveterate flash floods, is at the grinding edges of two tectonic plates, and has a microclimate tenacious of noxious oxides will have its priorities among the aspects of its environment that it attempts to control. For example, Los Angeles makes money catching water. In a few days in 1983, it caught twenty-eight million dollars' worth of water. In one period of twenty-four hours, however, the ocean hit the city with twenty-foot waves, a tornado made its own freeway, debris flows poured from the San Gabriel front, and an earthquake shook the region. Nature's invoice was forty million dollars. Later, twenty million more was spent dealing with the mountain debris.

There were those who would be quick—and correct—in saying that were it not for the alert unflinching manner and imaginative strategies by which Los Angeles outwits the mountains, nature's invoices at such times would run into the billions. The rear-guard defenses are spread throughout the city and include more than two thousand miles of underground conduits and concrete-lined open stream channels—a web of engineering that does not so much reinforce as replace the natural river systems. The front line of battle is where the people meet the mountains—up the steep slopes where the subdivisions stop and the brush begins.

Strung out along the San Gabriel front are at least a hundred and twenty bowl-shaped excavations that resemble football stadiums and are often as large. Years ago, when a big storm left back yards and boulevards five feet deep in scree, one neighborhood came through amazingly unscathed, because it happened to surround a gravel pit that had filled up instead. A tungsten filament went on somewhere above Los Angeles. The county began digging pits to catch debris. They were quarries, in a sense, but exceedingly bizarre quarries, in that the rock was meant to come to them. They are known as debris basins. Blocked at their downstream ends with earthfill or concrete constructions, they are also known as debris dams. With clean spillways and empty reservoirs, they stand ready to capture rivers of boulders—these deep dry craters, lying close above the properties they protect. In the overflowing abundance of urban nomenclature, the individual names of such basins are obscure, until a day when they appear in a headline in the Los Angeles *Times*: Harrow, Englewild, Zachau, Dunsmuir, Shields, Big Dalton, Hog, Hook East, Hook West, Limekiln, Starfall, Sawpit, Santa Anita. For fifty miles, they mark the wild boundary like bulbs beside a mirror. Behind chain links, their idle ovate forms more than suggest defense. They are separated, on the average, by seven hundred yards. In aggregate, they are worth hundreds of millions of dollars. All this to keep the mountains from falling on Johnny Carson.

The principal agency that developed the debris basins was the hopefully named Los Angeles County Flood Control District, known familiarly through the region as Flood Control, and even more intimately as Flood. ("When I was at Flood, one of our dams filled with debris overnight," a former employee remarked to me. "If any more rain came, we were going to have to evacuate the whole of Pasadena.") There has been a semantic readjustment, obviously intended to acknowledge that when a flood pours out of the mountains it might be half rock. The debris basins are now in the charge of the newly titled Sedimentation Section of the Hydraulic Division of the Los Angeles County Department of Public Works. People still call it Flood. By whatever name the agency is called, its essential tactic remains unaltered. This was summarized for me in a few words by an engineer named Donald Nichols, who pointed out that eight million people live below the mountains on the urban coastal plain, within an area large enough to accommodate Philadelphia, Detroit, Chicago, St. Louis, Boston, and New York. He said, "To make the area inhabitable, you had to put in lined channels on the plain and halt the debris at the front. If you don't take it out at the front, it will come out in the plain, filling up channels. A filled channel won't carry diddly-boo."

To stabilize mountain streambeds and stop descending rocks even before they reach the debris basins, numerous crib structures (barriers made of concrete slats) have been emplaced in high canyons—the idea being to convert plunging streams into boulder staircases, and hypothetically cause erosion to work against itself. Farther into the mountains, a dozen dams of some magnitude were built in the nineteen-twenties and thirties to control floods and conserve water. Because they are in the San Gabriels, they inadvertently trap large volumes of debris. One of them—the San Gabriel Dam, in the San Gabriel River—was actually built as a debris-control structure. Its reservoir, which is regularly cleaned out, contained, just then, twenty million tons of mountain.

The San Gabriel River, the Los Angeles River, and the Big Tujunga (Bigta Hung-ga) are the principal streams that enter the urban plain, where a channel that filled with rock wouldn't carry diddly-boo. Three colossal debris basins—as different in style as in magnitude from those on the mountain front—have been constructed on the plain to greet these rivers. Where the San Gabriel goes past Azusa on its way to Alamitos Bay, the Army Corps of Engineers completed in the late nineteen-forties a dam ninety-two feet high and twenty-four thousand feet wide—this to stop a river that is often dry, and trickles most of the year. Santa Fe Dam, as it is called, gives up at a glance its own story, for it is made of boulders that are shaped like potatoes and are generally the size of watermelons. They imply a large volume of water flowing with high energy. They are stream-propelled, stream-rounded boulders, and the San Gabriel is the stream. In Santa Fe Basin, behind the dam, the dry bed of the San Gabriel is half a mile wide. The boulder-strewn basin in its entirety is four times as wide as that. It occupies eighteen hundred acres in all, nearly three square miles, of what would be prime real estate were it not for the recurrent arrival of rocks. The scene could have been radioed home from Mars, whose cobbly face is in part the result of debris flows dating to a time when Mars had surface water.

The equally vast Sepulveda Basin is where Los Angeles receives and restrains the Los Angeles River. In Sepulveda Basin are three golf courses, which lend ample support to the widespread notion that everything in Los Angeles is disposable. Advancing this national prejudice even further, debris flows, mudslides, and related phenomena have "provided literary minds with a ready-made metaphor of the alleged moral decay of Los Angeles." The words belong to Reyner Banham, late professor of the history of architecture at University College, London, whose passionate love of Los Angeles left him without visible peers. The decay was only "alleged," he said. Of such nonsense he was having none. With his "Los Angeles: The Architecture of Four Ecologies," Banham had become to this deprecated, defamed, traduced, and disparaged metropolis what Pericles was to Athens. Banham knew why the basins were there and what the people were defending. While all those neurasthenic literary minds are cowering somewhere in ethical crawl space, the quality of Los Angeles life rises up the mountain front. There is air there. Cool is the evening under the crumbling peaks. Cool descending air. Clean air. Air with a view. "The financial and topographical contours correspond almost exactly," Banham said. Among those "narrow, tortuous residential roads serving precipitous house-plots that often back up directly on unimproved wilderness" is "the fat life of the delectable mountains."

People of Gardena, Inglewood, and Watts no less than Azusa and Altadena pay for the defense of the mountain front, the rationale being that debris trapped near its source will not move down and choke the channels of the inner city, causing urban floods. The political City of Los Angeles—in its vague and tentacular configuration—actually abuts the San Gabriels for twenty miles or so, in much the way that it extends to touch the ocean in widely separated places like Venice, San Pedro, and Pacific Palisades. Los Angeles County reaches across the mountains and far into the Mojave Desert. The words "Los Angeles" as generally used here refer neither to the political city nor to the county but to the multinamed urban integrity that has a street in it seventy miles long (Sepulveda Boulevard) and, from the Pacific Ocean at least to Pomona, moves north against the mountains as a comprehensive town.

The debris basins vary greatly in size — not, of course, in relation to the populations they defend but in relation to the watersheds and washes above them in the mountains. For the most part, they are associated with small catchments, and the excavated basins are commensurately modest, with capacities under a hundred thousand cubic yards. In a typical empty reservoir — whatever its over-all dimensions may be — stands a columnar tower that resembles a campanile. Full of holes, it is known as a perforated riser. As the basin fills with a thick-flowing slurry of water, mud, and rock, the water goes into the tower and is drawn off below. The county calls this water harvesting.

Like the freeways, the debris-control system ordinarily functions but occasionally jams. When the Genofiles' swimming pool filled with cars, debris flows descended into other neighborhoods along that part of the front. One hit a culvert, plugged the culvert, crossed a road in a bouldery wave, flattened fences, filled a debris basin, went over the spillway, and spread among houses lying below, shoving them off their foundations. The debris basins have caught as much as six hundred thousand cubic yards in one storm. Over time, they have trapped some twenty million tons of mud and rock. Inevitably, sometimes something gets away.

At Devils Gate — just above the Rose Bowl, in Pasadena — a dam was built in 1920 with control of water its only objective. Yet its reservoir, with a surface of more than a hundred acres, has filled to the brim with four million tons of rock, gravel, and sand. A private operator has set up a sand-and-gravel quarry in the reservoir. Almost exactly, he takes out what the mountains put in. As one engineer has described it, "he pays Flood, and Flood makes out like a champ."

It was assumed that the Genofiles were dead. Firemen and paramedics who came into the neighborhood took one glance at the engulfed house and went elsewhere in search of people needing help. As the family remained trapped, perhaps an hour went by. They have no idea.

"We didn't know why it had come or how long it was going to last."

They lost all sense of time. The stuck horn went on blaring, the directional signal eerily blinking. They imagined that more debris was on the way.

"We didn't know if the whole mountain was coming down."

As they waited in the all but total darkness, Jackie thought of neighbors' children. "I thought, Oh, my gosh, all those little kids are dead. Actually, they were O.K. And the neighbors thought for sure we were all gone. All our neighbors thought we were gone."

At length, a neighbor approached their house and called out, "Are you alive?"

"Yes. But we need help."

As the debris flow hit the Genofiles' house, it also hit a six-ton truck from the L.A.C.F.C.D., the vigilant bureau called Flood. Vigilance was about all that the L.A.C.F.C.D. had been able to offer. The patrolling vehicle and its crew of two were as helpless as everyone else. Each of the crewmen had lived twenty-six years, and each came close to ending it there. Minutes before the flow arrived, the truck labored up Pine Cone Road—a forty-one-per-cent grade, steep enough to stiff a Maserati. The two men meant to check on a debris basin at the top. Known as Upper Shields, it was less than two years old, and had been built in anticipation of the event that was about to occur. Oddly enough, the Genofiles and their neighbors were bracketed with debris basins—Upper Shields above them, Shields itself below them, six times as large. Shields Debris Basin, with its arterial concrete feeder channels, was prepared to catch fifty thousand tons. The Genofiles' house looked out over Shields as if it were an empty lake, its shores hedged about with oleander. When the developer extended Pine Cone Road up into the brush, the need for Upper Shields was apparent. The new basin came in the nick of time but—with a capacity under six thousand cubic yards—not in the nick of space. Just below it was a chain-link gate. As the six-ton truck approached the gate, mud was oozing through. The basin above had filled in minutes, and now, suddenly, boulders shot like cannonballs over the crest of the dam, with mud, cobbles, water, and trees. Chris Terracciano, the driver, radioed to headquarters, "It's coming over." Then he whipped the truck around and fled. The debris flow came through the chain-link barrier as if the links were made of paper. Steel posts broke off. As the truck accelerated down the steep hill, the debris flow chased and caught it. Boulders bounced against it. It was hit by empty automobiles spinning and revolving in the muck. The whole descending complex gathered force with distance. Terracciano later said, "I thought I was dead the whole way." The truck finally stopped when it bashed against a tree and a cement-block wall. The rear window shattered. Terracciano's partner suffered a broken leg. The two men crawled out through the window and escaped over the wall.

Within a few miles, other trapped patrols were calling in to say, "It's coming over." Zachau went over—into Sunland. Haines went over—into Tujunga. Dunsmuir went over—into Highway Highlands. As bulldozers plow out the streets after events like these, the neighborhoods of northern Los Angeles assume a macabre resemblance to New England villages under deep snow: the cleared paths, the vehicular rights-of-way, the parking meters buried within the high banks, the half-covered drift-girt homes. A street that is lined with palms will have debris berms ten feet up the palms. In the Genofiles' front yard, the drift was twelve feet deep. A person, without climbing, could walk onto the roof. Scott's bedroom had a few inches of space left at the top. Kimberlee's had mud on the ceiling. On the terrace, the crushed vehicles, the detached erratic wheels suggested bomb damage, artillery hits, the track of the Fifth Army. The place looked like a destroyed pillbox. No wonder people assumed that no one had survived inside.

There was a white sedan under the house eaves crushed to half its height, with two large boulders resting on top of it. Near the pool, a Volkswagen bug lay squashed. Another car was literally wrapped around a tree, like a C-clamp, its front and rear bumpers pointing in the same direction. A crushed pickup had boulders all over it, each a good deal heavier than anything a pickup could carry. One of the cars in the swimming pool was upside down, its tires in the air. A Volkswagen was on top of it. Bob Genofile— owner, contractor, victim—walked around in rubber boots, a visored construction cap, a foul-weather jacket, studying the damage,

mostly guessing at what he couldn't see. A big, strongly built, leo-
nine man with prematurely white hair, he looked like a middle line-
backer near the end of a heavy day. He wondered if the house was
still on its foundation, but there was no telling in this profound
chaos, now hardening and cracking like bad concrete. In time, as his
house was excavated from the inside, he would find that it had not
budged. Not one wall had so much as cracked. He was uninsured,
but down in the rubble was a compensation of greater value than
insurance. Forever, he could say, as he quietly does when he tells
the story, "I built it, man."

Kimberlee's birthday came two days after the debris. She was a
college student, turning nineteen, and her father had had a gift for
her that he was keeping in his wallet. "I had nineteen fifty-dollar
bills to give her for her birthday, but my pants and everything was
gone."

Young Scott, walking around in the wreckage, saw a belt sticking out of the muck like a night crawler after rain. He pulled at it,
and the buried pants came with it. The wallet was still in the pants.
The wallet still contained what every daughter wants for her birthday: an album of portraits of U.S. Grant, no matter if Ulysses is wet
or dry.

The living room had just been decorated, and in six minutes the
job had been destroyed — "the pale tangerines and greens, Italian-
style furniture with marble, and all that." Jackie Genofile continues
the story: "We had been out that night, and, you know, you wear
your better jewelry. I came home like an idiot and put mine on the
dresser. Bob put his on the dresser. Three weeks later, when some
workers were cleaning debris out of the bedroom, they found his
rings on the floor. They did not find mine. But — can you believe
it? — a year and a half later Scott was down in the debris basin with
one of his friends, and the Flood Control had these trucks there
cleaning it out, and Scott saw this shiny thing, and he picked it up,
and it was my ring that Bob had given me just before the storm."

Before the storm, they had not in any way felt threatened. Like
their neighbors, they were confident of the debris basins, of the concrete liners of the nearby stream. After the storm, neighbors moved
away. Where Pine Cone Road swung left or right, the debris had
made centrifugal leaps, breaking into houses. A hydrant snapped

off, and arcing water shot through an upstairs window. A child
nearly drowned inside his own house. The family moved. "Another
family that moved owned one of the cars that ended up in our pool,"
Jackie told me. "The husband said he'd never want to live here
again, you know. And she was in real estate."

After the storm, the Genofiles tended to wake in the night, startled and anxious. They still do. "I wake up once in a while really
uptight," Bob said. "I can just feel it—go through the whole thing,
you know."

Jackie said that when rain pounds on a roof, anywhere she happens to be, she will become tense. Once, she took her dog and her
pillow and went to sleep in Bob's office—which was then in Mon-
trose, down beyond Foothill Boulevard.

Soon after the storm, she said, "Scotty woke up one night, and
he had a real high temperature. You see, he was sixteen, and he kept
hearing the mud and rock hitting the window. He kept thinking it
was going to come again. Kim used to go four-wheeling, and cross
streams, and she had to get out once, because they got stuck, and
when she felt the flow of water and sand on her legs, she said, she
could have panicked."

Soon after the storm, the family gathered to make a decision.
Were they going to move or were they going to dig out their house
and rebuild it? Each of them knew what might have happened. Bob
said, "If it had been a frame house, we would be dead down in the
basin below."

But it was not a frame house. It was the fort. "The kids said
rebuild. So we rebuilt."

As he sat in his new living room telling the story, Bob was
dressed in a Pierre Cardin jumper and pants, and Jackie was beside
him in a pale-pink jumpsuit by Saint Germain. The house had a
designer look as well, with its railings and balconies and Italianate
marbles under the tall dry trees. It appeared to be worth a good deal
more than the half-million dollars Bob said it might bring. He had
added a second story and put all bedrooms there. The original roof
spreads around them like a flaring skirt. He changed a floor-length
window in the front hall, filling the lower half of it with cement
block.

I asked what other structural changes he had made.

He said, "None."

The Genofiles sued Los Angeles County. They claimed that Upper Shields Debris Basin had not been cleaned out and that the channel below was improperly designed. Los Angeles settled for three hundred and thirty-seven thousand five hundred dollars.

From the local chamber of commerce the family later received the Beautification Award for Best Home. Two of the criteria by which houses are selected for this honor are "good maintenance" and "a sense of drama."

Mike Davis

In 1990, when Mike Davis (b. 1946) published *City of Quartz*, his pessimistic view of Los Angeles and its future was at odds with Mayor Tom
Bradley's notion of "a glorious mosaic." But in the wake of the L.A. riots
two years later, Davis began to look like a prophet. A dissection of the hidden assumptions underlying the city's urban planning, *City of Quartz* (represented here by its preface) has become one of the most influential pieces
of social criticism ever written about Los Angeles. A contemporary coun-
terpart to such contrarian thinkers as Carey McWilliams and Louis
Adamic (to both of whom he has paid tribute), Davis was born in Fontana,
a working-class community just west of San Bernardino, and worked as a
truck driver and meat cutter before publishing his first book, *Prisoners of the
American Dream*, in 1986. The recipient of a 1998 MacArthur grant, his subsequent books include *Ecology of Fear* (1998), *Magical Urbanism* (2000), and
Late Victorian Holocausts (2001).

from

CITY OF QUARTZ

The best place to view Los Angeles of the next millennium is
from the ruins of its alternative future. Standing on the sturdy
cobblestone foundations of the General Assembly Hall of the Socialist city of Llano del Rio—Open Shop Los Angeles's utopian
antipode—you can sometimes watch the Space Shuttle in its elegant
final descent towards Rogers Dry Lake. Dimly on the horizon are
the giant sheds of Air Force Plant 42 where Stealth Bombers (each
costing the equivalent of 10,000 public housing units) and other,
still top secret, hot rods of the apocalypse are assembled. Closer at
hand, across a few miles of creosote and burro bush, and the occasional grove of that astonishing yucca, the Joshua tree, is the advance guard of approaching suburbia, tract homes on point.

The desert around Llano has been prepared like a virgin bride
for its eventual union with the Metropolis: hundreds of square miles
of vacant space engridded to accept the future millions, with
strange, prophetic street signs marking phantom intersections like

'250th Street and Avenue K'. Even the eerie trough of the San Andreas Fault, just south of Llano over a foreboding escarpment, is being gingerly surveyed for designer home sites. Nuptial music is provided by the daily commotion of ten thousand vehicles hurtling past Llano on 'Pearblossom Highway'—the deadliest stretch of two-lane blacktop in California.

When Llano's original colonists, eight youngsters from the Young Peoples' Socialist League (YPSL), first arrived at the 'Plymouth Rock of the Cooperative Commonwealth' in 1914, this part of the high Mojave Desert, misnamed the Antelope Valley,[1] had a population of a few thousand ranchers, borax miners and railroad workers as well as some armed guards to protect the newly-built aqueduct from sabotage. Los Angeles was then a city of 300,000 (the population of the Antelope Valley today), and its urban edge, now visible from Llano, was in the new suburb of Hollywood, where D. W. Griffith and his cast of thousands were just finishing an epic romance of the Ku Klux Klan, *Birth of a Nation*. In their day-long drive from the Labor Temple in Downtown Los Angeles to Llano over ninety miles of rutted wagon road, the YPSLs in their red Model-T trucks passed by scores of billboards, planted amid beet fields and walnut orchards, advertising the impending subdivision of the San Fernando Valley (owned by the city's richest men and annexed the following year as the culmination of the famous 'water conspiracy' fictionally celebrated in Polanski's *Chinatown*).

Three-quarters of a century later, forty thousand Antelope Valley commuters slither bumper-to-bumper each morning through Soledad Pass on their way to long-distance jobs in the smog-shrouded and overdeveloped San Fernando Valley. Briefly a Red Desert in the heyday of Llano (1914–18), the high Mojave for the last fifty years has been preeminently the Pentagon's playground. Patton's army trained here to meet Rommel (the ancient tank tracks are still visible), while Chuck Yeager first broke the sound barrier over the Antelope Valley in his Bell X-1 rocket plane. Under the 18,000 square-mile, ineffable blue dome of R-2508—'the most important military airspace in the world'—ninety thousand military training sorties are still flown every year.

But as developable land has disappeared throughout the coastal plains and inland basins, and soaring land inflation has reduced access to new housing to less than 15 per cent of the population, the militarized desert has suddenly become the last frontier of the Southern California Dream. With home prices $100,000 cheaper that in the San Fernando Valley, the archetypical suburban fringe of the 1950s, the Antelope Valley has nearly doubled in population over the last decade, with another quarter million new arrivals expected by 2010. Eleven thousand new homes were started in 1988 alone. But since the Valley's economic base, not counting real-estate agents, consists almost entirely of embattled Cold War complexes — Edwards Air Force Base and Plant 42 (altogether about eighteen thousand civilian jobs) — most of the new homebuyers will simply swell the morning commute on the Antelope Valley Freeway.

The pattern of urbanization here is what design critic Peter Plagens once called the 'ecology of evil.'[2] Developers don't grow homes in the desert — this isn't Marrakesh or even Tucson — they just clear, grade and pave, hook up some pipes to the local artificial river (the federally subsidized California Aqueduct), build a security wall and plug in the 'product.' With generations of experience in uprooting the citrus gardens of Orange County and the San Fernando Valley, the developers — ten or twelve major firms, headquartered in places like Newport Beach and Beverly Hills — regard the desert as simply another abstraction of dirt and dollar signs. The region's major natural wonder, a Joshua tree forest containing individual specimens often thirty feet high and older than the Domesday Book, is being bulldozed into oblivion. Developers regard the magnificent Joshuas, unique to this desert, as large noxious weeds unsuited to the illusion of verdant homesteads. As the head of Harris Homes explained: 'It is a very bizarre tree. It is not a beautiful tree like the pine or something. Most people don't care about the Joshuas.'[3]

With such malice toward the landscape, it is not surprising that developers also refuse any nomenclatural concession to the desert. In promotional literature intended for homebuyers or Asian investors, they have started referring to the region euphemistically as 'North Los Angeles County.' Meanwhile they christen their little pastel pods of Chardonnay lifestyle, air-conditioned and overwatered, with scented brand-names like Fox Run, Mardi Gras, Bravo, Cambridge, Sunburst, New Horizons, and so on. The most hallucinatory are the gated communities manufactured by Kaufman and Broad, the homebuilders who were famous in the 1970s for exporting Hollywood ramblers to the suburbs of Paris. Now they have brought back France (or, rather, California homes in French drag) to the desert in fortified mini-*banlieus*, with lush lawns, Old World shrubs, fake mansard roofs and *nouveaux riches* titles like 'Chateau.'

But Kaufman and Broad only expose the underlying method in the apparent madness of L.A.'s urban desert. The discarded Joshua trees, the profligate wastage of water, the claustrophobic walls, and the ridiculous names are as much a polemic against incipient urbanism as they are an assault on an endangered wilderness. The *eutopic* (literally no-place) logic of their subdivisions, in sterilized sites stripped bare of nature and history, masterplanned only for privatized family consumption, evokes much of the past evolution of tract-home Southern California. But the developers are not just re-packaging myth (the good life in the suburbs) for the next generation; they are also pandering to a new, burgeoning fear of the city.

Social anxiety, as traditional urban sociology likes to remind us, is just maladjustment to change. But who has anticipated, or adjusted to, the scale of change in Southern California over the last fifteen years? Stretching now from the country-club homes of Santa Barbara to the shanty *colonias* of Ensenada, to the edge of Llano in the high desert and of the Coachella Valley in the low, with a built-up surface area nearly the size of Ireland and a GNP bigger than India's—the urban galaxy dominated by Los Angeles is the fastest growing metropolis in the advanced industrial world. Its current population of fifteen million, encompassing six counties and a corner of Baja California, and clustered around two super-cores (Los Angeles and San Diego–Tijuana) and a dozen major, expanding metro-centers, is predicted to increase by another seven or eight million over the next generation. The overwhelming majority of these new inhabitants will be non-Anglos, further tipping the ethnic balance away from WASP hegemony toward the polyethnic diversity of the next century. (Anglos became a minority in the city and county of Los Angeles during the 1980s, as they will become in the state before 2010.[4])

Social polarization has increased almost as rapidly as population. A recent survey of Los Angeles household income trends in the

1980s suggests that affluence (incomes of $50,000 plus) has almost tripled (from 9 per cent to 26 per cent) while poverty ($15,000 and under) has increased by a third (from 30 per cent to 40 per cent); the middle range, as widely predicted, has collapsed by half (from 61 per cent to 32 per cent).[5] At the same time the worst popular fears of a generation ago about the consequences of market-driven overdevelopment have punctually come true. Decades of systematic under-investment in housing and urban infrastructure, combined with grotesque subsidies for speculators, permissive zoning for commercial development, the absence of effective regional planning, and ludicrously low property taxes for the wealthy have ensured an erosion of the quality of life for the middle classes in older suburbs as well as for the inner-city poor.

Ironically the Antelope Valley is both a sanctuary from this maelstrom of growth and crisis, and one of its fastest growing epicenters. In the desperate reassurance of their gated subdivisions, the new commuter population attempts to recover the lost Eden of 1950s-style suburbia. Older Valley residents, on the other hand, are frantically trying to raise the gangplanks against this ex-urban exodus sponsored by their own pro-growth business and political elites. In their increasingly angry view, the landrush since 1984 has only brought traffic jams, smog, rising crime, job competition, noise, soil erosion, a water shortage and the attrition of a distinctively countrified lifestyle.

For the first time since the Socialists left the desert (in 1918 for their New Llano colony in Louisiana) there is wild talk of a 'total rural revolution.' The announcement of several new megaprojects — instant cities ranging from 8,500 to 35,000 units, designed to be plugged into the Valley's waiting grid — have aroused unprecedented populist ire. On one recent occasion, the representative of the Ritter Ranch project in rustic Leone Valley was 'ambushed by an angry mob . . . screaming and bitching and threatening to kill [him].' In the Valley's two incorporated municipalities of Lancaster (the international headquarters of the Flat Earth Society) and Palmdale (the fastest growing city in California for most of the 1980s), more than sixty different homeowners' associations have joined together to slow down urbanization, as well as to contest the state's plan for a new 2,200-bed prison for Los Angeles drug and gang offenders in the Mira Loma area.[6]

Meanwhile the myth of a desert sanctuary was shattered shortly after New Year's Eve 1990 when a stray bullet from a gang member's gun killed a popular high-school athlete. Shortly afterwards, the trendy Quartz Hill area, advertised as the emergent 'Beverly Hills' of the desert, was wracked by a gun-battle between the local 5 Deuce Posse and some out-of-town Crips. The *grand peur* of L.A. street gangs suddenly swept the high desert. While sheriffs hunted fugitive teenagers with dogs—like escapees from a Georgia chain-gang—local businessmen formed the semi-vigilante Gangs Out Now (GON). Intimidated by official warnings that there were six hundred and fifty 'identified gang members' in the Valley, the local high school attempted to impose a draconian dress code banning 'gang colors' (blue and red). Outraged students, in turn, protested in the streets.[7]

While the kids were 'doin' the right thing,' the local NAACP was demanding an investigation of three suspicious killings of non-whites by sheriffs' deputies. In one case the deputies gunned down an unarmed Asian college student while in another a Black man accused of wielding a three-pronged garden tool was shot eight times. The most egregious incident, however, was the slaying of Betty Jean Aborn, a homeless middle-aged Black woman with a history of mental illness. Confronted by seven burly sheriffs after stealing an ice-cream from a convenience store, she supposedly brandished a butcher's knife. The response was an incredible volley of twenty-eight rounds, eighteen of which perforated her body.[8]

As the desert thus announced the arrival of the *fin de siècle* with a staggering overture of bulldozers and gunfire, some old-timers— contemplating the rapidly diminishing distance between the solitude of the Mojave and the gridlock of suburban life—began to wonder out loud whether there was any alternative to Los Angeles after all.

THE MAY POLE

Class war and repression are said to have driven the Los Angeles Socialists into the desert. But they also came eagerly, wanting to taste the sweet fruit of cooperative labor in their own lifetimes. As Job Harriman, who came within a hair's-breadth of being Los Angeles's first Socialist mayor in 1911, explained: 'It became appar-

ent to me that a people would never abandon their means of liveli-
hood, good or bad, capitalistic or otherwise, until other methods
were developed which would promise advantages at least as good as
those by which they were living.' What Llano promised was a guaranteed $4 per day wage and a chance to 'show the world a trick they
do not know, which is how to live without war or interest on money
or rent on land or profiteering in any manner.'[9]

With the sponsorship not only of Harriman and the Socialist
Party, but also of Chairman W. A. Engle of the Central Labor
Council and Frank McMahon of the Bricklayers' Union, hundreds
of landless farmers, unemployed laborers, blacklisted machinists,
adventurous clerks, persecuted IWW soapbox orators, restless
shopkeepers, and bright-eyed bohemians followed the YPSLs to
where the snow-fed Rio del Llano (now Big Rock Creek) met the
edge of the desert. Although they were 'democracy with the lid off
... democracy rampant, belligerent, unrestricted,' their enthusiastic
labor transformed several thousand acres of the Mojave into a small
Socialist civilization.[10] By 1916 their alfalfa fields and modern dairy,
their pear orchards and vegetable gardens—all watered by a complex and efficient irrigation system—supplied the colony with 90
per cent of its own food (and fresh flowers as well). Meanwhile,
dozens of small workshops cobbled shoes, canned fruit, laundered
clothes, cut hair, repaired autos, and published the *Western Comrade*.
There was even a Llano motion picture company and an ill-fated
experiment in aviation (the homemade plane crashed).

In the spirit of Chautauqua as much as Marx, Llano was also
one big Red School House. While babies (including Bella Lewitzky,
the future modern dancer) played in the nursery, children (among
them Gregory Ain, the future modern architect) attended Southern
California's first Montessori school. The teenagers, meanwhile, had
their own Kid Kolony (a model industrial school), and adults
attended night classes or enjoyed the Mojave's largest library. One
of the favorite evening pastimes, apart from dancing to the colony's
notorious ragtime orchestra, was debating Alice Constance Austin's
design for the Socialist City that Llano was to become.

Although influenced by contemporary City Beautiful and Garden City ideologies, Austin's drawings and models, as architectural
historian Dolores Hayden has emphasized, were 'distinctively femi-

nist and California.' Like Llano kid Gregory Ain's more modest 1940s plans for cooperative housing, Austin attempted to translate the specific cultural values and popular enthusiasms of Southern California into a planned and egalitarian social landscape. In the model that she presented to colonists on May Day 1916, Llano was depicted as a garden city of ten thousand people housed in graceful Craftsman apartments with private gardens but communal kitchens and laundries to liberate women from drudgery. The civic center, as befitted a 'city of light,' was composed of 'eight rectangular halls, like factories, with sides almost wholly of glass, leading to a glass-domed assembly hall.' She crowned this aesthetic of individual choice within a fabric of social solidarity with a quintessentially Southern California gesture: giving every household an automobile and constructing a ring road around the city that would double 'as a drag strip with stands for spectators on both sides.'[11]

If Austin's vision of thousands of patio apartments radiating from the Bonaventure Hotel–style Assembly Hall, surrounded by socially owned orchards, factories and a monumental dragstrip sounds a bit far-fetched today, imagine what Llanoites would have made of a future composed of Kaufman and Broad *chateaux* ringed by mini-malls, prisons and Stealth Bomber plants. In any event, the nine hundred pioneers of the Socialist City would enjoy only one more triumphant May Day in the Mojave.

> The May Day festivities of 1917 commenced at nine o'clock in the morning with intra-community athletic events, including a Fat Women's Race. The entire group of colonists then formed a Grand Parade and marched to the hotel where the Literary Program followed. The band played from a bunting-draped grandstand, the choral society sang appropriate revolutionary anthems like the 'Marseillaise', then moved into the Almond Grove for a barbecue dinner. After supper a group of young girls injected the English into the radical tradition by dancing about the May Pole. At 7:30 the dramatic club presented 'Mishaps of Minerva' with newly decorated scenery in the assembly hall. Dancing consumed the remainder of the evening.[12]

Despite an evident sense of humor, Llano began to fall apart in the later half of 1917. Plagued by internal feuding between the General Assembly and the so-called 'brush gang,' the colony was assailed from the outside by creditors, draft boards, jealous neighbors, and the Los Angeles *Times*. After the loss of Llano's water rights in a lawsuit—a devastating blow to its irrigation infrastructure—Harriman and a minority of colonists relocated in 1918 to Louisiana, where a hard-scrabble New Llano (a pale shadow of the original) hung on until 1939. Within twenty-four hours of the colonists' departure, local ranchers ('who precariously represented capitalism in the wilderness') began to demolish its dormitories and workshops, evidently with the intention of erasing any trace of the red menace. But Llano's towering silo, cow byre, and the cobblestone foundation and twin fireplaces of its Assembly Hall, proved indestructible: as local patriotic fury subsided, they became romantic landmarks ascribed to increasingly mythic circumstances.

Now and then, a philosophical temperament, struggling with the huge paradox of Southern California, rediscovers Llano as the talisman of a future lost. Thus Aldous Huxley, who lived for a few years in the early 1940s in a former Llano ranch house overlooking the colony's cemetery, liked to meditate 'in the almost supernatural silence' on the fate of utopia. He ultimately came to the conclusion that the Socialist City was a 'pathetic little Ozymandias,' doomed from the start by Harriman's 'Gladstone collar' and his 'Pickwickian' misunderstanding of human nature—whose history 'except in a purely negative way . . . is sadly uninstructive.'[13]

Llano's other occasional visitors, lacking Huxley's vedic cynicism, have generally been more charitable. After the debacle of 1960s–70s communitarianism (especially the deadly trail that led into the Guyanese jungle), the pear trees planted by this ragtime utopia seem a more impressive accomplishment. Moreover, as its most recent historians point out, Huxley grossly underestimated the negative impact of wartime xenophobia and the spleen of the Los Angeles *Times* upon Llano's viability. There but for fortune (and Harry Chandler), perhaps, would stand a brave red *kibbutz* in the Mojave today, canvassing votes for Jesse Jackson and protecting Joshuas from bulldozers.[14]

THE DEVELOPER'S MILLENNIUM?

But, then again, we do not stand at the gates of Socialism's New Jerusalem, but at the hard edge of the developers' millennium.

Llano itself is owned by an absentee speculator in Chicago who awaits an offer he cannot refuse from Kaufman and Broad. Setting aside an apocalyptic awakening of the neighboring San Andreas Fault, it is all too easy to envision Los Angeles reproducing itself endlessly across the desert with the assistance of pilfered water, cheap immigrant labor, Asian capital and desperate homebuyers willing to trade lifetimes on the freeway in exchange for $500,000 'dream homes' in the middle of Death Valley.

Is this the world-historic victory of Capitalism that everyone is talking about?

On May Day 1990 (the same day Gorbachev was booed by thousands of alienated Moscovites) I returned to the ruins of Llano del Rio to see if the walls would talk to me. Instead I found the Socialist City reinhabited by two twenty-year-old building laborers from El Salvador, camped out in the ruins of the old dairy and eager to talk with me in our mutually broken tongues. Like hobo heroes out of a Jack London novel, they had already tramped up and down California, but following a frontier of housing starts, not silver strikes or wheat harvests. Although they had yet to find work in Palmdale, they praised the clear desert sky, the easy hitchhiking and the relative scarcity of La Migra. When I observed that they were settled in the ruins of a *ciudad socialista*, one of them asked whether the 'rich people had come with planes and bombed them out.' No, I explained, the colony's credit had failed. They looked baffled and changed the subject.

We talked about the weather for a while, then I asked them what they thought about Los Angeles, a city without boundaries, which ate the desert, cut down the Joshua and the May Pole, and dreamt of becoming infinite. One of my new Llano *compañeros* said that L.A. already was everywhere. They had watched it every night in San Salvador, in endless dubbed reruns of *I Love Lucy* and *Starsky and Hutch*, a city where everyone was young and rich and drove new cars and saw themselves on television. After ten thousand day-dreams like this, he had deserted the Salvadorean Army and hitch-hiked two thousand five hundred miles to Tijuana. A year later he was standing at the corner of Alvarado and Seventh Streets in the MacArthur Park district near Downtown Los Angeles, along with all the rest of yearning, hardworking Central America. No one like him was rich or drove a new car—except for the coke dealers—and the police were as mean as back home. More importantly no one like him was on television; they were all invisible.

His friend laughed. 'If you were on TV you would just get deported anyway and have to pay some *coyote* in Tijuana $500 to sneak you back to L.A.' He argued that it was better to stay out in the open whenever possible, preferably here in the desert, away from the center. He compared L.A. and Mexico City (which he knew well) to volcanoes, spilling wreckage and desire in ever-widening circles over a denuded countryside. It is never wise, he averred, to live too near a volcano. 'The old gringo *socialistas* had the right idea.'

I agreed, even though I knew it was too late to move, or to re-found Llano. Then, it was their turn to interrogate me. Why was I out here alone, amongst the ghosts of May Day? What did *I* think of Los Angeles? I tried to explain that I had just written a book. . . .

Notes

1. Despite the incautious claims of Lynne Foster in her recent Sierra Club guide (*Adventuring in the California Desert*, San Francisco 1987), there is absolutely no evidence that 'many thousands of pronghorn antelope roamed the area' in the nineteenth century. On the contrary, small numbers of pronghorn were introduced in the Space Age, partially to allow the Valley to live up to its name!

2. 'Los Angeles: The Ecology of Evil,' *Artforum*, December 1972.

3. Los Angeles *Times*, 3 January 1988; Antelope Valley *Press* 29 October 1989.

4. For demographic projections, see Southern California Association of Governments (SCAG), *Growth Management Plan*, Los Angeles, February 1989. To the rather arbitrary five-county SCAG area I have added projections for San Diego and Tijuana.

5. County research quoted on KCET-TV's 'A Class by Itself,' May 1990.

6. Los Angeles *Business Journal*, 25 December 1989; *Press* 14 and 19 January 1990.

7. Ibid., 17 and 19 January.

8. *Daily News*, 4 June 1989. (It was months before the Los Angeles *Times* reported the Aborn murder in its main edition.)

9. Harriman quoted in Robert Hine, *California's Utopian Colonies*, San Marino, Calif. 1953, p. 117; and Dolores Hayden, *Seven American Utopias*, Cambridge, Mass. 1976, pp. 289–90.

10. Llano chronicler Ernest Wooster quoted in Nigey Lenon, Lionel Rolfe, and Paul Greenstein, *Bread and Hyacinths: Job Harriman and His Political Legacy*, unpublished manuscript, Los Angeles 1988, p. 21.

11. Cf. Hayden, pp. 300–1 (on Austin's design); and Sam Hall Kaplan, *L.A. Lost and Found*, New York 1987, p. 137 (on Ain's attempts to design for cooperative living).

12. Hines, p. 127.

13. 'Ozymandias, The Utopia that Failed', in *Tomorrow and Tomorrow and Tomorrow* . . . , New York, 1956, pp. 84–102.

14. Of course I deliberately beg the question of the Joshuas ploughed away to build Llano (ominously they have never grown back), not to mention what would have come of Austin's car in every red garage or where the water for 10,000 singing tomorrows would have been 'borrowed' from.

Lynell George

In "City of Specters," Lynell George (b. 1962) evokes a phantasmic Los Angeles, a haunted place where bits of the past swirl through the present to reemerge at unexpected moments, reminding us of who and what we used to be. A staff writer for the *Los Angeles Times* (and former staff writer for *LA Weekly*), George grew up in Culver City and now lives in Echo Park. Her book *No Crystal Stair: African-Americans in the City of Angels*, in which "City of Specters" appears, was published in 1992.

CITY OF SPECTERS

A teacher here recently gave a vocabulary test in which she asked her students to provide the antonym of youth. Over half the class answered death.

Truman Capote, "Hollywood"

They worship death here. They don't worship money they worship death.

Raymond Chandler on Hollywood

Death is only a word, it is an abrupt absence that has reality.

John Clellon Holmes

Some mornings, from a majestic set of sooty garret windows, Moss will watch downtown's concrete fall then slowly rise. With black coffee in hand and Joe Turner sassing on the stereo, he daily makes note of the city's slow progress—aborted elaborate projects, radically altered plans. Most evenings he is mesmerized by the strict configuration of windows, light, and ledges that metamorphose into surreal though solemn faces. Like sacred ceremonial masks, they loom stoic and unblinking in the vast night sky.

This warehouse space squats unobtrusively beneath a black argument of electric lines and is cordoned off by a set of railroad tracks that seem to wander nowhere. It's been years since I've settled down on these scarred wood floors, since Moss has opened the door, his mouth, or his heart to friends.

778

When I first met Moss through his girlfriend Inez, he was new to town. I'd met Inez while I was still shelving and selling best sellers to attorneys and junior film executives at a small bookstore in Century City. Some evenings when I worked late, I'd see her draping mannequins in expensive, exotic clothes. She stopped me one afternoon when she saw me carrying a slim portfolio, while waiting in line for lunch. "Student?" she asked glancing through black-and-white still lifes. I nodded. "Good stuff. It'll get better." She had given up on photography—the smell, the cost. After hours she dressed windows for a chain of Westside department stores; from dawn to dusk she fretted over huge canvases in her downtown loft. With time she offered the use of her forsaken darkroom as well as a critical eye.

In those days, Moss had only just begun curiously prowling empty side streets at all hours, carefully sidestepping limp bodies of homeless women and men. He would stoop to check a pulse at the temple or the rhythm of halting, shallow breaths—once leaning over to share his air with a little girl whose lips and lids had gone blue. This ritual continued until he was shaken down at dusk near Al's Bar at Traction. Now he seldom talks or slows his stride for any thing or one.

Some say now he is a ghost. Standing a shade over six feet, rail-like, from a short distance within dusk's half-light, Moss looks like nothing more than a haphazard stroke mark leaning against a gray wall. He hasn't the need for a telephone; even an urgent knock at his door goes unanswered. I've often wondered how, within this shroud of secrecy, of ambient solitude, he spends the measure of his days.

There used to be busy, intricate structures occupying floor-to-ceiling space at four corners of this reconverted warehouse. Dark, heavy pieces of menacing industrial sculpture, fabricated from found fragments of iron, steel, aluminum, old hubcaps or wire hangers. He welded works of art together from piles of castaway remains. On ambitious days, he'd take long rides as far south as Long Beach or as far north as Goleta on "collecting trips." Since there are no trees, he waited to hear the rustle of newspaper skidding across asphalt before beginning his evening's work. At street side, three stories below, you could catch occasional sparks, a warm glow, and flickering shadows as they moved along the farthest wall.

Not much remains of those days: Just a few blistered spots in the floor where the heat became too intense, and a faint gray scar running the length of Moss's arm, starting just above the wrist and terminating at the bend of his elbow.

Only once was I asked along on one of Moss's elaborate scavenger hunts. The invitation surprised me, since he was generally mysterious about his work and seldom had words for me. I'd been downtown working in the darkroom and visiting Inez, who'd been floored with the flu. Moss kept bringing in burnt slices of wheat toast, which Inez rejected with a regal flutter of the hand. When she drifted off to sleep, I gathered my things to head back west. "Where you off to?" he asked over a sink of dishes. "I think I need a second set of eyes." We drove out to the beach, taking congested surface streets, Moss chewing gum and twisting radio knobs all the way. Finding a place a half-dozen blocks from the shore, he pulled out a net, some soiled-stiff work gloves, and slipped out of his shoes. With each step we sank deeper into white hot sand. He rescued odd bits of metals that peeked out from just beneath the surface. The bounty was scarcer than he would have liked; it seemed hardly worth the ride through smog and traffic. "It'd been nice," he said with his eyes on the road ahead, "to save a little bit more."

There was the occasional show. There were modest local reviews. There was a community opening up within the shadow of City Hall, as local artists moved from studio spaces near the sea to work spaces just east of Little Tokyo. They settled within a collection of dark suspicious streets—Traction, Rose, Third, Second, Center, Vigness, Santa Fe—that made up an ersatz SoHo, populated by blue- and orange-haired Otis Parsons and Art Center grads.

Moss immigrated from Illinois by hand-me-down Ford Falcon. He flopped in a hole-in-the-wall motel on the easterly fringes of Sunset Strip, with the hourly rates hastily scrawled in pencil and posted on the back of the door. Being an emigré was not information Moss offered freely, but cowboy tans or "pulling calves" would occasionally swirl to the surface in toxically induced reveries. At clear moments he offered instead his sober, polished line: "I was surely dead in Illinois."

Shedding small-town shyness, Moss relaxed gleefully into big-town anonymity, carefully collecting a shimmering cluster of friends. His closest was a painter named Aaron, a native, who had an infectious booming laugh which began somewhere deep inside his five-foot-six-inch frame and ended in a high, maniac titter. Moss met him on a midnight constitutional. Both frequently waged battles with insomnia; they rose at small hours to walk off jangled nerves. In a thin-lapeled, antique tuxedo and black Converse high-tops laced with glittered strings, he would drag Moss to boring Hollywood parties—"B.H.Ps," he called them—where they would stand around in tight private circles laughing and tossing copper pennies into heated turquoise pools. He would then spirit him off again in his pumpkin-colored Rambler to a "real" celebration in Echo Park or Silver Lake where the music, heavy on bass and drum, made the floorboards groan and tremble and the hot air floating in smelled heavy-sweet like ancient gardenias.

Moss lived a few buildings away from the neighborhood's sole celebrity—singer/songwriter Peter Ivers, the flamboyant host of the cult cable show "New Wave Theater." Ivers, a Harvard graduate in classics, came to L.A. in 1971 to try to break into the music business. Eleven years later, and still far from a household word, he settled into a sixth-floor loft downtown, where he sometimes entertained friends with his own blues harmonica stylings or on a whim invited a random mix of musicians over for a rooftop twilight jam session. He spent many quiet afternoons in meditation or engaged in yoga. Among friends and casual acquaintances he was known as carefree, idealistic, and above all trusting. The first time I saw Ivers, Moss pointed him out at a cramped and smoky downtown party. He was shrugging out of a too-small tailored jacket, as someone put a friendly arm around his shoulder, then ushered him into a distant, darkened room. Moss would often brush against him at noisy openings, or exchange a quick nod behind black shades while traveling in daylight down Traction. The next time I saw Ivers, his grainy face filled the front page of an L.A. free weekly—he had been found on March 3, 1983, bludgeoned to death in his sleep. His body tangled within the folds of sheets damp with his own blood.

Daily patterns changed. An unspoken, unofficial neighborhood curfew was quickly imposed. Residents traveled in loud packs at nightfall, and thin voices offering comfort crossed over thinner telephone wires. People traded stories: about the forty-five minutes it took for police to arrive; about the failure to seal off the murder scene; about the cheap lock on Ivers's front door. Neighbors waited silently for murder motives, for officers to assemble follow-up clues.

But Aaron grew tired. Moss remembers a bristling, electric impatience. After a handful of weeks he was bored with sipping black coffee with friends, waiting to hear if it was safe to roam neighboring side streets at night. After a noisy display, Aaron ventured out of the neighborhood, to the beach, "for inspiration"; his body was found the following morning in a littered alley behind a dumpster, a few blocks from the Venice boardwalk. He'd been relieved of $20, a cracked Timex, and his glittered shoestrings.

Most agreed the streets had gotten mean. "The romance went out of it after that," Moss recalls, "I mean you felt kinda foolish trying to hang on to any of it." The neighborhood began to change after the city re-zoned these industrial work spaces as live-ins. Downtown became a neighborhood in transition. Earthquake proofing and proper plumbing made these last refuges for many local artists financially out of reach. Moss sublet his place to one of the many up-and-coming actors who was venturing into the neighborhood for a "funky place" to throw a memorable grand fete. He rented a U-Haul, packed slides of his work, Levis, T-shirts, hot plate, and books into the trunk of his Falcon and headed east.

"I stopped sculpting," Moss says as he pulls proof sheets, prints, and negatives from black boxes, then spreads them on a gray blanket close to the light. I recognize some faces: Inez, her cotton-white hair pulled away from her face with a foamy smoke-colored scarf, scowls out of frame; Aaron, at the beach in shabby thrift-store layers, shivers through a huge gap-toothed grin.

Moss says, flipping through proofs, that he roamed New York without the energy to pester a soul. He first took a train to Chicago then rented a truck and traveled to Evanston, Illinois, where he says he sat on the day-porch with his father smoking cigarettes, reveling in the scented silence. This was life for a while.

"Just couldn't seem to work with my hands. They just wouldn't cooperate. And when I did it seemed I'd have dreams. Angry dreams. That's why I stay awake."

We wade through more photos. Box upon box of matte-finished black and white images—people, buildings, sky, ragged terrain. Some have amoebalike ocher stains where the fixer wasn't completely rinsed away. Most are underdeveloped and have a somber gray cast. Lack of color, Moss explains, provides necessary distance. "Otherwise it's all too confrontational."

Since these photos remain in narrow black boxes parked beneath his bed, I ask Moss what he does for money. Odd jobs: drawing espresso at local coffee bars, pumping gas, working in darkrooms at professional photo labs in Hollywood. He's grown accustomed to the isolation. "If you drop out of sight in L.A., people don't always assume you're dead, I've learned. Rather they assume you've only moved out of carphone service distance. Or that you're busy . . . thus happy and healthy."

I talk him into taking a walk, to move out of the shade of his living quarters. Maybe pick up a roast beef sandwich at Philippe's, or a warm sake in Little Tokyo—just like old times. We walk along deserted but wide-open stretches of Alameda—the same path we'd take to Aaron's summer evenings just before nightfall. We move slowly toward the cluster of wispy palm trees and stucco clock tower denoting Union Station in the distance. We pass a lone transient with a rusted shopping cart filled with a careful selection of grimy rags and broken glass. He has stripped completely nude. His hair has clustered into a dry forest of auburn dreadlocks, his skin so smooth and dark it looks more like cool onyx than charred flesh. He blesses the corner of Alameda and Second with a wave of open palms, then bends head first toward the sidewalk in an extended stretch that looks more like a mystic yoga posture. Moss and I stand motionless as he pauses for a moment, raises his arms, and shouts into the sun.

In junior high school we went to more funerals than weddings. My friend J. remembers solemn autumn rosaries that began just after sunset, giving us little time to climb out of dusty chinos and Earth Shoes and into more somber, respectful attire.

These deaths were often careless accidents; macho posturings or random, mercuric moves made in fits of anger, that most times followed a red blur of words. Best friends played fatal games with

loaded guns, and Cuban "car club" members met with grisly, mysterious demises that drastically rewrote the lives of survivors.

The first funerals my classmates attended were for close friends,
all under eighteen. "I didn't go to an old person's funeral until my
grandfather died," J. recalls. By then it was a ritual that had grown
darkly familiar. For shortly before her grandfather slipped away,
her stunned family buried her older brother, the summer of his sixteenth year.

Around campus, J. was often mistaken for a blond-haired, blue-
eyed Cuban, since her circle of friends, except for me, was almost
exclusively Latino. Like the "homegirls," she adopted a belligerent
slur to her speech, a fluid ease to her style. In her I saw an inner
calmness, a worry-free veneer that I worked hard to master. Yet
she, too, like me, possessed an eager, insatiable curiosity. We both
had grand though pragmatic aspirations of being well respected yet
quite possibly only modestly successful writers. We spent weekends
outside of Culver City, a quiet, tidy community just on the edges of
L.A. proper, exploring what lay beyond. We gathered ideas to store
in looseleaf notebooks. We collected city color.

Summer '77, J. and I abandoned Venice Beach and took to tangled Sunset Boulevard. Of that summer, I remember an odd jumble
of mismatched details—a wash of faces and light that bloomed on
either side of the wide stretch of boulevard. Music was changing on
the radio and in the streets. Heavy distorted guitars and epic song-
cycles were being replaced by frail, tinny strings backed by even
flimsier English voices. These were the new British coif bands that
my friend Larry was hyped to join. They would be his magic ticket
out of L.A. Others were simply looking to mobilize within city limits, resurrecting junked husks of automobiles to rebuild and eventually call their own. My summer's master plan, to read, eat hothouse
tangerines, and watch Lucille Ball four times a day in various sitcom
incarnations, was undermined by my parents, who quickly filled
afternoons with piano lessons at USC and art classes in the hills
above Hollywood where I learned to use a potter's wheel.

What I don't remember about that summer were important
details. J.'s actual words—what they were or in what order they
were spoken. Those have all blurred and faded with years and nu-

merous tellings and retellings. What has stubbornly remained is the flat tone of her voice—distant, matter of fact—as if she were reporting what was playing at the Culver Theater or reading a list of prices from a coffee-shop menu.

She passed on what little information she had at the time—that her brother's battered body had been found within the tall yellow grass in the canyons behind UCLA just above Sunset. Years later I learned that he had been shot full of heroin and that the coroner found several bullets lodged near his heart.

No arrests were ever made.

At the time I mutely sifted through comfort words. I'm not all that sure if I said that I was sorry, or if I even knew that I was supposed to. For the first time in our friendship, I felt a frustrating, sinking sense of helplessness, uselessness. For I had no words or Lucy Ricardo/Ethel Mertz scheme to change the circumstances or erase this reality. I felt in an unforgivable way that I was letting her down. There was some elusive thing to say, floating and swirling just out of reach, that would, if not change things, alleviate some of the confusion and grief. But I was at a loss to find it.

Her brother remains vague in my mind—an adolescent indifference, an impatient grunt, and a closed bedroom door. His death at sixteen sat uncomfortably within my newly formed fourteen-year-old perceptions of life. Old and very sick people died, not sixteen-year-olds. I assumed they were all mistaken, all wrong. I think in the back of my mind I truly believed that he would reappear and laugh the laugh that softened his eyes into slender crescents like his father's. I never told J. this, but I persistently thought it. Sixteen-year-olds didn't die. They still had too much to do.

Over the years, I know that J. found strength in caring for others, her instinctive need to be strong for everyone else. I'd always been reluctant to ask her how she felt about what happened, but she'd always come to mind when my brother had his own unsettling series of near misses: slipping fifteen feet down an abandoned coal shaft in Colorado; falling asleep at the wheel early one Easter morning just before slamming into a telephone pole. Four A.M. waking nightmares that only confirm how tenuous it all is.

Only recently, just a handful of days before our ten-year high-school reunion—with J. married and with me easing my way into a commitment to journalism—did I sense that there was the distance to beg for closure. Her thoughts materialized slowly in murky fragments, like Moss's jumbled scrapbook stowed in a box: a procession of priests in whispering robes; doves nesting in a front-lawn shade tree; her mother losing a single stone in a ring representing the lives of her children; a teacher who brought by classroom poetry penned in her brother's awkward hand.

With this event, she separates childhood from adulthood. It is her jagged break with innocence. "Because it has to be." It has taken some time, but I realize that I do as well. That it has quickened my pace, skewed my view of the world. Sometimes I run so fast that nothing at all comes into focus. And at times amid my mind's white noise, I hear well-intentioned but threatening comfort words: "Slow down, you. We've got to slow you down."

J., who's grown weary of being strong for everyone else, in marriage has found an anchor. A peace. Sitting in summer skirts, in winter sun, staring out into the gray sea, I remember J. attempting to call up an image of her brother. "I know he'll never be here the same way I knew him. And not a day goes by that I don't think about him." But sometimes, she confides, no matter how hard she tries, it's difficult to resurrect a face, a form. "It's more like a feeling. A presence. Not a physical shape. More a spirit, I hope to never lose."

Tonight they are dropping poison from the sky. Around the neighborhood there are Xeroxed notices hastily taped to the windows of all my favorite morning haunts—the bookstore near Franklin Avenue, the coffeehouse on Vermont—"Come to the Anti-Malathion Rally at Pioneer Market!" boxy, black letters implore.

At 6:00 P.M. there's a less-than-impressive assembly shaking angry placards at motorists stopped in gridlocked traffic near Echo Park Avenue. By 7:00 P.M., not even remote traces of minor civil disobedience remain. Commuters speed by with air-conditioners blasting. Some pause at the corner and slip folded bills through a narrow opening in the window to purchase plastic covers from sidewalk vendors for their cars.

I wake to the voice of a rabid crackpot who's been doing double duty on the radio recent mornings. He drank down a tumbler full of the solution diluted in water a handful of years ago and is still alive to tell of it. He can't understand why a city whose skies are often a brown smear of smog would be so testy over "a little bug repellent" that just *might* save the state's crop. But as my friend Donna pointed out as I was trying rather unsuccessfully (and against the wind) to tape down a makeshift plastic cover over my car, "Ever notice they never spray in Beverly Hills." I hadn't made the conscious connection, not that I was surprised.

I live above one of the less-glamorous stretches of Sunset Boulevard, just after it snakes belligerently, in fits and starts, off its course from the shore to downtown. Outside my picture window a decapitated yet otherwise seemingly healthy palm tree looms. At night when the state helicopters aren't spraying insecticide, city choppers track the trail of elusive fugitives with great shafts of white light. During the uncomfortable heat, brought on by a lingering tropical storm named Fausto, helicopters clip through evening stillness well into the first cool of morning. These are the summer evenings, the uncomfortable waves of heat, that usually don't wrestle with us until the final days of August or early September. I spend early evening bent over a weary rotary fan ten years my senior and listen to the humid voice of Billie Holiday. At night the jasmine, thriving in abundant clusters near my bedroom window, blooms so strong that it often enters my dreams.

Friends call late at night without apologies because with the heat they have lost all hope for sleep. We prepare for the late summer months when acquaintances from out of town will descend. At their request, we embark on macabre foot tours: to the site where a lovely starlet expired after leaping from her elevated perch atop the Hollywood sign; or to the barstool at Musso and Frank where F. Scott Fitzgerald swam in his dry martinis. They want to see just where the nocturnal specter takes its noisy ride down Sierra Bonita; where Marilyn Monroe ate Nembutal and crawled into a final, dreamless slumber. There is the ride through Silver Lake as it dips into Atwater, offering a idyllic panoramic view of Forest Lawn Memorial Park in Glendale. For others there is the obligatory stroll along Hollywood Boulevard near the stretch where anxious throngs still fit their soles within grooves set in cement at Mann's Chinese; or those who instead choose to stare into the now equally famous blank eyes of runaways tirelessly parading the boulevard.

Whipping through the canyons, clipping hairpin turns through arroyo-gashed hills on Mulholland Drive, I explain to my disappointed charges that James Dean didn't take his fatal spill along this stretch of road. They accept with little argument, though I sometimes catch them surreptitiously searching for invisible skid marks in the asphalt ahead. Instead we end up in Griffith Park with the rest of the straw-hatted tourists and bored teens on cheap dates, staring up at the bronze James Dean bust just west of the observatory. They study the inscription, snap a few shots, then ask to move on.

There is a dead-man's curve with which I am more familiar. The one that reckless students risk on any given weekend. Because it is not yet world-famous it is not the one that houseguests ask to see. This sinister, serpentine stretch of gray concrete between Pacific Palisades and Brentwood offers blind curves that open up onto glimmering, startling city views. Sunset becomes a densely foliated backwood pass, and one of the drives most negotiated—tanked up and flying—on a dare. The other, "Top of the World," is a narrow ribbon of road leading up to a flat mesa, where students smoke pot, drink, then extend the rush by driving full speed down this narrow curving grade.

"They are consumed with having fun. Having a good time," local teachers have explained. Many seem oblivious to consequence. "They just want to have a good time. It is their impression of 'The Good Life.'"

A couple of years ago the cover of the *Los Angeles Times* Metro section featured a shot of Palisades High School students slumped in hysterical tears. Four members of the student body had been killed in a automobile accident on Halloween night. The driver had been drinking and ran headlong into a tree on San Vincente Boulevard. The car exploded into a forest of flames that lit the night sky. Those standing close by could hear the screams, but the heat was too fierce to admit assistance. Astonished onlookers heard the cries grow faint then die away.

Most student deaths recorded on this campus perched high above Malibu's palm-lined strand are often fatalities stemming from instances of violence. Too many are DUIs—either unlucky victims or blind perpetrators. Former Palisades administrator Roselynd Weeks puts the average at about five a year: "The Halloween accident seemed to be the most traumatic. There was a longer mourning period. But by junior/senior prom time it was back to business as usual." Bronze plaques go up along main corridors, memorial pages are set aside in class annuals, and classroom discussions spawn promises to mend old ways, but old habits are slow to change.

They've begun bringing wrecked automobiles onto campus to startle errant students, to shock them into some semblance of responsibility. They've placed them conspicuously in the quad for the day—crumpled masses of wrecked and charred metal, that once represented shining pride. They sit stoically in the sun like precious museum pieces on loan. Some students fall by to marvel at the remains, to imagine the condition of bodies pulled from the amorphous mass. At first some parents and faculty wondered about the appropriateness of this gesture. Some saw it as a tasteless sideshow sensation rather than a drunk-driving deterrent. After a more recent fatality, no one blocked the way.

It is sometimes difficult for teachers and administrators to determine whether or not some of these accidents are simply an elaborate way to camouflage a flirtation with suicide. Like an elderly shut-in's failure to take life-sustaining medication, it could be a passive, covert form of taking one's own life.

Teachers and administrators keep careful watch on troubled students and their black moods. They intermittently explore precarious emotional states in constant flux. Close friends will sometimes duck in to alert a trusted teacher or counselor about the words and needs of a distraught friend.

Creative expression is often a key, a hairline artery leading deep inside—a bleak poem composed in a writing class or a brooding pen-and-ink sketch handed in at an art workshop may have subtle allusions to death eloquently stowed between the lines or intricately laced within its borders.

Deep depressions bloom out of everyday disillusionment—disappointment in love, low self-esteem, lack of attention from significant loved ones. These dark moods expand, color existence a sooty gray. Eventually thoughts move from vague indistinct meditations on depression to concrete contemplations of quick ways out.

For many young people of this generation, the concept of life has never been more ephemeral, the scope of a life-span more abstract. Worries hover around the planet—environmental and international issues and the future of the human species. More and more, adolescents construct a blueprint for the future that doesn't carve out a place for spouse and/or children. "They see the big picture more," explains Roselynd Weeks, "how the system works. And in that sense they are much more mature than generations preceding them."

There is, despite the abundance of sunshine and wealth, an oppressive sense of doom about an indifferent and chaotic world. A profound emptiness and a gray despair are both cradled snugly within this vast lap of luxury. For some, it only becomes increasingly apparent every day—there is not the need nor time to pace and fret over a future that may never be.

Taking the Harbor Freeway south, the 91 east, I watch a fine drizzle fall. It is the first gray day in months. On the radio, newscasters impart strange tales that seem to wander in from remote dreamscapes: A Latina, after unloading the morning groceries, steps outside of her Huntington Park home and sets herself afire. Across town another woman walks toward a car and into the whirl of smoke and hot flame engulfing it. A skull and bones are found beneath a condemned building along the Wilshire corridor. Another Medfly discovered, this time in the Compton area. To protect the season's crop, there are plans to send helicopters into these skies in strict, arrowhead formation.

Along Santa Fe, in Compton, the sidewalks and structures rising from them emerge in monochromatic grays. These wide stretches of open road and industrial buildings don't offer much consolation. Traveling north, I watch warehouses unfold into boarded-up apartment buildings, then to chain-link fences enclosing lots of full of rust and weeds, and finally plot upon plot of tiny churches boasting grand and inspirational names: Living Water Fellowship, Compton/ Samoa Seventh Day Adventist, Mount Pilgrim Baptist, New Jerusalem Church of God and Christ.

For some time the papers ignored this community and others much like it across the Southland. They ignored the residents who, to avoid a stray bullet, curled near the baseboards to find sleep. They ignored children who stepped over stiff, bloodied bodies on their way to homeroom. They ignored young mothers who worked themselves to the quick to keep their children in private schools, off the street and hidden from harm.

They ignored the survivors.

Both of my parents taught in these inner-city classrooms. Some Mondays the police would stop by with stills of the most recent "Jane Doe" for my mother to identify. She'd stare at the face, search for a familiar glimmer in the eyes, then shake her head. With a nod of thanks they would quickly depart.

"Those were the most resilient kids," she often recalls. "They all seemed to be blessed with short memories. Life would jump up and slap them down but they'd quietly collect themselves. They were always ready to take more."

Two years ago, when the "Gang Problem" spilled out of the ever-widening circumscription media-labeled "South-Central L.A.," and into the affluent community of Westwood near UCLA, the papers finally took notice. Police were unleashed on these neighborhoods by the hundreds, to "sweep" the streets clean. City government responded by looking into other vague "emergency programs" —all Band-Aid efforts to cure only one of the many problems that have been chipping away at this community for decades.

In spite of the efforts, the statistics remain chilling: the black infant mortality rate is the highest in the country. Black males in the United States between the ages of fourteen and twenty-five have a one in twenty chance of being shot. In 1990, 364 gang-related homicides were reported in this city alone, almost doubling in 1991.

As a reporter, I've sat in on community meetings held within exquisite eighty-year-old church sanctuaries. After bowing their heads in prayer, the congregation furrows brows and searches sagacious eyes for the answers. From AIDS to random drive-by shootings, they are a people besieged. Some only shrug shoulders. Others whisper genocide.

Here it is sometimes difficult to gauge what is feared most—the ominous threat of death or the uncertain properties of life. "Some put up a front, a bravado, to get them through," I've listened to teachers muse. "They will tell you they're not afraid. I think some of them fear death. Those with conventional values. A good number of them have the loftiest of ambitions—doctors, lawyers, actors, singers, athletes—but then there's also the element that has nothing to lose. Those who simply exist."

You see those empty eyes, those clouded, spiritless faces all over. Yet I'm still struck by the chill that returns a well-intentioned smile. Along this stretch of East Compton Boulevard, this chill moves through to the core. More gray buildings, more steely faces; the only splashes of color I see for blocks are the Moorish and Byzantine structures containing the mausoleums of Angeles Abbey Memorial Park.

"We've lost the ability to love, especially the black race. We just can't seem to love ourselves," says Jean Sanders, who is vice president/general manager of Angeles Abbey, the second black cemetery west of the Mississippi.

Sanders, on a busy week, sees ten to twelve families in her small, orderly office papered with inspirational messages clipped from magazines, and color snapshots of various government dignitaries. The winter months are the hardest, she says. Especially Christmas. "The joyous times are often the saddest. People just can't cope. The county stats go way high."

Sanders, whose grandfather was a mortician in Arkansas, carries the tradition a third generation. She is the first black woman to be appointed to the state's Cemetery Board. She digs graves, works in the crematory, and when short-handed, operates the tractor, but most importantly she explains, her purpose is to listen and console.

She's grown used to the fact that when families arrive they are often surprised to see her. Those grieving expect instead a grim old man in an ill-fitting gray suit, but when he fails to greet them, they seldom bother to hide their amazement. Soon their faces will relax with her presence, with the gentle cadence of her voice and the sincerity of her eyes.

"I have women who come in to work on their sons' graves. In the process, they will be able to accept their child's death. It's taken one woman seven years. A seven-year death. She's just beginning to focus in on her family. People here die slowly, inwardly for a long, long time."

It wasn't too long ago that finding a plot of soil to bury a black body posed a problem in Los Angeles. In some areas, private charters blocked these interments as late as 1966. African-American families, in black veils and ash-gray suits, loaded caskets onto streetcars and rode to Evergreen Cemetery in East L.A. It is where three generations of my family have been laid to rest. Sanders remembers hearing those stories. She has watched this neighborhood change three times—from predominately white until Watts went up in flames in '65, then predominately black, and now Latino.

Angeles Abbey has had to adjust to the community's changing face: the Gypsies who throw noisy feasts and roast pigs in honor of the newly departed; the Vietnamese who fill caskets with the loved one's earthly possessions, then decorate the grounds with ripe fruit and flora. The gang funerals she says, despite what you read in the dailies, have been low-key and uneventful. "They come in, do their thing, and then they leave.

"These kids are more afraid of the known than the unknown," Sanders explains. "They live with the known every day. Live with a father on crack or a mother on welfare, maybe a brother in the gangs. They take their hostility out on buildings—mark it up with graffiti, break windows. They take their hostility out on people. They take human lives."

Staring in the face of all this can spiritually drain you, Sanders tells me. It is a job which is difficult to term "enjoyable," but Sanders admits she does what she can to strengthen and uplift. She likes people. She gives them hope. "I had a lot of babies coming in recently. A *lot* of babies, and that's hard. Young adults with gunshot wounds—victims of violent crime. The hatred and hostility is troubling. These dying spirits. I sometimes stop and ask them what they're hungry for. And when they answer, it seems so basic, so simple when you stop to think about it—happiness. That's all they want. 'Happiness in the house.'"

My old roommate from my days north has recently moved in to town. She is just beginning to get a grip on the rhythm of the city, but its heat and size still daunt her. Just as she traveled two buses with me to buy a proper winter fedora for February's gusts and lightning storms, I carefully instruct her to place cool compresses on her pressure points—at her wrists and temples—then to lie in a darkened room "cadaver still."

We often share notes for survival.

She has taken a movie job, a low-budget travesty that required a scene in a cemetery. The crew set up on a patch of green and started digging a shallow grave. After a while they turned up dry bones. Caretakers turned their heads. The remains glowed ivory white in the dusky earth.

My mind's eye quickly processes these spare details into flickering clips from campy fifties' horror movies; an endless montage shot from oblique angles and captured in powdery half-light. I visualize men and women intently lobbing sun-scorched bones. Tibias and ulnae sail gently through cloudless skies. Yet as in the movies, in varying shades of gray, the eyes don't look so urgent or frightened, the expressions not nearly as desperate as they would, or often do, in real life.

As my friend imparts her tale, we stand in front of "The Original" Miceli's Italian on Las Palmas. We wait along with a small cluster of others for a table near the bar upstairs where a graying rhythm section runs through an impressive collection of standards — "Night and Day," "Stella by Starlight," "Body and Soul." A bewildered drifter, with upturned palms, slows his pace as he nears the line forming near the front doors. Muttering, he works his way north toward the neon and noise of Hollywood Boulevard, shaking his head, his face stretched into a wild, delirious smile, he is saying, "I'm not dead yet, I'm not dead yet. *I'm not dead yet.*"

July 1990

Walter Mosley

In his six novels about the detective Easy Rawlins, Walter Mosley (b. 1952) has created a long, multi-volume novel of manners about African-American life in Los Angeles in the years after World War II: a place, he writes, "where a black man can dream, but he has to keep his wits about him." The mechanics of plotting, although deftly handled, are subsidiary to Mosley's rare gift for social portraiture. Starting with *Devil in a Blue Dress* (1990), the Easy Rawlins novels map the sprawling community of South Central Los Angeles as a self-contained culture within the larger city, with its own code of ethics and way of life.

from

DEVIL IN A BLUE DRESS

John's place was a speakeasy before they repealed Prohibition. But by 1948 we had legitimate bars all over L.A. John liked the speakeasy business though, and he had been in so much trouble with the law that City Hall wouldn't have given him a license to drive, much less to sell liquor. So John kept paying off the police and running an illegal nightclub through the back door of a little market at the corner of Central Avenue and Eighty-ninth Place. You could walk into that store any evening up until three in the morning to find Hattie Parsons sitting behind the candy counter. They didn't have many groceries, and no fresh produce or dairy goods, but she'd sell you what was there and if you knew the right words, or were a regular, then she'd let you in the club through the back door. But if you thought that you should be able to get in on account of your name, or your clothes or maybe your bankbook, well, Hattie kept a straight razor in her apron pocket and her nephew, Junior Fornay, sat right behind the door.

When I pushed open the door to the market I ran into my third white man that day. This one was about my height with wheat-brown hair and an expensive dark blue suit. His clothes were disheveled, and he smelled of gin.

"Hey, colored brother," he said as he waved at me. He walked straight toward me so that I had to back out of the store if I didn't want him to run me down.

"How'd ya like t'make twenty dollars fast?" he asked when the door swung shut behind him.

They were just throwing money at me that day.

"How's that?" I asked the drunk.

"I need to get in here . . . lookin' fer someone. Girl in there won't let me in." He was teetering and I was afraid he'd fall down. "Why'ont you tell'em I'm fine."

"I'm sorry, but I can't do that," I said.

"Why's that?"

"Once they tell you no at John's they stick to it." I moved around him to get into the door again. He tried to turn and grab my arm but all he managed was to spin around twice and wind up sitting against the wall. He put up his hand as if he wanted me to bend down so he could whisper something but I didn't think that anything he had to offer could improve my life.

"Hey, Hattie," I said. "Looks like you got a boarder out on your doorstep."

"Drunk ole white boy?"

"Yep."

"I'll have Junior look out there later on. He can sweep'im up if he still there."

With that I put the drunk out of my mind. "Who you got playin' tonight?" I asked.

"Some'a your homefolks, Easy. Lips and his trio. But we had Holiday, Tuesday last."

"You did?"

"She just come breezin' through." Hattie's smile revealed teeth that were like flat gray pebbles. "Must'a been 'bout, I don't know, midnight, but the birds was singin' wit'er 'fore we closed for the night."

"Oh man! Sorry I missed that," I said.

"That'a be six bits, baby."

"What for?"

"John put on a cover. Cost goin' up an' he tryin' t'keep out the riff-raff."

"And who's that?"

She leaned forward showing me her watery brown eyes. Hattie was the color of light sand and I doubt if she ever topped a hundred pounds in her sixty-some years.

"You heard about Howard?" she asked.

"What Howard?"

"Howard Green, the chauffeur."

"No, uh-uh. I haven't seen Howard Green since last Christmas."

"Well you ain't gonna see him no more — in this world."

"What happened?"

"He walked outta here about three in the mo'nin' the night Lady Day was here and wham!" She slammed her bony fist into an open palm.

"Yeah?"

"They din't hardly even leave a face on'im. You know I tole'im that he was a fool t'be walkin' out on Holiday but he didn't care. Said he had *business* t'see to. Hmm! I tole him he hadn't oughtta left."

"Killed him?"

"Right out there next to his car. Beat him so bad that his wife, Esther, said the only way she could identify the body was cuz of his ring. They must'a used a lead pipe. You know he had his nose in somebody's nevermind."

"Howard liked to play hard," I agreed. I handed her three quarters."

"Go right on in, honey," she smiled.

When I opened the door I was slapped in the face by the force of Lips' alto horn. I had been hearing Lips and Willie and Flattop since I was a boy in Houston. All of them and John and half the people in that crowded room had migrated from Houston after the war, and some before that. California was like heaven for the southern Negro. People told stories of how you could eat fruit right off the trees and get enough work to retire one day. The stories were true for the most part but the truth wasn't like the dream. Life was

still hard in L.A. and if you worked every day you still found yourself on the bottom.

But being on the bottom didn't feel so bad if you could come to
John's now and then and remember how it felt back home in Texas,
dreaming about California. Sitting there and drinking John's scotch
you could remember the dreams you once had and, for a while, it
felt like you had them for real.

"Hey, Ease," a thick voice crackled at me from behind the door.

It was Junior Fornay. He was a man that I knew from back
home too. A big, burly field hand who could chop cotton all day
long and then party until it was time to climb back out into the
fields. We had had an argument once, when we were both much
younger, and I couldn't help thinking that I'd've probably died if
it wasn't for Mouse stepping in to save my bacon.

"Junior," I hailed. "What's goin' on?"

"Not too much, yet, but stick around." He was leaning back on
a stool, propping himself against the wall. He was five years older
than I, maybe thirty-three, and his gut hung over his jeans, but
Junior still looked to be every bit as powerful as when he put me on
the floor all those years before.

Junior had a cigarette between his lips. He smoked the cheapest, foulest brand that they made in Mexico—Zapatas. I guess that
he was finished smoking it because he let it fall to the floor. It just
lay on the oak floor, smoldering and burning a black patch in the
wood. The floor around Junior's chair had dozens of burns in it. He
was a filthy man who didn't give a damn about anything.

"Ain't seen ya 'round much, Ease. Where ya been?"

"Workin', workin', day and night for Champion, and then they
let me go."

"Fired?" There was hint of a smile on his lips.

"On my ass."

"Shit. Sorry t'hear it. They got layoffs?"

"Naw, man. It's just that the boss ain't happy if you just do your
job. He need a big smack on his butt too."

"I hear ya."

"Just this past Monday I finished a shift and I was so tired I
couldn't even walk straight . . ."

"Uh-huh," Junior chimed in to keep the story going.

". . . and the boss come up and say that he need me for an extra hour. Well I told him that I was sorry but I had a date. And I did too, with my bed."

Junior got a kick out of that.

"And he got the nerve to tell me that *my people* have to learn to give a little extra if we wanna advance."

"He said that?"

"Yeah." I felt the heat of my anger returning.

"And what is he?"

"Italian boy, I think his parents the ones come over."

"Man! So what you say?"

"I told him that my people been givin' a little extra since before Italy was even a country. 'Cause you know Italy ain't even been around that long."

"Yeah," Junior said. But I could see that he didn't know what I was talking about. "So what happened then?"

"He just told me to go on home and not to bother coming back. He said that he needed people who were willing to work. So I left."

"Man!" Junior shook his head. "They do it to ya every time."

"That's right. You want a beer, Junior?"

"Yeah." He frowned. "But can you buy it with no job and all?"

"I can always buy a couple'a beers."

"Well then, I can always drink'em."

I went over to the bar and ordered two ales. It looked like half of Houston was there. Most tables had five or six people. People were shouting and talking, kissing and laughing. John's place felt good after a hard day's work. It wasn't quite legal but there was nothing wrong with it either. Big names in Negro music came there because they knew John in the old days when he gave them work and didn't skimp on the paycheck. There must've been over two hundred regulars that frequented John's and we all knew each other, so it made a good place for business as well as a good time.

Alphonso Jenkins was there in his black silk shirt and his foot-high pompadour hairdo. Jockamo Johanas was there too. He was wearing a wooly brown suit and bright blue shoes. Skinny Rita Cook was there with five men hanging around her table. I never did understand how an ugly, skinny woman like that attracted so many men. I once asked her how she did it and she said, in her high whiny voice, "Well, ya know, Easy, it's only half the mens is int'rested in how a girl look. Most'a your colored mens is lookin' for a woman love'em so hard that they fo'gets how hard it is t'make it through the day."

Mary Helen Ponce

Early on, the San Fernando Valley city of Pacoima was known for its citrus fruits and vineyards. During World War II, it was one of the few
Southern California communities where both African-Americans and Chicanos could achieve middle-class prosperity. In her memoir *Hoyt Street:
Memories of a Chicana Childhood* (1993), Mary Helen Ponce (b. 1938) recalls
her family's life in Pacoima throughout the war years and beyond. The
author of *Recuerdo: Short Stories of the Barrio* (1983), *Taking Control* (1987),
and the novel *The Wedding* (1989), Ponce teaches literature and creative
writing at the University of California, Santa Barbara.

LAS VISTAS

Although Pacoima was twenty-odd miles from Los Angeles and
close to San Fernando, a town with three movie theaters, I
rarely went to the movies. I accompanied my sisters when they
shopped in town, but not to the movies. They liked to go on a Saturday night, when anyone who counted would show up. But the show
was too expensive for large families such as ours. I had to be content
with films shown at school, most of which were old, cracked, and
boring, and the black-and-white movies screened at the church hall.

I attended las vistas, as the church-sponsored movies were
called, with Doña Luisa, who although she was as poor as a church-
mouse, paid my way. The movies were part of the parish activities
organized by Father Mueller. He disapproved of gambling, so he did
not organize bingo games. Nor was he fond of church-sponsored
dances; he claimed that young people danced much too close, which
led to "occasions of sin." The movies he showed were considered a
harmless and proper way to bring people together, and they gener-
ated money for the school fund. For me they were great fun.

The movies were held on Sunday evenings, right after the
rosary. Following benediction Father Mueller reminded all parish-
ioners about the show that was to benefit the parish. He never gave
the movie title, but mumbled something about a new, wonderful

801

movie with leading Hollywood actors. He feared that people might recognize the title of some ancient movie. Folks in the neighborhood attended the movies out of respect and also because there was nothing else to do on Sunday evenings.

My mother, who constantly reminded us to speak proper Spanish, called the movies las películas. Doña Caridad hated words that might indicate she was uncultured and insisted that the correct word for motion pictures was *el cine*. Depending on how well they spoke el inglés, my friends liked to say they were going to el "chow." I called the movies *las vistas*, out of loyalty to Doña Luisa, who used words said to be muy rancheras.

At first I attended the church movies with a group, or with Doña Luisa. Trina refused to join us, saying they were too dull for her taste; she was a teenager. She and her friend Sally preferred the San Fernando movies. They played Frank Sinatra records on Sally's chipped record-player (you could hear the music all the way to Hoyt Street) and pretended to swoon. They experimented with "slow dancing," a style popular in the Los Angeles dancehalls, which allowed couples to hold each other close and to slide back and forth in time to the sultry music. Now and then the girls jitterbugged, twirling away for hours, until they fell to the floor from exhaustion. Once they had rested, back they went to dancing the very latest and most "hip" steps.

When she saw me changing my dress for las vistas, Trina would just snicker. "I wouldn't be caught at them old movies. It's not hep!"

"I like em."

"That's cause you're a square."

She tossed back her page boy, arched her eyebrows (just like Joan Crawford), then locked herself in the bathroom to check her makeup. In time las vistas were identified with los santuchos, the overly religious, and kids like me.

The movies were mostly westerns—old westerns, in black and white. Father Mueller drove to "Los," as we called Los Angeles, to pick up the films and assorted reels. He never explained why western movies were all he got; I figured he knew a cowboy. But since that was all he ever came up with, that's what we saw. In spite of his efforts and enthusiasm, it was difficult to mask our disappointment with the old movies.

Among my favorite western heroes were Hopalong Cassidy and Roy Rogers. El Cassidy, as Doña Luisa called him, was sort of pure. He wore a dark cowboy shirt with a fancy design and a white cowboy hat. Not only was he the "good guy," who neither swore nor started a fight, but he never kissed women! He held their hands, gazed into their blue eyes, then smiled, tipped his white hat, and rode off into the sunset. He left behind some pretty and puzzled women.

El Cassidy fought the "bad guys": Mexican bandits in torn shirts, with huge mustaches and shifty eyes. Their filthy, matted hair hung across their sweaty faces. He fought Indians too, men with swarthy complexions and sweaty bodies, who wore buckskin and feathers, and who wielded tomahawks and shot bloody arrows in battle. El Cassidy saved the ranch from the banker, the cattle from the cattle rustlers, the townspeople from the outlaws, and fair maidens from Indians.

El Roy Rogers was cute and much younger than Hopalong. His slanted eyes crinkled when he smiled, which was often, and his straight hair escaped from under his cowboy hat to land on his wide brow. He was slender, not as husky as el Cassidy, but in his high-heeled boots, astride a horse, Roy Rogers looked strong, even mighty. His partner was Dale Evans, a pretty woman who wore western clothes and rode a frisky horse. Like el Cassidy, Roy Rogers treated women like sisters; he never looked at Dale Evans with lovesick eyes.

Roy Rogers lived somewhere in the West, where he fought Indians and bandidos. Whenever he whistled, his horse Trigger would trot to him, then off they would ride. Other than look pretty on her horse, Dale Evans never did much.

Before the movie began, Father Mueller and the Holy Name Society members, who were in charge of the event and felt terribly important, dusted the folding chairs stored in back of the hall, then lined them up in neat rows, leaving a narrow space to the right. The stage curtains were pulled apart; the movie screen came down. Sodas were laid out in tubs filled with chipped ice, oil for popcorn was heated, and boxes of assorted candy were stacked inside the kitchen.

When el chow was scheduled, rosary ended promptly at seven thirty. I found it miraculous that Father Mueller ended prayers so soon on a movie Sunday. He never dared to skip a Mystery, but prayed at a fast clip; often he skipped the Litany of the Saints, thinking no one would notice. As soon as he had blessed the congregation, he bolted into the sacristy to change his skirt. While Don Crispín locked the church and snuffed out the candles, our pastor dashed into the church hall to prepare for las vistas. Within minutes people began filtering in. Some still clutched holy beads; women with scarves over their hair quickly took them off, stuffed them in a pocket, and looked around for a seat.

"Did the chow start yet?"

"Todavía no."

"Is he chowing el Cassidy?"

"Neh, es el Roy Rogers."

The hall kitchen teemed with activity. People went in and out, arms laden with boxed candy and Cracker Jacks, everyone's favorite treat. Others sorted the candy: Milk Duds, Baby Ruths, and Milky Ways, which sold for five cents, por un cinco. At the front counter (actually a half door that swung open), young girls kept busy measuring oil and popcorn into the popcorn maker. In the stretches when they weren't performing this loathsome chore, they pried open the caps on strawberry and orange sodas and made change. Eyes bright and expectant, they elbowed each other, vying for position, as behind them the popcorn machine spat out white fluffy chivitas and the church hall filled with the delicious smell of hot popcorn.

I wanted to help sell popcorn, but the teenage girls, all of whom acted superior, monopolized the counter. They licked their red lips, fluffed their dark hair, and told me to sit down. As soon as the boys lined up, they acted sweet and passive, fluttering their eyelids in perfect rhythm. They flirted outrageously, elbowing each other in the ribs, while pretending to sell el esquite.

"May I help you?"

"You chure can."

"Don't act smart! Whadda ya want, popcorn or . . ."

"He wants a kiss!"

"I'm gonna tell Father . . ."

My primary job at las vistas was to translate the movies for Doña Luisa and her friends. While they understood what was taking place, many things in the show escaped them. It was up to me to fill them in on what had or was about to occur. In return for this, Doña Luisa and the Trinidads (all but Doña Caridad, who was stingy), would give me money to spend. I would have preferred to be with my friend Elena, near the boys, but sat with Doña Luisa out of loyalty.

I sat in the middle, between Doña Luisa and Doña Magda, who sat next to Doña Cari. Doña Clarissa rarely went to the movies, saying her eyes were too weak. Once el rosario let out, the ladies staked the third row for themselves and their reluctant interpreter.

As soon as the movie started, I immediately began to translate. In an effort to impress the señoras and earn a nod of approval from Doña Caridad, I would search my mind for the most appropriate and similar Spanish words to reflect the action taking place, then whispered them to the women, all of whom sighed with relief. Often I became flustered at my lack of Spanish, and took too long to respond.

"Que está pasando?" Doña Cari had to know what was happening.

"Nada."

I paused when appropriate; when the action picked up, I too accelerated. I tried not to lag behind, and in an effort to see everything, would practically fall off my seat. I hated to lose sight of the action, and I feared mixing up the "good guys" with the "bad guys."

El Cassidy rarely spoke. He merely grunted, tipped his hat to the ladies, then dug his silver spurs into his horse and rode off. El Roy Rogers spoke only to Trigger or Dale Evans. Mostly he smiled a lot, his eyes squinting in the sun. His movies all ended on the same note. He would whistle to Trigger, jump into the leather saddle, then ride off, leaving behind swirls of dust.

At times the movies were too long, the plot too predictable. I would tire of my job and yearn to sit in front with Elena. By now I had spent the money given me by Doña Luisa and the Trinidads. As the show dragged on, I fidgeted in my seat, edging toward Elena. Once I had collected más cincos, I sought ways to escape from the boring job of translating an old cowboy movie. One usually worked.

"Qué están diciendo?" Doña Magda would hiss, her breath hot on my face, eager to know what the actors had said.

"Que la va a matar."

"No es posible!" Doña Caridad screeched, about to fall off her seat. Even when flustered she spoke in precise, proper Spanish. In the darkened hall her myopic eyes searched for mine; her chins quivered in agitation. She leaned across Doña Magda, her eyes probing mine. "It's not possible," she hissed in Spanish, then covered her eyes with a linen hankie she kept in her pocket. Doña Cari would not accept that El Cassidy, who had just saved the pretty girl from the bandits, was planning to kill her.

"Sí. He's gonna kill her just the same." I pulled at the hem of my dress, then crossed my arms in front of my chest, daring her not to believe.

Doña Luisa (who always knew when I was fibbing) was not about to feed me to the lions. In a voice hoarse from yelling at me, she volunteered her opinion. "*Hmmm, puede ser.* It could be," she lied, her dark eyes glued to the movie screen.

I remained unruffled, my fist tight around the nickels I had earned, as I pushed my way toward Elena. Around me the thoroughly confused women sat in wonder at this sudden turn of events. They squabbled, each wanting to believe only what they had seen on the white screen, until told to "hush" by those sitting in back.

I joined Elena, who had saved my seat, knowing how resourceful I could be. She welcomed me with a knowing grin. I stuffed myself with the popcorn and Milk Duds bought with my earnings, then giggled at the cute boys sitting next to me.

On the way home, the Trinidads discussed the movie, el Cassidy, and the translation that did not fit the action. I pretended not to hear and moved away from the prying eyes of Doña Caridad, the sour breath of Doña Magda. The heated discussion was led by Doña Caridad, who even in the dark had a commanding presence, and easily intimidated Doña Magdalena. As she picked her way between the many rocks on Hoyt Street, she voiced her concern about her idol, el Cassidy.

"Ay, Dios mío!" Her chest rose and fell in agitation. Doña Caridad would not give up on the aging, white-haired cowboy.

"El Cassidy would not do a thing like that," hissed Doña Magda, knowing that this is what Doña Cari wanted to hear. She pulled her rebozo around her head, then shuffled on down the street.

"Pues, yo sí," said Doña Luisa, throwing caution to the winds. She yanked me by the arm, then propelled me toward home.

"Hmmm, pos hoy en día no hay respeto," concluded Doña Cari, adjusting her wool shawl around her ample shoulders. "Today there is no respect." This ended the argument.

At times I felt guilty about the translation and the nickels, especially when the señoras began to bicker among themselves. My guilt would last until the following Sunday, when once more I might recite an original version of an old western.

Sandra Tsing Loh

The San Fernando Valley has served as the punchline for more than a few Los Angeles jokes, so it's perhaps appropriate that one of L.A.'s best humor writers, Sandra Tsing Loh (b. 1962), should be a longtime Valley resident. Loh began to write about what she calls the "lesser Los Angeles" in the early 1990s as a columnist for the now-defunct *Buzz* magazine. Before that, she was a performance artist known for such pieces as playing a concerto for spawning fish on a beach in Malibu. The author of four books—the essay collection *Depth Takes a Holiday* (1996), the monologue *Aliens in America* (1997), the novel *If You Lived Here, You'd Be Home By Now* (1997), and *A Year in Van Nuys* (2001), a send-up of Peter Mayle's best-selling *A Year in Provence*—she is perhaps best known for her weekly radio commentary "Loh Life," on Santa Monica station KCRW.

COMING HOME TO VAN NUYS

It can be hard, sometimes, to come home to Van Nuys.

Especially via LAX, when you've just gotten off the plane from New Mexico or Minnesota or some other faraway place where pale green cornfields shiver under a cobalt sky. . . .

So unlike Airport Parking Lot C, really, where Burger King debris sucks up around your ankles and rows and rows of battered automobiles sulk beneath an oily sun. You step over a smashed Michelob bottle and suddenly you remember your life: you're poor, you're anonymous, and you drive a shitty car.

You think about the scenic drive ahead, deep into the Grid of the sweltering Valley, home of a hundred King Bear Auto Centers, a thousand Yoshinoya Beef Bowls, and ten thousand yard sales, some consisting of no more than a couple of "Disco Lady" T-shirts flung out on a scabrous lawn like some kind of SOS. You want to close your eyes and say, "There's no place like home." But, in fact, you *are* home.

On my last return to L.A., the mantra I put to myself as I wandered the grim expanse of Parking Lot C, looking for my 1973 VW with its bad clutch, was: "What do I love about Van Nuys? What do I love about Van Nuys?" Twenty minutes later, when I found the car (in section Ss), I had an epiphany.

What's great about living in Van Nuys is that we, uh . . . we have a pretty good variety of take-out. Maybe that doesn't sound like much, but it's something they sure don't have in Minnesota.

And besides, we're talking a whole world of take-out possibilities. My kitchen drawer is bursting with menus that must have been hurled onto my front porch in the dead of night. Within five minutes of my house I can get at least a dozen different kinds of "ethnic" food—including 100 percent authentic soul food, Thai, Chinese, Salvadoran, East Indian, Northern Italian, Spanish (the chef is from Barcelona, not Mexico), Israeli, Cajun, German, and Japanese.

Ah, yes. You're imagining the vivid cadences of exotic languages. The bustle of wonderful bazaars and open-air markets full of kiosks, and street cars, and flapping geese, and bicycle bells. French guys with fresh baguettes roller-skating in Gene Kelly pants, mariachi music, an honest cobbler from Istanbul, and a very wise man from Tibet who can tell you everything about yaks.

The problem, of course, is that this joyous melting pot doesn't describe Van Nuys at all. Walt Disney never made it over here to redecorate. The notion of "ethnic charm" is a hoary old Americanism from the seventies. There are few vibrant ethnic enclaves in the Valley; what I didn't tell you is that for each nationality I've named, there is exactly one restaurant. One. Marooned by itself in a tiny strip mall, generally sandwiched between an X-rated video store and a Sally for Nails salon. Not all of them do very well.

The take-out places that do flourish here are ones that dispense terrific food at terrific speed. At one of my favorites, Golan Restaurant, the employees wear perpetual scowls as they hurl peppers and falafel into paper bags with deadly urgency. And the folks at Thai Koon Café, another find, do a mean delivery—clocking in at something like twelve minutes from their door to mine—no doubt having knocked down a few Domino's delivery guys on the way.

More common are the ethnic restaurants that are slowly dying on the vine. They have a certain lost quality I can identify with. No one seems to understand what they're doing here. It is the way of the Grid.

One example. About three years ago an Egyptian restaurant opened in a strip mall not far from here. And I don't mean your generic Middle Easternish Pita Hut chain. I mean *Egyptians.* I'm not sure if this place ever had a name. The location's previous take-out tenant was a Chicken Delight franchise, and the sign, featuring a startled yellow bird, remained up for a while even though the Egyptians didn't sell chicken. Nor was there much cause for delight; the place was always empty. You could see the young cook through the window, sitting by himself in an orange plastic chair, smoking cigarettes, reading the paper.

About two months later, suddenly a crudely lettered sign that simply read KABOB went up. Still nothing. Soon after, the management decided to abandon the idea of using English at all; KABOB came down, and energetic banners in Arabic flew up around the windows.

It was at this point that I really became interested. (I'm the worst kind of consumer: small income and exacting standards. You have to do a lot to get my attention, because when I let go of twelve dollars, I don't do it lightly.) Aha! I thought. They're only communicating with their own people. Something really fabulous must be going on.

But still the masses failed to flock. Why wasn't the Egyptian community (wherever it was) catching on to this? An eager visit to the restaurant revealed the answer. The authentic Egyptian-food experience turned out to be an overpriced (paper) plate of stringy beef, instant rice, and runny tomatoes. Three more dollars earned you a trip to the salad bar—featuring Lady Lee peas, which the cook poured expressionlessly from the can. They made a gentle splattering sound as they slid into the copious salad-bar vat.

What inspires some folks to relocate halfway around the world to the San Fernando Valley in order to feed bad food on paper plates to their own people? Perhaps the chef really did not want to be in the food industry at all. Perhaps his family pushed him into it, like my own Chinese father pushed me to be an aeronautical engineer. (He believed I was destined to shine in the Advanced Tactical Weapons Division at Hughes Aircraft Company. He was wrong.)

But the take-out place that makes me feel the worst is the one in the strip mall on my corner—the home of Royal India. I've come to know the owner; his name is Shah. Unfortunately, I've also come to know his troubles. Like many Indian restaurants languishing in the Valley, the food is in-credible: there's rich vindaloo, tikka masala like red paint, lamb sag delicately aromatic in its gleaming metal dish. The interior, too, is embarrassingly classy for a place flanked by an "All-Nite" liquor store. There are white tablecloths, napkins stuffed in wineglasses like bouquets, and two bow-tied waiters who speak in perfectly modulated British accents. And it's going out of business. It kills me. I want to write the owner a note:

> Dear Shah, I can't afford to spend twenty-five dollars on dinner every night, but I want to keep you in my neighborhood. You are a culinary genius. I wish I could help!

But I don't. Instead, I slide another frozen dinner into the microwave. One block away, Shah peers out of Royal India's red curtains, watching for invisible customers on what is called Victory Boulevard. Up above him, a neon COIN LAUNDRY sign blinks on and off.

James Ellroy

Although he now lives in Kansas City, James Ellroy (b. 1948) remains among the most visible of contemporary Los Angeles crime novelists. His work, most notably the *L.A. Quartet* comprising the novels *The Black Dahlia*, *The Big Nowhere*, *L.A. Confidential*, and *White Jazz*, imagines Los Angeles as a nightmarish underworld, where no one is innocent and everybody pays. Ellroy's interest in crime has starkly personal roots. When he was ten, his mother, with whom he had been living in the San Gabriel Valley suburb of El Monte, was brutally murdered, and the case was never solved. For many years afterward, Ellroy battled alcoholism and drug addiction before finding a way out by means of the literature of noir. In "The Tooth of Crime," he spends some time with the detectives of the Sheriff's Homicide Bureau as they try to clear their year-end books.

THE TOOTH OF CRIME

Captain Dan Burt looks and talks like an enlightened fast-track Republican. He's midsized, tan, and groomed. If he wasn't running the Los Angeles County Sheriff's Homicide Bureau he'd be saving America from both Bill Clinton and right-wing yahoos within his own party. He knows how to talk, inspire loyalty, and wear a dark-blue suit.

Today he's riffing on the Simpson case and its lessons for homicide detectives. Six team heads and two administrative aides pack his office SRO.

Burt says: "We can cop an attitude behind the O.J. thing or we can learn from it. I'm glad it wasn't our case, but I want to make damn sure we all go to school on it."

He's got seven lieutenants and one sergeant by the short hairs. He lays out a dizzying spiel on crime-scene containment, evidence chains, and the need to recognize the media magnitude of celebrity murders at the outset, think them through from an adversarial attorney's perspective, and evaluate and define every investigatory aspect as they progress. The pitch is tight and inside, with a slow-breaking kicker: The LAPD took the grief on this one, and *we* reaped the benefit.

A handsomely crafted ceramic bulldog sits on a table beside the captain's desk, replete with a Sheriff's Homicide baseball cap and a rubber turd behind its ass. Burt pats the beast and wraps up the briefing.

"This unit has flourished because we've made an effort to stay open-minded and learn from our mistakes. We've never let our reputation turn us arrogant. If we continue to assess the Simpson case and incorporate what we learn into our procedures, we'll make something good out of one big goddamn mess."

Murder is a big, continuous twenty-four-hour-a-day mess. Murder spawns a numbingly protracted investigatory process that is rarely direct and linear—chiefly because it overlaps with more and more murder, taxing the resources of the investigative agencies involved and inundating detectives with interviews, courtroom appearances, reports to be written, and next-of-kin to be mollified and cajoled into intimate revelations. Murder seldom slows down and never stops; murder stays true to its Motivational Trinity: dope/sex/money.

The L.A. Sheriff's Department investigates all murders, suicides, industrial-accident fatalities, and miscellaneous sudden deaths within the confines of Los Angeles County—the vast, unincorporated area in and around the L.A. city limits. The LAPD's jurisdiction snakes inside, outside, and through the LASD's turf— city/county borders are sometimes hard to distinguish. The county consists mainly of lower-middle-class suburbs and rat's ass towns stretching out ninety-odd miles. This is the big bad sprawl visible from low-flying airplanes: cheap stucco, smog, and freeway grids going on forever.

The LASD Homicide Bureau is housed in a courtyard industrial park in the city of Commerce—six miles from downtown L.A. Sheriff's Homicide is individually subcontracted by numerous police departments inside the county—if you get whacked in Norwalk or Rosemead, the LASD will work your case.

Sheriff's Homicide investigates about 500 snuffs a year. The L.A. District Attorney's office has publicly acknowledged its investigators as the best in southern California. Police departments nationwide send their prospective homicide dicks to the LASD for two-week training programs. LASD detectives teach well because theirs is regarded as the pinnacle assignment—one bestowed after a minimum of ten years in jail work, patrol, and other Detective Division jobs. The mid-forties median age says it all: These people have put the rowdier aspects of police work behind them and have matured behind the gravity of murder.

Former sheriff Peter Pitchess dubbed his homicide crew "the Bulldogs"—a nod to their tenacity and salutary solved-case rate. In truth, bulldogs are lazy creatures prone to breathing disorders and hip dysplasia. The vulture should replace the bulldog as Homicide's mascot.

Vultures wait for people to die. So do homicide cops. Vultures swoop down on the recently dead and guard the surrounding area with sharp claws and beaks. Homicide cops seal crime scenes and kick off their investigations with the evidence culled within.

Sheriff's Homicide is a centralized division. Its basic makeup is six teams of fourteen detectives apiece, bossed by lieutenants Derry Benedict, Don Bear, Joe Brown, Dave Dietrich, Ray Peavy, and Bill Sieber. Two adjunct units—Unsolved and Missing Persons—work out of the same facility. The teams handle incoming murders on a rotating, forty-eight-hour on-call basis.

On-call detectives carry beepers and sleep very poorly, if at all. Beeper chirps signify death and additions to their already strained caseloads. Late-night beeps are only marginally preferable to what the old-timers called "trash runs": call-outs for obvious suicides and pro forma viewings of the poor fucker who got decapitated by an exploding boiler.

The bureau is furnished in the white-walled, metal-desked, policework moderne style. All incoming calls originate in the "Barrel," a desk counter rigged with telephones, memo baskets, and boards for charting murders and assigned personnel. The Barrel adjoins the main squad room—ninety desks arranged in lengthwise rows. The team lieutenants' desks sit crosswise at the far end, next to a shelf jammed with Sergeant Don Garcia's bulldog trinkets.

You can purchase bulldog watches and T-shirts at Sergeant Garcia's cost. A bulldog wall clock will set you back $39.95. Dig the bulldog lapel pin—the giant tongue and spiked collar detailing are worthy of Walt Disney on angel dust. Don's been running the concession for years. He buys the stuff bulk from various manufacturers. He's just acquired a new item: a bulldog neon sign to light up your wet bar!

The Unsolved and Missing Persons units reside in separate rooms off the squad bay. The sign on Unsolved's door reads "UN- LOVED." Unsolved is charged with periodically reviewing cold cases and investigating any new leads pertaining to them. The crew— Dale Christiansen, Rey Verdugo, Louie "the Hat" Danoff, John Yarbrough, and Freddy Castro—is the faculty of the College of Unresolved Justice. Their curriculum is the file library that Louie the Hat has lovingly preserved. Louie says the files talk to him. He's on a spiritual trip and runs his "no body" cases by psychics once in a while.

A corridor links Unsolved to a room lined with computers. A dozen screens glow green all day every day—dig the dozen clerks running record checks on permanent overdrive. The clerks—mostly women—hog the lunchroom from noon to 2 P.M. daily. They watch soap operas and pine for the candy-ass male stars—right down the hall from the ugly bulldog wall plaque.

Note to Sheriff Sherman Block: Vultures are more charismatic than bulldogs.

It's early December. Deputies Gil Carrillo and Frank Gonzales have tickets for the annual Sheriff's/LAPD fistfest. They're primed for an evening of charity boxing—until Lieutenant Brown tells them they're the first on-call team up.

It's a given: Some geek will get murdered tonight and fuck up their fun.

Carrillo and Gonzales decide to stay home and rest. Gil lays some comedy on the deskman, Sergeant Mike Lee: I want a good night's sleep and an indoor crime scene near my pad about 10 A.M. tomorrow. Joe Brown says he'll place the order, ha! ha! ha!

Gil and Frank retire to their cribs. Gil's about six foot three and massively broad. The earth shakes whenever he walks. He co-bossed the LASD's end of the Richard Ramirez "Night Stalker" serial killer task force back in the eighties, ran against Sherman Block in the last sheriff's election, and glommed 17 percent of the vote. Frank's picture should appear in every dictionary on earth, next to the words "Latin lover." He is one handsome motherfucker. Carrillo and Gonzales bring vulture charisma to every case they work—but they're pissed that they blew the fights off for nothing.

Because Gil's wish comes true. His beeper beeps at 10 A.M.—it's an indoor crime scene ten minutes from his pad.

The victim is Donna Lee Meyers, female Caucasian, age 37. She's dead at her house in Valinda, a downscale San Gabriel Valley town.

She's facedown on a green shag rug in the bathroom. She's nude. She's been stabbed between twenty and forty times. Defensive wounds on her hands and arms indicate an extended struggle with her killer.

Patrol deputies responded to the 911 call. The informant was Donna Lee Meyers's father. He came to pick up his 3-year-old grandson and found the back door unlocked and the house filled with gas fumes.

The boy coughed and led him to the body. Every gas burner in the kitchen had been turned on and left unignited.

Carrillo and Gonzales arrive at the scene and get a rundown from the deputies. Their first collective hypothesis: The killer didn't have the stones to ice a little child up front, so he juiced up the gas before he split. Their first collective instinct: The murder was unpremeditated, with a sharp instrument used as a weapon of opportunity. Their first collective decision: Stay outside and let the criminalists do their work first—don't risk contaminating the crime scene.

The serologist takes blood samples off the rug and the surrounding area. The print man dusts and comes up with smudges and smears. A technician prowls with an Electrostatic Dust Lifter—a vacuum sealer–like device that transfers the outline of footprints to a cellophane dust-catching sheet. The coroner remains on hold—to remove the body when Carillo and Gonzales give the word.

Carillo and Gonzales canvass the neighborhood. The word on the street: Donna Lee Meyers did cocaine—and used to deal small quantities of it. Carillo and Gonzales take notes, write down names for backup interviews and compile a list of Donna Lee Meyers's known associates. A friend of the victim's shows up at the house—and appears to be genuinely shocked that Donna Lee is dead.

THE TOOTH OF CRIME 817

Carillo and Gonzales take the man to a nearby sheriff's substation and question him.

He tells them that he dropped by to pay Donna Lee back some coin, and cops to being a casual coke user. The man vibes totally innocent. Carillo and Gonzales let him go and hotfoot it back to the crime scene.

They view the body. A deputy tells them that the killer left the TV on for the kid. Coroner's assistants take Donna Lee Meyers to the L.A. County Morgue.

The follow-up begins.

Carillo and Gonzales attend the autopsy and hear the cause of death confirmed. They locate the father of Donna Lee Meyers's son and dismiss him as a suspect. A psychologist assists them in their dealings with Donna Lee's little boy. The boy's memories of that day are hellishly distorted. Gentle questioning elicits ambiguous responses.

Early December becomes mid-December. Carillo and Gonzales interview Donna Lee Meyers's known associates and come up short on hard suspects. It's becoming a long, hard one—the kind you solve or don't solve while other cases accumulate.

It's creeping up on Christmastime. The bureau lunchroom is draped with red and green banners and packed with an assortment of sugar-soaked treats.

Bulldog-vultures swoop by and chow down—pecan pies and toffee clusters hook you on the first bite.

Talk flows. Food disappears. Nineteen ninety-four is winding down in a swirl of rapid-fire conversation.

Bill Sieber's midway through his standard epic pitch: how a friend's daughter was murdered in Olympia, Washington, and boy did the cops screw up the case! Bill's a primo monologuist. He's got his audience hooked—even though every detective has heard the story six dozen times. Lieutenant Frank Merriman's interjecting punch lines, smiling his standard shit-eating grin. Frank grins 96 percent of the time. Somebody should transpose his brain waves to TV, so the whole world could cut in on the laughs.

Cheryl Lyons zips by. She's got electric turquoise eyes—or she's wearing electric turquoise contact lenses. The late Jack Hoffenberg bootjacked Cheryl's persona for the female lead in his novel *The Des-perate Adversaries*. Cheryl the 1973 narc became Cheryl of the Paper-back Pantheon. Cheryl's pensive today—will the county notch in eight more murders and top its all-time yearly high of 537?

Ike Sabean thinks it's a lock. Ike works Juvenile Missing Per-sons—and must be considered a certified genius.

You've seen his work on milk cartons—the photos of missing kids and the number to call if you spot them. Ike developed the idea in cahoots with a Chicago dairyman. He got a total of sixty-seven dairies and industrial firms to display the pix—and ran up a 70 per-cent local found rate until the public became inured to the photos. Ike's also a board-licensed mortician. He explains the allure of his moonlighting job thusly: "I like to work with people."

Jerome Beck lingers by the chocolate-chip-cookie plate. Beck was the technical adviser on the flick *Dead Bang*. He also wrote the story. Guess what? The director of that movie named the Don Johnson–portrayed lead character "Jerry Beck."

Big Gil Carrillo walks in. The floor shakes; a serving bowl full of Jell-O jiggles. Gil buttonholes Louie the Hat and runs the Donna Lee Meyers crime-scene pix by him.

They discuss defensive wounds and blood-spatter trajectories. Louie's got a spaced-out woman in tow—a psychic he consults every so often.

They call him "the Hat" because he always wears a Tyrolean porkpie with a feather in the band. If you fuck with Louie's hat, Louie will fuck with you. A few years ago, some LAPD clown snatched Louie's hat and goofed on Louie's shaved head. Louie un-hesitatingly popped him in the chops.

Big Gil walks off. Louie hobnobs with his psychic. Don Garcia tacks a notice to the bulletin board: Bulldog wristwatches make wonderful Christmas gifts!

The computer women look pissed. All this holiday bonhomie is drowning out the volume on their soap opera.

The boss is teething on the Guevara case. His ceramic bulldog is teething at the fur ball on the tip of his Santa Claus cap—Dan Burt likes to dress the beast in seasonal headwear.

Ray Peavy's crew got the job—a double abduction/murder way the hell out in Lancaster. Deputy Liova Anderson and Sergeant Joe Guzman caught the first squeal—one baffling whodunit.

Peavy's laying out a chronology for Dan Burt. It's an informal captain's office confab—and the open door encourages kibitzers.

Anderson got the initial call on Wednesday, November 30: a body dump out in the desert. Liova drives up to Palmdale/Lancaster and views the stiff: a male Latin with his hands, face, and crotch scorched.

The victim was wrapped in a baby blanket, doused with a flammable agent, and burned. Liova picks up a strong vibe: The genital scalding indicates some sort of sex murder.

Liova has to work solo for the first seventy-two hours—Joe Guzman, a nationally known expert on gang violence, is off giving a lecture in Texas. She knuckles down and *hauls*.

She attends the postmortem on Friday. The doctor pulls a bullet out of the dead man's head and tags the cause of death as a "gunshot wound." He cuts the dead man's fingers off, rehydrates them, and rolls a clean set of prints.

On Sunday, Liova hears a radio news broadcast. A Latin couple named Carlos and Delia Guevara have been reported missing in Lancaster. She gets another strong vibe: Her dead man is Carlos Guevara.

She calls the Antelope Valley Sheriff's Missing Persons unit. An officer tells her that Sergeant Jim Sears and Deputy Jerry Burks of Sheriff's Homicide have already been assigned to the case —because a bullet hole was found in Carlos and Delia Guevara's living-room wall.

Joe Guzman returns from Texas. Liova drives him up to Lancaster and explains the case en route. The team meets up with Burks and Sears at the Guevara house. Sears drops a belated bomb: Delia Guevara's body was discovered in Yermo over the weekend.

The woman had been shot and similarly dumped—in San Bernardino County, sixty miles from the spot where Guzman and Anderson's body was found.

Liova checks the Guevaras' family records stash and finds a fingerprint ID card on Carlos. She takes it to the L.A. County crime lab and has a technician compare it to the rehydrated digits cut off her victim.

The prints match.

Burks and Sears work the Delia side of the case. Anderson and Guzman stick with Carlos.

Liova's original vibe simmers: This is a sex or sexual-revenge killing. She begins an extensive background check on the Guevaras.

She learns that Delia worked at a local Burger King and Carlos worked at a local appliance store. She learns that the couple had emigrated from Mexico illegally and were living above their means. She learns that Delia had been receiving menacing phone calls at work and that Carlos loved to talk lewd in mixed company—even though it made his friends and neighbors uncomfortable. Carlos was also known for chasing women outright.

Joe Guzman finds numerous toys in a sealed-off bedroom at the Guevara house. It is a striking anomaly. The Guevaras were childless and had often told friends they did not intend to have children. The motive takes circumstantial shape.

Two killings. Vengeance perpetrated by a cuckolded lover or the parents of an abused child.

Ray Peavy wraps his account up. Anderson and Guzman, Burks and Sears are *still* on the case—which remains one baffling whodunit.

Sergeant Jacque Franco pokes her head in the door and eavesdrops. Deputy Rick Graves sidles by for a listen; Dan Burt shoots him an attaboy for his work on that drowning case off Catalina Island.

Ray Peavy says, "It never ends."

Jacque Franco says, "We're still six short of breaking the record."

Dan Burt pats his fat ceramic bulldog.

Sergeant Bob Perry and Deputy Ruben "B. J." Bejarano get called out on Christmas Eve. It's cold, dark, and rainy—good indoor mayhem conditions.

They roll to a video store near the Century Sheriff's Station. A Taiwanese woman named Li Mei Wu lies dead on the floor behind the counter.

The weather has kept rubberneckers to a minimum. Patrol deputies have rounded up eyewitnesses and sequestered them at the station. A sergeant lays things out for Bejarano and Perry.

Three black teenagers entered the store around closing time. They gave the victim some verbal grief, split, and returned a few minutes later. One of them shot Li Mei Wu with a rifle. They ran outside and disappeared on foot.

The victim is positioned faceup. There's a live .22-caliber round and a .22 ejected casing behind the counter. A coroner's assistant lifts the body, notes the exit wound, and points to a projectile tangled up in Li Mei Wu's clothes. He says the shot probably tore out the woman's aorta.

The assistant finds $300 in Li Mei Wu's pockets. Perry and Bejarano note the untouched money and the full cash register and tentatively scratch robbery as a motive. The patrol sergeant tells them what eyeball witnesses told him: The perpetrators bopped to a coin laundry a few doors down before they bopped back and bopped Li Mei Wu.

The body is hustled off to the county morgue. B. J. diagrams the video store in his notebook, zooms down to the laundry, and quicksketches the floor plan. A deputy from the crime lab arrives. He begins snapping crime-scene shots and dusting both the video store and the coin laundry.

Bob and B. J. secure the location and drive to Century Station. Two witnesses are waiting; three have signed preliminary statements, left their phone numbers, and gone home.

B. J. and Bob conduct interviews. They go over minute points of perspective and indoor and outdoor lighting repeatedly. Questions are phrased and rephrased; answers are cross-checked against the three preliminary statements. A single short narrative emerges.

At 8:20 P.M., three black teenagers enter the video store. They behave in a raucous fashion; Li Mei Wu tells them to leave. The kids peruse the skin-flick section and touch numerous *fingerprint-sustaining surfaces*. They walk to the laundry, behave in a raucous fashion, return to the video store and approach Li Mei Wu. One boy says, "Give me your money, bitch!" One boy pulls a rifle from under his clothes and shoots Li Mei Wu—just like that.

It's Christmas morning now. Yuletide greetings, Bulldogs—your new case is senseless blasphemy on this day of peace and joyous celebration.

Days pass. Bejarano and Perry work the Li Mei Wu snuff.

They interview four more witnesses and get their basic scenario confirmed. They run mug shots by the witnesses and come up empty. They run a previous-incident check on the video store—and hit just a little bit lucky.

The place was robbed in November, while Li Mei Wu was working the counter. The perpetrators: three black teenagers.

The same kids robbed a nearby pizza joint that same November night. Li Mei Wu ID's one boy as the grandson of one of her customers. Deputies went by the family pad to grab him—but Junior was long gone.

B. J. and Bob think the December incident report through. One fact stands out: Li Mei Wu hit the silent alarm when she was robbed in November—but did not rush for it on the night of her death. *She obviously did not recognize the kids as the kids who robbed her the previous month.* Bejarano and Perry get their gut feeling confirmed: The murder was committed by local punks. The killers ran away on a rainy night—they didn't have a car and got soaked dispersing back to their pads. One robbery threesome; one trio of killers. Word would be out in the neighborhood—and loose talk would give them a good shot at solving the case.

While other cases accumulate.

There's a big post-Christmas murder lull. Entire on-call shifts are rotating through sans killings. The lunchroom tree is wilting under the weight of decomposed fake snow.

Bulldog eyes are bloodshot. Bulldog waistlines have expanded. High-octane coffee can't jolt Bulldog talk out of a desultory ripple.

Rey Verdugo's recalling other murder lulls. A few years ago the County of Los Angeles went nine days without a single murder. One of Rey's buddies put a sign reading KILL! in the squad-room window. Sheriff's Homicide notched twelve righteous whack-outs over the next twenty-four hours.

Dave Dietrich's showing off some threads he got for Christmas. His wife reads men's fashion mags and shops for him accordingly.

You'd call him "Dave the Dude"—if he didn't look so much like a college professor.

Bill Sieber's drinking Slim-Fast in anticipation of his New Year's diet. He's monologuing between sips—in an uncharacteristically subdued fashion. Ray Peavy and Derry Benedict are discussing the Christmas party at Stevens Steak House. Ray worked the bash as a disc jockey—between his regular off-duty deejay gigs.

Talk shifts to famous unsolved murders. Derry brings up his favorite: the 1944 Georgette Bauerdorf job. When he retires he's going to write a novel about the case.

Louie Danoff and Rey Verdugo compare shaved heads. Gary Miller pokes at a cookie like it's a hot turd.

The killers of Carlos and Delia Guevara, Donna Lee Meyers, and Li Mei Wu are still at large. Soon the year's murder tally will stop—and a new list will begin.

Nineteen ninety-four winds up three short of the all-time murder high. Gunfire rings in 1995—celebratory shots all over the county.

Gunshots and firecracker pops start to sound alike. The locals get used to the noise but expect it to diminish before January 2.

Five shots explode at 6:45 New Year's night. The location is California and Hill, in the city of Huntington Park.

The shots are very loud. The shots in no way, shape, matter, or form sound like anything short of heavy-duty gunfire.

The shots have a gang-killing timbre—maybe the H.P. Brats and H.P. Locos are at it again. A dozen people on Hill Street call the Huntington Park PD.

Huntington Park rolls a unit over. Patrolmen find the body of Joseph Romero, male Latin, DOB 5/11/69. He's dead behind the wheel of his car, ripped through the torso by five AK-47 rounds.

Spent shells rest near the curb. One round blew straight through Romero and out the driver's-side door.

Sheriff's Homicide is alerted. Lieutenant Peavy, Deputy Bob Carr, and Sergeant Stu Reed make the scene.

Carr and Reed are short, heavyset, and fiftyish. They joined the department back in the '60s. Reed's an expert wood-carver; Carr sports the world's coolest handlebar mustache. Both men talk as slow and flat as tombstones.

A crowd forms. Huntington Park cops seal the people out with yellow perimeter tape. Coroner's assistants remove the body; a sheriff's tow truck hauls Romero's car off to the crime lab.

Reed and Carr eyeball the scene. They hit on a hypothesis fast.

Romero was sitting in the car by himself. He was parked six doors down from his pad. He was waiting for somebody.

The passenger-side window was down. "Somebody" walked up, stuck the gun in, and vaporized him.

The crime vibes "gang vengeance" or "dope intrigue," or somebody fucking somebody's girlfriend or sister. The cops have got some witnesses on ice—just dying to offer their interpretations.

Reed and Carr interview them at the H.P. station. Three solid-citizen types tell similar stories: shots fired and two male Latins running off in divergent directions. One man was short; one man was tall—their descriptions match straight down the line. Reed and Carr go over their statements from every conceivable angle.

It's an exercise in spatial logic and a master's course in the plumbing of subjective viewpoints. It's the culling of minutiae as an art form—and Carr and Reed are brilliant cullers.

It's starting to look like another neighborhood crime. The shooter and his accomplice fled on foot and were probably safe at home within minutes.

Reed and Carr interview a Mexican kid named Paulino. Paulino denies being a gang member and states that he hasn't done dope since he got out of rehab. He says he saw the tall male Latin fifteen minutes after the shooting. The guy was waving to a babe leaning out a window in that beige apartment house on Salt Lake Avenue.

A fifth witness independently corroborates the story. He saw the tall man running toward that same building moments after the shooting.

It's coming together. Reed and Carr decide to wait and not hit the building tonight—too many things could go wrong. They agree: Let's check with the HPPD Gang Squad when they come on duty. We'll find out who lives in that building and move accordingly.

Three non-eyewitnesses remain: Joseph Romero's uncle, aunt, and brother. Carr and Reed talk to them gently, and phrase all intimate questions in a deferential tone. The family responds. They say Joe was a nice kid trying to put dope and gang life behind him.

They supply names: Joe was tight with a dozen male Latins in the neighborhood.

Reed and Carr do not mention the beige apartment house. They do not know who the family knows and might feel compelled to protect.

The family leaves. Reed and Carr drive home to get a few hours' sleep. They look old and cumulatively exhausted—like they never had a chance to get caught up while murders accumulate.

The holidays are over. Bob Perry and Jacque Franco are bullshitting at their desks.

Bob says he just notched a score on the Li Mei Wu case. The kids arrested turn out to be the punks who robbed the video store a month before the murder. The suspects are 13, 13, and 16.

Stu Reed sidles by. Jacque asks him how the Romero job is going. Stu says they've got one shooter ID'd but can't find him. Jacque says, "Don't worry—he'll come back to the neighborhood to brag."

Gil Carrillo sits down. He straightens a mimeographed sheet of paper he keeps pressed to his desk blotter.

"The Homicide Investigator" jumps out in bold black print. A single paragraph is inscribed below it:

"No greater honor will ever be bestowed on an officer or a more profound duty imposed on him than when he is entrusted with the investigation of the death of a human being. It is his duty to find the facts, regardless of color or creed, without prejudice, and to let no power on earth deter him from presenting these facts to the court without regard to personality."

Gil blows the motto a kiss. His eyes take on that "Don't mess with me, I'm deep in a reverie" look. You see why people voted for the man. He cares way past the official boundaries of the job. Jacque says, "This job is still Disneyland to you, isn't it?"

Gil tilts his chair back. "It's not Disneyland when you get called out at 3 A.M., but when you get to the murder scene it's like you're coming up on Disneyland and you can see the Matterhorn ride in the distance. It's not Disneyland when you see all the ugliness, but it's Disneyland at the trial when the jury foreman says 'Guilty' and you break down crying just like the victim's family."

※

The holidays are long gone.

Dan Burt's bulldog has gone back to his baseball cap.

Burt tosses a gun catalogue in his wastebasket. He's a lifelong gun fancier pushed to the point of apostasy.

"My gun collection sickens me now," he says. "It makes me feel like I'm part of some mass illness."

Ray Peavy coughs. "We found Carlos Guevara's car at the Greyhound Terminal downtown. The crime lab's got it."

Burt points to a sheet of paper on his desk blotter—a mockup of the condolence letter the bureau sends to murder victims' families.

"We can't send that to Guevara's wife, because she's dead too. I guess all we can do is pray and work the case."

While other cases accumulate.

July 1995

Garrett Hongo

Los Angeles's clash of cultures is often played out most vividly among its students, as they circle one another warily in the city's schools. In this excerpt from his memoir *Volcano*, the Japanese-American poet Garrett Hongo (b. 1951) describes his own experience going to school in Southern California in the mid-1960s. Hongo is the author of two poetry collections, *Yellow Light* and *The River of Heaven*, which was the 1987 Lamont Poetry Selection of the Academy of American Poets and a finalist for the Pulitzer Prize. Born in Volcano, Hawaii, he moved with his family at an early age to South Central L.A.

from

VOLCANO

What I cared about was the inner city, about my teenage life brooding on the social complexities of my integrated high school—unusual in that it was a third white, and a third black, and a third Japanese American. I cared about what it was I *didn't* see a whole lot of where I'd grown up. *Compassion*. I cared about what the family could give that the city did not. I cared that the complete brutality of ghetto life was not compensated for by anything I'd ever witnessed, by anything I could yet imagine.

Once, when I was about thirteen, I'd climbed up on the roof of my parents' house because I'd heard that there was a riot going on in the other side of the city. I was told that you could see fires burning, smoke rising, from the rooftops of our neighborhood. Watts was only a few miles away—across the freeway and down some— and my schoolmates told me to watch the riot from my roof. I climbed up there and saw a red glow, miles off, under a little cover of smoke clouds.

I thought of a classmate—a little guy who'd been caught with a small-caliber pistol on the junior high school bus one day. I'll call him Gerald. The gun wasn't his, but was being passed around from seat to seat, person to person. It was with him when the driver caught up with its illicit migrations. Gerald was busted. He was put out of school on detention, on probation, on expulsion. He went to "joovie," a state-run reform school, where he was raped, repeatedly, by the older, bigger black kids. The Chicanos left him alone. The whites knifed him. He came back, no longer somber and reflective, no longer full of jokes and smiles in gym class. He carried a brief-case now, in which he kept a switchblade, a Filipino dagger, a hunt-ing or a Swedish filleting knife. He was sullen, quiet, and marched quickly between buildings from class to class. If someone laughed too hard or too long close by him now, he'd fix the laughing school-mate with a stare. If the laughter stopped, nothing would happen. If it did not, we'd soon hear someone was "knifed" in the lavatory, and Gerald would spend the next day full of malicious smiles. It made us cautious about ridicule, real or perceived. I learned about paranoia, about retribution, and little about forgiveness. Watts burned, and all I could see was a red wound across the city and smoke pouring from it. In my dreams that night, I saw my old friend Gerald smil-ing, a wound opening wider and wider under his own rib cage as he lay on the ground. His eyes did not blink.

Another time, I was riding bikes with my friends from junior high school. But it was summer—hot, smoggy, with no classes and flies in the air around all the Dumpsters in the alleyways we rode through, dodging cars pulling out of their garages in South Los Angeles. We wanted to meet girls, to learn some dances like the big-ger guys. We rode around with transistor radios dangling from the handlebars of our Schwinn Sting-rays, from the nose-sprocket shock absorbers of our clunky Hornets. We listened to the "soul" stations—the black AM channels that played rhythm and blues, the new Motown tunes by the Temptations and the Supremes, the Stax/Volt sides from Memphis by Aretha Franklin and Sam and Dave. We wanted to be "baad" and have soul—like the black kids in our school, the kids who knew all the dances, who did the Slauson and the Twine and the Jerk and the Duck-in-the-Wall. We did wheelies in the streets on our Sting-rays and tried to figure a way to get a girl to teach us something. We decided to call one up. We rode from the public library where we met every day and biked a few blocks over toward the apartment house where a "new" girl lived with her parents. She'd know dances from the part of town she came from, she'd be willing to teach us things. She'd want to be accepted. She'd want to make friends.

We biked over to a Laundromat around the corner from where we knew she lived, where we thought a pay phone might be. I was elected to make the call. We stopped by a booth. The phone was broken. The glass in the booth was all broken. The phone book's pages flapped in the wind from passing delivery trucks and automobiles and tanker trucks hauling gasoline around our city. A little gravel showered on my shoes. I had to do something.

I went into the little bungalow next to the phone booth, where I thought the Laundromat was. It was cool, dark inside. There was no sign on the front. I went through a short entry hallway, then turned into a large, darkened room.

There were round tables, and chairs, with people sitting inside. There was a long bar with stools. People sat on the stools. There was a mirror, shiny bottles along a shelf in front of the mirror, a stainless steel cash register, a few plants. All of the people were women. Some were in sweatshirts and some were in leather jackets. None of them wore dresses that I could see. They had haircuts like men—crew cuts and butch cuts, and hair slicked with pomade. A couple of them were in a booth by the side kissing each other. One would open her mouth, and I could see the gold fillings of her teeth sparkle a little with saliva in the soft light of a table lamp. Then it would be dark, her shining mouth eclipsed, swallowed by the black disk of another woman's mouth, the one who sat in her lap, who squirmed in it and fondled her partner's breasts under her loose shirt. I turned away.

I said something to the bartender, a heavyset woman wearing a garish aloha shirt. I might have asked for the *pay phone*. I might have asked for change. She ordered me out, saying I had to be *older*, I had to be *twenty-one*. I drifted out of the bar, stumbling back over the little chicane of darkness through the entryway, appearing in the bright, smoggy light and pneumatic rushing sounds of the large Los Angeles boulevard.

My friends awaited me. They were laughing, grinning. It was "a dyke bar!" they were saying. "A bar full of dykes!"

"What's a *dyke*?" I asked.

"A lezzie," someone said. "A *homo* woman!"

Two pranced and did the Funky Chicken in the dirt of the vacant lot where we stood next to the bar.

They hopped on their bikes, and I pursued. We went over to the new girl's apartment house without calling. We knocked on the door. She let us in. She had lots of records. Stacks of 45s. She taught us the Philly Dog, a cha-cha, the Hole-in-the-Wall. I got to *hold* her. I got to feel a slender teenage girl's flesh under a cotton blouse and summer shorts. I knew approval and I knew disapproval, but, to be human, I knew nothing of what I needed to know.

FRATERNITY

It was high school in Gardena. I was in classes mostly with Japanese American kids—*kotonks*, Mainland Japanese, their ethnic pet name originated, during the war, with derisive Hawaiian GIs who thought of the sound of a coconut being hit with a hammer. Sansei *kotonks* were sons and daughters of the Nisei *kotonks* who had been sent off to the concentration camps during World War II. School was tepid, boring. We wanted cars, we wanted clothes, we wanted everything whites and blacks wanted to know about sex but were afraid to tell us. We "bee-essed" with the black kids in the school parking lot full of coastal fog before classes. We beat the white kids in math, in science, in typing. We ran track and elected cheerleaders. We *ruled*, we said. We were dumb, teeming with attitude and prejudice.

Bored, I took a creative writing class with an "academically mixed" bunch of students. There were Chicanos, whites, a black woman, and a troika of Japanese women who sat together on the other side of the room from me. They said nothing—*ever*—and wrote naturalistically correct *haiku*. Suddenly among boisterous non-Japanese, I enjoyed the gabbing, the bright foam of free talk that the teacher encouraged. An aging man in baggy pants that he wore with suspenders, he announced he was retiring at the end of the year and that he wanted no trouble, that he was going to read "Eeebee White" during our hour of class every day, that we were welcome to read whatever we wanted so long as we gave him a list ahead of time, and that we could talk as much as we wanted so long as we left him alone. We could read, we could write, we could jive each other all class long. It was freedom. And I took advantage.

I sat next to a Chicano my age named Pacheco and behind a white girl a class younger than me named Regina. Behind us was a curly-headed white guy who played saxophone in the marching band. He'd been in academic classes with me, the only Caucasian among Japanese, a Korean, and a few Chinese. He was a joker, and I liked him, but usually stayed away—we didn't fraternize much across the races, though our school was supposed to be an experiment in integration.

Gardena H.S. wasn't so much a mix or blend as a mosaic. Along with a few whites and blacks, Japanese were in the tough, college-prep, "advanced placement" scholastic track. Most whites and blacks were in the regular curriculum of shop, business skills, and a minimum of academic courses. The "dumb Japs" were in there with them. And the Chicanos filled up what were called the *remedial* classes, all taught imperiously only in English, with no provision for language acquisition. We were a student body of about three thousand, and we walked edgily around each other, swaggering when we could, sliding the steel taps on our big black shoes along the concrete outdoor walkways when we wanted to attract a little attention, making a jest of our strut, a music in the rhythm of our walking. Blacks were bused in from Compton; the whites, Japanese, and Chicanos came from around the town. Girls seemed to me an ethnic group of their own too, giggling and forming social clubs, sponsoring dances, teaching some of us the steps.

Crazes of dress moved through our populations—for Chicanos: woolen Pendletons over thin undershirts and a crucifix; big low-top oxfords; khaki work trousers, starched and pressed; for the *bloods*: rayon and satin shirts in metallic "fly-ass" colors; pegged gabardine slacks; cheap moccasin-toed shoes from downtown shops in L.A.; and for us *Buddhas*: high-collar Kensingtons of pastel cloths, Al tapered "Racer" slacks, and the same moccasin shoes as the bloods, who were our brothers. It was crazy. And *inviolable*. Dress and social behavior were a code one did not break for fear of ostracism and reprisal. Bad dressers were ridiculed. Offending speakers were beaten, tripped walking into the john, and set upon by gangs. They *wailed* on you if you fucked up. A girl was nothing except pride, an ornament of some guy's crude power and expertise in negotiating the intricacies of this inner-city semiotic of cultural display and hidden violence. I did not know girls.

I talked to Regina, saying "white girl" one time. She told me not to call her that, that she was *Portuguese* if anything, that I better *know* that white people were *always* something too. From vague memories of Hawai'i, I reached for the few words in Portuguese that I knew. I asked her about the sweet bread her mother baked, about heavy donuts fried in oil and rolled in sugar. I said *bon dea* for "good day" to her. I read the books she talked about—Steinbeck, Kesey, Salinger, and Baldwin. Her mother brought paperbacks home from the salon she worked in, putting up other women's hair—*rich* women's. We made up our reading list from books her mother knew. I wanted desperately to impress her, so I began to write poetry too, imitating some melancholy rock and country-and-western lyrics. She invited me to her house after school. It was on the way, so I walked her home. It became a practice.

Her father was a big, diabetic man from Texas. With his shirt off, he showed me how he shot himself with insulin, poking the needle under the hairy red skin on his stomach, working it over the bulge of fat around his belly. He laughed a lot and shared his beer. There were other guys over too—white guys from the football team, a Filipino, and one other Japanese guy who played left tackle. They were tough, raucous, and talked easily, excitedly. I stood alone in the front yard one day, holding a soft drink in my hand, the barbecue party going on around me. Regina and her mother were baking bread inside. No one knew exactly what was going on, and I was still trying to pretend all was casual.

I took photographs of her. We had a picnic on the coast by the lighthouse near Marineland, on the bluffs over the Pacific. It was foggy, mist upon us and the tall, droopy grasses in the field we walked through, but we made do. She wrapped herself in the blanket she'd brought for us to sit on. We were in the tall grasses of the headlands far from the coast road. She posed. I changed lenses, dropping film canisters, other things. She waved to me, unbuttoning the blouse she was wearing, her body full of a fragrance. The warm, yeasty scent of her skin smelled like bread under bronze silk.

We couldn't be seen together—not at the private, car-club-sponsored Japanese dances out in the Crenshaw District, not at the whites-dominated dances after school in the high school gym. Whites did not see Buddhas, and Buddhas did not see bloods. We were to stay with our own—*that* was the code—though we mixed some in the lunch line, in a few classes, on the football field, and in gym. We segregated ourselves.

Regina and I went to the Chicano dances in El Monte. Pacheco introduced us to them. Regina, tanned Portuguese, passed for Chicana, so long as she kept her mouth shut and her lashes long. Pacheco showed her what skirts to wear, his quick hands fluttering through the crinolines and taffetas in her closet at home. He advised me to grow a mustache and let my black hair go long in the back, to slick it down with pomade and to fluff it up in front, then seal it all in hair spray. I bought brown Pendletons and blue navy-surplus bell-bottoms. I bought hard, steel-toed shoes. We learned trots and tangos. We learned *cuecas* and polkas. We *passed*, *ese*, and had a good time for a couple of months.

One day, Regina got hurt. She was stopped by one of the football players at the beach. She was stepping onto a bus when he came up behind her and grabbed her arm. She tried to twist away, and the arm snapped. She crumpled. Everyone ran. She rode in a friend's car to the hospital that day and had the arm set. She didn't call me.

I heard about it after school the next day, crossing the street against the light. It was summer, and I was taking classes while Regina spent her days at the beach. I'd see her weekdays, stopping at her house on the way home. I was going to her when, just outside the gates of our school, a guy I knew taunted me with the news. He was Japanese, and it was strange to hear him say anything about Regina. I hadn't realized anyone from my crowd knew about us.

I wanted to run the rest of the way to her house. I crossed over a rise of bare earth, then down to a bedded railway—a strip line so that scrap steel and aluminum could be shipped from the switching stations and railyards downtown to steel and aeronautical factories near our school. Brown hummocks rose above eye level and masked the track of crossties, steel rails, and the long bed of gravel. I was set upon there by a troop of Japanese boys. A crowd of them encircled me, taunting, then a single gangly fellow I recognized from gym class executed most of the blows. They beat me, grinding my face in the gravel, shouting epithets like *inu* ("dog"), *cow-fucker*, and *paddy-lover*.

I've seen hand-sized reef fish, in a ritual of spawning, leave their singular lairs, gathering in smallish, excitable schools—a critical mass—and, electrified by their circling assembly, suddenly burst the cluster apart with sequences of soloing, males alternating, pouncing above the finning group, clouding the crystalline waters above the circle with a roil of milt.

All spring and summer, I'd been immune, unaware of the enmity of the crowd. I hadn't realized that, in society, humiliation is a force more powerful than love. Love does not exist in society, but only between two, or among a family. A kid from Hawai'i, I'd undergone no real initiation in shame or social victimization yet and maintained an arrogant season out of bounds, imagining I was exempt. It was humiliating to have been sent to Camp. The Japanese American community understood their public disgrace and lived modestly, with deep prohibitions. I was acting outside of this history. I could cross boundaries, I thought. But I was not yet initiated into the knowledge that we Japanese were *not* like anyone else, that we lived in a community of violent shame. I paid for my naïveté with a bashing I still feel today, with cuts that healed with scars I can still run my fingers along. I can still taste the blood, remember the split skin under the mustache on my upper lip, and feel the depth of an anger that must have been *historical*, *tribal*, arising from fears of dissolution and diaspora.

Separated societies police their own separations. I was hated one day, and with an intensity I could not have foreseen. I was lifted by my clothes, the hands of my schoolmates at the nape of my shirt collar and the back of the waistband of my trousers, and I was hurled against the scrawny trunk of a little jacaranda tree and beaten there, fists cracking against my arms as I tried to cover my face, thumping along my sides and back, booted feet flailing at my legs. I squirmed, crawled, cried out. And I wept. Out of fear and humiliation and a psychic wounding I understand only now. I was *hated*. I was high and needed lowering. My acts were canceled.

Regina was canceled. Both by our own peoples, enacting parallel vengeances of their own, taking our bodies from us.

Our trystings were over, and, later that summer, Regina simply moved away. Her father was retiring, she said, and had found a nice trailer park up by Morro Bay. She wouldn't see me before she left. I had to surprise her at a Laundromat one Saturday. She gave me a paperback book. She laughed, made light of everything, but there was a complete *fear* of me that I felt from her, deeply, one I had not felt before — at least, it had never registered. *Race*. It is an exclusion, a punishment, imposed by the group. I've felt it often since. It is a fear of *fraternity*. A fraternity that is forbidden. I wept, but let her go.

Pico Iyer

In the early 1990s, Pico Iyer (b. 1957) spent a week at Los Angeles International Airport (or, more commonly, LAX) and described the experience in "Where Worlds Collide," an essay originally published in *Harper's* in 1995 and later expanded for *The Global Soul: Jet Lag, Shopping Malls, and the Search for Home* (2000). Iyer is one of a new breed of travel writer: smart, opinionated, and interested not only in exotic landscapes but also in how we all live in an increasingly interconnected world. Born in England to Indian parents, Iyer moved to Los Angeles as a seven-year-old, although he later returned to England and was educated at Eton and Oxford. He is the author of the novel *Cuba and the Night* (1995) and five travel books, including *Video Night in Kathmandu* (1988) and *The Lady and the Monk: Four Seasons in Kyoto* (1991).

WHERE WORLDS COLLIDE

They come out, blinking, into the bleached, forgetful sunshine, in Dodgers caps and Rodeo Drive T-shirts, with the maps their cousins have drawn for them and the images they've brought over from *Cops* and *Terminator 2*; they come out, dazed, disoriented, heads still partly in the clouds, bodies still several time zones—or centuries—away, and they step into the Promised Land.

In front of them is a Van Stop, a Bus Stop, a Courtesy Tram Stop, and a Shuttle Bus Stop (the shuttles themselves tracing circuits A, B, and C). At the Shuttle Bus Stop, they see the All American Shuttle, the Apollo Shuttle, Celebrity Airport Livery, the Great American Stageline, the Movie Shuttle, the Transport, Ride-4-You, and forty-two other magic buses waiting to whisk them everywhere from Bakersfield to Disneyland. They see Koreans piling into the Taeguk Airport Shuttle and the Seoul Shuttle, which will take them to Koreatown without their ever feeling they've left home; they see newcomers from the Middle East disappearing under the Arabic script of the Sahara Shuttle. They see fast-talking, finger-snapping, palm-slapping jive artists straight from their TV screens shouting incomprehensible slogans about deals, destinations, and drugs.

Over there is a block-long white limo, a Lincoln Continental, and, over there, a black Chevy Blazer with Mexican stickers all over its windows, being towed. They have arrived in the Land of Opportunity, and the opportunities are swirling dizzily, promiscuously, around them.

They have already braved the ranks of Asian officials, the criminal-looking security men in jackets that say "Elsinore Airport Services," the men shaking tins that say "Helping America's Hopeless." They have already seen the tilting mugs that say "California: a new slant on life" and the portable fruit machines in the gift shop. They have already, perhaps, visited the rest room where someone has written, "Yes on Proposition 187. Mexicans go home," the snack bar where a slice of pizza costs $3.19 (18 quetzals, they think in horror, or 35,000 dong), and the sign that urges them to try the Cockatoo Inn Grand Hotel. The latest arrivals at Los Angeles International Airport are ready now to claim their new lives.

Above them in the terminal, voices are repeating, over and over, in Japanese, Spanish, and unintelligible English, "Maintain visual contact with your personal property at all times." Out on the sidewalk, a man's voice and a woman's voice are alternating an unending refrain: "The white zone is for loading and unloading of passengers only. No parking." There are "Do Not Cross" yellow lines cordoning off parts of the sidewalk and "Wells Fargo Alarm Services" stickers on the windows; there are "Aviation Safeguard" signs on the baggage carts and "Beware of Solicitors" signs on the columns; there are even special phones "To Report Trouble." More male and female voices are intoning, continuously, "Do not leave your car unattended" and "Unattended cars are subject to immediate tow-away." There are no military planes on the tarmac here, the newcomers notice, no khaki soldiers in fatigues, no instructions not to take photographs, as at home; but there are civilian restrictions every bit as strict as in many a police state.

"This Terminal Is in a Medfly Quarantine Area," says the sign between the terminals. "Stop the Spread of Medfly!" If, by chance, the new Americans have to enter a parking lot on their way out, they will be faced with "Cars left over 30 days may be impounded at Owner's Expense" and "Do not enter without a ticket." It will cost them $16 if they lose their parking ticket, they read, and $56 if they park in the wrong zone. Around them is an unending cacophony of antitheft devices, sirens, beepers, and car-door openers; lights are flashing everywhere, and the man who fines them $16 for losing their parking ticket has the tribal scars of Tigre across his forehead.

The blue skies and palm trees they saw on TV are scarcely visible from here: just an undifferentiated smoggy haze, billboards advertising Nissan and Panasonic and Canon, and beyond those an endlessly receding mess of gray streets. Overhead, they can see the all-too-familiar signs of Hilton and Hyatt and Holiday Inn; in the distance, a sea of tract houses, mini-malls, and high-rises. The City of Angels awaits them.

It is a commonplace nowadays to say that cities look more and more like airports, cross-cultural spaces that are a gathering of tribes and races and variegated tongues; and it has always been true that airports are in many ways like miniature cities, whole, self-sufficient communities, with their own chapels and museums and gymnasiums. Not only have airports colored our speech (teaching us about being upgraded, bumped, and put on standby, coaching us in the ways of fly-by-night operations, holding patterns, and the Mile High Club); they have also taught us their own rules, their own codes, their own customs. We eat and sleep and shower in airports; we pray and weep and kiss there. Some people stay for days at a time in these perfectly convenient, hermetically sealed, climate-controlled duty-free zones, which offer a kind of caesura from the obligations of daily life.

Airports are also, of course, the new epicenters and paradigms of our dawning post-national age—not just the bus terminals of the global village but the prototypes, in some sense, for our polyglot, multicolored, user-friendly future. And in their very universality—like the mall, the motel, or the McDonald's outlet—they advance the notion of a future in which all the world's a multiculture. If you believe that more and more of the world is a kind of mongrel hybrid in which many cities (Sydney, Toronto, Singapore) are simply suburbs of a single universal order, then Los Angeles's LAX, London's Heathrow, and Hong Kong's Kai Tak are merely stages on some great global Circle Line, shuttling variations on a common global theme. Mass travel has made L.A. contiguous to Seoul and adjacent to São Paulo, and has made all of them now feel a little like bedroom communities for Tokyo.

And as with most social trends, especially the ones involving tomorrow, what is true of the world is doubly true of America, and what is doubly true of America is quadruply true of Los Angeles. L.A., legendarily, has more Thais than any city but Bangkok, more Koreans than any city but Seoul, more El Salvadorans than any city outside of San Salvador, more Druze than anywhere but Beirut; it is, at the very least, the easternmost outpost of Asia and the north-ernmost province of Mexico. When I stopped at a Traveler's Aid desk at LAX recently, I was told I could request help in Khamu, Mien, Tigrinya, Tajiki, Pashto, Dari, Pangasinan, Pampangan, Waray-Waray, Bambara, Twi, and Bicolano (as well, of course, as French, German, and eleven languages from India). LAX is as clear an image as exists today of the world we are about to enter, and of the world that's entering us.

For me, though, LAX has always had a more personal resonance: it was in LAX that I arrived myself as a new immigrant, in 1966; and from the time I was in the fourth grade, it was to LAX that I would go three times a year, as an "unaccompanied minor," to fly to school in London—and to LAX that I returned three times a year for my holidays. Sometimes it seems as if I have spent half my life in LAX. For me, it is the site of my liberation (from school, from the Old World, from home) and the place where I came to design my own new future.

Often when I have set off from L.A. to some distant place— Havana, say, or Hanoi, or Pyongyang—I have felt that the multi-cultural drama on display in LAX, the interaction of exoticism and familiarity, was just as bizarre as anything I would find when I ar-rived at my foreign destination. The airport is an Amy Tan novel, a short story by Bharati Mukherjee, a Henry James sketch set to an MTV beat; it is a cross-generational saga about Chang Hsieng meet-ing his daughter Cindy and finding that she's wearing a nose ring now and is shacked up with a surfer from Berlin. The very best kind of airport reading to be found in LAX these days is the triple-decker melodrama being played out all around one—a complex tragi-comedy of love and war and exile, about people fleeing centuries-old rivalries and thirteenth-century mullahs and stepping out into a fresh, forgetful, born-again city that is rewriting its script every moment.

Not long ago I went to spend a week in LAX. I haunted the airport by day and by night, I joined the gloomy drinkers listening to air-control-tower instructions on earphones at the Proud Bird bar. I listened each morning to Airport Radio (530 AM), and I slept each night at the Airport Sheraton or the Airport Hilton. I lived off cellophaned crackers and Styrofoam cups of tea, browsed for hours among Best Actor statuettes and Beverly Hills magnets, and tried to see what kinds of America the city presents to the new Americans, who are remaking America each day.

It is almost too easy to say that LAX is a perfect metaphor for L.A., a flat, spaced-out desert kind of place, highly automotive, not deeply hospitable, with little reading matter and no organizing principle. (There are eight satellites without a center here, many international arrivals are shunted out into the bleak basement of Terminal 2, and there is no airline that serves to dominate LAX as Pan Am once did JFK.) Whereas "SIN" is a famously ironical airline code for Singapore, cathedral of puritanical rectitude, "LAX" has always seemed perilously well chosen for a city whose main industries were traditionally thought to be laxity and relaxation. LAX is at once a vacuum waiting to be colonized and a joyless theme park — Tomorrowland, Adventureland, and Fantasyland all at once.

The postcards on sale here (made in Korea) dutifully call the airport "one of the busiest and most beautiful air facilities in the world," and it is certainly true that LAX, with thirty thousand international arrivals each day — roughly the same number of tourists that have visited the Himalayan country of Bhutan in its entire history — is not uncrowded. But bigger is less and less related to better: in a recent survey of travel facilities; *Business Traveller* placed LAX among the five worst airports in the world for customs, luggage retrieval, and passport processing.

LAX is, in fact, a surprisingly shabby and hollowed-out kind of place, certainly not adorned with the amenities one might expect of the world's strongest and richest power. When you come out into the

Arrivals area in the International Terminal, you will find exactly one tiny snack bar, which serves nine items; of them, five are identified as Cheese Dog, Chili Dog, Chili Cheese Dog, Nachos with Cheese, and Chili Cheese Nachos. There is a large panel on the wall offering rental-car services and hotels, and the newly deplaned American dreamer can choose between the Cadillac Hotel, the Banana Bungalow (which offers a Basketball Court, "Free Toast," "Free Bed Sheets," and "Free Movies and Parties"), and the Backpacker's Paradise (with "Free Afternoon Tea and Crumpets" and "Free Evening Party Including Food and Champagne").

Around one in the terminal is a swirl of priests rattling cans, Iranians in suits brandishing pictures of torture victims, and Japanese girls in Goofy hats. "I'm looking for something called Clearasil," a distinguished-looking Indian man diffidently tells a cashier. "Clearasil?" shouts the girl. "For your face?"

Upstairs, in the Terrace Restaurant, passengers are gulping down "Dutch Chocolate" and "Japanese Coffee" while students translate back and forth between English and American, explaining that "soliciting" loses something of its cachet when you go across the Atlantic. A fat man is nuzzling the neck of his outrageously pretty Filipina companion, and a few Brits are staring doubtfully at the sign that assures them that seafood is "cheerfully served at your table!" Only in America, they are doubtless thinking. A man goes from table to table, plunking down on each one a key chain attached to a globe. As soon as an unsuspecting customer picks one up, touched by the largesse of the New World and convinced now that there *is* such a thing as a free lunch in America, the man appears again, flashes a sign that says "I Am a Deaf," and requests a dollar for the gift.

At a bank of phones, a saffron-robed monk gingerly inserts a credit card, while schoolkids page Jesse Jackson at the nearest "white courtesy telephone." One notable feature of the modern airport is that it is wired, with a vengeance: even in a tiny, two-urinal men's room, I found two telephones on offer; LAX bars rent out cellular phones; and in the Arrivals area, as you come out into the land of plenty, you face a bank of forty-six phones of every kind, with screens and buttons and translations, from which newcomers are calling direct to Bangalore or Baghdad. Airports are places for connections of all kinds and *loci classici*, perhaps, for a world ruled by IDD and MCI, DOS and JAL.

Yet for all these grounding reminders of the world outside, everywhere I went in the airport I felt myself in an odd kind of twilight zone of consciousness, that weightless limbo of a world in which people are between lives and between selves, almost sleepwalking, not really sure of who or where they are. Light-headed from the trips they've taken, ears popping and eyes about to do so, under a potent foreign influence, people are at the far edge of themselves in airports, ready to break down or through. You see strangers pouring out their life stories to strangers here, or making new life stories with other strangers. Everything is at once intensified and slightly unreal. One L.A. psychiatrist advises shy women to practice their flirting here, and religious groups circle in the hope of catching unattached souls.

Airports, which often have a kind of perpetual morning-after feeling (the end of the holiday, the end of the affair), are places where everyone is ruled by the clock, but all the clocks show different times. These days, after all, we fly not only into yesterday or this morning when we go across the world but into different decades, often, of the world's life and our own: in ten or fifteen hours, we are taken back into the twelfth century or into worlds we haven't seen since childhood. And in the process we are subjected to transitions more jolting than any imagined by Oscar Wilde or Sigmund Freud: if the average individual today sees as many images in a day as a Victorian saw in a lifetime, the average person today also has to negotiate switches between continents inconceivable only fifty years ago. Frequent fliers like Ted Turner have actually become ill from touching down and taking off so often; but, in less diagnosable ways, all of us are being asked to handle difficult suspensions of the laws of Nature and Society when moving between competing worlds.

This helps to compound the strange statelessness of airports, where all bets are off and all laws are annulled—modern equivalents, perhaps, to the hundred yards of no-man's-land between two frontier crossings. In airports we are often in dreamy, floating, out-of-body states, as ready to be claimed as that suitcase on Carousel

C. Even I, not traveling, didn't know sometimes if I was awake or asleep in LAX, as I heard an announcer intone, "John Cheever, John Cheever, please contact a Northwest representative in the Baggage Claim area. John Cheever, please contact a service representative at the Northwest Baggage Claim area."

As I started to sink into this odd, amphibious, bipolar state, I could begin to see why a place like LAX is a particular zone of fear, more terrifying to many people than anywhere but the dentist's office. Though dying in a plane is, notoriously, twenty times less likely than dying in a car, every single airline crash is front-page news and so dramatic—not a single death but three hundred—that airports are for many people killing grounds. Their runways are associated in the mind's (televisual) eye with hostages and hijackings; with bodies on the tarmac or antiterrorist squads storming the plane.

That general sense of unsettledness is doubtless intensified by all the people in uniform in LAX. There are ten different security agencies working the Tom Bradley Terminal alone, and the streets outside are jam-packed with Airport Police cars, FBI men, and black-clad airport policemen on bicycles. All of them do as much, I suspect, to instill fear as to still it. "People are scared here," a gloomy Pakistani security guard told me, "because undercover are working. Police are working. You could be undercover, I could be undercover. Who knows?"

And just as L.A. is a province of the future in part because so many people take it to be the future, so it is a danger zone precisely because it is imagined to be dangerous. In Osaka's new $16 billion airport recently, I cross-examined the Skynet computer (in the Departures area) about what to expect when arriving at LAX or any other foreign airport. "Guard against theft in the arrival hall," it told me (and, presumably, even warier Japanese). "A thief is waiting for a chance to take advantage of you." Elsewhere it added, "Do not dress too touristy," and, "Be on your guard when approached by a group of suspicious-looking children, such as girls wearing bright-colored shirts and scarves." True to such dark prognostications, the side doors of the Airport Sheraton at LAX are locked every day from 8:00 P.M to 6:00 A.M., and you cannot even activate the elevators without a room key. "Be extra careful in parking garages and stairwells," the hotel advises visitors. "Always try to use the main entrance to your hotel, particularly late in the evening. Never answer your hotel room door without verifying who is there."

One reason airports enjoy such central status in our imaginations is that they play such a large part in forming our first (which is sometimes our last) impression of a place; this is the reason that poor countries often throw all their resources into making their airports sleek, with beautifully landscaped roads leading out of them into town. L.A., by contrast, has the bareness of arrogance, or simple inhospitability. Usually what you see as you approach the city is a grim penitential haze through which is visible nothing but rows of gray buildings, a few dun-hued warehouses, and ribbons of dirty freeway: a no-colored blur without even the comforting lapis ornaments of the swimming pools that dot New York or Johannesburg. (Ideally, in fact, one should enter L.A. by night, when the whole city pulses like an electric grid of lights—or the back of a transistor radio, in Thomas Pynchon's inspired metaphor. While I was staying in LAX, Jackie Collins actually told *Los Angeles* magazine that "Flying in [to LAX] at night is just an orgasmic thrill.") You land, with a bump, on a mess of gray runways with no signs of welcome, a hangar that says "Trans World Airlines," another broken sign that announces "Tom Bradl y International Ai port," and an air-control tower under scaffolding.

The first thing that greeted me on a recent arrival was a row of Asians sitting on the floor of the terminal, under a sign that told them of a $25,000 fine for bringing in the wrong kinds of food. As I passed through endless corridors, I was faced with almost nothing except long escalators (a surprisingly high percentage of the accidents recorded at airports comes from escalators, bewildering to newcomers) and bare hallways. The other surprise, for many of my fellow travelers, no doubt, was that almost no one we saw looked like Robert Redford or Julia Roberts or, indeed, like anyone belonging to the race we'd been celebrating in our in-flight movies. As we passed into the huge, bare assembly hall that is the Customs and Immigration Center here, I was directed into one of the chaotic lines by a Noriko and formally admitted to the country by a C. Chen. The man waiting to transfer my baggage (as a beagle sniffed around us in a coat that said "Agriculture's Beagle Brigade" on one side and "Protecting American Agriculture" on the other) was named Yoji Yosaka. And the first sign I saw, when I stepped into America, was a big board being waved by the "Executive Sedan Service" for one "Mr. T. Ego."

For many immigrants, in fact, LAX is quietly offering them a view of their own near futures: the woman at the Host Coffee Shop is themselves, in a sense, two years from now, and the man sweeping up the refuse is the American dream in practice. The staff at the airport seems to be made up almost entirely of recent immigrants: on my very first afternoon there, I was served by a Hoa, an Ephraim, and a Glinda; the wait-people at a coffee shop in Terminal 5 were called Ignacio, Ever, Aura, and Erick. Even at the Airport Sheraton (where the employees all wear nameplates), I was checked in by Viera (from "Bratislavia") and ran into Hasmik and Yovik (from Ethiopia), Faye (from Vietnam), Ingrid (from Guatemala City), Khrystyne (from Long Beach, by way of Phnom Penh, I think), and Moe (from West L.A., she said). Many of the bright-eyed dreamers who arrive at LAX so full of hope never actually leave the place.

The deeper drama of any airport is that it features a kind of interaction almost unique in our lives, wherein many of us do not know whom we are going to meet or whom others are going to meet in us. You see people standing at the barriers outside the Customs area looking into their pasts, while wide-open newcomers drift out, searching for their futures. Lovers do not know if they will see the same person who kissed them good-bye a month ago; grandparents wonder what the baby they last saw twenty years ago will look like now.

In L.A. all of this has an added charge, because unlike many cities, it is not a hub but a terminus: a place where people come to arrive. Thus many of the meetings you witness are between the haves and the hope-to-haves, between those who are affecting a new ease in their new home and those who are here in search of that ease. Both parties, especially if they are un-American by birth, are eager to stress their Americanness or their fitness for America; and both, as they look at each other's made-up self, see themselves either before or after a stay in L.A.'s theater of transformation. And so they stream in, wearing running shoes or cowboy hats or 49ers jackets, anxious to make a good first impression; and the people who wait for them, under a halfhearted mural of Desertland, are often American enough not to try to look the part. Juan and Esperanza both have ponytails now, and Kimmie is wearing a Harley-Davidson cap backwards and necking with a Japanese guy; the uncle from Delhi arrives to find that Rajiv not only has grown darker but has lost weight, so that he looks more like a peasant from back home than ever.

And the newcomers pour in in astonishing numbers. A typical Sunday evening, in a single hour, sees flights arriving from England, Taiwan, the Philippines, Indonesia, Mexico, Austria, Germany, Spain, Costa Rica, and Guatemala; and each new group colors and transforms the airport: an explosion of tropical shades from Hawaiian Air, a rash of blue blazers and white shirts around the early flight from Tokyo. Red-haired Thais bearing pirated Schwarzenegger videos, lonely Africans in Aerial Assault sneakers, farmers from changeless Confucian cultures peering into the smiles of a Prozac city, children whose parents can't pronounce their names. Many of them are returning, like Odysseus, with the spoils of war: young brides from Luzon, business cards from Shanghai, boxes of macadamia nuts from Oahu. And for many of them the whole wild carnival will feature sights they have never seen before: Japanese look anxiously at the first El Salvadorans they've ever seen, and El Salvadorans ogle sleek girls from Bangkok in thigh-high boots. All of them, moreover, may not be pleased to realize that the America they've dreamed of is, in fact, a land of tacos and pita and pad thai—full, indeed, of the very Third World cultures that other Third Worlders look down upon.

One day over lunch I asked my Ethiopian waitress about her life here. She liked it well enough, she said, but still she missed her home. And yet, she added, she couldn't go back. "Why not?" I asked, still smiling. "Because they killed my family," she said. "Two years back. They killed my father. They killed my brother." "They," I realized, referred to the Tigreans—many of them working just down the corridor in other parts of the hotel. So, too, Tibetans who have finally managed to flee their Chinese-occupied homeland arrive at LAX to find Chinese faces everywhere; those who fled the Sandinistas find themselves standing next to Sandinistas fleeing their successors. And all these people from ancient cultures find themselves in a country as amnesiac as the morning, where World War II is just a rumor and the Gulf War a distant memory. Their pasts are escaped, yes, but by the same token they are unlikely to be honored.

It is dangerously tempting to start formulating socioeconomic principles in the midst of LAX: people from rich countries (Germany and Japan, say) travel light, if only because they are sure that they can return any time; those from poor countries come with their whole lives in cardboard boxes imperfectly tied with string. People from poor countries are often met by huge crowds—for them each arrival is a special occasion—and stagger through customs with string bags and Gold Digger apple crates, their addresses handwritten on them in pencil; the Okinawan honeymooners, by contrast, in the color-coordinated outfits they will change every day, somehow have packed all their needs into a tiny case.

If airports have some of the excitement of bars, because so many people are composing (and decomposing) selves there, they also have some of the sadness of bars, the poignancy of people sitting unclaimed while everyone around them has paired off. A pretty girl dressed in next to nothing sits alone in an empty Baggage Claim area, waiting for a date who never comes; a Vietnamese man, lost, tells an official that he has friends in Orange County who can help him, but when the friends are contacted, they say they know no one from Vietnam. I hear of a woman who got off and asked for "San Mateo," only to learn that she was meant to disembark in San Francisco; and a woman from Nigeria who came out expecting to see her husband in Monroe, Louisiana, only to learn that someone in Lagos had mistaken "La." on her itinerary for "L.A."

The greetings I saw in the Arrivals area were much more tentative than I had expected, less passionate—as ritualized in their way as the kisses placed on Bob Barker's cheek—and much of that may be because so many people are meeting strangers, even if they are meeting people they once knew. Places like LAX—places like L.A.—perpetuate the sense that everyone is a stranger in our new floating world. I spent one afternoon in the airport with a Californian blonde, and I saw her complimented on her English by a sweet Korean woman and asked by an Iranian if she was Indian. Airports have some of the unsteady brashness of singles bars, where no one knows quite what is expected of them. "Mike, is that you?" "Oh, I didn't recognize you." "I'd have known you anywhere." "It's so kind of you to come and pick me up." And already at a loss, a young Japanese girl and a broad, lonely-looking man head off toward the parking lot, not knowing, in any sense, who is going to be in the driver's seat.

The driving takes place, of course, in what many of the newcomers, primed by video screenings of *L.A. Law* and *Speed*, regard as the ultimate heart of darkness, a place at least as forbidding and dangerous as Africa must have seemed to the Victorians. They have heard about how America is the murder capital of the world; they have seen Rodney King get pummeled by L.A.'s finest; they know of the city as the site of drive-by shootings and freeway snipers, of riots and celebrity murders. The "homeless" and the "tempest-tost" that the Statue of Liberty invites are arriving, increasingly, in a city that is itself famous for its homeless population and its fires, floods, and earthquakes.

In that context, the ideal symbol of LAX is, perhaps, the great object that for thirty years has been the distinctive image of the place: the ugly white quadruped that sits in the middle of the airport like a beached white whale or a jet-age beetle, featuring a 360-degree circular restaurant that does not revolve and an observation deck from which the main view is of twenty-three thousand parking places. The Theme Building, at 201 World Way, is a sad image of a future that never arrived, a monument to Kennedy-era idealism and the thrusting modernity of the American empire when it was in its prime; it now has the poignancy of an abandoned present with its price tag stuck to it. When you go there (and almost nobody does) you are greeted by photos of Saturn's rings and Jupiter and its moons, by a plaque laid down by L.B.J. and a whole set of symbols from the time when NASA was shooting for the heavens. Now the "landmark" building, with its "gourmet-type restaurant," looks like a relic from a time long past, when it must have looked like the face of the future.

Upstairs, a few desperately merry waiters are serving non-alcoholic drinks and cheeseburgers to sallow diners who look as if they've arrived at the end of the world; on the tarmac outside, speedbirds inch ahead like cars in a traffic jam. "Hello All the New People of LAX—Welcome," says the graffiti on the elevator.

The Theme Restaurant comes to us from an era when L.A. was leading the world. Nowadays, of course, L.A. is being formed and reformed and led by the world around it. And as I got ready to leave LAX, I could not help but feel that the Theme Building stands, more and more, for a city left behind by our accelerating planet. LAX, I was coming to realize, was a good deal scruffier than the airports even of Bangkok or Jakarta, more chaotic, more suggestive of Third World lawlessness. And the city around it is no more golden than Seoul, no more sunny than Taipei, and no more laid-back than Moscow. Beverly Hills, after all, is largely speaking Farsi now. Hollywood Boulevard is sleazier than 42nd Street. And Malibu is falling into the sea.

Yet just as I was about to give up on L.A. as yesterday's piece of modernity, I got on the shuttle bus that moves between the terminals in a never-ending loop. The seats next to me were taken by two tough-looking dudes from nearby South Central, who were riding the free buses and helping people on and off with their cases (acting, I presumed, on the safe assumption that the Japanese, say, new to the country and bewildered, had been warned beforehand to tip often and handsomely for every service they received). In between terminals, as a terrified-looking Miss Kudo and her friend guarded their luggage, en route from Nagoya to Las Vegas, the two gold-plated sharks talked about the Raiders' last game and the Lakers' next season. Then one of them, without warning, announced, "The bottom line is the spirit is with you. When you work out, you chill out and, like, you meditate in your spirit. You know what I mean? Meditation is recreation. Learn math, follow your path. That's all I do, man, that's all I live for: learnin' about God, learnin' about Jesus. I am *possessed* by that spirit. You know, I used to have all these problems, with the flute and all, but when I heard about God, I learned about the body, the mind, and the flesh. People forget, they don't know, that the Bible isn't talkin' about the flesh, it's talkin' about the spirit. And I was reborn again in the spirit."

His friend nodded. "When you recreate, you meditate. Recreation is a spiritually uplifting experience."

"Yeah. When you do that, you allow the spirit to breathe."

"Because you're gettin' into the physical world. You're lettin' the spirit flow. You're helpin' the secretion of the endorphins in the brain."

Nearby, the Soldiers of the Cross of Christ Church stood by the escalators, taking donations, and a man in a dog collar approached another stranger.

I watched the hustlers allowing the spirit to breathe, I heard the Hare Krishna devotees plying their wares, I spotted some Farrakhan flunkies collecting a dollar for a copy of their newspaper, *The Final Call*—redemption and corruption all around us in the air—and I thought: welcome to America, Miss Kudo, welcome to L.A.

Bernard Cooper

In "Burl's," originally published in *Truth Serum* (1996), a collection of auto-biographical essays, Bernard Cooper (b. 1951) explores what he calls "the hazy border between the sexes" with fluidity and grace. Recalling the origins of desire in a string of bewildering childhood episodes, Cooper offers vivid snapshots of Los Angeles locales ranging from the neon-and-chrome exuberance of a streamlined Hollywood diner to the rather pompous lobby of the Downtown Athletic Club. Cooper's first book of essays, *Maps to Anywhere*, won a 1990 PEN/Ernest Hemingway Award; he is also author of the novel *A Year of Rhymes* and a volume of short stories, *Guess Again*. A former instructor of writing at Otis/Parsons Institute of Art and Design and Antioch University Los Angeles, he is now art critic for *Los Angeles* magazine.

BURL'S

I loved the restaurant's name, a compact curve of a word. Its sign, five big letters rimmed in neon, hovered above the roof. I almost never saw the sign with its neon lit; my parents took me there for early summer dinners, and even by the time we left—Father cleaning his teeth with a toothpick, Mother carrying steak bones in a doggie bag—the sky was still bright. Heat rippled off the cars parked along Hollywood Boulevard, the asphalt gummy from hours of sun.

With its sleek architecture, chrome appliances, and arctic temperature, Burl's offered a refuge from the street. We usually sat at one of the booths in front of the plate glass windows. During our dinner, people came to a halt before the news-vending machine on the corner and burrowed in their pockets and purses for change.

The waitresses at Burl's wore brown uniforms edged in checked gingham. From their breast pockets frothed white lace handkerchiefs. In between reconnaissance missions to the tables, they busied themselves behind the counter and shouted "Tuna to travel" or "Scorch that patty" to a harried short-order cook who manned the grill. Miniature pitchers of cream and individual pats of butter were extracted from an industrial refrigerator. Coca-Cola shot from a glinting spigot. Waitresses dodged and bumped one another, as frantic as atoms.

My parents usually lingered after the meal, nursing cups of coffee while I played with the beads of condensation on my glass of ice water, tasted Tabasco sauce, or twisted pieces of my paper napkin into mangled animals. One evening, annoyed with my restlessness, my father gave me a dime and asked me to buy him a *Herald Examiner* from the vending machine in front of the restaurant.

Shouldering open the heavy glass door, I was seared by a sudden gust of heat. Traffic roared past me and stirred the air. Walking toward the newspaper machine, I held the dime so tightly, it seemed to melt in my palm. Duty made me feel large and important. I inserted the dime and opened the box, yanking a *Herald* from the spring contraption that held it as tight as a mousetrap. When I turned around, paper in hand, I saw two women walking toward me.

Their high heels clicked on the sun-baked pavement. They were tall, broad-shouldered women who moved with a mixture of haste and defiance. They'd teased their hair into nearly identical black beehives. Dangling earrings flashed in the sun, as brilliant as prisms. Each of them wore the kind of clinging, strapless outfit my mother referred to as a cocktail dress. The silky fabric—one dress was purple, the other pink—accentuated their breasts and hips and rippled with insolent highlights. The dresses exposed their bare arms, the slope of their shoulders, and the smooth, powdered plane of flesh where their cleavage began.

I owned at the time a book called *Things for Boys and Girls to Do*. There were pages to color, intricate mazes, and connect-the-dots. But another type of puzzle came to mind as I watched those women walking toward me: What's Wrong with This Picture? Say the drawing of a dining room looked normal at first glance; on closer inspection, a chair was missing its leg and the man who sat atop it wore half a pair of glasses.

The women had Adam's apples.

The closer they came, the shallower my breathing. I blocked the sidewalk, an incredulous child stalled in their path. When they saw me staring, they shifted their purses and linked their arms. There was something sisterly and conspiratorial about their sudden closeness. Though their mouths didn't open, I thought they might have been communicating without moving their lips, so telepathic did they seem as they joined arms and pressed together, synchronizing their heavy steps. The pages of the *Herald* fluttered in the wind; I felt them against my arm, as light as batted lashes.

The woman in pink shot me a haughty glance, and yet she seemed pleased that I'd taken notice, hungry to be admired by a man, or even an awestruck eight-year-old boy. She tried to stifle a grin, her red lipstick more voluptuous than the lips it painted. Rouge deepened her cheekbones. Eye shadow dusted her lids, a clumsy abundance of blue. Her face was like a page in *Things for Boys and Girls to Do*, colored by a kid who went outside the lines.

At close range, I saw that her wig was slightly askew. I was certain it was a wig because my mother owned several; three Styrofoam heads lined a shelf in my mother's closet; upon them were perched a pageboy, an empress, and a baby doll, all in shades of auburn. The woman in the pink dress wore her wig like a crown of glory.

But it was the woman in the purple dress who passed nearest me, and I saw that her jaw was heavily powdered, a half-successful attempt to disguise the telltale shadow of a beard. Just as I noticed this, her heel caught on a crack in the pavement and she reeled on her stilettos. It was then that I witnessed a rift in her composure, a window through which I could glimpse the shades of maleness that her dress and wig and make-up obscured. She shifted her shoulders and threw out her hands like a surfer riding a curl. The instant she regained her balance, she smoothed her dress, patted her hair, and sauntered onward.

Any woman might be a man; the fact of it clanged through the chambers of my brain. In broad day, in the midst of traffic, with my parents drinking coffee a few feet away, I felt as if everything I understood, everything I had taken for granted up to that moment —the curve of the earth, the heat of the sun, the reliability of my own eyes—had been squeezed out of me. Who were those men? Did they help each other get inside those dresses? How many other people and things were not what they seemed? From the back, the imposters looked like women once again, slinky and curvaceous, purple and pink. I watched them disappear into the distance, their disguises so convincing that other people on the street seemed to take no notice, and for a moment I wondered if I had imagined the whole encounter, a visitation by two unlikely muses.

Frozen in the middle of the sidewalk, I caught my reflection in the window of Burl's, a silhouette floating between his parents. They faced one another across a table. Once the solid embodiments of woman and man, pedestrians and traffic appeared to pass through them.

There were some mornings, seconds before my eyes opened and my senses gathered into consciousness, that the child I was seemed to hover above the bed, and I couldn't tell what form my waking would take—the body of a boy or the body of a girl. Finally stirring, I'd blink against the early light and greet each incarnation as a male with mild surprise. My sex, in other words, didn't seem to be an absolute fact so much as a pleasant, recurring accident.

By the age of eight, I'd experienced this groggy phenomenon several times. Those ethereal moments above my bed made waking up in the tangled blankets, a boy steeped in body heat, all the more astonishing. That this might be an unusual experience never occurred to me; it was one among a flood of sensations I could neither name nor ignore.

And so, shocked as I was when those transvestites passed me in front of Burl's, they confirmed something about which I already had an inkling: the hazy border between the sexes. My father, after all, raised his pinky when he drank from a teacup, and my mother looked as faded and plain as my father until she fixed her hair and painted her face.

Like most children, I once thought it possible to divide the world into male and female columns. Blue/Pink, Roosters/Hens. Trousers/Skirts. Such divisions were easy, not to mention comforting, for they simplified matter into compatible pairs. But there also existed a vast range of things that didn't fit neatly into either camp: clocks, milk, telephones, grass. There were nights I fell into a fitful sleep while trying to sex the world correctly.

Nothing typified the realms of male and female as clearly as my parents' walk-in closets. Home alone for any length of time, I always found my way inside them. I could stare at my parents' clothes for hours, grateful for the stillness and silence, haunting the very heart of their privacy.

The overhead light in my father's closet was a bare bulb. Whenever I groped for the chain in the dark, it wagged back and forth and resisted my grasp. Once the light clicked on, I saw dozens of ties hanging like stalactites. A monogrammed silk bathrobe sagged from a hook, a gift my father had received on a long-ago birthday and, thinking it fussy, rarely wore. Shirts were cramped together along the length of an aluminum pole, their starched sleeves sticking out as if in a halfhearted gesture of greeting. The medicinal odor of mothballs permeated the boxer shorts that were folded and stacked in a built-in drawer. Immaculate underwear was proof of a tenderness my mother couldn't otherwise express; she may not have touched my father often, but she laundered his boxers with infinite care. Even back then, I suspected that a sense of duty was the final erotic link between them.

Sitting in a neat row on the closet floor were my father's boots and slippers and dress shoes. I'd try on his wing tips and clomp around, slipping out of them with every step. My wary, unnatural stride made me all the more desperate to effect some authority. I'd whisper orders to imagined lackeys and take my invisible wife in my arms. But no matter how much I wanted them to fit, those shoes were as cold and hard as marble.

My mother's shoes were just as uncomfortable, but a lot more fun. From a brightly colored array of pumps and sling-backs, I'd pick a pair with the glee and deliberation of someone choosing a chocolate. Whatever embarrassment I felt was overwhelmed by the exhilaration of being taller in a pair of high heels. Things will look like this someday, I said to myself, gazing out from my new and improved vantage point as if from a crow's nest. Calves elongated, hands on my hips, I gauged each step so I didn't fall over and moved with what might have passed for grace had someone seen me, a possibility I scrupulously avoided by locking the door.

Back and forth I went. The longer I wore a pair of heels, the better my balance. In the periphery of my vision, the shelf of wigs looked like a throng of kindly bystanders. Light streamed down from a high window, causing crystal bottles to glitter, the air ripe with perfume. A make-up mirror above the dressing table invited my self-absorption. Sound was muffled. Time slowed. It seemed as if nothing bad could happen as long as I stayed within those walls.

Though I'd never been discovered in my mother's closet, my parents knew that I was drawn toward girlish things—dolls and jump rope and jewelry—as well as to the games and preoccupations that were expected of a boy. I'm not sure now if it was my effeminacy itself that bothered them so much as my ability to slide back and forth, without the slightest warning, between male and female mannerisms. After I'd finished building the model of an F-17 bomber, say, I'd sit back to examine my handiwork, pursing my lips in concentration and crossing my legs at the knee.

One day my mother caught me standing in the middle of my bedroom doing an imitation of Mary Injijikian, a dark, overeager Armenian girl with whom I believed myself to be in love, not only because she was pretty, but because I wanted to be like her. Collector of effortless A's, Mary seemed to know all the answers in class. Before the teacher had even finished asking a question, Mary would let out a little grunt and practically levitate out of her seat, as if her hand were filled with helium. "Could we please hear from someone else today besides Miss Injijikian," the teacher would say. *Miss Injijikian.* Those were the words I was repeating over and over to myself when my mother caught me. To utter them was rhythmic, delicious, and under their spell I raised my hand and wiggled like Mary. I heard a cough and spun around. My mother froze in the doorway. She clutched the folded sheets to her stomach and turned without saying a word. My sudden flush of shame confused me. Weren't boys supposed to swoon over girls? Hadn't I seen babbling, heartsick men in a dozen movies?

Shortly after the Injijikian incident, my parents decided to send me to gymnastics class at the Downtown Athletic Club, a brick relic of a building on Grand Avenue. One of the oldest establishments of its kind in Los Angeles, the club prohibited women from the premises. My parents didn't have to say it aloud: they hoped a fraternal atmosphere would toughen me up and tilt me toward the male side of my nature.

My father drove me downtown so I could sign up for the class, meet the instructor, and get a tour of the place. On the way there, he reminisced about sports. Since he'd grown up in a rough Philadelphia neighborhood, sports consisted of kick-the-can, or rolling a hoop down the street with a stick. The more he talked about his physical prowess, the more convinced I became that my daydreams and shyness were a disappointment to him.

The hushed lobby of the Athletic Club was paneled in dark wood. A few solitary figures were hidden in wing chairs. My father and I introduced ourselves to a man at the front desk who seemed unimpressed by our presence. His aloofness unnerved me, which wasn't hard considering that no matter how my parents put it, I knew that sending me here was a form of disapproval, a way of banishing the part of me they didn't care to know.

A call went out over the intercom for someone to show us around. While we waited, I noticed that the sand in the standing ashtrays had been raked into perfect furrows. The glossy leaves of the potted plants looked as if they'd been polished by hand. The place seemed more like a well-tended hotel than an athletic club. Finally, a stoop-shouldered old man hobbled toward us, his head shrouded in a cloud of white hair. He wore a T-shirt that said INSTRUCTOR, but his arms were so wrinkled and anemic, I thought I might have misread it. While we followed him to the elevator—it would be easier, he said, than taking the stairs—I readjusted my expectations, which had involved fantasies of a hulking drill sergeant barking orders at a flock of scrawny boys.

We got off the elevator on the second floor. The instructor, mumbling to himself and never turning around to see if we were behind him, showed us where the gymnastics class took place. I'm certain the building was big, but the size of the room must be exaggerated by a trick of memory, because when I envision it, I picture a vast and windowless warehouse. Mats covered the wooden floor. Here and there, in remote and lonely pools of light, stood a pommel horse, a balance beam, and parallel bars. Tiers of bleachers rose into darkness. Unlike the cloistered air of a closet, the room seemed incomplete without a crowd.

Next we visited the dressing room, empty except for a naked, middle-aged man. He sat on a narrow bench and clipped his formidable toenails. Moles dotted his back. He glistened like a fish.

We continued to follow the instructor down an aisle lined with numbered lockers. At the far end, steam billowed from the doorway that led to the showers. Fresh towels stacked on a nearby table made me think of my mother; I knew she liked to have me at home with her—I was often her only companion—and I resented her complicity in the plan to send me here.

The tour ended when the instructor gave me a sign-up sheet. Only a few names preceded mine. They were signatures, or so I imagined, of other soft and wayward sons.

When the day of the first gymnastics class arrived, my mother gave me money and a gym bag (along with a clean towel, she'd packed a banana and a napkin) and sent me to the corner of Hollywood and Western to wait for a bus. The sun was bright, the traffic heavy. While I sat there, an argument raged inside my head, the familiar, battering debate between the wish to be like other boys and the wish to be like myself. Why shouldn't I simply get up and go back home, where I'd be left alone to read and think? On the other hand, wouldn't life be easier if I liked athletics, or learned to like them? No sooner did I steel my resolve to get on the bus, than I thought of something better: I could spend the morning wandering through Woolworth's, then tell my parents I'd gone to the class. But would my lie stand up to scrutiny? As I practiced describing phantom gymnastics—*And then we did cartwheels and, boy, was I dizzy*—I became aware of a car circling the block. It was a large car in whose shaded interior I could barely make out the driver, but I thought it might be the man who owned the local pet store. I'd often gone there on the pretext of looking at the cocker spaniel puppies huddled together in their pen, but I really went to gawk at the owner, whose tan chest, in the V of his shirt, was the place I most wanted to rest my head. Every time the man moved, counting stock or writing a receipt, his shirt parted, my mouth went dry, and I smelled the musk of sawdust and dogs.

I found myself hoping that the driver was the man who ran the pet store. I was thrilled by the unlikely possibility that the sight of me, slumped on a bus bench in my T-shirt and shorts, had caused such a man to circle the block. Up to that point in my life, lovemaking hovered somewhere in the future, an impulse a boy might aspire to but didn't indulge. And there I was, sitting on a bus bench in the middle of the city, dreaming I could seduce an adult; I showered the owner of the pet store with kisses and, as aquariums bubbled, birds sang, and mice raced in a wire wheel, slipped my hand beneath his shirt. The roar of traffic brought me to my senses. I breathed deeply and blinked against the sun. I crossed my legs at the knee in order to hide an erection. My fantasy left me both drained and changed. The continent of sex had drifted closer.

The car made another round. This time the driver leaned across the passenger seat and peered at me through the window. He was a complete stranger whose gaze filled me with fear. It wasn't the surprise of not recognizing him that frightened me; it was what I did recognize—the unmistakable shame in his expression, and the weary temptation that drove him in circles. Before the car behind him honked, he mouthed "hello" and cocked his head. What now? he seemed to be asking. A bold, unbearable question.

I bolted to my feet, slung the gym bag over my shoulder, and hurried toward home. Now and then I turned around to make sure he wasn't trailing me, both relieved and disappointed when I didn't see his car. Even after I became convinced that he wasn't at my back (my sudden flight had scared him off), I kept turning around to see what was making me so nervous, as if I might spot the source of my discomfort somewhere on the street. I walked faster and faster, trying to outrace myself. Eventually, the bus I was supposed to have taken roared past. Turning the corner, I watched it bob eastward.

Closing the kitchen door behind me, I vowed to never leave home again. I was resolute in this decision without fully understanding why, or what it was I hoped to avoid; I was only aware of the need to hide and a vague notion, fading fast, that my trouble had something to do with sex. Already the mechanism of self-deception was at work. By the time my mother rushed into the kitchen to see why I'd returned so early, the thrill I'd felt while waiting for the bus had given way to indignation.

I poured out the story of the man circling the block and protested, with perhaps too great a passion, my own innocence. "I was just sitting there," I said again and again. I was so determined to deflect suspicion from myself, and to justify my missing the class, that I portrayed the man as a grizzled pervert who drunkenly veered from lane to lane as he followed me halfway home.

My mother listened quietly. She seemed moved and shocked by what I told her, if a bit incredulous, which prompted me to be more dramatic. "It wouldn't be safe," I insisted, "for me to wait at the bus stop again."

No matter how overwrought my story, I knew my mother wouldn't question it, wouldn't bring the subject up again; sex of any kind, especially sex between a man and a boy, was simply not discussed in our house. The gymnastics class, my parents agreed, was something I could do another time.

And so I spent the remainder of that summer at home with my mother, stirring cake batter, holding the dustpan, helping her fold the sheets. For a while I was proud of myself for engineering a reprieve from the Athletic Club. But as the days wore on, I began to see that my mother had wanted me with her all along, and forcing that to happen wasn't such a feat. Soon a sense of compromise set in; by expressing disgust for the man in the car, I'd expressed disgust for an aspect of myself. Now I had all the time in the world to sit around and contemplate my desire for men. The days grew long and stifling and hot, an endless sentence of self-examination.

Only trips to the pet store offered any respite. Every time I went there, I was too electrified with longing to think about longing in the abstract. The bell tinkled above the door, animals stirred within their cages, and the handsome owner glanced up from his work.

I handed my father the *Herald*. He opened the paper and disappeared behind it. My mother stirred her coffee and sighed. She gazed at the sweltering passersby and probably thought herself lucky. I slid into the vinyl booth and took my place beside my parents.

For a moment, I considered asking them about what had happened on the street, but they would have reacted with censure and alarm, and I sensed there was more to the story than they'd ever be willing to tell me. Men in dresses were only the tip of the iceberg. Who knew what other wonders existed—a boy, for example, who wants to kiss a man—exceptions the world did its best to keep hidden.

It would be years before I heard the word *transvestite*, so I struggled to find a word for what I'd seen. *He-she* came to mind, as lilting as *Injijikian*. *Burl's* would have been perfect, like *boys* and *girls* spliced together, but I can't claim to have thought of this back then.

I must have looked stricken as I tried to figure it all out, because my mother put down her coffee cup and asked if I was OK. She stopped just short of feeling my forehead. I assured her I was fine, but something within me had shifted, had given way to a heady doubt. When the waitress came and slapped down our check — "Thank you," it read, "dine out more often" — I wondered if her lofty hairdo or the breasts on which her nametag quaked were real. Wax carnations bloomed at every table. Phoney wood paneled the walls. Plastic food sat in a display case: fried eggs, a hamburger sandwich, a sundae topped with a garish cherry.

William T. Vollmann

The 1992 Los Angeles riots were among the worst civil disturbances in American history, a three-day outbreak of looting, violence, and arson in which 55 people died, more than 2,300 were injured, and 1,100 buildings were damaged at an estimated cost of nearly a billion dollars. The riots were remarkable for the speed with which they swept across the city, affecting neighborhoods from South Central to Beverly Hills. In this excerpt from his prose collection *The Atlas* (1996), William T. Vollmann (b. 1959) refracts the riots through the prism of a dinner party, and manages to say a great deal about the events in barely more than a page. Vollmann, an ambitious and idiosyncratic writer, likes to stake out the extremes of experience and the fringes of society, from war in Sarajevo to prostitutes in San Francisco's Tenderloin. Born in Los Angeles, he is the author of twelve books of fiction and nonfiction, including the monumental *Seven Dreams* cycle, which, when finished, will reimagine the history of North America as a clash between European and indigenous populations.

from

THE ATLAS

Los Angeles, California, U.S.A. (1992)

To the ancient ones who lived behind horse-headed gates, people like him and her would have been appalling. Those two thought themselves at home everywhere, and so they had no home.

Long before Magic Mountain the greasy-gray air had begun to smell like burning tires. Three patrol cars sped past. Through his window he saw one of those skeletal-trailered trucks used to haul racks of new automobiles to the dealers' lots; it was carrying nothing but police cars. He and she both had sore throats by the time they passed the Pico Canyon exit. The air smeared itself more and more thickly over the mountains ahead. To the east, no mountains could even be seen. She drove rapidly. They continued to descend. His eyes began to water.

I've never seen it this bad, she said.

They passed another car. The driver was looking where the road led and shaking his head. Two men in the next car were gesturing to one another.

He had a terrible headache. Ahead, the air was a featureless curtain, opaque and purplish-gray. The hills nearby were paradoxically clear, their greenery standing out on the chalky eroded walls. It is always like that in a fog; the very clarity of one's immediate surroundings points up the obscurity ahead.

The sun was large, pale yellow and soft in the turbid sky.

She clenched the steering wheel. — Do you think they burned Uncle's store?

I don't know. I hope not. I like your uncle.

They were close enough to see the black smoke now. Another patrol car screamed past.

Later they were at a dinner in the expensive hills where the smell of burning was not so bad. A white woman said: You know, I was a student at Kent State. I was there when the National Guard shot Allison Krause and those other students. I saw it! I saw the blood! I breathed it all in . . .

Somebody was coughing.

And I—I *knew* the pigs were the enemy, the woman said. No question about it. They were the pigs. And tonight, well, tonight I'm thinking that the police are *protecting* me. Thank God the police are standing between me and the enemy! And I'm trying to understand what changed. Because I don't feel that I'm any different; the police sure aren't any different—

His throat ached. He said: Do you mean that the blacks are your enemy?

She put down her wineglass and he thought that she might cry. She said: Yes, they are. It's not fair that I have all the nice things I have and they have nothing. I understand that, I really do. Once I had black friends. But I'm afraid. And I hate them because they make me afraid. And that truck driver, the way they dragged him out and beat him half to death . . .

Another guest had come in quietly from the pool while they were talking, and he was black.

The black man said: So you've hated me for a week. I've hated you for half a thousand years. Nothing personal.

My friends, my *friends!* cried the host, waving his hands. Don't *listen* to what you're both saying; it's just the stress and this awful air . . .

D. J. Waldie

Many Angelenos have little good to say about the instant tract developments of the early 1950s, but in *Holy Land: A Suburban Memoir* (1996) D. J. Waldie (b. 1948) creates a kind of deadpan epic out of this landscape. A city official in his hometown of Lakewood, Waldie is an anomaly among Southern Californians; he still inhabits the same house he was born in, purchased by his parents in 1946. Composed of more than three hundred brief chapters, *Holy Land* weaves together strands of personal and social history to imbue ordinary suburban life with eccentric poignancy.

from

HOLY LAND

E very family speaks its own language. The language I learned had the flavor of big cities in it.

Sometimes my mother, brother, and I ate lunch at the counter in the Woolworth's in the shopping center. Sometimes the waitress would comment on the way we spoke, and ask us if we were English.

I live on Graywood Avenue.

The next street west is Hazelbrook. The first street east is Faculty. These three streets, with about 140 houses, are bounded by Hedda Street and South Street.

All of my friends came from within the rectangle of these three blocks that I could reach without crossing at an intersection.

From age six to thirteen, I spent part of nearly every day and nearly all summer in the company of my brother and other boys who lived in houses like mine.

The character of those seven years is what makes a suburban childhood seem like an entire life.

✻

My brother and I played Monopoly with the boy across the street and the three brothers who lived one block east.

We would begin the game on the morning of one day. It might end—after long breaks and arguments and reconciliations—two days later in someone else's house.

We made the rules up as we went along, to keep the game going as long as possible.

When we played Monopoly, we stretched out the game by doubling the money in the bank from other sets. We let players go in debt, ignored fines, allowed players to mortgage properties to each other, and forgave rents.

Late in the afternoon on the last day of one of these games, we would lose the point of playing. We moved the metal tokens around the board and realized that no one could win under these rules.

By consent, the game ended when the first player was finally called to dinner.

Chevron's real estate division decided to auction off the street names in its new subdivision as a fund raiser for the YMCA.

Several city council members bid successfully for a street name of their own. One city officials paid to have a street named after his daughter.

I paid $200 to have a street named after my family.

The street is a cul-de-sac at the border of the city. There are eighteen houses on the dead-end street. The houses there are more than double the size of mine.

Behind them, beyond a high cinder-block wall, is a trailer park built on a landfill in the city of Long Beach.

As a boy, I made cities in the dirt behind my house.

After school, and on summer afternoons, Billy C and I knelt on the grass at the edge of my mother's garden, under the window to the room I shared with my brother.

We played where my mother's enormous rose bushes hung over our heads.

We laid out roads, parking lots, and rows of roofless houses with pale dirt walls. Sometimes Billy and I uncovered a bone or half of the smooth white jaw of a cat buried beneath the roses.

Billy C and I made garages for the metal trucks my mother bought at the big Woolworth's store in the shopping center.

The rows of dirt garage walls, as high as the width of a boy's palm, would harden in the two or three hours we played.

Some of the trucks were cast from dies made before the war. The trucks preserved the aerodynamic designs of the 1930s. They were painted in primary colors—blue, yellow, and red.

Sometimes we left a truck in the dirt, and it would disappear before we returned another day to dig.

The lost trucks turned up, sometimes years later, in the garden. They had nearly no paint. Their wire axles were rusted, and the rubber tires were gone.

The dirt in my backyard is part sand and part clay. It's part of the Chino soil series.

In 1917, the Bureau of Soils of the Department of Agriculture classified most of the soil now covered by houses and lawns as Chino clay loam.

This soil had been carried away from the San Gabriel Mountains only ten thousand years ago.

As late as 1914, the runoff from foothill canyons was allowed to flow unchecked into the vague rivers of the coastal plain. They dropped new sand and clay over soil deposited by older rivers during the late Pleistocene.

The rivers of the coastal plain found new beds almost every winter. Every summer, the rivers disappeared.

Where the ground dipped slightly, as it does here, the rivers concentrated alkali. It made mediocre land for wheat or barley, but it was good enough for growing sugar beets.

When sugar beet production declined in the 1920s, the truck farmers who leased the land from the Montana Land Company alternated crops of carrots, lima beans, and alfalfa.

Most of the farmers, before 1942, were Japanese.

My mother came to Southern California in 1943, while my father was serving as gunnery officer on the destroyer *Bradford*. The *Bradford*'s home port was Long Beach. My mother worked there as an escrow clerk in a bank.

The *Bradford*'s duty throughout the war in the Pacific was to serve as an escort ship for carrier operations. The *Bradford* directed fighter aircraft, monitored radar, and screened carriers from Japanese submarines and torpedo planes.

The *Bradford* also collected downed Navy flyers whose planes were too damaged or low on fuel to reach the carriers from which they were launched.

The crew members of the *Bradford* never lost a pilot they were sent to find.

In two years of bitter fighting, no sailor on board was killed in enemy action. In the battles for Iwo Jima and Okinawa, where kamikaze aircraft sank or damaged more than thirty ships, the *Bradford* was unharmed.

The war ended, and my parents stayed in Southern California.

They stayed a continent away from my father's mother in New York City.

They bought a house on a street that ended, for a few years, in bean fields.

Don Rochlen, the publicist who promoted the new suburb, told reporters from Los Angeles newspapers that the house lots in the new suburb were made small by design so that the streets could be wider.

The houses are close enough so that you might hear, if you listened, a neighbor's baby cry, a father arguing with a teenage son, or a television playing early on a summer night.

Most things here are close enough for comfort.

❊

Once, my father and I watched a rerun of *Victory at Sea* in the small middle bedroom where my parents kept the television set.

It was early evening, and my father had just come home from work at the Gas Company offices in Los Angeles.

He sat next to me on the bed. I was ten or eleven years old.

I already knew my father had been in the Navy in the war, because I had seen his officer's uniform in a suitcase in the attic.

The episode of *Victory at Sea* was about the invasion of Okinawa. We looked at the black-and-white images of ships in formation before the battle. He said we might see the *Bradford*, the ship he had been on.

We saw Japanese fighters and torpedo planes attack the ships. We saw the air around the ships fill with the small, black-and-white explosions of antiaircraft shells. We saw kamikaze planes burst into flames—in the air, as some struck the water, and when one hit an American ship.

We didn't see the *Bradford*.

David Thomson

Mulholland Drive, a 21-mile stretch of winding dirt and blacktop that extends from the Cahuenga Pass to Leo Carrillo State Beach, is best known for its movie-star mansions and scenic viewpoints. In "Beneath Mulholland," David Thomson (b. 1941) casts the road as a metaphor for the city itself. A regular contributor to *Film Comment* and *The New Republic*, Thomson is one of the most influential film writers of recent decades. His books include *A Biographical Dictionary of Film* (1975), *Rosebud: The Story of Orson Welles* (1996), and the novels *Suspects* (1985) and *Silver Light* (1990).

BENEATH MULHOLLAND

It is a drive and a highway, running east-west, the supreme vantage point for the entirety of Los Angeles and the San Fernando Valley. You can stand up there and feel like Christ—or the Devil. Mulholland Drive allows both roles.

Like any road, it has an A and a B that it connects. But Mulholland is more concerned with being up there than with destination. Few travel its length, except as explorers; and as it makes that winding automobile journey it is several different roads and moods, going from *Shampoo* to *Shane*. Mulholland is a phenomenon of Los Angeles, both an idealized spectacle and a place from which to survey the classic city of visibility. Even as you drive, the panorama turns into a model for grace and dread.

Imagine Marilyn Monroe, fifty miles long, lying on her side, half-buried on a ridge of crumbling rock, the crest of the Santa Monica Mountains, with chaparral, flowers and snakes writhing over her body, and mists, smog or dreams gathering in every curve. You'd need a certain height to recognize that intricate course as a body. But that's Mulholland, and you can drive it whenever you've got an hour and a half to spare, pursuing the ridge between Cahuenga and the Pacific. It's about as long as an old movie, and as full of scents and half-grasped fears and splendors as Marilyn's drowsy state.

Play with that fancy. Her toes twitch at the Hollywood Freeway, vaguely disturbed by the furious traffic of gnats. From the knob of her ankle you can look down on the Hollywood Bowl, turn east to the HOLLYWOOD sign or see downtown skyscrapers looming in the steam like guns in a Turkish bath. As the legs become thighs, Mulholland enters its richest stretch, full of designer security systems for houses hiding from the road, of sprinklers hissing at the bougainvillea and the blinding roses, of glamorous real estate, the Mulholland where young giants of the city live, some of them with views north and south, of San Fernando's pimento suburbia and the gray daytime swell of L.A., which at night goes MTV in black fur and diamond lights. At that most precious, privileged part of the body, where the thighs widen and foliage starts, you can find the secret mansion of Warren Beatty, high on its own escarpment, guarded by trees and Bauhaus bars.

There are those who think of only this Mulholland, who would not go beyond the low belt that is the San Diego Freeway. But there's much more to find. A little west of the freeway, Mulholland becomes a dirt road for nearly eight miles, as far as Topanga Canyon Boulevard. In a minute of driving, you give up the serene sway from one curve to another for a violent, jolting surface and roadside weeds so dusty their short season of green looks like the color of dollars.

This must be the belly of the beast, grumbling at what it has eaten. There are no houses or telephones, none of the firehouses from the wealthy, worried section. If you broke down, you would be stranded. To the north you can see the sharkskin surface of the Encino Reservoir, but to the south there are only empty concertina folds of hillside where hawks spin in the mauve and gold dust of sunset. You could lose a Live Aid concert down in Topanga State Park. How much easier for a few desperate people to lurk there. The dirt road section of Mulholland is a place for paranoia—eerily empty on weekdays at noon, a bikers' track on weekends and a place for furtive love and dealing. You sometimes come upon a parked car with talk too delicate to approach. And there are mattresses dying in the brush where who knows what trysts were enjoyed, or how long ago.

Just as you think you are lost, the hard-top resumes and you slide into a little patch of community before the last long section — the ribs, the breasts, the shoulders and throat. This rolling country-side contains a distant dewdrop green golf course, a ranch where stunts are filmed, riding trails, the homes of solitaries, artists and eccentrics, a mock Alpine section, a trashy trailer park, the three satellite dishes of a Jewish recreation center, hillsides burnt black by the latest fires and, at last, the highest number on Mulholland, 35375, a camp for blind children set among eucalyptus trees. Then there's the sea, a beach named after actor Leo Carrillo, sidekick to the Cisco Kid, and platinum surf like Marilyn's hair in her last pictures.

Some say the road was built for that journey, so that the sweaty poor of Bunker Hill and Fairfax secretaries could get to the sea for relief. There are faster ways now, of course, on the freeways or Santa Monica Boulevard. And even in 1923–24, when Mulholland was built, the road was more a gesture of triumph and philosophy than a means of transport.

That's why it was named after William Mulholland (1855–1935), the superintendent of the L.A. Water Department, who designed and presided over the scheme that sucked water from the Owens Valley, 250 miles away, to make Los Angeles fertile, flush-friendly and be-pooled. No water tanks need more pumping than those on Mulholland, and the well-watered thighs still bloom in William's honor. Mulholland is regarded now as a robber baron and an ecological rapist: this is the "Bless me for I have sinned" the Angeleno murmurs whenever he enters the shower or drops into the copper sulphate pools that fill every navel and armpit along Mulholland. In other words, no one is sending the water back to the parched and desolate Owens Valley. They're keeping it, along with the casual guilt.

"There it is — take it" is what Mulholland is supposed to have said, of the water and the brutal advantage of clout. Mulholland Drive still lives on that advice, just as Hollywood taught us to cherish scoundrels. The road is like a location in a film, chosen and dressed for its magnificent vantage and for the juxtaposition of inane civilization and a dangerous wilderness. This is where the desert touches Gucci and Mercedes, where pet chihuahuas can be eaten by coyotes. Mulholland has buildings that could topple into the canyons: the John Lautner Chemosphere stands on one concrete stem, and there is a tennis court on stilts. It has rich homes that might be descended on at night by anarchists, murderers or nightmare Apaches. There is even a Manson Avenue that runs off Mulholland: you have to wonder whether it was scripted tribute or magical impromptu.

Mulholland is a pinup and an idea: it has Brancusis in some groomed gardens, and beer bottles shattered from target practice a few miles farther on. Its function is to embody that contrast: it is a highway made for narcissism and envy, an example of privilege, luxury and airy superiority that whispers, "Look at me—take me, if you can." The road, the drive, the highway all thrill to the way man has commanded natural power and beauty here and turned them into a property or a story. That HOLLYWOOD at the eastern end, letters fifty feet high, is a title, a caption: it's there to tell us the landscape is a kept woman as well as collapsing topography. And the road is called Mulholland Drive so that you know you should be wary of anyone on foot.

Sources and Acknowledgments

Great care has been taken to trace all owners of copyright material included in this book. If any have been inadvertently omitted or overlooked, acknowledgment will gladly be made in future printings.

Helen Hunt Jackson, *from* Echoes in the City of the Angels: *Glimpses of California and the Missions* (Boston: Little, Brown, 1902).

Mary Austin, The Land: *Lost Borders* (New York: Harper & Brothers, 1909).

Stewart Edward White, *from* The Rules of the Game: *The Rules of the Game* (New York: Grosset & Dunlap, 1910).

Harris Newmark, *from* Sixty Years in Southern California 1853–1913: *Sixty Years in Southern California 1853–1913* (New York: The Knickerbocker Press, 1916).

Vachel Lindsay, California and America: *The Art of the Moving Picture* (New York: The Macmillan Company, 1922). Revised edition of the book first published in 1915.

Louis Adamic, *from* Laughing in the Jungle: *Laughing in the Jungle* (New York: Harper & Brothers, 1932). Copyright © 1932 by Louis Adamic, renewed 1960 by Stella Adamic. Reprinted by permission of HarperCollins Publishers Inc.

Aldous Huxley, Los Angeles. A Rhapsody: *Jesting Pilate: An Intellectual Holiday* (New York: George H. Doran, 1926). Copyright © 1926 by the Estate of Aldous Huxley. Reprinted by permission of The Huxley Literary Estate.

H. L. Mencken, Sister Aimée: *A Mencken Chrestomathy* (New York: Knopf, 1974). Copyright © 1916, 1918, 1920, 1921, 1924, 1926, 1927, 1929, 1932, 1934, 1942, 1949 by Alfred A. Knopf, a division of Random House, Inc. Reprinted by permission of Alfred A. Knopf, a division of Random House, Inc.

Upton Sinclair, *from* Oil!: *Oil!* (New York: Albert and Charles Boni, 1927). Copyright © 1926, 1927 by Upton Sinclair, renewed 1954 by David Sinclair. Reprinted by permission of the University of California Press.

Carroll & Garrett Graham, *from* Queer People: *Queer People* (Carbondale: Southern Illinois University Press, 1976). This novel was first published in 1930. Copyright © 1930 by Carroll & Garrett Graham.

Arna Bontemps, *from* God Sends Sunday: *God Sends Sunday* (New York: Harcourt, Brace and Company, 1931). Copyright © 1931 by Harcourt Brace & Company, renewed 1958 by Arna Bontemps. Reprinted by permission of Harold Ober Associates Incorporated.

Edmund Wilson, The City of Our Lady the Queen of the Angels: *The American Earthquake: A Documentary of the Twenties and Thirties* (Garden City, NY: Doubleday, 1958). Copyright © 1958 by Edmund Wilson, renewed 1986 by Helen Miranda Wilson. Reprinted by permission of Farrar, Straus and Giroux, LLC.

James M. Cain, Paradise: *The American Mercury*, March 1933. Copyright © 1933 by James M. Cain. Reprinted by permission of Harold Ober Associates.

William Faulkner, Golden Land: *Collected Stories* (New York: Random House, 1950). Copyright © 1935 by Random House, Inc. Used by permission of Random House, Inc.

875

M.F.K. Fisher, Pacific Village: *Westways*, 1935. Copyright © 1935 by M.F.K. Fisher. Reprinted by permission of Lescher & Lescher, Ltd. A Thing Shared: *The Gastronomical Me* (New York: Duell, Sloan & Pearce, 1943), Copyright © 1943, 1954 by M.F.K. Fisher; reprinted in *The Art of Eating*, by M.F.K. Fisher, copyright © 1990 M.F.K. Fisher. All rights reserved. Reproduced here by permission of Wiley Publishing, Inc.

Cedric Belfrage, *from* Promised Land: *Promised Land* (London: Left Book Club, 1938). Copyright © 1938 by Cedric Belfrage.

Raymond Chandler, Red Wind: *Dime Detective*, January 1938. Also appears in *The Simple Art of Murder*. Copyright © 1950 by Raymond Chandler, renewed 1978 by Helga Greene. Reprinted by permission of Houghton Mifflin Company. All rights reserved.

John Fante, *from* Ask the Dust: *Ask the Dust* (New York: Stackpole Sons, 1939). Copyright © 1980 by John Fante and reprinted by permission of Black Sparrow Press.

Nathanael West, *from* The Day of the Locust: *The Day of the Locust* (New York: Random House, 1939). Also appears in *Miss Lonelyhearts & The Day of the Locust*. Copyright © 1939 by Estate of Nathanael West. Reprinted by permission of New Directions Publishing Corp.

Christopher Isherwood, *from* Diaries: Katherine Bucknell (ed.), *Diaries, Volume One: 1939–1960* (New York: HarperCollins, 1997). Copyright © 1996 by Don Bachardy. Reprinted by permission of HarperCollins Publishers Inc.

F. Scott Fitzgerald, Last Kiss: Matthew J. Bruccoli (ed.), *The Short Stories of F. Scott Fitzgerald* (New York: Scribner, 1989). Copyright © 1949 by The Crowell-Collier Publishing Company, renewed 1976 by Frances Scott Fitzgerald Smith. Copyright © 1989 by Charles Scribner's Sons. Reprinted by permission of Scribner, a division of Simon & Schuster, Inc.

Charles Reznikoff, *from* Autobiography: Hollywood: Seamus Cooney (ed.), *Poems 1918–1975: The Complete Poems of Charles Reznikoff* (Santa Barbara, CA: Black Sparrow Press, 1977). Copyright © 1977 by Marie Syrkin Reznikoff. Reprinted by permission of Black Sparrow Press.

Budd Schulberg, A Table at Ciro's: *Some Faces in the Crowd* (New York: Random House, 1941). Copyright © 1941 by Budd Schulberg. Reprinted by permission of Miriam Altshuler Agency, on behalf of Budd Schulberg.

Bertolt Brecht, Landscape of Exile, Hollywood Elegies, Californian Autumn, The Democratic Judge, The Fishing-Tackle, Garden In Progress: John Willett and Ralph Manheim (eds.), *Poems* (London: Methuen, 1979). Reproduced by permission of Routledge, Inc., part of the Taylor & Francis Group. *from* Journals: John Willett (ed.), *Journals 1934–1955*, translated by Hugh Rorrison (New York: Routledge, 1993). Copyright © 1973 by Stefan S. Brecht; translation copyright © 1993 by Stefan S. Brecht. Reproduced by permission of Routledge, Inc., part of the Taylor & Francis Group.

Chester Himes, *from* If He Hollers Let Him Go: *If He Hollers Let Him Go* (Garden City, NY: Doubleday, Doran and Company, 1945). Copyright © 1945 by Chester Himes. Reprinted with permission of Roslyn Targ Literary Agency.

Carlos Bulosan, *from* America Is in the Heart: *America Is in the Heart: A Personal History* (Seattle: University of Washington Press, 1973). First published in 1946. Copyright © 1943, 1946 by Harcourt, Brace and Company Inc.

Carey McWilliams, *from* Southern California Country: An Island on the Land: *Southern California Country: An Island on the Land* (New York: Duell, Sloan & Pearce, 1946). Copyright © 1946, 1973 by Carey McWilliams. The book is available from Gibbs Smith, Publisher. Reprinted by permission of Harold Ober Associates. *from* North from Mexico: Blood on the Pavements: *North from Mexico: The Spanish-Speaking People of the United States* (Philadelphia: J.B. Lipincott, 1948). Copyright © 1948, renewed © 1975 by Carey McWilliams. Reprinted by permission of Greenwood Publishing Group, Inc.

Simone de Beauvoir, *from* America Day by Day: *America Day by Day*, translated by Carol Cosman (Berkeley: University of California Press, 1999). Copyright © 1954 by Editions Gallimard, Paris, translation copyright © 1999 by The Regents of the University of California. Reprinted by permission of University of California Press.

Truman Capote, Hollywood: *Local Color* (New York: Random House, 1950). Copyright © 1950 by Truman Capote. Used by permission of Random House, Inc.

Evelyn Waugh, Death in Hollywood: *Life*, September 29, 1947. Copyright © 1947 by Evelyn Waugh. Reprinted by permission of Sterling Lord Literistic, Ltd.

Octavio Paz, *from* The Labyrinth of Solitude: *The Labyrinth of Solitude: Life and Thought in Mexico*, translated by Lysander Kemp (New York: Grove Press, 1961). Copyright © 1961 by Grove Press, Inc. Used by permission of Grove/Atlantic, Inc.

Ray Bradbury, The Pedestrian: *The Golden Apples of the Sun* (Garden City, NY: Doubleday & Company, 1953). Copyright © 1951 by the Fortnightly Publishing Company, renewed 1979 by Ray Bradbury. Reprinted by permission of Don Congdon Associates, Inc.

Tennessee Williams, The Mattress by the Tomato Patch: *Hard Candy* (New York: New Directions, 1954). Also appears in *The Collected Stories of Tennessee Williams*. Copyright © 1948 by The University of the South. Reprinted by permission of New Directions Publishing Corp.

Ross Macdonald, *from* The Barbarous Coast: *Archer in Hollywood* (New York: Alfred A. Knopf, 1967). *The Barbarous Coast* was first published in 1956. Copyright © 1956 by Ross Macdonald. Reprinted by permission of Alfred A. Knopf, a division of Random House, Inc.

Jack Kerouac, *from* On the Road: *On the Road* (New York: Viking, 1957). Copyright © 1957 by John Sampas, Literary Rep. Reprinted by permission of Sterling Lord Literistic, Inc.

Lawrence Clark Powell, *from* "Ocian in View": *"Ocian in View"* (Santa Barbara, CA: Capra Press, 1987). Copyright © The Regents of the University of California, successor to the copyrights of the late Lawrence Clark Powell. Reprinted with permission.

Gavin Lambert, The Slide Area: *The Slide Area: Scenes of Hollywood Life* (London: Hamish Hamilton, 1959). Copyright © 1959 by Gavin Lambert. Reprinted by permission of the author.

Lawrence Lipton, *from* Slum by the Sea: *The Holy Barbarians* (New York: Julian Messner, 1959). Copyright © 1959 by Lawrence Lipton. Reprinted by permission of The Estate of Lawrence Lipton, James Lipton, Executor.

Norman Mailer, *from* Superman Comes to the Supermarket: *The Presidential Papers* (New York: Putnam, 1963). Copyright © 1963 by Norman Mailer. Reprinted by permission of the Wylie Agency.

Randall Jarrell, The Lost World: *The Complete Poems* (New York: Farrar, Straus and Giroux, 1969). Copyright © 1969, renewed 1997 by Mary von S. Jarrell. Reprinted by permission of Farrar, Straus and Giroux, LLC.

Tom Wolfe, The Kandy-Kolored Tangerine-Flake Streamline Baby: *The Kandy-Kolored Tangerine-Flake Streamline Baby* (New York: Farrar, Straus and Giroux, 1965). Copyright © 1964, renewed © 1993 by Tom Wolfe. Reprinted by permission of Farrar Straus and Giroux LLC.

Jules Siegel, Goodbye Surfing, Hello God!: *Record* (San Francisco: Straight Arrow Books, 1972). Copyright © 1967 by Jules Siegel. Copyright © renewed 1995 by Jules Siegel. Reprinted by the permission of Russell & Volkening as agents for the author.

Joan Didion, Los Angeles Notebook: *Slouching Towards Bethlehem* (New York: Farrar, Straus and Giroux, 1968). Copyright © 1966, 1968, renewed © 1996 by Joan Didion. Reprinted by permission of Farrar Straus and Giroux LLC. The Getty, Quiet Days in Malibu: *The White Album* (New York: Simon & Schuster, 1979). Copyright © 1979 by Joan Didion. Reprinted by permission of Farrar Straus and Giroux LLC. Fire Season: *After Henry* (New York: Simon & Schuster, 1992). Copyright © 1992 by Joan Didion. Reprinted with the permission of Simon & Schuster, Inc.

Charles Bukowski, Waiting: *The Last Night of the Earth: Poems* (Santa Rosa, CA: Black Sparrow Press, 1992). Copyright © 1992 by Charles Bukowski and reprinted by permission of Black Sparrow Press. Betting on Now: *Betting on the Muse: Poems and Stories* (Santa Rosa, CA: Black Sparrow Press, 1996). Copyright © 1996 by Linda Lee Bukowski and reprinted by permission of Black Sparrow Press. The Death of the Father: *Hot Water Music* (Santa Barbara, CA: Black Sparrow Press, 1983). Copyright © 1983 by Charles Bukowski and reprinted by permission of Black Sparrow Press.

Salka Viertel, *from* The Kindness of Strangers: *The Kindness of Strangers* (New York: Holt, Rinehart and Winston, 1969). Copyright © 1969 by Salka Viertel. Reprinted by permission of Henry Holt and Company, LLC.

Reyner Banham, *from* Los Angeles: The Architecture of Four Ecologies: *Los Angeles: The Architecture of Four Ecologies* (New York: Harper & Row, 1971). Copyright © 1971 by Reyner Banham. Copyright © renewed 1999 by Mary Banham. Reprinted by permission of the University of California Press.

Charles Mingus, *from* Beneath the Underdog: *Beneath the Underdog: His World As Composed By Mingus*. Edited by Nel King. (New York: Alfred A. Knopf, 1971). Copyright © The Estate of Charles Mingus. Reprinted with permission.

Marc Norman, *from* Bike Riding in Los Angeles: *Bike Riding in Los Angeles* (New York: E. P. Dutton, 1972). Copyright © 1971, 1972 by Marc Norman. Reprinted by permission of the author.

Cees Nooteboom, Autopia: Charles G. Salas and Michael S. Roth (eds.), *Looking for Los Angeles* (Los Angeles: Getty Institute Publications, 2001). Translated by Philipp Blom. First published in Dutch in 1973. Copyright © 1973, 2002 by Cees Nooteboom. Reprinted with permission of the author.

Umberto Eco, The City of Robots: *Travels in Hyperreality* (New York: Harcourt Brace Jovanovich, 1986), translated by William Weaver. First published in Italian in 1975. Copyright © 1973, 1976, 1983 by Gruppo Editoriale Fabbri-Bompiani, Etas S.p.A. English translation by William Weaver copyright © 1986 by Harcourt, Inc., reprinted by permission of Harcourt, Inc.

David Hockney, *from* David Hockney by David Hockney: *David Hockney by David Hockney*, edited by Nikos Stangos (London: Thames & Hudson, 1976). Copyright © 1976 by David Hockney. Reprinted by permission of the David Hockney Studio.

Jan Morris, Los Angeles: The Know-How City: *Destinations: Essays from Rolling Stone* (New York: Oxford University Press, 1980). Copyright © 1980 by Jan Morris. Reprinted by permission of A.P. Watt Ltd. on behalf of Jan Morris.

John Rechy, *from* The Sexual Outlaw: *The Sexual Outlaw* (New York: Grove Press, 1977). Copyright © 1963 by John Rechy. Used by permission of Grove/Atlantic, Inc.

John Gregory Dunne, Eureka!: *Quintana & Friends* ((New York: Dutton, 1978). Copyright © 1978 by John Gregory Dunne. Reprinted by permission of the author.

Art Pepper, *from* Straight Life: *Straight Life*, by Art and Laurie Pepper (New York: Da Capo, 1994). This book was first published in 1979. Copyright © 1979 by Laurie Pepper. Reprinted by permission of Laurie Pepper.

Lawrence Weschler, *from* Seeing Is Forgetting the Name of the Thing One Sees: *Seeing Is Forgetting the Name of the Thing One Sees* (Berkeley: University of California Press, 1982). Copyright © 1982 by The Regents of the University of California. Reprinted by permission. L.A. Glows: *The New Yorker*, February 23, 1998. Copyright © 1998 by Lawrence Wechsler. Reprinted by permission of the author.

Robert Towne, Preface and Postscript to Chinatown: Text provided by the author. This essay appeared in a slightly different form in *Chinatown* (Santa Barbara, CA: Neville Publishing, 1983). Copyright © 1983 by Robert Towne. Reprinted by permission of the author.

Carol Muske, August, Los Angeles, Lullaby: *An Octave Above Thunder: New and Selected Poems* (New York: Penguin, 1997). Copyright © 1997 by Carol Muske. Reprinted by permission of Penguin, a division of Penguin Putnam Inc.

Wanda Coleman, Angel Baby Blues: *Heavy Daughter Blues: Poems and Stories 1968–1986* (Santa Rosa, CA: Black Sparrow Press, 1987). Copyright © 1987 by Wanda Coleman. Reprinted by permission of Black Sparrow Press.

Mona Simpson, *from* Anywhere But Here: *Anywhere But Here* (New York: Alfred A. Knopf, 1986). Copyright © 1986 by Mona Simpson. Reprinted by permission of Alfred A. Knopf, a division of Random House, Inc.

Gary Snyder, Night Song of the Los Angeles Basin: *Mountains and Rivers Without End* (Washington D.C.: Counterpoint, 1996). Copyright © 1996 by Gary Snyder. Reprinted by permission of Counterpoint Press, a member of Perseus Books, L.L.C.

Carolyn See, *from* Golden Days: *Golden Days* (New York: McGraw-Hill, 1986). Copyright © 1986 by Carolyn See. Reprinted by permission of the author.

Charles Willeford, *from* I Was Looking for a Street: *I Was Looking for a Street* (Woodstock, VT: Countryman Press, 1988). Copyright © 1988 by Charles Willeford. Reprinted by permission of JET Literary Associates, Inc.

Rubén Martínez, Going Up in L.A.: *The Other Side: Notes from the New L. A., Mexico City, and Beyond* (New York: Vintage Books, 1993) Copyright © 1993 Rubén Martínez. Reprinted by permission of Verso.

John McPhee, *from* The Control of Nature: *The Control of Nature* (New York: Farrar, Straus and Giroux, 1989). Copyright © 1989 by John McPhee.

Reprinted by permission of Farrar Straus and Giroux LLC. Published in Canada by Macfarlane Walter & Ross, Toronto.

Mike Davis, *from* City of Quartz: *City of Quartz* (London: Verso, 1990). Copyright © 1990 by Verso Press. Reprinted by permission of Verso.

Lynell George, City of Specters: David Reid (ed.), *Sex, Death and God in L.A.* (New York: Pantheon Books, 1992). Copyright © 1992 by Random House, Inc. Reprinted by permission of Pantheon Books, a division of Random House, Inc.

Walter Mosley, *from* Devil in a Blue Dress: *Devil in a Blue Dress* (New York: W.W. Norton & Co., 1990). Copyright © 1990 by Walter Mosley. Reprinted by permission of W.W. Norton & Co., Inc.

Mary Helen Ponce, Las Vistas: *Hoyt Street: An Autobiography* (Albuquerque: University of New Mexico Press, 1993). Copyright © 1993 by Mary Helen Ponce. Reprinted by permission of The University of New Mexico Press.

Sandra Tsing Loh, Coming Home to Van Nuys: *Depth Takes a Holiday* (New York: Riverhead Books, 1996). Copyright © 1996 by Sandra Tsing Loh. Reprinted by permission of Riverhead Books, a division of Penguin Putnam, Inc.

James Ellroy, The Tooth of Crime: *Crime Wave* (New York: Vintage Books, 1999). Copyright © 1999 by James Ellroy. Reprinted by permission of Vintage Books, a division of Random House, Inc.

Garrett Hongo, *from* Volcano: *Volcano* (New York: Alfred A. Knopf, 1995). Copyright © 1995 by Garrett Hongo. Reprinted by permission of Alfred A. Knopf, a division of Random House, Inc.

Pico Iyer, Where Worlds Collide: *Harper's*, August 1995. Copyright © 1995 by Harper's Magazine. All rights reserved. Reproduced from the August 1995 issue by special permission.

Bernard Cooper, Burl's: *Truth Serum* (Boston: Houghton Mifflin, 1996). Copyright © 1996 by Bernard Cooper. Reprinted by permission of Houghton Mifflin Company. All rights reserved.

William T. Vollmann, *from* The Atlas: *The Atlas* (New York: Viking, 1996). Copyright © 1996 by William T. Vollmann. Reprinted by permission of Viking Penguin, a division of Penguin Putnam Inc.

D. J. Waldie, *from* Holy Land: *Holy Land* (New York: W.W. Norton & Co., 1996). Copyright © 1996 by Donald J. Waldie. Reprinted by permission of W.W. Norton & Co., Inc.

David Thomson, Beneath Mulholland: *Beneath Mulholland* (New York: Alfred A. Knopf, 1997). Copyright © 1997 by David Thomson. Reprinted by permission of Alfred A. Knopf, a division of Random House, Inc.

THE LIBRARY OF AMERICA SERIES

The Library of America fosters appreciation and pride in America's literary heritage by publishing, and keeping permanently in print, authoritative editions of America's best and most significant writing. An independent nonprofit organization, it was founded in 1979 with seed money from the National Endowment for the Humanities and the Ford Foundation.

SPECIAL ANTHOLOGIES

CHILLICOTHE & ROSS CO. PUBLIC LIBRARY

3 7925 1024 5597 4

A

M8

810.8   Writing Los Angeles : a
WRIT   literary anthology /

                              10/16/02

MAIN